US LABOR IN TROUBLE AND TRANSITION

US LABOR IN TROUBLE AND TRANSITION:

The Failure of Reform from Above, the Promise of Revival from Below

————————————◆————————————

KIM MOODY

VERSO

London • New York

First published by Verso 2007
© Kim Moody 2007
All rights reserved

1 3 5 7 9 10 8 6 4 2

VERSO
UK: 6 Meard Street, London W1F 0EG
USA: 180 Varick Street, New York, NY 10014-4606
www.versobooks.com

Verso is the imprint of New Left Books

ISBN: 978-1-84467-154-0 (pbk)
ISBN: 978-1-84467-155-7 (hbk)

BRITISH LIBRARY CATALOGUING IN PUBLICATION DATA
A catalogue record for this book is available from the British Library

LIBRARY OF CONGRESS CATALOGING-IN-PUBLICATION DATA
A catalog record for this book is available from the Library of Congress

Typeset by Hewer Text Uk Ltd, Edinburgh
Printed and bound in the USA by Courier Stoughton Inc.

CONTENTS

Acknowledgments   vii

List of Tables   ix

List of Acronyms   xi

1 A Message about the Future from the Present   1

2 The Great Transformation   11

3 The Changing Industrial Geography   37

4 The Changing Industrial Demography   58

5 Lost Decades   79

6 The End of Militancy, the Surrender of the Workplace, and the
   Origins of Decline   98

7 Winning to Change: The Failure of Reform from Above   121

8 The Politics of Defeat—One More Time   143

9 The Split: Reform from Above Again   169

10 Beneath the Split: Resistance and Change from Below   198

11 Paths to Power, Roads Not Taken   224

Notes   249

Index   279

ACKNOWLEDGMENTS

A special acknowledgment goes to my partner Sheila Cohen, with whom I have worked out many of my ideas and from whom I have borrowed more than a few. Her collaboration and support have been invaluable. The past and present staff and the many close associates of *Labor Notes* might all take more than a little credit for the facts, analysis, ideas, and experiences that went into this book. My many years on the *Labor Notes* staff were an in-depth apprenticeship in the life and realities of the labor movement in the United States and a few other countries as well. This project continues to educate thousands of the activists and grassroots leaders who make the labor movement possible. As any look at my endnotes will reveal, *Labor Notes* was a key source of information on trends in working-class organization and activity. The hundreds of union and community activists I have known through my work at *Labor Notes* have also contributed to this book through what I have learned from them. Only a few of them actually appear in the book, but they have all helped to shape my thinking. I add to this list the staff and students at the Cornell labor studies program in New York City.

The Centre for Research in Employment Studies at the University of Hertfordshire provided me with some of the much-needed time it took to complete my research and pull this book together. Finally, I wish to thank the editors and staff at Verso, for whom this is my third book, for their suggestions and patience.

TABLES

2.1 Average Rate of Profit, 1950–73
2.2 Indicators of Global Economic Integration
2.3 US Foreign Direct Investment Outflow: Total and Manufacturing as a Percentage of Total
2.4 Foreign Direct Investment in Manufacturing: Outflows and Inflows, 1984–2004
2.5 US International Trade: Exports and Imports of Goods, 1984–2004
2.6 Real Private Nonresidential Fixed Investment, 1991–2004
2.7 Manufacturing: Real Fixed Assets per Production Worker, 1990–2004
2.8 The 57-second Work Minute: Value Added in Manufacturing, 2002
3.1 Real GDP by Type of Product 1980–2005; Services as a Percentage of GDP
3.2 Employees in Nonfarm Industries, 1990–2005
3.3 Real Value Added in Manufacturing: South and US
3.4 Foreign Direct Investment in the US and US South, 1990–2003
3.5 Construction Contracts by Value, US and the South, 1990–2003
3.6 Mergers, Acquisitions and Divestitures, 1985–2003
4.1 Industrialization Indices, 1870–1920
4.2 Women in the US Civilian Labor Force, 1950–70
4.3 Changes in Population in the Northeast and Midwest, 1950–70
4.4 Civilian Labor Force by Gender and Race, 1975–2004
4.5 Immigrant Population, 1995–2004
4.6 Latin American Legal Immigration by Decade
4.7 Percentage of Employed Asians and Latinos in Major Occupational Groups, 2003
5.1 Real Average Weekly Wages (1982 dollars) for Production and Nonsupervisory Workers

5.2   Private Sector Health Care and Pension Benefits Coverage, 1979–2003

5.3   Median Real Family Income by Race/Ethnicity, 1979–2003

5.4   Real Family Income Growth 1947–2000 by Income Level

5.5   CEO Pay Top Ten: Compensation and Total Stock Options, 2004

5.6   Top Ten Recent CEO Annual Retirement Packages

5.7   Family Income Growth and Shares, 1963–2003

5.8   Income Growth by Source, 1990–2004

6.1   Strikes, Strikers, and Percentage of Employed, 1945–81

6.2   Union Membership and Density, Selected Years, 1953–2005

6.3   Unions that Lost 100,000 Members or More, 1976–83

6.4   Financial Assets and Receipts of Selected Unions, FY2005

6.5   Claimed Union Membership of the Largest Unions, 1999 and 2004

7.1   Indicators of Union Well-Being, 1992–95

7.2   Union Members, 1995–2005

7.3   NLRB Representation Elections, FY 1997–2005

7.4   Industrial Distribution of Representation Elections 2005

7.5   NLRB Representation Elections, 1950–80

8.1   Union Household and White Union Member Democratic Presidential Vote, 1948–2004

8.2   Labor PAC Expenditures and Changes in Congress, 1996–2004

11.1 Average Hourly Manufacturing Wages in Selected States, 2003

11.2 Real Hourly Wages in Food Processing by Industry Sector and Region, 1982–92

ACRONYMS

ACTWU   Amalgamated Clothing and Textile Workers Union
AFGE   American Federation of Government Employees
AFA   Association of Flight Attendants
AFL   American Federation of Labor
AFL-CIO   American Federation of Labor-Congress of Industrial
   Organizations
AFSCME   American Federation of State, County, and Municipal Employees
AFT   American Federation of Teachers
AIFLD   American Institute for Free Labor Development
ALPA   Airline Pilots Association
AMFA   Aircraft Mechanics Fraternal Association
APWU   American Postal Workers Union
ATU   Amalgamated Transit Union
AUD   Association for Union Democracy
AWU   Airline Workers United
BLET   Brotherhood of Locomotive Engineers and Trainmen
BMWE   Brotherhood of Maintenance of Way Employees
BWFJ   Black Workers for Justice
CBTU   Coalition of Black Trade Unionists
CILS   Center for International Labor Solidarity, AFL-CIO
CIO   Congress of Industrial Organizations
CIW   Coalition of Immokolee Workers
CLC   Central Labor Council
CLUW   Coalition of Labor Union Women
CNA   California Nurses Association
COLA   Cost of Living Adjustment
COPE   Committee on Political Education, AFL-CIO
CSEA   Civil Service Employees Association
CSWA   Chinese Staff and Workers Association
CTV   Venezuelan Confederation of Labor

CTW   Change to Win Federation
CWA   Communications Workers of America
DC 37   District Council 37, AFSCME
DRUM   Dodge Revolutionary Union Movement
EPI   Economic Policy Institute
FDI   Foreign Direct Investment
FIRE   Finance, Insurance, and Real Estate
FLOC   Farm Labor Organizing Committee
GCIU   Graphic Communications International Union
GDP   Gross Domestic Product
GM   General Motors Corporation
GNP   Gross National Product
GPS   Global Positioning System
HERE   Hotel Employees, Restaurant Employees International Union
HMO   Health Maintenance Organization
IAM   International Association of Machinists
IBEW   International Brotherhood of Electrical Workers
IBT   International Brotherhood of Teamsters
ILGWU   International Ladies Garment Workers Union
ILA   International Longshoremen's Association
ILWU   International Longshore and Warehouse Union
IUE   International Union of Electrical Workers
LIUNA   Laborers International Union of North America
LWC   Longshore Workers Coalition
M&As   Mergers and Acquisitions
MTA   Metropolitan Transit Authority (New York State)
NAFTA   North American Free Trade Agreement
NALC   National Association of Letter Carriers
NCF   National Civic Federation
NEA   National Education Association
NED   National Endowment for Democracy
NLRB   National Labor Relations Board
NMFA   National Master Freight Agreement
NUHHCE   National Union of Hospital and Health Care Employees
NUMMI   New United Motor Manufacturing Inc.
NWA   Northwest Airlines
OCAW   Oil, Chemical and Atomic Workers International Union
OECD   Organization for Economic Cooperation and Development
OI   Organizing Institute
OPEC   Organization of Petroleum Exporting Countries
OPEIU   Office and Professional Employees International Union
OSHA   Occupational Safety and Health Act
OTOC   Omaha Together One Community

PACE   Paper, Allied-Industrial, Chemical and Energy Workers International Union

PATCO   Professional Air Traffic Controllers Organization

PEAC   Progressive Educators for Action

PMA   Pacific Maritime Association

PAC   Political Action Committee

PSC   Professional Staff Congress

RICO   Racketeer Influenced and Corrupt Organization Act

ROC   Restaurant Opportunities Center

RWDSU   Retail, Wholesale and Department Store Union

SEIU   Service Employees International Union

TDU   Teamsters for a Democratic Union

TNC   Transnational Corporation

TQM   Total Quality Management

TWU   Transport Workers Union

UAW   United Automobile Workers of America

UBC   United Brotherhood of Carpenters and Joiners of America

UE   United Electrical, Radio and Machine Workers

UFT   United Federation of Teachers

UFW   United Farm Workers of America

UFCW   United Food and Commercial Workers

UMWA   United Mine Workers of America

UNITE!   United Needletrades, Industrial and Textile Employees

UNITE-HERE   See UNITE and HERE

UPIU   United Paperworkers' International Union

UPS   United Parcel Serviced

URW   United Rubber Workers

USWA   United Steel, Paper and Forestry, Rubber, Manufacturing, Energy, Allied-Industrial and Service Workers International Union

UTU   United Transportation Union

WTO   World Trade Organization

1

A MESSAGE ABOUT THE FUTURE
FROM THE PRESENT

The 2005 split of organized labor in the United States into two federations, the old American Federation of Labor-Congress of Industrial Organizations (AFL-CIO) and the new Change to Win Federation (CTW), was a response to the long-term decline of the unions, both as a percentage of the workforce and in absolute numbers of members. Few would dispute this. Looked at from the vantage point of 2005 or later, this decline appears as a prolonged and gradual descent. Yet, when looking at the drop in membership, organizing activity, strikes, or most other measures of union activity, the decline has a definite turning point that is often ignored. That turning point was during the years 1980–81. It was then that membership began its fall in absolute numbers, that new organizing efforts dropped by half, that concessions became a major mode of collective bargaining, and that the labor movement as a whole let the air traffic controllers (PATCO) go down to defeat without lifting a finger. In the years that immediately followed, unions turned to labor–management cooperation schemes in hopes of saving jobs and to an acceleration in union mergers as a means to institutional salvation. All of the defensive reactions were in response to economic changes and increased employer aggression, but they nevertheless compounded the crisis of decline.

There was, to be sure, an earlier economic turning point with the major worldwide recession of 1974–75 that will be discussed in later chapters. It brought in train a series of changes in the US and world economies that have made labor's ability to fight more difficult. As I argued in my 1997 book, *Workers in a Lean World*, these were global trends. But labor's turning point, only a few years after the recession of 1974–75, occurred before many of the industrial, economic, and demographic developments that further disoriented organized labor had unfolded. So, while economic changes certainly provided limits to labor's response, many of the major trends often cited as among the leading causes of labor's decline only gathered force after the sudden and severe retreats of 1980–81. This strongly implies a failure of leadership and of the institutional framework and ideology on which that leadership rested.

The quarter century-old retreat that followed the turning point of the early 1980s has left a trail of declining living and working standards for union and nonunion workers alike. It has turned collective bargaining on its head—from a front for economic and social gains across a broad range of issues to a means of retreat, sometimes orderly, sometimes not. Far from taming the lion of employer aggression, it has encouraged still more demands for lower labor costs and the slumping living standards that follow. Unions as institutions, with notable exceptions here and there, have failed their members and proved unable to recruit new ones in sufficient numbers to slow down, let alone reverse, a deteriorating balance of class forces in American society that has created a capitalist class of super-rich individuals whose wealth is unprecedented in history. The cost of this is a working class that has lost ground in virtually every field of social and economic life. This, in turn, generates from time to time in one place then another acts of rebellion and resistance. It is in these acts, or rather their accumulation and eventual explosion, that the hope of union revival lies. To get some idea of what such rebellion and resistance might bring, we look at a few recent examples. Here, perhaps, are some messages about the future to be found in the voices of the present.

Within the space of a little more than a year, from early 2005 through early 2006, four events occurred, each of which spoke to the future of organized labor in the United States. The message of each was different, but they were related by the changing economic and social context in which they took place and by the social class they represented; namely, the working class. These were visible events in a time and place where work and workers are usually invisible—not the stuff of the six o'clock news or the daily tabloids. These events forced their way on to the corporate media's reluctant attention, however briefly, because each represented something that seems rare in the US these days—the specter of workers' power. Just to write or read these last two words arouses skepticism. Power in an era of American labor's decline and retreat? Power when the remains of this movement are splitting? Power from a class torn by racial and national division? Yet, as implausible as it might seem to many, each of these events reflected power both real and potential.

The four events, in order of their occurrence, were: the March 2005 victory of the Coalition of Immokolee Workers over Taco Bell and its giant corporate parent, Yum! Brands; the December New York City transit strike; the December split in the AFL-CIO; and the giant outpouring of immigrant workers in April and then on the 1 May "Day Without Immigrants." These were, to be sure, events of very different magnitudes and even of lasting impact. Yet, each tells us something about labor's recent past and each speaks, sometimes in cloudy Delphic ways, to the future. The cast of characters is crucial because it reflects the labor movement, not just the unions, from bottom to top: the poorly paid, perhaps undocumented and nonunionized immigrant farm workers in the South; the "traditional" fairly well-paid unionized blue-collar workers in New York's transit system; the squabbling and much better paid union "bosses" of the AFL-CIO and Change to Win Coalition; and the millions of immigrant workers and families demanding simply the right to live and work in the United States. Without any reference to one another, each of these groups was trying, through their actions, to leave behind a problem-ridden past and find a way to a better future. What were the distinct pasts each addressed? How did they interrelate? What did they say about the future?

The farm laborers who picked tomatoes in Immokolee, Florida had experienced just about every indignity American society can dish out. They came mostly from Mexico, Guatemala, and Haiti with different languages and distinct cultures—all different from those dominant in their new "home." Like other immigrants in other parts of the country, they had faced racism, anti-foreigner sentiment, government harassment, employer abuse, and earnings that no one would describe as a "living wage." It is not surprising that they began to organize themselves or that they called one of their first actions an "anti-slavery campaign."[1] But there was also something about these workers that made them emblematic of the way work was being organized in the US. They labored not only at the bottom of the American fast food chain, but in a chain that ran up through Taco Bell restaurants to the headquarters of their huge parent corporation, Yum! Brands. Despite its ridiculous name, Yum! Brands is big global business. In 2005 it pulled in $9.3 billion in revenues worldwide.[2] The workers, who formed the Coalition of Immokolee Workers (CIW) in 1995, looked into things and found that out. CIW staffer and farm worker Lucas Benitez said:

> . . . the power is beyond the growers. There are big corporations that are controlling the agricultural industry because they consume a majority of its products. So when we saw this new direction that the industry was going, we decided to focus on one of the major corporations that buys the products we pick.[3]

How could a few hundred farm workers in Florida beat this corporate giant? They leveraged their power, so to speak. For these workers, the "community" and the workplace are virtually one and the same. CIW staffer Julia Perkins said:

> What's important about the boycott is that it comes directly from the community and from the workers. The workers are spearheading it and leading it. Even though we have a national campaign, we don't want to lose our base in the community.[4]

With the help of a nationwide network of similar organizations called worker centers, along with church groups, students, and unions, they launched a national boycott similar to those used in the past by the United Farm Workers and the Farm Labor Organizing Committee. They picked Taco Bell as their target and in April 2001, after Taco Bell refused to respond to their demands, they began the boycott. Boycotts are notoriously hard to organize and sustain. And while it got support all around the country, it was the persistence of the Immokolee workers that sustained it and spread it with "truth tours" across the country all the way to Taco Bell headquarters in Irvine, California. In March 2006, they won everything they asked for (see chapter 10). So, what the Immokolee workers are saying to "big labor" is that you need a strong base where you work and live, particularly when those things overlap. Building on that, you also need solidarity, the concrete aid of others, not just resolutions, but actions that inflict damage on capital that values cheap labor and will fight to keep it. Victory also brings self-confidence and now the Immokolee workers plan to take on McDonalds![5]

New York City transit workers are in a different situation. There are 35,000 of them in one city and when they strike their impact is big and swift. In short, their union, Transport Workers Union Local 100, has a lot of power. But, for a quarter of a century, the leaders of Local 100 chose not to use it. Of course, it is illegal for them, as public employees, to strike and the consequences are severe. So, the last strike was in 1980. That, too, had consequences. When, at my request, a well-known member of Local 100 addressed a class of apprentice electricians just days before the new strike, he began by saying (more or less), "I am of a generation of trade unionists that has known only retreat." He meant that his union, like so many others, had made concessions to management over the years and that conditions on the job had gone from bad to worse. He was not explaining passivity, but why the members would mostly strike given half a chance. For many, the time had come to draw the line, to use the power they knew they had. After years of indignity and insults they demanded their leaders fight back. The point that most infuriated them was management's insistence on a two-tier pension plan, one that would stiff the next generation of transit workers. To this final insult they said no, even if it was not clear they could win. They knew, too, that other city workers were getting lousy contracts and that their actions just might change things for others and hence for all down the line. Here, it was those in the stronger position whose actions could aid those with less leverage, the next generation as well as other city workers—this was the other end of the solidarity chain from the Immokolee workers.

The "big" labor movement event in 2005, of course, was the split in the AFL-CIO. This had been long in the making and I will tell that story in chapter 9. The issue was organizing the unorganized, itself a question of future power. If unions failed to change their ways and organize by the hundreds of thousands, the dissidents argued, organized labor would disappear as a force in American life. The challengers had a point. Unions had shrunk to 12.5% of the workforce in 2005, only 7.8% in the private sector and there were few signs of improvement. The leaders of the Change to Win Coalition demanded that the federation should rebate as much as 50% of per capita dues the affiliated unions paid to it for unions that took organizing seriously. No agreement could be reached and the split, already almost a fact, became formal. Within weeks, the Change to Win Federation was organized. While the issue was clearly labor's power *vis ^ vis* corporate America and in the political arena, here the future was murkier. Could the Change to Win unions deliver on their promise? What kind of unions would result if they did? What would the remaining AFL-CIO unions do, particularly those that did have an ambitious organizing program? And, always in the thoughts of the historically minded: was this another CIO like the 1930s—a prelude to massive organizing? Whether it was or not, it was clear that a challenge had been issued that could not be ignored. Organized labor must grow or die.

Then, in April and May 2006, the immigrant workers who were sometimes the object of unionization and sometimes, like the Immokolee workers, self-organized, spoke. Perhaps five million or more participated in the outpouring of 1 May—the "Day Without Immigrants." Meatpacking plants in North Carolina went silent. The huge port of Los Angeles/Long Beach ground to a halt as 80–90% of truck traffic stopped due to the work stoppage of most of the port's 12,000 immigrant "troqueros."[6] Countless smaller workplaces closed down for the day all across the country. The immigrants and their supporters were demonstrating and striking against a bill in Congress that would severely limit their rights to live and work in the US. But, it was a show of economic and social power as well as of outrage and political resolve. It was a message not only to Congress and politicians, but to the unions. Here was a huge section of the workforce that, while at the bottom of the economic totem poll, had considerable power. Not only did much of the economic growth in services rest on the shoulders of these immigrant workers, but so did the production of huge factories and the movement of goods through major ports. There was more potential power here than many had reckoned with.

The most basic message is not about adding up these events and actions along with others like them in the hope that such a calculation will give us a sum greater than the parts; that is, a new social movement with the power needed to bring real change. This kind of social math is common among progressives today. We will return to this approach, but first I want to examine the deeper message of our four examples. What these stories share is both what drives the actors in them to fight, organize, and split and what seems to pose the greatest barriers to just those actions. The barriers are all too clear. Globalization destroys or moves jobs and with them union leverage. The far-reaching reorganization of the workforce and of work itself that is one consequence of globalization, deregulation, etc. disorients unions and their members. Enhanced corporate size and power make the extraction of concessions easier and resistance more difficult. All of these, it is said, make organizing harder throughout much of the economy. Corporate money thwarts political efforts to level the playing field or alleviate misery. Competition for jobs, housing, and education enhances racism, which divides and re-divides us. Massive immigration is caught in that long-standing divide and is in no way the cause of it. Corporate America exploits this in both brutal and subtle ways. The barriers are substantial.

The very barriers thrown up by capital and its world-wide reorganization of production and work, however, are the consequence of the same forces that propel these different groups of workers to fight in the first place, that make labor leaders seek new ways to organize, and that lead many groups of workers to find new ways to fight and find allies. For three decades capital has faced problems with profitability that have led it to seek cheap labor at home and abroad; to reorganize and intensify work; to merge, downsize, and outsource; to pressure governments to deregulate, open their treasuries to business, and repress labor. In all these cases, it is the workers and the working class that have paid—in wages, health, taxes, uprooted lives, unaffordable housing, dumbed-down education, and more. On the other hand, it is the same employer–employee relationship intensified and brutalized and its extension into other spheres of life that compel resistance now in one place, then in another. As we will see, the living and working conditions of the working class and virtually all its various sections have worsened. It is the era of lean production, extended subcontracting, brutal work intensification, falling real wages, and concessionary demands. These are both barriers to and causes of struggle. It is capital's drive to save itself that forces more and more groups of working-class people at work and in their communities to resist in new and old ways.

What our four examples also show is that the search for more effective forms of resistance, whether old or new, has joined the recurrent fact of resistance. While no predictions of immediate or near-term upheavals will be made here, it is worth noting that most periods of working-class or social upsurge involve not simply more of the same, but new types and forms of struggle and/or organization. When these types of organizations are appropriate to the era, as the industrial unions were in the 1930s or the wildcat strikes and rank-and-file caucuses were in the 1960s and 1970s, the compulsion of capital's relentless pressure on work and livelihood is joined by the hope and belief that an effective way has been found to alter the balance of social/political power and force concessions on capital. These "new" forms of organization don't have to be new in history. What matters is that such new types of organization as worker centers, non-majority unions, union reform and democracy movements, worker-based organizing drives, and deeply rooted workplace organizations are important, not because they have never happened before, but because they are "new" to this era, in that they have been too long abandoned or simply not tried until recently. What is ultimately important about new forms of organization is precisely their ability to disrupt at crucial times. Pressure is never enough to change the balance of forces. If we have learned anything from the 1930s and the 1960s, it is that movements must make "business as usual" untenable at key times and places. Organizations that simply become institutionalized and bureaucratized, as have our unions, often lose this ability. New types of organization may have that potential.[7]

One fairly common view of how the labor movement will turn things around was mentioned above as being a sort of social math: the adding of various social movements (old or new), organizations, and campaigns to a (one hopes) growing version of the existing trade unions. This view is a kind of coalitionism writ large. Naturally, coalitions and hopefully a convergence of the various working class-based social movements and organizations are desirable and important. It is hard to imagine much in the way of improved and expanded union organizing efforts without steps in that direction. But a real convergence of movements, each of which after all has its own agenda and goals, is not likely on a massive scale without something bigger to compel such a convergence. We can look back on the 1960s at the opportunity for a full-scale alliance between organized labor and the civil rights movement. We can even see moments and events that seemed pregnant with this possibility. But it didn't happen in more than rhetoric. We can name many factors that prevented it, one of which was the retreat of the labor leadership in the face of the militancy of their own members, but what was missing were the underlying conditions for a general upsurge like the 1930s when the unemployed joined the employed and neighborhoods and other unions often provided a logistical support for workplace action. To put this another way, it is not convergence that brings upsurge, but upsurge that makes convergence possible. And an upsurge of the magnitude necessary to change the balance of class forces in the US today will be rooted in capitalism's most fundamental relationship, that between labor and capital in the heart of production.

What then are the forces that have pushed organized labor into years of retreat that have now led to a split among the unions over how to organize? What has pushed New York City transit workers and many others like them into risky strikes they were not certain to win in any clear way? What, indeed, has compelled so many to find ways to resist even when a traditional strike didn't seem feasible? What is it that made the most vulnerable workers assert themselves in hundreds of local fights like that in Immokolee and then to emerge as a national force? Is each simply explained by local and specific causes or are there bigger forces at work and if so, what are they? The rest of this book will try to answer these and other related questions. It will look at the underlying forces and at the various responses to them. While its focus is on the United States, its underlying assumption is that global capitalism has pushed so hard for so long to save its profit margins amidst an uncontrolled world of cut-throat competition it created itself, that it necessarily compels resistance and struggle in one place after another.

Since much of the recent debate on the future of organized labor has focused on organizing, this book will conclude with some thoughts on that as well as some other key issues that will affect the future. Just as the decline of unions had a definite turning point, so union revival is certain to come as a result of a social upheaval. Upsurges, however, cannot be predicted or manufactured. But neither can today's activists, leaders, and organizations sit and wait for such a development. What is done today may well shape tomorrow's possibilities. If our organizations settle for bureaucracy over democracy, for servicing over mobilization, will they be ready for bigger things? If our leaders embrace partnership with capital over conflict, will the potential that still exists in most unions be squandered? If the workplace is surrendered to the employer in the hopes of hanging on, what source of enduring power will the movement have? If the unions turn their backs on 21 million foreign-born workers can they really hope to organize the unorganized? And what about labor's historic Achilles' heel: the South?

To answer these and other questions confronting labor and the US working class, we turn to the sweeping changes in the US economy and society that have so disoriented unions and workers. It is hoped that, by the end, a clearer picture of what has brought the labor movement to where it is, what people are saying and arguing about that and what can be done about it, and just where the movement might focus, will emerge. In broad brushstrokes, the picture that will emerge is that an epic change in the US and world economies that began in the 1970s has fundamentally altered and worsened working-class life in America. The causes and results of this change are not always the ones most frequently cited by mainstream or even pro-labor sources. This change has affected not only collective bargaining and union density, but the nation's politics as well. In this maelstrom of change, organized labor has taken false paths to security and failed to mount effective resistance or new organization. An attempt to reform the unions from above failed, leading to the 2005 split. Resistance, however, is persistent and has taken both old and new forms. Here lies the hope and potential of the future of the working class in the United States.

The analysis and argument of this book falls into three main parts. In chapters 2 through 5, the enormous changes that have occurred in the past thirty or more years will be examined critically. They include the sweeping economic, social, geographic, and demographic shifts that have altered working life dramatically and disoriented organized labor. Many of these trends are associated with "globalization," but they include changes in domestic industrial location and the reversal of working-class living standards that has occurred in the US since the mid-1970s. The second part, chapters 6, 7, and 8, deals with organized labor's responses to these changes and the crisis they have brought to the unions. Here is the retreat into concessions, partnerships, and mergers following the long period of militancy from the mid-1960s through the late 1970s. This was a retreat not only from confrontation, but from new organizing—a retreat that laid the basis for labor's seemingly unstoppable decline. In this part, we will examine the attempts to reverse this decline by top-down reform and the hope for salvation from above through labor's traditional political strategy of dependence on the Democratic Party. Finally, we will examine the 2005 split in the labor movement; the limits and potential of that top-down split; and the grassroots alternatives that point to roads not taken in the quest for union renewal. The voices from the near present outlined above present samples and hints of these alternatives. They and the many other examples and proposals in the final two chapters are the hope upon which the growth of labor's numbers and power can be built.

2

THE GREAT TRANSFORMATION

In the thirty years from the mid-1970s to the mid-2000s, the world of the worker in the United States was turned upside down. The industrial centerpieces of the US economy shrank or reorganized and the cities, towns, and unions based on them went into decline and/or dramatic changes in make-up. The industrial "heartland" became the rust belt. The "industries" that appeared to replace them were low-wage and mostly nonunion. Technology, "deployed with ferocity" in a more competitive world, as one economist put it, eliminated some jobs and intensified others.[1] The loss of union density turned into an absolute loss of union members. The institution of collective bargaining was turned from a phalanx of advance to a line of retreat. The upward trend in real wages of the previous thirty years reversed into a prolonged downward spiral. The decline in economic inequality that began during World War 2 stopped and inequality accelerated with each decade. The New Deal liberal consensus that had dominated politics for over three decades was drowned in a sea of money and replaced by an aggressive neoliberalism that called itself conservative. The underpinnings of American labor ideology were invalidated, though union leaders clung tenaciously to the old tenets. Greed became good. Business values took center field. What had been national became global. Globalization, in turn, became the reason or excuse for every move against the working-class majority.[2] Whether one lived through the whole period or was born or migrated into it, the new world of work that emerged was not only unfriendly to working people but had become one in which polarities had switched and the compass failed.

Economists Bennett Harrison and Barry Bluestone entitled their investigation of the early stages of this transformation *The Great U-Turn*. Writing in the late 1980s, they saw the common denominator behind the new trends that were reversing the economic conditions of the majority as a concerted business effort at "zapping labor." Among the many new devises they listed for "zapping labor" were contract concessions or give-backs, two-tier wage schemes, the growth of part-time and contingent work, and "union avoidance."[3] Today, this list is not just familiar and by now part of the routine of "collective bargaining," but incomplete. At the least we would have to add two-three-many-tiered pension plans as well as pension erosion or cancellation; all manner of cost shifting of health benefits costs and/or the avoidance of such benefits; alternative work schedules scarcely dreamed of in the 1980s; longer hours; a plethora of employee participation programs associated with lean production; and lean production without employee participation. In this era business practices that had been simply aspects of production, notably outsourcing or work relocation, became weapons in bargaining and union-busting. Others, like turning workers into independent contractors and, hence, expelling them from the realm of labor law protection, became widespread. Indeed, labor law was turned into its opposite. Traditional union structures and strategies were rendered ineffective. New ones, even when tried, didn't work much better; for example, mergers didn't add muscle, corporate campaigns couldn't save lost strikes, and jointness or partnership programs didn't make employers considerate, much less generous. If everything seemed to be in flux and confusion about the future was almost universal, one thing remained constant—employer aggression. Not just aggression in bargaining, but in everything to do with work and the way the production of goods and services was organized and business conducted. Aggression in politics and legislation. Aggression in world affairs. What, then, was at the root of all this change and all this aggression?

Profitability and the Crisis of the 1970s

The "Great U-Turn" began in the mid-1970s when the economies of world capitalism ground to a halt in the 1974–75 recession. The twenty-four richest countries saw their growth rates go from 5% in 1973 to zero in 1975. Europe's industrial economies dropped from 6% growth to minus one percent. In the US, the gross domestic product dropped by one percent from 1973 through 1975, while industrial production fell by 10%.[4] It was the worst economic slump since the Great Depression of the 1930s and would open the door to all the changes mentioned above. But what had brought it on? Signs of economic trouble had been everywhere. Inflation was on the rise. Productivity was slumping. The international monetary system was out of whack. In 1971 Nixon had disconnected the dollar from gold. In early 1973, the system of currencies pegged to the dollar was abandoned altogether. Later that year, OPEC quadrupled the price of crude oil.[5] Couldn't all of these factors explain what had gone wrong with the undeniable economic expansion of the thirty preceding years? At the time, the "external shock" of oil prices was popular as an explanation, but the impact of price increases came too late to explain the fall in production. In any case, the earlier recession of 1971 indicated something deeper. Inflation was often a sign of an overheated economy headed for recession, but seldom thought to be a cause of slump. Productivity did drop in 1974, but this was a result of recession, not a cause.[6] Clearly, there was something deeper that underlay the economic turnaround.

The something that underlay the recession of the mid-1970s and many other problems was systemic: a long-term decline in the rate of profit. This recurring glitch in the accumulation of capital flows not from high wages or low productivity growth, as many economists argued at the time. Although these factors can have an impact, the deeper problem of falling returns on capital flows from the nature of capitalist competition itself. The actual figures for the period leading up to the 1974–75 recession illustrate the problem. Put simply, it is that the accumulation of capital deployed in the context of intensified competition tends to outrun the surplus created by productive labor. So, as Table 2.1 shows, using figures developed by economists Anwar

Table 2.1   **Average Rate of Profit, 1950–73**

	1950	1959	1960	1964	1969	1973
Surplus (S)	165.3	278.4	286.5	364.5	523.8	719.8
Fixed Capital (K)	438.7	738.0	755.7	872.3	1320.9	1940.3
Rate of Profit = S/K	.38	.38	.38	.42	.40	.37
Average S/K 1950s			.38			
Average S/K 1960–64				.40		
Average S/K 1964–68					.42	
Average S/K 1969–73						.38

Source: Shaikh and Tonak, *Measuring the Wealth of Nations: The Political Economy of National Accounts*, 1994.

Shaikh and Ahmet Tonak, from 1950 through 1959 the surplus (S) from which profits are drawn grew at an average annual growth rate of 7.3%, while fixed nonresidential capital (K) grew by almost the same rate, 7.2%. Hence the profit rate, the ratio of S to K (S/K), remained more or less stable at 38%. From 1960 through 1964, however, S grew by 7.3% a year, while K grew by only 3.8% per year, resulting in higher profit rates, averaging 40% for those years.[7] But then things changed.

From 1950 through the mid-1960s the course of profit rates, with some fluctuations, had been upward from about 38% a year to 42%, an increase of over 10%. After the mid-1960s, however, the annual profit rate (S/K) dropped to 37% in 1973, just before the onset of recession. The average for the years 1969 through 1973 was 38%. In these years, the surplus had actually grown faster than before, averaging 10.8% a year. But the value of fixed capital grew even faster at 13.6% a year. This was due to a high annual average growth rate of 9% in new fixed capital from 1960 through 1973. All during this period, S, K and real wages rose. To put it another way, it was not labor costs that caused the decline in profit rates or even a slump in productivity, which generally rose, but a shift in the value composition of capital toward fixed capital. Hence the ratio S/K, the profit rate, fell.[8] This is not just a matter of arithmetic. Something had happened that caused US industry to maintain a high rate of investment in fixed capital. That something was the growth of competition, particularly of international competition for the first time since World War 2.

The 1960s saw an acceleration of international trade. From 1960 through 1973, exports from the developed nations (the OECD countries) grew by over 9% a year and most of these went to other wealthy countries. US imports of goods increased by just under 7% a year during the 1950s, but during the 1960s they grew by almost 15% a year.[9] As a percentage of the Gross National Product originating in manufacturing, imports rose from 10.8% in 1959 to 13.9% in 1969 and then to 37.8% in 1979.[10] While, after World War 2, German and Japanese firms were building for export production, US firms continued their old strategy of building abroad inside foreign markets. This meant very little export capacity, on the one hand, and the rise of imports, on the other. Not surprisingly, the decline in profitability hit manufacturing the hardest. According to Robert Brenner, using somewhat different calculations than Shaikh and Tonak, profit rates in manufacturing fell by 43.5% from 1965 to 1973, compared with about 30% for non-manufacturing.[11] The imports hit some of the country's major and most capital intensive manufacturing industries especially hard. For example, imported cars, first from Germany and later Japan, reached 9% of the US market by 1967 and jumped to

16% during the oil embargo of the mid-1970s. This was, of course, an acceleration of what would become known as globalization and of the central role of the US economy in that process.

The effect of the competition which flowed from this acceleration was precisely to increase the use of technology and hence of fixed investment. This competition was not only with foreign car makers, but between US companies as well. Looking at two of the major industries of that era, one study carried out in the late 1970s concluded that innovations in the production process were more important in competitive strategy than product innovation. Speaking of major appliance and auto companies in the 1960s, William Abernathy wrote:

> This changing mode of competition has had a pronounced effect on the development of the industry. As costs and productivity have become more important, the rate of major product innovation has decreased, and process innovation has increased in competitive importance.[12]

Capitalist competition is all about the growth and expansion of capital—its accumulation. While, as we will see later, there are a number of ways to do this, the major means to expansion is investment in fixed capital. Competition, in fact, grows out of accumulation itself since, under most circumstances, a firm cannot expand without increasing market share (or finding new markets) and, hence, undercutting other firms.[13] So, the dynamics of accumulation intensify competition, which, in turn, compels further investment. Under conditions of growing competition this can mean a defense of one's market share and profits by the same means. This is what happened in the US in the 1960s and 1970s. During the 1980s, even though there was some recovery in the second half, the average profit rate was only 32.5%.[14] Clearly, something besides more of the same was needed. Thus, in the decades that followed the recession of 1974–75, American capital turned to alternative means of recovering profitability and improving competitiveness.

Globalization: Where Did the Jobs Go?

There is no doubt that the worldwide economic crisis of the mid-1970s sparked the acceleration of global economic integration. I have argued this before in *Workers in a Lean World* and won't repeat the entire argument here.[15] But a few figures will illustrate this acceleration. As Table 2.2 shows, virtually every indicator of international economic integration grew faster than world GDP from the early 1980s to the early 2000s. While trade grew faster than the world economy as a

Table 2.2   Indicators of Global Economic Integration

(Worldwide in $ billions)

	1982	1990	2005	(+)
GDP	10,899	21,898	44,674	(309%)
Exports*	2,247	4,261	12,641	(463%)
FDI Outflows	28	230	779	(2,682%)
Outward Stock**	600	1,791	10,672	(1,679%)
TNCs	37,000	60,000	77,000	(108%)
TNC Foreign Affiliates	170,000	500,000	770,000	(353%)
Assets of Foreign Affiliates	2,100	6,000	45,600	(2,071%)
Cross-border M&As	n/a	151	716	(374% 1990, –2005)

* Exports of goods and non-factor services
** Accumulated FDI
Source: UNCTAD, World Investment Report, United Nations, 1993, 1995, 2004.

whole, the most striking characteristic of globalization since the 1970s is rapid growth of foreign direct investment (FDI); that is, investment abroad in building or buying facilities as opposed to "portfolio" investment in stocks or bonds without an intention to own, control, or produce anything. The growth in FDI occurred in phases. From 1960 through 1973 the accumulated stock of FDI doubled. But from 1973 through 1993 it grew tenfold. We have already noted that one characteristic of the economic strategy of most US manufacturing companies in the immediate post-WW2 period was to build and produce inside foreign markets rather than exporting goods as did Japan and Germany. Today, everyone does both. Consequently, not only has the number of TNCs grown, but more importantly, so have the number of overseas affiliates and sales in foreign markets, both at more than twice the rate of growth of the world economy.[16] Hence, huge corporations operating in many countries. Until the late 1980s most of this growth in worldwide FDI was in manufacturing, the site of the fastest falling profit rates in the US in the prior period.[17] Did this lead to the loss of some 4 million US manufacturing jobs since 1980?

There is no doubt that both "free trade" and the growth in overseas investment eliminated jobs in US manufacturing. The North American Free Trade Agreement, the World Trade Organization, and the many other "liberalization" agreements have made the flow of capital around the world easier. Given this, there is no reason to doubt that US capital sought low-cost production sites abroad wherever feasible. The Economic Policy Institute estimates that NAFTA alone was responsible for a net loss of 879,280 US jobs, mostly in manufacturing, from 1993 through 2002.[18] The evidence in auto is clear to anyone who has visited the "maquiladora" towns along the US–Mexican border, where big parts plants bear names like General Motors, Ford, United Technologies, Lear, etc. An IUE local at one General Electric plant in Massachusetts told *Labor Notes*, "We've lost one-third of our jobs to NAFTA."[19] And the instances could go on. As I spelled out in *Workers in a Lean World*, international production chains cross borders and tend to be clustered in one of the three "Triad" zones: North America; Japan and East Asia; Western and Eastern Europe. These three regions alone accounted for 60–70 per cent of all inward FDI in 2005.[20] Specific work is exported, particularly within these regions, in the search of higher profits and its disruptive effects on the lives of the displaced workers, their communities, and unions are enormous. But the question remains as to whether or not the export of capital from the US has been proportionately big enough to explain the huge net loss of manufacturing jobs in the US that has occurred in the last twenty years. If not, what is the most likely cause or set of causes?

The outflow of US capital, measured by outgoing FDI, rose very little in the 1960s. Its ascent began in the 1970s. As Table 2.3 shows, after the 1980–81 recession US FDI would rise interrupted only by recessions and the 1987 stock market slump. From 1984 through 2004, outgoing FDI grew by over 17 times, compared with 3 times for the US GDP. Even when adjusted for inflation, FDI outgrew GDP over 12 to 1 times. But after the late 1980s, much of this growth went to the facilities for financial and professional services sold abroad. Manufacturing FDI grew by 6 times from 1984 through 2004, or over 4 times in real terms. The portion of total FDI that went to manufacturing shrank from decade to decade as services became more important.[21]

Economists at the Economic Policy Institute argue that "the very large increases in direct investment (i.e., plant and equipment) flows to other countries have meant reduced investment in the domestic manufacturing base . . ."[22] This was no doubt the case, but their impact on total employment is less clear. First is that one of the main reasons for investing abroad is the fall in domestic profit rates. In manufacturing, according to Robert Brenner's calculations, profit rates went flat and then fell in the second half of the 1990s and, as we would predict, manufacturing FDI rose.[23] Again manufacturing FDI rose during the stagnant years of the early to mid-2000s. Profit rates are the regulator

Table 2.3   US Foreign Direct Investment Outflow: Total and Manufacturing as a Percentage of Total

(FDI in $ millions)

Year	Total FDI	Manufacturing FDI	M/T%
2004	229,294	54,202	22.3
2003	119,406	27,825	23.3
2002	134,946	32,277	23.9
2001	124,873	25,871	20.7
2000	142,627	43,002	30.2
1999	209,392	39,672	18.9
1998	131,004	23,122	17.7
1997	95,769	28,326	29.6
1996	84,426	24,325	28.8
1995	92,074	44,472	48.3
1994	73,252	23,989	32.8
1993	77,247	18,522	24.0
1992	42,647	16,868	39.6
1991	32,696	12,914	39.5
1990	30,982	16,532	53.4
1989	37,604	17,201	45.7
1988	18,599	8,928	48.0
1987	30,154	13,204	43.8
1986	19,641	6,234	31.7
1985	13,388	6,283	46.9
1984	13,045	7,488	57.4
1983	9,525	3,390	35.6

Source: Bureau of Economic Research, *U.S. Direct Investment Abroad: Balance of Payments and Direct Investment Position Data*, www.bea.gov; Bureau of Economic Research, *National Data, A. Selected NIPA Tables*, www.bea.gov; Council of Economic Advisors, *Economic Report of the President 2005*, Washington DC, US Government Printing Office, 2005, p. 220.

of investment and there is no reason to believe these funds would have been invested in US manufacturing capacity given slumping profit rates and other more profitable opportunities inside as well as outside the country. That is the nature of capitalist accumulation and competition.

One problem in measuring any actual shifts of work performed in the US abroad, that is, "offshoring" in the narrowest sense, like that from the GE plant mentioned above, is that the government doesn't track them. The Bureau of Labor Statistics "reported" some 4,633 private sector jobs leaving the US from January through March 2004, but this was absurdly low. Most of the recent estimates focus on IT and call center work and are done by financial or other business consulting firms such as Forester Research, Deloitte Research, or Global Insight. Their estimates range from a few hundred thousand IT jobs lost over a few years to millions of service jobs over a decade.[24] The most helpful study of offshoring is the Cornell/UMass study done by Kate Bronfenbrenner and Stephanie Luce in 2004. Based on media coverage of actual work relocations from US facilities to ones abroad during the first quarter of 2004, it estimates that 406,000 jobs were moved abroad for that entire year. This is only 0.03% of the employed workforce of 2004, but 2.8% of manufacturing jobs. Furthermore, this was up from 204,000, found in a similar study conducted by Brofenbrenner and Luce in 2001. This is a big jump over three years. Additionally, the lost work would have a "ripple effect" on suppliers. From 2001 to 2004, however, there was somewhat of a shift away from manufacturing to IT and financial service jobs. In 2001 almost all of the lost jobs counted in the sample period were manufacturing jobs, while in 2004 17% were service or IT jobs, particularly those going to India and China.[25] Even at that, if the rate of "offshoring" continued to double every few years, it would have a major impact on manufacturing jobs. At the same time, however, these figures tend to show that the actual replacement of existing US jobs in manufacturing by ones overseas cannot explain the extent of lost jobs in manufacturing from the early 1980s through 2004. Up to that point, "offshoring" was simply too small to account for so many lost jobs. It did, however, impact union jobs disproportionately. With private sector union density just below 8% and that for manufacturing at 12.9% in 2004, 39% of the jobs lost during the first quarter of 2004 to "offshoring" were union jobs according to Bronfenbrenner and Luce.[26] While the total loss may have been relatively small, its disorienting impact on union workers was significant.

Also, from 1980 through 2004 real manufacturing output in the US doubled. It might well have grown even faster *if* US producers had not invested abroad, but the growth itself makes implausible the idea

Table 2.4   Foreign Direct Investment in Manufacturing: Outflows and Inflows, 1984–2004

($ millions)

Years	FDI Outflow	FDI Inflow	Difference
2001–04	$140,175	$111,044	-$29,131
1992–00	$262,298	$414,009	$151,711
1990–91	$29,446	$24,340	-$5,106
1984–89	$39,338	$122,931	$63,593

Source: Bureau of Economic Analysis, *U.S. Direct Investment Abroad: Capital Outflows; Foreign Direct Investment in the U.S.: Capital Flows, 1984–2004*, www.bea.gov.

that overseas investment underlies the actual drop in the number of US production workers by about 4 million over those years. In fact, for most of the last twenty years, except in periods of recession, the flow of foreign investment *into* manufacturing in the US has outrun the outflow, as Table 2.4 shows. Only during the recessionary or slow growth periods of 2001–04 and 1990–91 did the outflow of FDI in manufacturing exceed the inflow. Over the entire twenty years, the flow of investment into US manufacturing outstripped outward-bound capital by 43%. An indicator of the impact of the inflow of FDI into US manufacturing was that the percentage of value added in US industry by foreign companies grew steadily, except in recessionary years, from 3.8% in 1988 to 5.9% in 2000. The employment effect was reported to have grown from 3.1 million employees to 5.7 million, a gain of 2.5 million jobs. About one third of these were in manufacturing, meaning an increase of about one million manufacturing jobs. Eighteen-point-four percent of these jobs were union, compared with 15.4% in US-owned companies. Thirty percent of all these jobs were located in the South.[27] This incoming FDI has an important implication in altering what David Harvey calls the "space economy," i.e., the geographic distribution of production and labor that has left communities destroyed and so disoriented unions and working people, but it runs counter to the argument that FDI, as such, accounts for the millions of lost jobs.[28] Since net inflow of manufacturing FDI exceeded outflow, there must have been a net increase in employment. Another possible explanation for lost manufacturing jobs might be found in the volume of imports that globalization has brought.

The growth of world trade in recent years is largely a function of the growth of FDI and TNCs. Trade is statistically reported as that between nations, but most of it is actually between or within companies. About 35% of US imports and exports, are intra-firm; i.e., within the

Table 2.5   US International Trade: Exports and Imports of Goods, 1984–2004
($ billions)

Year	Exports	Imports	Balance	E/I %
2004	$807.5	$1,472.9	$665.4	55
2003	$713.1	$1,260.7	$547.6	57
2002	$681.6	$1,164.7	$483.1	58
2001	$718.7	$1,145.9	$427.2	63
2000	$772.0	$1,224.4	$452.4	63
1999	$684.0	$1,030.0	$346.0	66
1998	$670.4	$917.1	$246.7	73
1997	$678.4	$876.5	$198.1	77
1996	$612.1	$803.1	$191.0	76
1995	$575.2	$749.4	$174.2	77
1994	$502.9	$668.7	$165.8	75
1993	$456.9	$589.4	$132.5	78
1992	$439.6	$536.5	$96.9	82
1991	$414.1	$491.0	$76.9	84
1990	$387.4	$498.4	$111.0	78
1989	$359.9	$477.7	$117.8	75
1988	$320.2	$447.2	$127.0	72
1987	$250.2	$409.8	$159.6	61
1986	$223.3	$368.4	$145.1	60
1985	$215.9	$338.1	$122.2	64
1984	$219.9	$332.4	$112.5	66

Source: US Census Bureau, Bureau of Economic Analysis, News, CB05-82, BEA05-26, June 10, 2005, www.bea.gov; Council of Economic Advisors, Economic Report of the President 2005, Washington DC, US Government Printing Office, 2005.

same company.[29] Some of this is the result of international outsourcing or "offshoring." Whatever the specific route or origin of trade, there is no doubt that imports have exceeded exports since the mid-1970s. By the 1980s the trade deficit was dire and by the 1990s even worse as the ratio of exports to imports shrank and the balance grew more and more negative, as Table 2.5 shows. While the US generally held its own in food, capital goods, and industrial materials and supplies, it lost significantly in consumer goods. Textiles, apparel, and electronic goods lost out heavily among consumer goods. And, of course, these industries saw significant employment declines over the years. Indeed, textiles and apparel alone lost over half a million jobs between 1997 and 2002 *before* the Multi-fiber Agreement that protected them expired on January 1, 2005.[30] From 1990 through April 2005, 2.9 million manufacturing jobs were lost. Sixty percent of those were in nondurable production and 54% of that (942,600) was in textiles and apparel alone. Chemicals lost another half million jobs and primary metals over 200,000. In other words, the loss of jobs on a large scale that is linked to imports was somewhat concentrated in a few industries. Others, like transportation equipment, including auto, experienced major geographic and structural reorganizations within the country as a result of competition, outsourcing, and the decision of former rivals Germany and Japan to build and operate in the US, but not, at least until the big layoff announcements of 2006, dramatic net job losses.[31]

No discussion of the impact of trade can avoid the rising presence of China. China appears to be for the twenty-first century what most people thought Japan would be in the late twentieth. Between 1996 and 2003 imports from China, measured in value, grew by 73% in real terms, while total imports actually dropped in real value by 8%. As a proportion of imports they nearly doubled, rising from 6.5% to 12.1%.[32] Chinese imports far outstripped US exports to China, which remain negligible despite the promises of the Clinton Administration when China was admitted to the WTO. According to calculations used by the Economic Policy Institute, the average annual value in real terms of Chinese imports rose from $6.4 billion from 1989–97 to $10 billion in 1997–2001, and then to $25 billion a year in 2001–03. From these figures, they extrapolate that "job displacement soared to 234,000 per year" as a result of imports from China.[33] That would be about 12% of the net job losses in those years, almost all of which are accounted for by manufacturing jobs. The EPI's projection of the total net loss of "job opportunities" due to imports from China from 1997 through 2003 is 677,000 jobs. This would account for 23% of all jobs that actually disappeared during those years, again almost all from manufacturing. Given that China's proportion of total imports was between 6.5% and 12% during those years, this seems highly implausible. An additional reason to believe that Chinese imports are not at the root of job-loss is that, as one study put it, "a large share of US imports from China is actually imports that used to come from other countries—instead of being produced in the United States." Most of these former importers were also Pacific Rim nations.[34]

The problem here is that the EPI estimates are not actual counts of lost jobs based on clear causation, but a projection of the possible effects of imports on the loss of "job opportunities." That is, jobs that might have been if there had been no imports *and* US firms had been dedicated to a higher level of domestic production in those industries affected.[35] While this may help us understand the potentially negative effects of this aspect of globalization as well as the rise of China as an industrial power, it doesn't actually resolve the problem of why so many jobs disappeared. Here we repeat that decisions by capital to build, maintain, or expand productive capacity in one or another place or industry are based on estimates of profitability and the state of the competition. Profit rates in manufacturing took a nosedive after 1997 and were adversely affected by the recession that began in 2000, making it unlikely that US manufacturing firms would invest domestically. Even when Chinese imports reached 12% of total imports in 2003 their value was the equivalent of only about 3% of total manufacturing sales in the US, including all imports ($152.4 billion/$4,824.2 billion = 3.2%).[36] In a broader sense, total imports or imports in specific industries do affect profits by restraining prices as the fight for market share becomes more intense. This would, in turn, impact profit rates, particularly if US firms fought back by investing in newer technology. But the impact on employment is indirect and it may well be that the actual loss of jobs in manufacturing is more the result of the competitive strategies adopted by employers than of the imports themselves. If this is the case, there are strong implications for labor's response.

Capital, Technology, and Labor Costs in the Great Transformation

One of the characteristics of the crisis that began in the 1970s was "stagflation," a period of slower growth, dragging productivity rates, and higher inflation. Since inflation is supposed to be associated with rapid growth, there was much speculation about the reasons for this. The most frequent culprit was productivity. How to get the same number or even fewer workers to produce more? While employers would turn to many strategies to wring this increased productivity from their workers, such as lean production, the most basic way to increase output per hour has always been to apply machinery and improved technology. This involves increased capital investment. This was the age-old way to deal with the competition, domestic or foreign. The "stagflation" of the 1980s actually made this impractical as prices and interest rates remained high, although there was considerable investment in computers as their prices fell. The 1990–91 recession tamed the inflation and interest rates. So, in the 1990s, business in general, including manufacturing, turned to the cornucopia

Table 2.6   **Real Private Nonresidential Fixed Investment, 1991–2004**

(billions of chained $2000)

Year	Total	Structures	Equipment	E/T %
2004	$1,225.6	$239.7	$996.6	81.3
2003	$1,110.8	$237.4	$879.2	79.2
2002	$1,075.6	$251.6	$826.5	76.8
2001	$1,180.5	$306.1	$874.2	74.1
2000	$1,232.1	$313.2	$918.9	74.6
1999	$1,133.3	$293.2	$840.2	74.0
1998	$1,037.8	$294.5	$745.6	71.8
1997	$934.2	$280.1	$658.3	70.5
1996	$833.6	$261.1	$578.7	69.4
1995	$762.5	$247.1	$523.1	68.6
1994	$689.9	$232.3	$467.2	76.7
1993	$631.9	$228.3	$417.4	66.1
1992	$581.3	$229.9	$371.1	63.8
1991	$563.2	$244.6	$345.9	61.4
1990	$595.1	$275.2	$355.0	59.7

Source: *Statistical Abstract of the United States*, 2004–2005, p. 210.

of new technologies. The proportion of capital spending from borrowing grew from about 8% in the early 1990s to over 25% by the end of the decade, with about half that going to real capital investment, indicating a strong desire to gain productivity through technology.[37] As a result, real private fixed nonresidential investment grew rapidly in the 1990s. From a low-point in 1991 it increased by 119% through 2000, more than doubling—compared with a growth of 37% over the 1980s.[38] There was a slight decline in 2001 and 2002 as a result of the recession and stock market meltdown of those years, but then it moved up again through 2004. Fixed investment has two components: structures and equipment. Growth in structures would indicate an expansion of capacity through new facilities, and hence a growth of employment, while that in equipment generally means efforts to gain productivity through new technology or machinery, which would tend to decrease employment wherever it was applied. Equipment grew by 188% from 1991 through 2004 compared with an actual decline after 2000 for structures. Thus, the proportion of fixed investment that

Table 2.7   Manufacturing: Real Fixed Assets per Production Worker,
1990–2004.

(Real assets in millions chained $2000, except per worker)

Year	Production Workers	Real Assets	Per Worker
2004	10,083,000	$1,905,639	$188,677
2000	11,943,646	$1,805,818	$151,749
1995	12,253,100	$1,333,804	$104,203
1990	12,232,700	$1,112,034	$86,204
1985	12,174,400	$959,333	$78,634
1980	14,214,000	$840,745	$59,207

Sources: Bureau of Economic Affairs, *Fixed Asset Table: Current-Cost Net Stock of Private Fixed Assets By Industry Group*, 1973–2004, www.bea.gov; Council of Economic Advisors, *Economic Report of the President 2005*, Washington DC, US Government Printing Office, 2005; US Department of Commerce, *Statistical Abstract of the United States*, 2001, 2002, 2004–2005; *Monthly Labor Review*, April, 2006, p. 68; US Census Bureau, *2002 Economic Census*, Manufacturing, General Summary, p.1.

went to equipment rose steadily from 61% in 1991 to 81% in 2004. Real fixed assets per worker rose by 119% from $86,204 in 1990 to $188,677 in 2004, partly as a consequence of this investment and partly as the number of workers declined. Clearly, the investment strategy of capital was to increase productivity per worker. And it did. From 1990 through 2000 average annual productivity grew by 4.5% in manufacturing, about twice the rate of the business sector as a whole. After slumping to 2.2% in 2001, it rose again to 7.2% in 2002 and 5.1% in 2003, compared with 5% and 4.4% for the whole business sector in those last two years. Altogether output per hour rose by two-thirds from 1990 through 2003, while production rose by 72%. Thus productivity accounts for over 90% of the growth in manufacturing output in those years.[39] In other words, the decline of the manufacturing production workforce from 1990 through 2004 was largely explained by capital's increased investment and the relatively high level of productivity growth it produced.

All of this was done without increasing unit labor costs significantly. With such productivity gains, it would be expected that real wages would rise. Real hourly compensation (wages and benefits) in manufacturing did rise 24% from 1990 through 2003, most of it in the second half of the 1990s, but productivity gains practically cancelled out any rise in real costs. By 2003, unit labor costs were a mere 1.5% above where they had been in 1990.[40] A workforce with almost three million fewer workers was producing much more with only modest gains in wages and almost no additional cost to capital. All of this was a function of the dynamics of real capitalist competition, domestic and international, as well as the struggle to keep up profit rates. The irony, basic to the system, was that all this investment produced yet another drop in profit rates after 1997, contributing to the causes of the recession of 2000. The inability, despite all the success in increasing productivity and holding down labor costs, to stave off either competition or declining profit rates meant that increasing the ratio of capital to worker was not enough. The fight to maximize profits would require an effort right at the point of production itself—lean production gone leaner.

War in the Workplace: Technology and Concessions

The effect of technology is not quite that simple, however. Technology is a tool in increasing the rate at which workers produce a surplus, or, to put it another way, reduce the amount of time it takes for them to produce their own wage and benefit costs and, therefore, increase the time and surplus devoted to the employer. The application of new technology for the purpose of extracting greater productivity and reducing the workforce in relation to output involves conflict. Referring to the role of technology in competition J.K. Galbraith put it well when he wrote:

> . . . technology is not a gentle mist descending from heaven to the benefit of all. It is instead a competitive weapon, with which one set of economic organizations wrests markets and incomes from another. In our time, this weapon has been deployed with ferocity.[41]

Here Galbraith is referring to the struggle between firms, but also to the fact that the economic impact on firms that provide technology (winners) and those who use it (losers) is different. Income has tended to accrue disproportionately to firms that provide it. This effect is relevant here because most of the industries that destroyed jobs since the 1970s fall into the loser category of those who use the technology to attempt to compete with one another and with foreign firms in the same line of business. Among these are automobiles, steel and other primary metals, machinery, food and clothing, low-tech consumer goods, etc.[42] These are the industries where job-loss, wage restraint, speed-up, and other weapons in the struggle for productivity and a greater surplus, the struggle between worker and employers, were sharpest from the late 1970s. For the most part, these were not the lowest wage industries, which is one reason why capital's first extra-technological attack on labor costs took the form of concessions.

The rehearsal for contract concessions covering wages and working conditions was arguably in the public sector in New York City during the 1975 fiscal crisis, where the unions went along with minimal resistance. Here the unions not only made wage concessions and eventually put their pension funds up for ransom, but formalized the idea that future wage increases would be tied to productivity gains. This was followed rapidly by a similar demand for concessions in Atlanta in 1977, where Mayor Maynard Jackson fired striking members of the American Federation of State, County, and Municipal Employees.[43] But it was the 1979 Chrysler bailout that opened the floodgate of concessions. Wage and other concessions cascaded through the auto industry after 1979, on to steel, and then just about every major industrial employer. Soon the concessions trend was given another boost in 1981 when Ronald Reagan broke the Professional Air Traffic Controllers' strike. Negotiated wage increases for the first year of new contracts in the private economy fell from 9.8% in 1981 to 1.2% in 1986. In manufacturing, the average dropped from 7.2% to −1.2% over those years. Wage concessions were accompanied by a wide range of work rule changes, speed-up, job loading, and longer hours. These latter being enabled by and sometimes enabling the introduction of new technology and related work reorganization. For the most part, union leaders went along.[44] Resistance would come and a few high profile strikes would catch people's imagination. The strike of Latino workers at Watsonville Canning in California and of meatpackers at Hormel in Austin Minnesota became causes célèbre in the mid-1980s. But mostly there was retreat. From their high point in 1972, real weekly wages of production and nonsupervisory workers throughout the economy would fall by nearly 20% by 1993, even as inflation declined. As a Ford executive explained at the time, what they wanted was "a bending of the labor cost trend line." They got it. Whereas real hourly compensation in the nonfarm business economy had grown an average of 2.6% a year from 1960 to 1973, a period of rising inflation, it grew by only about 1% a year from 1973 to 1999 as inflation subsided. One institutional casualty was pattern bargaining; this had collapsed in auto, steel, meatpacking, the airlines, and other traditional strongholds of unionism.[45] Clearly, this represented a "bending" of collective bargaining as it had been known and, along with large-scale job-loss, another source of disorientation for union leaders and members.

Concessions dealt with an increasing range of issues. Health care costs, for example, became a high-profile issue at NYNEX in 1989, where the CWA waged a successful strike to stop cost shifting. They were an issue in many of the strikes of the 1990s and the early 2000s, including at General Electric and Verizon.[46] Two-tier wage schemes began in the 1980s and were still major bargaining issues into the 2000s. In 2003, GM and Ford spin-offs Delphi and Visteon imposed a two-tier wage structure whereby new hires would get paid only $10 an hour and the union would accept gradual downsizing. In the same year, the workers in those companies were cut adrift from the pattern set by the Big Three auto companies, contributing to the multi-tier wage set-up that now characterized the auto industry as a whole.[47] That same year, the growing auto parts supplier Metaldyne, a DaimlerChrysler spin-off, got a wage cut from $25 an hour to $12.50 for production workers with the backing of the United Auto Workers International leadership.[48] Increasingly in the 1990s and 2000s issues associated with lean production, such as staffing levels, work time, and outsourcing, became important.

By the mid-2000s pensions became a major target of concessionary demands. Companies had under-contributed to pension funds in the late 1990s when soaring stock prices artificially filled corporate coffers. When the boom ended in 2000, many turned to aggressive restructuring and even bankruptcy in order to impose concessions *and* to renege on pensions. In 2004, this was tried at United Airlines, Goodyear Tire & Rubber, and LTV Corporation. The idea was to dump pension obligations on the government's already overtaxed Pension Benefits Guarantee Corporation.[49] While some companies had attempted this in the early 1990s, it became a flood in the mid-2000s. As *Labor Notes* summed it up:

> A number of bankrupt companies have been able to renege completely on pension payments by either using the threat of court-ordered abrogation of their labor contracts (US Steel, LTV, US Airways, and Northwest Airlines) or, in the case of United in 2005—where militant mechanics voted down a tentative agreement—using the court to unilaterally impose the default.[50]

In 2005, Delphi would join the bankruptcy bandwagon and demand a wage cut from all its workers from $26 an hour to $10 as well as threatening to terminate its pension plan.[51] The pension issue would hit the public sector as well.

War in the Workplace: Technology and Lean Production

Concessions were not the only "labor zapping" innovation of the 1980s and 1990s. This was also the era of "lean production." Before discussing the specifics of lean production and the labor–management cooperation programs associated with it, it is necessary to look more closely at the technology applied by industry in the years following World War 2. The development of the computer made possible a "command-and-control" technology alongside management techniques such as operations research first developed by the military during World War 2 and expanded during the Cold War. Important among the new technologies was programmable numerically controlled machinery. As it developed, largely under Navy contracts, the programming and operation of the computer were put in the hands of engineers and other specialists, while the workers who operated the machines were excluded from this knowledge.[52] These modern methods of the control of man and machine and their interactions became understood and deployed as extensions of Taylorism—the measurement and control of labor and, above all, the removal of the knowledge of the labor process from the shop floor and the hourly workforce to the exclusive domain of management. As one expert put it, "Automation shares the same goal as Taylorism—to establish management control over a knowledge domain that serves as the basis for a division of labor that is minimally dependent upon skills or disposition of a (shrinking) workforce."[53] By the 1980s, the computer was liberated from the mainframe and was available as an independent center of control virtually anywhere. In office work this meant the rapid diffusion of the desk-top personal computer and subsequently the Local Area Network which transformed much white-collar work.[54] Far from creating the more skilled jobs envisioned by some, for the majority it brought more de-skilling. Charlie Richardson describes how it affected some service and retail jobs:

> Computers gather information on how the job is done, and then use that information to standardize and control the work process. Automated teller machines lead to automated check-in at the airport and automated check-out at the supermarket, with fewer workers doing more work controlled by more machines.[55]

It also created new possibilities for more flexible forms of production in industry. But a more flexible system of production calls for a more flexible workforce—one that can be deployed and redeployed, replaced and reduced as needed. That is where lean production comes in.

Lean production had it origins in Japan in the 1960s, pioneered at Toyota by Taichii Ohno, among others. The original idea is to reduce and even eliminate "waste" in production. Waste, in this definition, not only includes excessive parts, mistakes, or buffers, but excessive labor. "Waste" is discovered by removing resources without reducing production. Can a job previously done by five workers be done in the same or even less time by four? When one phase of production is tightened up those that follow in sequence must also be re-calibrated. For this reason Mike Parker and Jane Slaughter have called the system "management-by-stress," since the labor process is constantly stressed and re-calibrated. The process by which this is done is called *Kaizen*, meaning constant improvement in which the workers themselves participate. Once the labor input has been reduced it is built into the "command-and-control" technology and there is no going back without a struggle. The tension between and the re-calibration of phases of production that are geographically separated are regulated by "just-in-time" delivery of parts, semi-finished materials, etc., and these days finished products to retail outlets such as Wal-Mart. In this system logistics become key, allowing for the geographic dispersion of production.[56] In this context, outsourcing becomes more and more central to lean production, but far less territorially bound than in its 1960s Japanese origins. This, in turn, allows for the introduction of lower-cost labor into the overall production system—even crossing borders.

At different times and places lean production has had a number of other characteristics, notably in early times the right of workers to stop the assembly line. The purpose of this was not to relieve pressure on the workers, but to reveal weaknesses or problems in the system. This has tended to fade out as work measurement has increased in sophistication or been more universally applied. Another feature important to its implementation and to the application of new technology was the many forms of employee participation or involvement, or team concept. In the original lean production system, teams were the major way of implementing constant improvement. Teams would meet to discuss ways to improve, that is increase, production by reducing waste. In Japan workers were promised life-time job security to eliminate the threat of job-loss, which was modified or abandoned as Japan's miracle economy ran into trouble in the 1990s. In the US, this was turned on its head and fear of job-loss itself provided the motivation for accepting this in many situations. Implementing lean production was not always simple. For example, several piecemeal efforts at Chrysler didn't stop that corporation from losing market share and profits in the 1990s. So, in 1997 it introduced the Chrysler Operating System (COS) with a remarkable resemblance to the Toyota Production System. As one Chrysler worker put it, COS was "the latest in a long series of schemes by which Chrysler management seeks to raise productivity."[57] In addition to increasing productivity and the ideological effort to convince workers of their shared interest with the business, team concept was a means to get the workers' knowledge of the production system into management's hands, where it could then be incorporated into their programmable control systems.[58]

Increasingly, however, employee participation gave way to more frankly top-down systems of measurement and management, notably Total Quality Management (TQM) programs. More often than not teams were eventually eliminated and/or their previous functions considered redundant. Mike Parker and Jane Slaughter of *Labor Notes* described this change:

> The attention to workers' needs began to fade with the rise of *Total Quality Management* in the 1990s. TQM was straightforwardly a method of managing, a way for management to insure that the whole organization worked more effectively for the goals of the company. The emphasis was on top management setting the course; "strong leadership" became the rage again, rather than the softer consensus style of the 1980s.[59]

Increasingly, "objective" measurement of work, never a real science, was employed and standards such as "benchmark metrics" and "cycle time analysis" introduced to obtain higher levels of worker performance.[60] Along with TQM came reengineering, an up-front means of reducing the workforce, often by eliminating steps in the production or service-providing process through the application of new technology. Again, as Parker and Slaughter describe it, "The emergence of reengineering in the 1990s, with once again a prominent role for technology, is partly because the technology itself has greatly expanded and improved."[61] Reengineering became one of many tools for the other craze of the 1990s and beyond, downsizing.[62] By the mid-1990s lean production methods, if not the entire package, TQM, reengineering, etc. had spread from factories to offices, hospitals, airlines, indeed, just about every type of work that called for a large workforce and considerable capital investment. In manufacturing, at least, one study of "high performance work systems" that include many of the practices listed above, concluded, "In general, organizational changes at the shop-floor level make plants more productive and enable them to produce a greater volume of output or a qualitatively superior or more varied output with a given amount of resources."[63] So, lean production also contributed to long-term job-loss in manufacturing.

Another central aspect of lean production is outsourcing. While chains of supplier firms have always been part of mass production, the effort to reduce the number and proportion of higher-paid workers at the final assembly production stage of manufacturing unquestionably increased beginning in the 1980s. Outsourcing is another way of lowering labor costs by substituting lower-paid workers in smaller supplier firms for the better-paid "core" workers. Historically, most of what gets outsourced are administrative and other peripheral functions. So, for example, a 2002 survey of 410 "global executives" by consultants Michael F. Corbett & Associates found that 75% of the firms surveyed outsourced food and maintenance services, 66% legal services, 53% payroll, 52% internet services, 45% data processing, and 41% telemarketing. Still, 62% of those surveyed reported outsourcing production of manufactured components.[64] While comprehensive figures don't exist for manufacturing, the symbol of this change was the reduction of "in-house" work done at General Motors from 70% in 1990 to 49% only a few years later.[65] Not surprisingly, the proportion of nonunion workers, employed in smaller second-tier suppliers, grew over the years. In the auto industry, which tends to be the pace-setter in work and production reorganization, another virtual revolution occurred in the late 1990s with the introduction of "modular production." The President of the United Auto Workers at that time, Steve Yokich, called modular "nothing but outsourcing."[66] In fact, it was something more.

This system, whereby first-line supplier firms provided assembled modules, like the entire interior or cockpit rather than dozens of pieces, forced a basic reorganization, bringing first-line suppliers under tight control by the big assembly corporations. In one case, the number of parts delivered to GM by a major supplier dropped from 75 to 1. One result was the rapid growth in the size of first-line suppliers. Whereas in 1993 there had been only five supplier firms with revenues more than $2 billion a year, by 1997 there were thirteen. Further down the supply chain, smaller firms produce for the now larger first-line companies. Again upping the ante on outsourcing, both GM and Ford spun-off their own parts producing divisions, Delphi and Visteon respectively. Even before its 1999 spin-off, Delphi had increased its sales by 35% since 1992 to $28.5 billion, while reducing its workforce by 45%.[67] The reorganization of an industry by a few top corporations became possible, like long-distance just-in-time and international production, because of the "command-and-control technology" mentioned earlier. What appeared as the decentralization of production through outsourcing was, in fact, enabled by a growth in centralized power. As Bennett Harrison noted, power relations between the huge "core" companies and the descending tiers of supplier or "peripheral" firms were "asymmetrical," with the big assembler outfits dominant. He wrote, "*Production* may be decentralized into a wider and more geographically far-flung number of work sites, but *power, finance,* and *control* remain concentrated in the hands of the managers of the largest companies in the global economy."[68]

This system of extended lean production called for a further means of control of the logistics that held it together. Beyond the factory or any job with a stationary workplace came new technologies for the tracking and control of workers on the move. If capital had developed incredible technologies for domination of traditional workplaces, they had yet to find a way to similarly keep track of and speed-up the work of truck drivers, field repair and maintenance people, and others who work beyond the immediate reach of supervision. As with early operations research and numerical control it was the military that developed Global Positioning Systems (GPS), where satellites thousands of miles above earth track moving objects or persons. By the 2000s, Charlie Richardson wrote, "The Postal System, UPS, utility companies, open pit iron ore mines, and large freight companies are a few of those putting GPS to work."[69] Given the growing importance of logistics and transportation to the geographically extended systems of production mentioned above, GPS becomes the long-distance equivalent of the latest track and spy workplace technology.

The renewed importance of logistics in both trade and lean production has led to other technological changes in transportation. For example, as railroads have again become important, due in part to containerization in sea transport, new efforts to reduce and control labor have developed, such as Remote Control Operation (RCO) of trains in the rail yard and single-person operation over long distances. Automatic trackside detectors and Centralized Traffic Control are eliminating brakemen, rear flagmen, and on-board maintenance crews. As one railroad worker wrote in *Labor Notes*, "Taken together, these and other technologies have reduced the responsibilities of the train crews."[70] Clearly, those who had thought that lean production, employee involvement, TQM, and the associated technology somehow meant the end of Taylorism and the arrival of greater job satisfaction or worker control were dead wrong. The growth of real fixed assets mentioned earlier was a means not only of increasing productivity and eliminating jobs, but of increasing control *over* the workforce as well.

Lean production also brought new ways to organize and extend work time. Across the economy there has been a growth of less-than-full-time work. Nonstandard or contingent forms of work such as part-time, temporary, and "self-employed" contract work have increased significantly. The growth of these types of jobs in absolute and proportional terms began in the mid-1970s as part of the *Great U-Turn*. In the case of part-time work, almost the entire increase is attributable to "involuntary" part-time employment. By the mid-1990s, according to the Economic Policy Institute (EPI), 34% of women and 25% of men worked in one or another type of non-full-time, irregular employment. This would shrink somewhat as the economy expanded after 1995, but rise again with the onset of recession and slow growth in the early 2000s. Three things can be said about most forms of nonstandard work: the majority of workers in these jobs are women; they pay less per hour than full-time work and provide fewer benefits; and their hours are determined by the employer, not the workers in most cases. The EPI found that in all forms of nonstandard work, the employers set the schedule in over half the cases. Instances in which employees have the dominant say range from 1.3% for single mothers to no higher than 5.4% for married men. The flexibility involved with these jobs is more often than not the employer's flexibility, not the employee's. These types of jobs not only provide employers with "flexibility" and a buffer at layoff time, but reduce the possibility of more full-time jobs. As the Economic Policy Institute reports, "Firms are relying more on part-time and temporary workers and overtime from existing workers to meet the ebbs and flows of demand—practices that preclude the hiring of more permanent full-time workers."[71] And, of course, they are paying less for this service.

Two other important developments in working time associated with lean work reorganization are longer hours, often due to increased overtime, and "alternative work schedules." In manufacturing the average worker put in nearly two weeks more in 2002 than in 1982. That is, annual hours rose from 1,898 in 1982 to 1,977 in 2000.[72] Like nonstandard work, overtime has become a buffer for employers during times of recession. So, from July 2000 through July 2003, as manufacturing employment (including nonproduction employees) fell by nearly two million workers, average overtime hours rose by an hour to 4.7 hours a week. Overtime also plays a key part in the "alternative work schedules" (AWS). An AWS does away with the standard 8-hour day, Monday to Friday week. Instead of day and night shifts, the workforce is divided into three crews. Each crew works a ten- or twelve-hour day, usually four days a week, sometime three days on and three off. Two of the "weeks" are stretched over the weekend. In most cases, the workers rotate crews. Some workers, usually younger ones, like the longer day, shorter week. But both the longer day and the constant rotation have severe consequences for health. One is that the longer day is more exhausting. Another is that rotation plays havoc with sleep—it interrupts the body's natural circadian rhythms. Yet another is that since OSHA exposure limits for various chemicals and materials are based on an 8-hour day, the longer days increase exposure past those limits.[73]

For the masters of lean production, work is not only measured by hours or even minutes, nor by the length of the workday or week, and the production made in those times. Its intensity is measured within the minute in seconds or even nanoseconds. Increasing the intensity is the purpose of *Kaizen*, of course. The Toyota standard for work performed within a minute was 57 seconds. That is, only three seconds

Table 2.8 **The 57-second Work Minute: Value Added in Manufacturing, 2002**

Value Added per Worker's Hour	= $92.30
- Hourly Labor Cost	= -$16.48
Surplus Value Added	= $75.82
SVA per 8-hour day	=$606.56
SVA per Minute	$1.26
SVA per Second	$ .021
Old 45-second minute	
New 57-second minute	
Gain 12 seconds x $ .021	= $ .25 per minute
+ $1.26	= $1.51 new 57-second minute
x 60 minutes	= $90.60 SVA per hour
Average annual hours per worker	= $1,977
New SVA per year per worker	= $179,111
Old SVA per year per worker	= $149,896
Increase per worker	= $29,215

Source: US Census Bureau, *2002 Economic Census*, Manufacturing, p.1.

of "rest," or non-performance are allowed. The beachhead for this standard in America was the joint GM–Toyota venture, the NUMMI plant. The old GM practice produced only 45 seconds of actual work during each minute. So, in the re-tooled NUMMI plant, according to Parker and Slaughter, "work standards are *kaizened* upward so that team members work fifty-seven out of sixty seconds."[74] The concept of shrinking one's breathing time to 3 seconds per minute is mind-blowing. The time lost for this tiny respite from physical effort can only add to the stress already present in most types of work. To give a rough idea of the value of these extra 12 seconds of effort to the employer, I reproduce in Table 2.8 a version of a handout I prepared for students at Cornell's labor studies program in New York City.

Altogether, the fight for greater profitability through the lean reorganization of work in the era of the Great Transformation produced a shrinking workforce in manufacturing, a brutal intensification of work, a basic reorganization of the country's industrial geography, longer and more irregular working time, and greater control over the labor process and most, if not all, of the workers in it. It spread far beyond manufacturing to impact work across the US economy. By the early twenty-first century, the footprint of lean production could be found in organizations from medical centers to Wal-Marts.

It was no wonder people seemed somewhat more willing to strike. Earlier in 2005, the BNA had reported that more employers were looking for concessions in a wide area of issues. Ninety-five percent were "very confident" or "fairly confident" they would get what they wanted. Over half wanted to shift more health care costs on to their workers, while over a quarter wanted more freedom to outsource, hire temps, and use more overtime.[75] Apparently more workers were willing to try to thwart those goals. In the 2000s those who chose to resist fought their battles on a shifting industrial terrain. Not only had the nature of work changed, so had what it produced or moved around and where it did so. If the Great Transformation of work had been confusing and disorienting for workers and their unions, so had the changing industrial landscape.

3

THE CHANGING INDUSTRIAL GEOGRAPHY

Globalization, concessions, and lean production were not the only disorienting changes that took place in the years following World War 2. The most frequently cited change in the US economy is the shift from goods-producing industries and employment to service-producing industries and jobs. This shift is an old one. In fact, there never was a time in the US when goods-producing labor outnumbered service-producers in the nonagricultural workforce. The high point was from 1890 through 1900 when those who produced goods composed 48% of the non-farm workforce.[1] By 1959, the farmers had all but disappeared and those employed in goods-producing industries shrunk to 36% of nonagricultural employees. By 1980, they were 27%, by 1990 22% and by 2004 only 17%. The numbers of employees in goods-producing industries rose, reaching a high of 24,997,000 in 1979. So, since then it has not only been a matter of the growth of service-producing jobs, but of a net loss in goods-producing employment of just over 3 million jobs from 1979 through 2004. Manufacturing lost over 5 million in those years, while construction employment grew by over 2 million. The absolute growth in service-producing employment in those years was a staggering 44.5 million jobs. Government employment over those years dropped from about 18% of the total to 16% by 2004, while the number of government workers grew by about 5 million, mostly in state and local government.[2] The shock to unionism, based as it was so heavily in goods-producing industries, was enormous.

Did this enormous shift in employment mean that the US had become simply a service economy? Was it now a "post-industrial" society that simply imported goods, while a handful provided financial services to the world and the majority took in each other's laundry, so to speak? While, as I argued in *Workers in a Lean World*, globalization has meant a change in the world division of labor, this has not created a *rentier* economy despite the growth of finances as part of the world

Table 3.1   Real GDP by Type of Product 1980–2005, Services as a Percentage of GDP

(billions of chained $2000)

	1980	1990	2000	2005
GDP	$5,161.7	$7,112.5	$9,817.0	$11,134.8
Goods	$1,567.1	$2,252.7	$3,449.3	$3,954.9
Structures	$627.8	$718.3	$942.1	$1,054.2
Services	$3,004.2	$4,170.0	$5,425.6	$6,138.9
% of Total	58.2	58.6	55.3	55.1

Sources: *Economic Report of the President 2005*, pp. 218, 221, 224, 225; Bureau of Economic Analysis, *National Data, Selected NIPA Tables*, May 2006; *Gross Domestic Product-by-Industry Accounts*, May 26, 2006, www.bea.gov.

economy. To look more carefully at just what has changed, we will look first at the actual production of real Gross Domestic Product and what has changed.

Table 3.1 shows the production of goods, structures, and services. This represents the GDP divided by product type, rather than industries. A commonly cited figure for the division by industry would put service-producing industries at two-thirds of GDP. In understanding the structure of the economy, however, it is the commodity that matters. When we look at what products or commodities the economy generates, the result is rather different. This is largely because the establishments surveyed by the Bureau of Labor Statistics (BLS) in a given industry do not necessarily produce a single product: "the establishment may also engage in the production of a secondary commodity,"[3] notes a BLS study. So, a more accurate view of what the US economy actually produces is found in the figures in Table 3.1. What they reveal, surprisingly, is that as a proportion of real GDP "services" have actually declined somewhat in the last quarter of a century. Had we gone back further, the proportion of the GDP generated by services would have been 57% in 1960 and 60% in 1970. In almost whatever year one picks in the 1970s, 1980s, or 1990s, services average about 58% of real GDP. As Table 3.1 shows, this proportion is down somewhat in the 2000s. This probably reflects the fact that the rate of inflation (chained $2000) has been somewhat higher in services than goods; indeed the prices of durable goods fell by nearly 10% from 2000 to 2003, while prices for services rose by about 12%.[4] What these figures reveal in a longer sense, however, is that the ratio of service output to goods and structures, as the government measures these, has not changed much in almost half a century. The matter of the true proportion of actual production to services has a strategic side to it. The industrial core remains the sector on which the majority of economic activity is dependent. Hence it is the power center of the system. Yet, much of it is actually more vulnerable to worker action than are some major services or retail trade.

If we were to look not just at the division between goods and services, but at that between industrial production and service production, the role of services diminishes even more. For example, the Federal Reserve System, which prepares the Industrial Production Index that measures the growth of industrial output, includes utilities in the Index. If we moved the 2005 real value added by utilities of $205.4 billion out of the service column and combine it with goods and structures to get closer to an industrial sector, services shrink slightly to 53.3% of GDP from the 55.1% in Table 3.1. If we went a step further and included transportation and warehousing in the new "Industrial" column, services slip to 50.3%. There is, however, a deeper reason that all the growth in service employment does not produce the sea change in output many imagine. Much of the labor that goes into producing services is devoted to administration or the distribution and redistribution of value rather than its creation. Here we have to make one more distinction: that between productive and nonproductive labor; i.e., between labor that produces value and that which doesn't. Mostly, this distinction is between the realm of production, be it of goods or services, and that of circulation or distribution. As a capitalist economy expands, from local to national, from national to global, the problems of circulating capital, distributing goods, and determining which firms get what share of the total profits produced require more and more labor time. These are often necessary for the fulfillment of production and the final sale of the commodity, but in and of themselves they don't produce new value.

In the 1970s Harry Braverman pointed out that, as capitalist production grew and spread, its administration necessarily became more complex. There was in the late nineteenth century a shift from personal direction by the owner to professional managers of giant corporations. So, managers grew from about 7% of the workforce in 1910 to almost 15% in 2000. Then came the development of marketing as competition became more intense and then the extension of production to specialist suppliers to cut fixed costs. Accounting, sales, legal services, and other internal and external matters of record became essential. Hence, the proportion of professional and technical employees rose from 4% in 1910 to 23% in 2000. Increasingly, each business had to handle the work of moving capital and money around as well as transporting, storing, and selling goods. This brought on a large clerical workforce in addition to managers, sales persons, and professionals of various kinds. Thus, clerical workers increased from a little over 5% of the labor force in 1910 to 18% in 2000.[5]

Globalization, of course, makes administration even more complex, whether it is centralized or decentralized, and calls forth more professional and clerical workers. So, by the 1980s in manufacturing about 30% of the workforce was engaged in administration or the realm of circulation of one sort or another. More generally, the growth in the proportion of clerical workers accelerated in the 1960s, but leveled off in the 1980s as computers increasingly did their work. Professionals, on the other hand, continued to accelerate as a proportion of the workforce after 1960.[6] So far we are talking about occupations. As we saw, however, corporations began outsourcing many of these necessary, but non-productive (of value) functions after World War 2. As Saskia Sassen has argued, globalization has increased these "Producer Services" as independent "industries." These are not services ordinary people buy, like haircuts or dry cleaning. They are purchased by other businesses, much like a manufacturer purchases components. Sassen lists such services:

> Producer services cover financial, legal, and general management matters, innovation, development, design, administration, personnel, production technology, maintenance, transport, communications, wholesale distribution, advertising, cleaning services for firms, security, and storage.[7]

The Professional and Business Services sector of the employed workforce that performs many of these activities rose from 6.7% of the total in 1959 to 12.5% in 2004. Employment in financial services, necessary to investment, grew from 4.6% to 6.1% of all employees in those years.[8] Until the late 1980s, employment in consumer-oriented and business-oriented services grew at about the same rate, each accounting for about a third of the workforce, but beginning in the early 1990s, at the end of the recession, business services took off. By 2000, businesses purchased 48% of the output of all services. The largest purchaser of business services was the catch-all "services" sector itself. The second largest consumer of business services, however, was manufacturing, at $127 billion in 2000, reminding us that much of the service sector rests not only on business in general, but on the production of material commodities.[9]

Services also grew as more activity once performed at home, informally, or outside the cash economy became commodified and brought under the control of capital. Over time, they accounted for a growing share of real GDP. Braverman pointed out that food preparation, making and cleaning clothes, the care of the elderly or sick, and even entertainment all came under the reign of business organization for profit.[10] So, personal services grew as well as producer services. Wholesale and retail employment also grew rapidly as increasingly people had to buy more commodities, whether goods or services, on the market. Employment in health care accelerated after 1970 as it became more and more a business. Globalization increased transportation as production of goods grew and business executives strode the world. A wealthier class of professionals attached to many of these global industries required more and better restaurants, theaters, clubs, and housing. And so, services that are commodities increased and with them the low-paid workers needed to produce or perform them. These workers increased more rapidly than the value of the services themselves or than workers in the goods producing sectors because many of these jobs are less susceptible to automation and because service workers are employed for shorter hours. In 2005 and early 2006, manufacturing workers put in over 40 hours a week, while those in retail did about 30 hours, in business services a little over 34 hours, in education and health services 32 hours, and in leisure and hospitality just over 25 hours a week.[11] As we saw in the last chapter, part-time and temporary workers have increased in number and most are in service jobs. Indeed, the fastest growing element of business services was in temporary employment agencies that grew by 2.5 million workers between 1988 and 2000.[12]

One more thing needs to be said about the shift to service industries. As much of the decline in profit rates after the mid-1960s occurred in manufacturing, it follows that over the long run capital would tend to seek sectors where higher or at least more predictable profits could be made. This is not a simple matter. Businesses with high levels of fixed capital will tend to use these for as long as possible. Nevertheless, with manufacturing profits in trouble, following the recession of the mid-1970s investment in the FIRE sector, where quick gains could be made through speculation, soared. As Brenner notes:

> Between 1975 and 1990, the proportion of total private plant and equipment investment devoted to FIRE (finance, insurance, and real estate) doubled, from around 12–13% to 25–6%; between 1982 and 1990 almost a quarter of all private plant and equipment investment was in FIRE.[13]

FIRE's profits also rose as a proportion of the total in those years. Profit rates in manufacturing are typically higher than those in the private sector as a whole or in non-manufacturing industries. But the rapid collapse of manufacturing profit rates after the mid-1960s, made these lower, but more stable rates of return attractive. Again, as Brenner reports, "In the face of much reduced opportunities for profitable investment in manufacturing, there was, from the start of the 1980s,

Table 3.2   Employees in Nonfarm Industries, 1990–2005

(in thousands)

Industry*	1990	2000	2005**	% +/-
Total Nonfarm	109,487	131,781	134,376	22.7
Total Private	91,072	110,996	112,498	23.5
Mining/Nat. Resources	765	599	644	15.8
Construction	5,263	6,787	7,416	40.9
Manufacturing	17,695	17,263	14,222	-19.6
Transport & Utilities	4,216	5,011	4,932	17
Wholesale Trade	5,268	5,933	5,784	9.8
Retail Trade	13,182	15,280	15,300	16.1
Information	2,688	3,631	3,066	14.0
Prof. & Business Services	10,848	16,666	17,121	57.8
FIRE	6,614	7,687	8,233	24.3
Education & Health	10,984	15,109	17,507	59.4
Health Only	8,211	10,858	12,436	51.5
Leisure & Hospitality	9,288	11,862	12,898	38.9
Other Services	4,261	5,168	5,386	26.4
Government	18,415	20,790	21,878	18.8
Local Government	10,914	13,139	14,129	29.5

* NAICS classifications
** December 2005
Sources: *Statistical Abstract,* 2005, pp. 400–403; BLS, *News;* The Employment Situation: April 2006, USDL 06–777.

a sharp lurch toward the service sector." This was so in many developed countries, but especially so in the US where service industries were largely nonunion and labor relatively cheap.[14] Naturally, shifts in employment followed from changes in the direction of investment.

As Table 3.2 shows, from 1990 through 2005 the overall shift from goods-producing work to service employment was significant. There were exceptions such as construction and transportation and utilities. But for the most part the fastest growers, those that grew more than the average for total employment, were health and education, professional and business (i.e., producer) services, leisure and hospitality, FIRE, and local government. Among these some have a union presence that is above the 7.8% average for the private sector. Within the information classification telecommunications (21.4%), motion pictures (15%), publishing (8.8%), and broadcasting (8.6%) are all at least slightly above average although still low. Local government is by far the best organized at almost 42%. But the fact remains that millions of workers in the growth sectors do not have union representation. With the exception of health care, the unions do not seem to have a plan or even show much interest in many of these industries.

As we noted above, however, a significant portion of the employment that the government categorizes as service-producing is actually part of the traditional industrial workforce. So, again, if we shift transportation and utilities out of the service column, the industrial workforce rises from 19.8% to 24% for 2005. In 1990, however, the same proportions were 26.1% and 30.7%. So, the shift away from industrial production and employment was real even though the conventional calculations reduce the industrial workforce by about four percentage points.

In a period of about thirty years, the workforce had been transformed in industrial and occupational terms. This was a polar development in which both very highly paid and poorly paid jobs grew, while many in the middle including the lost manufacturing jobs, shrank. Professionals sporting credentials, the badge of their higher education and qualifications, as we saw now composed 23% of the workforce, more than the 17% employed in goods-producing firms. At the other end of the new workforce were millions producing or performing services or selling or moving products for far less money or benefits. This reshaped labor force was polarized by race and gender as well. Both ends worked in areas never deeply penetrated by unions.

Spatial Shifts

Not only did the industrial mix of the US economy change in the decades after World War 2, so did the location of a significant portion of economic activity within the United States. In the post-World War 2 era, meatpacking, for example, went through two dramatic spatial reorganizations. First, the Big Four packing companies closed their yard and slaughterhouses in Chicago and other urban centers and moved to smaller cities and towns in the Great Plains states, where production was rationalized and specialized between beef, pork, and others. The workforce was reduced rapidly. For the most part the unions, the United Packinghouse Workers and the Amalgamated Meatcutters, were able to follow this move and in 1968 they merged, or rather the UPW was absorbed into the Amalgamated. In 1979, the Amalgamated became a junior partner to the Retail Clerks when the two merged to

Table 3.3   **Real Value Added in Manufacturing: South and US**

(millions $ 1982)

	1947	1963	1972	1989	1999	2003
SOUTH	43,304	113,915	208,638	332,962	474,532	442,002
US	327,273	633,937	936,492	1,172,135	1,551,497	1,437,964
South % of US	13.2	18.0	22.3	28.4	30.6	30.7

Growth of Real Value Added In South and US 1947–2003

	1947–72	1972–1989	1989–1999	1999–2003
SOUTH	383%	60%	43%	6.9%
US	186%	25%	32%	-7.3%

Sources: Donald B. Dodd, *Historical Statistics of the States of the United States: Two Centuries of the Census 1790–1990*, Westport, CT, Greenwood Press, 1993, p. 442; Department of Commerce, *Statistical Abstract of the United States, 2001*, p. 620, *2006*, p. 648; US Census Bureau, *2002 Economic Census*, General Summary, Subject Series, p. 24, www.census.gov.

create the UFCW. The merger strategy would not work. A second restructuring, conducted this time by aggressive nonunion newcomers like Iowa Beef Products (IBP), broke the union's bargaining pattern, thwarted its organizing drives, and defeated a heroic effort by workers at Hormel's Austin, Minnesota plant (UFCW Local P–9) to stop the concessions trend in the mid-1980s. By the 1990s wages were down and the industry was more and more nonunion.[15] The shift from Midwest to Great Plains, from urban to semi-rural had been more than the unions could handle and, if anything, the mergers only weakened their resistance.

Far greater than the shift of manufacturing to rural areas in the North or abroad was the move of goods production and all the economic activities that follow it to the US South. As used here, the South refers to the eleven states of the former Confederacy plus Kentucky. There is no doubt that some of the jobs that move to the US South don't stay there. As Jefferson Cowie has shown in his study of RCA, *Capital Moves*, or William Adler in *Mollie's Job*, some of the jobs that move South at one time later continue the journey on to Mexico and more recently to China.[16] With the end of the Multi-fiber Agreement, the exodus of textile jobs from the South to China and elsewhere will accelerate. The search for cheap labor is more or less endless. It is limited in many cases by the relative immobility of accumulated capital, the size and weight of the product, the need in many cases to be near to the market, transport and transaction costs, etc. So, despite the reality of the "global assembly line," its impact is neither universal nor absolute.

As Table 3.3 shows, the shift of value added produced in US manufacturing to the South since World War 2 was substantial, rising from about 13% of national output to over 30%. The period of fastest growth was from 1947 through 1972 at an average of almost 16% a year. This slowed during the years 1972 through 1989 to 3.8% a year and then increased to 4.8% from 1989 to 1999—all faster than average growth for the US as a whole. With the recession of 2000, growth turned to decline, with Southern output dropping at a slightly slower rate than for the US. Even with the drop, the South held on to nearly 31% of US value added in manufacturing. Over the long period, the proportion of US manufacturing workers in the South rose from 21% in 1962 to 27% in 1972, 31% in 1989, 32% in 2000. Even as manufacturing jobs continued to increase nationally up to 1980, Southern jobs grew faster, meaning a geographic transfer of perhaps a million jobs. When the total number declined after 1980, while manufacturing jobs in the South continued to rise, there was another substantial regional shift in manufacturing work. With the recession, Southern manufacturing jobs fell to 31% in 2003, losing a little ground to the rest of the country.[17] But it is clear that the enormous shift in employment from mostly unionized regions in the Northeast, Midwest, and West Coast to the South was another disorienting experience for organized labor. In a later chapter we will discuss organizing the South, labor's ancient and unheeded cry. Here, we simply note that union leaders throughout this period, with a few exceptions, talked themselves into the idea that these jobs were going overseas when, in fact, at least half of them just moved down the Interstate.

The automobile industry provides a clear and tragic example of this. Much of the growth in Southern manufacturing from the late 1970s on was in auto assembly and parts production. The leader in this growth was Nissan, which located an assembly plant in Tennessee in the late 1970s, though production didn't start until 1984. GM followed with its Saturn plant, which was located in Tennessee in the mid-1980s and opened in 1990. The supplier plants followed. By 1997 Tennessee was the fourth largest auto producing state in the country. The German companies followed in the 1990s with Mercedes (now DaimlerChrysler) locating in Alabama and BMW in South Carolina. All are near Interstates and all drew supplier firms in their trail. In Tennessee, the number of supplier firms grew from 49 in 1977 to about 500 in 1997. Employment in those plants rose from under 26,000 workers in 1977 to 100,000 in 1997. Across the South, Asian

Table 3.4   Foreign Direct Investment in the US and US South, 1990–2003

($ millions)

	1990	1995	2000	2002	2003
Total South	178,034	232,706	356,429	289,818	344,988
Total US*	578,355	769,491	1,175,628	1,016,004	1,239,214
South %	30.8	30.2	30.3	28.5	27.8

* Includes PR and other US territories.
Sources: *Statistical Abstract*, 2004–2005, p. 804; 2006, p. 825; US Bureau of Economic Analysis, *International Economic Accounts*, "Foreign Direct Investment in the US: Gross Property, Plant, and Equipment of Nonbank US Affiliates by State, 1993–2003," www.bea.gov.

and European companies now have 10 assembly plants employing 50,000 or more workers, all nonunion. Altogether the motor vehicle industry in the South employed over 200,000 workers by mid-2006. So, while the textile plants may go, the auto industry in Dixie, with its large sunk investment, seems set to stay.[18] So far, none of the major plants is under union contract. Fewer than 20% of auto parts workers in the entire US are now in unions, down from over 50% in 1979.[19]

As the auto industry indicates, a significant part in the development of Southern industry comes from foreign investment in the US. As we saw in the last chapter, incoming FDI outstripped outgoing investment for the US for most years. As Table 3.4 shows, just under a third of incoming FDI went to the South, rising from 1990 to 2000 and then slumping somewhat with the recession after 2000 to 2002. In 2003, this foreign investment rose again, although it remained a somewhat smaller proportion of the US total. About 30% of the jobs created by cumulative incoming FDI were in the South. But in manufacturing the proportion is 34%. In fact, of the eight regions defined by the Bureau of Economic Analysis, the Southeast runs ahead of all the others including even the traditionally industrial Great Lakes region. In 2003, 493,300 manufacturing jobs in the South were due to the operations of foreign companies, while in the Great Lakes region it was 402,900 jobs.[20] This is in part due to the fact that firms going into the South are somewhat more likely to be greenfield plants than is the case in the other regions.[21]

With all this investment going into the South, it would follow that construction there would also increase in value and as a proportion of that in the nation. Indeed, a look at construction activity shows a similar trend to manufacturing and FDI. Table 3.5 shows the proportion of construction contracts measured by their dollar value for the South and the US from 1990 through 2003. The value of construction work

Table 3.5   **Construction Contracts by Value, US and the South, 1990–2003**

($ millions)

	1990	1995	2000	2003
South	$71,449	$106,518	$171,431	$196,148
US	$246,022	$306,527	$472,965	$526,996
South %	29.0	34.8	36.3	37.2

Source: *Statistical Abstract*, 2001, p. 595; 2004–2005, p. 598.

in the South rose from 29% in 1990 to just over 37% in 2003. It follows, of course, that if the South was taking a bigger share of the nation's material output, it would need more homes, factories, and offices. The growth of Southern construction as a proportion of total US output meant that the South accounted for about two-thirds of job growth in construction in the 1990s. A fair amount of this is due, no doubt, to the rapid growth of cities like Atlanta, Houston, Charlotte, Nashville, Miami, and others.[22]

With a growing proportion of the country's economic activity in the South and the simultaneous rise of international trade, it stands to reason that the South has come to play a special role in the insertion of the United States into the world economy. As production has become more spatially decentralized, transportation has taken on a bigger role in production and circulation. The nation's busiest airport is now Atlanta. Some of the nation's biggest trucking companies, such as Overnite (now UPS Freight) and J.B. Hunt, are southern-based companies gone national—remaining largely nonunion. And, seven of the nation's ten largest ports, measured by tons of traffic, are located in the South.[23] Some of these will have been hurt by Hurricane Katrina, but they are likely to be refurbished and modernized due to their importance in Latin American, Pacific, and Atlantic trade. The question of transportation and logistics, however, goes beyond the role of the South in altering the nation's economic landscape. So, we will look more broadly at these essential aspects of the US economy and its global position.

Move It Or Lose It

Time is money, goes the old saying. For capitalism this is doubly true. Fixed capital that sits idle is "devalued" while earning nothing. Intermediate goods traveling from one factory to another or final goods destined for market that sit in a warehouse cost money—more of it as time goes on. Important unsigned papers stuck in an airport fail to close the deal. All of these and countless more aspects of production and sales call forth ever faster means of transportation and communication capable of handling more—more information, more goods, more producer services, etc. Capital must be invested in these activities. Some of this is part of production itself—the trucks or railroad or ships or planes that move things from one production site to another and then to market. Some produces no new value but is necessary: moving executives around the country or world by air; transmitting legal briefs across oceans electronically or by air; locating customer service call centers in India or elsewhere. Whether part of production or part of circulation, transportation has become more important and more efficient.

A quick look at some figures will give us an idea of the growing importance of transportation. By volume (tons) freight traffic in the US increased by 51% from 1980 through 2000. Not remarkable. But trucking freight volume grew by 98%, rail by 206%, and domestic air freight by 300%. Measured by dollar outlays, freight traffic within the US rose by seven-and-a-half times from 1970 through 2000 or 88% in real terms (chained $2000). The transportation workforce grew by 27%, or nearly a million employees, from 1990 through 2000, while real weekly earnings fell by 10%.

Gross private fixed investment in transportation equipment over those same years increased by almost nine times or 173% in real terms.[24] Notice that real costs of freight movement, as well as real wages, were lower than the increase in volume and much lower than the real fixed investment in transportation equipment. The investment, increased volume, and falling real wages were making freight transportation cheaper.

As discussed above, the US government categorizes all transportation as a service. But, as David Harvey argues:

> Certain costs also attach to the circulation of capital. Commodities have to be moved from their point of production to their final destination for consumption. Marx treats these physical movements as part of the material production process and therefore as productive of value.[25]

So, as we did above, we will consider the transportation of goods to market, but also between different points of the production process, as part of production. Other aspects of transportation might also be considered part of production, but for the moment this will do. From a trade union point of view, its significance is that freight movement is a key point of vulnerability in production systems and retail systems *à la* Wal-Mart—even more so since the development and spread of just-in-time delivery. This, of course, has implications for organizing now nonunion sectors like the auto parts industry, big box retailers, and the big nonunion truck outfits. To get a better idea of how the changes in transportation have both disoriented unions in many cases and provided new points of pressure and leverage for workers, we look more closely at the transformation of a key part of transportation in the global era.

The major shift in transportation in the US over these years was the development of inter-modal transportation. This simply refers to the fact that today sea and land transport are linked into one continuous flow. The change began with the containerization of seagoing freight as early as the 1950s. Containerization radically changed the nature of shipping, the character and geography of longshore work, and the organization of land transportation across the US. The container is a railroad car-sized steel box that can be carried by ship, rail, or truck. Prior to containerization, ships held cargo in their "hold" where longshoremen loaded and unloaded the cargo in gangs, passing the cargo to other gangs onshore. A container ship, however, has no hold, only a flat bed. Its crew is minimal. Only a handful of dockers work the ship, lashing and unlashing containers in "gangs" of two. Onshore, huge cranes lift containers from ship to truck or train. The nature of the work changed and the system of job dispatch from the union hall that prevailed on the West Coast under the old set-up was thrown into crisis. This led to a 134-day strike in 1971–72, although the issue was not resolved until the 1978 contract. On the West Coast, the truckers who move freight from dock to track are "independent contractors" denied union representation. They are almost all immigrants. As we will see in a later chapter, they are a powerful group and on May 1, 2006 they closed down the Port of Los Angeles as part of the "Day Without Immigrants." The breakdown of containers no longer happens on the waterfront, but typically inland at break-bulk centers. The work is now more isolated and mechanically dominated, union representation fragmented, and the old social connotation of "the waterfront" long gone.[26] But this is only the beginning of the changes brought on by containerization and inter-modal transport.

The advantage of the container is that it moves seamlessly from one port to another and then by truck, train or truck again to its final destination. This is the inter-modal system. It is driven by globalization. In the case of the US, with its large and growing trade deficit, the direction of this freight is inward, from abroad to one or another location in the country. So, today, with the exception of the Port of South Louisiana, every major US port deals mostly with imports.[27] But not all imports remain imports. As container ships have grown in size they have outgrown the Panama Canal. Hence, it has become cheaper for Asian or European companies to move freight imported into one coast across country by rail or truck to a port on the other coast and then by ship to its final destination. Stan Weir, a former longshoreman, described this "landbridge system" when he wrote:

> Japanese shippers are now discontinuing use of the Panama Canal. Containers from Yokohama are put ashore at Oakland, California, railroaded to Newport News, Virginia, put on ships, and taken to European destinations. The landbridge works from Atlantic to Pacific and to and from the Gulf as well. Also, containers loaded in or bound to any American city can be put aboard the landbridge at any one of a number of freight stations.[28]

The landbridge has become part of a larger system of logistics affecting transportation, but dominated by giant corporate producers and/or retailers. This is what is called "supply chain management" (SCM) in which cutting-edge communications technology guides and times the movement of products from one point of production to another and finally to the market. This includes phases of production and final sales around the world. GPS mentioned above is a piece of this, but it is the movement of goods within a just-in-time framework that is central. Logistics becomes an alleged science designed to produce Marx's famous "annihilation of space by time." Big outfits like UPS have developed their own Logistic units, while other companies turn to newer "third party logistics" firms like Pacer Global Logistics or Exel. Not only manufacturing firms command such supply chains, but the big box retailers, above all Wal-Mart, now stand at the end of such logistically controlled "pull" systems of delivery.[29]

Globalization, containerization, the landbridge system, and supply chain management have impacted all forms of goods-moving transportation, but perhaps most severely in trucking. The major changes in the trucking industry have been consolidation as smaller firms were driven out of business and the simultaneous decline in union representation in freight. As truck freight traffic became increasingly coast-to-coast and after NAFTA, border-to-border, Class 1 trucking firms that wanted to stay in the game had to grow and invest. The consolidation was enabled by deregulation, which began as an administrative policy of the Interstate Commerce Commission in the late 1970s and was codified with the passage of the Motor Carrier Act of 1980. Entry to the industry and to routes was eased and competition encouraged. At first the number of trucking companies increased, but recession and competition, particularly from nonunion entrants, led to bankruptcies and eventual consolidation. The entrance of new firms and the closing of less profitable routes by traditional carriers also meant a loss of union density as early as the 1980s. By 1985, the number of workers covered by the Teamsters' National Master Freight Agreement had dropped from over 300,000 in 1970 to as low as 160,000. As in other industries the result was a long string of concessionary contracts. By 2001 there were only 100,000 Teamsters covered by the National Master Freight Agreement, half the number at UPS alone.[30]

The consolidation that followed in the 1990s and 2000s not only produced giant merged freight carriers like Yellow-Roadway, but a blurring of the distinction between the freight industry, package delivery, and airfreight as mergers produced integrated transportation companies. As the Teamsters for a Democratic Union's paper *Convoy-Dispatch* summarized it:

> Mergers and acquisitions are the name of the game in the new trucking industry as companies scramble to compete against one another in all sectors of the market: LTL (less-than-truckload) freight, parcel delivery and global logistics.[31]

The symbol of the new industry with its eye on logistics as well as simple transport was the UPS buyout of the huge nonunion trucking firm Overnite (now UPS Freight) for $1.25 billion. *Convoy-Dispatch* warned, "UPS's acquisition of Overnite poses a threat to UPSers, freight Teamsters, and to the retirement security of all members covered by Teamster benefit plans." Nonunion FedEx's freight division was already worth $3 billion a year. So, competition was likely to become even more brutal. TDU called for an all-out effort to organize Overnite.[32] All these changes, from the 1970s on, had kept the union on the defensive. The Carey administration had taken a big step to turn this around with the 1997 UPS strike, but the Hoffa administration that followed dropped the ball at UPS and went on to lose a poorly prepared strike at Overnite.[33]

Globalization and deregulation hit other sections of transportation as well. The major airlines were by 2005 mostly in bankruptcy and their unions still making and in some cases resisting concessions. Rail, too, had changed with the unions making concessions. These, like trucking, were growing industries, but ones faced with new competition, including that from other modes of transportation, new technology, rising fuel prices, and other problems. In all cases, they turned first to their workers to solve those problems through work reorganization, wage cuts, and increasingly concessions from health and pension benefits. For unions built over the decades on the habits of business unionism and the belief that contracts were a fire wall against retreat, the new situations were disarming. The new ideas that were tried, stock ownership, "partnership," employee participation, worked only for the employer when they worked at all. But companies under pressure from ever more intense competition at home and abroad would do even more to save or expand their business and their profits. To geographic shifts and changes of operation must be added the other great strategy of capital, one we've already seen just above, consolidation through mergers and acquisitions.

The Concentration and Centralization of Capital: M&A

Competition, as we saw, is rooted in the accumulation process itself. As a firm grows and expands through accumulation it necessarily bumps up against the market share of its rivals. The competition, in turn, drives each firm to expand through more accumulation, perhaps in the form of new technology. This investment requires more market share to justify the cost. This process reflects the concentration of capital, or rather of the successful capitals, into ever-larger units. Hence the development of the modern corporation and by the period we are looking at, the multinational or transnational corporation (TNC). In this highly competitive world, this is a risky approach to increasing market share and hence one's share of profits. It is likely to be most successful when there is a new product, technology, or more efficient form of organization. The contemporary examples of this are Microsoft and Wal-Mart. There is, however, an old, well-established short-cut: the merger, buy-out, or acquisition of a firm in the same line of production, a "horizontal" merger. Through mergers and acquisitions a corporation can expand its market share, while at the same time rationalizing its capital structure and workforce. This strategy is particularly suited to industries where new technological breakthroughs or products are unlikely or where rationalization is called for, as in the producer services discussed earlier. This particular strategy does not always work any more than any other competitive strategy, but is nonetheless tried again and again. It can also be tried for defensive reasons—to prevent market loss. Another reason to merge or acquire is to buy up a supplier firm, a "vertical" merger or acquisition. This, of course, only makes sense if the acquired supplier's output is cheaper than what the purchasing firm could produce the same things for. So, we also see divestitures such as GM/Delphi and Ford-Visteon. In any case, mergers and acquisitions (M&As) have grown in number, size, and value over the last three decades as companies fight for position.

Table 3.6 shows the major M&A activity since 1985. From 1985,

Table 3.6   Mergers, Acquisitions and Divestitures, 1985–2003

Year	1985	1990	1995	2000	2003
Number	1,719	4,239	4,981	11,169	7,743
$ Value (Bil.)	$149.6	$205.6	$895.8	$3,440	$1,318
US Acquisitions Abroad					
Number	91	392	317	746	398
$ Value (Bil.)	$3.7	$21	$63	$136	$106
Foreign Acquisitions of US Companies					
Number	259	773	80	741	321
$ Value (Bil.)	$27.9	$56	$4	$335	$58

Source: *Statistical Abstract*, 2001, p. 493; 2004–2005, p. 499.

with ups and downs determined by the business cycle, M&As grew by twenty-two times by 2000, while GDP grew by just over one-and-a-half times. In real dollars the respective growth rates were M&As fifteen times (350%), GDP by 62%. Obviously, consolidation or vertical integration were strong competitive strategies in those years. The number and value slump with the recession that began in 2000, but were still well above 1985 through 1995. The upward trend returned, however, in early 2006. Thomson Financial, which tracks mergers and acquisitions, announced that US merger activity in the first quarter of 2006 at $333.7 billion was the highest ever except for the first quarters of 1999 and 2000.[34] The mergers and buyouts of the 1990s and 2000s were different from those of the 1980s, many of which were fueled by "junk bonds" and directed at asset-stripping to enrich corporate raiders. The M&As of the 1990s and later were about consolidation, on the one hand, and control of supply-chains, on the other. The enormous acceleration was partly the result of globalization and the deregulation of transportation, banking and finance, telecommunications, and other industries since 1980.[35] Mergers, buyouts, and divestitures present big problems for unions used to bargaining with one company or a group of firms in a particular industry. The UPS acquisition of Overnite is a clear example.

Consolidation and vertical integration or disintegration are not even across the economy. In the late 1990s and early 2000s, some of the industries most hit by M&As were banking and finance, real estate, oil and gas, electrical and medical equipment. In the 2000s, business services entered the M&A fray. Not all of these had much of a union presence, although some might be targets of future organizing. One industry that was swept by mergers and buyouts that was a union stronghold was telecommunications.[36] For decades the CWA had fought to create a national contract for workers in the giant AT&T/Bell system that once controlled most telephone traffic in the US. As the result of a 1983 consent decree, in 1984, AT&T was broken up into seven Regional Bell Operating Companies (RBOC), with AT&T limited to long-distance traffic. Massive downsizing followed with some 44,000 hourly workers laid off. The CWA now faced eight or nine separate bargaining units. The RBOCs reduced their combined net workforce by 72,000 jobs between 1984 and 1992. In the meantime, nonunion outfits began to grow and proliferate.[37]

All of this was bad enough, but then came the Telecommunications Act of 1996, which set in motion the deregulation of the industry. In anticipation of the Act, AT&T spun off its Lucent manufacturing arm and NCR, a computer firm it had purchased earlier. As one study noted, "Within months of the AT&T trivestiture announcement and weeks after the Telecommunications Act of 1996 was signed into law, the number of regional Bells decreased from seven to five."[38] The number would sink to four, most of which now engaged in every aspect of telecommunications, as mergers and acquisitions continued. In 2005 SBC, already a product of mergers, agreed to acquire AT&T for $16 billion, making it one of the largest multi-service companies in the industry. Alltel Corp, already the sixth largest cellular company, was to buy Western Wireless which owned Cellular One, for $4.4 billion. Sprint agreed to buy NEXTEL for $35 billion. Cingular bought AT&T Wireless for $41 billion. Verizon, already a national giant as the result of several mergers, proposed to acquire MCI in 2005. In addition, most of these companies have developed new divisions to deal with new services.[39] The CWA has held on to its core constituency and beaten back most major concessions, but it exists in a rising sea of nonunion outfits in an industry that has become highly competitive and aggressive toward its workforce.

Lean "Production" comes to Retail: Wal-Mart

The big economic news of the early twenty-first century was Wal-Mart, subject of many articles, books, and documentaries, and lots of campaigns. It has altered the landscape of retailing as it has spread from its humble Arkansas roots in 1962, to become by far the biggest retailer in the country in less than two decades, with its stores still springing up across the nation and world. It has changed, too, the "downtown" of many small and mid-sized towns and cities as it drives smaller competitors out of business. It has pushed many of yesterday's big grocery chains to the wall. It is the country's biggest employer, and it has no unions in its US stores. Wal-Mart has been in the lead of a sea change in retailing: the shift from department stores and supermarkets to warehouse stores and supercenters or "big box," one-stop shopping behemoths. In 1997 there were 1,530 such establishments with sales of $81.9 billion in the US, by 2002 there were 2,915 big box retailers with $189.6 billion in sales. While the sales of the supercenters were more than doubling in those years, those of department stores, discount outfits, and grocery supermarkets were flat or falling. The top four supercenter chains accounted for 84% of stores and 92% of sales.[40]

The top of the top four was, of course, Wal-Mart. Although the "bigness" of the superstores with their magnification of consumerism may seem quintessentially American, the trend actually originated in France in the 1960s with Carrefour, which is still the second largest retailer in the world. It passed through the Price Club in California and various membership warehouse retailers in the 1970s into the 1980s when the French firm Euromarché partnered with Super Value to create the first real US supercenter in 1984, appropriately named Biggs.[41] Kresge "dime stores" became K-Marts and, then, out of the South came Wal-Mart. Since then Wal-Mart has led, indeed imposed, the "big box" format on the industry.

Nelson Lichtenstein sees Wal-Mart as the corporate "template" for today, just as GM was for the mid-twentieth century.[42] But Wal-Mart could not be what it has become without the revolution in manufacturing and logistics brought by lean production. The tightly controlled chain of suppliers, the just-in-time movements of goods, and the logistical and telecommunications technology that pulls it all together came from Toyota and GM. The Taylorized work patterns, the utter uniformity (one best way) of everything, and the use of the term "associates" instead of employees or workers are also well-worn pieces of lean production. Their object is to eliminate "waste" and constantly lower costs. Wal-Mart's significance is that it has become the dominant retailer by pulling together many of the strains we have discussed: just-in-time delivery techniques, advanced logistics to match, advanced IT inventory system, control over its suppliers, and globalization big time—meaning, above all, China. To this, Lichtenstein points out, it has added a level of central control and management loyalty beyond what most corporations achieve.[43] It would have been the envy of Soviet economic planners. Of course, Wal-Mart also engages in the seamier side of lean production à la GM, breaking labor laws, discriminating, abusing immigrant workers, etc. So powerful have these techniques been in their application to retailing and so successful in trimming costs and, hence prices, that it has forced those who would compete to follow suit, just as Toyota and GM forced other car makers to imitate them. For the same reasons, Wal-Mart has been able to grow without the route more typically taken by corporate America, the merger or acquisition. The exception is overseas where Wal-Mart buys up stores and chains, such as Asda in Britain.[44] In the US Wal-Mart grows in the old-fashioned way, the simple expansion of capital, the wringing of tax concessions from local and state governments, the greasing of palms, and so on.

The one thing that most makes it the leader to be imitated is its ability to keep prices low. It does this both by keeping its direct labor costs low, by the control it has over its suppliers by virtue of its sheer size, and by extensive purchasing from China in particular.[45] But cost-cutting through such lean methods isn't that new. What is new is its scale and market breadth. While Wal-Mart may be a "template" for corporations on the make or on the defensive, it is also important to understand it as a product of the bigger changes in production methods, supplier control, management strategies, and geographic expansion as well as its being a leader in applying those trends to its own industry.

In any case, for Wal-Mart to maintain its strategy and lead it has to keep costs down at its US stores as well as at its overseas suppliers. This, of course, is why it is so anti-union and has been since Sam Walton founded it in the 1960s. In the 1970s, a decade of a significant labor upsurge and union growth, Wal-Mart faced wildcat strikes just like GM and attempts to unionize some of its discount centers. They were crushed and no union took up the fight.[46] For now, it is clear that Wal-Mart's need to shave every penny by keeping wages low and benefits minimal, and breaking overtime and minimum wage laws in order to sustain its growth and lead in the industry will guarantee a bitter anti-union attitude, making its unionization difficult. Its sheer size and geographic scope magnify that difficulty. To force Wal-Mart to accept unions will take more than law suits, NLRB cases, demonstrations, and other pressure tactics. It will take a deeper strategic look at industry in the US.

A Changed and Changing World

Any one of the massive changes discussed above would have thrown the best of unions off base. But the unions that confronted them were mostly stuck in business union practices and ideas from another era. The changes, what is more, were all of a piece, interconnected by the dynamics of the system driven by capital's incessant need to accumulate, and the competition that flows from that need. The context was global but the shifts within the US were shaped by domestic trends as well:

the shift to producer services brought on by accumulation in industry; the changing pattern of employment; the economic growth of the South; and the transformation of transportation, business consolidation, and the rise of Wal-Mart. Many of these trends were enabled by equally dramatic political changes. Intertwined with these changes were the historic demographic changes that altered the composition of the working class and workforce to a degree not seen since the decades leading up to World War 1.

4

THE CHANGING INDUSTRIAL DEMOGRAPHY

During the three decades following the deep recession of 1974–75, the gender, racial, and ethnic composition of the US workforce changed as dramatically as the economic context in which it labored. This was the third great demographic transformation of working-class structure since the end of the Civil War. Each transformation underlines the fact that the working class, or for that matter any social class born of capitalism, must change as the system itself transforms old social structures, introduces new technology and organization, expands both economically and geographically, and draws more of humanity into the machinery of production. Class in capitalism is not a fixed thing, not a layer in a sociological chart. Although the individuals and families that are drawn into the working class throughout its history experience this personally, as on their own migration or entrance into the labor market, most are pushed and pulled into this class by forces beyond their control. Because this class necessarily changes over time, its "borders" are fuzzy, often hard to delineate. I will leave that exercise for another time. Here we review some of the history of working-class formation and transformation in the United States.

Looking at the period following the Civil War we can identify three major periods of demographic change in the US working class. The first, running roughly from the 1870s up to 1920 was the period of the ascendancy of industrial capitalism in the United States. Though one can trace the development of capitalism and the working class back further, it is really in these decades that the transformations from simple manufacture to giant industry, from farm to city, from continental expansion to the beginnings of global empire take place. It is the period of the formation of the modern US working class in which there is somewhat of an improvement in living standards for many, but the loss of stability for most. The second transformation takes place during the 1940s and 1950s, and into the 1960s. This is the maturation of American capitalism, the apex of its industrial development, and its rise to preeminent world power. It is the period in which "prosperity" appears to be most widespread, although it is in reality quite uneven. The third is the one that takes place during the period we are focusing on, from the mid-1970s to today (the mid-2000s). Although it appears to many as the height of American world power, it is, in fact, the era of declining industrial power, the increasing burden of empire (at home as well as abroad), and stagnant or declining living standards for working-class people. The symbol of decline, as we will see, is precisely capital's insatiable demand for cheap and cheaper labor. In each of these transformations the composition of the class and the workforce on which it rests changes significantly. We'll review the first two periods briefly and then turn to the current era.

1870–1920: Industrialization, Immigration, and Segregation

From 1870 to 1920, the US economy took on the basic industrial and corporate organizational form it would have for the next half-century. This period of industrialization was incredibly rapid and intense. This was the era of the start of the formation of the modern industrial working class in the US. But it was anything but a smooth process. It saw huge depressions in 1873 and 1893 and lesser ones leading up to World War 1. Unlike industrialization in much of Europe, it did not draw mainly on a domestic agricultural workforce, but on the peasantry of what David Montgomery described as "a vast agricultural domain in which capitalist development shattered long-established patterns of economic activity," a rural periphery that ranged from southern and eastern Europe, Scandinavia, Southern China and Japan, across Mexico and into the American South.[1] Thus, capitalism, already on the way to impacting most of the world, began the "push" of propertyless masses off the land in search of work. By the millions they came to the United States and made the workforce grow as it could not have by drawing solely on the displaced farmers of the US. Of the more than 26 million who came during this period, as Table 4.1 shows, almost 88% came from Europe, mostly from its southern and eastern rural periphery. If they had been pushed from Europe by economic and political changes, they were "pulled" to the US by the phenomenal growth of industry there.

In these years, real GNP grew by 10% a year on average, while manufacturing output grew by over 13% a year. The number of production workers in manufacturing grew by an annual average of over 6%, while the workforce as a whole grew by a little over 5% a

Table 4.1   Industrialization Indices, 1870–1920

Year	1870	1900	1920	Annual Avg. % Growth
Real GNP	$23.1 billion	$76.9 billion	$140.0 billion	10.0
Manufacturing. Index	25	100	192 (1914)	13.4
Manuf. Prod. Workers (000)	2,054 (1869)	5,098 (1989)	8,465 (1919)	6.2
Nonagricultural Workers	6,557,000	18,691,000	23,482,000	5.2
Agricultural Workers	5,949,000	10,382,000	10,666,000	1.6
Real Annual Wage	$375	$573	$672	1.6
Urban Population	9,903,000	22,106,000	54,253,000	8.9
Rural Population	28,656,000	45,998,000	51,768,000	1.6

Immigration	1871–1900	1901–1920	1871–1920
Total	11,902,032	14,599,259	26,502,291
Europe	10,713,960	12,582,632	23,296,592
% Europe	90.0	86.2	87.9

Sources: US Bureau of the Census, *Historical Statistics of the United States: Colonial Times to 1970*, Washington, DC, USBOC, 1975, Parts 1 & 2, pp. 22, 127, 164–165, 224, 667; Jacqueline Jones, et al. *Created Equal: A Social and Political History of the United States*, Volume II from 1865, New York, Longman, 2003, p, 550.

year.[2] But this growth was turbulent and uneven and for virtually all who were drawn into this class in the making the experience was one of disruption and upheaval. The immigrants had been torn from their land and entered a strange and hostile country. The native-born workers saw their skills debased and their jobs lost or broken by new technology and giant corporations. The nation was transformed into an urban society with vast slums in one lifetime. To many of the native-born, even those who were sons and daughters of earlier immigrants, the new immigrants seemed an economic and cultural threat.

While this industrialization was also reshaping much of Western Europe, what was unique to the US was the geographic scale of development. Montgomery describes how two great industrial belts developed in the years after the Civil War. One ran across the Great Lakes from Buffalo to Chicago and Milwaukee, the other from Pittsburgh down the Ohio River to Louisville. By the 1880s both met on the Mississippi at St. Louis.[3] In the decade that followed another strip of industry developed in the Western mountains that ran from Canada to Mexico. A unique labor radicalism was born that led to the formation of the IWW in 1905.[4] Huge cities were built in short order across all these new industrial areas. As Table 4.1 shows, the urban population more than doubled by 1900 and by 1920 surpassed the rural population. But this was also a population on the move. For millions, the typical housing arrangement was not even the tenement, but the boarding house. As Montgomery wrote, ". . . the rates of labor turnover and geographical mobility were notoriously high."[5]

The organization of business also changed radically from the end of the Civil War to 1900. After experiments with the "pool," the "trust," and the "cartel" burgeoning American capital settled on the giant corporation. The gigantic scale of these enterprises was achieved by the most rapacious methods as the "Robber Barons" created, destroyed, bought, merged, and cheated their way to the modern corporation. The number of mergers sauntered along between 26 and 303 a year for much of the 1890s and then, in 1899, exploded to 1,208 in a single year, valued at over $2 billion.[6]

The term "class formation" lends itself to the idea of a continuous process of growth. While the numbers rose more or less constantly, the waves of migration and the geographic scale, along with the technological and organizational transformation of industry, itself not a simple forward process, meant constant disruption in the lives of millions. As historian Paul Le Blanc wrote:

> In the five decades from 1870 to 1920, wave upon wave of immigrant labor inundated industrializing America, helping to decompose and recompose the US working class in ways that disrupted and fragmented labor organization and class consciousness . . .[7]

The native-born workers often contributed to the "fragmented labor organization" by refusing to admit into their unions or organize immigrant workers as they did African Americans. Though, as Howard Zinn argued, these years "were marked by the most bitter and widespread labor troubles that had yet been seen in the United States," permanent trade union organization proved difficult in the new industries.[8] The exceptions were the craft unions in construction and local transport, both sheltered from the economic storms of industry by the phenomenal and unbroken growth of the cities. Despite deep recessions, the number of construction workers grew steadily from 795,000 in 1870 to 2.7 million in 1910. These unions excluded most new immigrants as well as Blacks and composed a solid base in the AFL for Samuel Gompers and the development of business unionism.[9] By the end of this period efforts would be made to organize immigrants in steel, meatpacking and elsewhere, but these would not succeed until the 1930s.

One other feature of this period put its stamp on the future of organized labor in the US. This was the near total segregation of the African American population from the formative development of the industrial working class. With the failure and abandonment of Reconstruction in the South, the vast majority of African Americans remained trapped on the land as tenant farmers or sharecroppers, socially segregated, and denied the vote. In 1900, 87% of Blacks lived in the South and 83% of those on the land. In the Northeast only 2.2% of the urban population was African American, in the North Central region 3.2% and out West 4%.[10] For the white workers who poured into the factories and mills of the North, whether immigrant or native-born, Blacks scarcely existed even where they were not excluded by discrimination. Only with the Great Migration that began during World War 1, at the very end of this period, did this change significantly. The experience of Black and white toilers could hardly have been more different. The identification of "whiteness" with working-class status, long established as David Roediger has pointed out, was reinforced by this regional segregation as well as the segregation imposed on African Americans everywhere in the country whether by law or custom.[11] Only toward the end of this period, with the outbreak of war in Europe, did Blacks begin to leave the rural South for the urban North. Between 1910 and 1920 the number of Southern-born Blacks living in the North grew by 322,000, concentrated mainly in industrial cities.[12]

The other segregation, this one limited to the labor market and workplace, was between men and women. Women, of course, worked. Mostly they worked in the home, not just as homemakers but as the person who ran the ubiquitous working-class boarding house, and who grew vegetables and sewed the family's clothes, whether they lived in the city or the country. All this in addition to their traditional caring roles. But a fifth of women were also counted in the paid labor force by 1900. Over a million worked as domestic servants, half of them immigrants, a quarter Black. By 1900 over half a million worked in the clerical jobs created by the growth of business organization, marketing, and retailing. They composed almost 30% of the workforce in the new telephone industry. They labored in garment, food processing, and steam laundry plants. Some could be found in steel mills. Like Blacks, they were routinely excluded from the craft unions, but they struck, as in Lawrence in 1912, and formed some of the first industrial unions, as in apparel—although men would run these unions. But if 20% were in the labor force, 80% were not.[13] That change would come later. So, in this sense, too, the modern working class had only partially been formed.

It was in this period that the US took its first major step to becoming a world power. In 1898, the US took Puerto Rico and the Philippines as a result of war with Spain. It also annexed Hawaii. Deeply involved in the China market, in 1900 the US government issued the "Open Door" notes to the major powers demanding that it be entitled to as much of a piece of China as Japan and the Europeans. Although the notes were largely ignored, this laid the basis for American foreign policy for decades to come. In 1902 the US, through a bogus internal rebellion, seized Panama and began the construction of the Panama Canal. Then, in 1904, President Teddy Roosevelt pronounced his Corollary to the Monroe Doctrine declaring that the US had the right to intervene anywhere in the Western Hemisphere to exercise "an international police power."[14] This was used by President Wilson in 1913 when he invaded Mexico, then in the midst of its revolution. Along with this new imperial role came the notion of the "white man's burden," reinforcing racism at home and increasing anti-foreign sentiment at a time when millions of immigrants were entering the workforce. During much of this period the AFL was openly anti-immigrant and called for restrictions on immigration from southern and eastern Europe.[15] This direction also began the process of integrating the labor leadership into America's imperial project. Although Gompers had opposed the annexation of the Philippines, he and much of the AFL leadership would be enthusiastic supporters of US entry into World War 1. It was during the war that the government attacked both the IWW and Socialist Party, including imprisoning the party leader Gene Debs. The result was the crippling of the left wing of organized labor.[16]

While there were scores of examples of worker unity across race, ethnic, and gender lines in the midst of class conflict, the impact of immigration along with race and gender segregation, regionally and in most workplaces, made the process of class formation in this period a flawed and incomplete one. In half a century, the average annual real wage of nonagricultural workers had risen only 79% in an era of rapid industrial growth and the amassing of great fortunes. Clearly, America's new imperial foreign policy had not benefited the working class. By contrast, from 1873 through 1899, the wealth of the richest ten people in America had doubled or tripled. In 1905, the *New York Times* first listed the word "millionaire" in its index. Shortly after that, John D. Rockefeller became the nation's first billionaire.[17] It would take a period of settling down following the Great Migration in the 1920s to lay the basis for the labor upheaval of the 1930s and the organization of the industrial unions of the CIO. Even then, regional, racial, and gender segregation remained dominant until World War 2 and the next great transformation.

The Second Transformation, 1941–1970

At the end of World War 2, an enormous strike wave swept the country. Over seven-and-a-half million workers struck during 1945 and 1946, 4.6 million in the last year alone. In that year, five cities saw general strikes as unions supported one another. This was the culmination of a wave of wildcats and "quickie" strikes that began as early as 1942 despite a wartime no-strike pledge by the CIO unions.[18] Labor was feeling its power. Union membership had jumped from 6.5 million in 1939 to 12.3 million in 1945. By 1975 there would be over 22 million union members in the US, the highest number ever. Private sector membership would peak at 16.9 million in 1970 and public sector members at almost 6 million in 1976. Union density peaked in 1953 at 32.5% of the non-farm workforce. But in 1975 it was still 28.9%. In manufacturing, the figures were 42.4% and 36.6% in those years. Many of the big unions didn't hit their membership peak until fairly late in this period: the Steelworkers in 1973, Teamsters in 1974, the Auto Workers and Machinists in 1969.[19] The loss of density was underway and the decline in membership was beginning, but there was not yet a sense of lost power. Indeed, the 1950s had seen a very high level of strike activity, culminating in the 116-day steel strike in 1959, the biggest in US history.[20] In the 1960s strikes, many of them unofficial, would rise even more, continuing through the 1970s. Indeed, the period from 1966 through 1979 was one of widespread labor upheaval, a piece of the turbulent 1960s that is often overlooked.[21]

The workforce that carried out these strikes and struggles was in many ways different from that which organized the CIO unions in the 1930s. There were more women, Blacks, and Latinos among these strikers and union members. By the mid-1960s the spirit of the civil rights movement had infused many unions and aided the organization of the public sector which brought more women and people of color into unions. In California, the United Farm Workers gave Latino workers a high profile. In Detroit, radical Black workers in DRUM alerted the Auto Workers' leaders to the new militancy among Black workers. It was, of course, the era of the new social movements when women, Blacks, Latinos, and others asserted their rights and made new demands on a society that was experiencing a fairly long period of economic growth. With it came the rise of consumption as things once done in the home increasingly had to be purchased. Those who were locked out of this prosperity fought to get their share. Underlying this social explosion were deep demographic as well as economic changes.

Table 4.2   Women in the US Civilian Labor Force, 1950–70

Year	1940	1950	1960	1970
Total	55,640	62,208	69,628	82,715
Women	13,840	17,795	22,516	31,233
% of Total	25	29	32	38
Married	5,040	9,273	13,485	19,799
% of Women	36.4	52.1	59.9	63.4

Source: *Statistical Abstract*, 1972, pp. 216, 219.

One of the most important of these changes was the entrance of married women into the workforce in large numbers, beginning in the 1950s. As Stephanie Coontz writes, "Wives and mothers first started to work in great numbers during the 1950s in order to supplement their families' purchasing power; expansion of household comforts came 'at the cost of an astronomical indebtedness.'"[22] Another change in this period was that married women were not just taking on paid work when the children had left home as had sometimes been the case in the past, but precisely at the time in the family lifecycle when expenses were highest: namely when there were adolescent children in the home. This was particularly true among jobs that were "lower status;" i.e., working class. It was economic compulsion at work.[23]

As Table 4.2 shows, the proportion of women rose from 25% of the civilian workforce in 1940 to 38% by 1970. Even more remarkable is the percentage of married women in the workforce, which rose from 36.4% of all women in the labor force in 1940 to 63.4% in 1970. There had, of course, been the brief time during WW2 when married women entered industry in large numbers, but that was short-lived. The post-war trend was to be permanent and continuous. In the 1960s these women would play a key role in the organizing of the public sector, although women could be found in growing numbers in almost all industries, including "nontraditional" jobs in steel mills, auto plants, and coal mines. Between 1960 and 1974 1.3 million women joined unions, providing 37% of total union growth in that period. By 1974 women were 21% of all members, up from 18% in 1960.[24] It was almost certainly lower than this before 1960, but figures are not available. In any case, the unions were still predominantly male in numbers, leaders, and culture. This, plus the gains, led women trade unionists to organize the Coalition of Labor Union Women in 1974. Feminism found roots in the unions as well as in the middle class, forming what was often called the "working women's movement."[25]

Table 4.3   Changes in Population in the Northeast and Midwest, 1950–70

Year	1950	1960	1970	+ 1950–70
Total	69,877,230	80,902,843	89,293,179	19,415,949
Black	3,821,880	5,913,468	8,217,058	4,395,178
% Black	5.5	7.3	9.2	+28
"Other"	113,483	213,636	605,482	491,999
% "Other"	0.2	0.3	0.7	+115
% Nonwhite	5.7	7.6	9.9	+343

Source: *Statistical Abstract*, 1972, p. 28.

Another demographic change of historic dimensions during this period was the migration of African Americans from the rural South to the urban North. This began during WW2 when about 10% of the Southern Black population moved north, but it was the mechanization of Southern cotton culture that pushed millions off the land and heading North in search of employment.[26] As Table 4.3 shows, over four million African Americans moved into the industrial Northeast and Midwest from 1950 to 1970, increasing their share of the population there from 5.5% to 9.2%. Their presence in the nonagricultural workforce of the whole country increased by over two-and-a-half-million, growing from 9.8% to 10.8% of that workforce. Those living in central cities increased from 44% in 1950 to 58% in 1970.[27] The growing Black presence in many industries did not mean a smooth transition to more influence in organized labor. For one thing, a couple of the previous strongholds of Black labor, the United Packinghouse Workers and A. Philip Randolph's Brotherhood of Sleeping Car Porters and Maids, experienced decline as the industries they were based on restructured. Even where the numbers of African American workers grew, such as in auto or steel, they had to fight their way to any kind of influence on union affairs. In this period a variety of organizations emerged to fight for a place at the table of the unions.

The Trade Union Leadership Council in Detroit was among the many such groups of Black unionists around the country in the late 1950s. Many of these came together under Randolph's leadership to form the Negro American Labor Council in 1960. There was a bitter fight within the AFL-CIO between Randolph and federation president George Meany. To ameliorate or, perhaps, co-opt some of the pressure coming from Black unionists the AFL-CIO set up the A. Philip Randolph Institute in 1965. A few years later, in 1972 the somewhat more independent Coalition of Black Trade Unionists was formed. The presence of African American workers as both rebels inside and leaders of growth came in 1968 with the strike led by DRUM at the Dodge Main plant in Detroit and the strike of Memphis sanitation workers during which Martin Luther King, Jr. was murdered.[28] Both symbolized in different ways the important role that Black labor now played in the economy, but also the continued second-class status on the job and in the unions. But unlike the earlier period discussed above, African Americans were now at the center of the working class.

The other great demographic change was the increase of Latino workers in industry and in the urban areas of the Southwest and Northeast. The US already had a significant Latino population: Mexicans in the Southwest, since that was seized in the 1846–48 war, and Puerto Ricans on the island, since that was seized in 1898. But these populations still lived mostly on the agricultural periphery. From the 1940s on this changed. Lichtenstein summarizes the reason:

> Economic change in both Puerto Rico and Mexico had crippled labor-intensive agriculture, forcing millions of Latinos with few economic resources into northern cities. These massive population movements took place at precisely the time that industry was fleeing to the exurbs and rural regions, stripping central cities of more than a million jobs.[29]

This was definitely the case in New York City where the bulk of Puerto Ricans went. Also in meatpacking, where Blacks and Latinos had worked in Chicago. But the industrial jobs in Gary, Pittsburgh, Detroit, and elsewhere would not disappear until the end of this period. One of the experiences that brought both Puerto Rican and Mexican male workers to the mainland and across the border was service in the US Army during World War 2. Many Puerto Ricans served in the all-Puerto Rican 65th Infantry, saw military action and assumed they had some rights in the US. Mexican Americans also served in the US Army. Juan Gonzales writes of their experience in the war:

> It transformed the thinking of a whole generation of Mexican men who served in it, just as it did Puerto Ricans. More than 375,000 Mexican Americans saw active duty in the US armed forces, many in critical combat roles.[30]

Like African Americans and Puerto Ricans who served, they returned with the idea they deserved something better than what their people had had before. In Puerto Rico this took the form of a revival of nationalism. In the South and Southwest it gave momentum to the civil rights and nationalist movements that would arise in the 1950s and 1960s. It put Chicano farm workers in a frame of mind that led to the organization of the United Farm Workers in the 1960s under the leadership of César Chavez.[31] As with women and Blacks, Latinos also organized within the unions for a better deal. In 1971, a Chicano Caucus was set up in the Steelworkers, while in 1973 Latino union leaders founded the Labor Council for Latin American Advancement (LCLAA).[32]

By 1975 there were 6.7 million people of "Spanish Origin," as the bureau of the Census put it. By 1980 there were 8.4 million by official count. While the government didn't specify Hispanics until later, the "Other" category in Table 4.3 would be mostly Latino. The growth of this population in the Northeast and Midwest, while much smaller than that of Blacks, was very rapid, reaching over 600,000 by 1970. In New York, Puerto Ricans filled not only low-paid service jobs, but many of the remaining manufacturing jobs. Puerto Rican women became dominant in the garment industry in those years. Although these jobs were in decline or on the move, the "ethnic queue" effect, whereby older Jewish and Italian workers left the industry, as Roger Waldinger argues, opened jobs to Latino newcomers for a time.[33] By 1980, Latinos composed over 6% of the US civilian labor force. This would rise dramatically later on as immigration accelerated, but as the class took shape in the years after World War 2, Latinos were firmly planted as a recognizable part of the working class. Altogether, by 1980, when both manufacturing employment and union membership hit their peak, the US civilian workforce was 46% female, 11% African American, and 6% Latino. White males, who had been by far the largest and dominant component of the workforce in the earlier period of transition and during the 1930s, were now a minority. In the unions, however, at least two-thirds of members were still white males.[34] The change would come later.

This period was also the height of the Cold War and the Vietnam era. America's role in the world during and following World War 2 made it one of the two great superpowers. Until Vietnam became a major engagement and debacle, the Cold War had seemed to work for the US economy, which grew at a healthy clip. It even seemed to benefit the working class as real wages doubled from 1947 through 1967.[35] But a price was being paid in more ways than one that would help to disarm the unions when the economy turned sour, as it did during the Vietnam War. The first price was a pact with the devil, an organized effort to do the US government's Cold War dirty work overseas. In the early 1960s, the AFL-CIO set up a series of "institutes" funded by government and even CIA money, to promote tame anti-Communist labor unions in the Third World. They were launched in cooperation with some of the worst anti-union corporations, notably

W.R. Grace and Rockefeller interests, although this became so embarrassing that business eventually withdrew from the boards of the AFL-CIO institutes. Notable among these were the American Institute for Free Labor Development (AIFLD), which functioned in Latin America, the African American Labor Center, and the Asian-American Free Labor Institute. These aided labor federations and unions that were more pliable by US corporate interests investing abroad.[36] This took place just as US corporations were looking more to overseas markets and investments. The institutes became part of the "Wall Street Internationalism" of the period. They became partners in America's Open Door policy, built into Cold War strategy from the start, battering down barriers to US investment first in Europe then in the Third World. In doing so, these institutes helped lay the basis for the export of jobs from the US.[37] All this was done without the knowledge of union members, at least until they were exposed. Thus, this alliance with corporate America, the CIA, and the foreign policy establishment contributed to the lack of democracy in US unions.[38]

This alliance with corporate America for foreign policy goals also reinforced the schizophrenic idea, so deeply imbedded in business union ideology, that you can simultaneously be partners and adversaries with capital. It reinforced the leaders of the AFL-CIO in the view that social upheaval was bad, even when it was a white working-class or trade union upsurge, much less when it was Black people. In the Cold War context, social conflict made America look bad—it was grist for the Communist mill they so hated. Social conflict also disrupted the normal rhythms of routine collective bargaining and of the corporate well-being on which it was based. Thus, corporate interests, at home and abroad, were to be protected. It never occurred to the leaders of the AFL-CIO, who kept this trade union colonialism close to their chests, that it could turn against the unions as it would in the 1980s and beyond. Partners in "Wall Street Internationalism," they went along even when many union leaders objected.

The Third Transformation: Harvest of Empire

Following the recession of the mid-1970s, along with all the other changes described in the preceding two chapters, the workforce again saw a major demographic change. If the biggest change of the 1950s and 1960s had been the increase in Blacks and married women in the paid labor force, the big change of the 1980s, 1990s, and early 2000s was the rapid growth of Latinos as a proportion of the civilian workforce. From 1975 to 2004, Latinos went from 4.4% to 13.1% of the labor force, as Table 4.4 shows. This was a growth of 15 million people.

Table 4.4   Civilian Labor Force by Gender and Race, 1975–2004

Year	1975	%*	1985	1995	2004	%
Total	93,775	100	115,461	132,304	147,401	100
Male	56,299	60	64,411	71,360	78,980	53.6
Female	37,475	40	51,050	60,944	68,421	46.4
White	82,831	88.3	99,926	111,950	121,086	82.2
Black	9,263	9.9	12,354	14,817	16,638	11.3
Latino	4,171	4.4	7,696	12,267	19,272	13.1
Asian					6,271	4.3

*percentages do not equal 100 due to overlap and rounding
Sources: *Monthly Labor Review*, Current Labor Statistics, Vol. 129, No. 5, May 2006, pp. 59–60; *Statistical Abstract*, 2006, p. 388; 2000, p. 404; 1990, p. 380; 1984, p. 406.

From 1995 to 2004 over 7 million Latinos joined the workforce. In fact, they composed 46% of all the 15 million additional people looking for work in those years. By 2004, although the proportion of Blacks also grew, Latinos had surpassed African Americans in numbers. Such rapid growth could not be explained by birth rates. In fact, many of the Latinos that entered the workforce after 1985 were immigrants. Before looking at Latino workers in more detail, it is necessary to examine immigration into the US since the 1970s.

The 1965 Hart-Cellars Act ended the highly discriminatory national quota system and opened the door, within limits, to Third World immigration, particularly for those with relatives already in the US or with sought-after professional skills.[39] While immigration did increase somewhat after that, it was not until the mid-1980s that it began to take off, hitting its high point in 1991 when 1.8 million people were "admitted" into the country as legal permanent residents. The level of annual documented entry has remained high ever since.[40] The figure for those "admitted," however, overstates the level of legal immigration since only 45% of the 4.3 million people "admitted" between 1995 and 2005 were actually new arrivals. The rest were people already in the country who had an "adjustment of status." The pattern of immigration has changed over the decades since the end of WW2. In the 1940s, while Europe was only recovering from the war and its economies were still weak, the largest number of immigrants still came from there. In the 1960s, however, the inflow of people from Mexico, the Caribbean, and Central and South America surpassed that of Europe. Asia also grew rapidly, with the Philippines supplying the largest group. In the 1970s, 1980s, and 1990s, European immigration

Table 4.5   Immigrant Population, 1995–2004

Estimated Legal Permanent Resident Imigrant Population, 2004	
Total	11.6 million
Country of Origin	
Mexico	3.1 million
Philippines	0.5 million
India	0.5 million
China	0.4 million
Dominican Republic	0.4 million
Vietnam	0.4 million
Canada	0.3 million
El Salvador	0.3 million
Korea	0.3 million
United Kingdom	0.3 million
Cuba	0.3 million
Estimated Undocumented Immigrant Population:	
1996	5.0 million
2000	7.0 million

Source: Department of Homeland Security, Office of Immigration Statistics, *Population Estimates*, February 2006, p. 4; Immigration and Naturalization Service, *Estimates of the Unauthorized Immigrant Population Residing in the United States, 1990 to 2000*, "Executive Summary," January 31, 2003, www.uscis.gov.

continued to decline in absolute numbers despite an increase in the early 1990s from former Communist countries. It was in the 1980s that immigration into the US exploded, with the inflow from Mexico, Central America, and the Caribbean, already significant at 1.5 million for the whole decade of the 1970s, almost doubled in the 1980s to just under 3 million. This immigration remained high through the 1990s and grew somewhat again from 2000 to 2005, averaging about 350,000 a year. Unlike the majority of Asian immigration, which has also increased, that from Mexico, Central America and the Caribbean is not based on "employment preferences" which favor educated professionals. These were poor people fleeing the wreckage of globalization.[41]

As Table 4.5 shows, as of 2004 there were 11.6 million legal permanent resident immigrants in the US, according to the Department of Homeland Security. Legal permanent residents are those with "green cards." Of these 3.1 million were of Mexican origin, by far the largest group. The next largest groups were from the Philippines and India with half-a-million each; followed by China, the Dominican Republic, and Vietnam, each at about 400,000. In addition, according to estimates by the Department of Homeland Security, there were 10.5 million "unauthorized" or undocumented immigrants in the US in January 2005, 3.1 million of whom arrived after 2000. Altogether over 80% had arrived since 1990.[42] Between those with "green card" status and the undocumented are several million with temporary or indefinite status, from holders of temporary work permits to those with student visas. These are immigrants whose status is always in danger of expiration. So, the figures on legal permanent residents tell only a part of the story of how many Latin Americans actually live in the US. The leap in the census figures for the Latino population, although they don't distinguish between citizens and immigrants, suggests the immigrant population is nearly twice the official immigration figures. By official estimate based on census figures, the total foreign-born population in the US was 34.2 million by 2004, of which about 21 million were not citizens. The foreign-born workforce was 21.4 million in 2004, of whom almost 12 million were not citizens.[43]

The list of major countries of origin is suggestive of the most basic causes of such growth in immigration in recent years. With the exception of India, all of these countries have established trails of immigration that go back to US economic and/or military involvement in these nations. In the case of Mexico, China, Cuba, and the Philippines, this goes back to the initial period of US empire-building just over a hundred years ago, but it also reflects, with the exception of Cuba, the deep contemporary involvement of US business in these areas. Korea, of course, entered the US orbit during the Korean War in the early 1950s. Vietnam and the Dominican Republic trace back to US military interventions, albeit on a very different scale, in the 1960s. El Salvador, Korea, and Cuba, with 300,000 each, are all sites of US intervention within the last half century. Canada and the United Kingdom also fall in the 300,000 legal resident range, but clearly represent something else.[44] Along with India, immigration from these two countries tends to be composed in its majority of college-educated professionals, managers, and technicians.[45] In the cases of Mexico, the Dominican Republic, and El Salvador, the correlation between the impact of globalization, US foreign policy, and accelerated emigration from those countries to the US is all too clear.

Like the Caribbean, Central America became part of the US "backyard" after the Spanish-American War. By the 1920s, US business had more invested in all of Latin America, mostly in Central America and the Caribbean, than in Europe. In the 1920s and 1930s, the US military intervened throughout the region scores of times to protect American business interests there. As Sidney Lens wrote some years ago, "There was never a day from 1919 to 1933 when American marines did not intervene in or occupy the sovereign territory of another country." [46] After WW2 this practice was resumed with interventions in the Western Hemisphere, sometimes covert, in Guatemala (1954), Cuba (1960), Brazil (1964), the Dominican Republic (1965), Chile (1973), Grenada (1983), and Panama (1989).[47] In all but one case, Cuba, they were directed against elected officials or governments.

In the case of the Dominican Republic immigration traces back to the US military invasion of that island in 1965 for the purpose of suppressing a popular uprising in favor of Juan Bosch, who had been elected president two years earlier but deposed by the local military. Lyndon Johnson, already escalating the war in Vietnam, sent in 26,000 troops and crushed the revolt. The inflow of Dominicans to the US leaped by almost ten times from the 1950s to the 1960s, reaching its high point of a quarter of a million during the 1980s.[48] In Central America it was the 1980s that sent thousands to the US. In Guatemala, Nicaragua, and El Salvador, the Reagan Administration backed far right forces in bloody wars against rebellious peasants. El Salvador was perhaps the bloodiest with its ruthless Death Squads. By 1984, it is estimated that 500,000 Salvadorans had moved to the US, despite efforts by the Reagan Administration to detain thousands. The Salvadoran population of Los Angeles grew from 30,000 in 1979 to 300,000 in 1983. The legal residents from El Salvador "admitted" during the 1970s had totaled a little over 30,000. In the 1980s the number shot up to 213,539.[49] The interventions, *coups*, and death squads had all received the support of the AFL-CIO and often the active involvement of AIFLD.

It wasn't just military intervention, overt or covert, that pushed millions of Latin Americans from their homelands. It was that other favorite policy of Corporate America and virtually every administration of the last half-century or more—free trade. "Free Trade," as a policy, isn't just about trade, it's about opening nations, all nations, to investment by the big corporations. To put it another way, it's about finding ways for these corporations to exploit low-wage labor without government intervention. "Free Trade" is *not* simply about the market doing its thing. Because many nations developed their domestic industry by protecting it from imports and foreign ownership, free trade policy required that these nations abandon that development strategy. An opening was first found by US capital through a policy change in which Puerto Rico and Panama, both under US control, developed the first free trade zones (FTZ). The FTZs suspended government regulations and gave the corporations a free hand. Next came the border development program in northern Mexico, with its *maquiladora* plants, in principle similar to a FTZ. In 1985, the Reagan Administration negotiated the Caribbean Basin Initiative, which opened countries in the region to this type of investment. Such imports as occurred were usually components that went into products then imported back into the US—contributing to the trade deficit and costing US jobs. By 1992, there were 200 FTZs in Mexico and the Caribbean, housing more than 3,000 plants employing 735,000 workers. All of this was only a rehearsal for NAFTA, which did more of the same as we saw earlier.[50]

This, however, was only one side of "free trade." The other was investment by the banks in New York, London, etc. in the Third World. In Latin America this meant, above all, the New York City banks—Wall Street. When oil money poured into these banks in the early and mid-1970s, they promoted low-interest loans to Third World countries. But then, inflation and high interest rates took hold and by the early 1980s, countries throughout Latin America were increasingly unable to pay even the annual interest. This became the Third World Debt Crisis. The debt became the lever by which the US and other industrial powers, with the help of the International Monetary Fund, not only ended barriers to their investment, but literally forced the redesign of many Third World economies. This would be carried out by the countries' political leaders, but the compulsion involved, though economic, was more powerful than anything the US Marines could have pulled off. Mexico is a prime example. Here's how I described the remake of the Mexican economy about ten years ago:

> The transformation wrought under the administrations of Miguel de la Madrid (1982–1988) and Carlos Salinas de Gortari (1988–1994) amounted to a basic redesign of the Mexican economy and of the corporatist practice of PRI (ruling Institutional Revolutionary Party) rule as well. In the eight years leading up to the announcement of NAFTA in 1990, prices of many necessities were raised, wages frozen, the re-privatization of the banks begun, wholesale privatization of productive enterprises carried out, the General Agreement on Tariffs and Trade signed (1986), long-standing tariffs and investment restrictions lifted or drastically reduced, and some 25 industries deregulated in the American manner.[51]

Not surprisingly, the result was what any corporation would desire; real wages dropped drastically by 67% from 1982 to 1991, those of Mexico's slightly better paid industrial workers by 48%. Four dollars a day became the wage along the Mexican border as well as in the Dominican Republic.[52] Foreign investment in agri-business and plantation farming, another side of "free trade," also served to drive

Table 4.6   Latin American Legal Immigration by Decade

Decade	1971–80	1981–90	1991–00	2001–05
World Total	4,493,314	7,338,062	9,083,386	4,902,056
Americas*	1,812,796	3,455,287	4,293,994	2,029,593
% of Total	40.3	47.1	47.3	41.4
Annual Average Americas*	181,280	345,529	429,399	405,913

*Not including Canada.
Sources: INS, *1997 Statistical Yearbook of the Immigration and Naturalization Service*, October 1999, p. 26; DHS, *Yearbook of Immigration Statistics: 2005*, Table 3, www.uscis.gov.

millions off the land in Mexico, Central America, and the Caribbean with no hope of work in their own lands. So, Mexican legal immigration into the US rose from 640,294 in the 1970s to 1,655,843 in the 1980s, 3,541,700 in the 1990s, and 876,823 from 2001 through 2005.[53] In all likelihood, undocumented entry to the US in those years was as high as legal immigration. Neither laws nor police nor giant fences will be able to stop this flow of humanity in search of survival.

The question raised then is did this immigration, reflected in the rapid growth of the numbers and proportion of Latinos in the workforce, have a negative impact on wages, as some would claim? In any overall sense, the answer has to be no, because the timing would be wrong. For any type of increase in the labor force to depress wages would take a while to work its way through the economy. As we will see in the next chapter, real weekly wages of production and nonsupervisory workers began their descent in 1973, well *before* the major upswing in immigration numbers or Latino labor force participation that occurred in the 1980s and 1990s. Indeed, some 60% of the immigrant population and 80% of the undocumented population in the US as of 2004 had arrived since 1990.[54] The causes of that fall in wages were the recession of 1974–75, the "stagflation" that followed well into the 1980s, and the wage concessions that began nationally with the 1979 Chrysler bailout and spread throughout industry from the early 1980s onward. Furthermore, if there was to be a negative impact on wages, one would expect it to come in the wake of the enormous increase of immigration from the mid-1980s through the mid-1990s. This would presumably raise unemployment and depress wages. But, in fact, unemployment rates fell and real wages rose after 1995 until the recession of 2000.[55]

Table 4.7   Percentage of Employed Asians and Latinos in Major Occupation Groups, 2003

Occupation	Total (000s)	%Asian	%Latino
Total	137,739	5,785 (100%)	17,355 (100%)
Managerial, Professional	47,929	3,588 (45%)	2,924 (17%)
Service	22,086	928 (16%)	4,108 (24%)
Sales and Office	35,496	1,313 (23%)	3,834 (22%)
Construction, Maintenance & Natural Resources	14,205	227 (4%)	3,026 (17%)
Production & Transport	18,020	703 (12%)	3,424 (20%)

Source: *Statistical Abstract*, 2005, pp. 385–388.

To get a better idea of just where the new immigrant groups fit in the workforce, we will look at the occupational distribution of the two immigrant groups that have grown fastest in recent years: Latinos and Asians. By 2005, foreign-born workers composed 15% of the labor force. Almost half (49%) were Latinos, while 22% were Asians.[56] Both groups have had a long presence in certain industries and occupations going back decades or further. Nevertheless, the rapid growth in numbers of both groups gives them a special place in the changing demographics of the US working class. Table 4.7 shows the percentage among the major occupational groupings of each of the two ethnic groups, both native-born and foreign-born.

Both the ethnic and occupational groups here are very broad, so some care is required in interpreting them. Also note that these are figures for employed people, which can differ from occupational statements given by immigrants upon arrival in the US and also from civilian labor force figures. So, for example, a person from India with a PhD or an MD might end up driving a taxi in New York City for some time. In that sense, these occupational figures are a more accurate reflection for the groups as a whole since they describe what people actually work at.

The first thing to be noticed when figuring out the percentage of the ethnic group that works in an occupational grouping is that 45% of Asians are in the managerial and professional category compared with 17% of Latinos. To some extent this reflects the fact that while 15% of legal immigrants in 2005 fell into the "employment-based preference" category, 33% of Asians entered or had visas renewed on that basis. Still, there are also the New York taxi drivers from the Indian subcontinent and the garment sweatshop workers in New York and Los Angeles from China. Nevertheless, it is clear that Latinos, in particular, fall into many of the poorer-paying working-class occupational groups. Latinos have high percentages in many building trades occupations, as well as in building maintenance, food preparation, housekeeping, apparel, and other low-paying jobs. In one occupation, drywall installers, they are almost half the national workforce at 47%.[57] What seems clear is that Latino workers, whether native-born or immigrant, have fitted into and possibly stuck in some of the lower-paying occupations. Some of this is because of the "ethnic queue" phenomenon described earlier. That is, Latino workers are entering jobs abandoned by other groups so that competition is minimal.

While Latino immigrants can be found almost anywhere in the US, including, for example, meatpacking plants on the Great Plains and deep South, as can Asians, they tend to be concentrated in large numbers in a few urban areas, notably New York, Los Angeles, Chicago, and Miami.[58] The major Latino ethnic groups in these cities are different: Dominicans and Puerto Ricans in New York; Mexicans and Central Americans in Los Angeles and Chicago; Cubans in Miami, etc. By 2000, 27% of the population in New York and 47% of the population in LA was Latino. By most accounts, the new immigrant populations have contributed to economic revitalization in areas like LA and New York hit by de-industrialization in the 1970s and 1980s.[59] It would be naïve to deny that there is some level of competition between newer immigrant groups and other working-class people. Space in these giant cities is finite and the transition from one group to another in a given neighborhood is full of friction. While employment levels are more flexible, there can be friction here too. Yet, what appears to be the case is that there is a strong tendency today, as there was over a hundred years ago, for the various ethnic immigrant groups to concentrate in particular occupations or industries in a given geographic region. So, in LA, for example, the building maintenance workers are heavily Mexican and Central American, as are the dry wall installers, and the truckers on the waterfront. In New York, Latino immigrants are found in greengrocer stores and restaurant kitchens, but also construction, Indians and Pakistanis are found driving cabs, etc.

As we will see later, all of the groups just mentioned have been involved in strikes and efforts to organize some kind of union. Ruth Milkman, in the introduction to a recent study of immigrant organizing reached the following conclusion:

A key finding from this analysis is that recent immigrants (those arriving in 1990 or later) are the least likely to be unionized, whereas those who have been in the United States the longest (arriving before 1980) have unionization levels roughly double those of newcomers, and in California over four times as great.

She goes on to say, "In fact, for the nation's most settled immigrants, union membership is as likely—and for most subgroups more likely— as for native workers."[60] In other words, as time goes on and immigrants become more accustomed to their new home or establish documented status, they are as or more likely to join or organize a union than native-born Americans. The outpouring of millions of immigrant workers on May 1, 2006 was certainly a signal that they will fight for a better life even in the face of repression and possible job-loss. These signs are extremely important as they can lay the basis for current and future organizing. One of the problems we saw in the period from 1870 to 1920 was that many of the AFL unions shunned immigrant workers. Although US unions have a history of anti-foreigner attitudes and practices, that has begun to change. In addition, immigrants are already attempting to organize in a variety of ways. The question is, are the strategies and structures of today's unions fit for the job? Are they even looking at some of the immigrant groups with the most potential bargaining power?

5

LOST DECADES

In the 1970s, thirty years of economic gains for working-class people stopped and began to go into reverse. Underlying the long-term economic decline in working-class living standards were the big trends discussed in chapters 2 and 3: concessions, lean production, outsourcing, major shifts in employment to lower-paying jobs, international competition, and a political atmosphere that will be discussed in a later chapter. Free trade, footloose capital, cut-throat competition all led US capital to put the brakes on working-class living standards and working conditions in the 1970s and 1980s and then to attempt to solve the problem of slumping profit rates by pushing back such gains as labor had made since the end of World War 2. These efforts were all too successful. Organized labor seemed incapable of stopping this assault. Although there were a few years, notably the second half of the 1990s, when wages and incomes recovered slightly, the most basic measure of working-class income, average weekly wages, remained far below the high point achieved in the early 1970s by early 2006. Neither longer hours nor increased productivity could save the day.

As Table 5.1 shows, average real weekly wages reached their high point in 1972 at $315.44. They began an unbroken twenty-year descent to $254.87, the low point, in 1993. After that, real weekly wages would go up and down, but never come anywhere near their all-time high. The 11% increase gained from 1993 to 2001 was wiped out after 2003. By early 2006, the average production and nonsupervisory worker was stuck with 1960s buying power, the reward for longer hours and intensified work. Real weekly wages were 13% below their 1972 level. Perhaps all this could be blamed on inflation, a constant rise in the prices of what we buy. This was plausible during the 1970s when inflation was out of control—the period of "stagflation." But prices grew more slowly in the 1980s, slower still in the 1990s and into the 2000s.[1] One culprit was the hourly wage. The average annual

Table 5.1   **Real Average Weekly Wages (1982 dollars) for Production and Nonsupervisory Workers**

Year	Weekly Wage
1950	$212.52
1972	$315.44 High Point
1982	$267.26
1992	$254.99
1993	$254.87 Low Point
1994	$256.73
1995	$255.07
1996	$255.73
1997	$261.31
1998	$268.32
1999	$271.25
2000	$271.96
2001	$275.38
2002	$278.83
2003	$278.75
2004	$277.82
2005	$273.93 March
2006	$274.49 March

Sources: Labor Research Association-Online March 2001; *Economic Report*, 2005, p. 266; US Bureau of Labor Statistics, USDL 06-694, April 19, 2006, Table 1, www.bls.gov.

rate at which the dollar value of the hourly wage grew slowed down from decade to decade: 1970–79 8.6%; 1980–89 4.3%; 1990–99 3.2%; 2000–04 3.0%. With this deceleration of hourly wage growth, it took a smaller amount of inflation to knock down real hourly rates. Average real hourly wages went from $8.99 in 1972 to a low point of $7.52 in 1993. After that they rose to a high of $8.27 in 2003, but by March of 2006 were down to $8.19, still about 9% below the 1972 rate. In manufacturing, where the trend was the same, workers attempted to make up for this loss in real hourly wages by working longer hours. In the 1970s and 1980s workers put in an average of 3.2 hours of overtime a week. In the 1990s it was up to 4.5 hours a week. From 2000 through 2004, despite slow economic growth, the average weekly

overtime hit 5.4 hours.[2] Employers had long ago discovered that given
the costs of benefits, it was cheaper to have existing employees work
overtime than to hire new ones. This increase in hours does explain
at least some of the actual increase in real weekly wages in the 1990s
and early 2000s. Without the overtime, real weekly wages would have
fallen even more. Yet, even longer hours could not recover a 1970s
wage.

Wages, of course, are not the same for everyone. Race and gender
still affect what a worker will earn on average. So in 2003, according
to economists at the Economic Policy Institute, whites made $16.82
an hour, Blacks $12.23, and Latinos $10.67. Over the period 1989–
2000 when there was a slight increase in real wages, whites and Blacks
made small gains, while Latinos actually lost ground slightly. Over
that period the gap in real hourly wages between Blacks and whites
scarcely changed: 72.4% to 72.7%. But the gap between Latinos and
whites actually widened from 67.3% in 1989 to 63.4% in 2003. The
gap between male and female wage earners continued to decline, though
it did not disappear. In 1989, women on average made 73.1% of a
man's hourly wage. By 2003 it had gone up to 81%.[3] Despite some
improvement for women and Blacks, a falling real wage would impact
women and people of color even more seriously.

With all the talk about the high cost of health care benefits, you
might think that the benefits piece of total compensation, not included
in the wage figures above, might have brought increased indirect buying
power. Not so—at least in the private sector. From 1989 through
2000 the annual real dollar value of all benefits (health, pensions,
payroll taxes, etc.) in private sector compensation fell by almost one
percent a year, or about 10% for that period. It rose from 2000–03
by 2.5% a year, making up most of the value lost during the 1990s,
but not yet representing any real progress.[4] But even these figures hide
the problem faced by millions in terms of lost benefits. Table 5.2
shows the declining coverage of both health care insurance and pensions.
On both fronts everyone lost. Again, however, coverage was unequal
across race and gender from the beginning and did not improve, except
for some groups in the 1990s. Here the impact of immigration can
be seen in the very low coverage rate for Latinos, particularly after
1979. Immigrants, especially of course undocumented workers, are
much less likely to get health care or pension benefits because of the
jobs so many hold. Indeed, workers in high-wage jobs are much more
likely to have a pension plan (73.3%) than low-wage workers (14.6%).[5]

The coverage rates only begin to tell the story of the erosion of
benefits over the years. In terms of pensions, even those who remain
covered have seen significant changes in the last decade or two. One
of the biggest changes is that from defined benefits plans to defined

Table 5.2   **Private Health Care and Pension Benefits Coverage, 1979–2003**

Employer-Provided Health Insurance Coverage			
Year	1979	1989	2000	2003
All Workers	69.0%	61.5%	58.9%	56.4%
Men	75.4%	66.8%	63.2%	59.7%
Women	59.4%	54.9%	53.3%	52.3%
White	70.3%	64.0%	62.7%	60.3%
Black	63.1%	56.3%	55.4%	54.3%
Latino	60.4%	46.0%	41.8%	39.3%
Employer-Provided Pension Coverage			
All Workers	50.6%	43.7%	48.3%	45.9%
Men	56.9%	46.9%	50.3%	47.2%
Women	41.3%	39.6%	45.8%	44.3%
White	52.2%	46.1%	53.7%	51.1%
Black	45.8%	40.7%	41.3%	40.9%
Latino	38.2%	26.3%	27.5%	25.8%

Source: Mishel, et al., *The State of Working America, 2004/2005*, pp. 138–139.

contribution plans. Under the traditional defined benefit plan a worker could know how much retirement income he or she could expect. Under a defined contribution program this is no longer the case and benefits are up to the vagaries of the market. In 1992–93, 32% of employees had defined benefits plans, while 35% participated in defined contribution programs. By 2005, defined contribution plans accounted for 42% of all plans and defined benefits programs for only 21%. Aside from the uncertainty, most defined contribution plans require employee contributions, something defined benefit plans seldom did. In 2003, 36% of these plans required a 100% contribution, over 80% called for 50% or more by the employee. So, this becomes one more way workers lose income. Rates of participation in these different plans differed by types of employment. So, 64% of white-collar workers had defined contribution plans in 2005 compared with 50% of blue-collar workers. Those covered by a union contract were far more likely to have a defined benefit plan in 2005: 73% compared with only 16% of nonunion workers.[6]

According to BLS figures, the real value of benefits dropped from $2.41 an hour in 1987 to $2.19 in 2000. Health insurance value fell from a high of $1.77 in 1992 to $1.36 in 2000. After that it rose to $1.52 largely on the basis of a surge in medical costs.[7] The percentage of people working in medium or large companies covered by medical plans fell from 97% in 1980 to 76% in 1997, the last year for which the BLS published these figures. The percentage required to make a contribution rose from 26% in 1980 to 69% in 1997 for individuals and from 46% to 80% for family coverage in those years. The amount of the average monthly contribution for individuals rose from $11.92 in 1984 to $39.14 in 1997. For families it went from $35.93 to $130.07 in those years.[8] This, of course, does not cover co-pays and other items that have risen in more and more plans over the years. All of this comes out of the monthly wage, so that the decline in real weekly wages discussed above only begins the story of declining buying power.

According to mainstream economic theory, real wage increases are financed by increases in productivity. In order to prevent a hasty struggle over slices of the economic pie, labor should strive to increase its output per hour, thus expanding the size of the pie itself so all can have more. This is not only a matter of faith for most economists, but has long been a piece of the ideology of the American labor leadership. If this were truly the case, real wages should have risen significantly over the years since productivity did rise. From 1980 to 1990 productivity in the nonfarm business economy rose by an average of 1.7% a year. This is not great, but it was an increase, whereas real wages fell. In the 1990s, productivity averaged 2.2%. Still not great, but apparently enough to allow for a real wage increase of less than one percent a year from the low point of 1993 to 2000. From 2000 to 2004 productivity jumped by an average of 4% a year, but after a slight increase of 2.5% for two years up to 2002, real wages again slipped by almost 2% down to early 2005. In fact, as the Economic Policy Institute noted, although the long period from the mid-1970s to 1995 was usually thought of as one of a "productivity slowdown" compared with the three decades before, throughout the entire period from 1973 to 2003, "productivity growth far outpaced that of compensation" (wages plus benefits).[9] Clearly, somebody else received the gains from productivity.

Part of what underlay the slow growth of wages was a shift in employment noted in chapter 3. Gone were four million or so manufacturing jobs, many union jobs, that paid better than the service and retail jobs that replaced them and became the main source of employment for millions entering the labor market after 1973. Things do not look much better for the future. In its growth projections from 2002 to 2012, the Bureau of Labor Statistics projects 27 "Largest Job Growth" occupations. Of these, 16 comprising almost two-thirds of the total of 8.9 million new jobs providing the largest growth are among the two lowest paying categories, almost all requiring no more than "Short-term on-the-job training." In short, dead-end jobs. The lowest paid group would earn *up to* $19,600 a year, while the next category would earn up to $27,380.[10] The fact that two-thirds of the occupations providing the largest job growth require so little training also puts the lie to the idea that the job problem can be solved with more training and education of individuals. Indeed, back in the 1990s, Jack Gordon, editor of *Training* magazine, noted that companies were dumping their more experienced workers and concluded, "companies getting rid of their more experienced employees are not looking for higher skills. They're looking for younger workers, people who'll work cheaper."[11] And so it seems. The future does not look much brighter than the recent past.

Given the long-term fall in real wages, one might expect family or household income to decline as well. For some it did, but the median income of all families rose until 2000 and then slumped for the three largest racial groups. The gap between white incomes and those of Black families closed somewhat until after 2000, while that between whites and Latinos grew steadily. Again, the poor growth of Latino income reflects their place on the job ladder, but also the growing proportion who are immigrants and likely to be stuck with the worst entry-level jobs. While all three groups saw income rise, the rates were different. Median white real family income rose by 18% from 1979 to 2000 and then fell by 1.6%. Black family income rose 32.4% in that period, almost twice the rate of whites, but then fell by 4.5%, over three times the rate of whites. Latino family income increased by 10.6% by 2000, the slowest of the three groups, and then fell by 6.8% in 2003, the deepest fall. It seems fairly clear that the income drops were due to the recession and rising unemployment which affected each group differently. The unemployment rate for whites went from

Table 5.3 **Median Real Family Income by Race/Ethnicity, 1979–2003**

($ 2003)

Year	1979	1989	2000	2003
White	$47,990	$51,539	$56,645	$55,768
Black	$27,175	$28,952	$35,972	$34,369
% White	56.6	56.2	63.5	61.6
Latino	$33,268	$33,589	$36,790	$34,272
% White	69.3	65.2	64.9	61.5

Source: Mishel et al., *The State of Working America, 2004/2005*, p. 48.

2.6% in 2000 to 4.3% in 2003, while that for Blacks went from 5.4% to 8.3% and that for Latinos from 4.4% to 6.4%.[12] Still, we have to ask why family incomes, despite the drop from 2000 to 2003 and possibly more after that, nonetheless, remained above the 1970s levels.

The major explanation lies in increased working time. Not just the overtime in manufacturing mentioned earlier. We saw in an earlier chapter that the average annual work time of a manufacturing production worker rose from 1,898 hours in 1982 to 1,977 in 2002, an increase that nearly equaled an additional two weeks in the working year.[13] That didn't affect weekly wage rates, but it must have had some small effect on annual income. For example, by 2002 this would have added $557.66 to the average production worker's annual wage; that is, not much. The real explanation, however, lies not in the increased hours of individual workers, but the increased work time of most families. The term "working families" has come into common use not only to dodge the more suggestive "working-class families," but because the phenomenon of families in which both adults and sometimes older offspring all work for wages has become the norm. We saw that married women began entering the labor market in large numbers as far back as the 1950s. Since the 1970s, however, not only their numbers but the hours they put in have risen significantly. Husbands also put in more hours, but the increase was much smaller as most already worked a regular workweek. It is no surprise, furthermore, that those in lower income groups have extended their work time more. Wives in the lowest fifth of the income ladder increased their work time by 61.1% from 1979 through 2002; those in the second lowest fifth by 69.5% and those in the middle fifth by 54.5%. Wives in the top two fifths, representing most of the middle and upper classes, increased their hours by 33.1% and 30.8% respectively. Thus, from 43.5% to 52.7% of the increased income of families in the bottom three fifths of the population was due solely to increased work time, according to EPI. The decline from 2000–02 was similarly due to decreased work time as the economy slowed. It is clear that had the hours of wives not increased as rapidly as they did, family incomes would have fallen almost as drastically as real weekly wages. Indeed, in married households where the wife was not in the paid labor force, the real family income did fall slightly from 1979 to 2003.[14]

By now, married women working for wages is hardly news. The so-called "family wage," by which the male breadwinner was supposedly able to support the entire family is long gone.[15] Married women with children working for wages is not news either, but it is a very difficult proposition in this country. Almost 60% of women with children under six work for wages, while 76% of those with children from ages

6 to 17 are also active in the labor force.[16] To do this, mothers must leap many barriers and deal with endless problems. Jody Heymann summarized some of these in her book *The Widening Gap* when she wrote:

> The overwhelming majority of children in this country are raised in households in which every adult works at a wage or salary job. Yet, in spite of this, school days are usually two-thirds as long as typical workdays, the school year has 30 percent fewer days than the work year, and the need for out-of-school care far outstrips its availability. Leave from work to care for their children's health or to address critical educational issues is unavailable to tens of millions of Americans.
>
> Affordable, decent care for preschool children is available to fewer families than paid leave. Care for preschool children costs more than a state university education—with far more limited financial aid.[17]

As Heymann goes on to show throughout her book, most employers offer little in the way of flexibility and women lose jobs when they have to take time off for family emergencies. Children must be left alone at times. Those whose parents are both away at work frequently have problems at school, etc. The Family Medical Leave Act of 1993 has been some help. But again, as Heymann points out, "Most of the reasons parents needed to take leave from work to help school-age children were covered neither by the FMLA nor by existing programs serving school-age children."[18] A society in which so many leaders and opinion-makers talk of family values does little to actually aid the working family.

Taking the long view, it becomes clearer that the majority of Americans, roughly the working class, has seen a reversal of fortune in the last half century. Table 5.4 shows the real family income growth by population fifths (quintiles) from 1947 to 1973 and 1973 to 2000. What is apparent here is that during the years after WW2 and up to the recession of 1974–75 almost everyone saw their family's income double or nearly so. In fact, the top fifth did a little worse than the rest, while the poorest in the bottom fifth did the best. This was the

Table 5.4   **Real Family Income Growth 1947–2000 by Income Level**

Years	Lowest 5th	2nd 5th	3rd 5th	4th 5th	Top 5th
1947–1973	116.1%	97.1%	98.2%	103.0%	84.8%
1973–2000	12.1%	18.3%	26.6%	36.5%	66.9%

Sources: Mishel et al., *The State of Working America 2004/2005*, p. 71.

era of faster economic growth, less "free trade," more manufacturing, Great Society programs, and stronger unions. From 1973 to 2000, incomes slowed down, but much more so for the lower three fifths and even the fourth fifth. Those in the top fifth did much better. From 2000 to 2003, the lowest three fifths all saw a drop in family income, meaning that some though not all of the gain up to 2000 was wiped out.[19] So it is that over the last thirty years or so workers have lost wage income, while their families have struggled to keep heads above water by extending their working time, not to mention working harder under today's lean and mean regime. Productivity, though not up to earlier standards until after 2000, nevertheless ran ahead of wages. What had shaped up was a transfer of income and wealth from the working class to capital and its owners. What emerged was a society of extremes—the haves having more, the have-nots growing in number.

Poverty: the Competition of Capitals, not of Workers is Primary

The official poverty rate in the US fell from 22.4% in 1959 to 11.1% in 1973. After that it rose again, with some ups and downs, reaching 12.5% in 2003. The decline, of course, was due to the growing incomes of the earlier period as well as various anti-poverty programs, notably Medicaid and Medicare. It was also due to the migration of Blacks from the South in the 1950s and 1960s; i.e., from rural poverty to urban-based industrial jobs for many. The resurgence of poverty was due to stagnating incomes in the bottom fifth of the population, itself a product of industrial shift. In 1973 when the poverty rate hit its historic low point there were 22,973,000 people officially poor. In 2003, that number was 35,861,000.[20] In 2003, there were more whites in poverty than African Americans, Asians, and Latinos combined: 24,272,000 (67.7%) to 19,233,000. Yet, racism and discrimination in employment, housing, and education among other things, make poverty the great discriminator. In 2003, 10.5% of whites were counted poor, while 24.4% of Blacks, and 22.5% of Latinos earned below the poverty line. The ratio of Black or Latino poverty to white has declined somewhat over the years. Back in 1980, the percentages were 10.2% for whites, 32.5% for African Americans, and 25.7% for Latinos. Nevertheless, the gap remains large. In 2003, the rates for foreign-born whites (18.8%) and Latinos (23.1%) were higher than those for the native-born. For Blacks, it was the opposite. Native-born Blacks had a poverty rate of 25.1%, compared with 16.0% for foreign-born Blacks, reminding us that despite all the racial changes and well-advertised multiculturalism of the country, African Americans remain the number one target of discrimination and racism. It was also due to the fact that the loss of industrial jobs hit African Americans particularly hard, as it was blue-collar employment that brought many who moved North out of poverty in the first place. The reversal of this can be seen in the fact that Black poverty was higher in the industrial Midwest (24.9%) than in the South (22.3%) in 2003.[21] The question remains why in the richest nation in the world is there so much poverty?

It is easy to say that poverty stems from unemployment and low wages. On top of that there is the lack of government policies that could alleviate poverty. But there are deeper reasons found in the economic system that make poverty, at one or another level, inevitable. First is what Marx called the reserve army of labor. That is the unemployed, the displaced, those not counted in the labor force but who are looking for work, and those who might be forced back into the labor market by adversity. Most recently this would include many of the millions forced off welfare. A rough count for 2004 would give a core reserve army of 8.1 million unemployed plus 2.1 million "not in the labor force" but looking for work, for a total of 10.2 million.[22] But the latent reserve army, including married women not yet working, many of the disabled, teenagers leaving school, etc., is much larger. Immigration feeds this army at times, but is no larger a piece of it than the others. This reserve army pulls down on the general wage level, particularly among the least skilled and lowest paid. It is constantly fed by the displacement of workers from their current jobs, which will tend to ratchet down wages even among the once well-paid.

The reserve army, however, exists in a context. It has a disciplining effect on workers in general, and on specific industries as workers are displaced by technology, plants closing, or business reorganization, but it can't by itself explain the wide discrepancy in wage levels. As economist Howard Botwinick has argued, the basic mechanism is not simply the skills of the individuals competing in the labor market. Rather it is the competition between capitals that leads to this "persistent inequality." Competition pushes capitals to mechanize and automate, thus creating different profit rates within and between industries. Those with lower profit rates will attempt to lower labor costs. Over time this ongoing competitive process will lead to wage differentials, partly through de-skilling as well as through worker displacement. At the extremes, wage differentials are greatest between capital intensive and labor intensive industries. The return of sweatshops, the rise of low-wage contracting, and industrial homework that characterize much of the garment and electronics industries in the US are clear examples that brutal competition between marginal capitals, in particular, necessarily produces poverty-level wages. It is the competition of capitals, not just the competition among workers, that is determinant.[23]

Some nine million adults, 43% of the total, living in official poverty work. Millions more just above the official poverty line are also compelled to take such work as they can get. Of course, the whole shift of employment from capital intensive manufacturing to labor intensive service jobs we saw earlier guarantees the continuance of a large low-wage workforce—at least until these jobs are unionized. Displacement tends to move workers from better-paid jobs to worse ones. For example, in 2004 the government counted 5.3 million workers displaced from jobs they had held for three or more years in 2001 by plant or company closings (46.5%), slack work (28.3%), or the abolition of the job (28.6%). These were workers laid off in 2001 and 20% still had no job by 2004. In that year, 57% of these displaced workers made less than they had in their old job.[24] Looking at the layoffs of some 16,000 workers in southern California due to industrial restructuring in the 1980s, Fernandez Kelly argued that this displacement laid the basis for the growth of low-wage employment in the nearby electronics industry.[25] So it is that the so-called creative destruction by which capitalism replaces one industry with another is also part of the mechanism that reinforces low wages and poverty and recruits to the reserve army of labor.

Historically, organized labor fought for programs that would both alleviate the impact of unemployment and underemployment and reduce pressures on the labor market. Programs like unemployment insurance and "welfare" were won by organized labor in the 1930s precisely to alleviate this impact. But "welfare" is all but gone, with the number of people receiving Temporary Assistance for Needy Families having dropped from 13.2 million in 1995 to 5.2 million in 2002, while only about 38% of the unemployed are insured these days.[26] The other major piece of government policy labor fought for was the minimum wage. This still exists, but its purchasing power and hence its protective value have shrunk over the years. The minimum wage reached its highest real value in 1979 when it was worth $6.81 in 2003 dollars. Despite five increases in the dollar value over the years since, its real value plunged to $5.50 in 2000 and $5.15 in 2003. As a percentage of the average hourly wage, the minimum wage rose to over 50% in the late 1960s and then fell, with minor ups and downs, to 34% in 2003. Only a little more than half a million hourly workers get the $5.15 minimum, but another 1.5 million actually make less according to the official figures.[27] This does not include the millions of invisible workers who toil in the nation's growing underground or informal economy. So, America's already minimalist, now shredding welfare state does little to head off poverty or low wages more generally.

Wealth: Capital Wins, Labor Loses

While working-class families were seeing real wages fall and their incomes hold up only by working longer hours, members of the capitalist class saw their incomes soar and their wealth accumulate. The best known example of this is the annual compensation of Corporate America's CEOs. The AFL-CIO notes that the ratio of CEO pay to that of the average workers rose from a mere 42 times in 1980 to a high of 531 times in 2000. With recession and the slump in stock prices, it went down to 431 times in 2004. The federation reports that the average compensation of a CEO in the Standard & Poor 500 was $11.75 million in 2005.[28] If you look only at the top 100 companies it goes up to $17.9 million, which was reported to be a 25% jump over 2004.[29] But these are only averages. Just as some do worse, others do better, much better. William McGuire, CEO of UnitedHealthcare, pulled in $1.5 billion, as medical costs soared across the nation.[30] This, as you will see below, was up from $819 million in 2004. Then there was James Kilts who pulled in $150 million for selling his company, Gillette, to Proctor & Gamble. Just down the pay scale was CEO David H. Brooks who earned $70 million and whose defense contracting company, DHB, allegedly sold the Marines defective body armor.[31] By the way, the average compensation of CEOs at the top 34 defense contractors was $11.6 million in 2004. And while David Brooks was the star earner in that group, Van Honeycutt, whose firm, Computer Sciences, does police training in Iraq, made almost $20 million in 2004.[32]

Typically, the big bucks come from stocks and stock options. Executive compensation is figured in different ways. A common way to figure total compensation is to add to the cash salary, bonuses, incentives, restricted stock awards that must be cashed in within a certain time period, and stock options already exercised. This, of course, understates the actual value of the annual pay package since the unexercised options are not included. In Table 5.5, I reproduce selected examples from *Business Week*'s 2005 "BW 50 Executive Compensation" survey of both compensation, figured as above, and total stock option value for 2004. It is clear that a CEO who was paid anything like this kind of money over time would become a billionaire before too long. Indeed, over fifteen years, the country's top ten CEOs accumulated $11.7 *billion* among them.[33]

The theory behind the big switch from mere large cash salaries to big chunks of stock goes back to the early 1990s when two academics,

Table 5.5   CEO Pay Top Ten: Compensation and Total Stock Options, 2004

CEO	Company	Compensation	Total Value of Options
William McGuire	UnitedHealth	$10.0 million	$806 million
Irwin Mark Jacobs	Qualcom	$3.1 million	$407 million
Margaret Whitman	eBay	$2.9 million	$305 million
John Chambers	Cisco Sys.	$1.9 million	$263 million
Terry Semel	Yahoo!	$601,980	$290 million
John Thompson	Symantec	$2.7 million	$214 million
Kevin Rollins	Dell	$2.5 million	$210 million
Ray Irani	Occidental	$30.9 million	$181 million
Edwin Crawford	Caremark	$1.8 million	$171 million
James Tobin	Boston Sci.	$2.0 million	$98 million

Source: "BW 50 Executive Compensation," *Business Week Online* April 4, 2005,
www.businessweek.com

Michael Jensen of Harvard and Kevin Murphy of Rochester University,
argued that the executives of that day were not sufficiently focused on
profits and dividends. They acted like corporate bureaucrats, not
entrepreneurs. To shake them out of their bureaucratic lethargy, these
two proposed that they get stocks to align their interests with those
of shareholders.[34] The executives took their advice and did, in fact,
become more focused on earnings. Dividends soared past "retained
earnings" during the 1990s and beyond. Companies bought back shares
to increase their value and borrowed heavily to do it.[35] As the CEOs
and other executives accumulated stocks, stock price surpassed all other
indicators as their goal.[36] This led to other new and creative tactics.
One, which was more or less legal, was to have the company announce
the presumably good earnings for the quarter just after the stock options
were granted so that their value would rise and the CEO could cash
them in for a big gain. A 2006 examination by the watchdog group
The Corporate Library of ten top S&P 500 companies revealed "24
occasions out of 37 where the timing of press releases increased the
value of recently-awarded stock options."[37] Another way to do the same
thing is to make sure that the stock options are granted when the
company's stock price is unusually low. Still more creative and more
illegal is backdating the option. Mr. McGuire, who we met above,
was accused by shareholders of doing just this.[38] At its most extreme
this sort of entrepreneurialism leads to Enron-style fudging of company
finances.

Table 5.6   **Top Ten Recent CEO Annual Retirement Packages**

CEO Senior	Company	$ Value of Package
Lee Raymond	ExxonMobil	$8,187,200
Henry McKinnell	Pfizer	$6,518,459
Edward Whitacre	AT&T	$5,494,107
William McGuire	UnitedHealth	$5,092,000
Robert Nardell	Home Depot	$4,612,500
Samuel Palmisano	IBM	$4,550,000
Ruben	Colgate-Palmolive	$3,700,000
Brian Roberts	Comcast	$3,600,000
Kenneth Lewis	Bank of America	$3,486,425
Richard Davidson	Union Pacific	$2,700,000

Source: AFL-CIO, Corporate Watch, www.aflcio.org.

The accumulation of outsized wealth doesn't end when the CEO retires. The public became aware of the practice of granting of huge "pensions" to retiring CEOs when in the midst of his divorce proceedings, former GE CEO Jack Welsh, who made $123 million in his last year on the job, was to get $2 million a year in retirement funds and benefits.[39] By 2005 the practice was common and the $2 million more like a minimum. Table 5.6 shows the retirement packages for the top ten CEO seniors. We cannot help but notice that William McGuire, who keeps showing up, is among the most favored corporate retirees. In any case, none of the top twenty-five on the AFL-CIO broader list was to get less than $2 million a golden year.

The rationale for all this pay and pensions is that these invaluable individuals brought their company and its shareholders more value. Sometimes this is the case, but a 2006 study by The Corporate Library found that while ten companies that recorded $82.7 billion in stockholder gains over five years paid their top executives $190 million over that period, another ten paid their CEOs $865 million for losing $640 billion in shareholder value.[40] Another rationale for this high pay is that once you pay one CEO this much, you have to pay others more or less the same or they'll fly the coop. Who would leave a job that pays millions regardless of performance? If this is really about performance, how is it that the US economy did much better back in the days of the six-figure bureaucrats that Jensen and Murphy so despised than it has done in the hands of the bold multimillion dollar marketeers? In any case, the real reason for all of this is something else. Paul Krugman writes:

The key reason executives are paid so much now is that they appoint the members of the corporate board that determines their compensation and control many of the perks that board members count on. So it's not the invisible hand of the market that leads to those monumental executive incomes; it's the invisible handshake in the boardroom.[41]

The perks, for this part-time job, have been on the rise. In 2005, the average compensation for a director at a large corporation rose by 14% in one year to $144,000 a year. The average estimated time on the job for a director was 191 hours in 2005, for an hourly rate of $753.00. For smaller S&P 500 companies the average annual compensation for board members was $56,500, or $296 an hour. The result of this invisible handshake was described by Daniel Steininger, chair of Catholic Funds Investments, when he said, "I think they're more tolerant of nonperformance. Directors paid that kind of money are not going to ask hard questions."[42] But, there's more. Also very often in the act is a consultant. These are hired by the CEO. And like the directors, they are paid a lot to do a little. Typically, they recommend as much or more than other CEOs are getting. So, the money heading for the top all goes up.[43] But does it matter?

Apologists for this set-up say no. In fact many Americans who have no hope of ever seeing this kind of money say no. "What does it matter what William McGuire gets? I won't see any of it," is an answer you might hear. But it's wrong. As economist Krugman put it directly, "if the rich get more, that leaves less for everyone else."[44] Each year, the working class generates only so much surplus. If CEOs and investors keep taking more, then each year there will be less for the rest. And that is just what has been happening. If the incomes of the wealthier grow faster than those lower down the income scale, the wealthy will keep getting a larger share—and less will be available for the rest.

Table 5.7 **Family Income Growth and Shares, 1973–2003**

Growth	Bottom 5th	2nd 5th	3rd 5th	4th 5th	Top 5th
1973–2000	12.1%	18.3%	26.6%	36.5%	66.9%
2000–2003	-2.0%	-1.2%	-0.3%	0.2%	-0.2%
Share 1973	5.5%	11.9%	17.5%	24.0%	41.1%
2000	4.3%	9.8%	15.5%	22.8%	47.4%
2003	4.1%	9.6%	15.5%	23.3%	47.6%

Sources: Mishel et al., *The State of Working America 2004/2005*, pp. 67–71.

Table 5.7 looks at growth rate for income fifths of families from 1973 to 2000 and at the shares for the same years. The top fifth of families saw their income grow much faster than any other group and ended up with a bigger share of a bigger pie. Everyone else lost ground over the long haul. It is true that the real incomes of all groups grew to one degree or another, but the lower on the ladder the slower the growth. From 1947 through 1973 the trend was the opposite, the top fifth grew more slowly than the others and, hence, the real living standards of the majority rose fairly rapidly. Then came the "Great U-Turn."

The richest got richer not only because of outsized CEO or director compensation. It was also because of the sources of their income. It grew from accumulated wealth—assets that produce claims on the surplus like stocks, bonds, land, etc.

What matters is which class owns the bulk of these claims on profits and assets *and* which class is *excluded* from such property rights in capital as well as from daily management. This exclusion is as safe today as it was in the heyday of private ownership. As of 2004, there were $109.2 trillion in financial assets, i.e. all claims on capital, in the US. Of this total, $13.1 trillion rests safely in the hands of non-financial businesses (mostly the corporations themselves), while another $8.5 trillion is held by commercial banks. Excluding private and public sector pension funds, which we will deal with later, another $25.1 trillion is held by financial businesses other than banks (investment houses, insurance companies, mutual funds, etc.)—all safely outside the grasp of the working class. Another $9.3 trillion is held outside the country, almost certainly in the hands of capitalists and corporations elsewhere. Thus, at least $56 trillion or 51.3% of financial assets are in the hands of capitalist institutions. Various levels of government hold $6.4 trillion or 5.9%, which, while not directly controlled by capitalists, are out of the reach of the workers.[45]

Continuing this look at the distribution of financial assets, those owned directly by households amount to $36.8 trillion or another 33.7% of the total. The richest 1% owned 33.6% of all stock by value. The next 9% owned 43.3%. Thus, the wealthiest 10% owned 76.9% of all stock held by households. The middle class would share 12.4%. Altogether the bottom two-thirds of households in the US (over 200 million people), more or less the working class, owned a mere 10.7% of all personally held financial assets. So, excluding pension funds and government held assets, capital and its collective institutions owned roughly $84.3 trillion or 77.2% of financial assets. Far from moving in the direction of broader ownership, 75% of the growth in stock ownership from 1989 through 2001 was accounted for by the top 10% of all households.[46]

Public and private pension funds amounted to $7.5 trillion or 6.9% of total financial assets in 2004. Pensions are regarded as deferred wages, although recently we see that corporate pension funds are deliberately under-funded and sometimes defaulted on. In any case, most pension funds are run by the corporations that provide them or by professional business managers in order to maximize their return. The idea that the stocks and bonds in these funds at any given moment "belong" to the workers in any real way is largely a fiction. What belongs to the workers and what they have claims on are the retirement benefits, the deferred wages, negotiated by the union, unilaterally set by the employer, or determined by the markets. The only types of pension funds on which workers have even an indirect influence, and it is very indirect, are the so-called Taft-Hartley plans such as those negotiated by the Teamsters, Mine Workers, and building trades unions. Even here, the workers don't have much say. One advocate of improved pension fund governance explained it this way:

> To summarize, unionized Taft-Hartley plans, which are collectively bargained, jointly managed plans and by far the smallest of plan assets, are the only categories in which owners—that is workers—have a say in the management of the funds. The others, which contain more than $4 trillion of pension fund assets, although nominally owned by workers and retirees, are in fact managed with little employee involvement. Although close to $2 trillion is invested in DC (defined contribution) plans in which individuals select broad asset allocations, participants in fact often exercise little real choice, because the range of choices and fund investment decisions are determined without their input.[47]

In fact, as this same author goes on to explain, corporations routinely "integrate pension finance decisions with corporate decisions." This is a rather polite way of saying that corporations routinely raid their pension funds, particularly in the 1990s when stock prices inflated the value of these funds, to improve their quarterly earnings figures— there's that CEO maximizing his stock options again! They also plunder them by charging high fees and salaries for their managers and trustees. Pension assets even play a role in leveraged buyouts and mergers and in this way are actually used against the workers. If there really is any "ownership" or control of these funds by the workers, it would be hard to explain that, while the value of the funds increased by 413% from 1979 to 1998, the average benefit actually fell by 33% in the same period.[48] No capitalist owner of a mutual fund, trust, hedge fund, or other form of collectively held assets would suffer so little control or have to face such a fall in returns when the value of assets was swelling in a bull market that rose by 900% in those years. They would, at the very least, take their money elsewhere, something the workers cannot do with "their" pension assets.

If we look at the distribution of all net financial assets, including bonds, commercial paper, etc. minus debt, we see that the top 10% control 80%, while the other 90% of households in the US share only 20% among them and that quite unequally as well. Back in 1962, the top 10% controlled 62% of net financial assets, leaving more for the middle class. This makes it clear that, as a social class, capital is well in control of the ownership of the nation's means of production. The differing claims on various assets such as stocks, bonds, loans, commercial paper, etc. are claims within the capitalist class and the circuits of capital. Furthermore, at the very pinnacle of the capitalist class, the top 1% of the population, these claims are themselves run like businesses in a variety of collective institutions that perpetuate the fortunes of old money families and expand those of the newcomers. Much of this was described by Domhoff in the 1980s. Kevin Phillips has updated this. Writing of the American old rich as a hereditary elite, he says, "Elaborate trusts, well-staffed family offices, and professional financial management had combined into the US equivalent of the entail and primogeniture that kept the landed wealth intact and concentrated in eighteenth and nineteenth century Britain." Quoting *Forbes* magazine, he notes that the forty-three living descendants of Cornelius Vanderbilt, one of America's earliest rail tycoons, are to this day all wealthy people. He shows as well that from the early 1980s through 1999 the wealth of both old money families and high tech parvenus grew by a factor of ten, at the very least, to fortunes ranging from the $7 billion of the old line Phipps family and $8 billion of the Rockefellers, up to the slightly weightier $13 billion of the DuPonts all the way to neophyte Bill Gates' $85 billion stash. Old and new alike would be hit significantly by the stock market slide that began in the summer of 2000 and accelerated two years later. Few at the very top, however, would even lose their billionaire status let alone descend into the middle class. Gates, for example, slipped to $55 billion as of 2001.[49]

The secret of unequal incomes lies very largely in the totally one-sided nature of who owns the claims on America's businesses and on the surplus produced by their workers from which profits are derived. The rich have done better than the rest because the returns on these claims have grown much faster than wages and benefits.

Table 5.8 shows the growth rates for different types of income. With the exception of net interest, most forms of income to capital or the wealthy grew at a much faster rate than worker income. If inflation were figured in the difference would be even greater. Overall, the different income types as well as outcomes brought about a shift

Table 5.8 Income Growth by Source, 1990–2004

Source	1990	2004	% Growth
Corporate Profits ($ bil.)	$438	$1,021	133
Dividends	$169	$444	163
Stock Price (NYSE Index)	$1,939.5	$6,612.6	241
Net Interest	$442	$548	24
Chained $2000 Index	81.6	108.3	33
Average Weekly Wages	$349	$529	52
CPI-U	131	189	44
Income Shift from Labor to Capital			
Capital Income	13.9%	19.1%	18.1
Labor Income	75.6%	71.8%	72.1

Sources: *Economic Report of the President*, 2005, pp. 242–243, 266, 279, 315, 320–321; EPI, *The State of Working America 2004/2005*, p. 93.

of the nation's income away from labor to capital. In fact, the figures in Table 5.8 understate this shift because executive salaries would be included in the "labor" figure. So, as important as the outrageous compensation for CEOs has become, the bigger problem lies in the ability of the wealthy to accumulate assets that keep them rich even when there is a problem with the stock market or the economy. The CEO pay, of course, reinforces this as it creates more billionaires owning huge clumps of stock. This money doesn't just buy multiple mansions, yachts, jet planes, etc. It buys the political system, as we will see later, which in turn makes sure the wealthy are not taxed as they once were, that labor law remains ineffective or worse, that poverty goes unaddressed, and more. For America's workers, the years since the 1970s have been lost decades. Income has been lost as society's wealth moves upward, jobs have been lost by the millions, power has been lost as unions decline and retreat.

THE END OF MILITANCY, THE SURRENDER OF THE WORKPLACE, AND THE ORIGINS OF DECLINE

Union membership reached its high point around 1980 when organized labor could claim over 20 million members. By 2005, there were 4.5 million fewer union members. In terms of union density, the proportion of union members to the number of workers, the slide began much earlier. Density peaked in 1953 at 32.5% of the nonagricultural workforce and continuously slipped to 12.5% in 2005. All of this is by now well known. What is cited slightly less frequently is that between 1970 and 2005 organized labor lost almost 9 million members in the private sector. To put this another way, in the heart of the economy where society's wealth is extracted, the unions lost over half their members. The peak in membership for all private sector unions was hit in 1970 at just under 17 million. Density had already fallen from 35.7% in 1953 to 29% in 1970, but most of the big unions did not see membership slippage until that time and could afford to ignore such a warning sign. The Auto Workers and Machinists reached their peak in 1969, while the Steelworkers grew or stabilized until 1973 and the Teamsters until 1974.[1] These and most other unions had grown in the momentous struggles of the 1930s, through the wartime strikes, during the huge post-war strike wave when membership grew by a couple of million, and into the 1950s, during which unions sustained a high level of strike activity through 1955.[2] In terms of numbers of members, the high point for private sector unionism was 1970—just before what I have argued was the turning point of so many trends in US society and economy. They sustained growth through the upsurge of the 1960s when strike figures almost surpassed the great 1945–46 strike wave. As Table 6.1 shows, strike activity dropped somewhat from the mid-1950s through the early 1960s. By the mid-1960s, it was rising by most indicators, peaking in the number and percentage of workers striking in 1970 and in the

Table 6.1   Strikes, Strikers, and Percentage of Employed, 1945–81

Year	# Strikes	# Strikers	% of Employed
1945	5,750	3,470	8.2
1946	4,985	4,600	10.5
1947	3,693	2,170	4.7
1948	3,419	1,960	4.2
1949	3,606	3,030	6.7
1950	4,843	2,410	5.1
1951	4,737	2,220	4.5
1952	5,117	3,540	7.3
1953	5,091	2,400	4.7
1954	3,468	1,530	3.1
1955	4,320	2,650	5.2
1956	3,825	1,900	3.6
1957	3,673	1,390	2.6
1958	3,694	2,060	3.9
1959	3,708	1,880	3.3
1960	3,333	1,320	2.4
1961	3,367	1,450	2.6
1962	3,614	1,230	2.2
1963	3,362	941	1.1
1964	3,655	1,640	2.7
1965	3,963	1,550	2.5
1966	4,405	1,960	3.0
1967	4,595	2,870	4.3
1968	5,045	2,649	3.8
1969	5,700	2,481	3.5
1970	5,716	3,305	4.7
1971	5,138	3,280	4.6
1972	5,010	1,714	2.3
1973	5,353	2,251	2.9
1974	6,074	2,778	3.5
1975	5,031	1,746	2.2
1976	5,648	2,420	3.0
1977	5,509	2,040	2.4
1978	4,230	1,623	1.9
1979	4,827	1,727	1.9
1980	3,885	1,366	1.5
1981	2,568	1,081	1.2

After 1981 the BLS only reported on strikes of 1,000 or more workers.
Source: *Historical Statistics*, Part 1, p. 179; *Statistical Abstract*, 1982–83, pp. 410.

number of strikes not until 1974 when the recession hit, but remaining well above the average of the 1955 through 1965 level throughout the decade. As Cal Winslow wrote in a paper for a 2005 UCLA conference on rank-and-file movements of the "long 1970s":

> There were 298 major strikes in 1977, involving 1,212,000 workers. In 1979 there were 235 strikes, still involving more than a million workers. It was in the 1980s that the annual average fell to 83, in the 1990s to 34. I believe ending this story in 1974 is a mistake; it leaves out much that is important; it also makes the outcome seem overly determined.[3]

Winslow has used the narrower measure of "major" strikes involving 1,000 or more workers, but the broader figures in Table 6.1 show the same pattern. Unfortunately, this broader measure was discontinued by the Reagan Administration after 1981.

Many of the strikes of the 1960s and 1970s were wildcats, initiated by rank-and-file activists usually against the will of union officials. Most were over working conditions and about power in the workplace as management tried to redress slumping profit rates through increased

Table 6.2   Union Membership and Density, Selected Years, 1953–2005

Year	Membership	Density	Private Membership	Density
1953 (T)	16,310,000	32.5%*	15,540,200	35.7%
1962 (T)	16,893,100	30.4%	14,731,200 (T)	31.6%
1970 (G)	19,381,000	27.3%	16,978,000* (T)	29.1%
1977 (G)	19,335,000	23.8%	16,166,800 (T 1976)	25.1%
1980 (G)	20,095,000*	23.0%	15,264,000 (L)	20.6%
1983	17,717,000	20.1%	13,142,600 (T)	17.8%
1993	16,627,000	16.0%	9,517,536	11.2%
1995	16,360,000	14.9%	9,432,000	10.4%
2000	16,258,000	13.5%	9,110,000	9.1%
2005	15,472,000	12.5%	8,227,000	7.9%
2006	15,359,000	12.0%	7,981,000	7.4%
(T) Troy, 1986; (G) Goldfield, 1987; (L) Lewin, 1986 * Denotes peak				

Sources: Troy in Lipset, *Unions in Transition*, 1986, p. 81; Lewin in Lipset, p. 244; Michael Goldfield, *The Decline of Organized Labor in the United States*, 1987, pp. 10–11; BLS, *Women In the Labor Force: A Data Book*, 2005, p. 81; BLS, *News*, Union Members in 2005, USDL 06-99, January 20, 2006, Tables 1 and 3; BLS, *News*, Union Members in 2006, USDL 07-0113, January 5, 2007, Tables 1 and 3, www.bls.gov.

productivity. In 1970, the *New York Times* noted the rebellion, especially among younger workers: "at the heart of the new mood, the union men said, there is a challenge to management's authority to run its plants, an issue that has resulted in some of the hardest-fought battles between industry and labor in the past."[4] In those years, public sector workers stormed into unions inspired by the social movements and the militancy of labor as a whole. But in the heat of the militancy of the period private sector unions had also grown by over 2 million workers as Table 6.2 shows. Organizing efforts, measured by NLRB representation elections, soared from about 4,000 a year in 1960 to over 8,000 in the mid-to-late 1970s and then after 1980 dropped dramatically and suddenly to fewer than half that number.[5] The simultaneous drop in strikes and organizing was hardly a coincidence.

Most discussions of union decline focus on the decline and/or restructuring of the old basic industries on which the CIO unions were largely based. But here it is worth pointing out that unions grew in the years when they displayed militancy. They grew when they fought for something and in particular, as in the 1960s and early 1970s, when they fought to sustain or increase power in the workplace. These days, the notion that growth and militancy have any connection, except possibly a negative one, is angrily dismissed precisely by those who lay the greatest claim to strategies for growth—namely the leaders of the Change to Win Federation and, above all, of the SEIU. We will return to this in a later chapter, but it is important to keep in mind that in the history of American labor there is a strong correlation between the general level of strike activity and other forms of militancy and growth. It is equally true that decline, for example in the 1920s, was accompanied by passive and conservative leadership and attempts to accommodate employers. But first we will look at the economic and industrial trends.

Table 6.1 makes very clear that decline of union membership began earlier than 1980 in the private sector. Public sector unionism has held its own since it made its great gains in the 1960s and 1970s. The first big drop in overall union membership came in the short period from 1980 through 1983 when 2.4 million members disappeared in three years. Underlying this was a drop of 3 million private sector union members from 1977 to 1983. From 1980 to 1983 alone, however, over 2.1 million private sector union members disappeared—over two-thirds of the total loss. After 1983, through the 1980s and 1990s, the decline continued but in the 1990s at a slower rate. So, to figure out what happened in the private sector we have to look beyond the overall figures. The most obvious place to look at first is manufacturing. Wage and salary employment in manufacturing hit its high point in 1979 at 19.4 million employees. By 1983, when the recession had just

Table 6.3   Unions that Lost 100,000 Members or More

Union	1976	1983	Net Loss
USWA	1,300,000	707,000	-593,000
IBT	1,946,000*	1,523,400	-422,600
UAW	1,358,000	1,010,000	-348,000
IAM	917,000	596,000	-321,000
ACTWU	502,000	253,000	-249,000
LIUNA	627,000	444,000	-183,000
ILGWU	365,000	258,000	-107,000
URWA	211,000	108,000	-103,000
Total Net Loss			-2,235,600
*1974			

Sources: *Statistical Abstract*, 1981, p. 411; 1986, p. 423; Troy, p. 92.

bottomed out, there were 17 million jobs, a loss of 2.4 million manufacturing jobs.[6] A loss of this magnitude would certainly explain some of the loss of private sector union jobs.

Looking more narrowly at only production workers and over a longer period to allow for recovery we can see that 80% of the manufacturing jobs lost from 1980 to 1990 were lost in *just three industries*: primary metals, textiles, and apparel. In these three industries alone a total of 1.25 million jobs disappeared in that decade.[7] And, sure enough, as Table 6.3 shows the Steelworkers (USWA), the Ladies Garment Workers (ILGWU) and the Amalgamated Clothing and Textile Workers Union (ACTWU) lost heavily for a total of almost a million members from 1976 to 1983 and they would continue to lose ground afterward. So, for those unions the loss of jobs to plant closings, workforce reductions, overseas competition, etc. seems an adequate explanation. But how are we to explain the heavy loss of members in unions such as the Auto Workers, Rubber Workers, Teamsters, Laborers, or, a special case, the Packinghouse Workers, whose membership had fallen from 103,600 in 1954 to 73,300 by 1960—all in industries with stable or growing employment.[8] The number of production workers in the automobile industry rose from 575,000 in 1980 to 617,000 in 1990 and 770,000 in 2000. Yet the UAW lost members from the late 1960s onward. The trucking industry grew from 1,024,000 in 1974 when the IBT hit its membership peak to 1,249,000 in 1979, then saw a slump during the recession of 1980–82, but grew again from 1,189,000 in 1982 to 1,395,000 in 1990 and continued to grow. The Packinghouse Workers had seen their members shrink so drastically in the 1960s that they had merged with the old AFL Amalgamated Meat Cutters in 1968 and when that didn't stop membership decline, with the even more conservative Retail Clerks to form the UFCW in 1979. Yet, industry employment rose from 298,000 production workers in 1980 to 359,000 in 1990 and 429,000 in 2000. Tire production and construction also grew as the United Rubber Workers and Laborers declined.[9] The problems faced by the Packinghouse Workers, Auto Workers, Rubber Workers, Laborers, and Teamsters all involved one or another version of industrial restructuring often with a geographic dimension such as that discussed in chapter 3. The restructuring was in response to new forces of competition, domestic or global, which took the form of an effort to break the union's pattern bargaining contract set-up that kept wages relatively high or to simply escape the union altogether. Here, I can only give a brief sketch of what were fairly complex processes.

In meatpacking, the change involved both the rise of new companies and the intensification of competition and the closing of the huge integrated plants in Chicago, Kansas City, and Sioux City. The old "Big Four" (Swift, Armour, Wilson, and Cudahy) were challenged first by newcomers Morrel, Hormel, Oscar Mayer, and Hygrade, engaged primarily in pork with plants spread around the Midwest and Great Plains. The Big Four closed their big city plants by the mid-1950s, which shattered the union's militant, and half Black base. By 1964, the Packinghouse Workers membership in the Big Four was cut in half to about 26,000. By the 1960s, a new group of packers, Cargill, ConAgra, and IBP, came along with new packing methods and technology, again spreading plants around mostly rural areas. The carefully constructed "chains" that upheld the pattern agreements in the industry came under heavy attack. By the time the Packinghouse Workers had dissolved into the UFCW, the union had adopted an "orderly retreat" of concessions. When Local P-9 at the Hormel plant in Austin, Minnesota tried to resist the falling wages, the UFCW leadership opposed and eventually ended the strike. By the mid-1980s meatpacking wages, which had been ahead of those in manufacturing generally since 1960, fell increasingly behind—$8.73 compared with $10.84 in 1990.[10]

As we saw in chapter 3, the auto industry also restructured along geographic lines, with much of its production shifting to the South. Although the shift to the South began in the 1960s and 1970s with GM's "Southern Strategy," the UAW did succeed in organizing those plants. The real Southward momentum began later in the 1980s with the opening of the Nissan and Saturn plants in Tennessee. By 1990, over 318,400 or 39% of auto industry employees were in the South.[11]

It was also in the 1980s that the shifting of parts production to the *maquiladora* plants of northern Mexico took place, where auto employment rose from 7,500 in 1980 to 135,000 by 1992.[12] But the UAW's slip began in 1969 from 1.4 million to 903,800 by 1983 before the next wave of geographic restructuring when Big Three plants closed on the East and West Coasts and the move South accelerated. There was, however, a less noticeable restructuring of the industry during the 1960s and 1970s. This was set off largely by the fact that the US proportion of world auto production plummeted from 47.9% in 1960 to 27.2% by 1975.[13] The response of the Big Three assemblers was to launch their well-documented rush to automation and speed-up in the 1960s and 1970s—the speed-up that sparked so many of the wildcats of that era. In addition, they increased outsourcing of parts manufacturing to lower-cost independent parts suppliers. Most of these were in the northern states where the industry was located, although as I said above, GM initiated its "Southern Strategy" in this period. The result was that the UAW's share of the workers in the parts industry fell from 50% to about a third by 1990. Density in the industry as a whole fell from 85% in 1978 to 60% by the early 1990s. Altogether, the Big Three shed some 300,000 workers from 1978 to 1990.[14] The major conclusion by the UAW concerning membership decline was the union's failure to follow the work and organize the independent suppliers. It, therefore, entered the concessionary era that began with the Chrysler bailout in 1979 in a weakened position. What had appeared to be a return to some level of official militancy in the late 1970s, when UAW President Doug Fraser gave his famous "one-sided class war" speech, rapidly turned into a rout and the retreat into concessions, "jointness," and labor–management cooperation. The industry wage pattern, already tattered by the 1970s, came to cover fewer workers.[15]

The decline of the Teamsters also involved the unraveling of a system of pattern bargaining, this one centered around the National Master Freight Agreement (NMFA) that had been established by Jimmy Hoffa in the 1950s and 1960s. During this period, Hoffa had brought 600,000 new members into the Teamsters. By 1970, over 300,000 truckers and dock workers were covered by the NMFA, which in turn set the pattern for other jurisdictions such as car hauling. But the industry was already seeing the rise of nonunion carriers competing directly with those covered by the NMFA. The volume of freight carried by union companies declined by 20–25% from 1967 to 1977. The leaders that followed Hoffa after 1967 were, if anything, more corrupt and certainly less competent. Thus even before deregulation came into effect in 1980, the union was losing ground. Under competitive pressure, companies began withdrawing from the master agreement. By 1977, the short-haul agreement had fallen apart. From 1970 to 1979 the number of Teamsters covered by the

NMFA fell from 306,000 to 277,000. After deregulation it dropped even further to as low as 160,000 by 1985. By 2006, the Teamsters reported only 80,000 members in their freight division.[16]

The fate of the Rubber Workers, a former CIO industrial union, and the Laborers, an old AFL building trades union, had a geographic aspect, though like the unions it was quite different. By most accounts, the United Rubber Workers reached their high point in numbers, at 211,000, and bargaining success in 1976 when they struck the "Big Four" tire makers and won a $1.35 wage increase over three years, plus substantial gains in COLA and pensions.[17] But, as with so many of the basic industries, rubber began its restructuring shortly thereafter. As one industry description of the subsequent troubles put it rather brutally:

> The Rubber Workers organized labor in their field and rose to such prominence that in 1976 the union could shut down the North American tire industry until it got the contract it wanted. That also signaled the high-water mark for the United Rubber Workers. Tire production migrated to the non-union South. Recessions, consolidation, foreign ownership, automation and imports since then cut the union's clout and membership ranks.[18]

By 1991, they were down to 89,000 members. In 1995, the United Rubber Workers were absorbed by the United Steelworkers.

The story of the Laborers involves the entire construction industry. In this industry the drop in union density came earlier and faster than in manufacturing. In 1953 84% of construction workers were in unions; by 1966 this had fallen to half that at just over 41%.[19] This virtual collapse came even before the formation of the Construction Users Anti-Inflation Roundtable, forerunner of the Business Roundtable, by the big industrial corporations and leading nationwide contractors such as Bechtel and Brown and Root (now part of Halliburton) in 1969.[20] In any case, the Laborers lost far more members than the more skilled building trades unions. As we saw in chapter 3, construction activity followed manufacturing to the South after WW2. There it would be easy to replace the unskilled laborer with local nonunion talent. But the other geographic shift that cost the laborers union jobs was the acceleration of suburbanization following WW2, the main cause of the huge drop in density after 1953. This was highly subsidized by the government through GI loans, highway construction, etc. Not only did this trend encourage manufacturing to move out of cities, it also shifted construction work to the suburbs. As one urban historian wrote, "In the 1970s suburban population increased by 12 percent while that of central cities decreased by 4.6 percent; over half the nation's retail dollars and two-thirds of the housing construction dollars were spent in the suburbs."[21]

What is more, the construction was of a different type than urban construction. In the hands of William Levitt and sons, right after the war wooden track houses were now produced in huge numbers using mass production techniques. Judd and Swanstrom describe the process:

> The Levitts broke down the complex process of building a house into 26 operations, and then assigned each step to a separate contractor. Because each contractor did the same job over and over again, it was possible to achieve incredible speed. Levitt avoided unions and used piecework incentives to speed the process even more.[22]

The laborer had typically been a hod carrier, moving bricks, mortar, and other heavy materials around a building site. Now much of the work was done in factories and lumber yards and little brick or stone was used at all in the new suburban tracts. For foundations the ready-mix cement truck made moving wheel barrels of cement obsolete. An even more modern problem for the Laborers Union in some large urban settings was the rise of nonunion and even off-the-book demolition and repair work once done by the Laborers.[23]

In these ways, the 1970s through the recession of the early 1980s saw the big slump in private sector union membership that underlay the fall from the overall high point in 1980. While the rate at which unions lost members would decrease somewhat, the decline continued. Only in two years during the 1990s did the number of union members rise: by 100,000 in 1998 and by 266,000 in 1999. These promising starts soon vanished, except for a one-year blip in 2001, as absolute decline continued up to 2005 when once again a small gain of a little over 200,000 was registered. As welcome as any growth was, it was clear this level of increase would not solve labor's problem. While industrial shift and restructuring underlay the falling numbers in many cases, it was clear that the unions had failed to follow the geographic shifts from city to suburb, North to South. This failure would continue into the 1990s and beyond. The evidence of this failure of policy and action is the virtual collapse of NLRB elections after 1980–81.

The End of Militancy, the Surrender of the Workplace, and the New Survival Strategies

The opening of the 1980s saw the end of the wave of militancy that had come from the ranks beginning in the 1950s and emerging as a visible trend in the mid-1960s. Two recessions had taken the wind out of some of the rank-and-file movements, the persistent opposition of the leadership out of others. The battle for the workplace was turning into a retreat. There continued to be rebellions into the late 1970s, as with the 1978 miners' strike and the Steelworkers Fight Back campaign of Ed Sadlowski, also in 1978, but the strike wave and most of the reform and radical movements in the unions and workplaces of the nation were losing momentum. There would, of course, be strikes after 1980–81, but their incidence decreased and their purpose changed from an effort to expand the frontiers of labor's power in the workplace and economy to the defense of what had already been won. Something else had changed as well. The trade union leadership, long bureaucratized and conservatized, had opposed most of the upsurge. In the course of this, they had abandoned their own previous selective militancy; that is, their willingness at critical points to use the strike weapon to win or preserve things they thought essential to collective bargaining, which had included workplace organization. As mentioned earlier, the 1950s saw a high level of strike activity led by even some of the most bureaucratic leaders, for example, the 1959 steel strike led by "Tuxedo Unionist" David McDonald to preserve a "past practice" contract clause that was key to shop floor power. The 1960 GE strike against Bulwareism—take it or leave it bargaining—was another example. The Rubber Workers 1976 strike yet another. Even the 1970 UAW–GM strike, although certainly directed at "letting off steam" and regaining control over a militant membership, revealed that the union leaders still believed they had to win something in order to do that. The "30-and-Out" early retirement clause won in the 1970 contract was significant because it was a major demand of the main opposition group, the United National Caucus. This was traditional business unionism. Somewhere in this period this idea was abandoned or at least took a back seat to other ideas and strategies aimed not at securing gains or workplace power, but at defending the institution of collective bargaining *per se*.

The incident I usually associate with this change is the 1979 Chrysler bailout. There was already a precedent in the give-backs made by the public sector unions during New York City's 1975 fiscal crisis. Additionally the Chrysler bailout would be followed by the high-profile firing of the PATCO air traffic controllers by Ronald Reagan.[24] But I think the roots of this rapid conversion to a new bargaining paradigm in 1979–80 had been prepared more broadly across the manufacturing sector in the leadership's resistance to and suppression of the rank-and-file upheaval of the previous period. In several cases, this meant above all the suppression of Black militancy in the workplaces of several industries. The August 1973 incident where the UAW leadership broke a wildcat strike at Chrysler's Mack Avenue stamping plant by assembling a thousand or so union officials and Administration Caucus loyalists to force the strikers back to work revealed the extent to which they would go to stop the wave of militancy.[25] This was only the most visible sign of the UAW leadership's efforts to regain control. The result was all too clear. As Heather Thompson summarized it:

> Although labor leaders successfully mounted yet another assault on shop-floor dissent to secure their leadership position in August 1973, their victory soon rang hollow as well. Labor liberals hoped to use their newly secured power to win greater gains from auto companies, but this did not happen. In fact, after 1973, auto companies mounted their own increasingly aggressive attack on the bargaining prerogatives of the UAW, and having already killed off much of its militant base, the union leadership was in no position to resist this assault. As a result of leadership decisions made between 1967 and 1973, between 1973 and 1985, Detroit's labor movement suffered a tremendous setback at the hands of management for which workers paid dearly.[26]

If the case of the UAW was the most extreme, it was not unique in its purpose. Leadership resistance to rank-and-file militancy was apparent in the Teamsters, Steelworkers, the Communications Workers after the 1971 New York Telephone strike, the New York City public sector unions after 1975, and in many others as well. This weakened the rank-and-file base of the union and laid the basis for concessions that would affect the entire labor movement. In the course of all this, the leadership of a growing number of unions adopted new strategies, not to make gains, deal with the growing problems of the workplace, or to grow the union, but to preserve the union as an institution and the leadership's position in it. They would at times be forced into strikes, but these would be highly defensive and more selective than ever. The three major survival strategies they turned to as the new period unfolded were concessions, labor–management cooperation and then partnership, and mergers as a substitute for new organizing. These became not temporary expedients in troubled times or industries, but permanent features that would spread from manufacturing to virtually all other industries, including sectors not under pressure of foreign competition. By the mid-1980s, these strategies had spread throughout the labor movement. The suppression of rank-and-file militancy in the 1970s and the surrender of the workplace, along with the subsequent or simultaneous abandonment of their traditional selective militancy as a key tool to making gains, meant that new organizing, particularly in the South, was out of the question since that would require a great deal of militancy and conflict, the active support of the membership, the ability to win gains, and a direct confrontation with racism they were in no way prepared to have. The new strategies did not require militancy, membership support, or an attack on America's racial divide. They specifically involved abandonment of any fight over workplace power as concessions and labor–management cooperation ceded long contested authority to management. The deregulation that took hold in the late 1970s and the Reagan era that followed reinforced practices already well underway.

The surrender of the workplace to management was a long process. Most unions had granted management sweeping powers as long ago as the late 1930s or 1940s in "management rights" and no strike clauses, but members had fought desperately to maintain power nonetheless. Concessions and cooperation would carry this retreat to the level of surrender, not by the ranks in the workplace itself, where resistance would rise and fall only to rise again. Although this surrender by the top leadership was necessarily gradual, it had its symbolic moments and key concessions. The 1970 GM strike was certainly a landmark, but one that still had a foot in the old ways. The crushing of the 1973 Detroit Chrysler wildcats was a clearer milestone. For auto, the institutionalized symbol was the "living agreement" of 1982, discussed below in the context of "jointness." For Teamsters, it was the surrender in 1970 of the "24-hour strike" clause. This was a clause that was meant to limit wildcats by giving management the right to fire anyone who struck during the life of the contract for more than 24 hours. Naturally, stewards and militants in many IBT locals learned to use the 24-hour strike to maintain or expand their control over conditions. So, its surrender by Frank Fitzsimons was a blow to the rank-and-file militants. It was one cause of the 1970 nationwide teamster wildcat.[27] In steel it was the Experimental Negotiating Agreement (ENA) signed in 1973 just before the 1974 contract negotiations. With the ENA USWA President I.W. Able gave up the right to strike over the contract. It would later be abandoned by the industry in favor of efforts to break the industry pattern, which succeeded by 1986.[28] Nevertheless, it gave management increased power. The less visible, because so common, "jointness," team concept, employee involvement, and other such programs were the landmarks in scores of industries. For the ranks it was a retreat, for the leaders a surrender, in a fight that could never end no matter how many white flags went up. It was, no doubt, with unintended irony that in 1979 UAW President Doug Fraser complained of "one-sided class war."[29]

By the mid-1980s, concessions had become an institutional part of collective bargaining. As we saw earlier, wage settlements had decreased to the point of near disappearance by that time and benefits soon began to erode. This was a change—a change in the very nature of collective bargaining. For all the caution and bureaucracy that characterized the American labor leadership, collective bargaining had meant winning something new or improving something already won. Even corrupt leaders like Hoffa understood it this way. There were mobsters here and there who didn't care, but the most run-of-the mill labor officials before the 1980s thought it was their duty to bring home the bacon. The key to that had been the notion of "taking labor out of competition" through various forms of industry or area-wide pattern agreements. This now gave way to a much more company-centered bargaining often directed at improving the competitive position of the company and, hence, placing labor back in competition. Nelson Lichtenstein describes the impact of the Chrysler bailout this way:

> The Chrysler bailout therefore had a twofold consequence: the concessionary bargaining in what had once been a flagship firm of American industry offered a powerful model that quickly spread to other firms, where blue-collar wages fell; of equal import, the fragmentation of the collective-bargaining process implicit in the bailout gave to many union-management relationships a quality not far different from that of Japanese enterprise unionism, in which workers are given powerful incentives to identify their economic well-being with the fate of their own firm and its management.[30]

To put it slightly differently, concessions led logically to the second strategy: labor–management cooperation. For the leadership, who always thought of themselves as a sort of partner in the industry, this was a simple step. But as Lichtenstein notes above, there was also an economic incentive for rank-and-file workers to go along: the constantly reiterated threat of plant closings, downsizing, failure to "get a product" for your workplace, etc. This became not only the mantra of management, but of the labor leader as well. It was not only or even primarily wages that were surrendered but working conditions and shop floor organization and power.[31]

The next step, taken in the 1980s, was formal labor–management programs. They might be called team concept or employee involvement or participation, but their purpose was to get the workers to identify with the economic plight or well-being of the company. While these had a compelling logic in industries like auto, rubber, or steel that did face foreign competition, they were nonetheless applied with equal vigor in industries that could neither relocate nor simply choose to close facilities at random. We have already discussed team concept in the context of lean production. Here I want to look briefly at different types of labor–management cooperation schemes because these types of bigger "partnerships" are still in the air.

"Jointness" came to the auto industry in the wake of the reopening of the GM contract in 1982 for the purpose of making more concessions.

It was pioneered at GM, but would be adopted by Ford and Chrysler as well. Its ostensible purpose was to jointly figure out ways "for improving operational competitiveness in order to enhance job security." This might be done through improving product quality, retraining workers, or improving productivity. In its original form in 1982 it consisted of five levels of joint committees running from company headquarters down to the local union. By the late 1980s it was composed of a mind-boggling array of joint committees designed to bypass the grievance procedure, among other things. Eventually, jointness would produce armies of "clipboard people" in the plants chosen from among the union members by union officials with company approval to encourage pro-company sentiment and discourage grievances. The jointness partners were not to engage in negotiations or compromise, but to arrive at agreement through consensus.[32]

This last point is crucial. Behind negotiations and compromise, traditional collective bargaining methods, always lay the potential use of force—the strike. Without that the inherently unequal power relationship between capital and labor could not be redressed. Consensus precluded the use of force and, hence, embodied the unequal relationship between the corporation and the union. It was, therefore, a piece of the departure from traditional business union bargaining. It might have amounted to nothing more than a way to tie-up union officials in endless meetings, but the 1982 auto contracts included letters of agreement that gave the union and management the power to change conditions in any plant without the permission of the local union or membership. This was new. It was called the "living agreement" and was, in fact, used to alter working conditions, including the removal of work from a plant.[33] It was the formal document of unconditional surrender of union control over working conditions by the leadership. In any event, jointness did not stop the workforce reductions or the spin-off of GM's Delphi parts division.

The Communications Workers of America bought into a similar program with AT&T in 1993. Called the Workplace of the Future, it was "to secure the future—the future for the company, but also the future for the employees and the unions."[34] The Workplace of the Future, with its multiple layers of joint committees, did not secure the future for tens of thousands of employees who lost their jobs in wave after wave of layoffs and downsizing throughout the 1990s, all without notifying the union.[35] In April 1997, the AFL-CIO and several unions announced a partnership with the huge HMO Kaiser Permanente that was supposed to make Kaiser Permanente "the preeminent deliverer of health care in the United States" by improving quality and showing that "labor–management cooperation produces . . . market-leading competitive performance." The deal was actually proposed by AFL-

CIO President John Sweeney. The unions would "market" Kaiser to other unions. All of this and some "guarantees" similar to those at AT&T, GM, and elsewhere were supposed to save union jobs at Kaiser. No layoffs were to come as a result of the partnership, it was said. In fact, Kaiser had been closing hospitals in California. And even as the agreement was being announced, the California Nurses Association were on strike against Kaiser for reducing staff and undermining care. A year earlier several SEIU locals had threatened to strike over the same issues. Yet, the SEIU and other AFL-CIO unions rushed into this partnership apparently agreeing with SEIU Local 250 President Sal Rosselli that, "We can convince Kaiser to compete on the basis of quality, not price."[36]

Sweeney, who had proposed the Kaiser deal, went on to propose a different sort of partnership. In 1998, he discussed with GE CEO Jack Welch the formation of a sort of economy-wide partnership in the form of the "Economic Leadership Dialogue on Citizenship." This "dialogue" was to include top business and labor leaders. In a letter proposing the new organization Sweeney warned that a failure to achieve "common purpose threatens to leave our nation a future that neither of us will proudly claim as our legacy to the next generation." To avert this Sweeney called for a "deepening of the participants' understanding of the unities and differences between leaders of labor and leaders of business on issues related to our nation's strategic interests."[37] This sort of thinking would lead Sweeney, as a member of President Clinton's business-dominated Advisory Committee for Trade Policy, to sign along with many CEOs a letter endorsing Clinton's World Trade Organization policy just weeks before the big anti-WTO demonstrations in Seattle.[38]

Jointness and partnership, like team concept, had two consequences. The most obvious was to convince leaders and workers to drop the old union idea of a conflict of interest. Since job security rested on the fate of the company in a highly competitive world, the interest of the union and management must be the same. There could be differences over this or that, but the clear priority was the competitive health of the company. The second consequence flows from the first. Since not all workers would or did buy into this new set-up and its ideology, there would now be conflict between members focused not on the real issues faced by workers, but over jointness itself. A whole new topic to take up the time and energy of the members and such officials as opposed or questioned partnership. In the case of Kaiser, conflict arose between unions representing workers at Kaiser, between the California Nurses and the SEIU. In other words, if the ideology didn't convince everyone, it would at least change the subject. Consensus, ideological confusion over the very purpose of the union, internal and inter-union conflict over a program that could not possibly gain the workers anything were the harvest of this approach.

Jointness, partnership, and team concept, nevertheless, all faced opposition from various quarters. Perhaps the symbol of the failure of labor–management cooperation to win the hearts and minds of all workers was its defeat at GM's state-of-the-art team concept Saturn plant in Tennessee. Saturn was not a runaway plant. It was designed with the cooperation of the UAW leadership to be the latest word in employee participation and union cooperation in "growing the business." The car was to be of Japanese quality in order to compete in its home market. Saturn never made a profit and is now history, but for over a decade it was held up as *the* model of the high performance workplace. In fact, while selling the Kaiser partnership the head of the Oregon Nurses Association had said in 1997, "We've seen it work at Saturn and at Levi Strauss and it will work at Kaiser Permanente."[39] Had she been speaking two years later she might have noticed that things had not worked out so well: Saturn workers were in revolt and Levi was about to close its last US plant. In 1999, UAW Local 1853 members at Saturn threw out chief company cheerleader and local union President Mike Bennett and his Vision Team by a two-to-one vote, indicating they wanted a more independent and aggressive union. Working conditions, it turned out, were not good.[40] All throughout the following year, the workers at Saturn knocked down one "partnership" pillar after another until in December 1999 they voted up a new contract by 89%. The new contract was in almost every respect a traditional GM "adversarial" contract.[41] Partnership had taken a big hit in the southland.

One other institutional change in collective bargaining that accompanied the retreat from militancy deserves mention. That is the tendency of contract terms to become longer. In the 1940s, most CIO unions had one-year contracts. In 1948, the Auto Workers signed a three-year agreement and in 1950, UAW's President signed an unprecedented five-year contract, all in hopes of stabilizing labor relations. This would fall apart after three years, but the trend toward three-year agreements was set.[42] By 1957 a third of all contracts were three years long and by the end of the 1960s they were standard. The onset of concessions, however, brought another lengthening of contracts. The number of three-year deals fell from 70% of all contracts in 1985 to 49 per cent in 1997. Those with longer terms rose from a mere 4% to 37% in those years.[43] Meant to stem or at least postpone new demands for concessions, the longer contracts simply eroded both workplace power and union democracy even further. If concessions, partnerships, and longer contracts had not stopped the loss of jobs and the deep reorganization of manufacturing or the restructuring of other industries such as health care, they did not stop the loss of union members and the decline of density either. The leaders of one union after another turned to another panacea, seeking institutional salvation through mergers.

The Return of "Big Labor"?

Back in the 1940s and 1950s, people talked about Big Government, Big Business, and Big Labor. Two world wars and the New Deal had, indeed, made government big. Business, as we saw, had become big long ago. When the unions emerged from World War 2 with more members than at any time in US history and struck almost every major industry, organized labor, too, became officially "big." Few would use that term today. But a sort of *faux* bigness has been in the making as unions merge to survive and/or to gain political clout, presumably from their "new" numbers. The latest giant to emerge was the appropriately named United Steel, Paper and Forestry, Rubber, Manufacturing, Energy, Allied Industrial and Service Workers International Union. It now claims to be "the largest industrial union in North America," although a union with so many jurisdictions hardly matches the traditional industrial union idea of "one industry, one union." The term industrial, apparently, was to distinguish the 800,000-member union from the much bigger SEIU, Teamsters, and UFCW. It has about a dozen major jurisdictions, including some not mentioned specifically in its new name: aluminum, petroleum refining, copper mining and refining, health care, public employees, etc., etc.[44] Every AFL-CIO president from George Meany to John Sweeney encouraged mergers, but it was the decline in membership that pushed the trend.

The AFL-CIO had dropped from 135 unions when it was formed in 1955 to 53 in 2006. Part of the drop was due to the exit of the unions that founded or later joined the Change to Win Federation, but most of this consolidation was due to mergers, absorptions, or affiliations. From 1955 through 1979 there were 60 mergers or between 2 and 3 a year. After 1979, however, the rate accelerated, with 35 taking place between 1980 and 1989 and 39 between 1990 and 1999, well over 4 a year on average.[45] Almost all the early ones were absorptions of small unions by larger ones. From 1985 through 1994, there were 46 mergers, or between 4 and 5 a year. Almost half those mergers were accounted for by four unions: the SEIU (9), the IAM (4), the UFCW (4), and the CWA (5).[46] During John Sweeney's first nine years in office, up to early 2005, there were 31 more mergers.[47] The rate had slowed down a bit as the number of remaining unions dwindled. It was clear, however, that after 1979, mergers, not new organizing, were to be *the* strategy for organizational survival. It was, of course, as the timing makes clear, accompanied by the two other strategies for institutional survival, concessions and cooperation.

Most of the unions that stand out as among the few that are growing have done so largely or in part through mergers and absorptions of smaller unions. From 1980 through 1993, the SEIU alone took in over 100 national, regional, or local unions representing 180,000 additional members.[48] This included 7 state employee associations.[49] Since he took office in 1996, Andy Stern notes that the SEIU has doubled in size to 1.8 million members. Most of this is through new organizing, but about 350,000 have come in as absorptions or affiliations, including in recent years a union of security guards, a school employees' union in Washington State, the Connecticut State Employees Association, and the General Workers' Union (UGT) of Puerto Rico.[50] The SEIU's biggest absorption was the 45,000 members of 1199 that it gained in 1989, and more later when the New York 1199 joined. Altogether, about 150,000 1199 members would go to SEIU when New York 1199 joined SEIU in 1998, arguably the event that put SEIU on track to becoming the pre-eminent union of health care workers.[51] The UFCW, born of its 1979 merger between the 550,000 member Amalgamated Meat Cutters and the 600,000 member Retail Clerks, started its new life with 1,150,000 members. As of 2004, it had 1,358,723, an increase of 208,700 over a quarter of a century. A partial listing of mergers since 1979 shows a gain of 260,200 via that route alone. A report issued in 2004 by REAP, a reform group in the UFCW, says, "the UFCW has been and continues to be a hodgepodge of many union mergers."[52] The Teamsters took this path more recently after Hoffa "junior" took over. The Brotherhood of Locomotive Engineers joined the Teamsters as of January 1, 2004 and were followed within a year by the Brotherhood of Maintenance of Way Employees. In 2004, the Teamsters went after the Graphic Communications International Union (GCIU). With the GCIU membership voting narrowly in favor, the merger became official on January 1, 2005.[53] The Communications Workers have also grown through mergers. Those absorbed include the International Typographers Union, the Newspaper Guild, Association of Flight Attendants, the Connecticut Union of Telephone Workers, and the International Union of Electrical Workers (IUE).[54]

In most of these cases, the membership of the absorbed union has voted in favor of the merger, convinced that this would bring them new resources, power, and political clout. But does it? Sometimes it does. The affiliation of the Connecticut Union of Telephone Workers with the CWA in 1998 brought resources that helped them win a strike and an improved contract in that year.[55] In cases like this, mergers can strengthen the position of both unions sharing a common industrial jurisdiction. But the list of failed struggles in which affiliation didn't help or even hindered is too long not to bring this into question. Among the failed strikes by merged unions are those by former Mine-Mill workers in the USWA at Phelps Dodge in the early 1980s, UFCW Local P-9 at Hormel in the mid-1980s, Allied Industrial Workers at A.E. Staley in 1993–95 (absorbed by the Paper Workers), Rubber Workers at Bridgestone/Firestone in 1993–95, the Detroit Newspaper workers in 1995–2000. The point is not that the mergers were themselves responsible for all these defeats, though in the cases of the Hormel and Staley strikes they were. Rather, it is that such mergers do not necessarily change the balance of forces in a given industry. There are basically three reasons for this.

The first is that many mergers make no industrial or strategic sense and, therefore, change little. What were the small independent textile and garment unions that joined the UFCW in the mid-1990s supposed to gain? What were the workers at a corn processing plant (Staley) to get from the Paper Workers and now the Steelworkers? Or for that matter, what sense did the merger between the Paper Workers and the OCAW that produced PACE make industrially? To mention a few others without strategic value: Woodworkers in the Machinists; Leather Workers or Firemen and Oilers in the SEIU; New York Retail Workers (District 65) or graduate students in the UAW; Puerto Rican baseball players in the UFCW; newspaper or electrical manufacturing workers in the CWA; or HERE with UNITE!. In most cases, the small unions are simply buried in the bigger one. In others, the absorbing union becomes a sort of mini-federation with a variety of semi-autonomous divisions representing jurisdictions that have little in common industrially. The divisions continue handling bargaining much as they did before. This is the structure of the SEIU, CWA, UFCW, and many others. How well this works varies from union to union, but it clearly does not bring a strategic focus or renewed industrial power.[56]

The second is that mergers sometimes do the opposite of what is usually claimed for them as unions compete for members. Because mergers have become a central strategy for survival, the big unions seeking new affiliates sometimes contribute to the actual fragmentation of bargaining in an industry. SEIU has become the biggest union in health care, but in doing so it actually split the growing National Union of Hospital and Health Care Employees in 1989 when it fought AFSCME (or AFSCME fought SEIU) for the affiliation. In the end the 76,000-member NUHHCE was split with 13 districts going to SEIU and 5 to AFSCME.[57] Today, health care workers can be found not only in those two unions but in the CWA, USWA, UAW, and others, largely the result of absorptions. As health care becomes more and more of a national industry with a huge for-profit core, this fragmentation becomes more of a problem. While railroad workers were traditionally divided by craft unions, they are now divided by major affiliation. Two rail unions are now in the Teamsters, while the United Transportation Union, itself the result of earlier mergers, remains independent. Newspaper and publishing workers are similarly fragmented by affiliation in related industries dominated by national chains. Mergers in these cases have, if anything, hurt bargaining power.[58]

The third problem relates to structure, resources, and democracy. Union mergers are necessarily top-down affairs. By the time the members get to vote on the deal, all the details of structure, finances, and leadership have been carefully worked out by the top leaders. The notion that the merger brings new resources is misleading. It combines the resources, to be sure, but there isn't really anything new. What is the case, is that the central leadership of the bigger union is almost certain to have control over these combined resources. These can be used for more organizing, as is the case with SEIU, or simply to increase the top-down power and pay of the central leadership as in the UFCW and many other unions. One trend that affects this is that over the years the bigger unions have accumulated wealth that is independent of dues income. This is true not only of those unions with a record of frequent mergers, but mergers definitely increase this source of assets and income available to the bureaucracy. The UFCW is a good example. In 2003 the UFCW had total receipts of $229.8 million. Of this $145.6 million came from dues and another $3.8 million from "affiliate transmittals." Fully $50.7 million came from the sale of assets, investments, and supplies; interest, dividends, or rent. In other words, 22% of the union's income, equivalent to 35% of dues income, came from various accumulated investments and business transactions. The REAP report described the working of the leadership in relation to these assets and receipts as follows:

> Two-thirds of the delegates at International Union conventions are full-time, highly paid officers and staff comprised primarily of white males . . . the largest 50 local unions could out-vote the remaining 450 local unions . . . The 50-some International Union Executive Board members [elected at conventions–KM] turn their authority over to the five-member International Union Executive Committee. The five-member International Union Executive Committee members turn their authority over to the International Union President.[59]

Under the UFCW Constitution, the president has control over all assets of the union. In other words, the president has direct control

Table 6.4   Financial Assets and Receipts of Selected Unions, FY2005

($ millions)

Union	Assets	Receipts	Interest, Dividends, Rent, Sale of Assets/Investments	% of Total
IAM	$243.2	$109.9	$21.5	19.6
AFSCME	$56.7	$148.9	$12.2	8.2
SEIU	$164.7	$258.8	$38.1	14.8
CWA	$474.8	$546.9	$257.1	47.0
USWA	$346.4	$1,125.9	$789.3	70.1
Carpenters	$209.0	$86.4	$39.4	45.6

Source: US Department of Labor, LM2 (revised) for Fiscal Year 2005, www.dol.gov/esa.

of $50 million not dependent on the membership. As Table 6.4 shows, the UFCW is not an extreme case. Many unions, particularly those with a history of mergers, have accumulated income-bearing assets that give the leadership a certain financial independence. The degree of income not from members will vary from year to year according to whether there is a large sale of assets, as was the case with the USWA and CWA in FY2005 and the drop in non-dues receipts by the UFCW from FY2003 to FY2005. Nevertheless, the existence of a significant source of income totally independent from the membership is bound to increase the autonomy of the top leadership.

The other major, in fact more frequent, claim for a merger is that it will bring increased political clout. In forming the alliance with PACE in 2004 that would lead to the merger in 2005, USWA President Leo Gerard said, "first and foremost, we're gaining political strength."[60] At that time, both unions had lost members. From 1999 to 2004 PACE was down 10% or 262,786 members and the USWA by 20% or over half a million members. In other words, the allied union would bring to the 2004 election over three-quarters of a million fewer members than it had during the 2000 election.[61] Coordinated activity in political action may be a good thing and may increase effectiveness, but this has little to do with the notion that merging what were in reality two weaker organizations brings increased political power. We will look more closely at labor's role in politics later.

The final consideration in examining the triptych of defensive strategies is whether or not mergers have actually discouraged new organizing for many unions or provided a substitute for it. What is most striking about the period of concessions, partnership, and mergers is the near collapse in the number of NLRB elections after 1980. As mentioned earlier, in the 1970s unions had pursued an average of about 8,000 such elections a year. After 1980, that number fell by more than half to a little over 3,000 elections a year within a year or two and it never recovered.[62] Mergers did, indeed, become a substitute for new organizing in the period of retreat. Many unions do some organizing, but for most it is still a low priority. Here we will look at several of the biggest unions to see if they have grown in recent years. If a union has grown more than can be explained by mergers, then it should be considered as organizing. If it has shrunk or remained stagnant despite mergers, it will not make the grade as an organizing union. Table 6.5 shows claimed membership figures for the thirteen largest unions, those with half a million or more members, from 1999 through 2004 in order of their size in 2004. A loss in membership does not necessarily mean that the union does no organizing, but it would not qualify as an organizing union. A look at the Teamsters website, for example, will reveal a long list of organizing successes for the past few years. Most of these however, like those of the labor movement as a whole, are small units not big enough to off-set membership losses in other units.[63] One of the revealing aspects of the declining membership figures for most of these large unions is that many of them also experienced mergers or affiliations during those years. These include the IBT, USWA, and the UFCW. Two of the unions with substantial growth rates over this period, the SEIU and the CWA, leading protagonists on each side of the 2005 split in the AFL-CIO, grew mostly from new organizing. In the case of the AFT, it is hard to tell how much of this might have come from joint affiliations with NEA locals. The AFT and NEA, for example, conducted a joint organizing drive among colleges in Washington State in 2004. Like other unions the AFT has expanded its organizing efforts to include non-teaching public employees and health care workers.[64] What seems clear is that with a handful of exceptions new organizing was practically abandoned with the retreat from militancy and far too little organizing is going on despite all the debate about it. What does go on remains unfocused for most unions and is directed mostly at tiny units, and much of it is unsuccessful.

The decline of militancy, the hostility to the militancy of the 1966–75 era that came from the leadership of most unions most of the time, and the turn to concessions, labor–management cooperation, and mergers as strategies for survival have failed to stem the tide of decline and are, in many ways, responsible for its continuation. More importantly, these new approaches have provided alternatives or substitutes for actions, strategies, organizing, and internal changes that might have stemmed the losses and turned things around. The failure,

Table 6.5   Claimed Union Membership of the Largest Unions, 1999 and 2004

Union	1999	2004	+/- Members	+/- %
NEA	2,495,826	2,679,396	+183,570	+7.4
SEIU	1,321,790	1,602,882	+281,092	+21.3
UFCW	1,391,399	1,358,723	-33,067	-2.4
AFSCME	1,300,000	1,350,000	+50,000	+3.8
IBT	1,400,700	1,328,000	-72,700	-5.2
AFT	686,518	816,300	+129,782	+18.9
LIUNA	774,696	743,957	-30,739	-4.0
IBEW	718,742	682,605	-36,137	-5.0
IAM	737,510	627,408	-110,102	-14.9
UAW	762,439	624,585	-137,854	-18.0
CWA	490,621	557,136	+66,515	+13.6
UBC	515,986	523,271	+7,285	+1.4
USWA	636,297	512,312	-123,985	-19.5

Source: Jack Fiorito, "Union Renewal in the UK and US," Florida State University, 2006.

if not its causes, is by now widely recognized in much of the labor movement. Indeed, the crisis that organized labor had stumbled into beginning in the 1970s, led many to call for change by the mid-1990s. This became the unusual rebellion at the top that seemed to promise change in 1995.

WINNING TO CHANGE:
THE FAILURE OF REFORM FROM ABOVE

If much of the 1980s had been rough on organized labor, 1989 seemed to bring hope. There had been two highly visible and successful strikes against concessions. The United Mine Workers had taken on Pittston, a multinational conglomerate, and won. Under the leadership of Rich Trumka, the miners had rallied the support of the labor movement, bringing thousands of union demonstrators to a remote corner of western Virginia in a major labor confrontation. Across the country, miners went out in support in wildcat strikes. Civil disobedience was frequent, despite efforts by the AFL-CIO to discourage illegal activities. In addition to mass mobilization, the miners had revived the labor tactic of the sit-in when they occupied a Pittston coal processing plant, Moss #3.[1] No doubt Trumka and others knew that striking one mine complex of a multinational conglomerate with many mines and businesses could not by itself bring Pittston to heel. The strategy was to create a political crisis in the state of Virginia through constant disruption. That is what they did and it worked. The Mine Workers of 1989 had come through a long period of democratization and internal struggle that went back to the victory of the Miners for Democracy in 1972. All this had been done in an industry that, like so many others, had gone through a drastic restructuring and consolidation. The coal tonnage controlled by the biggest operators had grown from 57% in 1976 to 77% in 1991. As with the Teamsters, the UMWA's national contract had been shrinking as coal operators pulled out of the "Bituminous Coal Operators Association" and the number of miners covered by the national contract fell from 135,000 in 1979 to 45,000 in 1992. But the union took a stand in 1989, employed unconventional tactics, and won, forcing Pittston to accept the national pattern.[2]

In New York and New England, the Communications Workers took on the "Baby Bell" NYNEX over its demands for cost-sharing of health benefits. In 1986, the CWA had been undermined by the IBEW's "me-too" agreement with NYNEX and by a mobilization effort that was "too little, too late." So, in 1988, the CWA began a mobilization program a full year before the contract expiration. The union brought thousands of local officials, stewards, and members into workplace committees and published a monthly *Mobilization Report*. This time, the IBEW was brought on board. The strike of 60,000 CWA and IBEW members began in August 1989 and was to last four months. The CWA used mobile pickets and high-profile public actions in New York and Boston, where they were joined by IBEW members. The union also went after the company at the New York State Public Service Commission, where NYNEX was asking for a rate increase. In the end, the company's cost-shifting demand was defeated. Like Pittston, this was a defensive strike in line with the changed atmosphere, but the militancy and membership involvement in both strikes seemed to portend a turnaround in labor's fortunes.[3] The impression was reinforced when also in 1989 the OCAW beat a five-year-old lockout by BASF. The union had built alliances with community groups, engaged in Pittston-style civil disobedience, and carried the struggle all the way to BASF's German headquarters with the help of the German Greens.[4]

An equally militant strike at Eastern Airlines would end in the collapse of the company. Eastern had been one of the many failed experiments in labor–management cooperation and employee ownership in which the workers made concessions but the plight of the airline continued. But then matters went from bad to worse when Frank Lorenzo of Continental bought Eastern with an eye to shifting assets to Continental.[5] To the Machinists who called the strike in 1989 and the other unions who honored the picket lines, a fight to the finish seemed preferable to massive give-backs and what they believed was the inevitable demise of the company at the hands of asset-stripper Lorenzo.[6] So, while it was no victory, it was not viewed as a defeat like so many others where give-backs were made.

The events that were to shake the Teamsters union did not start as a positive sign. In 1987, following the indictment of Teamster President Jackie Presser for embezzlement, the US Justice Department announced it was filing a suit under the Racketeer-Influenced, Corrupt Organizations Act (RICO) with the intention of placing the entire IBT under a federal trustee. In June 1988, the RICO suit was officially filed. The Teamsters waged a campaign against the suit, rejoined the AFL-CIO in hopes of improved respectability and protection. The AFL-CIO, in turn, opposed the suit.[7] It all might have been just one more piece of bad publicity for organized labor, but something else was already going on that would turn this into one of the biggest union reform efforts since the Miners for Democracy.

The Teamsters for a Democratic Union (TDU), a reform organization that had been founded in 1976, had launched a campaign in the fall of 1985 for the right of members to vote directly on the union's top officers. Volunteer organizers crisscrossed the US and Canada gathering signatures on a petition to be presented at the 1986 Teamster convention. They gathered support from independent-minded local officials, notably Sam Theodus of Local 407 in Cleveland. They made a splash at the convention, but had no hope of winning such a reform in that forum. When the first signs of a RICO or trusteeship became clear, TDU developed a position that was different from the Teamster leadership or the AFL-CIO. TDU opposed the idea of a government takeover of the union and its internal business, but did not oppose the suit *per se*. Instead, in April 1987 before the actual filing of the RICO suit, TDU National Organizer Ken Paff wrote a long letter to the assistant attorney general in which he made it clear that TDU opposed a takeover. He warned of the dangers of "absentee leadership" and argued for a direct election of officers under government supervision. He wrote, "Indeed, there is only one 'reorganization' under RICO that the government can effectively undertake: namely to direct the IBT to hold direct rank and file elections under government supervision for all International Officers."[8] And that is just what happened. When the suit was finally filed, in addition to many indictments of mob-connected officers, when the Justice Department and the IBT leader signed a consent decree in March 1989, it called for the court-appointed monitors to hold such an election. Under these circumstances, TDU became not just a dissident faction, but an opposition party in union politics.[9]

TDU, however, were not strong enough to challenge the IBT leadership alone. They sought a candidate with a reputation for honesty and militancy and with broad appeal. That candidate was Ron Carey, a former UPS worker and president of Local 804 in New York. In September 1989 Carey announced his candidacy to a cheering crowd of 2,000. This changed events from just another corruption scandal to a union reform crusade. The election didn't happen until the spring of 1991 when Carey beat the divided forces of a squabbling old guard with just 48% of the vote, but the year-and-a-half campaign was another sign that labor's fate might be taking a turn for the better.[10] In fact, Carey's victory took the Teamsters out of the AFL-CIO's most conservative and corrupt wing and placed it alongside the forces that would mount a challenge to the AFL-CIO old guard in 1995. Without the IBT votes, the New Voice Team could not have carried the 1995 AFL-CIO convention.

In 1989, union reform was in the air in a number of unions. For one thing, the United Mine Workers waging the unique struggle in

Virginia that year were the product of one of the country's most successful reform movements and Trumka himself, although he had introduced an element of centralism since the early 1980s, had been active in the Miners for Democracy.[11] He was viewed as a militant and would be a natural for what would become the New Voice slate in 1995. In the United Auto Workers the New Directions Movement had become a contending party in union politics. Led by Jerry Tucker, a former assistant director in the union's Region 5 where he had led a number of in-plant struggles that beat back concessions, New Directions spread from Region 5 across the union. Tucker had been denied election as Region 5 Director at the 1986 UAW convention by two tenths of a vote. He got a government-supervised rerun and won, but had only 12 months left to serve. He would lose a subsequent election narrowly. Nevertheless, New Directions came to the 1989 convention in high spirits supported by a number of presidents of large local unions. It was at this convention that New Directions declared itself a national organization and the second party, after the long-standing Administration Caucus, in the union. There was no chance of a direct election of top officers in the UAW as there was to be in the Teamsters, but there was a sense that the new caucus could impact on the union's attitude toward labor–management cooperation and workplace organization, and end its concessions-ridden contracts. 1989 was to be the crest for New Directions, but it saw itself as part of the events of 1989. One of its most important leaders, Dave Yettaw, president of the 11,000-member Local 599 at the Flint Buick complex, would go on to lead the first in a long series of local strikes that began in Flint in 1994 and ended there at two different local unions in 1998.[12]

In New York City's giant Transport Workers Union Local 100, the similarly named New Directions moved from being based mainly as a newsletter, *Hell on Wheels*, to also running for office in 1988. Their candidate, Tim Schermerhorn, got 22% of the vote. In 1989, TWU New Directions became a presence at the TWU's national convention. Here they allied with striking flight attendants from Eastern Airlines and dissidents from Pan Am locals to call for the establishment of a national strike fund. They didn't win, but the sense of momentum was real and New Directions would go on to eventually win the top office in Local 1000 in 2000.[13] There was a leadership challenge in the American Postal Workers Union and, for the first time, Black challengers won election in the Mail Handlers Union.

Nineteen-ninety also seemed to continue the trend. The SEIU's Justice for Janitors campaign in Los Angeles featured the same kind of militancy as the 1989 strikes and like them it won, in this case recognition by the building maintenance contractor ISS.[14] The embattled unions at the *New York Daily News* also took to the streets. Columnist Juan Gonzalez became de facto rank-and-file leader of this hard-fought struggle. If it was not a total victory, it did beat back some of the worst concessions. Milan Stone, who had presided over contract concessions for the Rubber Workers, was voted out of office in 1990.[15] *Labor Notes* even speculated that there was something of a "new directions" trend mostly from below that opposed concessions and cooperation. And so there was. It had, albeit in the context of a long economic upturn, helped to push first-year wage increases in new contracts up from their 1986 low-point of 1.2% for all nonfarm contracts and -1.2% for manufacturing up to 3.7% and 3.0% respectively.[16] But the trend was not strong enough to turn things around. And a new recession in 1990 made it harder to do so.

Things Get Worse

The hopes of 1989 didn't last long. Signs that many unions had not learned anything from Pittston or NYNEX appeared rapidly. A passive strike by the Amalgamated Transit Union against Greyhound headed for defeat and the union's third round of concessions in 1990 as the company recruited scabs. One striker told *Labor Notes*, "the union doesn't seem to do anything. All we do is stand around and wave all the buses in."[17] A more high-profile sign that the post-militancy mindset was still operating at the powerful UAW came in April 1992 when the UAW called off a five-month-old strike at Caterpillar when faced with scabs. The strike had gotten support from across the labor movement. A March rally in Peoria, Illinois had attracted 20,000 workers. South African and Belgian CAT workers held brief sympathy strikes. But there was no real mobilization, no Jerry Tucker-style in-plant strategy before the strike. Just a conventional strike. And then it was called off and the company imposed its own concessions-heavy settlement. Tucker, who was running for UAW president at the time, commented, "The leadership let the membership down because they didn't explore alternative strategies from the start."[18]

Caterpillar, previously a model of labor–management cooperation, was unrelenting in its demands. Later that year, the UAW did attempt an "inside/outside strategy" at Caterpillar and while it did reduce production somewhat, it was not enough to convince CAT to make an acceptable offer. Later in 1993 and 1994, there would be several wildcat strikes as the company harassed workers engaged in work-to-rule efforts. "It's hard to hold them back," commented one UAW staffer in 1994. In June 1994, the UAW would again call a strike at

CAT, only to call it off in December 1995 with no agreement.[19] Like CAT, other companies resumed their offensive in 1992 and 1993.

In 1992, A.E. Staley, a subsidiary of British sugar giant Tate & Lyle, handed Allied Industrial Workers Local 837 at its Decatur, Illinois plant a list of lean production-style demands that one Staley worker would later describe as "one long management's rights clause from end to end." This included twelve-hour rotating shifts.[20] The union had called in Jerry Tucker to run an in-plant campaign and Ray Rogers to conduct a corporate campaign. The inside campaign was hurting Staley production, but the company turned the tables and in June locked out and replaced the strikers. Rogers noted at that time that when you lock out "a well-organized membership, you give the union a full-time army of campaigners." Later that summer, Staley workers became "Road Warriors" carrying a plea for support and a message of solidarity to labor around the country.[21] The Staley struggle would be a highly active one in which strikers from CAT and later members of the United Rubber Workers at Bridgestone/Firestone, who went on strike in July 1994, would rally together with Staley workers in Decatur. Illinois was declared a "War Zone." They succeeded in getting Miller Brewers to cancel their contract with Staley, and turned next to Pepsi.[22] But one of the defensive strategies of this period intervened in the midst of the struggle. In 1994, the AIW had merged into the United Paper Workers International Union (UPIU). In late 1995, the UPIU ended the strike and the Staley workers narrowly ratified Staley's unilateral offer. The UPIU then engineered the defeat of the Local president, Dave Watts, replacing him with someone who had been calling for surrender for a long time.[23]

The Bridgestone/Firestone workers were not to escape any of the trends of the time. Their company had been recently bought by a foreign, in this case Japanese, outfit; their strike was over the same "lean" issues as Staley, and they would find themselves merged into another union even while on strike. In addition, the union was trying to uphold the industry pattern. The Rubber Workers had lost membership and were down to 98,000 and their president, Ken Coss, was looking for a partner to merge with. Discussions with the Oil, Chemical, and Atomic Workers had not worked out. In 1995, the Rubber Workers finally merged into the United Steelworkers. It had required a two-thirds vote of convention delegates and that passed by three votes. Even before the merger was formalized, the Steelworkers launched a "corporate campaign" to pressure the company into a settlement. In May 1995, however, the Rubber Workers called off the Bridgestone/Firestone strike, returning to work under the company's final offer. Although the Steelworkers negotiated a contract in November 1996 as a result of their campaign, the pattern was broken and the company had already implemented the "lean" work rule changes it wanted.[24] In December, the UAW called off the CAT strike to accept a company imposed deal that was a rout, virtually eliminating in-plant organization.[25]

In Detroit, in 1995 newspaper workers began a strike in a hopeful mood, with mass picketing at the *Free Press* printing plant in McComb County supported at times by hundreds of UAW members from nearby plants. The initial militancy, however, was soon discouraged by the leadership and then stopped once a court injunction against mass picketing came down. Though officially it dragged on until 2000, it had been lost when the mass pickets came down and nothing was put in their place. The three International Unions, IBT, CWA, and GCIU, provided money and staff, but no strategy other than a boycott of the Detroit papers. But the two national newspaper chains, Gannett and Knight-Ridder, could not be hurt by a boycott in one city. Misplaced faith was put in the NLRB. As *Labor Notes*' Jane Slaughter wrote in an assessment of what might have worked, "the unions' only hope was to create a political crisis in the city, one big enough that both the local power structure and the far-off CEOs would feel the heat." That, of course, had been the secret of victory at Pittston.[26]

The years since 1989–90 had been a disaster for most unions. The usual hope that a Democratic administration in Washington would change all that was soon dashed. Nelson Lichtenstein summarized the period succinctly:

> Management efforts to avoid or eliminate trade unionism hardly weakened as the Republican 1980s gave way to a new decade and a new administration. Long, bitter disputes at the *Detroit Free Press*, Caterpillar, Staley, Avondale Shipyards, Bridgestone-Firestone, Yale University, and the Port of Charleston testified to management self-confidence and the weakness of the contemporary labor movement.[27]

The results of these years and the defeats that accompanied them were clear. Real weekly wages actually reached their low point in 1993, as Table 7.1 shows, rose very slightly and leveled off until 1997 when they finally rose. But the whole time they remained well below their 1972 high point. First-year wage increases in new contracts, which had risen to 4% in 1990 as a result of the momentum of 1989, then fell again to the 1980s level of 2.6% in 1995. In each year these gains were exceeded by the rate of inflation. As noted in an earlier chapter, both health care and pension benefits were also further eroded in this period.

Of equal or greater concern was the continuing drop in membership. Neither concessions, cooperation, nor mergers had stopped the loss of

Table 7.1   Indicators of Union Well-Being, 1992–95

Year	Real Wages	1st Year Increase	CPI	Union Members	Density
1990	$262.43	4.0%	5.4%	16,776	16.0%
1991	$258.34	3.6%	4.2%	16,612	16.0%
1992	$254.99	2.7%	3.0%	16,418	15.7%
1993	$254.87	2.3%	3.0%	16,627	15.7%
1994	$256.73	2.0%	2.6%	16,748	15.5%
1995	$255.07	2.3%	2.8%	16,360	14.9%

Membership of the Big Unions, 1985–95

Union	1985	1995	Loss/Gain
IBT	1,523,400*	1,285,000	-238,400
AFSCME	997,000	1,183,000	+194,000
UFCW	989,000	983,000	-6,000
UAW	974,000	751,000	-223,000
SEIU	688,000	1,027,000	+339,000
UBC (Carpenters)	609,000	378,000	-231,000
USWA	572,000	403,000	-169,000
CWA	524,000	478,000	-46,000
AFT	470,000	613,000	+143,000
*1983			

Sources: *Economic Report of the President*, 2005, pp. 266, 283; BLS, *Women in the Labor Force: A Databook*, 2005, p. 81; *Statistical Abstract*, 1997, p. 436; Troy, p. 92.

members and the decline of density. Union density continued its unbroken fall down to 1995, while membership fell through 1992, slanted upward very slightly for two years and then dropped again. Most of the big unions continued to lose ground, despite the upsurge in mergers that began in the 1980s. Of the biggest, only the AFT, AFSCME, and the SEIU saw growth and at least some of that for the latter two was due to the merger with the 150,000 workers who went with the fragments of 1199. The realization that mergers would not make up for membership loss and that new organizing was necessary for survival of the movement as a whole became almost inescapable— at least to some. And that led to another inescapable conclusion.

Declining membership was one highly visible cause of labor's declining of political clout. The first two years of the Clinton Administration were the proof of that. The Administration bungled the Health Security Act, in part by pushing almost simultaneously for NAFTA. Labor attempted to support HSA, while opposing NAFTA at the same time. Their effort to convince Clinton to prioritize health care failed.[28] What they got, instead, was NAFTA. The fiasco around health care led to the 1994 Republican victory in the Congressional elections. It was obvious that money alone could not save labor's political efforts and that they had failed at least in part due to slumping numbers.[29] Since it was a movement-wide problem the natural focus became the AFL-CIO itself. Lane Kirkland had presided over the decline since 1979, so he would be the first target for change. With Lane Kirkland's term of office set to expire in October 1995 some began to think the unthinkable: of making a request that he step down and a challenge at the AFL-CIO convention if he didn't.

A Familiar "New Voice"

Conflict among top leaders of American labor is not new. In the old AFL, Samuel Gompers had to deal with a Socialist opposition. His successor, William Green, faced John L. Lewis and the industrial unionists who reluctantly took their fight outside the old federation to form the CIO. Within the CIO it was Cold War liberals versus Communists, until they kicked them out in 1949. And in the merged AFL-CIO, it was Reuther versus Meany until Reuther took the UAW out of the AFL. More generally, it was the ultra-Cold Warriors, led by Albert Shanker of the AFT, versus those leaders with a more liberal bent on questions of foreign policy, civil rights, and which wing of the Democratic Party to support. At least since the merger of 1955, what wasn't done during those fights, no matter how ferocious they seemed, was a public leadership fight for dominance of the AFL-CIO. But now, in 1995, you had an old guard Cold Warrior presiding over a declining organization with a "dinosaur" reputation and a failed political orientation.[30]

Lane Kirkland did not come up through the ranks. He belonged to a union for one moment during World War 2 when he was a deck officer in the merchant marines. After the war he went to work for the AFL as a researcher. Then he worked his way up through the hierarchy as a foreign policy enthusiast and Washington insider. In 1969, George Meany made him secretary-treasurer of the federation as a dependable foe of the radicalism of the era inside and outside the labor movement. Kirkland was the perfect post-militancy man. In 1979, this Cold Warrior, who had called himself "the oldest, established, permanent, floating heir apparent in history," was elected AFL-CIO president without any visible opposition.[31]

Kirkland's timing couldn't have been worse. AFL-CIO membership began its numerical slide soon after he took office. The Chrysler bailout opened the floodgates of concessions that very year. Ronald Reagan was elected president of the United States the next year. The PATCO strikers were fired following that. And so it went. As if his luck wasn't bad enough, as his second decade in office began the Cold War ended. He might have been saved by his other main focus, the Democratic Party, but as we have seen that turned into the fiasco, only fanning the flames of rebellion in the higher strata of the federation. Irony of ironies, one of Kirkland's accomplishments was to cost him his position. Following the merger strategy of the period, which he encouraged, he had successfully brought the UAW, the United Mine Workers, and the Teamsters back into the AFL-CIO during the 1980s.[32] It was the leaders of these unions, along with the AFSCME and the SEIU, that would provide the leadership and the bulk of the votes that convinced Kirkland to step down and then defeated his nominee, Secretary-Treasurer Tom Donahue.

Phase one of the rebellion was meant to be a more or less traditional palace coup. During a closed session of the February 1995 meeting of the AFL-CIO Executive Council in Bal Harbour, Florida, Gerald McEntee of the AFSCME, John Sweeney of the SEIU, Ron Carey of the Teamsters, and Rich Trumka of the Mine Workers asked Kirkland not to run for re-election at the October convention of the federation.[33] At first Kirkland refused to step aside. This brought reactions such as McEntee's comment, "There is a convention this October and if President Lane Kirkland does not resign, we'll resign him."[34] By this time Kirkland could do the math and see that the very unions he had brought back into the fold gave his opponents the votes to do it. Above all, the Teamsters, who prior to 1991 would almost certainly have backed Kirkland or his choice, were now, under Ron Carey, in the ranks of those demanding change. A rank-and-file rebellion in that union had played a key role in Kirkland's undoing. The IBT's votes tipped the scales. Kirkland said he would resign two months before the October convention and would appoint Donahue as his successor and surrogate candidate. The palace rebels of February had actually suggested that Donahue be the next in line, but now things had gone too far and by summer they began constructing a slate. John Sweeney would run for president and Rich Trumka for secretary-treasurer. They proposed a constitutional change adding a third top position, executive vice president, for which the AFSCME's Linda Chavez-Thompson would run. Lining up behind Donahue were the CWA, whose Barbara Easterling would be Donahue's running mate, the AFT, the UFCW, the Letter Carriers, the IBEW and most other building trades unions.[35]

The Sweeney slate became the "New Voice" team. Not only did they make an open challenge, but in an even more unusual move they publicly campaigned in the months leading up to the AFL-CIO convention. I remember at one of the giant demonstrations for the Detroit newspaper strikers in late summer 1995 Sweeney and Trumka addressing the rally as though they were campaigning for the votes of the strikers and their many supporters. Leaflets and placards were passed out promoting the "New Voice for Labor." Of course, the only people at the rally who would have a vote in October were the handful of other top union officials. It seemed as though the rebels wanted to stir things up. And, indeed, at the October convention Sweeney responded to Donahue's criticism of the SEIU Justice for Janitors campaign tactic of blocking a bridge in Washington, DC, saying, "I believe in building bridges, whenever the shelling lets up . . . But I believe in blocking bridges whenever those employers and those communities turn a deaf ear to the working families that we represent."[36]

The New Voice team was elected on the third day of the convention by 56% of the vote in which the unions, that is their presidents, cast their votes according to their paid per capita membership. Though the proceedings were unusually rowdy for an AFL-CIO convention, there was never any doubt about the outcome. There were, however, other issues. There had been vocal dissatisfaction with the whole contest from many Black union leaders. They had not been consulted by either side. William Burrus, executive vice president of the Postal Workers, had said earlier, "the current struggle in the AFL-CIO is by 12 white men. We don't want people to do for us. We want to do for ourselves." The Coalition of Black Trade Unionists had not endorsed either side, but had put forth eleven proposals for increasing diversity on the Executive Council. Just prior to the convention the federation's affiliated "support groups" met together for the first time ever and proposed an expansion of the Executive Council. These groups included: the CBTU, A. Philip Randolph Institute, Asian Pacific American Labor Alliance, Labor Council for Latin American Advancement, and the Coalition of Labor Union Women.[37]

The composition of the Council did, indeed, become a major issue at the convention. Donahue supporters proposed a Council composed of the presidents of all affiliated unions. This would have meant hardly any women or people of color. A compromise was worked out between the two camps behind the scenes in traditional style that expanded the Council from 35 to 51. They also proposed a "unity slate" for the new Council that included 9 African Americans, 6 women, 1 Latino, and 1 Asian. Some 654 delegates from Central Labor Councils and State Feds, far more than at any previous convention, claimed to represent the grassroots and provided much of the cheering and booing of the event. But observing the proceedings were thirty-five Staley workers who more nearly represented the rank and file and who had come to seek solidarity. Sweeney did promise support and even a "task force" to help win in Decatur.[38] This was two months before the Paper Workers pulled the rug out from under what was now UPIU Local 7837's campaign to get Pepsi to cancel its Staley contract.

In the new as in the old AFL-CIO it is the president who has the power. So, what did organized labor get in the person of John Sweeney? Writing in *Labor Notes*, New York labor journalist Laura McClure wrote, "Sweeney has never been known as a rebel and still doesn't come off like one." The exception being his "blocking bridges" remark.[39] Paul Buhle described him as "a middle-of-the-road union leader with a personal history somewhat muddied by the common (though still misguided) practice of double-dipping salaries for overlapping job . . .".[40] Under his watch the size of the second salaries of SEIU officers had grown. Then there was the fact that he, along with Lane Kirkland, was responsible for labor's dropping its support of a single-payer health insurance plan.[41] There was also the embarrassing reality of his home local 32B/J where the corrupt regime of Gus Bevona still ruled in 1995. Bevona had succeeded Sweeney as president of 32B/J when Sweeney became SEIU president. Bevona paid Sweeney a total of $400,000 over thirteen years to be his "adviser," while Sweeney made Bevona eastern regional director at $90,000 on top of his $400,000 32B/J salary.[42] As for union democracy, Sweeney seemed to think that was an intriguing, but distant possibility worth investigating. He told the *Wall Street Journal*, "I'm very interested in union democracy and rank-and-file involvement, but it can't be accomplished overnight."[43] Those who hoped for radical changes would be disappointed.

There was, of course, some reason to think he represented a departure from Kirkland. In his assessment of Sweeney, Buhle went on to point out that it was under his leadership that the Justice for Janitors campaigns had been initiated. In addition, Sweeney had presented resolutions on gay rights and AIDS at the 1983 AFL-CIO convention. What gave him additional credibility was that under his watch the SEIU had grown, as Table 7.1 above shows, to over a million members. Although some of this had been through mergers and affiliations, the SEIU had taken organizing more seriously than most. JfJ had recruited 33,000 new janitors by the time Sweeney took over the AFL-CIO.[44] Furthermore, the "New Voice" platform spoke of coalitions and of reaching out to non-union low-wage workers. It said unions "must organize at a pace and scale that is unprecedented, build a new and progressive political movement of working people." Sweeney hinted at a more grassroots approach when he wrote, "Revitalizing the labor movement is like weaving a seamless garment of activism."[45]

But, as Greg Mantsios pointed out, beneath the new rhetoric or even conviction remained the old business union philosophy crafted by Gompers and wielded by every AFL and AFL-CIO leader since. This ideology embraced not only capitalism in general, but the American system in particular: meaning the belief in persistent growth, the well-being of American business, the belief that high wages are in the interest of US capital, and, as Mantsios described it, the belief that labor and business should "remain partners in the broad scheme of such things as economic growth, international competition, and national prosperity." Speaking to a business group in 1996, Sweeney himself would express this philosophy:

> We want to increase productivity. We want to help American business compete in the world and create new wealth for your shareholders and your employees. We want to work with you to bake a larger pie which all Americans can share—not just argue with you about how to divide the existing pie. It is time for business and labor to see each other as natural allies, not natural enemies.[46]

From this flows the idea of a social compact between labor and business and the belief that, as Sweeney put it, "for almost 30 years after World War 2, we all prospered, because we prospered together. We were concerned with raising the standard of living for working Americans, not just accumulating enormous wealth for a fortunate few."[47] Erased from this picture were the titanic strikes of 1945–46, the relatively high strike levels from 1950 through 1955, the long steel and electrical strikes of 1959–60, and the upsurge from the mid-1960s through the 1970s. Gone was the fact that all of these struggles were waged against corporations seeking to undermine working conditions, shop floor organization, and wages when possible, and contain unionism. It was a rewrite of history needed to justify the post-militant era as well as the core beliefs of the American labor bureaucracy's business union philosophy. The "New Voice" did have some new things to say, but there was an all too familiar ring to the basic propositions on which they rested. We will see that this ideology persisted not only through the Sweeney "reform" era, but into the new world of competing labor federations as well.

The Sweeney Record: The Failure of Reform from Above

Lane Kirkland and Tom Donahue were gone, but four decades of sycophantic staff, bureaucratic structures, Cold War operatives, conservative practices, and political connections that would make "a new and progressive political movement of working people" impossible were still in place. The full-scale house cleaning that was needed was probably impossible. So, as Jeremy Brecher and Tim Costello described it:

> The organizational strategy outlined in the New Voice program was essentially to build a new AFL-CIO staff structure that largely by-passes the existing officers and departments. This responded to the need to address a new set of tasks, to avoid entanglement in structures that are poorly adapted to those tasks, and to circumvent the bureaucratic deadwood. While perhaps wise, this strategy risks building not a new labor movement but rather a new bureaucracy in the shell of the old.[48]

It was not just that the program's tactics for changing things involved more, not less bureaucracy, but that its focus, its center of power was to be in the AFL-CIO headquarters in Washington, DC. The rank and file didn't have much to do with it other than receiving such new services and campaigns as were devised at the top. As Suzanne Gordon wrote in *Labor Notes* of the New Voice program before it was put in place:

> For every union problem there's a new Washington solution—an institute, a task force, a monitoring project, a clearing house, a policy center, a training center, a center for strategic campaigns, a new organizing department (with an office of strategic planning), a strategic planning process ("Committee 2000"), two or three campaign funds, a labor advisory committee, and a "strike support team of top people" from various union staffs.[49]

So, upon taking office the New Voice team set about creating new organizations to carry out their program of organizing and increased political effectiveness. A document distributed at the 2005 convention by the "Winning for Working Families" caucus that supported Sweeney against the Change to Win opponents listed some of these:

- Created an AFL-CIO Organizing Department and merged the Organizing Institute into the federation.
- Began Union Summer . . .
- Expanded and rebuilt the AFL-CIO political program, . . . established the National Labor Political Training Center . . .
- Created the AFL-CIO's first Working Women's Department.
- Launched an AMERICA NEEDS A RAISE campaign . . .
- Created a new Corporate Affairs Department . . .
- Combined and streamlined many AFL-CIO programs and activities . . .
- Reorganized the federation's communications activities . . . .
- Formed Committee 2000 to examine issues of AFL-CIO structure and governance . . .[50]

There were, of course, many pages of campaigns, activities, conferences, etc. in the Winning for Working Families' document, but these were at the head of the list. They reveal not only the tactical side-step described by Brecher and Costello, but the old Washington focus spelled out by Gordon. The question here is not whether all of these things were bad, some no doubt would attempt to address real problems. The question is of the essentially top-down, bureaucratic view of change. What would not change was the notion of where power was to lie in the new AFL-CIO. Change would be administered from the center under control of the center in so far as possible. There was also the matter of the methods of change. Looking at this side of the Sweeney effort at revitalization, union democracy advocate Herman Benson wrote:

> Sweeney and his co-thinkers seek that aim by rhetoric, by lectures and classes, by teach-ins, by advertising, by devising clever slogans, by union-sponsored credit cards, by every gadget and gimmick of public relations. They look everywhere except to what is most effective: the free independent democratic activity of union members inside their own unions.[51]

What is revealed here is not so much bad intentions as bad habits: the habits of a labor movement captured by its long-standing distrust of the rank and file, even to the point where the new "strike support team" was to be composed of "top people." The thirty-five Staley workers waiting in the halls at Bal Harbour in 1995 had not been promised troops or actions from other unions but a "task force." And they didn't even get that.

This is not to say that the new AFL-CIO did nothing outside of "the Beltway." After some second thoughts, it has continued its support to Jobs with Justice. It initiated the Stamford (Connecticut) Organizing Project, which united four locals along with community and church support in organizing workers in that city.[52] Three of the four locals belonged to unions that went with Change to Win in 2005, but the project seems to have continued. The Union Cities program was launched in 1997 to revitalize the AFL-CIO's Central Labor Councils (CLCs) and stimulate their role in organizing. The AFL-CIO's website lists a number of cities in which the CLC's in the Union Cities program helped to coordinate multi-union organizing drives. These included: San Francisco, Baltimore, Charleston, SC, Chicago, Kansas City, Milwaukee, New York, Portland, OR, Seattle, and Syracuse. Union Cities projects were also meant to generate "Street Heat," "in support of workers' struggles" in "bargaining, organizing, and legislative efforts."[53] Coordinated organizing drives inspired by the Union Cities had some high-profile successes such as the HERE, IBT, building trades campaign in Las Vegas that brought in 20,000 new union members. But for the most part, Union Cities failed to transform CLCs composed of "service model" unions focused primarily on local politics.[54] There was also, of course, the Organizing Institute. By 2005 it was said to have trained 1,200 "potential" organizers in its three-day schools, according to the Winning for Working Families caucus.

But half of its $2.5 million budget was spent on "corporate-style campus recruitment," as one critic put it. Rather than recruit from the ranks the emphasis seemed to be on training college students to become organizers. Yet, even some of the accomplishments claimed by the pro-Sweeney forces at the 2005 convention seem to underline the weaknesses of his administration. For example, the boast that he had "increased direct expenses for organizing support from 22 percent to 24 percent of AFL-CIO budget," must not have seemed exactly dramatic to forces that were demanding much more.[55]

One change that seemed fairly dramatic was the creation of the Center for International Labor Solidarity (CILS) and the simultaneous abolition of the notorious regional Institutes. The worst of the Cold Warriors were sent packing. According to Barbara Shailor of the Machinists, who became head of CILS, the AFL-CIO's international work shifted focus to issues associated with globalization. Shailor said that until September 11, 2001, "the predominant focus of our work was the economics of globalization, and foreign policy issues were very much in the background." She went on, "the International Affairs Department, the Solidarity Center on the country level, the departments of corporate and public affairs, are focused on issues of how we deal with the reality of the neo-liberal model we're confronted with."[56] Hence the federation's involvement in the events in Seattle in November–December 1999. But there are still troubling signs. For example, the AFL-CIO's backing of the Venezuelan Confederation of Labor (CTV) whose strike appeared to lead-off the coup against Hugo Chavez. Here, the CILS claims they used money from the National Endowment for Democracy, the neo-conservative run government agency that funded AFL-CIO Cold War foreign activities since the early 1980s, to support progressive forces within the CTV. The AFL-CIO still takes NED money, but claims there are no strings attached. They will not report on where or for what the money is spent. They don't reveal what they do in most of the forty countries where CILS is active. The "Resolution on the Solidarity Center" for the 2005 AFL-CIO convention called for the continuation of government funding. Above all, they will not discuss the pre-Sweeney past. On the other hand, they have opposed the School of Americas and warned against

US military involvement in Colombia.[57] In short, it seems clear there has been a change. Just how deep or far this change has gone will be difficult to assess until the AFL-CIO brings its past and present overseas practices into the light of day. This situation led the California State AFL-CIO to propose a resolution for the 2005 AFL-CIO convention calling for a public review of the federation's past policies and a stop to accepting government funds for overseas activities. It was not accepted by AFL-CIO leaders.[58]

The Organizing Record

The issue at the heart of the 2005 split in the AFL-CIO, however, was organizing the unorganized. So, the record of the Sweeney years is crucial to understanding what happened and what is likely to happen in the future. The overall picture is fairly clear. As we saw in the last chapter, Table 6.2, total union membership fell from 16,360,000 in 1995 to 15,472,000 in 2005, a net loss of 888,000 members. All and more of this was accounted for by the 1,173,000 members lost in the private sector in those years. Before going on to the actual organizing, a closer look at the total figures from 1995 to 2005 should give us a better overall picture. Table 7.2 shows total and private sector union membership for each year over this period. In this 11-year period, the

Table 7.2 **Union Members, 1995–2005 (000s)**

Year	Total	Private
1995	16,360	9,432
1996	16,269	9,415
1997	16,110	9,363
1998	16,211	9,306
1999	16,477	9,419
2000	16,258	9,148
2001	16,289	9,141
2002	15,979	8,652
2003	15,776	8,452
2004	15,472	8,205
2005	15,685	8,255

Sources: *Statistical Abstract*, 2001, p. 411; 2004–2005, p. 419; BLS, *News*, Union Members in 2005, January 20, 2006, USDL 06–99, Table 3, www.bls.gov.

unions saw a net increase in only four years: 1998, 1999, 2001 (after a significant drop in 2000), and 2005. In only two of those, 1999 and 2005, did the private sector contribute to what growth there was. In 1999, the private sector gain was 113,000 or about 43% of the total gain. In 1999, 97% of the growth was accounted for by only 18 out of 66 affiliates.[59] Clearly the organizing message was not getting through to the majority of unions. The 2005 private sector gain of a mere 50,000 was not even a catch-up with the losses of 2004.

Here, a slight digression concerning the top two, virtually equal priorities (if that isn't an oxymoron) of the AFL-CIO and most affiliates: organizing and political action in the form of electing Democrats. The upward trend from the low in 1997 up through 1999, when a net gain of 367,000 members was made, was two-thirds wiped-out in 2000, with not even a tenth of that made up in 2001. The roots of this are all too easy to identify—the 2000 elections. As is usually the case in presidential election years, staff and volunteers are taken off organizing and other functions and as the election approaches put into voter registration, get-out-the-vote efforts, phone banks, and other election-related activities. In 2000, these efforts were fairly successful: the union household vote went from 18% of the total vote in the 1996 election to 26% in 2000 or about 26 million voters.[60] But a heavy price was paid in terms of organizing. As Table 7.3 shows, after a slight uptick in the number of NLRB elections from 3,307 in 1997 to 3,339 in 1998, this shift in activity resulted in a drop in NLRB elections to 3,162 in 1999 and 2,983 in fiscal 2000. Organizing efforts, at least via the NLRB, never returned to their previous level.

From the vantage point of the leaders of the AFL-CIO and most of its affiliates the shift to political activity seems completely natural, indeed, the only thinkable thing. It, nevertheless, reveals a tension between the *twin priorities* of new organizing and political action as most union leaders understand it. In terms of resources there is a real contradiction which is seldom acknowledged or perhaps even realized. It was in 1999, after all, that the AFL-CIO announced a goal of 1million new members a year, apparently unconscious that in the following year they would make that impossible.[61] So, it is not surprising that both the number of representation elections and membership fell again in fiscal 2004 when, if anything, labor made an even greater effort to elect a Democrat. The Change to Win Federation does not have a different approach to this problem. Indeed, in May 2006, the AFL-CIO and Change to Win announced they would work together on the 2006 Congressional elections, at least where they agreed on candidates.[62]

Given the drop in the number of NLRB elections from 1998 to

Table 7.3   NLRB Representation Elections, FY 1997–2005

Year	# Elections	% Won	# Employees	% & # in Won Elections	
2005	2,649	56.8%	176,919	48.3%	85,838
2004	2,719	50.8%	191,964	49.3%	94,565
2003	2,937	53.8%	196,557	44.5%	87,499
2002	2,604	55.8%	174,845	45.3%	79,114
2001	2,694	53.8%	207,139	38.2%	79,277
2000	2,983	51.8%	235,675	45.5%	107,177
1999	3,162	53%	244,260	42.6%	104,045
1998	3,339	56%	238,367	38.0%	90,658
1997	3,307	50.4%	223,634	38.6%	86,325
Total Gained					814,498

Note: NLRB Fiscal Year is from October 1 through September 30.
Source: NLRB, Annual Reports 2003–2005, Table 13; NLRB Election Reports, Fiscal Year 2002, Summary; Fiscal Year 2001, Summary; Fiscal Year 2000, Summary, www.nlrb.gov; Bureau of Labor Statistics, "National Labor Relations Board (NLRB) Union Representation Elections, 1998–2002," April 28, 2003, www.bls.gov; Labor Research Association, *LRA Online*, June 25, 2002, www.laborresearch.org.

2000, the turn of the century represented not a new thrust in organizing, but a continued decline in the effort to organize in the private economy. What is clear, is that the private sector has not been the site of most of such successes as there have been. While employer resistance and a negative political atmosphere pose real barriers, they don't explain the overall drop in attempts to organize. Although there have been new efforts to organize outside the increasingly ineffective NLRB procedures, such as neutrality and card-check agreements, the bulk of organizing drives in the private sector are still conducted through NLRB elections. So, it is worth a look at just how these have gone. The first thing that stands out is that only 814,498 new members have been won through the NLRB route in the private sector from 1997 through 2005, not enough to even make up for the net loss of 1,108,000 private sector members in that period.

For all but two of these years, labor gained fewer than 100,000 members in the private economy via the NLRB. While the unions won slightly over half the elections, they gained less than 50% of the eligible workers. We can see that the average number of workers in a unit with an election in 2005 was about 67 workers. In 1999, according to a study by Bronfenbrenner and Hickey, the average number per unit had been 192 eligible voters.[63] The private sector does not seem to have been much of a strategic focus since 1999. The idea that capturing a smaller number of larger high-visibility targets, such as the 10,000 US Airways reservation clerks organized by the CWA in 1997 or the 2005 campaign at merged Cingular/AT&T that brought in 11,000 new members, might advance organizing in all sectors seems to have been lost during the second half of the Sweeney era.[64] If anything, the unions had become less strategic in the private economy. In the NLRB elections of 2005 the SEIU was well represented as might be expected, as were the Teamsters, UFCW, and Carpenters, but so were the Machinists and Steelworkers. The surprise is the number of security and plant guard unions represented in the 2005 representation elections, a new focus of the SEIU, but hardly a strategic sector. Very few elections in 2005 were in the South. Table 7.4 gives an idea of the industrial distribution of elections in 2005. Of the top five industries in terms of concentration of elections, three are traditional blue-collar areas. The largest number of elections and of eligible voters was in manufacturing, but the success rate there was very low. By far the best success rate was in health care, which would indicate the strategic focus of the SEIU. Of course, organizing in manufacturing is much more difficult because employers can and do plausibly use the threat to move the plant to a lower wage area at home or abroad. As a study led by Kate Bronfenbrenner in the 1990s found, employers used plant-closing threats in 50% of the cases studied.[65] This is far less credible in health care or other services. Altogether, these top five sectors account for 64% of the members gained through NLRB elections in 2005, with health care bringing in the largest number of workers. It is worth noting, however, that "landlocked" wholesale

Table 7.4   Industrial Distribution of Representation Elections 2005

Industry	# Elections	Total Eligible	# Gained	% of Eligible
Total	2,674	179,812	86,247	48
Manufacturing	460	52,057	17,604	33.8
Health Care	411	41,008	25,162	61.4
Transportation	349	17,061	8,916	52.3
Wholesale/Retail	236	11,672	3,481	29.8
Subtotal	1,456	121,798	55,163	45.3
% of Total	55	68	64	

Source: NLRB, *Annual Report*, 2005, Table 16, www.nlrb.gov.

and retail had an even worse record than manufacturing, while transportation was well above average.

Finally, if we compare the number of elections held in recent years with the number held in the period when the unions still grew up to 1980, we can see why organizing is going so slowly today. After slumping in the 1950s the number of elections rose again during the period of militancy. The percentage of workers gained each year, however, fell as employer resistance grew and unions stuck to conventional organizing tactics. So, the number of elections was increased to about 8,000 a year. If unions today conducted 8,000 elections a year at current success rates the number of those unionized in the private sector in 2005 would have been just over a quarter of a million. The five-year gain might have been a million and a quarter, enough to off-set the losses of those years and expand the membership in the private sector to its 1995 level with a density of 10.4% rather than 7.9%. Since there were victories in the pubic sector, some quite big like the SEIU Home Health Care victory in Los Angeles, union density as a whole would have been significantly higher. This, of course, is all speculation. The organizing climate is, as is well known, far more difficult today than in the pre-1980 period. In any case, it didn't happen. In fact what happened was that the number of NLRB elections sought by unions dropped dramatically after 1980 from around 8,000 to about 3,500 on average in the 1980s, falling again in the 1990s. Similarly the number of votes cast in representation elections fell from over 400,000 a year in the 1970s to half that in the 1980s and 1990s, including, as we saw above, after John Sweeney became president of the AFL-CIO.[66] Under Sweeney, in so far as NLRB elections are still an indicator, organizing in the private sector was down, not up. The

Table 7.5   NLRB Representation Elections, 1950–80

Year	# Elections	% of Workers Won
1950	5,731	84
1955	4,372	73
1960	6,617	59
1965	7,776	61
1970	8,074	52
1975	8,061	38
1980	7,296	37

Source: Richard Freeman and James Medoff, *What Do Unions Do?* New York, Basic Books, 1984, p. 223.

results gave much credibility to the Change to Win Federation's arguments.

Organizing had been the major promise of the New Voice team and they were unable to deliver. Some of this was due simply to the fact that most organizing is necessarily done by the affiliates, not by the federation. The federation leaders could encourage it, as they did, but if they couldn't convince the leaders of the affiliated unions to commit the resources, stir up the members to do much of the organizing, agree to a resource shift, get a focus on who and how to organize in today's anti-labor climate, and otherwise transform their daily business union routine into something like a social movement, then they couldn't fulfill the promise. The sign that they would not live up to their promises was the 1998 firing of Richard Bensinger, the federation's organizing director, after only about a year and a half in office. It was said he was alienating union chiefs by pressuring them to get on the program. What the firing revealed was not Bensinger's strengths or weakness so much as the continuing inertia of many unions that did not want to change.[67] This bureaucratic counterweight to change could not be moved by more administrative solutions and bureaucratic programs at the center. To move the old guard and to organize the millions outside the unions would take an upsurge from below inside and outside the existing unions. While rebellion festered in many unions, it was not strong enough to alter the balance of forces. In any case, this was not a force that John Sweeney would or could turn to. He shared too many assumptions and old business union ideas and practices with his opponents to do what would have been needed. In this vacuum, those unions who wanted to organize, who were shifting resources, and who increasingly wondered just what all the money they sent to the AFL-CIO was buying organized the next effort at reform from above.

8

THE POLITICS OF DEFEAT—ONE MORE TIME

In the 2006 mid-term elections, the Democrats regained control of both houses of Congress for the first time since 1994. Given the high rate of incumbency in the House, the shift of 28 seats was particularly significant. The cause of the shift in both houses was a widespread disgust with the Bush Administration. Republican policy on the war in Iraq, as well as on issues of the economic plight of a majority of working-class people and related issues such as health care were the concerns of rebelling voters. Labor claimed a big part in the voter shift. While union members typically vote more Democratic in Congressional elections than in those for president, the 74% vote of union household members for Democrats was higher than usual.[1] The AFL-CIO claimed that union voters accounted for four-fifths of the Democratic margin in the House elections. The union get-out-the-vote efforts had been enormous, with volunteers knocking on 8.25 million union household doors, making 30 million calls, and sending out 20 million pieces of literature to union homes and 14 million to worksites.[2] All of this was done despite the 2005 split that had created two labor federations. But few believed that victory for the Democrats meant that many of the problems facing working people would be addressed any time soon. As impressive as the effort by the unions had been in its own terms, it remained caged in a strategy that had failed for over half a century.

Politics would not be the salvation of the labor movement or of the AFL-CIO itself. In discussing the idea of a "labor–management accord" after World War 2, historian Nelson Lichtenstein argues that whatever one imagines it to have been, it was the product of a defeat. He goes on to write, "That defeat has a name, a legal construct, an institutional expression: it is 'collective bargaining.'" This, of course, as he says, would "surprise" those who assume that contractual unionism is the *alpha* and *omega* of organized labor. The defeat he is referring to is labor's political defeat following WW2. From its endorsement of Roosevelt in 1936 through the formation of the CIO's Political Action Committee (PAC) in 1943, the new CIO forged the basics of what would be labor's central political strategy, one might say addiction, its alliance with and dependence on the Democratic Party.[3] In the course of the New Deal and World War 2, labor had abandoned the AFL's old voluntarist ideology and its pretense of the nonpartisan doctrine of "rewarding your friends and punishing your enemies" in favor of a semi-institutional alliance with the Democrats. By the late 1940s, the strategy had failed by almost any accounting. Even before the capture of Congress by the Republicans in 1946 and the passage of the Taft-Hartley Act the following year, labor met defeat in a Congress now dominated by the alliance of conservative Southern Democrats and Northern Republicans. As historian Robert Zieger put it rather modestly, "In 1946 and 1947 the CIO's political and legislative arms proved inadequate to the task of expanding the welfare state and preventing antilabor legislation."[4]

Despite its failure, the basics of the strategy would be embraced wholeheartedly by the AFL-CIO upon its birth by merger in 1955 when the Committee on Political Education (COPE) replaced PAC. Influence peddling and power brokering would be the specialty of federation president George Meany throughout the 1950s and 1960s. Stephen Amberg described both the hope and the result:

> Union leaders in this era of philosophical complacency focused on strategy and tactics for moving the Democrats, and through them the American polity, toward support for labor's policy proposals. It was not to be.[5]

Labor's ambitious postwar agenda was watered down or simply discarded by White House and Congress alike and ultimately by labor itself. The construction of the "private welfare state" of benefits through bargaining employer-by-employer or industry-by-industry for those lucky enough to be covered by a union contract became the substitute for political success.[6] The modern pattern of AFL-CIO intervention in politics became established in this period. The federation had two arms to carry this out: the Legislative Department, which conducted its lobbying efforts, and COPE, which did its electoral work and raised money for political contributions. It achieved a moment of modest success in the 1960s, when its leaders, notably Meany and Reuther, received considerable attention from Democratic leaders.[7] Even this, however, might well be credited to the civil rights, anti-war, and women's movements more than to the unions alone. In any case, it was short-lived. As one biographer of George Meany wrote:

Table 8.1   Union Household and White Union Member Democratic Presidential Vote, 1948–2004

Year	% of Union Household	% White Union Member	% White Working Class**
1948	80	79	76
1952	56	53	52
1956	53	50	44
1960	64	64	55
1964	83	80	75
1968	56	50	50
1972	43	40	32
1976	64	60	58
1980	55	48	44
1984	57	49	42
1988	59	53	43
1992	55	48	42
1996	59	69	55
2000	59	52*	n/a
2004	59	53*	n/a
* White Union Households ** Income from $15,000 to $30,000			

Sources: S. Amberg, in Kevin Boyle (ed.), *Organized Labor and American Politics 1894–1994*, 1998, p. 175; G. Pomper, in M. Nelson (ed.), *The Elections of 2004*, CQ Press, 2005, p. 49; M. Gottschalk, *The Shadow Welfare State*, 2000, p. 34; S. Greenberg, *The Two Americas*, 2005, p. 319.

Nor did the AFL-CIO's political and legislative operations retain their luster through the 1970s. Successful in helping to elect Democrats, COPE seemed unable to prevent the party from drifting ever rightward.[8]

The failure of the Democratic Party pressure strategy became apparent early on when in the 1946 Congressional elections union voter turnout was low even though 67% of union members voted Democratic. Then in the 1952 presidential election the union household vote collapsed from 80% for the Democrats in 1948 to 56% in 1952.[9] Table 8.1 shows the union household presidential vote from 1948 through 2004. With the exception of 1964 when the Goldwater candidacy represented the first serious challenge from the conservative right, the labor vote never fully recovered in presidential elections. This is not to say that there was a simple shift to Republicans by white union members and households, as is often argued. For one thing, union household support for Congressional Democrats remained significantly higher, from 60 to 72%, landing somewhere in between in most years. Thus, about two-thirds of union household members voted consistently Democratic in Congressional elections.[10] For another, until the 1970s the vast majority of union members would have been white so that the majority that continued to vote Democratic was white. What is apparent, however, is that after 1980 the gap between union household voting and white union member voting grew. The union household vote, still well below its historic high in the 1940s, was by then held up increasingly by African Americans and Latinos. For white working-class voters in the $15,000 to $30,000 income level, the percentage voting Democratic in the presidential elections was even lower, but nevertheless followed the ups and downs of the union household and white union members voters. In other words, there has long been a large section of the white working class that has voted Republican.

The further decline of both the union household and white union member vote came precisely as union membership also fell, meaning the total union vote had to decline. Both also occurred as Lane Kirkland took office. And while it went up and down, the union vote did not recover much ground. The 1994 Congressional off-year election which so alarmed the labor bureaucracy also saw the white union vote for Congressional Democrats drop from 63% in 1990 and 66% in 1992 to 61% in 1994.[11] During Sweeney's first ten years, the union household vote, though bigger numerically, remained at 59% for the Democratic candidate for president, as Table 8.1 shows.

Sweeney had promised to make labor's political intervention more effective. Staying within the sacrosanct strategic framework of Democratic dependence, he did make significant shifts in emphasis. Two major shifts were increased spending on issue ads and the increased mobilization of staff and member volunteers for get-out-the-vote. In 1996, the AFL-CIO spent $25 million on issue ads. Some of these targeted Republican voting records on issues of importance to union members, particularly in Congressional Districts with close races. Also in the 1996 elections, the federation attempted to recruit 100 permanent grassroots activists in these districts with an additional 2,500 in the final six weeks of the contest. In the 1998 off-year election the AFL-CIO put 300 full-time paid staff in the field, while volunteers made some 14.5 million phone calls. Seventy percent of union members reported that their union had contacted them about the election.[12]

By the 2000 election the shift took a new direction away from advertising toward even more emphasis on mobilization. As one study described it:

> In the 2000 presidential election, labor spent $40 million; however, less than one-quarter of that money was spent on broadcast advertising. Why did labor reduce its reliance on political advertising and what new strategy did it adopt between 1996 and 2000? Labor learned in 1998 that the greatest way to affect the election outcome and get its 13 million members to vote was not through broadcast communications, but through grassroots, person-to-person contact.[13]

"Labor" spending here refers to the AFL-CIO. In addition, the federation fielded thousands of coordinators and sent out millions of fliers urging members to register and vote. As a result, 2.3 million new union members were registered.[14] And organizing came to a virtual halt. It is remarkable to think that the idea of mobilizing union members for politics or other efforts was something new and exceptional. Hadn't labor's numbers always been a source of strength? For those at the pinnacle of the movement the answer had long been no, except as passive voters. So when the notion of "worker-to-worker" networks for political ends became the official line, it seemed unique. An April 2000 issue of the UAW's magazine *Solidarity* told of how enthusiastic members were about the new "worker-to-worker" program it had launched in 1999. It noted the allegedly unknown fact that, "when union activists talk to members at work, trust jumps to 81 percent."[15] They could have learned this lesson from the 1997 UPS strikers. The push to mobilize for 2004 was, if anything, stronger and more effective as union members from "Blue" states poured in to the "Battleground" states to defeat George W. Bush. The union household vote composed about 24 per cent of the electorate in 2004, slightly less than the 26% in 2000. The number of union household voters had increased by about 2 million in 2004, when altogether 17 million more people voted. In 2000 a little over 10 million of those union household voters had voted Republican, while in 2004 it was over 11 million.[16] Mobilization was not enough.

Table 8.2 compares the political action committee money spent by all of labor during the Sweeney years with the results of Congressional elections. One thing to be noted in terms of changes during the Sweeney years, is that not only is a much higher percentage of the money spent on mobilization, but it is more focused than during the Kirkland era. In 2000, for example, the AFL-CIO alone spent $40 million, but this and the mobilization it helped finance were targeted on 71 Congressional Districts in which there were competitive races for House seats. Indeed, 80% of campaign-related money went to competitive districts compared

Table 8.2   Labor PAC Expenditures and Changes in Congress, 1996–2004

($ millions)

Year	$ Spent	Democrats in House	Democrats in Senate
1996	$104.1	206	45
1998	$111.3	211	45
2000	$136.0	212	50
2002	$167.8	204	48
2004	$191.7	202	44
2006	n.a.	229	51*
* Includes two independents who caucus with the Democrats			

Sources: James Caeser and Andrew Busch, *Red Over Blue: The 2004 Elections and American Politics*, New York, Rowman and Littlefield Publishers, Inc., 2005, p. 144; *Statistical Abstract*, 2006, pp. 258, 266; *New York Times*, November 12, 2006, www.nytimes.com.

with only 54% under Kirkland.[17] The incumbency rate in the House has run at about 98% in recent years, meaning that most races are not competitive unless a Representative retires, dies, or loses a primary. So, the only way to switch the party balance in the House is to focus on the so-called "marginal" or swing Districts. But as Table 8.2 shows, the results were disappointing. For all its spending, mobilizing, and focusing, labor could not shift the balance in Congress or, after 1996, elect its presidential choice. Even in its new streamlined form, the old strategy failed in the Sweeney era as it had before. The problem was not so much Sweeney, who had pushed for new tactics like member mobilization, as the strategy itself.

This old strategy had not brought many victories when the Democrats briefly held both the White House and Congress from 1993 through 1994 in the pre-Sweeney era. The notable exception was the Family Medical Leave Act of 1993.[18] During Sweeney's first term, labor had two legislative victories of some note. In 1996, they squeezed an increase in the minimum wage from $4.25 to $5.15 out of the Republican Congress by targeting twenty-nine fairly vulnerable House Republicans with media blitzes after that party had voted for a 30% increase in their own pay. In 1997 and 1998, they helped defeat "fast track" trade legislation. But after these victories, it was all downhill. In 2002, for example, fast track was passed and then the trade treaty with China.[19] In 2004 the biggest electoral mobilization yet failed to counter the right-wing mobilization that elected Bush, this time with an actual majority. The strategy, modernized and mobilized, failed on its own terms once again. It failed because of the framework it accepted without reflection: electing and pressuring Democrats. If anything, it was even more bound to fail because the rules of the game had changed yet again.

The Deck Gets More Stacked

In the years between George Meany's last term of office and John Sweeney's first term, the rules of American electoral politics changed substantially. Feeling the pressure of falling profit rates, of world recession, and later of stagflation, in the 1970s big business organized politically as it had not done for some time. As one journalist noted, "During the 1970s, business refined its ability to act as a class, submerging competitive instincts in favor of joint, cooperative action in the legislative arena."[20] The centerpiece of this re-organization was the Business Roundtable, a coalition of America's biggest industrial, financial, and service corporations. Its agenda was what would become known as Reaganomics or more generally as neoliberalism: deregulation, privatization, cuts or restraints on social spending, deep tax cuts for business and the wealthy, and "free trade." Formed in 1972 out of an earlier effort to control costs in construction, the Business Roundtable was described by one journalist as "the political rearmament of the business community."[21] Unlike labor, it and its big business confrères would be highly successful no matter who filled the seats of Congress or who sat in the White House. From deregulation under Carter to the Reagan tax cuts to NAFTA under Clinton to the Bush tax cuts, corporate America ruled. Its agenda became America's agenda and labor, despite a few small victories here and there, was unable to stop the corporate juggernaut. The wheels of this juggernaut were greased by two major institutional changes that altered both the electoral and the legislative rules of the game. Both were delivered gratis in the mid-1970s, not by business-friendly Republicans, but by labor's duly rewarded "friends," the Democrats.

In the wake of Watergate, the Democrats swept the Congressional elections, increasing their majority in the House from 239 to 192 in 1973 upward to 291 to 144 in 1975 to 292 to 143 in 1977. With this huge majority they set about reforming both campaign finances and the internal structure of Congress itself. The urge to reform campaign finance was a reaction to the disclosure that Nixon had secretly raised some $20 million from rich friends and friendly corporations.[22] The effort to reform the committee system in Congress was meant to open up the committee set-up so long dominated by high seniority Southerners to the newcomers who composed much of the increased Democratic majority. Probably nothing was further from the minds of most of these well-meaning junior representatives and senators than handing Congress and the electoral system over to big business lock, stock, and barrel. But this is just what they did—a reminder of the law of unintended consequences in a system that tilts toward business in the best and worst of times. Whatever the innocence, naiveté, or intentions of the "class of '74," a rearmed corporate America knew just what to do.

The Federal Election Campaign Act of 1974 amended a 1971 act creating the Federal Election Commission to keep track of political money, to establish public funding for presidential nominating and general elections, set limits on campaign contributions, and require corporations and unions to set up political action committees (PACs) to collect and disburse funds. PACs, of course, were the invention of labor. Now they were required by businesses that chose to contribute to candidates or parties, which was most of them. The impact of these reforms was to draw business ever deeper into funding presidential and Congressional candidates. The number of PACs soared from 600 in 1974 to 4,000 in 1984 and 4,500 in 2001.[23] The number of labor PACs grew from 201 in 1974 to 388 in 1984 and then fell to 316 in 2000 as unions merged. It would increase again to 328 in 2004. Corporate PACs, however, increased from 318 in 1974 to 1,756 in 2004. "Trade, membership, and health" PACs, most of which were business-based, grew from 89 in 1974 to 986 in 2004. So-called "nonconnected" or ideological and issue PACs were virtually nonexistent in 1974; by 1978 there were 168 of these and by 2004 their number had increased to 1,650.[24] These latter would turn out to be critical as they would be dominated by right-wing and pro-business anti-labor groups.

Far more important than their numbers was the money that PACs put into the federal electoral process. In real terms, PAC spending on Congressional elections increased by six-and-one-quarter times from 1974 to 2002. This spending, however, was by no means distributed evenly by source. In 1974, labor had actually accounted for half of all PAC campaign contributions. By 2002 labor PAC contributions amounted to only 19% of the total. Corporate and trade PACs alone outspent labor by over three to one in real terms.[25] In nominal terms total PAC spending rose from $430 million in the 1995–96 election cycle to $843 million in 2003–04, almost doubling during Sweeney's reign. Labor's PAC expenditures rose from $100 million to $183 million over those years, a somewhat slower rate.[26] This was a race labor could not win. And it was only one lap of the race. Individual contributions became the largest part of campaign funding for Congressional candidates as parties, interest groups, candidates learned how to garner large numbers of individual contributions through direct mail and later the Internet. Corporate lobbyists and others would elevate the practice of "bundling," collecting individual contributions and giving them in bulk to candidates, reputedly developed by Mark Hanna in the pivotal 1896 election to beat Democrat William Jennings Bryan. In the 2002 off-year election "soft" money used for issue ads came to over $400 million. Altogether, in 2002 labor contributions amounted to just under 8% of the total. In the 2000 presidential elections soft money reached $500 million, until it was banned in 2002, only to be replaced by "527" money.[27]

If all this corporate and pro-business money went to Republicans, things might have been different. But it didn't. In presidential contests, business funds went disproportionately to Republicans. But in Congressional elections corporate and trade contributions typically went to incumbents in Congress, particularly those with important committee positions. This is where the second reform of the mid-1970s came in. To allow the many junior Democrats elected to Congress in 1974 and 1976 a bigger role, the majority Democrats expanded the committee and subcommittee system so more of them could have committee chairs. This meant more incumbents for business to make contributions to. Thus, for the better part of the half a century in which the Democrats held a majority in the House and the nearly as many years in the Senate, the Democrats were the recipients of a huge share of corporate and trade money. The percentage of corporate PAC funds going to incumbent Democrats in the House rose from 35% in 1978 to a high of 51% in 1994. The total of corporate PAC funds going to all Democrats in the House in those years rose from 45% in 1978 to 54% in 1994. When the Democrats lost the House it fell to 30–35% of the total from 1996–2002. For trade PACs the trend was similar with the proportion of funds going to Democrats in the House rising from 47% in 1978 to a high of 61% in 1990, hitting lows of 29% in 1996 and 28% in 2000. "Nonconnected" or ideological and issue-based PACs follow the same pattern for the House. This trend is less pronounced in the Senate where somewhat more corporate and trade money went to Republicans.[28] What this means, of course, is that particularly in the House of Representatives labor was not simply fighting off Republicans, but since the 1970s, was competing with big business for the loyalty of Democrats with funds that could not possibly match those from business. It is hardly a coincidence that the last flurry of pro-labor legislation, such as OSHA, came in the early 1970s.

Matters were made worse by the increasing weakness of the Democratic Party in relation to candidates that ran in its name. Increasingly, candidates ran as individuals with their own campaign organizations, raising their own funds. As one observer put it:

The skills that work in American politics at this point in history are those of entrepreneurship. At all levels of the political system, from local boards and councils up to and including the presidency, it is unusual for parties to nominate people. People nominate themselves.[29]

In doing so, of course, they must prove themselves capable of raising credible amounts of money and of gaining backing from people in power.[30] It is not an open process. The growing role of the media, the so-called "Air War," and the decline of the urban machines, part of the old "Ground War," meant that elections became more and more expensive and dependence on those with money all the greater. Consultants and pollsters entered the field to make things even more costly. The average amount raised by candidates for the House rose from $61,084 in 1974 to $756,993 in 2002, multiplying by over eleven times. For the Senate it grew from $455,515 to $4,460,206 in those years, a ten-fold increase.[31] Labor's decision under Sweeney to return to emphasis on the "Ground War" of member mobilization might have been the right one, but given the new rules of the game it simply left all these candidates more dependent than ever on business money.

The story doesn't end there, however. It's not just how they get into office, but how they are influenced once they are there. Enter the lobbyists. The soaring costs of election spurred the growth of the Washington-based lobbying corps into a major industry. Campaign contributions buy "access" to elected officials. While they might buy access for the individual giver if the donation is big enough, it is typically the lobbyist who collects on the access promise. Microsoft is a good example. In the 1999–2000 presidential election cycle Microsoft gave $4.6 million in campaign contributions, the fifth largest from a corporation. In 2000 it spent $6 million and in 2003 $10 million on lobbying to reap the benefits of its contributions. It maintained 16 full-time lobbyists of its own as well as the services of 20 lobbying firms.[32] Before the lobbying disclosure act of 1946, there were some 6,000 individuals and organizations registered as lobbyists. When the law took effect the number rose to almost 15,000. By 2005, under the somewhat stricter reporting qualifications of the 1995 Lobby Disclosure Act, there were 34,785 registered lobbyists in Washington DC. As of 2004, lobbyists had spent $2 billion in one year. Over 600 corporations maintain lobbying offices in Washington, but most business interests "outsource" their lobbying to one of Washington's lawyer-lobbyists, multiple-client firms, or mega-firms. These latter firms not only lobby Congress, but also federal agencies. They are the connectors in the famous "Iron Triangle" or "subgovernments" in which they maintain regular contact not only with representatives, senators, and their staffs on key committees, but with the agencies in the executive branch that are the counterpart of those committees. Lobbyists not only pressure to kill, pass, or amend legislation, they often draft it in the first place.[33]

The weakening of the parties and the rise of individual candidacies along with the Congressional reforms of the 1970s have opened the door wider than ever for well-heeled lobbyists. Weak party organization creates such openings. As one expert on lobbying put it:

> When political parties are unable to take clear responsibility for governing, and when they cannot maintain cohesion and discipline among those elected under their labels, special interests have opportunities to gain access to the key points of decision within the government.[34]

As noted above, these key points include not only Congress and its many committees, but federal agencies in the executive branch where much of the detail of regulation is finalized as well. The Congressional reforms of the 1970s come into this because the proliferation of committees and subcommittees they fostered created far more points of access. Although the Republicans cut the number of subcommittees after they took over in 1996, the 109th congress (2005–07) still had 20 standing committees and 91 subcommittees in the House and 16 standing committees with 71 subcommittees in the Senate. These are where the work of Congress is done, legislation amended, killed, or passed on for a vote. They are, as one text put it, the "workshops of Congress" and there are lots of them.[35] For labor with limited legislative resources this was a problem that not even its grassroots lobbying and district level Legislative Action Committees could overcome. For business with hundreds of its own lobbyists and thousands of "hired guns" to be had for the money, it was an opportunity. It was an opportunity that largely explained why the agenda laid out in the 1970s by the Business Roundtable had been passed down to the last detail by the mid-1990s even though the Democrats had dominated the House since 1954 and the Senate for most of that time. The deck was stacked against labor more than ever. New tactics could not transcend the permanently flawed nature of the whole strategy of dependence. To reshuffle the deck would take a mobilization of a different and far more massive type. It would not be sufficient just to increase the union household vote, although that was in bad repair. It was a matter of mobilizing a rainbow of working-class people who did not appear to think of themselves as, much less act like, a class. It was also a question of just what organized labor was to mobilize such a force for.

Why White Workers Vote Republican, or What's the Matter with America?

The backbone of the labor vote is above all the African American union membership and their families. Eighty-six percent of African American voters identify as Democrats and in the 2004 election they voted by 88% for Kerry, despite the misgivings many must have had. It is likely that the 2.1 million Black union members vote even more heavily Democratic. But as 14% of union members and 11% of voters (in 2004), the African American community cannot possibly carry national elections for the Democrats or any future progressive alternative unless a substantial majority of white voters and, above all, white union members, also vote for Democratic or progressive candidates. While I will argue later that voting Democratic is *not* a viable strategy for many of the reasons given above, or even an accurate measure of class identity, for the moment it is the only measure we have of how successful the political right is in colonizing the working-class vote. Given its utter lack of success among African Americans, the only slightly greater success among working-class Latinos, and the still overwhelming preponderance of whites in the voting population, one unavoidable question becomes, why do so many white working-class people and even union members vote Republican?

In one sense, there is nothing unusual about working-class people in the developed capitalist nations casting votes for conservative capitalist parties. The working class is not a homogeneous mass and has many fissures within it, including race, gender, region, religion, and nationality. At most times, class consciousness is uneven and contradictory—influenced by the dominant capitalist ideas of the time as well as by old traditional ideas. In Britain an average of about 25–30% of manual workers regularly vote Conservative, while in France in the 2002 election 21% of blue-collar workers voted for the center right parties and 18% for the far right.[36] What actually makes the United States unique is that its working-class voters almost *all* cast their ballots for capitalist parties, albeit that one was once considered "liberal" and in legislative terms "pro-labor." While the two parties are not identical and differ on key social issues, the Democratic Party is, after all, a capitalist party in every sense of the word: ideology, program, personnel, and funding. It is one of the oldest political parties in the developed world with roots in the politics of slavery and, until somewhere in the twentieth century, an official commitment to white supremacy. It favored "free trade" (low tariffs) long before Republicans embraced such a policy. Its conversion to modern liberalism was late and never complete. Not even during the New Deal did it dream of ending segregation in the South or constructing anything like the European social democratic welfare states that would come after WW2. In foreign affairs the party and all its presidential candidates and office holders have been committed to the advancement of US capital abroad as the central feature of US foreign policy which included aggressive use of the military and its expansion, by today, across the entire globe. Its subservience to big business is etched in its legislative record. What we have arrived at today, after three decades of the processes described above, is a solidly right-wing Republican Party, on the one hand, and a confused centrist-to-center-right Democratic Party, on the other hand. The picture is made richer only because of the remnants of the "new" social movements of the 1960s and 1970s, the dissident trends within organized labor, the enthusiasm of many young people for global justice, and the rise of genuinely new social movements within the working class—above all the new movement(s) of immigrant workers. So far, these movements new and old are waiting in the wings, as it were, and are the potential for something new and better. They are, as yet, a partly active but also partly latent force in American politics. In analyzing and judging organized labor's political strategy we are, for the moment, stuck with the traditional measures of success: how workers and especially union members and households vote (Democratic or Republican) and what legislation or other political achievements labor can claim for its efforts in the framework of this long suffering strategy. As we saw above, these latter are few on the legislative front.

As noted above, the labor vote collapsed long before the appearance of the Michigan Wallace voter, the Reagan Democrat, or the Kansas Bush defector. At the core of this Republican worker phenomenon are some of the old facts of American politics and history. For example, since the Civil War, white Protestants of every class have voted disproportionately Republican. A reasonable working-class example of this is Johnny Metzgar, the steelworker father of labor historian Jack Metzgar. In his book, *Striking Steel*, Jack Metzgar describes his father as a strong and loyal union man who had helped organize the United Steelworkers in Johnstown, PA, and became an aggressive "griever" (shop steward) after the union was established. Johnny Metzgar was "a lifelong Republican" who voted three times for Roosevelt and worked for Truman in 1948. For Johnny "being a Republican was less a reflection of his political views than it was a way a Protestant German family differentiated itself from the Catholics and 'foreigners' in the local Democratic machine."[37] In Johnny Metzgar's story you can see one side of the ethnic "traditions" and prejudices that shaped party politics in much of urban America in the twentieth century. You can also see the collapse of the labor vote as this Republican union activist ceased voting for Democratic presidential candidates. We can presume that much of the dazzling 80% Democratic presidential union vote in 1948 came from working-class Republicans who followed their union, rather than their traditions and prejudices, to the polls. They followed their union to the polls because they thought it would continue to make a difference and when it didn't and other issues arose, they reverted to tradition and prejudice.

Building and holding together a labor vote, that is a class vote, in the context of the two-party system was not easy even in the period of union upsurge in the 1930s and 1940s, running up as it did against the disenfranchisement of Blacks in the South and deep roots of racism and social conservatism within the white sections of the working class generally. When circumstances changed after the 1940s and again in the 1970s, it would be even more difficult in the context of the postwar strategic framework. Before looking at the changing circumstances, however, we have to look at the big factor that always looms beneath the surface, behind the scenes, or up front: race and racism. White workers, like other whites, are often pulled away from their economic self-interest by appeals to racial threat and/or racial solidarity. Sometimes this is perceived as a sort of defense of the marginally better economic position they have achieved, which they think is somehow threatened by "new" entrants to their piece of the labor market, housing, schools, etc.—Blacks in the 1960s, immigrants in the late nineteenth century and again today. This is a well-known recurrent theme in American history. In the realm of electoral politics, racism is often wrapped in a populist appeal. George Wallace was a master of this. Populism in America has always been cousins with racism; sometimes distant and feuding cousins as in the 1890s, sometimes kissing cousins, but never too far from the family. So, from Strom Thurmond's 1948 Dixiecrats, to Wallace's 1968 and 1972 runs, to Bush senior's 1988 Willie Horton ads, crime and other code words drag the permanent underlying racism into the high-profile world of political campaigning.[38] Whether just below the surface or in the light of day, appeals to racism pull hard on any progressive coalition and certainly on the labor vote.

By the end of the 1940s, other things also pulled at the labor vote. There was the Cold War, the expulsion of the Communist-led unions from the CIO, the failure of Operation Dixie, the Korean War, McCarthyism, revelations of union corruption, and the very prosperity experienced by many union members. All these things made the concept of class suspicious and lowered the esteem of unions and union leaders, what historian Nelson Lichtenstein calls the "erosion of the union idea."[39] There was also the merger of the AFL and CIO in 1955 which announced that the differences between the two federations had virtually disappeared and/or been swept under the rug. Business unionism had triumphed again. As labor historian Robert Zieger summarized it:

> The merger of the AFL and the CIO . . . marked an end not only to the conflict between the two wings of organized labor but to the period of experimentation and expansion that the birth of the CIO had inaugurated two decades earlier.[40]

For the new leaders of the AFL-CIO the labor vote was not a source of independent power, but a bargaining chip. Furthermore, it was a bargaining chip more in the game of candidate selection at quadrennial Democratic Party conventions than in the fight for improved working-class living standards or social justice more broadly. The merger took place in New York in December 1955 at the very moment the modern civil rights movement was born in Montgomery, Alabama. Yet, the new federation failed to deal with its own segregation problem: namely the exclusion of Blacks and others from several railroad and building trades unions. Race was again put on the back burner and one of the major fissures in the labor vote allowed to fester, while the potential for expansion into the South was killed for two generations.[41] This would lead to an enormous fight within the new federation only a few years later, characterized by the battle between A. Philip Randolph and George Meany, and to an internal weakening of labor as it entered yet another period full of challenges.

The period that followed, particularly that from 1964 through 1979, was one of vast social motion and enormous contradictions. This was the period of labor upsurge and militancy discussed earlier in this book. But it was also the time when civil rights became Black Power, a time of civil disorder not only in urban ghettoes but on campuses and even on the nation's highways, when both the Vietnam War and the anti-war movement escalated. It was a period that began at the height of the economic boom and ended in its crisis. The labor upsurge involved all kinds of workers, from the Latino farm workers in California in 1964 to the nationwide wildcats of 1970 and the young whites at Lordstown in 1972, but it was particularly a time of upsurge and organization for Black workers. In the economic boom they increased their numbers in the industrial unions and formed new unions in the public sector. Two events that symbolized the arrival of African American workers at the gates of union politics were the DRUM-led strike at Dodge Main in Detroit and the Memphis sanitation workers' strike where Martin Luther King was murdered, both in 1968.[42] But this was also the moment of the white backlash.

Sensing the uneasiness among many white workers, Nixon took a page from Wallace's hymn book and made law and order his re-election theme in 1972. Recognizing that the Democratic Party in the South was now filling up with African American voters seeking candidates of a type not seen since Reconstruction, he opened a new chapter in Republican strategy with a clear and loud message to the white South in 1972. He carried all the Southern states with majorities ranging from 65.8% to 78.2%. His message also targeted antiwar protesters as elite and anti-American, themes that would be picked up decades later by hardcore conservatives seeking working-class votes. Union households voted 54% for Nixon in 1972.[43] One reason, it is often argued, is that George McGovern was a weak candidate seen by many working-class people as the symbol of the very elite they were learning to distrust. Another was that labor itself was deeply split over all the issues that confronted America in those years. Under Meany's command, the AFL-CIO had refused to endorse McGovern because of his position against the war and his support from the social movements that Meany so hated. It was a *de facto* endorsement of Nixon. This rightward gesture certainly played into the hands of Nixon and all those who hoped to split the blue-collar vote along racial lines. Watergate drove the white working class and union household voters back to the Democrats in 1976 in droves, with the highest proportion of union household voters backing the Democrats since 1964, but as the Carter years would make clear the Democratic Party was already moving to the right. With a huge majority in Congress and a Democrat in the White House, labor leaders watched their prize legislative goals, labor law reform and common-situs picketing among others, go down to defeat while deregulation of trucking and airlines became law. Then came the Chrysler bailout, Ronald Reagan, the Democratic Leadership Council and a new period of retreat for labor.[44]

In this new era, the labor vote slumped and then rose. As a percentage of the total vote, the union household vote fell from 28% in the 1950s to 26% in 1980, 23% in 1984, 21% in 1988, and 18% in 1992. Labor's declining numbers had contributed to this. But it is also likely that many union household members just stopped voting for a while. How did this declining sector of the electorate cast its votes? We saw in Table 8.1 that the percentage of union household voters who voted Democratic fell from 64% in 1976 to 55% in 1980, the year of the Reagan Democrat. The Democratic percentage rose after Reagan's first term and then leveled off at 59% for the Democratic presidential candidates with union household voters making up 26% in 2000 and 24% in 2004. Whatever their turnout, union household members also remained about two-thirds Democratic in Congressional elections in this whole period. The figures are, of course, weaker among white union households, where, as of 2000 and 2004, the ratio was 53% for

Democratic presidential candidates compared with 59% for all union households.[45] So, it seems clear that the white union vote, although it appears to have a floor at about half, is basically unstable.

In *What's the Matter With Kansas?*, Thomas Frank shows how conservative Republicans have managed to turn class on its head and convince many working and lower middle-class white people that the Democrats are dominated by a bunch of elitists out of touch with the cultural mainstream and, above all, with America's (white) working folk. As Frank shows in the case of Kansas, these new conservatives honed their *Kulturkampf* class politics on the upper-class moderate Republicans who had dominated the state party. For national figures such as Ann Coulter, Bill O'Reilly, or Rush Limbaugh, as well as for the Kansans, it is the latte-drinking coastal Democrats that matter. Religion and race play key roles in all this, but the great sleight of hand is the inversion of class antagonism. To accomplish such an act of legerdemain, the right-wing culture warriors have erased the corporation from their picture of America. There is the efficient market and the deserving entrepreneur, but no giant Enron or GM or US Steel or other such creature that destroyed your pension, closed your mill or plant, wrecked your town, etc. As Frank argues:

> This makes sense when you recall that the great goal of the backlash is to nurture a cultural class war, and the first step in doing so, as we have seen, is to deny the economic basis of social class. After all, you can hardly deride liberals as society's "elite" or present the GOP as the party of the common man if you acknowledge the existence of the corporate world—the power that creates the nation's real elite, that dominates the real class system, and that wields the Republican Party as its personal political sidearm.[46]

Thus, in this picture, the very institutions that the conservatives target as the source of cultural decay, Hollywood and "the liberal media," for example, are not described as business corporations out for a profit, but as lairs of latte-liberalism that look down on working-class people. As Frank points out, they get away with this because in fact our culture and its media "have for decades insisted on downplaying the world of work."[47] In other words, the corporate-dominated (and so-called liberal) media, movies, music, etc. have played more than a small role in obscuring the social reality of work in American society. And, of course, many of the top Democratic politicians, fundraisers, celebrities, and ideologues, in fact, fit the elitist profile all too well, living often highly visible elite lifestyles. No less a person than SEIU President Andy Stern, when asked about the perception of the Democrats as "latte-drinking, Chardonnay-sipping owners of Volvos," replied this was not just a perception, but the reality.[48]

Another side of the explanation for why white working-class people, including a hefty percentage of union members and households, remain Republicans or shift that way in some elections is that they do in fact hold many conservative values. As any number of recent commentaries on the rise of the Republican majority will tell you, guns, god, gays, and guts (militarism) play a big role in the success of right-wing ideas and candidates among white blue-collar workers. Religion and racism are all mixed in with these "values," but they nonetheless have a life of their own. Consciousness, of course, *is* contradictory. What might surprise many people is that the attitudes of white union families are almost identical to those of African Americans on a great many of these "hot button" issues. On national security, immigration, abortion, attitudes toward big corporations, and government regulation of business, the proportions, pro or con, are very similar to those of African Americans and much more left-leaning than the average voter, according to the findings of pollster Stanley Greenberg. There are differences, for example, on guns. But the real difference is race. Regardless of one's "values" conservatives cannot make the same appeal to working-class Blacks. As among African Americans and Americans generally, there remains a consistent third or more of union household members with socially conservative views on family, gender, abortion, the military, etc.[49] The right latches on to these values and provides an alternative explanation of society and the plight of working-class people discussed in earlier chapters. Conservative commentator Gary Bauer says, "Joe Six-Pack doesn't understand why his world and his culture are changing, and why he doesn't have any say in it."[50] The right offers an explanation that appeals to select core values that this stereotypical worker holds and by implication, if not explicitly, to his race. The only possible way to appeal to these working-class families from the other side of the political spectrum is on the basis of class: to turn the conservative *Kulturkampf* version of class back on its feet, put the real economy back in the picture, and expose the real role of the corporations in the US and the world. The Democratic Party and most Democratic politicians and operatives could no more do this than run the red flag up the pole on the Capitol dome. They are, after all, the other well-funded sidearm of capital at home and abroad.

There is one more factor in explaining why so many working-class and union household voters cast their ballots for Republicans and generally buy the ideas that come from right-wing commentators like Rush Limbaugh or Bill O'Reilly. It is the sense of betrayal felt particularly by Rust Belt blue-collar workers over the loss of jobs, plants, and the towns that were supported by them. They might well blame the corporations that did this, but corporate action would not be a betrayal on the scale of those who were supposedly the workers' friends: Democratic politicians and union leaders. Beyond rhetoric, these two groups did little or nothing to stop the plant closings from which most other misfortunes flowed. One source of evidence for this feeling among Rust Belt working-class people came during the failure of an SEIU organizing drive at a nursing home in Western Pennsylvania. Although management did not put up the kind of resistance one expects these days, the union lost its first attempt to organize the facility. Upon looking deeper into why these workers voted against the union despite low wages, what the union organizers discovered was resentment toward unions. One aspect of this was about violence and corruption. But the two other reasons given were "do-nothing" unionism and "the experience of de-industrialization and job-loss" in the region. Many of the workers in the nursing home had worked for one or another of the big companies in the region that had closed up shop and moved on. They had watched the union be cozy with the company in hopes of stopping it and doing nothing when the plant finally closed. It was not uncommon for these workers to give the company and media line that the unions put the plants out of business with their high wages.[51] The unions did little to counter these arguments when the closing came. The Democratic politicians of the region, who the union leaders supported no matter what, also did nothing.

The shift toward the Republicans nationally, however, is not primarily due to the weaknesses in the labor vote as currently constituted. It is also a result of the shift of a majority of Southern whites from the Democratic Party to the Republicans that began in the 1970s. Until 1992, no Democratic presidential candidate was elected without carrying a big piece of the South. The shift to the Republican Party was bolstered by the demographic shift of population to the South and Southwest, which provided the South with more presidential electoral votes, House seats, and State legislative majorities. This, in turn, has allowed the Republicans in a number of states to redistrict Congressional seats in their favor. The most outrageous example of this being the 2003 Tom Delay-inspired redrawing of four Texas districts in favor of the Republicans, a year after the state legislature had already done a compromise redistricting. While both parties engage in such practices, the overall demographic shift has favored the Republicans. Demographics have also increased white Southern representation in the Senate. Once solidly Democratic (and conservative), as of 2004, there were only 4 Democratic Senators from the 11 states of the former Confederacy out of a possible 22.[52]

The answer to this, of course, lies in unionizing much of the South. Building a liberal political majority had been a major concern in the attempt to organize the South after World War 2. The Southern

Democrats had strengthened their position in Congress and were a roadblock to progressive legislation even before the 1946 election. Unionization would have helped to alter this, the CIO leaders thought correctly. The failure of "Operation Dixie" spelled the failure of the CIO's overall political strategy.[53] All the evidence is that membership in unions over time does shift the political thinking of a large body of members, even if not all. As with union members nationally, any shift in thinking in the South is going to require a genuine class appeal based on a real understanding of the economic forces that keep many Southern whites poor or below wage levels in the North, including the role of racism in this. It means struggle and conflict with employers and politicians as well as with existing consciousness. It is precisely the struggle that offers the opportunity to transform consciousness. The question here, as with the union vote in the rest of the country, comes down to, is the labor leadership capable of this level of struggle on a scale that could transform the region? Can today's union leaders or those waiting in the wings present a convincing class analysis that does not sweep race under the rug as the CIO mistakenly tried to do in the 1940s? Is the dominant ideology of American labor fit for such a fight?

The Ideological Heritage of Business Unionism

American labor is famously non-ideological in that the vast majority of its leadership and membership have historically rejected the explicit class and socialist views held by trade unionists in most other developed capitalist nations—no matter how diluted and reformist those views may have become. The absence of such ideas, however, has created a vacuum for other ideas that deny class as an operating principle or any grand goals that might follow from that. In general, it can be said that organized labor as a movement and then as a set of institutions in the United States adopted over the decades a version of modern liberalism; that is, the slightly left-of-center side of capitalist ideology. It has been shaped by larger developments in capitalist politics, notably the rise of "progressivism" in the years before World War 1 and the New Deal in the 1930s. But business union ideology has its own history as well.

"Pure and Simple Unionism," as it was first known, has its putative origins in the nascent socialism of 1870s America. Its grandfather, so to speak, was not Samuel Gompers, but his mentor Adolph Strasser. Like Gompers, Peter J. McGuire of the Carpenters, and so many others in the 1870s and early 1880s, Strasser began his trade union career as a Marxist. Deeply concerned about the ineffectiveness of unionism in America, he worked to bring greater organization and centralization to the craft unions, imposing the British structural model on his own Cigar Makers and successfully urging others to follow suit. His top-down centralizing model won him the nickname "the Prussian." In time he came into conflict with the socialists in his own union and eventually shed his Marxism. By 1883, two years before the formation of the AFL, he could tell a Senate committee:

> We have no ultimate ends. We are going from day to day. We are fighting only for immediate objects . . . We are all practical men.[54]

In 1966, Meany wrote in *The American Federationist*, "We avoid preconceived notions and we do not try to fit our program into some theoretical, all-embracing structure."[55] Ten years later, upon receiving, of all things, a Eugene V. Debs award, Lane Kirkland would echo the same ideas when he said the AFL-CIO had "no visionary world, no utopia, that we're working toward," just a society where "everybody has his chance."[56]

The abandonment of ultimate goals like socialism was not simply a gradual journey from Marxism for individuals like Strasser. The business unionism of the AFL was forged in a long and bitter fight within the labor movement *against* the socialists. This fight raged from the 1870s through the end of World War 1 by which time the business unionists had secured virtual hegemony. From the idea of limited goals and the rejection of socialism or any major social transformation came the acceptance of the subordinate position of the worker within the system and the classic idea of liberalism, improvement. By 1913 Gompers could say, "it is our duty to live our lives as workers in the society in which we live and not to work for the downfall or the destruction or the overthrow of that society, but for its fuller development and evolution."[57] The assumption being that the development and evolution of the system was a benign process.

Along the way, another bedrock idea of business unionism took shape, namely the idea that the union *is* a business and should be run like one. As early as 1896 Gompers wrote that the trade unions were "the business organizations of the wage-earners to attend to the business of the wage-earners." The next step, spelled out by an academic a few years later, specified the role of the union leader:

> The union should be run on just the same business principles as a business firm.
>
> The union needs a man to manage it just as much as a business house needs a manager. Then why not reward him as the business firm rewards its manager?[58]

And so was born the justification for a permanent bureaucracy and the well-paid union bureaucrats who ran it, as well as the *de facto* rejection of democracy as a central principle of organization. It is also hard not to notice that in all these quotes we find "practical men" working to get the union member "his" chance with the help of "a man" managing the union, much like an equally male-dominated corporation of the day. The gender bias would outlast its early years, giving business unionism a distinctly male culture.

Two more ideas became central to the practice of business unionism: its most basic economic belief and the concept of a basic community of interest with capital. I say economic belief because it does not amount to a theory. In the hands of professional economists of a Keynesian bent, it can rest alongside its more respectable theoretical enabler, but in itself it is more a matter of faith than science. As good a formulation as any came from Sidney Hillman, President of the Amalgamated Clothing Workers, in 1928 when he said:

> A high standard of living is no more a question of mere justice . . . It is essential to our system of mass production to create a consumers' demand for almost unlimited output.[59]

A more modern version was offered by Walter Reuther in a 1952 exchange between himself and a Ford executive during a tour of an "automated" engine plant:

> "You know, Walter," said the manager, "not one of those machines pays union dues."
> "And not one of them buys new Ford cars, either," replied Reuther.[60]

George Meany would repeat this idea in 1966 when he wrote, "Unless the ever-rising tide of goods that American enterprise can produce is matched by the increased real earnings of workers, these goods cannot be sold."[61] The clear implication is that it is in the interest of the employers to provide their workers with "a high standard of living" so they can uphold the economy through their consumption. Thus, a common macro-economic interest is allegedly established between labor and capital. This idea is key to the collaborative nature of business unionism also because it changes the focus of economic discourse from production and exploitation (where do those profits come from?) to consumption. As Thomas Frank noted above, the world of work is downplayed. Indeed, in business unionism's official economic idea, *presto chango*, it disappears. Notice that for Meany in 1966 it is not even the workers who produce the "rising tide of goods" any more, but "American enterprise." Yesterday's producers with all the issues on-the-job that affected them, from speed-up and long hours to health and safety, became today's consumers—individual citizens wandering the aisles of Wal-Mart in their effort to absorb "the rising tide of goods." Of course, the very name Wal-Mart tells us one reason why capital doesn't need to pay as much as before: cheaper products from elsewhere for cheaper workers here. The real reason employers don't want to fulfil Hillman's "essential" condition for mass production lies in the micro-level employer–employee relationship at the point of production where the surplus from which profits come is produced. Remember the 57-second minute? This embarrassing fact contradicts the notion of a community of interest and points beyond the limits of business unionism. So, the business unionist takes the consumerist path of least resistance to the shared interests of labor and capital.

Along that road lies partnership. This, too, goes back to the early days of trade unionism. Gompers was the first to travel this road all the way. He did it on a grand scale through the National Civic Federation (NCF) founded in 1900. The founding president of the NCF and director of its Industrial Department was none other than Mark Hanna, the "bundler" we met above who helped make the Republican Party dominant for the better part of three and a half decades. Most of its members and officers were leading capitalists of the day. Gompers and Mine Workers President John Mitchell were charter members. The NCF was set up in the midst of the great employers' open shop drive. It advocated the mutual interests of employer and employee, the end of strikes, and the overcoming of the "misunderstandings" between labor and capital. It engaged in private or company-based "welfare work" largely to get around unions and avoid state intervention. Gompers, Mitchell, and other labor leaders graced its committees more for the self-importance it seemed to bestow on them than for anything the unions ever got out of it. While the NCF could not end strife or strikes, it did help the employers stop the growth of unions after 1904. And, of course, it established the legitimacy of the partnership idea.[62]

We have already seen John Sweeney's view on this subject in 1996, after becoming AFL-CIO president. While Sweeney often seems to look back to some golden age of social compact, the SEIU's Andy Stern looks coldly at some aspects of today's economic reality and embraces them in his view of partnership. He bemoans the failure of employers to see the potential in partnership. He told one interviewer, "Employers need to recognize that the world has changed and that there are people who would like to help them provide solutions in ways that are new, modern, and that add value." Presumably, unions, or at least some unions, are among those who would help add value. Unions, he says, should allow employers "to operate more efficiently with better quality." This includes outsourcing. To ease the results of efficiency and outsourcing, his concept of partnership includes the idea that the union acts

> as an outsourcing vehicle that takes a whole series of services from employers . . . so that there are common benefit plans or common training programs or common ways to deal with workers who lose their jobs and need a bridge until they find new employment.

He says unions can be "labor contractors," perhaps providing hiring halls like the building trades.[63] It is an elaborate version of partnership that seems to envision an expansion of the "private welfare state" to be administered by the unions in order to soften the blows inflicted by outsourcing and the corporate world's idea of efficiency in general.

The alliance with the Democratic Party is the logical extension of business unionism to the political realm. The lack of ultimate or even long-range goals, the embrace of the system with some modifications, the business-like relation to limited goals (lobbying for legislation), the top-down nature of political decisions and tactical choices, the self-importance that comes from associating with those in power, the notion of measured advances through a semi-institutional partnership with those who administer the system; all of these features of business unionism fit well the alliance with the capitalist party most open to compromise.

The problem is that these very same attributes fit poorly with the notion of labor as a social movement based on class and class conflict. How to inspire African Americans or Latinos to vote in larger numbers for candidates that shrink from addressing their issues? How to turn immigrants into citizens and working-class voters? How to attract working-class whites, particularly low-income ones, to vote for their real interests? Clearly, the Democratic Party cannot do these things. But can a business union leadership that shares many of the same ideas, cautions, and fears of class conflict and mass mobilization?

One More Dead End: The Politics of the Deal

The failure of labor's central political strategy at the national level was repeated more often than not at the state and local level. Fiscal crisis and restraint have been the normal situation of most states and cities for the last thirty years. This has been in part a function of the US three-level system of intergovernmental finances which pushes economic problems downward to the cities. Local governments employ the most workers of any level of government and must supply *and pay for* the bulk of urban services. This is far less than most developed capitalist countries provide. In Britain the national government provided 54%, in Japan 40%, and in the Netherlands 80% of local revenues. What is more, beginning in earnest with Reagan, the federal government reduced aid to the cities. So, the US federal government provided 13% of local revenues in 1984 and 4.5% in 1992.[64] This put enormous pressure on city budgets and, hence, on public sector unions. A look at reputedly liberal New York City from the 1975 fiscal crisis reveals a working class facing deteriorating living standards and a public sector labor movement with twice the union density of the country on the defensive no matter who was mayor.[65] While the traditional strategy of backing Democrats remained the dominant practice in state and local politics as at the national level, the unions occasionally looked elsewhere in this atmosphere of retreat. One "new" tactic has been called the "politics of the deal." Deal-making at any level of politics is hardly new. Indeed, the old AFL slogan "reward your friends, punish your enemies" more or less implies a deal. What is somewhat new about the politics of the deal is that both the union's "bottom line" and the reward come upfront. It is also often a Republican who reaps the reward in the form of an endorsement and campaign contribution. Two high visibility examples of this both come from New York.

The first comes from Dennis Rivera, president of 1199/SEIU. Rivera has a reputation as a left-liberal and 1199's 240,000 statewide members were largely Black and Latino. Yet, in the 2002 governor's election in New York State, Rivera gave the conservative Republican incumbent, George Pataki, the union's endorsement over African American Democrat Carl McCall. The deal was embodied in the Health Care Worker Recruitment and Retention Act, which passed the state legislature under pressure from Pataki well before the election so that delivery seemed certain. The Act set aside $1.8 billion for raises for state health care workers. Pataki won the election.[66] The second example comes from AFSCME District Council 37, whose 56 local unions represent 125,000 New York City employees. In the 2005 mayoral election DC 37 endorsed incumbent Republican mayor Michael Bloomberg over Latino Democratic contender Freddy Ferrer by a narrow vote of its executive board. The deal had been worked out by DC 37 Executive Director Lillian Roberts who was under fire from dissident local union presidents for, among other things, negotiating a mediocre contract in 2004. The 2005 deal involved a 1% pay hike for DC 37 members. The 1% came from a provision in the 2004 agreement that allowed for an additional 1% if productivity gains had been made.[67]

It may well be that the politics of the deal is only a fluke. Yet, versions of it have appeared in different forms in recent years. In the late 1990s, the SEIU and AFSCME struck a deal with the Governor of Puerto Rico that essentially gave them bargaining rights for most of the island's public employees, even though many of them already had independent unions.[68] Endorsements of and contributions to state and local politicians are important to many unions, but they seem to have a special importance to the SEIU that relates to organizing and seems to qualify as the politics of the deal. The SEIU gives lots of money to governors of both parties. In Illinois, for example, SEIU gave $800,000 to Democratic candidate Rod Blagojevich in 2004 in return for collective bargaining rights for 37,000 home health care workers.[69] In North Carolina the SEIU contributed to the Democratic governor as well in hopes of easing the way to the affiliation of the state employees' association, although it has so far rejected direct affiliation.[70] Although the politics of the deal may bring an immediate advantage, it is clearly not a strategy for moving US politics in a more pro-labor direction.

During the Sweeney years, as before, the same old strategy with the tactical modifications discussed above was deployed again and again by almost all unions. The labor household vote was increased but still 40% of it went to George W. Bush. In a certain sense, the 2004 election was for Sweeney what 1994 had been for Kirkland. For all the efforts, the result was still failure—more votes for Bush and fewer Democrats in the House and Senate. Perhaps an even larger labor vote could have made a difference, but organizing had failed even to reach its 1999 high point for the movement as a whole. Dissatisfaction and disagreement at the top were on the rise. A fight was in the air as the 2005 AFL-CIO convention approached.

THE SPLIT: REFORM FROM ABOVE AGAIN

In the months leading up to the August 6, 2003 AFL-CIO executive council meeting, a group of five union heads formed a coalition meant to influence the federation and push it toward an organizing agenda. They called it the New Unity Partnership (NUP) and it included the SEIU, HERE, UNITE!, the Laborers, and the Carpenters. The Carpenters had left the federation in 2001 and had been preparing for their exit since 1998. So, as a caucus within the AFL-CIO it was unusual from the start. It was also unusual in that it put forward written documents outlining the changes in AFL-CIO structure it argued were needed to actually get the unions organizing. The five union presidents, Andy Stern (SEIU), John Wilhelm (HERE), Bruce Raynor (UNITE!), Terrance O'Sullivan (LIUNA), and Douglas McCarron (UBC) called for a thorough-going reorganization of the federation into a small number (fifteen and later twenty) of mega-unions based on broadly defined core jurisdictions. Some of these jurisdictions as defined in the documents clearly overlapped those of other unions: Carpenters and Laborers with other building trades unions, UNITE! with UFCW. The key was centralization. The federation would have the power to merge unions, while at the same time being stripped down itself. The Central Labor Councils were to be merged into the State Federations. And so it went.[1] The questions raised by this bombshell were legion. How was the federation to make these changes? Who would decide who would be in what union? Was such a structure workable at all?

Those who paid attention would have known that these ideas had been taking shape for some time. In 2002, the SEIU's Stephen Lerner, who had crafted the LA Justice for Janitors campaign, circulated a document called "Three Steps to Reorganizing and Rebuilding the Labor Movement." He argued that there were too many unions, too many of which were too small to organize effectively, with too many being "general worker unions" with no industrial focus. All pretty much undeniable. The answer, he argued, lay in increasing union density. Density brought power in bargaining and in organizing. The road to higher density was to consolidate the AFL-CIO's 66 unions into 10–15 industry/sector-based unions capable of achieving higher density and gaining power. A summary of this appeared in *Labor Notes* in December 2002 and was debated in that magazine over the next couple of months by labor activists and experts such as Kate Bronfenbrenner of Cornell, Suzanne Wall of the SEIU, David Cohen of the independent United Electrical Workers, and Ken Paff of Teamsters for a Democratic Union.[2] It would be published and/or discussed in *New Labor Forum, Union Democracy Review*, and other publications that dealt with labor issues.[3] A forum about it sponsored by the Queens College Labor Center was attended by over 500 people at the City University Graduate Center in New York. It featured a pro-and-con debate on the NUP proposals.[4] Almost everyone involved in this debate thanked the NUP for provoking debate, something the labor movement typically lacks. It was a debate, however, that did not go very deep into the ranks of labor.

The New Unity Partnership would continue to make these arguments, and others relating to the allocation of resources, through 2004. Then, as suddenly as it had appeared on the scene, the NUP disappeared by the end of 2004.[5] Shortly after the November 2004 presidential election, a new programmatic statement was posted on the internet by SEIU President Andy Stern entitled "United to Win: 21st Century Plan to Build New Strength for Working People." The new plan dropped some of the schematics of the Lerner proposal. Stern proposed that there be up to three "lead unions" in each industry or sector, that they get 50% of their per capita dues back from the AFL-CIO, and that they must spend an escalating percentage of their budget on organizing starting from 10% in 2006 and reaching 20% by 2010. The AFL-CIO would have the power to order or prevent mergers— more power, fewer funds. The emphasis on density remained.[6] But there was a shift from structural formulae to financial resource allocation. Aside from the more realistic nature of these proposals, something else intervened to undermine the clear industrial/sectoral emphasis of the NUP plan. For one, UNITE! and HERE merged, creating exactly the type of "general workers' union" Lerner had denounced. At the same time, the original NUP leaders turned with increasing interest to the Teamsters, the very model of a merging multi-jurisdictional union. As Teamster President James Hoffa put it, "We have from A to Z in our union, airline pilots to zookeepers." Hoffa, in fact, discontinued the focused organizing drives initiated by reform president Ron Carey in the 1990s when the union reached a high point of organizing 400 shops in one year. Under Hoffa mergers displaced organizing and by 2000 only about 200 new units were organized and that number stayed below 300 a year up to 2005. Industrial focus was lost as the IBT took in rail unions and the Graphic Communications International Union.[7] Both the timing and the modifications of the program indicated a shift in which industrial focus was taking a back seat to politics for the former NUPsters.

On June 15, 2005, the fight took another leap forward with the founding of the Change to Win Coalition. This time the presidents of the SEIU, UNITE-HERE, and the Laborers were joined by the Teamsters and the United Food and Commercial Workers, another large multi-jurisdictional union. About fifty top-level officials from the six unions adopted by-laws for the Coalition under which the programs they would push at the AFL-CIO convention in July could be carried out whatever the AFL-CIO did.[8] On June 27, Doug McCarron, president of the Carpenters, who were already outside the AFL-CIO, announced that they were joining the new coalition.[9] The Change to Win Coalition was clearly more than a caucus. Whether the CTW unions planned to stay and fight in the AFL-CIO if they achieved more of what they wanted is at least questionable. In any case the SEIU did not attend the AFL-CIO convention. The events at the July convention in Chicago, the federation's 50th anniversary, had more the character of collective bargaining than a fight over principle, and, like collective bargaining, most of the negotiations took place behind closed doors. With the Sweeney team hurriedly making concessions on sectoral focus, the differences seemed to come down to how much of a dues rebate unions would get for a real commitment to organizing. CTW demanded 50% back, Sweeney offered 25%. In the end, as in 1995, some thought it might really have been about who would run the federation. According to the USWA President Leo Gerrard, the CTW leaders were "willing to take a smaller rebate if they could pick Sweeney's successor."[10] It seems clear, however, that the CTW leaders were prepared to leave. On July 25, The SEIU and Teamsters announced that they were leaving the AFL-CIO, taking about 20% of the old federation's budget with them.[11] They would be followed by the other Coalition members and later joined by the United Farm Workers.

On September 27 in St. Louis, the Change to Win Federation was born. Seven unions claiming 6 million members sent 500 delegates to this founding convention. Its structure reflected more a corporation or a nonprofit organization than a labor federation. It would be governed by a ten-person board, called the Council, chaired by SEIU Secretary-Treasurer Anna Burger, with UNITE-HERE's vice president Edgar Romney as secretary-treasurer. It would have a full-time executive director, who is Greg Tarpinian, adviser to Hoffa and to New York

State's Republican governor George Pataki.[12] The language of the leaders had the sound of corporate-speak. The new federation would "grow the labor movement" through increased "market share" and "value-added integration."[13] This growth would be financed by putting three-quarters of the CTW budget toward organizing. Among the resolutions passed were some good ideas: concentration on "core" industries, multi-union drives, large national organizing targets like DHL and Wal-Mart, using actions in one area to support organizing and contract fights in another.[14] That CTW was serious about organizing seemed certain. The new organizing director was Tom Woodruff, the organizing director of the SEIU who gets much of the credit for its successes.[15] On March 20, the new federation held a huge conference of 2,000 organizers in Las Vegas to launch its "Make Work Pay" campaign, which will set up local cross-union teams to conduct and support organizing in their area. Secretary-Treasurer Romney explained it like this:

> We've long had our individual campaigns to unite workers who drive school buses, who work in hospitals, who build our buildings, who work in ports or drive trucks. But as we run these individual campaigns, we will tie our work together to make it all add up to something bigger.[16]

As Jerry Tucker pointed out in a *Labor Notes* report on the CTW founding convention, these unions tend to organize in those "landlocked" industries less affected by globalization or offshoring, which will give them an advantage over many AFL-CIO private sector unions.[17] Success rates in NLRB representation elections are a lot higher in hospitals than in factories. This would indicate that the CTW Federation may have a good deal of success in organizing as they see it. But much about the new federation's direction raises questions about strategy and power, the nature and purpose of unions, and what, in fact, is most effective in facilitating the organization of workers. These questions are not confined to the CTW unions since unions in both federations share many characteristics. It, nevertheless, seems clear that the lead union in CTW, the SEIU, is creating a model of unionism that is not only different from what exists. It is a model that seems to depart, as well, from what many critics of the bureaucratic business unionism that characterized much of the AFL-CIO have posed as a positive alternative direction for American labor. To get an idea of the prospects of this new attempt at reform from above, I will look at three questions: the relationship between overall strategy and power; the basic purpose of a union; and what works in organizing.

Strategy, Power and the Ranks

As noted above, the CTW unions focus mainly on the "landlocked" service and construction sectors. This makes a certain kind of strategic sense in that the threat and reality of relocation are minimal. But can a labor movement, as opposed to an individual union, based solely on these industries actually have the kind of power the CTW leaders speak of? Given the shape and structure of the economy described in earlier chapters, the answer would have to be no. When we look at goods production, utilities, and transportation as commodities in a capitalist market and as major sites of accumulation, they remain the bedrock of the US economy. Peter Olney framed the debate somewhat differently from the "capacity builders," as he called those who would form the NUP and then the CTW, when he wrote in 2002:

> Much of the growth in density has occurred among service sector workers, especially in health care. This growth is important because it builds unions among women and people of color who now represent a majority of the ranks of organized labor, and because health care in particular is the fastest growing sector in the economy. Yet a labor movement that wants to challenge the employers must be present in the means of production and distribution.[18]

The way Olney framed this was critical because he was not counterposing organizing industrial workers, those in goods production, communications, utilities, and transportation/logistics, to service sector workers. He was simply arguing that unionizing the nonunion majority in these strategic parts of the economy is essential to any challenge to capital in the US. Olney, in fact, pointed out that the emphasis on service sector organizing was already there in the AFL-CIO. Of the $28 million distributed by the federation's Strategic Organizing program, $9 million, almost a third, went to two unions: the SEIU and HERE.[19] While the CTW has unions crossing both industrial production and service sectors, a look at the 2005 NLRB elections reveals that with some exceptions, it was not the CTW unions that made manufacturing the sector with largest effort, but unions like the USWA, UAW, CWA, and Machinists.[20] Since there does appear to be a sectoral split between the rump AFL-CIO and the CTW each is faced with a critical question: for the AFL-CIO, how will they organize the rest of industry given their poor record in this area; for the CTW, how will they achieve the power they speak of by obtaining density only in the less strategic areas of the economy? The even bigger question is, how can each federation help the other achieve the power they both need?

Kate Bronfenbrenner makes a related point.

> The task of organizing in manufacturing, high tech, and other more mobile sectors of the economy must become the responsibility of the entire labor movement.
>
> Because absent that support, global capital will continue to use the threat of global outsourcing to push down wage and benefit standards, and break unions in the best jobs in our economy. If those jobs become substandard and go nonunion, service and public sector jobs will follow.[21]

She goes on to make the point that in order to organize in the globalized industries, the labor movement must find "ways to share resources and provide assistance to those unions who are attempting to organize large multinationals in the manufacturing and high tech sectors not just in this country but around the globe."[22] Can today's divided labor movement do something that yesterday's united federation couldn't? The answer to this lies partly in what one thinks the purpose of a union is.

In a speech given in 1997, labor expert Frank Emspak said:

> We need to see organizing from a different perspective. Workers organize in order to gain a measure of respect, better their standard of living, and achieve some stability in employment. *They do not join unions to maintain the union* . . .
>
> We therefore need to ask a different question: "What type of organization do workers want to create in order to accomplish their objectives?"[23]

This is not a question frequently asked by contemporary business unionists in either federation. First of all, their presumption is that workers don't create an organization. That already exists in "the union;" i.e., the institution for which business unionists work. But, in fact, if the workers involved don't create an organization at some level, as Bronfenbrenner and others have pointed out, "the union" will lose the election, fail to win a first contract, or simply lose the loyalty of dissatisfied members. Of course, what Emspak is saying here is that union officials and staffers will tend to look at the question of organizing in a very different way than the workers who are being organized. The labor professionals are concerned with the propagation of the institution. For them, power comes from growth, size, density, and the contract. It is a power that *they* exercise in negotiating and administering contracts, obtaining the reality or illusion of political influence, and expanding the union as an institution even more. But power that relies only on size, density, and the contract is shallow power, fragile power. Look at what happened to the pattern agreements in the high density sectors in the 1980s and beyond. There has to be another dimension: workplace or on-the-job power, deep power.

Bronfenbrenner notes that American unions seem to have "ceded control of the hours and pace of work" at a time, as we saw in chapter 2, when "American workers are exhausted by twelve-hour days, mandatory overtime, seven-day weeks, cross training, and job combinations." Lean production and longer hours, on the one hand, or shorter hours at less pay, on the other, these are the choices for many workers. Bronfenbrenner goes on to say that employers just might pay more to avoid a union, as they do in manufacturing in the South, "but if it is about regaining control over staffing, the quality of care, or the pace, scheduling, and hours of work—those are the issues that really can transform workers' lives and are worth fighting for, but unions will have to take the lead."[24] Sometimes unions do take the lead. That was what happened at UPS between 1995 and the strike of 1997, when "the union" worked with rank-and-file activists, including members of the reform group Teamsters for a Democratic Union, to build a coordinated strike structure in every workplace they could reach. The issues in the strike were workplace issues: workload, part-time to full-time jobs. That is what happened at UAW Local 599 in 1994, when the local leadership urged the members to organize and fight in preparation for a local strike over workload, staffing, hours, etc. UPS and GM managements have in common their absolute disrespect for the contract. These unions could not possibly enforce the contract solely from headquarters or by dispatching International Reps despite their high density in these companies. Bronfenbrenner notes that some of the SEIU's most important victories occurred when they paid attention to these issues. But workplace organization can't be just a temporary device for organizing or the occasional strike. Larry Cohen, now president of CWA, was right when he responded to the 2004 "Unite to Win" proposals by saying that the "inner life" of the union matters. Bronfenbrenner is quick to point out that "inner life" is not enough if unions become "too small to matter."[25] Obviously, both are true. The difference is that the membership on-the-job is the foundation of the whole structure. Dan La Botz in the 1991 *Troublemakers Handbook* observed, "Rank and file activism at the workplace is the foundation of the labor movement." He goes on to cite David Montgomery, who writes:

> Unions had their origins in the attempt to get some sort of collective control over the conditions of work, running all the way from wage rates

to work rules, in the 19th century. The workplace is both where the union movement had its birth, and where the daily conflict lies that makes it impossible to snuff the union movement out.[26]

It is a birth that is constantly reproduced. Move the organization toward the passive, professionally run AARP model of mass "organization" and you have a lobby with less and less influence, not a union with more power. Olney summarized this part of the debate as follows:

> Bringing in millions of new workers is important, but the quality of that organizing and the fate of those workers once organized is the key to building power. Furthermore, the sector in which these employees labor is also an important variable. Manufacturing and logistics remain crucial to labor's power.[27]

Union power is built on power on the job. This power must be extended, of course, beyond any one workplace in order to "take labor out of competition." In this sense the union becomes the chain that pulls these workplaces together. As with any chain, it is only as strong as its weakest link. So, sacrificing workplace power to the "shallow" power of two-dimensional density and size can only undermine the union's power as a whole. That is the history of business unionism, above all in the period of post-militancy, concessions, and cooperation. It is in this sense that the "quality of that organizing" and "fate of the workers once organized" matter a great deal.

The 1990 LA Justice for Janitors campaign remains the classic example. A creative and well thought-out strategy drawn up by staff along with a "tactical mobilization" of the workers won the day. A measure of power had been established in the buildings of Century City and elsewhere. But then the workers were thrown into Local 399, a large geographically spread-out multi-jurisdictional local with 25,000 members, 12,000 in health care, and a white president, Duke Zeller. The new members complained of out-of-touch leadership, neglect of day-to-day issues, and no role in decision-making. Their partially successful rebellion in union elections was met with a trusteeship by then president John Sweeney. They were eventually put in a larger building service local with Latino leadership.[28] What was lost was the mobilization, experience, and dedication of workers proud of the struggle they had waged and the victory they had achieved. Wages remained low, in fact declined in real terms, and turnover high into the late 1990s.[29]

The matter of workplace power inevitably leads to the question of the workers' power within the union itself, the question of union democracy. In the "Three Steps" document that formally initiated the debate over the AFL-CIO's future, Stephen Lerner was highly dismissive of internal union democracy. He wrote:

> Considering union democracy as only a question of how a union is governed is too narrow. We need to talk more broadly about how unions can be strong enough locally and nationally to win economic justice and democracy for workers.
>
> If only 10% of workers in an industry are unionized, it is impossible to have real union democracy because 90% are excluded. If unions are weak there is no democracy at the workplace.[30]

Considering union democracy as a matter of union governance may be *too* narrow, but democracy *is* about governance. And how a union is run makes a big difference. The petty dictator or slick bureaucrat who is in a position to shove a concessionary contract down the members' throats is not building power. If Lerner's 10% are in an undemocratic union, the remaining 90% will find themselves without power or influence in that union as they are organized into it. In *Democracy Is Power* Mike Parker and Martha Gruelle put forward several propositions about the relationship of union democracy and workplace power. Here are two:

- Union power *requires* democracy. Unions need active members to be strong, and people won't stay involved for long if they don't have control of the union's program.
- The workplace (not the union hall) is the starting point for union democracy, because the purpose of democratic control in the union is to make it more effective against the boss.[31]

The difference here is that Lerner sees union democracy in formalistic terms—simply a matter of internal union structure. Parker and Gruelle are arguing that it is about power. The workplace is where union members have power—real and potential. It is here, after all, that they produce the surplus on which accumulation is based no matter what sort of industry or occupation is involved. So, it is here they can slow down or stop the creation of that surplus. To maximize this power they must have influence over how the union behaves. If membership activity and involvement are discouraged, as is so often the case, the union is weaker and the workers' position in the workplace becomes weaker still. Worse, if unaccountable leaders are working at cross-purposes, for partnership instead of resistance for example, the workers' power is undermined. Parker and Gruelle go on to argue throughout *Democracy Is Power* that union democracy is not just about structures and procedures, although these are important. It is about developing a culture of activism, involvement, transparency in union governance, and openness in debate. It is from this kind of culture that big mobilizations become possible when needed because a certain level of organization, mobilization, and involvement is always there. This cannot be done by excluding the membership from decision-making power.[32]

The relationship of union democracy and the workplace is a two-way street. Power is rooted in the workplace, but it is often in the union that the ability to use that power is limited. So, Elaine Bernard takes the argument from the other end and writes:

> Unions need to become schools of democracy for workers who do not find democratic practice or rights in the workplace and increasingly are feeling isolated and powerless both inside and outside of the workplace. Unions, as the self-organization of working people for social and economic justice, need to be models of democratic practice in their activities.[33]

The link is the workplace organization of the union, whether official or not. Mostly this self-organization means a stewards' organization directly responsible to the members in the workplace. This is a kind of *direct democracy* in which rank-and-file power is at its maximum in relation to both the union and the employer. The further up the union structure, the more it becomes a representative democracy, in so far as it is democratic at all. This representative element is only likely to remain accountable and replaceable to the degree that *direct democracy* rules in the local union and its workplace organization. Most unions have formally democratic structures in that there are elections, usually indirect, and contract votes. But the power of the ranks to control or even influence the hierarchy depends on active direct democracy at the most basic level as much as or more than it does on the overall structure of the union at the regional or national level.

Not surprisingly, the "democracy is power" perspective is controversial. Lerner and Andy Stern are clear that it is irrelevant, an issue we will return to. One of the most serious criticisms is that this view neglects the question of leadership and, hence, where ideas and strategies come from. Teresa Sharpe, for example, raises this question when she writes:

> A second problem with the equation of democracy and power is the implicit assumption that strategic skills and new tactics arise spontaneously. Democracy advocates cannot explain how the rank and file creates winning campaigns in the absence of skilled leadership. Such leaders must eventually emerge from the rank and file, but without staff support and training at the front end, workers will find it difficult to generate effective strategy.[34]

The assumption that strategic thinking can come only from staff seems deeply flawed. One of the tenets of the "democracy is power" approach is that open debate among and between leaders, staff, and ranks within a union may actually produce better strategy than staff alone could. But, more important, is the implication here that the advocates of union democracy reject leadership, even or especially authoritative leadership.

Democracy, even the most direct shop floor democracy, involves leadership and is impossible without it. Here's what Parker and Gruelle, whom Sharpe cites, actually say about leadership, criticizing those who reject "the idea of leadership itself:"

> We see leadership differently—as a needed tool in a complicated world. Leaders help us make sense of things we do not understand ourselves. Union leaders need a combination of knowledge and vision, applied to the members' concerns. Good leaders have proposals to solve problems, and the guts to see them through. A democratic union culture requires more leaders, not fewer; stronger leaders, not weaker ones.[35]

They note that there are many types of leaders. They even allow that at times leaders must make decisions on the spot without consulting the members, as when Ron Carey called a quickie strike after UPS unilaterally raised the weight of packages that sorters and drivers would have to lift from 75 pounds to 150. The deeper question is what the relationship of leaders to members is.

There is another dimension to the relationship of democracy, workplace organization, and leadership. If leadership is something developed from above, where will new leaders come from when others go stale, "go bad," or retire, or when the need to expand leadership in a growing union arises? It should be clear that a leadership recruited and handpicked from above or from outside is not likely to reflect the membership or have the "street-fighting" experience today's rough and tumble world of work calls for. Leadership has to be constantly renewed if we are to have more than a parade of "Yes" men and women. To constantly renew and expand union leadership means to draw on those who hone their skills in the workplace, stewards and activists. Jeff Crosby, president of IUE/CWA Local 201 put it well when he wrote:

> What is needed most of all is a cultural transformation of labor organizations so that everything we do is geared toward the development of leaders from among our members. *The union steward, and his or her ability or lack of ability to solve problems, is the union to most of our members.* We need thousands of local and workplace leaders who can analyze problems, gain the trust of their members, explain and execute programs and create new ones. I

think of this as an entire concept of trade unionism, "*Leadership Development Unionism*", borrowing from our own history and the thinking of popular educators and other social movements.[36]

Union democracy, along with workplace organization, is the school for developing leadership, not the rejection of it.

This concept of developing leaders from the ranks becomes even more important as the gender, racial, and national character of the workforce changes. Increasingly, the membership is composed of a higher proportion of women, people of color, immigrants, and low-wage workers. The leadership of most unions, including those that make the greatest claim to organizing among these "newer" groups, remains, as the saying goes, "pale, male, and stale," or at least pale and male. A study of union leaders in California who entered the labor movement in the 1980s or earlier done in 2001 found some alarming facts. The authors of the study note that traditionally union leaders "began their career as rank and file members of the unions they later represented." In contrast, 32% of the 68 leaders they interviewed came from "outside" and had never been members of that union, a majority were college graduates, and 47% came from clearly middle-class backgrounds. Given the demographic changes of union members, some even more alarming facts were that only 14% were women, 16% Latino, and none was African American because the two Blacks in earlier interviews could not be interviewed in 2001.[37] In the 1980s, when these leaders were working their way up in the labor movement, two-thirds of union members were white males. In 2005, however, white men made up just 47% of members.[38] Clearly, if the next generation of leaders is to reflect more nearly the new membership, it will have to come from the ranks.

Involvement, mobilization, leadership, and democracy, including *direct democracy*, are also intimately connected to new organizing in this era of employer resistance and economic uncertainty. In the important 1998 book *Organizing to Win* Kate Bronfenbrenner and Tom Juravich concluded from their study of organizing drives in the 1980s and 1990s, that what the union did mattered more than the resistance of the employer. They concluded from their studies:

The results lend strong support to our hypothesis that whether there is a comprehensive union-building campaign that incorporates person-to-person contact, leadership development, escalating internal and external pressure tactics, and building for the first contract is more important in determining election outcome than whether the union uses individual tactics. The more union-building strategies are used during the organizing campaign, the greater the likelihood that the union will win the election even in a climate of intense employer opposition.[39]

In an earlier study, Bronfenbrenner had found, "that unions were more successful when they encouraged active rank-and-file participation in and responsibility for the organizing campaign, including developing a large rank-and-file committee representative of the different interest groups in the bargaining unit." That is part of what is meant by union-building. More recent findings in the 1990s confirmed these results. They cited campaigns run by UNITE! in the South, the SEIU in upstate New York, and the Teamsters under Ron Carey at Overnite as recent examples. This was not just a case of using volunteer rank-and-file union members, most unions use "member-organizers," but of giving the workers being organized some control over the campaign and encouraging them to act like a union in the workplace from the start, well before the representation election.[40] Indeed, in a study of organizing efforts at the end of the 1990s, Bronfenbrenner and Hickey found that along with the more extensive use of a combination of innovative tactics,

> Perhaps the single most important component of a comprehensive campaign is an active representative committee that gives bargaining unit members ownership of the campaign and allows the workers to start acting like a union inside the workplace, building trust and confidence among the workforce and counteracting the most negative aspects of the employer campaign.[41]

It is sometimes argued that creating an activist local union with membership involvement, leadership accountability, and strong workplace organization actually works against new organizing because the members will tend to resist shifting resources from "servicing" or internal organizing to external organizing. Bill Fletcher and Richard Hurd draw something like this conclusion in their study of several SEIU locals in the 1990s, as does Teresa Sharpe. One can point to local unions that have resisted change, but it would be more helpful to look at those that did make the change. Indeed, Fletcher and Hurd also point to an SEIU local that successfully convinced members to support a shift of resources to organizing by explaining how this would increase their power.[42] One of the best examples of a local union that managed to maintain and increase workplace power, expand organizing capacity, and have a high degree of democracy in the 1990s, was Teamsters Local 174 in Seattle, Washington. Local 174 is a multi-jurisdictional local with 4,000 members. In the early 1990s, a reform slate of TDU members led by Bob Hasegawa took over and worked to transform the culture of the local. They won a two-dollar a month special assessment for organizing and set up a permanent Organizing Committee composed of working rank-and-file members and stewards.

The Committee members, in turn, helped convince local members to maintain the special assessment. The local hired only two full-time organizers. In the first six years of the new culture, the local organized several hundred new members.[43] To be sure there was opposition from some members and an anti-Hasegawa slate did win control of the local for one term. The members soon discovered that it wasn't just the new organizing that got hurt, it was their conditions and the power they had accumulated. Hasegawa and the TDUers were re-elected. Incidentally, it was about 600 members of Local 174 who made up the bulk of the famous "Teamsters and Turtles" in the streets of Seattle in 1999. Local 174 also has an alliance with environmental groups. It's an organizing social movement unionist local. Hasegawa explained what a new member might experience upon joining:

> We've taken that (social movement unionism) on in initiates' meetings. We take a hundred dollars off their initiation fee to attend this meeting. And it's not what they expect. They expect to hear about their benefits, and we do talk about that, but we also give them the background on the movement and labor history. We talk about democratic unionism. All of a sudden, light bulbs start coming on.[44]

Local 174 is just one example of the relationship between democracy, member involvement, and organizing. At the other end of the country, CWA Local 1037 represents workers at New Jersey's Department of Youth and Family Services, The Board of Public Utilities, and some private non-profit agencies in a state where for years a Republican governor was determined to cut just such services. But Local 1037 didn't shrink or lose density. Quite the opposite. They aggressively organized outside their core jurisdiction at DYFS. The local grew from 4,000 members to 7,500 members over twenty-three years according to its president Hetty Rosenstein. This was not done with full-time organizers. And it was not done by neglecting the workplace. Again, quite the opposite. Local 1037 has over 300 stewards, that's one for every twenty-five members. The stewards get no stipend or perks. They pay close attention to the details of day-to-day work, helped stop privatization of some services, put caps on case loads, upgraded clerical jobs, etc. On top of all this, says Rosenstein, growth of the local "is attributable to organizing by shop stewards."[45] The lesson of Local 1037 is that shop stewards can be, should be, the rank-and-file backbone of workplace organization *and* the activists who mobilize people to organize others. Another example comes from SEIU Local 660 representing 3,500 workers at the Los Angeles County-University of Southern California Medical Center in Los Angeles. This local, not yet merged into a statewide one, had a stewards' council with forty-five stewards that met monthly. In particular, they had won the right to a "pre-meeting" before their monthly meeting with management, all on work time. The stewards' council set a long-term goal of having one steward for every fifteen members. Along the way, the council led a campaign to reduce the workload forced on nurses. Local staff and reps supported and aided the campaign. All members were rallied to support the nurses who, using a state law, refused to work over a certain load. Management was forced to back down. Local 660 also backs up its stewards with even more workplace organization in the form of a "union committee" composed of "union contacts" who assist stewards. The local encourages units to have as many stewards and union contacts as possible.[46]

Part of the problem with the debate over the role of local unions in organizing is that it has often been put in terms of an "organizing model" versus a "servicing model," or more recently as a choice between organizing and representation. A good example of this latter way of framing the problem is found in a study done by Fletcher and Hurd in the collection *Rekindling the Movement*. As in their earlier study cited above, they are concerned with how to shift local unions from the old "servicing" or representation emphasis to external organizing. This, they argue, requires a shift in limited resources that is often resisted by local leaders, stewards, and members alike.[47] Examining the existing set-up of representation in the most local unions this is, in fact, what one would find. And this is the problem with the "servicing" versus "organizing" or representation versus organizing dichotomy of much of the current debate. The deeper problem, which Fletcher and Hurd hint at but don't develop, is that the representation system that has evolved over the past sixty years or so is itself deeply flawed. Beginning in World War 2, at the very least, shop floor or on-the-job representation has been turned into a bureaucratized, legalized, and professionalized grievance set-up that reflects the union and management hierarchies and consciously removes conflict from the workplace or job to higher levels beyond the control of the workers themselves. This has been reinforced over the decades by no-strike and management's rights clauses as well as countless arbitration and other legal decisions far removed from the source of conflict. As Jack Metzgar summarized it, "Grievance systems became progressively more bureaucratic and legalistic after 1946."[48] Over the years the members, too, have come to see this set-up as part of the woodwork, the natural way of doing things. So, yes, it requires exactly the same kind of full-time professional personnel that organizing is thought to require. Without returning the grievance functions to the first line of defense in the workplace through strong stewards' organization and reducing professional representation to a minimum this dichotomy will seem the only choice.

But the other choice is to build power on the job, as IBT Local 174, CWA Local 1037, SEIU Local 660, and others have done, thus expanding the resources of the local union.

What workers in America face today is not so much a choice between federations, as between types of unionism. There is the old bureaucratic business unionism that exists as the norm in both federations. Whether it is labeled an "organizing" or "servicing" union, its leaders long ago surrendered the workplace to management, despite continuing resistance from the members. Representation was professionalized and removed from the immediate influence of the members, thus weakening the first line of defense. They accepted and/or imposed concessionary contracts, engaged in labor–management cooperation in one or another form, and often sought salvation through mergers or affiliations. The old management's rights and no-strike clauses go unquestioned as though they were the first two of the ten commandments of labor: Thou Shalt Not ten times. These unions exist in every sector of the economy, public or private, service or industrial. If they are not shrinking they are stagnating or disappearing into another shrinking union. The second type is represented by locals such as IBT 174, CWA 1037, or SEIU 660, but glimmers can be seen in small unions like the United Electrical Workers or the ILWU. Probably most major unions have some slice of this more grassroots type. This we call democratic social movement unionism. It is more a direction to be sought than either a reality today or a "model" for tomorrow. So far, it is the exception, the direction in which to look if labor is to regain its power and grow. In the last decade or so, a new type of union has arisen, or rather a new direction been taken, in whole or part, by a few unions. This we will call *bureaucratic corporate unionism*. Again, elements of it can be found in both federations. But this course has been most thoroughly charted and set to date by the Service Employees International Union.

SEIU: The Evolution of Corporate Unionism and Shallow Power

The SEIU is certainly one of the most dynamic unions in the US labor movement. You are more likely to see the squads and battalions of the "Purple Army," visible by their purple T-shirts and caps, in the streets of America's big cities than similar groups from other unions. Its positions on big social issues and matters like the war in Iraq place it on the left of organized labor. It maintains an active international program through a series of "global partnerships" with unions in its core jurisdictions. Its base in low-wage building maintenance, health care, and service occupations gives it a membership that is 60% women and 40% people of color, both native-born and immigrant.[49] As an institution it exudes self-confidence. Its leadership thinks in strategic and not simply tactical terms to a degree rare in US unions. As Janice Fine notes, the SEIU "is very disciplined and focused with its resources and maps out its plans to move into new labor markets years ahead of time."[50] All of these features contribute to its record of organizing. It nearly doubled its membership between 1996 and 2006 to 1.8 million.[51] It has staked a claim to the future of US labor and, whatever one thinks of the split, it is no surprise that it would be the instigator and leader of something so bold. But just what direction is it posing for current and future union members? What is one to make of its radical internal restructuring?

The SEIU of today is the product of a long and somewhat contradictory evolution that nevertheless has shaped its current structure, culture, and aggressive stance. In its early development from a craft union of building maintenance workers (the Building Service Employees International Union, it dropped the "Building" from its name in 1968) it followed a path not unlike other craft unions, drifting into other jurisdictions as its old membership base declined. In 1980, when John Sweeney became president, the union took a decided turn, characterized by four developments. The first was an aggressive turn toward growth, largely through absorptions and affiliations. As mentioned earlier, from 1980 through 1993, the SEIU took in over 100 national or local unions, including 7 state employee associations and 47 local unions. The largest, the California State Employees Association had 80,000 members at the time in 1984.[52] The character of the union had changed dramatically into a multi-jurisdictional general union. For the time being, however, it kept the decentralized structure with its emphasis on local autonomy. Yet, secondly, it also increased its staff size from 20 in 1980 to 200 in 1988 and fivefold from 1984 through 1992. Between 1984 and 1988 its dues were doubled from $4.00 a month to $8.00 to fund organizing. This reflected both a new emphasis on organizing as well as on affiliations and on bringing in-house many of the functions for which other unions use consultants.[53] Embodied in these changes was a sort of contradiction, rapid growth through diversification, on the one hand, and increased resources at the center, on the other. Both would be important to the future of the SEIU.

A third change that contributed to changing the culture of the union was the hiring of large numbers of radical activists and organizers from outside the union. The SEIU had "missed" the 1960s and 1970s in most respects. But during the 1980s and 1990s, Sweeney hired mostly college-educated veterans of the 1960s and 1970s from community organizing, industrial "colonizing," or union staff backgrounds. While most union leaders preferred to promote from within and, in any case, would not think of hiring leftists, Sweeney gambled on the dedication of such activists to make the union grow.[54] In 1981, Sweeney also affiliated 9-to-5, the women's clerical organizing group led by feminist Karen Nussbaum, as a district of the SEIU. While the relationship of 9-to-5 and the SEIU went back to 1976 in Boston, it was Sweeney who agreed to charter District 925 run "for women and by women." Other new left organizing projects also found shelter in the SEIU of the 1980s, including the Rhode Island Workers Association and the United Labor Unions.[55] Sweeney had not only hired dedicated organizers, but had bought a piece of the social movement culture of the 1960s and 1970s that would be important to the future image and elan of the SEIU. One of the 1970s community organizers who worked his way up inside the SEIU was Andy Stern.

John Sweeney is, as we have seen, somewhat of a paradox: looking forward to justice for low-paid janitors by blocking bridges one day and backward to a social compact with those who inflict poverty the next. So, the transformation of the SEIU on his watch also featured a step beyond mere business unionism to the corporatization of the union. Michael Piore in one of the few studies of the SEIU's internal transformation described it as it was by the mid-1990s as follows:

> But the organization now in place is not simply a product of the natural evolution of these earlier efforts. It is an integrated structure, self-consciously devised and instituted by Sweeney and his staff. The ideas that underlie it were drawn from the business management literature. The staff read widely in the business press and the more scholarly literature as well. Their single most important source was probably the *Harvard Business Review*. As noted, the union hired the American Management Association to do staff training.[56]

The union was not simply run, by analogy, as a business, but literally by the norms of a modern corporation. This is consistent with the essentially administrative view of reform that Sweeney later brought to the AFL-CIO. For the SEIU it would be the formative principle that would contest with the social movement culture he had also imported.

The social movement side also gained ground under Sweeney's leadership. During the 1980s the union's historic base in the building services had eroded in all but a handful of big cities as contracting firms replaced union members. To counter the trend Sweeney took the Justice for Janitors campaign that began in Denver and had some successes in Seattle and Pennsylvania, national. In 1988, JfJ was launched in Los Angeles where there had been both an office building boom and the growth of an enormous immigrant workforce that would be the base of the campaign. LA JfJ would employ militant mobilization tactics and a broad outreach to community groups, particularly among immigrants. The 1990 LA JfJ victory became the signature campaign that underwrote the SEIU's reputation as a militant socially minded union. The two mergers with national and then New York 1199 helped solidify this image. The LA Justice for Janitors campaign also underlined another of the SEIU's features, the attention to planning and strategy. Stephen Lerner was the architect of the "market share" strategy that carried the day in LA. As one account put it, "JfJ's basic strategy is to seek control over all the key players in a local labor market, with the goal of taking labor costs out of competition." Another aspect of the strategy was, as the same study noted, "perseverance." That is, the union committed to the long haul, which is often what it takes to win these days and what many unions don't do. Perseverance also means a long-term financial commitment, which is where the social movement union meets the corporate union. As detailed above, this meeting of the corporate and the militant is also what led to the LA janitors being thrown into Local 399, where they attempted a rebellion and were put in trusteeship.[57]

During the 1980s the turn to corporate organizational norms was by no means consistent. Local autonomy still ruled and, in fact, the first effort to increase organizing was to require locals to take on that task. It was in this period the now famous "organizing" versus "servicing" model debate arose. It first appeared in a 1988 AFL-CIO manual that noted, the "servicing model of local union leadership— trying to help people by solving problems for them," in contrast to the "organizing model—involving members in solutions." This dichotomy was taken up by Andy Banks and Jack Metzgar in 1989 in the then influential and now unfortunately defunct *Labor Research Review*. The idea was "to involve many more people and expand leadership roles." This among other things would take the burden off staff.[58] As Fletcher and Hurd discovered in their study of "organizing model" locals in the SEIU discussed above, there was or could be a tension between the internal member participation and activation and the external priorities of the national union leadership. The national priorities would trump the local "organizing model" during the reign of Andy Stern who took over when Sweeney moved on to the AFL-CIO.

When Sweeney moved up to the AFL-CIO at the end of 1995, the union's secretary-treasurer Richard Cordtz took over. Cordtz represented the old guard. He was friends with Teamster chief Jackie Presser. His running mate in the 1996 election to replace Sweeney was to be none other than Gus Bevona, and, in old guard style, he had held on to a second salary from SEIU Local 79 in Detroit where he had been president. In the face of a clear majority in favor of Andy Stern's "New Voice" slate at the April 1996 convention, Cordtz withdrew.[59] Shortly before the convention where Stern became president, the union's Committee on the Future issued a report. Pointed toward some of the directions the union would take under Stern were its "two critical areas": organizing and political action. The brief section on the workplace simply called for "greatly expanded SEIU support for union-led workplace participation programs." The report suggested that the union's top two officials be barred from receiving two salaries, but left the other fifty-plus vice-presidents and executive board members free to continue the practice. More indicative of the future, it also called for increased central control over dues and other local functions and opposed the idea of direct elections of International officers. Sal Rosselli, president of Local 250 and, at that time, a leader of the reform group Service Employees for Democratic Reform, pointed to a "paternalistic attitude throughout the report."[60] The Committee on the Future's report, however, scarcely guessed at just how drastic the changes that lay ahead would be.

By the turn of the twenty-first century, the structure of the SEIU began to change dramatically. Centralization and corporate organizational norms were already part of the union's culture and they would be intensified. For example, the SEIU would move toward eliminating regular newspapers or magazines in favor of issue-related leaflets or brochures, the union equivalent of the corporate memo.[61] It had also moved toward a focus on its four major or "core" jurisdictions: hospitals, long-term health care, building (later "property") services, and public services.[62] This is a somewhat flexible and expansive view of jurisdiction. So, recently security guards have become a new target added to the renamed "property services" division.[63] Eventually, SEIU leaders would speak of working toward national standards or patterns in each of these: all seeming to move toward an industrial union model for each major sector. For reasons of history, many of the SEIU's local unions were themselves multi-jurisdictional. So, in 2000 the SEIU adopted a program that would reorganize locals along jurisdictional lines.

Called the "New Strength Unity Plan," it increased the powers of the international over the locals. Among other things it removed corruption or malfeasance as the basis for the trusteeship of a local union.[64] Trusteeships as a tool of policy were not new. As one of the most serious studies of the LA Justice for Janitors campaign noted, "JfJ has frequently been exported through trusteeships, which were imposed on the San Diego, Atlanta, San Jose, and Santa Clara locals."[65]

But after 2000, the corporate side of the union's culture took off. What resulted was not simply a jurisdictional rationalization of locals, but the destruction of many in forced mergers driven solely from the national headquarters to create numerically and geographically enormous mega-locals. The International was given expanded powers to reorganize locals. In the case of reorganizations, according to Stern in a letter to California locals, "the SEIU Constitution and Bylaws do not require a membership election to approve such jurisdictional changes."[66] Indeed, Article XIV, Sections 3 and 4 give the International Executive Board the power to merge locals "upon the consent of the Local Union *or* [emphasis added] . . . after a hearing upon reasonable notice before the International Executive Board" or before hearing officers appointed by the IEB.[67] In practice, the International usually holds hearings by appointed officers and then an after-the-fact plebiscite, which usually passes.

The New Strength Unity Plan was to add geographic scope to industrial and market focus; as Stern described it in his letter to California locals announcing the IEB's new plan to merge locals there along industrial lines, "to build industry and geographic strength for members."[68] Old locals were dismantled or merged to create geographically enormous mega-locals or units. Local 32B/J, John Sweeney's old local, traditionally covered some 35,000 building service workers in New York City. This large local was itself the product of a merger between 32B and 32J engineered by Sweeney in 1977. It would be one of the first "New Strength Unity" mergers. The merger began in 2001 after the International had trusteed Local 32B/J in order to get rid of Gus Bevona. Under the new president, Mike Fishman, parachuted in as trustee in 1999 and then elected president in 2000, the local spread into New Jersey and absorbed locals in the Bronx, suburban Westchester County and Connecticut. By 2006, Local 32B/J covered six states, running from Connecticut to Philadelphia to Washington DC, with 85,000 members. The "local" is still headed by Fishman operating out of New York City.[69] New York City's powerful 125,000-member Local 1199, the historic birthplace of hospital unionism in the 1950s and 1960s, expanded into upstate New York in 2002, creating a 240,000-member state-wide local. By 2005 the mergers had extended all the way to Baltimore, creating "1199 Eastern District," still headed by New York's Dennis Rivera. It is expected that the newly merged Massachusetts state-wide Local 2020 will affiliate with 1199 Eastern Region.[70]

The trend continued into the Midwest. In early 2004, 4,000 building service members of Local 50 in St. Louis were transferred to Local 1, headquartered in Chicago. Local 1, the union's founding local in 1921, had 35,000 members in building maintenance, not only in Chicago and its suburbs but in northern Illinois and Milwaukee, Wisconsin as well. Local 50 was abolished, its remaining public sector members transferred in to other regional locals. Local 1 now ran from Wisconsin to Missouri, a distance of about 280 miles as the crow flies. The president of another St. Louis-based SEIU local put what he thought was a positive spin on the merger when he told the press, "It's not unlike what businesses will do with their core industries."[71] In California, health care-based Locals 399 (Southern California) and 250 (northern California) were merged to create the statewide United Healthcare Workers West with 137,000 members. San Francisco building service Local 87 was trusteed and merged into statewide local 1877, where the LA janitors had ended up.[72] Indeed, the extent of this top-down internal merger movement by mid–2006 was described by Stern in the letter mentioned above:

> Jurisdictional improvements like these have been implemented successfully in many other parts of the country—in Illinois, Massachusetts, Rhode Island, Pennsylvania, Ohio, Washington State, Florida, Michigan, Missouri, New York, and even previously in California in some instances.[73]

Altogether, the SEIU planned to reduce California's 35 local union to five mega-locals, presumably along jurisdictional lines.[74] While most mergers are eventually approved by a yes or no vote, the methods of producing such mergers are sometimes heavy-handed. Not surprisingly, some of these "jurisdictional improvements" face resistance.

The 3,500-member Local 87 in San Francisco voted almost two-to-one to decertify from the SEIU and set up the independent United Service Workers for Democracy Local 87. During the hearing held by the International, a majority of members of Local 87 had opposed the merger, but the International ignored them. The concerns of Local 87 members and officers were voiced by the local's vice president Ahmed Abozayd: "Our pay rate was $15.25 an hour, 1877's was between $7 and $9 an hour. We had full benefits, they had little or none." Local 1877 had also signed a five-year contract, whereas Local 87 had always had three-year agreements.[75] In other words, they feared with good reason that merger into the much larger Local 1877 with much lower pay and benefits locked into longer contracts would undermine theirs. Another California SEIU local, Local 415, was in negotiations with Santa Cruz County, having already called a one-day strike. The local's lead negotiator was fired and replaced by an IEB member. The local's five elected officers resigned in protest, opposing the merger. Resigned president Ian McFadden said ironically, "Unions are by nature grass-roots organizations, hence the word 'local.'"[76] In Rhode Island, a similar effort to force a merger with a Boston-based local through trusteeship of Local 134 ran into opposition. Eventually, workers from three units of Local 134 left to join the independent United Service and Allied Workers of Rhode Island, which had been formed 2003 by other former 134 members escaping trusteeship.

The attempt to force a merger of higher education locals in Massachusetts into one statewide local met opposition on the grounds of democracy and the imposition of a widely distrusted staffer, Susana Segat, as provisional president of the new Local 888. In this case, after trying to get some semblance of democracy, 2,300 SEIU members chose to leave the SEIU and go with the Massachusetts Teachers Association. Apparently not wanting the troublesome academics, the SEIU agreed to let them go. It is worth noting that there was already a statewide coalition of higher education unions which the SEIU chose to ignore, in effect, creating disunity where a coalition had existed— albeit not under SEIU control.[77] At least for some workers, forced mergers had led to greater fragmentation, rather than "industry and geographic strength."

There are at least four major problems with the type of organization the SEIU appears to be headed for. The first is economic. The giant statewide and multi-state units the leadership is creating do not conform to the density or market share approaches the SEIU has made its strategic centerpiece. Density can be measured in several ways: by local labor market; by industry or "sector;" or by corporate or business structure. The labor markets for most health care, building service and public sector jobs are local or metropolitan in nature, in most cases not even statewide let alone composed of several states. There are exceptions such as state employees or large hospital chains where both industry and corporate density are relevant. But, for building services, as the strategy that was the model for the Justice for Janitors campaign has shown, the labor market is metropolitan despite the international character of some of the contractors involved. To put it another way, the members of Local 87 were right to worry that their higher wages and benefits could be threatened by being thrown into a huge statewide local with both lower standards and a variety of standards around the state. Huge statewide and multi-state "locals" don't conform to any relevant market or industry. In addition, the long contract terms that seem to go with the new more "efficient" organizational norms lock in lower standards, preventing upward wage drift across localities or regions. In other words, setting higher standards requires "taking labor out of competition" in the relevant labor markets, something the SEIU's own strategists argue. If the goal is to create regional or even national standards or patterns it is hard to see why such gigantic units are called for. Most unions that do have national or regional patterns in specific jurisdictions do not have such structures, rather they tend to have districts, councils, or some other such intermediate organization that straddles the locals. There is no convincing economic logic to the destruction of locals and their replacement with giant administrative units.

Furthermore, this corporate-style centralization overlooks, misunderstands, or simply dismisses the *role* of the local union. Whether based on a single workplace, as with most locals of the former CIO industrial unions, or multiple job sites, as with the Teamsters, retail unions, or the building trades, the major job of the local is to regulate the conditions of work in the workplace or on-the-job in the local labor market. This goes back to what was argued above about the importance of the workplace as a site of power, indeed, the origin of the major source of power that workers possess. Here, the role of stewards and stewards' organization is key. Yet, what can possibly be the relationship of stewards to some massive geographically spread and bureaucratically run administrative unit? What is the relationship of stewards in St. Louis to leaders in Chicago or those in Philadelphia to New York? What would even be their relationship to the full-time "Delegates" who report to Chicago or New York or, for that matter, to Washington DC? Will they be relegated to powerless chapters or units? There is evidence that the SEIU leadership wishes to go farther than most unions in ridding itself of this problem over time. In Britain, where Andy Stern and the SEIU have an aggressive presence as part of their "global partnerships" with unions abroad, Stern is frequently quoted or paraphrased as telling his British counterparts that shop stewards are a bad idea.[78] Equally suggestive of where Stern is heading is his comment in a recent interview with *The McKinsey Quarterly*. Having already expressed his concern to form industry-based partnerships that "provide value" for employers he engaged in the following exchange:

> *Quarterly:* Is the model of a workers' organization that isn't based on the workplace a viable way to get past the traditional confrontation between management and labor?

> *Andy Stern:* Yes, and I think that trying to have some kind of broader, less work site-based sectoral and national relationships is one way to do this.[79]

Here, partnership trumps workplace organization. The emerging structure of the union seems all too consistent with this goal. Of course, the SEIU today has workplace-based stewards, stewards training, and a stewards' manual that says much what any such manual would say.[80] But the question arises: are stewards and workplace organization to become a thing of the past, like local unions? It is probably unnecessary to invent yet another sloganistic plan to diminish the role of stewards. It would be enough to let their role atrophy as grievances or other problems are handled in some more "efficient" manner by full-time "delegates" or reps from politically and often geographically distant headquarters—probably via some IT "solution." If this is, indeed, the direction taken, it will be one more step toward two-dimensional density and shallow power. Were we to put this in the language of the old debate, we would have to say that what seems to be taking shape in the SEIU is the last word in the top-down "servicing model" as far as the members are concerned.

A third and closely related problem is the purposeful penetration of corporate culture deeper into union life. If business unionism involves the colonization of unions by the business culture of the past, the development of corporate unionism is in part enabled by the absorption of contemporary corporate culture. America has itself become awash with formalistic "can-do" campaigns, entrepreneurial leadership style, the inevitability of markets, competitive norms, "customer service" devises, and a pseudo-psychological language that embodies business values without necessarily expressing them honestly. Partnership fits neatly with this business mindset. Another aspect, mentioned earlier, is the shift of workers from producers to consumers. Consumerism in unions is already a big problem. Too many members see themselves not only as passive individuals in the marketplace, but as consumers of union services. Too many union officials and reps see themselves as service providers—here we are back in the servicing versus organizing model debate of the 1980s and 1990s. By doing away with locals within reach of members and possibly with active workplace organization as well, the SEIU threatens to intensify the consumerist view of unions.

The union's emphasis on staff, captured in the corporate-like phrase "staffing up," meaning to increase staff, is another sign of its top-down direction. According to the International it employs 300 people in its Washington DC headquarters and another 400 around the country. In addition many larger locals maintain a staff, including organizers, as well as full-time officials. In fact, the union's LM–2 forms show a total of 913 International employees, including officers and part-timers on the payroll, in the fiscal year 2005. This is up from 516 in 2000, an increase of 77% over five years.[81] An indication of just how seriously the SEIU takes "staffing-up" is that the union's web site listed 204 job openings in July 2006.[82] In another piece of SEIU corporate-speak, hiring and maintaining staff is now known as "talent management." In early 2006, Chief of Staff Kirk Adams noted, "the union has reached a point where we need more expertise and focus in the Talent

Management area." To fix this, the SEIU hired human resources expert Bob Laggini "to implement an integrated, union-wide strategy for talent management."[83] The move away from workplace and local organization toward greater dependence on staff points toward another aspect of two-dimensional density. It is a density suspended from above by a layer of "talent" recruited mainly from outside the union rather than upheld from below by deep roots in the workplace and local union, a three-dimensional density.

The old structure of the SEIU was not particularly democratic, but like many unions it had its share of democratically run local unions. Local 509 in Massachusetts, 87 in the Bay Area, and 250 in northern California or 660 in southern California come to mind. These and many others have been caught up in the centralization process. What seems most obvious about the direction of the SEIU is that the new mega-locals cannot possibly be democratic in any way. Whatever formal structures they have, membership control of the central leaders, staff, and resources is impossible in the vast geographic areas they cover. Such meetings as there are will most likely devolve to geographically dispersed "chapters" with little ability to communicate *horizontally* with one another, and no real power over the new administrative centers. The sheer size also means, as I said above, the inability of such workplace organization as is allowed to continue to have the type of influence, let alone control, over the mega-local that could make it the link between members and leaders. The growth of mega-locals will also dampen democracy at the level of the International Union, as we saw in the case of the UFCW where a relatively small number of huge locals control a majority of votes at the union's conventions. It is precisely these mega-locals that are most likely to be "on the program" and, hence, loyal to the incumbent leadership should a rebellion develop. We have seen that Andy Stern doesn't have much use for stewards or democracy, which interfere with power as he sees it. Democracy and workplace organization are also threats to partnership with employers as they tend to promote conflict in the face of deteriorating conditions.

In place of real organization with depth in locals and the workplace is the magic of two-dimensional density and central control of both contracts and organizing. It is a shallow kind of power resting on staff and long contracts. Its results are not always the greater steps out of poverty that are promised. While there is no doubt that virtually any union representation brings an improvement over none, the quality of the difference matters. Here, we look only at the results of the SEIU's most famous victory, the LA Justice for Janitors campaign of 1990. Before the first contract, the average hourly wage for janitors in the Los Angeles-Long Beach area, as measured by the BLS *Area Wage Survey*, was $6.10 an hour. After the signing of the Century City contract, this average rose to $6.24, with much of the area still not under contract. By December 1995, with the whole area covered, the average wage was $6.85. This represented an increase of 12.3% over five years or 2.5% a year, somewhat below the national average of 3% per year for non-manufacturing private sector collective bargaining agreements in those years.[84] In real terms (1982–84=100), however, it was a *decline* of 4%, or almost 1% a year. The second five-year agreement with the contractors, which, contrary to the "market share" doctrine, did not have the same rates for all five contract areas in greater Los Angeles, scheduled an increase in the minimum wage for cleaners in the core downtown LA area from $6.80 in April 1995 to $7.20 in February 2000. This was an increase of 6% or a little more than 1% a year. Again, in real terms this was a *drop* of 6% over five years. This was the highest wage in the five covered areas and the only area with full health care and pension benefits as late as 2000.[85] Thus, over ten years, LA janitors with the best conditions saw their real wages fall 10%. In this period, 1990 through 2000, average real hourly wages in the US *rose* by 4.8%.[86] It is just possible that had the LA janitors been in their own local instead of in the big statewide Local 1877, with its low wages, minimal benefits, and long contracts, they could have pressured for more and set a better pattern for others. In 2000, after a long strike by the 8,500 LA janitors, Local 1877 won a 24% wage increase over three years in the core/downtown/Century City area and 22% for those in the other areas, according to the *New York Times*.[87] This would have meant, for the first time, wage increases well beyond the rate of inflation, more or less making up for the drop from 1990 to 2000. Nevertheless, this meant that even after three contracts real wages had stood still. The gap between those in the core and suburban areas was even greater in 2003 than in 2000, about 15% compared with 6% earlier. Despite talk of establishing a national pattern for building service workers, SEIU contracts still differed enormously from city to city. In Chicago, for example, as a result of the 2000 contract janitors would make $12.50 an hour by 2003, about 40–50% more than LA janitors.[88] This record, whether typical or not, certainly brings into question the automatic powers of density and central control—the elements of shallow power.

The trend to large locals and more centralization has also been taken up by some of the other Change To Win affiliates. For example, since the 2004 merger of UNITE-HERE, "more than 40 locals and affiliates have merged in the fastest consolidation of two unions' power ever seen in the movement," according to a union press release.[89] Here, again, we would point out that UNITE-HERE's important campaign to bring the nation's major hotel chains under common conditions does not require or even feature multi-state mega-locals, or even, for that matter, the merger with UNITE!. Rather, it is directed at helping locals in major cities to get common expiration dates. As of mid-2004, the union had succeeded in bringing 400 major hotels under similar expiration dates in 2006, not by partnership, but by strikes where necessary.[90] The Carpenters, pioneers in setting their own course, also explored reorganization even before the New Strength Unity Plan was put in place. The Carpenters didn't eliminate or merge locals, they simply made them powerless and irrelevant. The old city-based district councils that had coordinated bargaining before were superseded by regional councils that now had all the power to negotiate and administer contracts for a much larger geographical area. Members can no longer elect business agents or vote on contracts. The regional council's secretary-treasurer has the sole power to hire staff and business agents. The reasons given for the new structure were the growth of regional contractors and the need to eliminate old "fiefdoms" in locals. Union dissidents argued that while the regional councils might be a good idea, eliminating locals and membership control over business agents and contracts would simply elevate corruption and "fiefdoms" to a higher level.[91]

To the strategies of retreat in the 1980s and 1990s, we can now add the rise of bureaucratic corporate unionism and the embrace of shallow power. This new direction is a step beyond business unionism in its centralization and shift of power upward in the union's structure away from the members, locals, and workplace; its fetish with huge administrative units; and its almost religious attachment to partnerships with capital. We call it corporate unionism because its vision is essentially administrative, its organizational sensibility executive rather than democratic, and its understanding of power market-based and, hence, shallow. What we are confronting today in the US and world economies is a clash of social forces between labor and capital in which the power of labor, of the working class, must be derived from mass mobilization based on deep organization. This implies a very different direction than either federation offers at the moment.

What about the AFL-CIO and its remaining unions? All that has been said about the limits of business unionism and the failure of reform from above still applies. The unions that do organize, for example, the CWA, the AFSCME, and the Steelworkers, will continue to do so. What remains to be seen is whether the split will inspire a positive drive across the old federation to increase organizing efforts. There is some evidence that both the earlier debate and the specter of competition have done so. The UAW transferred $50 million from its strike fund for organizing. The AFSCME has raised dues by $3 a month and the AFT by 75 cents a month per member, both for new organizing. The CWA has set aside $24 million in a strategic fund that includes organizing, with the IBEW, Painters, and Iron Workers creating similar funds.[92] Will they do this new organizing by imitating the emerging corporate model or will at least some strike out in a more grassroots, genuinely social movement direction? The federation as a whole, stripped of resources and no doubt somewhat demoralized by the split, will have to redefine its purpose. There is no prediction here that it will actually do so. John Sweeney missed his chance a decade ago. Without some sign of new leadership arising from below it is hard to see how it can transcend the habits of half a century. If a guess were to be ventured it would be that at the federation level, the AFL-CIO will do what it has always done in hard times and turn even more to electoral politics and salvation by Democrats—solving nothing. In any case, it will not be at the federation level that the future of organized labor in the US will be determined. It will be by those unions that choose to act and by those workers inside and as yet outside the unions who force action and transformation on old unions or, perhaps, even create new ones where none exists or old unions fail to organize.

Reform from above has failed on two counts. We cannot afford to wait for "strike three." The future of unionism and of working-class power and living standards rests on developments more deeply rooted in capitalist social and economic relations. The real choice is not between two federations but between three types of unionism: the old business unionism, the new corporate unionism, or a democratic social movement unionism born of struggle with the employers. Whether this last direction arises in the context of existing unions, comes from outside, or from some combination of the two, it is the hope for the future. We turn now to look at those forces on the ground that can provide the alternative and some strategic directions that could turn things around.

BENEATH THE SPLIT: RESISTANCE AND CHANGE FROM BELOW

The 2005 split from the AFL-CIO proposed a more aggressive approach to organizing, but offered no alternatives to either labor's traditional political strategy or the norms of business unionism. If anything, some of the unions in the Change to Win Federation have taken these norms a step or two further toward an even more hierarchical corporate model. The major new strategic ideas when combined with these norms seem doomed to produce a type of shallow power based on two-dimensional density (length and breadth without on-the-job depth) and centralized control to the extent they are successful in organizing. It might well be argued that spreading unionism now and filling in its content in time is better than the current stagnation and decline most unions face. In so far as the SEIU model is the wave of the CTW's future, however, there is as yet no plan to fill in the missing depth of workplace and local organization down the road. If anything, the direction of its leading unions seems to drift farther from these essential "ramparts of resistance." Moreover, the CTW's "landlocked" strategy is too narrow to alter the larger balance of forces between labor and capital in the US, much less the world.

Still, great things can grow from flawed models. Didn't that old autocrat John L. Lewis and his highly bureaucratized and badly depleted United Mine Workers kick off the CIO upsurge that changed the balance of class forces for a time? Well, yes and no. Lewis and the other seven initial CIO leaders of existing unions responded to the challenge of a pre-existing upsurge. The assault on the commanding heights of US capital came from within the plants even if the Lewises of the day sometimes provided the national framework. In auto, rubber, electrical, trucking, and elsewhere there was no Lewis and the new frameworks came from below. Leaders were essential, but most rose from the ranks. If they had training and skills, they had been acquired in radical political parties or related organizations like the Brookwood Labor College. There was no OI. Aside from the Mine Workers and Steelworkers, there was little in the way of "staffing-up," which came later, and there were no union "talent managers" or HR specialists. None of the new or old unions of that era possessed the vast bureaucratic structures they would acquire during and after WW2 and which persist and have grown worse over time. If they had, it is unlikely the upheaval of the 1930s would have taken the shape it did. For those who prefer the top-down, political atmosphere interpretation of the CIO, however, it needs only be said that today no labor leader will be able to claim, no matter how speciously, that "the President wants you to join the union," nor is any US president in the foreseeable future likely to say, "Clear it with Andy." The analogy with the CIO doesn't hold much water.

There are, of course, rays of hope, glimmers of successful tactics and actions. They can be found in both federations. There are successful strikes conducted by the CWA, Steelworkers, Machinists and others as well as by the SEIU and UNITE-HERE. There are innovative experiments in "non-majority unionism" by the United Electrical Workers and the CWA. The Justice for Janitors' campaigns *are* good organizing strategy. So is the work of the Laborers' Eastern Region Organizing Fund among immigrant workers. There are some examples of community mobilizations such as Jobs with Justice or some of the Union Cities Central Labor Council programs.[1] It is a good sign that the CWA made workplace organization a point of pride in the recent split debate when it wrote:

> Democracy in the workplace is the basis for popular support for collective bargaining, provides the best foundation for union organizing, and should provide a framework for union infrastructure at the local and national level as well as for the AFL-CIO.[2]

For these examples to become general and others to become practice bigger changes are needed. For these changes we look not to the top leaders of the two federations or even of most unions, but to developments at the base, both inside and outside of the unions.

The Resistance

The failure of 1989 to become a turning point for the working class, did not mean that class conflict had disappeared. Whatever went on at the pinnacle of organized labor, at the base resistance continued as it always does, at one level of intensity and visibility or another. Many of the visible strikes of the 1990s were over one or another aspect of lean production. These included: the 1990 *New York Daily News* strike; the 1992 Caterpillar strike; the 1993–95 strikes at A.E. Staley and Bridgestone-Firestone, and again at Caterpillar; the 1995–2000 Detroit newspapers' strike; the series of over twenty strikes at General Motors plants that lasted from 1994 through 1998; and the 1997 UPS strike. All of these strikes involved staffing levels, workload, work schedules, and other lean issues as well as wages and health care costs. Most of these strikes were draws or defeats, but most of the GM strikes and the UPS won most of what they demanded even if the victories proved to be temporary. Most were initiated at lower levels of the unions. The GM strikes were initiated by the local unions, while the UPS strike involved both leadership and rank-and-file efforts.

The 1997 UPS was arguably the most successful of that period. It seemed to signify that labor's big guns might be willing to turn the situation around. It had the added significance that it was the new reform leadership of the Teamsters that provided the votes that put John Sweeney into the top chair at the AFL-CIO only a year and half before. The strike at UPS had been well prepared for and emphasized member mobilization. It had also been preceded by a two-year fight against a team concept plan, unilaterally imposed by UPS management. The union issued a video spoofing the so-called "Star" team program. Using materials developed by *Labor Notes*, members of the rank-and-file group Teamsters for a Democratic Union, with the support of the IBT leadership, led a successful campaign that forced UPS to drop their team work plan. The campaign also became an important organizing tool in preparation for the strike. The major issue in this highly successful strike, turning part-time jobs into full-time employment, was also a lean production issue.[3]

Three post-UPS struggles worth special mention are the 2002–03 contract fight of the ILWU, the 2003 southern California grocery strike, and the New York City Transit strike of 2005 mentioned in the opening chapter. First the California grocery strike. The 70,000 grocery clerks across southern California who worked for the big chains were pushed into a strike in 2003. The issues here, as in so many other strikes, were health care benefits, a two-tier wage set-up, and outsourcing. The companies wanted the workers to pay more toward health insurance and to turn their shelf-stocking work over to the vendors who delivered the goods. They demanded that new hires start lower and never reach the current top wage level. The strike lasted for over fours months and had strong moral support from communities, customers, and other unions, and some financial support from the AFL-CIO. But the one thing that could have won it, putting up pickets that would be honored by the Teamsters who delivered food to and from the warehouses, was rejected—not by the Teamsters, but by the leaders of the strikers' union, UFCW. Another possible move, extending the strike to northern California where contracts were soon due to expire, was also rejected. In other words, the UFCW leadership refused to use what potential power it had. The strike was lost and a two-tier contract with the other concessions on health care, pensions, and some outsourcing was signed.[4] Less than a year later grocery clerks in northern California had a concessionary contract handed to them by the UFCW. Members wondered why the union, with 1.4 million members, hadn't used some of its power to stem the tide of concessions in the grocery industry.[5]

The ILWU 2002 contract dispute was not a strike, but a lockout by the employers, who are represented by the Pacific Maritime Association (PMA). As the union of West Coast dockers who handle all the trans-Pacific trade, the ILWU had enormous power. But the context in which bargaining took place in 2002 made the use of this power problematic. The Bush Administration, touting its war on terror, was determined not to have a high-profile labor victory by a militant union on his watch. But, facing re-election in November, he didn't want a bloody strike that crippled global trade either. It was not the union that called his bluff, but the PMA when in September they locked the ILWU members out, thus closing down Pacific trade into and out of the US and Canada. They were, they said, responding to a slowdown by union members. For the first time ever, a president imposed a Taft-Hartley eighty-day cooling off period on the employers. A tentative agreement was reached in November and ratified by the members by 89% in January 2003. The union and, apparently the members, saw this as a victory, having beaten back a PMA health benefits cost-sharing demand—although the new contract would be six years long.[6]

The contract between Transport Workers Union Local 100, representing 33,000 transit workers, and the Metropolitan Transit Authority, a state entity which runs New York City's transit system and the suburban commuter lines, expired on December 15, 2005. Roger Toussaint, president of Local 100, was determined to avoid a strike if possible and no real preparations were made for one. A strike was illegal under New York State's Taylor Law. The union could be fined and each member would be docked two days' pay for each day on strike. But the MTA had a long list of give-back demands, including "broadbanding" or job loading, and, at the last minute, came in with a new one: a two-tier pension scheme in which new employees would pay more than current ones.[7] The membership was angry. On top of all the demands was the draconian disciplinary system that they had faced for years. In 2004, the MTA issued 15,200 disciplinary citations, up from the already outrageous 10,000 in 2002. They were ready to strike. With no motion from the MTA, Toussaint called the members out at 3:00 a.m. on December 20. But then, on the 22nd, he called the strike off. The members were fined and Toussaint served five days of a ten-day jail sentence. A tentative agreement shortly after the strike was narrowly rejected by the members. Almost five months later the same offer was accepted minus the two-tier pension, but with increased medical costs.[8]

Despite different outcomes, there was a certain similarity between these three struggles. In each case, the membership seemed willing to strike or do what was necessary to win. But, in each case, the leadership did not use the leverage available to them. To be sure, the context was a bad one, politically and even economically. But, those things that might have built on the UPS victory or the more limited gains at many GM plants, where the leverage had been used, were not deployed. Punches were pulled. This reflected the greater disorientation felt by so many in organized labor, and revealed the ambivalence of leaders, some thought to be among the more militant, to use the power they commanded. The question of when and where to use the power of the stronger groups within the working class can be difficult, but it is key if there is to be a turnaround and if millions are to be organized.

Strikes were frequent and covered many industries. Resistance appeared to grow by 2005. As Chris Kutalik of *Labor Notes* reported:

> According to the Bureau of National Affairs there were 271 work stoppages in the first three quarters of 2005 as compared to 227 in all of 2004. And the BNA's numbers do not include many high-profile strikes at the end of 2005 which involved roughly 70,000 workers: Northwest Airlines mechanics and cleaners, Boeing Aircraft manufacturing workers, California hospital workers, and Philadelphia and New York City transit.[9]

It wasn't just strikes that characterized the resistance. There were other signs as well. A new kind of grassroots solidarity took shape in a couple of industries where the heritage of craft unionism had left fragmentation and disunity. The continuation and even acceleration of concessions bargaining also encouraged some workers to seek alliances across union lines. At the University of California in the spring and early summer of 2005, three unions, the AFSCME, CWA Local 9119, and the Coalition of University Employees, struck, one after the other in their separate contract fights. What made these strikes different was that members of the other two unions walked the picket lines with whichever union was on strike.[10] Under enormous pressure for far-reaching concessions and job reorganization from private freight carrying railroads, the United Transportation Union and the Teamster-affiliated Brotherhood of Locomotive Engineers and Trainmen announced a solidarity pact in February 2006. The previous spring members from both unions had formed the Railroad Operating Crafts United, calling for "a merger based on our proposal for a democratic rank-and-file-based union."[11] In early 2006, three unions at Mesaba Airlines pulled together to fight a 19.4% wage cut and what they called a possible "sham" bankruptcy.[12] Alarmed at the massive cutbacks at Northwest Airlines and that company's attempt to impose "the worst contract in the history of airline labor" on the unaffiliated Airline Mechanics Fraternal Association, members of several unions from NWA, United and American came together in November 2005 to form Airline Workers United. AWU would push for unity among the different unions and work to build "rank and file networks to make unions democratic and keep leaders accountable."[13] These were cases of high union density, but low levels of unity. Mergers that had made sense for years were thwarted by larger affiliations or in the case of AMFA its independence. The cries for unity came from the ranks or the local leaders of the different unions, acting together and even forming cross-union organizations. To make this sort of unity powerful enough to resist employers the size of an airline or other major corporation would require bigger changes in the national unions. This, too, would be part of the resistance.

Rebels and Reformers

Contests between union critics and incumbent leaders are often viewed as "nothing but politics," the "outs" versus the "ins" with little more than a change of faces at the top as the outcome. And, often that is just what they are. Full-time union office carries perks and those running for local office may just be running away from the workplace and toward a softer life. Those contesting higher office may be driven by similarly opportunist motives—the low road to the high life. But often, union "politics" is about something much bigger: the employer! Or to put it another way, it can be about power. When union leaders don't "bring home the bacon" or don't defend conditions and jobs; when, in fact, they seem to be in the way with their commitments to cooperation or concessions, to save jobs of course, union politics can be about fighting the boss. Because of that, it can also be about making changes in more than leadership offices: in structures and practices that reduce the power and effectiveness of the union. Sometimes, as we saw in terms of the 1960s and 1970s, this internal conflict becomes general across much of the labor movement.

Early in the development of that period of upsurge in the mid-1960s, long-time labor activist and socialist Stan Weir wrote:

> The rank and file union revolts that have been developing in the industrial workplaces since the early 1950s are now plainly visible. Like many of their compatriots, American workers are faced with paces, methods, and conditions of work that are increasingly intolerable. Their union leaders are not sensitive to these conditions. In thousands of industrial establishments across the nation, workers have developed informal underground unions . . . These groups are the power base for the insurgencies from below that in the last three years have ended or threatened official careers of long standing.[14]

In fact, long incumbent leaders of the Steelworkers, Rubber Workers, the Oil, Chemical & Atomic Workers, and the International Union of Electrical Workers all went down to defeat in those years. A few years later, the leaders of the Mine Workers would follow suit. Most of those who succeeded them were little better. But these fights were not about individuals. They were about "the pace, methods, and conditions of work" that the union leaders were "not sensitive to." In the decades since, when conditions of work are even worse, the very nature of work has changed, and union leaders are still "not sensitive to" workplace issues, rebellion against the union leadership typically begins with the fight against the boss.

Although rank-and-file based rebellions, reform movements, and pressure groups emerged across the labor movement in the 1980s, 1990s, and the early 2000s, unlike those of the 1960s and 1970s they did not arise in the midst of a period of general labor upsurge. Quite the contrary, it was, as we have seen, a period of retreat and even defeat. This fact conditioned the nature and possibilities of such grassroots movements within organized labor just as it did those of the movement as a whole. Yet, the dynamics that have almost always given rise to rank-and-file movements, the clash of conditions with bureaucratic inertia, remained strong enough to push many union activists into opposition to incumbent leaders and to the policies, structures, and practices they backed and which allowed capital to intensify the pressure on conditions. The lack of a general upsurge limited the possibilities of transformation in most cases. Rank-and-file rebellions were mostly small and seldom achieved all they set out to accomplish. They were more likely to act as pressure groups than as full-blown oppositions. Yet, they remained widespread and persistent.

In the closing years of the old century and opening years of the new, organized grassroots opposition or pressure groups arose in the

Carpenters, Transport Workers, Amalgamated Transit Union Locals 732 and 1181, AFSCME DC 37, United Federation of Teachers, United Teachers of Los Angeles, Professional Staff Congress/AFT, Operating Engineers, Auto Workers, Elevator Constructors Locals 1 and 2, SEIU Locals 32B/J and 1000 (CSEA), Theatrical Stage Employees 798, New York Metro Area Postal Workers Union/APWU, Machinists District 143, UFCW, Plumbers and Pipe Fitters, International Longshoremen's Association, and Teamsters to mention only a few well recorded in the pages of *Labor Notes* and/or *Union Democracy Review*.[15] Here we will look at a few of the more recent reform or pressure efforts.

By the late 1990s, UAW New Directions had faded away, survived by a network of local-based rank-and-file-run websites that exchanged information, held annual meetings, and occasionally held actions, as in support of locked-out UAW Local 2036. Then, in 2005, rank-and-file UAW members at Delphi began holding mass meetings from St. Louis to Lockport, New York, with most in the industry's Midwest heartland. Each of these meetings was attended by over 150 workers. In the face of the threat of bankruptcy, loss of pensions, and a 50% wage cut by GM-spin-off Delphi, most meetings called for a work-to-rule across the company. The meetings were followed by rallies of hundreds, again across the Midwest, one Indiana meeting attracting over 1,000 workers and supporters.[16]

Far from the Rust Belt in Los Angeles, in March 2005 rank-and-file teachers overthrew an incumbent union leadership—the first time in thirty-five years this had happened. The United Teachers of Los Angeles represents 42,000 teachers in LA's giant unified school system. It is affiliated with both the American Federation of Teachers and the independent National Education Association. It is a potential power in both the school system and the communities its members serve. Yet, the old leadership had been reluctant to use that power to resist the mindless standardization that is sweeping schools across the country. The rebel United Action slate won all the posts it contested, gaining a majority on the 49-member executive board. It endorsed the independent candidate for president, A.J. Duffy, who won with 60% of the vote. The issues ran the gambit of contemporary education issues: reduced class size; teacher participation in curriculum formation and implementation; alliances with parents and other school workers; and less standardized testing. It also demanded protection of health benefits and salary increases. United Action was a coalition of reform-minded activists. It was made possible, however, by the existence of Progressive Educators for Action (PEAC), a rank-and-file caucus that had been active for two years before the election. PEAC had organized demonstrations against excessive testing and paperwork. PEAC's strategy for increasing the union's power was to build or rebuild the chapters in each school in order to activate a broader part of the membership. This would now become the challenge facing the new leadership.[17]

The Teamster reform movement had suffered two serious setbacks. The first was the overturning of the 1996 election and the eventual banning of Ron Carey from the union as a result of a money laundering scam on his behalf by members of his campaign staff. This put Hoffa in office and brought the momentum of reform and that of the 1997 UPS strike to a halt. The second was the decertification of Local 556, a TDU bastion at Tyson Foods meatpacking plant in Washington State. The Hoffa administration joined the company in denouncing the local's militant leader Maria Martinez. After the defeat of the decert first time around, the company got a rerun which it won by four votes.[18] Teamster reformers have an advantage that dissidents in other unions usually don't have: a seasoned, permanent organization with thousands of members, regular meetings and annual conventions, a newspaper, and even a small staff. So, despite these setbacks, the reform forces, led by TDU, continued to fight for better contracts, to defend pensions, and to complete the reform of the union. In the 2006 election for top officers, TDU backed Tom Leedham and the "Strong Contracts, Good Pensions" slate. Leedham, secretary-treasurer of Local 206 in Portland, Oregon, ran against Hoffa in 1998 when he got 39% of the vote and again in 2001 when he got 35%. Reform forces feel that Hoffa's record in the past few years has greatly reduced his credibility, increasing Leedham's and the reformers' chances of winning. Leedham is committed to a program of aggressive organizing and union democracy as well as contract and pension protection.[19] A victory for Leedham and the reform slate he heads would represent a major shift in Teamster politics with considerable impact on the movement as a whole.

The AFSCME's District Council 37, representing some 120,000 New York City workers, went through a period of retreat and crisis in the 1990s. What had been the flagship of American public sector unionism in the 1960s, paralyzed by the New York city fiscal crisis of 1975, had slid a long way toward run-of-the-mill business unionism and worse. First in 1995, Executive Director Stanley Hill signed the "two zeros" contract, with no wage increases in the first two years of the three-year agreement. Then in 1998, when revelations of widespread corruption came out, it was discovered that the vote had been rigged. Al Diop, president of Local 1549, found guilty of stealing $1 million from the union treasury, was also a major player in the stolen contract vote. The District Council was put into trusteeship by the International. At the same time, a group of reform-minded local leaders, some of them the people who had blown the whistle on corruption, organized the Committee for Real Change. One of their major demands was for the direct election of the District Council's top officials.[20] The reformers, running as the Unity Slate, attempted to replace Executive Director Lillian Roberts in 2004, but the voting system in DC 37 was stacked in the incumbent's favor. The reformers did take a majority of the Executive Board, but in elections for top officers locals vote according to the number of members they have, so that about four locals dominate any election. In October 2005, however, the proposal to change this was defeated by delegates from the Council's 56 local unions.[21] Up to this point the reformers were limited to local presidents and other officers. There was little rank-and-file involvement. In early 2006, however, a new movement for direct elections took shape involving some of the same local leaders, but this time directed at the ranks in the locals.[22] Whether this more grassroots course can succeed in overthrowing DC 37's rigged election system remains to be seen, but the dynamic that produces rank-and-file revolt would continue to move union members to action.

A strong challenge to the eternally corrupt leadership of the International Longshoremen's Association (ILA) arose from a fight against a non-union stevedoring company in Charleston, South Carolina, in which five ILA members, soon known as the Charleston Five, were arrested. After a vigorous campaign in South Carolina and across the country, the Charleston Five were cleared of felony charges. Ken Riley, the African American president of Local 1422 in Charleston, his brother Leonard and others went on to form a union-wide reform organization called the Longshore Workers Coalition in 1999. The LWC made a splash at the 2001 and 2003 ILA conventions. As one LWC activist described the 2003 convention, "It was like a fight for civil rights within the ILA for rank-and-file members, fighting against deeply established anti-democratic practices."[23] LWC members and leaders also participated in the ad hoc "Concerned ILA Members," which led a campaign to reject the 2004 master contract covering 15,000 workers on the East Coast. They got an unprecedented 45% "no" vote against the contract.[24] In December 2004, the LWC held a national meeting to plan a campaign for direct election of top officers and to discuss the eventuality of a RICO suit against the ILA.[25] Like TDU, the LWC has signed up thousands of members and is becoming a real organized force in locals up and down the East Coast. In the context of a government trusteeship, it is pushing hard for democratic reforms including the direct vote on top officers.[26]

Union reform movements face a recurring dilemma. It is never enough to change the faces at the top. What needs changing are the two fundamental relationships that define a union: the relationship of leaders to members and that between leaders (and the institution) and the employer. These relationships are themselves intricately intertwined.

The "business-like," routine bargaining relationship of the union leaders to the employer tempts the leaders to place some distance between themselves and their activities and the ranks of the union. To the extent that this becomes bureaucratized and institutionalized in the internal affairs of the union, the union leader is even freer to cut deals, exercise "partnership." The relationship of the employer to the members, i.e., their exploitation and, whenever possible, its intensification, on the other hand, tends to create on-the-job resistance or rebellion and, hence, to disrupt the "business-like" relation of leader to employer. This, in turn, increases the temptation of the leader to further insulate him or herself from rank-and-file influence. To break this pattern, a union reform movement must alter both the central relationships, if not simultaneously, certainly in rapid sequence. This is, of course, difficult to manage even with the best-organized movements in the best of circumstances. The task is further complicated by the persistence of a hierarchical culture that we learn from an early age. This culture lionizes authority, meaning top-down authority, and trains us to expect leaders to "do for us," a practice once criticized in the old debate over the "servicing" versus the "organizing" models. So, in addition to breaking up existing objective relationships at the top of the union, there is the task of altering the way union rebels and members view leadership in the first place. That is, replacing leadership from above with a notion of democratic, shared leadership coupled with grassroots authority. So, the burden of transformation is a heavy one, indeed; one that is likely to be even weightier in a period of retreat and in a movement that seems to put increasingly greater value on top-down leadership and centralized authority.

A tragic example of this problem unfolded in Transport Workers Union Local 100, whose strike was discussed above. For years, the opposition New Directions caucus organized workplace actions, and contract campaigns, fought for a more democratic structure, and challenged the old guard leadership in local union elections. New Directions went back to the mid-1980s when a group of militants founded the newsletter *Hell on Wheels*. Over the years it grew in numbers and credibility to the point where a direct electoral challenge was feasible. In the 1998 elections train driver and New Directions' candidate Tim Schermerhorn got 49.5% of the vote for president. All along the way, their proportion of Executive Board members rose. Finally in 2000, New Directions won. Its candidate Roger Toussaint beat old guard incumbent Willie James with 60% of the vote. A tone of militancy was adopted, a stewards' education program put in place, and other changes made. But Toussaint opted for one-man rule. He even told the independent New York civil service paper, the *Chief*, that he would centralize authority in the hands of a CEO—himself.

Toussaint's reign became almost paranoid as he demoted any of his former supporters who criticized his functioning or policy. Indeed, *Chief* editor Richard Steier wrote, "Mr. Toussaint has compounded his internal problems by taking harsh action against numerous former allies . . . The net effect has been to wind up running the union largely on the strength of his own will." With some sixty non-elected well-paid staff positions to wield as patronage and considerable constitutional authority, he held on to power even when former New Directions' leader and local recording-secretary Noel Acevedo ran against him.[27] The culture of hierarchy won and the relations between members and leaders and leaders and employers scarcely changed despite Toussaint's militant posture and reputation. The course of the three-day strike in December 2005 and its outcome revealed both continued determination in the ranks to change things and the existence of grassroots leaders prepared to mobilize that sentiment at key moments, but for the moment real change in the union as an institution had been thwarted.

Despite setbacks and defeats, rank-and-file rebellion does tend to offer an alternative view of unionism, to force changes even on reluctant leaders in many cases, and challenge the top-down culture of business unionism. Like struggle in general, it transforms many of those who take part. In the context of a broad upsurge, rank-and-file motion and organization will possess more power and legitimacy than in times of retreat—even though most union reform efforts of recent years are a response to that very retreat. Like other forms of resistance, rank-and file-union reform efforts can be understood as rehearsals for future struggles. They are also training grounds for future leaders. This function is crucial precisely because most unions provide little or no education or leadership training for rank-and-file workers. The experience of building rank-and-file-based organizations and engaging in union politics is a school in itself. Fortunately, such activists also have a number of organizations to turn to for education and various resources.

Resources for Reform

The oldest organization to provide aid to rank-and file-rebels and union reformers is the Association for Union Democracy. This organization traces its roots all the way back to the early 1960s when Herman Benson began publishing *Union Democracy in Action*. Benson was an experienced trade unionist and socialist who turned to helping union reformers by providing information about reform efforts and increasingly linking reformers up with sympathetic labor lawyers. In 1969, the Association for Union Democracy (AUD) was set up and in

1972, it took on a small staff. The newsletter became the *Union Democracy Review* and the staff and the literature it produced provided union activists with information on their rights. AUD would play an important role in the Miners for Democracy, Steelworkers Fight Back, and TDU as well as dozens of smaller reform groups in such unions as the Machinists, Painters, Laborers, Amalgamated Transit Union, the Transport Workers, Electrical Workers, Musicians, and many others. While a lot of its work involved litigation or dealing with the Department of Labor, it also conducted classes and held conferences on rank-and-file organizing and membership rights.[28]

Founded in 1979 as a monthly magazine for rank-and-file activists, *Labor Notes* has become another resource for those seeking to "put the movement back in the labor movement," as its original masthead stated. In addition to the magazine, it has published a series of how-to books, held weekend and day schools on many topics, and held biannual conferences that would draw around 1,000 labor activists. In addition to union democracy, *Labor Notes* has taken on a number of key issues since its founding. In a few cases it helped to frame the national debate on the topic. In the 1980s, it sought to educate union members about the nature and consequences of contract concessions, offering advice on how to fight them. This was done at a number of conferences and in a 1983 book by Jane Slaughter entitled *Concessions and How to Beat Them*. A few years later, the project entered the emerging debate about labor–management cooperation schemes, first with Mike Parker's 1985 *Inside the Circle: A Union Guide to QWL*, followed by *Choosing Sides: Unions and the Team Concept* by Parker and Slaughter in 1988. In 1994, these were updated with the publication of *Working Smart: A Union Guide to Participation Programs and Reengineering*, also by Parker and Slaughter. The books were accompanied by innovative weekend schools on employee participation and lean production that trained hundreds of activists in how to resist management-dominated programs. *Labor Notes* also published manuals on sexual harassment, free trade, and union democracy. Overall, *Labor Notes* projected an alternative view of unionism based on workplace power, membership mobilization, union democracy, independence from the employer, and alliances with other working-class organizations such as worker centers. Its biannual conferences became a showcase of trends and struggles that illustrated this vision of social movement unionism and inspired activists across the labor movement. By the 2000s they were bringing together union militants, worker center members, immigrant workers, and labor activists from many countries. Like AUD, *Labor Notes* continues to be a valuable resource for union activists fighting for a better labor movement.[29]

The vacuum of educational materials and events left by most unions was also filled by a number of other centers and publications. The

Union Communications Services provides mail order and internet links to a broad range of publications and sources of information. The journals *New Labor Forum* and *Working USA* both provide forums for analysis and debate over the future of organized labor, filling the vacuum left by the closure of *Labor Research Review*. Then there are the specifically labor-oriented websites, above all *Labour Start* out of Canada which provides access to union and working-class news in virtually every corner of the world. The Northland Poster collective provides materials for union and issue campaigns out of Minneapolis, while the Madison, Wisconsin-based cartoonists Gary Huck and Mike Konopacki produce remarkable labor-oriented cartoons. Finally, there are the literally thousands of workplace and local union newsletters and bulletins that are too numerous to mention but that provide information to members in countless workplaces.[30]

Immigrants on the March and on Strike

On May 1, 1886 hundreds of thousands of workers, many of them immigrants, struck across America for the eight-hour day, creating what would become International Workers Day almost everywhere in the world except the United States. One hundred and twenty years later on May 1, millions of immigrant workers struck and demonstrated for the right to work without harassment in the United States. It was called "A Day Without Immigrants," and many of the nation's worst-paying jobs would go unperformed for all or part of the day. If the estimates of 5 or 6 million participants are right, then perhaps as much as a quarter of the country's 21 million foreign-born workers took action of some sort. Unlike May 1, 1886, unions did not call this action and played only a supportive role in it. A network of some 600 advocacy and community organizations with strong backing from the Catholic Church served as the organizational backbone for May 1 and the March and April demonstrations that preceded it.[31] The turnout was all the more impressive because the organizers in different cities had different agendas. Some called for a boycott or stay-at-home, but others, like LA Cardinal Roger Mahony warned potential demonstrators not to risk their jobs.[32] Still, they turned out by the tens and hundreds of thousands in cities across the country.

Unions did play a supporting role. In Los Angeles, for example, they put up more than $80,000 and handled much of the logistics. SEIU and AFSCME leaders acted as liaison to the immigrant organizations and the Teamsters provided two 18-wheelers to lead off the march.[33] Labor support was aided by a dramatic change of policy by the AFL-CIO in 2000 when they embraced amnesty for undocumented workers. This, in turn, had been preceded by a demonstration of 15,000 in Washington, DC called by the National Coalition for Dignity and Amnesty. Indeed, this Coalition had been holding demonstrations on May 1 since 1999.[34] The growing interaction between immigrant groups and unions reached a high point when several unions went on to play a key role in the 2003 "Immigrant Workers' Freedom Ride," a caravan that crossed the country and ended in a mass demonstration in New York. This high visibility event helped to build self-confidence in going public with the issue of immigrants' rights.[35]

The actions on May 1 also revealed the often overlooked strategic position that immigrant workers have in some industries. The Mexican and Central American waterfront truckers in the nation's largest port, Los Angeles/Long Beach, discussed below, brought 90% of that port's activities to a standstill on May 1. The meat and poultry processing industry reported that 50% of its operations across the country had been halted on that day. The American Nursery and Landscaping Association said that 90% of its workers struck, as did a similar percentage of workers in garden supply warehouses. Construction was also heavily hit in many areas as immigrant workers, like the California drywall hangers discussed below, walked out for the day.[36] Thus, May 1, 2006 showed not only the strength of the immigrant workforce in significant parts of the US economy, but the willingness and ability of immigrant workers to act on their own despite the high risk of job-loss or even deportation. This fact is key to understanding the growth of both trade union and community-based organization among immigrants.

Workers in the new, post-1970s wave of immigration had been striking and organizing for some time—often on their own. While numbers of native-born union members have fallen over the years, those of immigrant workers have risen. The Migration Policy Institute estimates that the number of foreign-born workers belonging to unions rose steadily from about 1.4 million in 1996 to 1.8 million in 2003, and from 8.9% of union members to 11.4%.[37] In 1986, there had been a successful strike by Mexican women at Watsonville Canning that had become a *cause célèbre*. Though members of the Teamsters, they had drawn on their own resources and support from local officials and other unions to win.[38] But the strikes and self-organizing efforts of the 1990s and 2000s were different in important ways. Most of them occurred in industries that had once been unionized but had gone through a dramatic restructuring and/or work reorganization in the 1980s. The unions had declined or collapsed and with them wages and conditions. It is important to note, as Milkman and Wong show in their study of four such situations in southern California, that the exit of native-born workers came as a result of declining conditions and *not* as a result of the entrance of immigrant workers.[39] The immigrants filled mostly vacant and usually newly reorganized jobs. By the 1990s, the new workforce began unionizing, often on their own initiative.

If the carefully planned and centrally directed 1990 Justice for Janitors' strike was one of the first strikes by nonagricultural immigrant workers to capture public attention, the 1992 strike by some 4,000 drywall hangers in southern California pointed to something new. The strike was initiated and sustained by the immigrant workers themselves. While they would receive support from the Carpenters and eventually join that union, the immigrant construction workers organized and led the strike on their own terms, closing down the residential construction industry in much of southern California for five months. This was a piece of the residential construction industry that had gone non-union, like that in the rest of the country. In 1992, striking on their own, these drywallers would bring back the union—a union that had given up organizing this industry years before and was at first reluctant to bring the drywallers under contract. The organization of the strike initially came from immigrants from the town of El Maguey, Mexico, several hundred of whom worked in the industry. This pattern would be repeated in countless strikes and organizing drives.[40] The uniting of workers from the same place in new communities and in the same work had re-established links long broken for many native-born workers. As work and neighborhood became separated in the US over the years, Stan Weir noted, "Informal organization in the work process no longer has supplemental aid from informal organization in the neighborhood. Only as racial and ethnic minorities in the central city cores gain more employment in city industry does the advantage return."[41] The connection of common origin, shared neighborhood or community, and work provides a source of strength for immigrant organization in many cases. It had been a factor in the 1990s Justice for Janitors campaign.[42] It also helps explain much of the self-organization that has taken place among immigrant workers. A survey of efforts by immigrant workers to organize unions is beyond the scope of this book. But to get at the potential and dynamics of this key sector of the workforce, we will look at a few examples.

Like building services and construction in southern California, waterfront trucking had gone through a major restructuring in which Teamster jobs had been replaced by owner-operators and declining conditions in the 1980s. Once again, Latino immigrants filled the void. In 1988 and again in 1993, the truckers had struck with only informal organization. Though further organization was largely initiated by the workers themselves, Communications Workers of America Local

9400 offered to help. As owner-operators, the truckers had no rights to unionize or strike. Together, however, they planned a complex strategy that involved the creation of an "employer" and, in 1996, a strike. Unlike the drywallers' strike, the truckers' efforts failed, largely due to the massive efforts of the truck contractors and extensive legal barriers, but the potential of self-organization had shown itself once again.[43] The fight of the waterfront truckers, however, didn't end in the 1990s. In 2004 and 2005 they would strike again over government harassment and fuel prices. Then on May 1, the "Day Without Immigrants," they struck along with millions of others, once again closing the port of Los Angeles/Long Beach.[44]

This transformation from formerly unionized workers to owners or drivers who leased their equipment was common to other areas of transportation as well. Across the country in New York, both the taxi and "Black Car" or limousine services had been reorganized so that the fleet drivers ceased to be employees and became independent contractors who now had to lease their cars. In both cases, immigrant drivers organized themselves to resist the near-poverty earnings they made and the long hours they worked to make them. The reclassification of yellow cab drivers from employees working out of a fleet garage and earning a commission into independent contractors began in the 1970s. The last union, SEIU Local 3036, virtually disappeared in the 1980s and the traditional workforce moved on or retired. The proportion of truly owner-operated taxis with their own medallion, in effect the license required of every cab, dropped from 30% to 15% by the 1990s. The majority who had been employees earning a percentage of "the meter," now had to lease their cab and pay for their own fuel. They literally spent the first few hours of each day working off their daily lease-fee. In the 1990s, Asian drivers had organized an advocacy group to lobby for better conditions known as the Lease Drivers Coalition. Most of the drivers were now South Asians, mostly Indian or Pakistani, and the Coalition was ethnically based. In 1998, however, the group transformed itself into the New York Taxi Workers Alliance, open to all yellow cab drivers. In May 1998, the new organization surprised the city when virtually all 24,000 cab drivers struck for twenty-four hours. Although as independent contractors they have no collective bargaining rights, they have functioned as a union ever since with about 5,000 actual members. They scored an enormous victory in 2004 when they negotiated a fare increase with the city with 70% of the increase going to the drivers.[45]

The city's 12,000 "Black Car" drivers work for fleets that serve corporate customers who want the elegant cars for their executives and clients. But, like the taxi drivers, they are independent contractors who must lease these cars. After paying their lease fees and other expenses they make between $4.00 and $6.00 an hour. Most are South Asians, but there are also East Asians and Central Americans. In 1995, they began organizing themselves. In this case, through an acquaintance they approached District 15 of the Machinists. Unlike many unions in this sort of situation, the Machinists allowed the drivers to organize and lead their own local, Machinists' Lodge 340. In an unusual turn of events that does not seem to have been picked up by other unions, the Machinists won an NLRB case in 1997 declaring the drivers employees. In 1999, Lodge 340 won its first contract with one of the major companies. Resistance from employers was intense and because many drivers were Muslims they were frequently harassed by the Federal government after 9/11. Nevertheless, by 2005, Lodge 340 had 1,000 dues-paying members. The effort to organize the whole industry continues.[46] Unfortunately, unions are not always this attentive to those who try to organize themselves. When the mostly Mexican workers in New York's green grocery stores began to organize themselves in the 1990s, they were at first helped by UNITE! Local 169. In a jurisdictional dispute, however, they were passed on to UFCW Local 1500 which, by most accounts, was not particularly attentive to the needs of these immigrant workers. A similar case occurred with UFCW Local 338 in New York with African grocery store delivery workers who had also organized themselves before approaching the union.[47]

This phenomenon of common origin, community, and work doesn't only occur in big cities. The example of the Guatemalan workers at the Case Farms poultry plant in Morganton, North Carolina shows that it can work in a semi-rural area as well. These workers, Mayas from the same areas of Guatemala, composed the majority of the 500 workers in this plant. As in most poultry plants, the conditions were horrible and unsafe and in 1993 these workers staged a brief strike. This caused both the UFCW and the Laborers to look into this plant as a possible target for organizing. Although this was the UFCW's jurisdiction, it was the Laborers who won the trust of the Mayan workers, helping them through another strike in 1995 and on to union recognition. What was clear, however, is that the union found an organized group of workers. As one union representative put it, "We didn't organize anybody. There was a union there before the union got there." Unfortunately, neither the workers nor the Laborers' Union were able to force a first contract on the company. Rather than simply abandoning the Case workers, the Laborers agreed to fund the formation of a worker center that would be administered by the National Interfaith Committee for Worker Justice. The center would address the problems of the many Central American workers in that part of North Carolina.[48]

If it is true that union organizing among immigrants is often enabled by the overlap of place of national or ethnic origin, shared neighborhood or community, as well as common work, it should come as no surprise that much of the organizing that goes on among immigrants is community-based. This includes a very broad range of organizations providing services, advocacy, legal rights, education, political mobilization, and policy development. As we saw above, hundreds, of such organizations were involved in the massive mobilization of May 1, 2006. Many of these organizations serve or "do for" immigrants and are run by middle-class professionals focusing on broad issues of immigrant rights or social welfare. What concerns us here are those organizations that actually organize immigrant workers with a focus on their work, like the LIUNA-sponsored Workers Center in North Carolina.

Worker Centers and Non-Majority Unions

Worker centers differ from other community-based organizations in that they focus mainly, though not exclusively, on workplace issues. Most of them engage in a combination of service delivery, advocacy, and organizing. All three tend to focus on issues related to work: pay and failure to pay, health and safety, immigration status, various employment rights. It is the organizing function, however, that gives worker centers the potential to play an important role in the development of unionization and a broader social and political movement. As community-based organizations they are geographically bound. Most of the workplaces in which their members are employed are within or near the communities. In some cases, like those of day laborers or farm workers where the work itself may be distant, the center focuses on sites where workers obtain jobs (street corners, contractors, or agencies). In almost all cases it is the employer–employee relationship, the reality of exploitation, that gives the worker center its importance.[49]

The worker center phenomenon grows out of many of the changes in work itself that have taken place in the last thirty or so years, some of which were described earlier in the book. Subcontracting, sweatshops, exploding food service and hospitality industries, relocated/de-unionized industries, new retailers giant and small, etc. All of these sources of employment have in common low wages, poor benefits, and workers of color. Increasingly the latter are also immigrants. By 2005 there were, by one count, 137 worker centers, 122 of which dealt specifically with immigrant workers. Geographically, they reflect concentrations of immigration: 41 are in the Northeast; 36 on the West Coast; 34 in the South; 17 in the East North Central region; and the rest scattered around the West. Almost 80% of the workers involved are immigrants.

The relatively large number in the South tells us something about the geographic distribution of reorganized and subcontracted industries we have noted before. In terms of the regions of origin of those immigrant workers who participate in worker centers, about 40% come from Mexico and Central America, another 18% from South America, 15% each from East Asia and the Caribbean, 8% from Africa, 3% from Europe, and 1% from the rest of Asia.[50]

While the rise of worker centers has followed the rhythm of both work reorganization and immigration, it has come in three waves. The first group of centers began in the late 1970s and early 1980s, initiated by politically minded activists with some connection to union organization. One of the first was the Chinese Staff and Workers Association (CSWA) in New York City's Chinatown. The CSWA was born out of a 1978 drive by HERE Local 69 to organize the city's Chinese restaurants. Workers joined Local 69 but became disillusioned with the neglect they experienced. In 1979, those at Chinatown's huge Silver Palace voted to form their own union with the support of what became the CSWA. Others soon followed suit. CSWA organizers linked the independent unions to the community and went on to help workers not in unions as well and to deal with other neighborhood issues such as housing. One of their organizers explained their view of organizing:

> By organize, we don't just mean joining the union. We see the union as a means to organize something greater . . . We organize where we live and work.[51]

At least two other worker centers were formed around this time. La Mujer Obrera (the Woman Worker) in El Paso, Texas grew out of a garment workers' strike at Farah Clothing. Formed in 1981, it focused on women in the small garment shops on the border after the big outfits like Farah folded up or moved across the border and the unions left the area. The Black Workers for Justice based in Rocky Mount, North Carolina came out of a fight against discrimination at K-MART. It has been a pioneer of Non-Majority Unionism, the building of union organization in plants and workplaces where the union has yet to be recognized and have collective bargaining status. In the 1990s they joined with the United Electrical Workers (UE) to form UE Local 150 at the University of North Carolina. More recently, they joined with the Farm Labor Organizing Committee, which has successfully organized Latino farm workers in North Carolina, to form the Black–Latino Alliance.[52] Black Workers for Justice, the CSWA, and La Mujer Obera set the pattern of community-based worker organization for most of those that came after.

The second wave came from the late 1980s through the mid-1990s.

Many of these were driven by the wave of immigration from Central America as people fled the wars, death squads, and counter-revolutions that were largely the result of US foreign policy, as discussed in chapter 4.[53] One of the earliest second-wave worker centers was the Workplace Project based on suburban Long Island, New York. Founded in 1992, this was a spin-off of a Central American Immigrant service organization. The Workplace Project organized among those working in this suburban area's restaurant, construction, landscaping, and housekeeping jobs. Many of these workers were undocumented and were being paid well below the minimum wage. Often they worked as day laborers, gathering on street corners to be picked up by potential employers. The Project began by taking on legal cases to gain unpaid wages, which was a common problem for immigrants. But founder Jennifer Gordon realized this was not increasing the power or security of the workers. So, the Project hired Omar Henriquez, a Salvadoran, to help the workers organize to press their claims collectively, learning from the CSWA and La Mujer Obrera. In particular, day laborers who gathered on certain street corners organized and demanded a common wage and succeeded in increasing their earnings significantly.[54]

Another second-wave worker center is Make The Road By Walking located in Brooklyn's Bushwick neighborhood, one of New York's poorest. With new waves of immigrants in the 1980s and 1990s, Bushwick became a predominanutly Latino area. Make The Road is a multi-issue organization dealing with housing, education, community development, and even gay and lesbian issues as well as workplace problems.[55] The heart of its organizing program is Tabajadores en Acción, which focuses on local garment sweatshops and the area's retail stores which employ mostly immigrants at notoriously low wages. As in other worker centers, one of the main activities is recovering unpaid wages. In one year, they recovered $200,000 in back wages.[56] At one store, MiniMax, as organizer Deborah Axt explained:

> We won $65,000 in back wages. More important, though, was that the women were organizing to change the conditions of the workers who are there now. We were able to win paid sick days, an FMLA kind of coverage, and public posting of legal and workplace rights.[57]

Make The Road also worked with the Retail, Wholesale and Department Store Union to successfully organize a small athletic shoe chain, Footco, winning their first contract in January 2006.[58]

The third wave of worker centers came after 2000. According to Janice Fine, the leading academic expert on worker centers, more of these were connected to unions than in the past.[59] One example is the Restaurant Opportunities Center (ROC), set up in the wake of 9/11 by workers from the Windows on the World restaurant in the World Trade Center. Under pressure from displaced workers, HERE Local 100, to which the workers belonged, asked former workers to set up ROC as a self-help effort in 2002. Soon, however, it became an organizing project willing to work with those in restaurants the union hadn't approached in the past. Like other worker centers it helped non-union workers win back pay, paid days off, lunchbreaks and other improvements. ROC has its own Board composed mostly of immigrant workers, but still maintains a relationship with HERE Local 100, which acts as ROC's fiscal sponsor. Sometimes this is problematic. As one organizer put it, "HERE seems to have some trouble with letting go."[60] In part, ROC sustained itself by acting as a catering cooperative, but in 2005 it set up its own full service restaurant, "Colors."

While I cannot attempt a total survey of worker centers, no account would be complete without reference to the Coalition of Immokolee Workers (CIW) mentioned in the opening chapter. Founded in 1995, the Coalition of Immokolee Workers is a second-wave worker center. The CIW differs from most worker centers, however, in that it is rural and based mostly on farm labor, though workers from other low-wage industries also belong. Immokolee is a dirt-poor town in the midst of Florida's tomato fields. CIW members come mostly from Mexico, Guatemala, and Haiti. Although it is not affiliated with either the United Farm Workers or the Farm Labor Organizing Committee and does not regard itself as a union, it has used the same tactic as those unions to make major gains: the boycott. In fact, the CIW has used a number of tactics in its efforts to get Taco Bell, purchaser of most of the tomatoes the members grow, to pay a penny more per pound— enough to double their wages. They have organized three general strikes in the area, held a thirty-day hunger strike in 2003, and marched 240 miles across Florida to make their point. Some of these actions produced wage increases. It was, however, the boycott that finally won the amazing victory of several hundred farm workers over Taco Bell and its parent, fast food giant Yum! Brands, which also owns Kentucky Fried Chicken, Pizza Hut, Long John Silver's, and A&W. Like the UFW boycott in the 1960s and the FLOC boycott in the 1970s and 1980s, the Taco Bell boycott got widespread support from other organizations, including Jobs with Justice and church groups, and unions. Student "Boot the Bell" campaigns got Taco Bell kicked off twenty-two campuses by the time of the victory. Key to going national with their campaign was the network of other worker centers around the country that helped out. This reminds us that worker centers are becoming a nationwide force. What CIW won with this support would affect more than their own members. Yum agreed to double the percentage of the tomatoes' price going to the workers by a "pass-through" increase in what it pays.

Taco Bell agreed to buy only from growers who agree to the "pass-through." An enforceable code of conduct for fast food industry suppliers, with the CIW as a monitoring organization, was also part of the agreement. With the victory of the Immokolee workers and others that came before them like the Asian Women's Immigrant Association's victory over Jessica McClinock in the 1990s, worker centers have staked a claim as part of the American labor movement.[61]

Like any workers' organization, worker centers have their problems and limitations. Piven and Cloward long ago pointed out that the power of working-class people, including the poor, lies in "mass defiance," the ability to disrupt.[62] Potentially, worker centers have such power. Yet, while they can win things like back pay, at times help organize unions, and even unite to win a victory of national significance, they often lack real power in relation to the employers they are dealing with most directly. For the most part, they seldom have more than a few members in any one workplace, so that they do not have direct workplace power like a union. Direct disruption, therefore, is not possible. Thus, their tactics are usually pressure tactics. Often they are legal tactics dependent on lawyers. Furthermore, they are also dependent to a large degree on foundation funding and, hence, on professionals who write grant proposals as well as those who make the grant decisions. Yet, Steve Jenkins, a former organizer for Make The Road, who makes many of these criticisms in a thoughtful way, also notes:

> Worker's centers are an oasis of support and useful services for workers facing inhumane working conditions and who have few other resources available to them.
>
> Many are playing a central role in developing linkages between progressive unions and community-based organizing efforts that have the potential to strengthen both organizing arenas. It is possible that this will open up new strategies for organizing workers that improve upon traditional union-organizing models by broadening workplace struggles to involve the working class communities.[63]

A good example of just that was the successful campaign to organize four big meatpacking plants in Omaha, Nebraska. Here was the sort of situation we have discussed earlier in the book. The meatpacking industry had been drastically reorganized, the unions broken, and its new plants filled by recent immigrants from Mexico and Central America. It was the Omaha Together One Community (OTOC), a faith-based community organization affiliated with the Alinsky-inspired Industrial Areas Foundation, that first took notice of the plight of the packinghouse workers. In 1999 they held a mass demonstration of 1,200 people to protest these conditions. The OTOC, as a worker center, could spread the word and protest, but by itself it lacked the power to change things. Eventually, it decided that a union was needed and a joint plan to organize 4,000 workers was announced in June 2000. With the OTOC mobilizing the community as well as recruiting workers, the campaign was a success. This was a huge boost for the UFCW and a demonstration that this sort of alliance can bear fruit. There were, however, problems once the union began negotiating the contract. Basically, as we have seen before, the union officials didn't really listen to the workers. The contract they negotiated neglected many of the workers' most heartfelt workplace issues or the question of immigration status.[64] There is a gap between the cultures of most unions and many worker centers that needs to be addressed. In particular, union officials and staff need to see worker centers as part of the same movement, but with unique functions.

Perhaps the UFCW leaders have learned something from this. In 2003, they set up a worker center in North Carolina as part of their long-term effort to organize the 5,500-worker Smithfield hog-processing plant in Tar Heel, North Carolina. About 60% of the workforce are Latino immigrants and the UFCW has made a long-term commitment. Drawing on community leaders and activists, the union called a May 1, 2006 ("A Day Without Immigrants") rally and 5,000 people from many plants and communities showed up. Most plants had to shut down production for the day. In June, rallies were held in seven cities around the country. Here is where the union, the worker center, other community-based groups, and the national upsurge of immigrant workers came together.[65]

In August 2006, the AFL-CIO took a significant step toward greater unity of trade unions and worker centers when they reached an agreement with the National Day Laborer Organizing Network, a nationwide network of community-based day labor organizations, that would allow worker centers to affiliate with state and local labor councils. In late 2006, the New York Taxi Workers Alliance announced that it would affiliate with that city's Central Labor Council. These moves follow on other local efforts at cooperation between unions and worker centers, such as those described above and that between the Korean Immigrant Workers alliance and the building trades' Ironworkers Local 416 in Los Angeles in order to bring more immigrants into the union.[66] These recent developments represent a new direction in the way at least some of organized labor in the US sees itself.

Worker centers, in other words, have to be understood in the context of a broader *labor movement* of which they are one piece. Like unions trying new ways to organize and still not making huge breakthroughs, they need to be seen for their potential as much as for their current achievements and limitations. Their role is not so much in the direct exercise of power as in the gathering in of troops to highlight issues and aid in further organizing. Another idea of how they might play a role in new organizing tactics can be seen in another fairly new (for this era) approach to organizing, the non-majority or pre-majority union.

The typical failed organizing drive sees the union and its staff organizer leave town not too long after the defeat. A good union might offer legal assistance to workers fired during the drive, but for all practical purposes "the union" i.e., its institutional representatives and resources, have split the scene. Before there was an NLRB, unions often held on with only a minority of the workforce as members and no recognition except when it could force it. Today, this is what the non-majority union does. If it can't get the majority it needs to win an election or otherwise impose collective bargaining in its fullest sense, "the union," this time its members supported by the institution, stays on and represents the workers as best it can. It is a long-range strategy for unionizing an employer who has been able to thwart a particular organizing effort. Such an approach is mostly likely to be sustainable if it has support within the broader community as well as from the union.

A good example of this is found among the housekeeping workers at the University of North Carolina. Under North Carolina law, no state institution can engage in bargaining with a union. So, normal recognition is out of the question as are dues check-off or other union security measures. The Black Workers for Justice (BWFJ), one of the first worker centers, began organizing among the housekeepers, who are 88% Black and 70% women, in the 1990s. They formed the UNC Housekeepers Association, which in 1997 joined with other unionists in the independent North Carolina Public Service Workers Alliance, also largely a BWFJ project. Then, they affiliated with the United Electrical Workers to become Local 150 which would attempt to organize all 19,000 housekeeping workers on UNC's sixteen campuses. UE Local 150 hired Saladin Muhammed, BWFJ chair, as lead organizer. Without recognition Local 150 nevertheless proceeded to act like a union. It organized mass grievances and Grievance Brigades made up of workers, students, and community activists. "Walkthroughs" and pickets by community leaders also highlighted issues. Eventually, Local 150 won the right of workers to join the union without retaliation, to file regular grievances, and to "meet and confer" with management on issues. By 2003, Local 150 had signed up 3,000 dues-paying members, a "pre-majority" union, but a union nonetheless.[67] Other examples of pre-majority unionism include the Communications Workers of America's Washington Alliance of Technology Workers, WashTech, which works among high tech workers in that state, and the Alliance@IBM/CWA Local 1701, which has 6,000 members throughout IBM. These latter two make extensive use of the internet.[68] Pre-majority unions offer an example of what should be done almost as standard operating procedure for unions serious about organizing in difficult situations. If the SEIU offers some strong pointers on how to lead-up to an organizing drive, pre-majority unions give us an idea of what to do when it doesn't work out the first time.

Convergence or Upsurge?

The examples presented in the brief survey of working-class resistance, rebellion, and immigrant organizing are not meant to be proof of a coming upsurge or event. As argued in chapter 1, simply adding up labor and social movements is neither a formula for upsurge nor a strategy for changing the balance of forces in American society. It is the upsurge that is mostly likely to bring a convergence of movements, not the other way around. My purpose, once again, is to show that the very social and economic conditions that have disoriented organized labor also drive various pieces and sectors of the working class, union and yet-to-be union alike, to struggle in one form or another. These struggles can and do at times reinforce one another and can play an important role in organizing as yet unorganized or un-unionized workers. Upsurge, however, comes when more working-class people experience the pressures imposed by capitalism's insatiable drive to improve profitability in a competitive world. The other side of almost any upsurge we can look at in the past is a sign of hope: an improved type of organization suited to the times, fissures in the capitalist class itself, a string of exemplary victories, and so on. No one can predict these. But the organizations and movements that exist today can do their best to prepare themselves to take full advantage of any such breakthrough. This includes some sense of strategic thinking among union leaders and activists that goes beyond the "line of least resistance" orientation of following "landlocked" industries regardless of the actual social and economic forces they bring to the equation of power. It means looking at some of the trends discussed in earlier chapters and relating them to what has been said above.

PATHS TO POWER, ROADS NOT TAKEN

This chapter will ask how some of the economic changes discussed earlier point to key areas of strategic focus in terms of organizing the unorganized and how these can interface with some of the new forms of organization and key demographic and geographic trends. This will not be a recipe for success or a simple road map to power. Every possible path to power one can point to will have its own problems and barriers. A good starting point is with one of the more sensible contributions to the pre-split debate on the future of the unions. Titled "Democracy, Density and Transformation: We Need Them All," the challenge issued by IUE/CWA Local 201 President Jeff Crosby is worthy of our attention. He wrote, "It would be helpful at the start if all parties acknowledged the difficulties of finding a way to come up with solutions to the on-going decline of the movement we love."[1] The point he makes is that there are no panaceas. Density can be important, but it doesn't guarantee much of anything if power is not applied. In any case, as Crosby points out, there are different ways to measure density. Democracy matters because it helps mobilize members, develops leaders and keeps them in touch. Transformation is needed because none of our unions has got it right in all ways. None of these things is easy.

So, with this grain of salt in mind, I want to point up some directions that seem to me to lead to the kind of power organized labor, in the broad sense, needs if there is to be any change in the balance of forces that underlies the horrible economic, social, and political context in which working-class people and organizations are forced to function. Here I will look primarily at four dimensions: industry, geography, demographics, and strategy or tactics. None of this is to say that what I will focus on is all that needs to be done or that those organizing in other areas should drop everything and change direction. One of the lessons of recent years is that successful organizing is often a long-term proposition and those engaged in successful organizing should stick with it. In the final analysis every industry and occupation that can be organized should be organized. The movement as a whole, however, also needs priorities and focus if breakthroughs are to be made.

Making and Moving it in the South

As argued in chapter 3, this is still an industrial society. The making and moving of goods and other tangible commodities (energy, communications) remain at the heart of capital accumulation. Much of the service sector that has arisen in recent decades rests on the production of goods. It is the increasing complexity and global span of bringing these goods to completion and final sale that call forth rapidly growing service employment. Even so spectacular a retailing power as Wal-Mart is only a means of moving goods to market. It relies on the production of such goods and even when they are imported on their transportation to the place of final sale in the US. To seek the heart of power, the unions will need to go beyond the comparative safety zone of the landlocked service industries, to the multinational corporations that dominate the economy and the realm of politics as well. Looking at US multinational corporations, the giants who must be tamed by labor to affect power relations, we see that mining, utilities and manufacturing firms produced 52% of their domestic value added in 2000. That doesn't include construction or transportation. Retail trade, home to the mighty Wal-Mart, accounted for just under 7%. Major producer services barely 5%.[2]

As I also argued in chapter 3, in the past half a century industry has shifted to the South with the result that the region has gone through a significant industrialization making it the center of about 30% of manufacturing output, 37% of construction, about 28% of foreign investment, and an important focus of sea, land, and air logistics. As a consequence of this transformation, 36.8% of the region's workforce are employed in manufacturing, construction, utilities or transportation, slightly more than the US average of 35.8% as of 2003. In six Southern states this percentage is over 40%.[3] Yet, as Table 11.1 shows despite half a century of industrialization, hourly wages in manufacturing in most Southern states are well behind the national average and even further behind industrial states with higher than average union density. Only three Southern states are above the national average and one (Louisiana) above that of one of the four Northern industrial states (New York) with high union density. Indeed, union density in the South averages 5.8%, compared with 15.5% in the Northeast, 16.3% in the Midwest, and 16% on the West Coast.[4] By itself, this difference goes a long way to explaining the gap in manufacturing wages, while

Table 11.1   Average Hourly Manufacturing Wages in Selected States, 2003.

	Wage	# Production Workers
US	$15.74	
South		
North Carolina	$13.66	434,000
South Carolina	$14.19	212,000
Georgia	$14.08	330,000
Alabama	$13.56	205,000
Tennessee	$13.56	291,000
North		
Michigan	$21.28	506,000
Ohio	$18.00	596,000
Indiana	$17.84	408,000
New York	$16.78	398,000

Source: *Statistical Abstract*, 2006, pp. 648, 653.

the difference in benefits is, if anything, much greater. What, then, explains the lack of unionization in the South?

The simplest explanation in terms of the near past is that few unions have tried it. There have really only been two periods or moments of hopeful effort towards breaking the anti-union barriers posed by Right-To-Work laws, intense open racism, and a culture that has successfully defined unionism as the equivalent of Communism for many. The last such effort came toward the end of the 1960s when Martin Luther King turned his attention to economic inequality and the Poor People's Campaign. With the Memphis sanitation workers' strike in 1968, he came to see the unionization of the South as a key to ending poverty. Had he not been assassinated in Memphis he would have gone on to Charleston, South Carolina in support of 1199's efforts to win a contract for hospital workers there. Gains were made in the public sector in Southern cities, and later in textiles, but few unions took up the call, particularly after King's death.[5] The civil rights era, however, showed that changes in the South had made a mass movement possible. The mechanization of cotton culture, the beginnings of industrialization, and the migration of African Americans into Southern cities, as well as northward, changed the balance of forces. The Black rural population in the South plunged from 11.9 million in 1950 to 4.1 million in 1969. The cities became a power-base for the Black community.[6]

The first post-WW2 attempt to organize the South began in 1948 with the CIO's Operation Dixie. The twin self-made stumbling blocks upon which Operation Dixie eventually floundered were the CIO leaders' attitude toward race and their attitude toward Communism. They tried to avoid the race issue by focusing on textiles, in which most workers were white. By the time the campaign was launched the CIO "mainstream" leaders were already at war with the Communist leaders of several CIO unions. Their evasion of the race issue at the very moment it was heating up in the South was bound to fail. Their obsession with Communism undermined their ability to work with other unions in the region. The irony was that despite their efforts to circumvent the race question and exclude Communists from the drive, Southern employers and politicians labeled the CIO as Communist "race-mixers."[7] Although the South was changing even then, neither industrialization nor urbanization had yet undermined the power of the old rural oligarchy, nor their ideological hold over the white population. That would come with the civil rights movement.

The South today is not free of its history or the dominant white culture of the past, but neither is it the same. Its major metropolitan areas have grown, some spectacularly. Just to cite a few: the Atlanta Metropolitan Statistical Area grew by nearly 50% from 1990 to 2004; Charleston, SC by 40%; Raleigh, NC by 61%; Tallahassee, FL by 27%; Knoxville, TN by 20%; Memphis, TN and Montgomery, AL by 16%; Norfolk-Newport News by 13%; and so on.[8] Demographically, the South has become one of the most diverse areas of the country. It has always, of course, been home to a large part of the nation's African American population. As a proportion of the country's Black population, the South fell throughout the twentieth century. By 2000, however, the South stabilized as home to 48.1% of Blacks in the US and by 2004 this had risen slightly to 48.2%. Almost a third of the nation's Latinos are located in the South. Much of this population is concentrated in Florida and Texas, but it has been rising fast in other southern states due to immigration.[9] By 2005, almost 30% of the nation's foreign-born civilian non-institutional population (9.7 million) lived in the South. They also composed just under 30% of the employed workforce (6.4 million) throughout the region. The largest number were in the southern Atlantic coast states from Virginia to Florida.[10] The immigrant population of North Carolina grew by 274% from 1990 to 2000 and its Latino population by 394% in that decade.[11] This represents an enormous change in the demographics of the South.

Industry has gone well beyond the traditional "New South" triad of coal mine, cotton mill, and railroad. Steel and textiles are mostly gone, but others have come to take their place. As we saw in chapter

3, the South is now home to a healthy portion of the US auto industry. Another industry that has grown rapidly in the South in recent years is meat (including poultry) packing and processing. Nationally, meatpacking, including slaughtering and processing, has grown from a little over 300,000 production workers in the mid-1980s to between 430,000 and 440,000 by 2006. In the eight Southern states where it is important it has grown or remained stable for the last decade and a half. These eight states account for just under 60% of the industry's nationwide employment.[12] We looked at the changes in this industry earlier in relation to the declining membership of the UFCW. Since that time, this industry has gone through even more enormous changes. It has seen a geographic shift and concentration, a move to larger plants, a corporate consolidation, a change in employment demographics, and a dramatic fall in wages. According to a Federal Reserve study, from 1963 to 1992 the percentage of employment in poultry processing in the South rose from 58.6% to 72.9% of that nationwide. That of processed meats (sausage, bacon, etc.) from 15.4% to 32.8% and that of meat packing from 23% to 24.5%. The same study concludes "that the meat industry is moving into bigger plants at a very rapid pace."[13] The North Carolina Smithfield hog-processing plant being targeted by the UFCW employs 5,500.[14]

A report on the industry done by the UFCW reform group REAP also noted that the industry has gone through a severe corporate consolidation in recent years. The reports says:

> The meat packing industry has become highly concentrated as the actual production and sales have fallen into the hands of fewer and fewer companies. The four largest beef packers increased their share of the industry's slaughter and processing output from 25 percent in 1977 to 80 percent in 2002. Over the same period of time, the four largest hog packers increased their share of the hog slaughter from 36 percent to more than 65 percent.[15]

Ten companies controlled 80% of the sales of the entire industry. Smithfield Foods, Tyson, Cargill, and Swift & Co. dominate beef and pork, while Tyson, Gold Kist, Pilgrim's Pride, and ConAgra dominate poultry, controlling 50% of the industry.[16] A key result of concentration of the industry increasingly in the South, often in rural areas, has been stagnation or even a drop in real wages. Real hourly wages in slaughtering fell from $6.41 in 1993 to $6.30 in 2003, while those in meat processing rose slightly from $6.84 to $6.91 over that ten-year period.[17] Table 11.2 shows real wages in the three sectors of the industry for the South and the Midwest, where much of the industry is still located, though mostly in rural parts of that region. Real wages

Table 11.2   Real Hourly Wages in Food Processing by Industry Sector and Region, 1982–92.

Region	1982			1992		
Urban	Packing	Processing	Poultry	Packing	Processing	Poultry
MW	$15.44	$14.56	$8.18	$8.68	$10.79	$9.05
South	$10.62	$10.04	$7.05	$7.72	$9.01	$7.07
Rural						
MW	$15.43	$13.80	$7.94	$8.79	$9.78	$7.74
South	$10.07	$8.83	$7.20	$7.87	$7.69	$7.07

Source: Drabenstott, Henry, and Mitchell, *Economic Review*, Federal Reserve Bank of Kansas City, Third Quarter 1999, p. 80.

dropped in all but one sector, urban Southern poultry, where they rose by two cents. What the table also shows is that the differential between the Midwest and the South remains large. To some extent, this reflects the difference in unionization. Nationally, the industry as a whole has gone from 80% union in 1980 to less than 50% today. Most of that is in the Midwest or Great Plains, very little in the South.[18]

Meatpacking has been the major source of employment for the growing immigrant and Latino population in the South. The Case Farms plant in North Carolina was 80% Latino immigrant, while the Smithfield plant targeted by the UFCW is 60% immigrant, with Blacks accounting for another 30%.[19] The employment of immigrant workers has been a major feature of the reorganization of this industry across the country. Since the 1980s percentages such as those at Case or Smithfield have been typical in meatpacking plants from the Great Plains, where Asians also play a large role, to the South.[20] The immigrant workers in meatpacking exist in the context of a much larger immigrant population in the region, as we saw above. On May 1, 2006 immigrant workers in North Carolina brought a number of factories to a standstill. It seems very likely that they will play a key role in organizing meatpacking in the South.

Focusing on the auto industry might seem an odd choice given the current and recurring problems of General Motors, Ford, Delphi and others in the traditional core of the US industry. What has happened, however, is not so much a crisis or decline of the *industry* per se as its reorganization. In addition, of course, was the recession which caused new car and truck production to drop from an all-time high of 13 million in 1999 to 11.4 million in 2003 and then up to 12.1 in 2004. Domestic car and light truck sales fell from 14.5 million in 2000 to

13.3 million in 2003 and then went up to 13.5 million in 2004. Despite the drop, both sales and production were well above the level of the 1990s.[21] The recession combined with continued restructuring in the parts sector, however, did cause a net loss of 194,000 production jobs from June 2000 to June 2006, a loss of about 18%. Three quarters of this was in the parts sector, in large part due to corporate consolidation in that sector. Even with these losses, the number of production workers in mid-2006 (895,000) remained slightly above the average of the early 1990s. Announcements by GM in 2006 about cutting an additional 50,000 jobs and Ford another 25,000–30,000 will hurt the traditional sector of the industry even more.[22] The problem is that the traditional "Big Three" and some of their suppliers have lost ground not only to imports, that now make up 27% of the market, but to foreign-owned "transplants" in the US that now account for 30% of domestic motor vehicle production. According to one study, "by 2003, transplant factories employed nearly 53,000 people, with an additional 9,000 jobs expected by the end of 2006 as manufacturing capacity continues to expand." The foreign-owned domestic producers include: Honda, Toyota, Nissan, Hyundai, BMW, and Mercedes/ Daimler-Chrysler. Much of this new production is located in the South: Mercedes in Alabama, Nissan in Tennessee and Mississippi, BMW in South Carolina, Toyota in Texas, Hyundai in Alabama.[23] As we saw earlier, these assemblers, in turn, have attracted both their own and independent parts suppliers to the region, creating, in effect, a new auto industry. In the six Southern states where motor vehicle and parts production is significant, employment grew steadily through the 1990s up to mid-2006 when there were over 200,000 workers, the most recent figures available as of this writing.[24] There was no recession in the Southern auto industry. The very success of this part of the industry was part of what underlay the crisis of the traditional auto companies.

In strategic terms, it makes a great deal of sense to begin with a focus on auto and meatpacking in the South. Both have grown in the South; both are characterized by a high degree of corporate consolidation, presenting manageable targets, and both are partially unionized in other parts of the country. In the case of auto in the South this concentration is heavily based in foreign-owned companies. Both auto and meatpacking also rely heavily on transportation and logistics for both their production chains and the delivery of the final product to market. The auto industry, for example, lies largely along Interstate highway I-75, running as a spatial assembly line from Michigan to Florida intersected by various East–West Interstates. I-95 is another North–South artery connecting auto parts and assembly. The vertically integrated meatpacking industry of the South is similarly linked by major highway and rail connections. This points to a third major focus: transportation and logistics. Trucking and warehousing, the core of logistics, have grown steadily from an average of about 900,000 employees in the early 1990s to 1.3 million in mid-2006.[25] The obvious starting point here is southern-based, former Overnite, now UPS Freight. As with auto and meatpacking much of transportation is already union, including, of course, UPS. Logistics, however, involves more than transportation or even storage, it is the overall guidance of a system of moving goods in a timely or just-in-time manner. This involves computers and those who operate, design, and program them, who will be communications technicians and professionals. Perhaps there is a role for the CWA, which already has members throughout the South in telecommunications, and outside the South in non-majority organizations among these technical workers such as WashTech at Microsoft.

The unions that would be at the center of such a focused organizing effort would be the UAW, the UFCW, and the Teamsters. All three have made some efforts in this direction, but nothing that amounts to a major push. It seems fairly clear that if it were simply left to each individually, there would be no more progress than has already been made. Clearly, more of "more of the same" won't work. A much bigger operation involving many unions and organizations in various supportive as well as direct organizing roles is needed. The split in the labor movement, of course, raises serious questions about broader coordination. But first, let's look at what "assets" the labor movement, broadly defined, has in the South.

Southern Assets

The extremely low union density for the South, an average of 5.8% for the region, seems to indicate there isn't much to start with in the region itself. But looked at in a more strategic way, there are important pockets of unionism, some quite established and stable, from which to draw support. Unions such as the CWA in telecommunications, the two postal unions in that piece of communications, the Teamsters in many national trucking firms and in rail as well, are all to be found throughout the South; the ILA in the ports and the AFSCME, AFT, and ATU in various municipalities and the building trades in the growing urban centers. All these and others provide a core, particularly in major cities, of potential support. There are, after all, over 2 million union members in the twelve states we are counting as the South. Almost half these are in the states along the Atlantic coast.[26] If only 1% are activists, this is 100,000 to 200,000 people working in important sectors. If a real effort is made to activate a much larger proportion of the membership the potential force of rank-and-file organizers is even greater.

There are also the worker centers. Florida's Immokalee workers as well as the North Carolina meatpackers have already shown the potential of immigrant workers to organize and act. In the South Atlantic states there are twenty-four worker centers, seven in North Carolina alone. Some, such as North Carolina's Black Workers for Justice (BWFJ) and South Carolina's Carolina Alliance for Fair Employment (CAFÉ), which regards itself as a union for non-union workers, have already worked with unions to bring unions and workers' rights to their states.[27] Because of their presence in immigrant communities many worker centers have the ability to reach out to workers in targeted plants and legitimize the idea of unionism in their communities. Their emphasis on leadership training also offers potential for furthering the process of grassroots unionization. The worker centers have another key role to play: that of bringing Black and immigrant workers together. CAFÉ has done that and the BWFJ has worked with FLOC in North Carolina to form the Black/Brown Alliance.[28]

North Carolina, which has one of the lowest union densities of any state, presents an example of some of the problems and possibilities. In 2005 there were only 107,000 union members in the state. Almost half of these belong to the fairly conservative State Employees Association of North Carolina, which is being courted by the SEIU. The Teamsters have about 8,000 members and the CWA and Steelworkers about 6,000 each, not an impressive force by themselves. Furthermore, the 2005 split at first brought disunity in the state AFL-CIO and a number of Central Labor Councils.[29] At the same time, there is organizing going on in North Carolina. The United Electrical Workers Local 150 has been organizing cleaning staff at the University of North Carolina with the aid of the Black Workers for Justice and, as mentioned earlier, have recruited 3,000 members and won a grievance procedure and other gains.[30] There was also the 2004 victory of the Farm Labor Organizing Committee in North Carolina, winning the right to represent some 8,000 immigrant "guest workers" after signing up 4,000 of them and getting an agreement from the North Carolina Growers Association.[31] After losing union members since 2000, North Carolina gained 10,000 new union members in 2005, bringing membership up from 97,000 in 2004 to 107,000 in 2005. In 2006, the UAW won representation elections at three Daimler-Chrysler subsidiaries in the state. Furthermore, in 2006 the Teamsters were organizing among school bus drivers and, of course, the UFCW at Smithfield.[32] In 2006 several of the "disaffiliated" Change to Win locals accepted Solidarity Charters and re-affiliated with the state

AFL-CIO.[33] The example of North Carolina indicates that while new organizing is possible, it will really take more of a national effort focused on the South to turn these small victories into larger ones. It also points to a role for worker centers and other groups in the cases of both UE Local 150 and the Smithfield campaign.

There are plenty of good ideas out there about how to organize most effectively. Studies by Bronfenbrenner, Juravich, Hickey, Lopez, and others show again and again that the involvement of rank-and-file workers, worker-based organizing committees, acting like a union from the start, direct action, and the employment of a full range of tactics work. Yet, most unions avoid these approaches and tactics or use only some.[34] Beyond the question of the tactics and strategies of individual organizing drives, however, is the bigger question of creating momentum: the perception by more and more workers that organizing works and brings tangible gains in income, benefits, and conditions on the job. Here the Change to Win program offers some important ideas: "Multi-union organizing campaigns, and multi-union support for each other's organizing drives, strikes and other actions"; "coordinating committees for organizing and bargaining in specific core industries"; "actions, including strikes, in other cities or metro areas to support demands for recognition and contracts in one area" to mention a few cited in a November 2005 CTW press release.[35] Have these things been done?

Nothing sets people in motion like people in motion. Southerners of all kinds are much more likely to take up the risks involved in unionizing if union members around the country are on the move. I have argued that you can't simply create an upsurge or a mass movement. But when you have organizations with millions of members and hundreds of thousands of officials and activists, you can certainly create a sense of motion. This is something, however, that cannot simply be initiated, much less turned on and off, at the top. This is not just a matter of another "campaign" or occasional "street heat," but of giving people the power and responsibility to act in ways that will certainly challenge the norms of business unionism. That means organizing around the country, putting pressure on companies targeted in the South at their unionized facilities elsewhere, it means mobilizing and involving members on a scale not seen in decades.

What about Wal-Mart?

Wal-Mart is the 800-pound gorilla in the discussion of organizing. It is now the largest employer in the US, possibly the worst employer in the US, it is everywhere, and it is growing. As Lichtenstein argues it is the "template" for the model modern corporation with its "pull" power on suppliers, its high tech just-in-time systems, its low-wage cowed workforce, its seemingly unstoppable competitive advantage, and its Southern organizational culture. It is hard to imagine a revitalized and powerful labor movement in the US without a unionized Wal-Mart. There are, nonetheless, two reasons for *not* making Wal-Mart an immediate priority. The first is its size and scope. It cannot be organized store-by-store, almost everyone agrees. So, where to start? I believe the place to start, when the time comes, is the South—its homeland, administrative center, and power-base. To organize it will require a regional approach where unions can reach its workforce at home as well as at its stores. Furthermore, the industries that form key parts of its life-blood, transportation/logistics and local or regional food processing, are not yet unionized enough in the South or elsewhere to affect the big box giant. Right now, unionism is too weak in these areas in the South to take on such a project. Unlike auto, meatpacking, and transportation there is no union base in this company.

The second objection involves the major union and current strategy for attacking Wal-Mart. So far, the "strategy" has been external: demonstrations, lawsuits, efforts to stop the placement of new stores. Some are successful in their own terms, stopping new stores, inflicting wounds around discrimination, overtime cheating, etc. But these cannot organize Wal-Mart's *workers*. Related to all of this is the union with the jurisdiction, the United Food and Commercial Workers. The UFCW's record of lost strikes and failed organizing drives is too consistent and too visible to make this union the likely David to Wal-Mart's Goliath. A realistic long-term strategy would involve a coalition of unions and community groups capable of reaching Wal-Mart workers where they live and prepared for a long-distance run. It seems to me to make more sense to build unionism in the South in those areas discussed above and possibly others as well, forge a coalition of unions across AFL-CIO/CTW lines dedicated to supporting an all-out organizing drive (not just the external tactics now being deployed), and otherwise lay the basis for a future assault on this foundation of a low-wage economy.

What Kind of Labor Movement?

Motion is the quantity in the equation of power. But there must be quality as well if workers are to be attracted to unions in their millions. As I have argued, union power must be deep as well as broad and wide. That sort of power begins in the workplace or on-the-job and in the local union. Membership involvement, leadership accountability, and union democracy are indispensable elements of a power that can be exercised by millions in a place and manner that impacts capital. The occasional recognition or contract strike is important but not enough. The hand and mind of labor must not only be removed from the making, moving, and providing of the nation's goods and services at certain times, but must be there to regulate it at any time. This is a regulation in conflict with capital not in partnership with it. It is a power to regulate the flow of the surplus which is capital's lifeblood. This throttle cannot be controlled from insulated headquarters hundreds of miles from the scene. So, strong and vital workplace organization is the first principle of union revitalization and new organization.

The second and closely related principle is union democracy. We have seen how controversial the idea, let alone the practice, of union democracy is. Traditional business unionism, of course, has no use for it. But the newer, more aggressive organizing unionism of the SEIU and others is even more explicit in rejecting democracy not only as unnecessary, but, by implication, a barrier to effective action and organizing. We've dealt with this earlier and here will only briefly look at some of the major reasons why union democracy must be a central part in the rebuilding of organized labor in the United States. Drawing again on Parker and Gruelle's *Labor Notes'* book, *Democracy is Power*, here are some of the arguments in favor of union democracy. They state flatly, "internal union democracy is key to union power." Why? Because, they argue:

> First, a union will act in the interests of its members only if those members control the union.
> Second, the power of the union lies in the participation of its members, and it requires democracy to make members want to be involved.

Third,

> A union run by the members is also more likely to exercise power. When the members run the union, they have chances to measure their collective strength against the boss, and gain the confidence to use it.

Finally,

> when members are in the habit of using their heads to figure out the problems of running the union—handling disagreements among themselves, setting priorities for scarce resources, and learning each other's concerns—they have more effective ideas for dealing with management's assaults as well.[36]

This last point can hardly be over-emphasized and it is one that seldom appears in the literature of union revival or organizing. The old revolutionary Frederick Engels saw the democracy of the early trade unions in Britain as "the military schools of the workingmen," the place where workers learned the arts of class warfare. Later he saw the experience of workers "in the management of their colossal Trade Societies" as schools that made workers "fit for administrative and political work."[37] In managing unions, workers learn skills that apply not only to the conflict of day-to-day trade unionism and collective bargaining, but to bigger organizational, strategic, and political matters as well. Top-down bureaucratic unions can't serve that function. Since union members, singly and collectively, will make mistakes, just as officials do, they need to have a way of learning and correcting mistakes. That way is union democracy.

To amplify their power, unions need to reach out to one another, but also to the larger working class. Mainly, this involves organizing the as yet non-unionized majority. Even this, however, calls for more than an army of organizers, mobilized ranks, and a full quiver of tactics. There are other working-class organizations out there, as we have seen. Important among them are the worker centers discussed in the previous chapter. These can help introduce workers to the unions, legitimate them, and, hopefully, also get some support from the unions. Worker centers can be a way for unions to reach groups that are not always directly accessible, above all immigrant workers. We have seen examples of this from Brooklyn to North Carolina. The mass outpouring of May 1, 2006 indicates a good deal of existing organization in these communities, including but not limited to worker centers. Unions need to be aware and respectful of such organizations. Jobs with Justice provides a model of more or less permanent cross-union action that is part of the equation. There are also more *ad hoc* types of labor-based coalitions like the living wage campaigns that have provided a grassroots version of political action, usually independent of any party or candidate-based organization.

Living wage campaigns have brought unions and communities together that have never worked together before. What started in Baltimore in the mid-1990s has become a nationwide phenomenon, with seventy-seven cities passing living wage ordinances by 2002 and campaigns in another seventy cities underway.[38]

This brings us to the conception of social movement unionism. In its earlier use, it was derived from the practice of unions like those in South Africa and Brazil that played a leading role in the fight for democracy and had close links with the working-class communities their members lived in. They acted like movements, not just collective bargaining agents. But these unions, those of the CUT in Brazil and

COSATU in South Africa, were based first and foremost in the workplace which was the source of the cohesion and power that allowed them to lead the broader movements. They did not lean on the "community" so much as they led it. Today, the term social movement unionism has been adopted by a wide spectrum of people with very different views. It has lost much of its unique meaning. Often it seems to mean union + community + issue campaigns. There is sometimes the implication that the union increases its power from leaning on or allying with various community and issue groups. I think this misses the point about where power lies and how to amplify it. Unions should ally with community-based working-class organizations and should have a broad political agenda. But, the primary reason for this is that the unions bring both their organized numbers and their social-economic power to this agenda. It was CUT and COSATU that brought added power to the *favelas* and townships, not the other way around. Social movement unionism is above all a matter of how the union acts itself, not just who it is allied with. Unions act on a broader agenda not because workplace issues aren't political, they are, but because they cannot address the full range of issues that working-class life calls for. Social movement unionism attempts to draw together a broader range of groups to forward a class agenda. But it will be unable to do this if its neglects or bypasses the fundamental issues that affect the union's members. Necessarily, we always return to the first principle: the power the class possesses by virtue of its place at the heart of capitalist accumulation in the workplace or on-the-job.

The Harvest of Empire: Again

Globalization begins at home. We tend to see it as an external force: imports, low-wage labor abroad, outgoing and incoming foreign investment, immigrants from around the world, and so on. But much of what we call globalization centers on the expansion of the US economy and its corporations since the end of World War 2. Until fairly recently, the bulk of the transnational corporations (TNCs) that forged the world-wide markets were US-based. Long before globalization "invaded" the US with cheap products, US capital went out in search of profits to the far corners of the world and called forth global markets. Global markets, however, run two ways. The largest employer in the country, one that avoids immigrant workers, rests on globalization. I am speaking, of course, of Wal-Mart. Without its cheap imports it would be just another Sears. On the other hand, there are the industries that rest on the low wages of immigrant labor, from restaurants and greengrocers in New York to factories in Los Angeles to hog slaughtering plants in North Carolina. Many of these immigrants, as we saw, are the refugees from American corporate investment abroad and the foreign policy and military adventures that have backed it for a century. Then there is oil! Oil in Iraq, oil around the Caspian Sea, oil in Saudi Arabia, oil whose representatives seem to drive US foreign policy. Today, that foreign policy puts our military in over 150 countries, not only in the wars of the moment (Iraq, Afghanistan), but in a network of bases from central Asia, around the Caspian Sea and to the Persian Gulf, as well as in the Pacific and elsewhere. Along with super-costly hardware, much of which can never be used and some of which doesn't work, all this imposes a "defense" budget that drains national wealth and limits political possibilities as well as displacing people abroad. All of this corporate, political, and military expansion amounts to what is now virtually a global empire.[39] Globalization is the polite and neutral sounding name given to this empire and the lesser ones that clash with it. A labor movement at the heart of empire has no choice but to act in opposition to its expansion and perpetuation. This is a matter of deep self-interest as well as of international solidarity and simple morality.

What to do? The most obvious thing would be to develop links with workers and unions abroad who work in the same industries and transnational corporations. Indeed, some unions do this. The SEIU, CWA, USWA, UAW, UE, and others have forged more or less permanent ties to their counterparts in various countries with the advantage of sharing information and exchanging actual support of one sort or another.[40] This direct contact is in addition to whatever relations exist within the international trade secretariats, worldwide federations of national unions, for many major industries. There have also been unofficial links at a more grassroots level, such as those organized by the Transnational Information Exchange (TIE), discussed in my 1997 book *Workers in a Lean World*. These were efforts to organize face-to-face contact between workers in a number of industries, including automobile and telecommunications across borders in North America and Europe. This was done through cross-border meetings by industry as well as through more ongoing contact and information exchanges.[41] There are also *ad hoc* campaigns such as the CWA's efforts in support of Colombian workers and the boycott of Coca Cola organized by Corporate Campaigns, Inc., because of its support for the Colombian government and its suppression of trade union rights. But there is also much work to be done at home.

The cluster of policies and institutions that enforces open markets, unrestricted overseas investment, and globalization of economic activity in general is called the Washington Consensus. Its key policy elements are privatization; market liberalization/deregulation; national budget austerity for developing nations; and the free flow of investment. The enabling institutions are the World Bank, the International Monetary Fund, and, most recently, the World Trade Organization (WTO). Except for the WTO they are based in Washington and implement policies proposed by Washington, hence the name Washington Consensus. The role of the United States government, in particular the Department of the Treasury, is predominant. According to Nobel Prize winner and former World Bank chief economist Joseph Stiglitz, the Washington Consensus took shape in the 1980s; that is, under Reagan. Stiglitz sees this as a departure from the IMF/WB regulatory role of an earlier era which, he writes, "was replaced by the free market mantra of the 1980s, part of a new 'Washington Consensus'—a consensus between the IMF, the World Bank, and the US Treasury about the 'right' policies for developing countries . . ."[42] The net result of this consensus, as Stiglitz and others point out, is that most developing nations are locked into a debt trap that keeps them poor, imposes low wages, and promotes the export of low-cost goods. Needless to say, it also fuels the enormous human migration that has characterized the last two decades or more. The poor nations, the low wages, the cheap goods, and the human beings in search of a decent living are the harvest of the empire that rules from Washington.

A movement against this global set-up arose in the 1990s around the world. In the US it burst onto the political scene in Seattle in November/December 1999. The explosive events of those days were significant because of the alliance of usually disparate forces such as environmentalists, global justice activists, and organized labor. The AFL-CIO brought 30–40,000 union members and although the official labor march and rally avoided confrontation, a few thousand union members joined those determined to disrupt a key meeting of the world elite. In this they had some success and Seattle was followed by similar demonstrations around the world. It showed, once again, the power of disruption. The activists in Seattle, of course, didn't start this movement against the enablers of globalization. There had been strikes and mass actions in Third World countries and Europe for years.[43] But when forces in the US in the heart of the globalizing empire joined the opposition it was a great stride forward. Tragically, the terrorist attacks on September 11, 2001 took the wind out of the sails of the movement and its labor component in particular. Other movements, however, have arisen in the wake of US intervention in Iraq. US Labor Against the War had united union leaders and activists from many unions in opposition to this disastrous military adventure.

Politics: The Road Not Taken

In the history of American labor, the alternative view to business unionism's approach to politics has a name: a labor party. It is an idea that recurs in each period of upsurge and often in retreat as well. In most, it gained some following or credibility even in the highest strata of the unions. It is an idea that straddles the deep-rooted commitment to the system of the business unionist, the reform impulse of the same and of the dissidents as well, and the underlying reality of class in America. It simultaneously raises and avoids or puts off the question of "ultimate goals," because its statement of class allegiance implies something bigger than "liberalism" in an American context without necessarily stating the bigger goal. Each time it has failed for lack of institutional support, itself a consequence of the many ties of the leadership strata, institutional, financial, or legislative, national, state, and local to the Democrats and the institutions they run. For most labor leaders at most times, the idea of a break with the Democrats is like looking into a political abyss in which the bottom is not visible and the way across not yet clear. This is not simply a matter of the national level, but of local and state politics as well. Yet, the idea constantly returns.

It is as old as the Workingmen's Party of the Jackson era and the years just after the Civil War. The party exploded in 1886 in the midst of a major labor upheaval, winning many local elections and nearly taking New York City.[44] Perhaps its first large-scale emergence was in the early 1920s after the failure of the labor upheaval of 1918–19 and the splintering and collapse of the Socialist Party. Pushed at first by the Communists through the Trade Union Educational League, it achieved considerable popularity in many unions. While this effort failed, Labor and Farmer–Labor Parties arose in several states during the 1920s and 1930s.[45] It was prominent in the debates in the AFL in the 1930s before the CIO split and in 1936 at the UAW's 2nd convention when the delegates passed a resolution in favor of a labor party over the opposition of the leadership. These efforts along with the state-level third parties were marginalized by the appeal of the New Deal for most labor leaders, but the idea would return in the 1940s just after the war.[46] In his book, *The New Men of Power*, C. Wright Mills reported that 13% of AFL leaders interviewed in 1946 and 23% of CIO leaders favored formation of a labor party within the next two or three years. When the timeline was stretched out to "eventually," with an implication of ten years, those favoring a labor party rose to 23% for the AFL and 52% for the CIO.[47] Of course, the longer view is much easier than a commitment to the near term. It was this noncommittal approach that the UAW took in 1948 when, to counter the Communist-backed Progressive Party candidacy of Henry Wallace, they passed a convention resolution calling for a "genuine progressive political party" at some unspecified time after the 1948 election.[48] The deepening institutionalization of the Democratic Party orientation would all but kill labor party sentiment in the 1950s.

As the examples of the 1920s and 1940s suggest, the idea of a labor party as an alternative to the Democratic Party gets traction in periods of perceived political defeat or betrayal as well as in those of upsurge. It surfaced marginally in the 1960s and 1970s in some strikes and in the demands of some rank-and-file groups, for example, the United National Caucus in the UAW.[49] But, the idea of a labor party was eclipsed by social movements that owed little to labor, even when friendly, and sought other types of alternative political action from the Mississippi Freedom Democrats to the Peace and Freedom Party when they didn't simply embrace the Democrats. It arose again in the 1990s, clearly a time of retreat. The idea, or at least the push to popularize it, came from the late Tony Mazzocchi, secretary-treasurer of the Oil, Chemical and Atomic Workers (OCAW). Mazzocchi was a unique figure in US labor in the 1980s and 1990s whose career deserves far more attention than it has been given. Working within what was a fairly conservative union of relatively well-paid workers, he pushed the limits of business unionism on health and safety and other issues in the 1970s. In advocating for a labor party he pushed beyond the conventions of business unionism. Along with a new OCAW president, Bob Wages, Mazzocchi helped to change the political culture of his union in the 1990s, which became the leading organization in advocating for a labor party. They used a survey prepared by the Labor Institute with which Mazzocchi was affiliated to get the idea across and discovered widespread support. This union of mainly well-paid white workers, many in the Southern oil fields and refineries, would lead a creative coalition campaign against BASF to end a five-year lockout, forge long-term coalitions with environmental justice groups, and provide the cadres in Louisiana to fight the candidacy of racist David Duke. Through internal education and debate, the OCAW was won to the labor party position long advocated by Mazzocchi.

In 1996, with the initial backing of four national unions, Labor Party Advocates became the Labor Party at a convention in Cleveland. The four sponsors, OCAW, United Electrical Workers, Brotherhood of Maintenance of Way Employees, and the International Longshore and Warehouse Union, were soon joined by the United Mine Workers, the American Federation of Government Employees, the Farm Labor Organizing Committee, the California Nurses Association and dozens of local unions. With 1,367 delegates and 200 observers, the Labor Party seemed off to a good start. At the same time, the convention rejected the idea of running candidates, deciding the party would be a pressure and campaigning group for the time being.[50] Two years later, the Labor Party held its first Constitutional Convention in Pittsburgh, attracting 1,209 delegates and the same six national unions. Attempts were made to resolve the questions of running candidates and of the structure of the party. The emphasis, however, was to be on issue-based campaigning, particularly its new Just Health Care campaign for a national single-payer health care system.[51]

Although it still exists and runs a series of campaigns, the Labor Party did not take off as hoped. While there are many views on why this happened, my own is that it suffered from three major unresolved problems. The first was the central strategy for growth. As *Labor Notes'* Jane Slaughter reported in 1996, while much of the party's activist base came from the local chapters, "The leadership, however, feels that the key to growth is the affiliation of local and national unions."[52] The hope that more national unions would affiliate was simply unrealistic. Even though affiliation did not require a union to cease endorsing or working for Democrats, the leaders of most of the larger International Unions were too institutionally committed to various Democrats and too concerned with recapturing Congress and then the White House to associate with such an effort. Mazzocchi reported just before the founding convention that the biggest question on the minds of union officials was, will it hurt Clinton?[53] In effect, by the time of the 1998 convention, with six national unions, 177 local unions, central labor councils, and regional bodies, and a variety of endorsers (not affiliates), the Labor Party had reached the limits of the growth by this affiliation strategy. Many in the Labor Party favored a more "bottom-up" approach to organizing. Chris Townsend of the UE noted the problem of further affiliations when he told *Labor Notes*, "How do you build a Labor Party in a labor movement where so many unions are dominated by business unionism? We're (the UE) starting with the accessible activists at the shop and local level: the stewards, delegates, local officials." But only the OCAW, UE, and BMWE even conducted recruitment drives among *their own* locals.[54] Without an aggressive campaign among locals of other unions the party could not have grown further, and that would have required stepping on the toes of International Union leaders who would not appreciate efforts among their members. Even this strategy became more difficult when both the OCAW and BMWE were gobbled up in separate mergers with larger unions that did not share their commitment to the Labor

Party: the OCAW into what became PACE and then merged into the Steelworkers and the BMWE into the IBT.

A second problem was that of structure. Perhaps not surprisingly, the Labor Party reflected the hierarchical structural norms of the labor movement itself. The affiliated national and regional unions received the overwhelming share of votes at its conventions. Furthermore, the role and nature of the local chapters remained unresolved, with no connection to national or local unions. This gave the party the aura of two distinct organizations, with the chapters frequently dominated by the far left, on the one hand, and national and other official organizations by high level union leaders, on the other. Greater weight for local unions as well as more aggressive organizing among them might have filled in a middle part of the structure.

The biggest problem, however, was the question of engaging in electoral politics. Both the affiliation strategy of growth and the structure of the party weighed heavily against the new party running its own candidates in opposition to Democrats. While leaders from the UE, OCAW, and ILWU favored limited experiments in elections, Mazzocchi and most national union leaders did not. For example, both the political director and president of the affiliated American Federation of Government Employees were members of the Democratic National Committee in 1996 and clearly opposed running independent candidates.[55] Rich Trumka, by this time secretary-treasurer of the AFL-CIO and deeply involved in Democratic politics, would certainly have been opposed as well. So, even the modifications made at the 1998 convention, which opened the door a crack toward Labor Party candidates, were very restrictive. In fact, until an experimental campaign in South Carolina in 2005–2006, the Labor Party abstained from elections. For all the difficulties of running independent candidates, a party that abstains from the electoral process will not be seen as a party at all. As a pressure group it competes with thousands of other issue-oriented organizations, coalitions, and interest groups. In any event, as a pressure group it cannot really put forth the idea of a working class seeking power.

The nineties were not the best of times for such a project. Mergers still seemed a way to offset lost numbers. Partnership was still thought to bring a union some influence in company policies. There was still belief in Clinton and new hope in Sweeney. But the barriers to the success of the Labor Party within organized labor tell us much about the possibilities of independent class political action in the near future. The great barrier, it should be no surprise, is the business union bureaucracy. It is not simply that they don't like the idea, but that they have too much at risk. The remaining breadcrumbs of political influence. The last shreds of stable bargaining relationships. The importance of being "inside the Beltway." All these hold the business union leaders to the old political course.

If there are to be steps toward independent political action by unions, they will most likely have to come from somewhere besides the top levels of all but a handful of unions. Whether or not the existing Labor Party can provide a framework or support for experiments and efforts toward independent labor-based political action remains to be seen. The Labor Party probably surprised many when in the summer of 2006, it gathered some 16,000 signatures, more than enough to get on the ballot in South Carolina where the Longshore workers we met above along with a number of other unionists in that state decided it was time to try something new. They chose the Labor Party as their vehicle. Whether they achieve ballot status and/or do well in the elections remains to be seen, but the effort tells us not to be too sure about just what is impossible. It also reminds us that the South may offer some opportunities other regions may not.

A break with the two-party system will take more than the unions. It must appeal to the working class as a whole. But it is worth remembering what organized labor does have to offer a new class politics in the US. Dan Clawson summarized the importance of the labor movement succinctly when he wrote:

> Despite unions' decline, they remain perhaps the most powerful and diverse progressive force in the United States today. The 16.3 million union members include 6.7 million women, 2.4 million African Americans, and 1.6 million Latinos. Unions have more women than NOW (National Organization of Women), more black members than the NAACP, more members than the Sierra Club. If we include the families of union members, 40 million Americans are directly affected by union victories and defeats. Moreover, while many members of organizations are involved only via mailing lists, unions have more than thirty thousand locals and chapters with regular meetings and elected officers. Many of these are far from vibrant, but others have impressive programs and activities and an active political culture.[56]

Veteran union reformer Herman Benson puts the number of family members directly affected at 50 million and estimates "a cadre of perhaps 100,000 officers, organizers, and staffers."[57] To this we would add at least a few hundred thousand local union rank-and-file activists. What matters most is what is out there in terms of working-class organization with the potential, even very long-range potential, of pushing in that direction or even taking independent steps toward electoral engagement. Local unions are a source of strength and organization in politics as in collective bargaining and workplace conflict. Along with the other organizations and movements described earlier, they can lay the basis for a new class politics. Given the institutional barriers to such action, it seems most likely that the beginnings of an upsurge in *direct action* in workplaces and communities by a variety of groups will be a prerequisite to independent electoral action. Direct action, of course, takes place all the time both on the job and in a variety of communities. What is required is an increase in actions and their convergence into the bigger stream that amounts to a social movement inside and outside of unions, by the active elements of the many pieces of the working class. Leaders and unions cannot manufacture such an upsurge. But neither can they wait for it to happen. The actions of organizations and leaders today can help to lay the basis for bigger things to come, just as inaction, timidity, bureaucracy, or "more of the same" can stifle them.

Pulling the Strands Together

What has been argued in this book runs, to a certain extent, counter to many of the explanations for organized labor's decline and crisis in the United States. These cannot be explained, I have argued, by the rise of a post-industrial economy, the displacement of goods production by that of services, or even by imports or foreign competition more generally. The economy, I have argued, remains an industrial economy in terms of its final output despite the rise of service jobs. The rise of retail, finance, and producer service industries rests primarily on the growing complexity of both producing and circulating goods and the economic surplus produced by them, some of it generated by the crisis of profitability itself. The loss of manufacturing jobs, the only group of industrial jobs to decline, occurred almost entirely in three industrial groups: primary metals, textile products, and garments. Thus, the decline of unionism in such manufacturing industries as auto, rubber, machinery, electrical equipment, and food production, not to mention non-manufacturing industries such as construction, communications, and transportation, is largely explained by geographic shifts within the US and technological displacement, on the one hand, and the failure of the unions to follow the jobs and organize the now nonunion sectors of their industries, on the other hand.

The failure to organize is not a general one stretched over the post-WW2 years. Historians frequently quote George Meany's famous 1972 remarks that he was not worried about organizing, "Why should we worry about organizing groups of people who do not appear to want to be organized?"[58] This attitude certainly contributed to the problem of declining union density that had begun after 1953. But, the fact is that unions did attempt to organize in those years. The collapse of new organizing came almost a decade later at the crucial turning point of the recession of 1980–81 as did the fall in membership, the decline of strikes, and the simultaneous rise of concessions, labor–management cooperation schemes, and union mergers. The tight correlation of all these trends in a very short period of time points to a massive change in behavior by most unions. This was an institutional change. But it could only have been brought about so rapidly and completely by a leadership in command of the highly bureaucratic structures that characterized most unions that allowed leaders to turn on a dime at the start of the 1980s. As we saw, the rank-and-file upsurge of that epoch had lost most of its momentum by that time and the leaders regained their authority. They were, of course, encouraged in this direction by a deeply ingrained business union ideology and practice shared to some extent by those sections of the membership most closely tied to the leadership by a system of incentives and privileges that had evolved in the collective bargaining system—high salaries, full-time workplace reps, lost time, junkets, etc. The leadership and some of its close followers had opposed the militancy of the upsurge of 1966–78 and had abandoned their own tactical/occasional militancy. In doing so, they simultaneously abandoned new organizing, with NLRB representation elections falling to half their previous level in 1980–81 and declining after that with little or no recovery even in the Sweeney years. So, the problem underlying labor's crisis is one of leadership, ideology, and structure that has yet to be addressed.

Efforts by reform movements to address some or all of these problems have, so far, failed to have enough lasting impact to turn things around. The rise of immigrant organization, whether on the job or in the community, likewise has yet to gain the power to alter the direction of today's unions or create ones strong enough to by-pass them. Yet, these and other positive trends are precisely the types of forces and actions that can be magnified by a general upsurge. The ideas needed to change organized labor into a force powerful enough to alter the balance of class forces in the US are all there competing with the old ideas and practices of business unionism and the newer, not yet fully solidified, strain of corporate unionism. It is as well to remember that the upsurge of 1966–79 became "plainly visible," as Stan Weir wrote in 1966, suddenly after simmering since the 1950s. Just as the collapse of the leadership in 1980–81 was a sudden, unpredicted act, so was the rapid onset of the upsurge. The possibilities of that upsurge were both provoked and limited by the reaction of the leadership and, hence, the unions as institutions, just as they were limited by the fragmented activities and limited vision of the militants and rebels of that era. The hope for the next upsurge is that there is a clearer vision with a wide enough base and an experienced grassroots leadership to push beyond the limits of the ideology, practice, and personnel of business unionism in its old and new forms. If it is hard to imagine such an upsurge today, it will change minds and lives when it, like that last one, becomes "plainly visible."

NOTES

Chapter 1

1 Jane Slaughter (ed.), *A Troublemaker's Handbook 2: How to Fight Back Where You Work—and Win!*, Detroit, Labor Notes, 2005, p. 148.
2 Yum! Brands, "Earnings Release," February 6, 2006, www.yum.com.
3 Slaughter, p. 149.
4 *Ibid.*
5 *Labor Notes*, #330, September 2006, pp. 3–4.
6 *Labor Notes*, #327, June 2006, pp. 1, 6; #329, August 2006, pp. 1, 10–11.
7 This point was well and sharply argued in Frances Fox Piven and Richard A. Cloward, *Poor People's Movements: Why They Succeed, How They Fail*, New York, Vintage Books, 1979, *passim*.

Chapter 2

1 James K. Galbraith, *Created Unequal: The Crisis in American Pay*, Chicago, University of Chicago Press, 1998, pp. 129–131.
2 For accounts of this see Nelson Lichtenstein, *State of the Union: A Century of American Labor*, Princeton, Princeton University Press, 2002, pp. 212–245; Kim Moody, *An Injury to All: The Decline of American Labor*, New York, Verso, 1988, pp. 165–219.
3 Bennett Harrison and Barry Bluestone, *The Great U-Turn: Corporate Restructuring and the Polarizing of America*, New York, Basic Books, Inc., 1988, pp. 1–52.

4   Organization for Economic Cooperation and Development, *Historical Statistics, 1995 Edition*, Paris, OECD, 1995, p. 154; Council of Economic Advisors, *Economic Report of the President 2002*, Washington, US Government Printing Office, 2002, pp. 333, 370, 372, 381, 426 (Henceforth *Economic Report*, plus year).

5   Robert Brenner, *The Boom and the Bubble: The US in the World Economy*, New York, Verso, 2002, p. 27; Ernest Mandel, *The Second Slump: A Marxist Analysis of Recession in the Seventies*, London, New Left Books, 1978, p. 36.

6   Galbraith, pp. 76–78; *Economic Report*, 2005, p. 269.

7   Anwar Shaikh and Ahmet Tonak, *Measuring the Wealth of Nations: The Political Economy of National Accounts*, Cambridge and New York, Cambridge University Press, 1994, pp. 125–126. The "S" in Shaikh and Tonak's account stands for the total surplus created by productive labor. Profit, as reported by businesses and government, is actually only a portion of S, which must also cover management salaries, administrative costs, overheads, etc. This is why the profit rate seems so high compared with government statistics. Nevertheless, the S/K ratio gives us a better picture of the actual performance of the economy and the relationship of "living" to "dead" labor.

8   Shaikh and Tonak, pp. 125–127; *Economic Report*, 2005, pp. 208, 284.

9   Brenner, p. 46; *Economic Report*, 2005, p. 328.

10 Harrison and Bluestone, p. 9.

11 Brenner, pp. 13–14, 41, 56; Harrison and Bluestone, pp. 9–10.

12 William Abernathy, *The Productivity Dilemma: Roadblock to Innovation in the Automobile Industry*, Baltimore, Johns Hopkins University Press, 1978, pp. 38–39, 72–73.

13 For a thorough discussion of this dynamic see Howard Botwinick, *Persistent Inequalities: Wage Disparity Under Capitalist Competition*, Princeton, Princeton University Press, 1993, pp. 123–142.

14 Shaikh and Tonak, p. 127.

15 Kim Moody, *Workers in a Lean World: Unions in the International Economy*, New York, Verso, 1997, pp. 41–50.

16 United Nations Conference on Trade and Development, *World Investment Report*, New York, United Nations, 1993, p. xx; 1995, p. 1; 2004, pp. xvii, 9 (Henceforth *World Investment Report*, plus year).

17 Moody 1997, pp. 46–48.

18 Economic Policy Institute, *EPI Journal*, Winter 2004, p. 1.

19 *Labor Notes*, #298, January 2004, p. 9.

20 *World Investment Report*, 2006, p. 6.

21　Bureau of Economic Research, *U.S. Direct Investment Abroad: Balance of Payments and Direct Investment Position Data*, and *National Data, Selected NIPA Tables*, www.bea.gov; *Economic Report*, 2005, pp. 208, 221.

22　Lawrence Mishel, Jared Bernstein, and Sylvia Allegretto, *The State of Working America 2004–2005*, Ithaca NY, Cornell University Press, 2005, p. 179.

23　Brenner, p. 215.

24　Kim Moody, "The Offshore War," *New Politics*, Vol. 10, No. 2, Winter 2005, pp. 65–67.

25　Kate Bronfenbrenner and Stephanie Luce, *The Changing Nature of Corporate Global Restructuring: The Impact of Production Shifts on Jobs in the US, China, and Around the Globe*, Submitted to the US–China Economic and Security Review commission, October 14, 2004, pp. 1–2, 3–6, 26–28.

26　US Department of Labor, "Union Members in 2005," *News*, USDL 06–99, February 20, 2006, p. 1; Bronfenbrenner and Luce, p. 36.

27　William Zeile, "Operation of US Affiliates of Foreign Countries," *Survey of Current Business*, August 2004, pp. 192–205.

28　For Harvey's own summary of the concept see, David Harvey, *The New Imperialism*, New York, Oxford University Press, 2003, pp. 94–124.

29　*Economic Report*, 2005, p. 181.

30　*Statistical Abstract*, 2004–2005, p. 630; *Economic Report*, 2005, p. 332; *Labor Notes*, #311, February 2005, pp. 1, 14.

31　*Statistical Abstract*, 2001, pp. 393–394; Bureau of Labor Statistics, *Employment and Earning*, B–4, www.bls.gov.

32　*Statistical Abstract*, 2001, p. 803; 2004–2005, p. 814; *Economic Report*, 2005, p. 217.

33　Robert Scott, *U.S.–China Trade, 1989–2003: Impact on Jobs and Industries, Nationally and State-by-state*, Washington DC, Economic Policy Institute, 2005 pp. 5–8.

34　Kristin Forbes, "Comments at NABE's 2004 Washington Economic Policy Conference," March 25, 2004, p. 5.

35　Scott, p. 9.

36　*Statistical Abstract*, 2001, p. 802; 2004–2005, p. 814; Brenner, p. 215.

37　Brenner, p. 241.

38　*Statistical Abstract*, 2004–2005, pp. 208, 210, 218.

39　*Ibid.*, p. 407; *Economic Report*, 2005, p. 270.

40　*Statistical Abstract*, 2004–2005, p. 407.

41　Galbraith, pp. 129–131.

42　*Ibid.*, pp. 127–132.

43 Lichtenstein, pp. 231–232; for a detailed account of labor in the New York City fiscal crisis see Kim Moody, *From Welfare State to Real Estate: Regime Change in New York City, 1974 to the Present*, New York, The New Press, 2007.

44 Lichtenstein, pp. 233–234; *Labor Research Association—Online, March 2001;* Moody, 1988, pp. 165–187.

45 Moody 1988, pp. 165–187; *Economic Report*, 2005, p. 268.

46 *Labor Notes*, #292, July 2003, pp. 1, 14.

47 *Labor Notes*, #295, October 2003, pp. 1, 11; #320, November 2005, pp. 1, 8–9.

48 *Labor Notes*, #298, January 2004, p. 4.

49 *Labor Notes*, #306, September 2004, pp. 1, 14.

50 *Labor Notes*, #320, November 2005, pp. 8–9.

51 *Ibid.*, pp. 1, 8–9.

52 David Noble, *Forces of Production: A Social History of Industrial Automation*, New York, Oxford University Press, 1984, pp. 52–56, 240–241.

53 Tony Smith, *Technology and Capital in the Age of Lean Production: A Marxian Critique of the "New Economy"*, Albany NY, State University of New York Press, 2000, p. 35.

54 Joan Greenbaum, *Windows on the Workplace: Technology, Jobs, and the Organization of Office Work*, New York, Monthly Review Press, 2004, pp. 69–71.

55 *Labor Notes*, #307, October 2004, p. 8.

56 Edna Bonacich, "Pulling the Plug: Labor and the Global Supply Chain," *New Labor Forum*, Vol. 12, Issue 2, Summer 2003, pp. 41–48.

57 *Labor Notes*, #221, August 1997, p. 5.

58 For a more complete critical discussion of lean production and team concept see Mike Parker and Jane Slaughter, *Working Smart: A Union Guide to Participation Programs and Reengineering*, Detroit, Labor Notes, 1994, *passim*; for a positive view of "high performance work systems" see Eileen Applebaum et al., *Manufacturing Advantage: Why High-Performance Work Systems Pay Off*, Ithaca, Cornell University Press, 2000, *passim*; Moody 1997, pp. 85–113; Smith, pp. 1–91.

59 Parker and Slaughter, p. 3.

60 Moody 1997, pp. 90–92.

61 Parker and Slaughter, p. 4.

62 Moody 1997, p. 96.

63 Applebaum et al., p. 227.

64 Moody, 2005 p. 65.

65 *Ward's Automotive World*, April, 1996, pp. 3–5.

66 *Labor Notes*, #247, October 1999, p. 14.

67 *Labor Notes*, #245, August 1999, pp. 8–9.

68 Bennett Harrison, *Lean and Mean: The Changing Landscape of Corporate Power in the Age of Flexibility*, New York, Basic Books, 1994, pp. 47, 144–145.

69 *Labor Notes*, #264, March 2001, p. 12.

70 *Labor Notes*, #309, December 2004, p. 6.

71 Mishel, Bernstein, and Allegretto, pp. 256–273.

72 US Census Bureau, 2002 *Economic Census: Manufacturing*, General Summary, p. 1.

73 Kim Moody and Simone Sagovac, *Time Out! The Case for a Shorter Work Week*, Detroit Labor Notes, 1995, pp. 15–17, 33–34.

74 Mike Parker and Jane Slaughter, "Unions and Management By Stress," in Steve Babson, *Lean Work: Empowerment and Exploitation in the Global Auto Industry*, Detroit, Wayne State University Press, 1995, p. 45.

75 *Labor Notes*, #313, April 2005, p. 4.

Chapter 3

1 US Bureau of the Census, *The Statistical History of the United States: From Colonial Times to the Present*, New York, Basic Books, 1976, p. 139.

2 *Economic Report*, 2005, pp. 264–265.

3 Bill Goodman and Reid Steadman, "Services: Business Demand Rivals Consumer Demand in Driving Job Growth," *Monthly Labor Review*, Vol. 125, No. 2, April 2002, p. 7.

4 *Economic Report,* 2005, p. 221.

5 Harry Braverman, *Labor and Monopoly Capital: The Degradation of Work in the Twentieth Century*, New York, Monthly Review Press, 1988, pp. 41–48, 179–187, 203–245; Ian Wyatt and Daniel Hecker, "Occupational Changes During the 20th Century," *Monthly Labor Review*, Vol. 129 No. 3, March 2006, p. 36.

6 Wyatt and Hecker, pp. 38–48; *Statistical Abstract*, 2001, p. 393, 2005, p. 630; *Monthly Labor Review*, Current Labor Statistics, April 2006, p. 68.

7 Saskia Sassen, *The Global City: New York, London, Tokyo*, Princeton, Princeton University Press, 1991, p. 90.

8 *Economic Report*, 2005, pp. 264–265.

9 Goodman and Steadman, pp. 5, 11.

10 Braverman, pp. 188–196.

11 US Department of Labor, "The Employment Situation", *News,* USDL 06–777, May 5, 2006, Table B2.

12 Goodman and Steadman, p. 6.

13 Brenner, pp. 81–82.

14 *Ibid*, pp. 16–22, 40–41, 89–91.

15 Brian Page, "Rival Unionism and the Geography of the Meat-packing Industry," in Andrew Herod (ed.), *Organizing the Landscape: Geographical Perspectives on Labor Unionism*, Minneapolis, University of Minnesota Press, 1998, pp. 281–293; Roger Horowitz, *Negro and White, Unite and Fight: A Social History of Industrial Unionism in Meatpacking, 1930–90*, Urbana, University of Illinois Press, 1997, pp. 245–279; Moody 1988, pp. 314–327.

16 William Adler, *Mollie's Job: A Story of Life and Work on the Global Assembly Line*, New York, Scribner, 2000, *passim*; Jefferson Cowie, *Capital Moves: RCA's 70-Year Quest for Cheap Labor*, Ithaca, Cornell University Press, 1999, *passim.*

17 *Statistical Abstract*, 2001, p. 620; 2002, p. 393; 2006, p. 648; Donald Dodd, *Historical Statistics of the United States: Two Centuries of the Census, 1790–1990*, Westport CT, Greenwood Press, 1993, pp. 442–460.

18 Karsten Hülsemann, *Greenfields in the Heart of Dixie: How the American Auto Industry Discovered the South*, paper presented at "Second Wave of Southern Industrialization" Conference, Georgia Institute of Technology, June 5–6, 1998, pp. 1–19.

19 *Labor Notes*, #306, September 2004, p. 10; BLS, *State and Area Employment, Hours, and Earnings*, Customized Data Tables, September 16, 2006, www.data.bls.gov.

20 William Zeile, "US Affiliates of Foreign Companies: Operations in 2003," *Survey of Current Business*, Bureau of Economic Analysis, August 2005, pp. 206–207.

21 William Zeile and Kenneth Johnson, "Regional Patterns in the Location of Foreign-Owned US Manufacturing Establishments," *Survey of Current Business*, Bureau of Economic Analysis, May 1999, pp. 1–14.

22 *Statistical Abstract*, 2004–2005, pp. 26–28.

23 *Ibid.*, pp. 679, 685.

24 *Ibid.*, 2004–2005, p. 675, 676; *Economic Report*, 2005, pp. 218, 279.

25 David Harvey, *The Limits to Capital*, Chicago, University of Chicago Press, 1982, p. 86.

26 Herb Mills, "The San Francisco Waterfront: The Social Consequences of Industrial Modernization," in Andrew Zimbalist, *Case Studies on the Labor Process*, New York, Monthly Review Press, 1980 pp. 127–155; David Wellman, *The Union Makes Us Strong: Radical Unionism on the San Francisco Waterfront*, New York, Cambridge University Press, 1995, pp. 159–177; *Labor Notes*, #327, June 2006, pp. 1, 6.

27 Jean-Paul Rodrgue, "The Port Authority of New York and New Jersey: Global Changes, Regional Gains and Local Challenges," *Les Cahiers Scientifique du Transport*, February 2004, translated reprint, pp. 1–4; Stan Weir (edited by George Lipsitz), *Singlejack Solidarity*, Minneapolis, University of Minnesota Press, 2004, pp. 96–97.

28 Weir, pp. 102–103.

29 Bonacich, pp. 41–45; Moody 1997, pp. 68–73.

30 Charles Perry, *Deregulation and the Decline of the Unionized Trucking Industry*, Industrial Research Unit, The Warton School, University of Pennsylvania, 1986, pp. 75–110; Dan La Botz, *Rank and File Rebellion: Teamsters for a Democratic Union*, New York, Verso, 1990, pp. 196–207; *Labor Notes*, #274, January 2002, p. 8.

31 *Convoy-Dispatch*, #227, June 2005, p. 5.

32 *Ibid.*, pp. 1, 6.

33 *Labor Notes*, #278, May 2002, p. 10; #281, August 2002, p. 16.

34 Thomson Financial, "Mergers & Acquisitions Review," First Quarter 2006, http:–dR–banker.thomsonib.com.

35 Robert Pitofsky, Chairman of the Federal Trade Commission, "Mergers and Corporate Consolidation in the New Economy," before Committee on the Judiciary, US Senate, June 16, 1998, pp. 1–2.

36 *Statistical Abstract*, 2001, p. 493; 2004–2005, p. 499.

37 Jeffrey Keefe and Rosemary Batt, "United States," in Harry Katz (ed.), *Telecommunications: Restructuring Work and Employment Relations Worldwide*, Ithaca, Cornell University Press, 1997, pp. 33–43.

38 Keefe and Batt, p. 43.

39 Ivan Seidenberg, CEO, Verizon, Written Testimony to the US Senate Committee on the Judiciary, March 12, 2005, pp. 1–3; *Macomb Daily*, February 15, 2005, www.macombdaily.com.

40 Michael Strople, "From Supermarkets to Superstores: Employment Shifts to the One-Stop Shop," *Monthly Labor Review*, Vol. 129, No. 2, February 2006, pp. 40–43.

41 Strople, p. 39.

42 Nelson Lichtenstein, "Wal-Mart and the New World Order: A Template for Twenty-First Century Capitalism?" *New Labor Forum*, Vol. 14, no. 1, Spring 2005, pp. 21–25.

43 Lichtenstein, 2005, pp. 25–30.

44 Martin Vander Weyer, "The Bottom Line," *New Statesman*, 22 May, 2006, pp. 53–54.

45 Lichtenstein, 2005, pp. 21–23; Nelson Lichtenstein, "Wal-Mart's Tale of Two Cities: From Bentonville to Shenzhen," *New Labor Forum*, Vol. 15, No. 2, Summer 2006, pp. 9–18.

46 Lichtenstein, 2006, p. 13.

Chapter 4

1   David Montgomery, *The Fall of the House of Labor: The Workplace, the State, and American Labor Activism, 1865–1925*, New York, Cambridge University Press, 1987, p. 70.

2   US Bureau of the Census, *Historical Statistics of the United States: Colonial Times to 1970*, Washington, DC, USBOC, 1975, pp. 127, 232, 667.

3   David Montgomery, *Beyond Equality: Labor and the Radical Republicans, 1862–1872*, Urbana, University of Illinois Press, 1981, pp. 4–8.

4   Melvyn Dubofsky, *We Shall Be All: A History of the Industrial Workers of the World* (Abridged Edition), Urbana, University of Illinois, 2000, pp. 9–20.

5   David Montgomery, *Citizen Worker: The Experience of Workers in the United States with Democracy and the Free Market During the Nineteenth Century*, New York, Cambridge University Press, 1995, p. 158.

6   Robert Heilbroner and Aaron Singer, *The Economic Transformation of America: 1600 to the Present*, New York, Harcourt Brace Jovanovich Publishers, 1984, pp. 202–205.

7   Paul Le Blanc, *A Short History of the U.S. Working Class: From Colonial Times to the Twenty-first Century*, Amherst, New York, Humanity Books, 1999, p. 51.

8   Howard Zinn, *A People's History of the United States, 1492–Present*, New York, Harper Perennial, 1995, pp. 276–277.

9   Montgomery 1987, pp. 50–57, 176.

10 *Historical Statisitics*, p. 22.

11 David Roediger, *The Wages of Whiteness: Race and the Making of the American Working Class*, New York, Verso, 1991, *passim*.

12 Philip Foner, *Organized Labor and the Black Worker, 1619–1973*, New York, International Publishers, 1974, pp. 129–132.

13 Barbara Mayer Wertheimer, *We Were There: The Story of Working Women in America*, New York, Pantheon Books, 1977, pp. 209–233; Roger Waldinger, "Another Look at the International Ladies' Garment Workers' Union: Women, Industry Structure, and Collective Action," in Ruth Milkman (ed.), *Women, Work and Protest: A Century of U.S. Women's Labor History*, Boston, Routledge & Kegan Paul, 1985, pp. 86–105.

14 Jones et al., pp. 629–635, 665–666; William Appleman Williams, *The Tragedy of American Diplomacy*, New York, W.W. Norton, 1972, pp. 35–57.

15 Philip Foner, *History of the Labor Movement in the United States,* Vol. 2, New York, International Publishers, second edition 1975, pp. 361–364; Philip Foner, *History of the Labor Movement in the United States,* Vol. 7, pp. 102–117.

16 Foner, Vol. 7, pp. 102, 292–337.

17 Kevin Phillips, *Wealth and Democracy: A Political History of the American Rich,* New York, Broadway Books, 2002, pp. 49–59.

18 George Lipsitz, *Rainbow at Midnight: Labor and Culture in the 1940s,* Urbana, University of Illinois Press, 1994, pp. 99–117; Moody 1988, pp. 17–18.

19 Leo Troy, "The Rise and Fall of American Trade Unions: The Labor Movement from FDR to RR," in Seymour Martin Lipset, *Unions in Transition: Entering the Second Century,* San Francisco, ICS Press, 1986, pp. 80–92.

20 Jack Metzgar, *Striking Steel: Solidarity Remembered,* Philadelphia, Temple University Press, 2000, pp. 11, 17–58; Jeremy Brecher, *Strike!,* Boston, South End Press, 2000, pp. 249–271; Moody 1988, pp. 83–94.

21 Moody 1988, pp. 83–95; *Statistical Abstract,* 1972, p. 244.

22 Stephanie Coontz, *The Way We Never Were: American Families and the Nostalgia Trap,* New York, Basic Books, 1992, p. 38.

23 Johanna Brenner, *Women and the Politics of Class,* New York, Monthly Review Press, 2000, p. 68.

24 *Statistical Abstract,* 1976, p. 384.

25 Moody 1988, pp. 275–277 Milkman, pp. 307–318.

26 Foner 1974, pp. 271–272; Lichtenstein, pp. 72–73.

27 *Statistical Abstract,* 1972, p. 216.

28 Foner 1974, pp. 232–254, 370–424.

29 Nelson Lichtenstein, *State of the Union: A Century of American Labor,* Princeton, Princeton University Press, 2002, p. 195.

30 Juan Gonzales, *Harvest of Empire: A History of Latinos in America,* New York, Penguin Books, 2000, pp. 86–87, 102–105.

31 *Ibid.,* pp. 102–107.

32 Priscilla Murolo and A.B. Chitty, *From the Folks Who Brought You the Weekend: A Short, Illustrated History of Labor in the United States,* New York, The New Press, 2001, pp. 261–262.

33 Roger Waldinger, *Still The Promised City? African Americans and New Immigrants in Postindustrial New York,* Cambridge, MA, Harvard University Press, 1996, pp. 18–32.

34 *Statistical Abstract,* 2001, p. 367; Mike Parker and Martha Gruelle, *Democracy is Power: Rebuilding Unions from the Bottom Up,* Detroit, Labor Notes, 1999, p. 69.

35 Lichtenstein, 2002, p. 99.

36 Paul Buhle, *Taking Care of Business: Samuel Gompers, George Meany,*

Lane Kirkland and the Tragedy of American Labor, New York, Monthly Review Press, 1999, pp. 150–154; Daniel Cantor and Juliet Schor, *Tunnel Vision: Labor, the World Economy, and Central America*, Boston, South End Press, 1987, pp. 41–49.

37 Cantor and Schor, pp. 49–63; Williams, pp. 258–275.

38 Beth Sims, *Workers of the World Undermined: American Labor's Role in U.S. Foreign Policy*, Boston, South End Press, 1992, pp. 28–40.

39 Min Zhou, "Chinese: Divergent Destinies in Immigrant New York," in Nancy Foner (ed.), *New Immigrants in New York*, New York, Columbia University Press, 2001, p. 145.

40 Department of Homeland Security, Office of Immigration Statistics, *Yearbook of Immigration Statistics: 2005*, Table 1, www.uscis.gov.

41 *Ibid.*, Tables 3 & 10; US Department of Justice, Immigration and Naturalization Service, *1997 Statistical Yearbook of the Immigration and Naturalization Service*, October 1999, pp. 25–26, www.uscis.gov.

42 Michael Hoefer, Nancy Rytina, and Christopher Campbell, "Estimates of the Unauthorized Immigrant Population Residing in the United States: January 2005," *Population Estimates*, Department of Homeland Security, August 2006, p. 1.

43 *Statistical Abstract*, 2006, pp. 45, 395; Bureau of Labor Statistics, "Foreign-Born Workers: Labor Force Characteristics," *News*, USDL 06–640, April 14, 2006, Table 4, www.bls.gov.

44 Department of Homeland Security, Office of Immigration Statistics, *Population Estimates*, February 2006, p. 4.

45 DHS, *Yearbook*, Table 10, www.uscis.gov; INS, *1997 Statistical Yearbook*, pp. 40–41.

46 Sidney Lens, *The Forging of the American Empire*, New York, Thomas Y. Crowell Company, 1971, pp. 269–271; Gonzales, pp. 58–60.

47 Sims, p. 6; Gonzales, p. 77.

48 Gonzales, pp. 117–119; INS, *1997 Statistical Yearbook*, p. 26.

49 Gonzales, pp. 138–139; INS, *1997 Statistical Yearbook*, p. 26.

50 Kim Moody and Mary McGinn, *Unions and Free Trade: Solidarity vs. Competition*, Detroit, Labor Notes, 1992, pp. 1–11; Gonzales, pp. 228–229.

51 Kim Moody, "NAFTA and the Corporate Redesign of North America," *Latin American Perspectives*, Vol. 22, No. 1, Winter 1995, pp. 95–103.

52 Moody 1995, p. 102; Gonzales, p. 239.

53 INS, *1997 Statistical Yearbook*, p. 26; DHS, *Yearbook*, Table 3, www.uscis.gov.

54 *Statistical Abstract*, 2001, pp. 44–45; 2006, p. 46; DHS, *Population Estimates*, 2006, p. 5.

55 *Statistical Abstract*, 2001, p. 386; *Labor Research Association-Online March 2001*.

56 Bureau of Labor Statistics, "Foreign-Born Workers: Labor Force Characteristics in 2005," *News* USDL 06–640, p. 1.

57 *Statistical Abstract*, 200–2005, pp. 385–388.

58 Louise Lamphere, Alex Stepick, and Guillermo Grenier (eds.), *Newcomers in the Workplace: Immigrants and the Restructuring of the Workplace*, Philadelphia, Temple University Press, 1994, pp. 1–19.

59 David Halle, Robert Gordon, and Andrew Beveridge, "Residential Separation and Segregation, Racial and Latino Identity, and Racial Composition of Each City," in David Halle, *New York & Los Angeles: Politics, Society, and Culture, a Comparative View*, Chicago, University of Chicago Press, 2003, pp. 150–159.

60 Ruth Milkman (ed.), *Organizing Immigrants: The Challenge for Unions in Contemporary California*, Ithaca, Cornell University Press, 2000, p. 13.

Chapter 5

1 *Economic Report*, 2005, p. 283.

2 *Ibid.*, p. 266; Bureau of Labor Statistics, *News*, USDL 06–694, April 19, 2006, www.bls.gov.

3 Mishel *et al*, pp. 166–167.

4 *Ibid.*, p. 117.

5 *Ibid.*, p. 141.

6 Stephanie Costo, "Trends in Retirement Plan Coverage Over the Last Decade," *Monthly Labor Review*, Vol. 129, No. 2, February 2006, pp. 58–61.

7 Mishel et al., pp. 135–137.

8 Current Labor Statistics, *Monthly Labor Review*, Vol. 129, No. 5, May 2006, Table 34, www.bls.gov.

9 Mishel et al., pp. 149–150; *Statistical Abstract*, 2006, p. 423.

10 *Statistical Abstract*, 2006, p. 406.

11 Quoted in Mike Parker and Jane Slaughter, "Advancing Unionism on the New Terrain," in Bruce Nissen (ed.), *Unions and Workplace Reorganization*, Detroit, Wayne State University Press, 1997, p. 213.

12 *Statistical Abstract*, 2004–2005, p. 396.

13 US Census Bureau, *2002 Economic Census: Manufacturing*, General Summary: 2002, p. 1.

14 Mishel et al., pp. 56, 102–105.

15 Nanette Page, "Working Class Women and Work," in Paula

Dubeck and Katheryn Borman, *Women and Work: A Reader*, New Brunswick NJ, Rutgers University Press, 1996, pp. 13–16.

16　*Statistical Abstract*, 2006, p. 393.

17　Jody Heymann, M.D., *The Widening Gap: Why America's Working Families are in Jeopardy—and What Can Be Done About It*, New York, Basic Books, 2000, p. 2.

18　*Ibid.*, p. 30, *passim*.

19　Mishel et al., p. 69.

20　*Ibid.*, p. 313.

21　*Statistical Abstract*, 2006, p 475.

22　*Ibid.*, pp. 400, 409.

23　Howard Botwinick, *Persistent Inequalities: Wage Disparity Under Capitalist Competition*, Princeton, Princeton University Press, 1993, pp. 95–122.

24　Bureau of Labor Statistics, "Worker Displacement, 2001–2003,", *News* USDL 04–1381, July 30, 2004, www.bls.gov.

25　Cited in Botwinick, p. 98.

26　*Statistical Abstract*, 2006, pp. 362, 413; 2001, p. 354.

27　Mishel et al., pp. 198–199; *Statistical Abstract*, 2006, p. 430.

28　AFL-CIO, "2005 Trend in CEO Pay,", *Corporate Watch* www.aflcio.org.

29　Jeffrey Pfeffer, "How to End CEO Pay Envy," *Business 2.0 Magazine*, June 1, 2006, www.cnnmoney.com.

30　Bernie Kohn, "Cashing In On a New Sure Thing," *Baltimore Sun*, June 11, 2006, www.sun-sentinel.com.

31　Jeanne Sahadi, "CEO Pay: Sky High Gets Even Higher," *CNN/Money*, August 30, 2005, www.cnnmoney.com.

32　Sarah Anderson, John Cavanagh, Scott Klinger, and Liz Stanton, *Executive Excess: Defense Contractors Get More Buck for the Bang*, Institute for Policy Studies and United for a Fair Economy, August 30, 2005, pp. 30–31.

33　Sahadi, "CEO Pay" www.cnnmoney.com.

34　*New York Times*, April 3, 2005, Section 3, p. 9.

35　*Economic Report*, 2005, p. 315; Brenner, pp. 150–151.

36　David Harvey, *A Brief History of Neoliberalism*, New York, Oxford University Press, 2005, p. 16.

37　The Corporate Library, "Report Analyzes Potential Coincidences Surrounding Stock Option Grant Dates and the Timing of Financial Press Releases," June 6, 2006, www.thecorporatelibrary.com.

38　Kohn.

39　Paul Krugman, "For Richer," *New York Times Magazine*, October 20, 2002, www.pkarchive.org.

40　The Corporate Library, "$865MM in CEO Compensation While Shareholders Suffer $640BN in Losses," March 31, 2006; "82.7BN in Stockholder Gains for Only $190MM in CEO Compensation—Sounds Like a Bargain," June 12, 2006, www.thecorporatelibrary.com.

41   Krugman.

42   Andrew Countryman, "Average Compensation for Board Directors Reached $144,000 in 2005," *Chicago Tribune*, April 30, 2006, www.sen-sentinel.com

43   Irwin Stelzer, "Executive Pay Watch," January 24, 2006, CBS NEWS, www.cbsnews.com.

44   Krugman.

45   *Statistical Abstract*, 2006, p. 758.

46   Mishel et al., pp. 290–292; *Statistical Abstract*, 2006, p. 758.

47   Teresa Ghilarducci, "Small Benefits, Big Pension Funds, and How Governance Reform Can Close the Gap," in Archon Fung, Tessa Hebb, and Joel Rogers, *Working Capital: The Power of Labor's Pensions*, Ithaca, Cornell University Press, 2001, pp. 166–167.

48   Ghilarducci, pp.159–161.

49   Phillips, pp. 114–125.

Chapter 6

1   Troy, 1986, pp. 81, 92; David Lewin, "Public Employee Unionism in the 1980s: An Analysis of Transformation," in Lipset, p. 244; Bureau of Labor Statistics, *Women in the Labor Force: A Data Book*, 2005, p. 81; BLS, "Union Members in 2005", *News*, USDL 06–99, Table 1, www.bls.gov.

2   For accounts of these *periods*, see: Metzgar, Lichtenstein, 2002; Jeremy Brecher, *Strike!*, Boston, South End Press, 1997; Moody, 1988; for union membership figures, Troy, p. 82.

3   Calvin Winslow, "A Decade of Strikes," unpublished paper submitted to the Conference on "Rank and File Movements of the Long 1970s," Center for Social Theory and Comparative History, UCLA, November 2005.

4   Cited in Brecher, pp. 249–251.

5   Henry Farber and Bruce Western, "Round Up the Usual Suspects: The Decline of Unions in the Private Sector, 1973–1998," Working Paper # 437, Princeton University, Industrial Relations Section, April 2000, p. 9.

6   *Economic Report*, 2005, p. 264.

7   *Statistical Abstract*, 2001, pp. 393–395.

8   Horowitz, p. 254.

9   Horowitz, pp. 258–264; *Statistical Abstract*, 2001, pp. 393–395.

10   Horowitz, pp. 247–276.

11   Bureau of Labor Statistics, "State and Area Employment, Hours and Earnings," 1990–2006, http:–dR–data.bls.gov.

12   Stephen Herzenberg, "Regulatory Frameworks and Development in the North American Auto Industry," in Frederick Deyo, *Social Reconstructions of the World Automobile Industry: Competition, Power and Industrial Flexibility*, New York, St. Martin's Press, 1996, pp. 276–277.

13   Deyo, p. 4.

14   Herzenberg, pp. 266–267.

15   Moody 1988, pp. 148–168.

16   Charles Perry, *Deregulation and the Decline of the Unionized Trucking Industry*, Philadelphia, Industrial Research Unit, Wharton School, University of Pennsylvania, 1986, pp. 44–48, 59–68, 99–110; International Brotherhood of Teamsters, "Freight Division," www.teamsters.org.

17   United Steelworkers, "Timeline of Rubber and Tire," www.usw.org.

18   *Rubber News*, "Rough Seas Ahead for Rubber Workers New Skipper," June 22, 2006, www.rubbernews.com.

19   Troy, p. 87.

20   Moody 1988, pp. 127–128.

21   Morris Zeitlin, *American Cities: A Working Class View*, New York, International Publishers, 1990, p. 116.

22   Dennis Judd and Todd Swanstrom, *City Politics: The Political Economy of Urban America*, New York, Pearson Longman, 2006, pp. 278–279.

23   Saskia Sassen-Koob, "Growth and Informalization at the Core: A Preliminary Report on New York City," in Michael Peter Smith and Joe Feagin (eds), *The Capitalist City: Global Restructuring and Community Politics*, Cambridge MA, Blackwell, 1987, pp. 147–148.

24   Lichtenstein, 2002 pp. 225–234.

25   Moody 1988, pp. 92–93.

26   Heather Ann Thompson, *Whose Detroit? Politics, Labor, and Race in a Modern American City*, Ithaca, Cornell University Press, 2001, p. 193.

27   Samuel Friedman, *Teamster Rank and File: Power, Bureaucracy, and Rebellion at Work and in a Union*, New York, Columbia University Press, 1982, pp. 21, 136–168, 190.

28   Garth Mangum and R. Scott McNabb, *The Rise, Fall, and Replacement of Industry-wide Bargaining in the Basic Steel Industry*, Armonk, NY, 1997, pp. 12, 80–92.

29   Moody 1988, pp. 148–149.

30   Lichtenstein 2002 p. 234.

31   Moody 1988, pp. 174–185.

32   Elly Leary and Marybeth Menaker, *Jointness at GM: Company Unionism in the 21st Century*, A New Directions Region 9A Publication, ca. 1992, pp. 31–42.

33   *Ibid.*, pp. 41–42.

34   AT&T, "A Report on the Workplace of the Future Conference," March 8, 1993, pp. 1–2.

35   Moody 1997, p. 93.

36   *Labor Notes*, #219, June 1997, pp. 5–6.

37   *Labor Notes*, #235, October 1998, pp. 1, 12.

38   *Labor Notes*, #249, December 1999, pp. 1, 14.

39   *Labor Notes*, #219, June 1997, p. 5.

40   *Labor Notes*, #241, April 1999, pp. 1, 11.

41   *Labor Notes*, #251, February 2000, pp. 1, 14.

42   Lichtenstein, 1995, pp. 279–281.

43   *Labor Notes*, #228, March 1998, pp. 13, 16.

44   USWA, "Leo Gerard, International President," no date, www.usw.org.

45   Gary Chaison, "Union Mergers and Union Revival," in Lowell Turner, Harry Katz, and Richard Hurd, *Rekindling the Movement: Labor's Quest for Relevance in the 21st Century*, Ithaca, Cornell University Press, 2001, pp. 239–240. Chaison, who counts 37 in the 1990s, leaves out at least one merger in that decade, that of the Allied Industrial Workers into the UPIU.

46   Lisa Williamson, "Union Mergers: 1985–94 Update," *Monthly Labor Review*, February 1995, pp. 18–19.

47   David Moberg, *The Nation*, March 14, 2005, p. 12.

48   Kim Moody, "When the Sum is No Greater Than Its Parts," *New Labor Forum*, Spring/Summer 2002, p. 43.

49   Chaison, p. 241.

50   SEIU, "SEIU History" Press Releases, January 15, 2002, January 9, 2003, September 2, 2005, www.seiu.org.

51   Williamson, pp. 20–21.

52   REAP, "A General Review of UFCW Structure," October 1, 2004, www.reapince.org.

53   Members for Democracy, "Teamsters Suck in Another Union—GCIU," no date, www.ufcw.net; *Labor Notes*, #298, January 2004, p. 4, #301, April 2004, pp. 5–6.

54   CWA, Website, www.cwa-union.org; *Labor Notes*, #260, November 2000, p. 2.

55   *Labor Notes*, #236, November 1998, pp. 1, 14.

56   Moody 2002, pp. 44–45.

57   *Labor Notes*, #124, July 1989, p. 3.

58   Moody, 2002, pp. 45–46.

59   REAP, pp. 4–5.
60   *Pittsburgh Tribune-Review*, June 5, 2004, www.pittsburghlive.com.
61   Jack Fiorito, "Union Renewal in the UK and US," 2006, Florida State University, Powerpoint slides.
62   Farber and Western, p. 9.
63   IBT, www.teamsters,org.
64   AFT, www.aft.org.

Chapter 7

1   Murolo and Chitty, p. 295; *Labor Notes*, #123, June 1989, pp. 1, 15; #125, August 1989, pp. 1, 14; #126, September 1989, pp. 1, 15; #128, November 1989, pp. 1, 14; #132, March 1990, pp. 1, 14.
2   Anna Zajicek and Bradley Nash Jr., "Lessons from the UMWA," in Tillman and Cummings, pp. 225–234.
3   Steve Early, "Holding the Line in '89: Lessons of the NYNEX Strike," Somerville MA, Labor Resource Center, September 1990, pp. 1–41.
4   *Labor Notes*, #131, February 1990, pp. 1, 14.
5   Joseph Blasi and James Gasaway, "The Great Experiment: Labor—Management Cooperation at Eastern Airlines," in Peter Cappelli (ed.), *Airline Labor Relations in the Global Era: The New Frontier*, Ithaca, Cornell University Press, 1995, pp. 190–198.
6   *Labor Notes*, #130, January 1990, p. 11.
7   La Botz, pp. 288–294.
8   *Ibid.*, pp. 290–291.
9   *Ibid.*, pp. 321–322.
10   *Labor Notes*, #127, October 1989, pp. 1, 13; Tillman, "Reform Movement in the Teamsters and United Auto Workers," in Tillman and Cummings, pp. 141–143.
11   Zajicek and Nash, pp. 228–234.
12   Tillman, pp. 150–163.
13   Downs and Schermerhorn, pp. 167–177; *Labor Notes*, #263, February 2001, pp. 1, 15.
14   *Labor Notes*, #137, August 1990, p.16.
15   *Labor Notes*, #140, November 1990, p. 4.
16   *Labor Notes*, #130, January 1990, pp. 7–10.
17   *Labor Notes*, #139, October 1990, p. 10.
18   *Labor Notes*, #158, May 1992, pp. 1, 11–12.
19   *Labor Notes*, #164, November 1992, pp. 1, 14; #175, October 1993, p. 5, #183, June 1994, pp. 1, 14; #187, October 1994, pp. 13, 16; Kim Moody, "American Labor: A Movement Again?"

in Ellen Meiksins Wood, Peter Wood, and Michael Yates (eds), *Rising from the Ashes? Labor in the Age of "Global" Capitalism*, New York, Monthly Review Press, 1998, p. 68.

20   *Labor Notes*, #169, April 1993, p. 16.

21   *Labor Notes*, #173, August 1993, pp. 1, 7; #174, September 1993, pp. 1, 10.

22   *Labor Notes*, 181, April 1994, p. 3; #191, February 1995, pp. 12–13; #193, April 1995, p. 3.

23   *Labor Notes*, #203, February 1996, pp. 1, 11.

24   Stephen Franklin, *Three Strikes: Labor's Heartland Losses and What They Mean for Working Americans*, New York, The Guilford Press, 2001, pp. 117–124, 232–238; Kate Bronfenbrenner and Tom Jurovich, "The Evolution of Strategic and Coordinated Bargaining Campaigns in the 1990s," in Turner, Katz, and Hurd, pp. 229.

25   *Labor Notes*, #195, June 1995, pp. 1, 3; #202, January 1996, p. 16.

26   *Labor Notes*, #263, February 2001, pp. 8–9.

27   Lichtenstein, 2002, p. 17.

28   Marie Gottschalk, *The Shadow Welfare State: Labor, Business, and the Politics of Health Care in the United States*, Ithaca, Cornell University Press, 2000, pp. 143–146; Lichtenstein, 2002, pp. 251–255.

29   Buhle, p. 244.

30   For a sweeping view of this history see Buhle, *passim*.

31   Buhle, pp. 205–223.

32   Lichtenstein, 2002 p. 249.

33   *Labor Notes*, #193, April 1995, p. 3.

34   *Labor Notes*, #194, May 1995, p. 7.

35   *Labor Notes*, #196, July 1995, pp. 1, 14.

36   Lichtenstein, 2002, p. 257.

37   *Labor Notes*, #199, October 1995, p. 16.

38   *Labor Notes*, #201, December 1995, pp. 1, 10, 11.

39   Ibid., p.1.

40   Buhle, pp. 244–245.

41   Gottschalk, pp. 138–139; *Labor Notes*, #196, July 1995, p. 14.

42   Robert Fitch, *Solidarity for Sale: How Corruption Destroyed the Labor Movement and Undermined America's Promise*, New York, Public Affairs, 2006, pp. 302–303.

43   Moody 1998, p. 72.

44   *Labor Notes*, #196, July 1995, p. 14.

45   Gregory Mantsios, "What Does Labor Stand For?" in Gregory Mantsios (ed.), *A New Labor Movement for the New Century*, New York, Monthly Review Press, 1998, pp. 49–51.

46   *Ibid.*, pp. 52–53.

47   *Ibid.*, p. 54.
48   Jeremy Brecher and Tim Costello, "A 'New Labor Movement' in the Shell of the Old?" in Mantsios, pp. 40–41.
49   *Labor Notes*, #199, October 1995, pp. 12–13.
50   Winning for Working Families, "Changes in the AFL-CIO 1996–2005," April 2005, p. 18.
51   Benson, p. 211.
52   Slaughter, pp. 188–189.
53   AFL-CIO, "Union Cities," www.aflcio.org.
54   Stanley Aronowitz, "Labor on Trial: Assessing Sweeney's Record," *Working USA: The Journal of Labor and Society*, Vol. 5 No. 2, Fall 2001, pp. 12–16.
55   Winning for Working Families, p. 24; Steve Early, "Member-Based Organizing," in Mantsios, p. 82.
56   Tim Shorrock, "Toeing the Line? Sweeney and US Foreign Policy," *New Labor Forum*, No. 11, Fall–Winter 2002, pp. 10–11.
57   Shorrock, pp. 11–13; *Labor Notes*, #316, July 2005, pp. 7–8.
58   *Labor Notes* #316, July 2005, p. 7.
59   Peter Olney, "The Arithmetic of Decline and Some Proposals for Renewal," *New Labor Forum*, No. 10, Spring/Summer 2002, p. 9.
60   *Labor Notes*, #263, February 2001, pp. 5, 14.
61   Olney, p. 7.
62   *The Detroit News*, May 10, 2006, www.detnews.com.
63   Kate Bronfenbrenner and Robert Hickey, "Changing to Organize: A National Assessment of Union Strategies," in Ruth Milkman and Kim Voss, *Rebuilding Labor: Organizing and Organizers in the New Union Movement*, Ithaca, Cornell University Press, 2004, p. 25.
64   *Labor Notes*, #224, November 1997, pp. 1, 14; #322, January 2006, pp. 1, 14.
65   Kate Bronfenbrenner, "Organizing in the NAFTA Environment: How Companies Use 'Free Trade' to Stop Unions," *New Labor Forum*, No. 1, Fall 1997, pp. 53–55.
66   Farber and Western, p. 9.
67   *Labor Notes*, #233, August 1998, p. 2.

Chapter 8

1   *New York Times*, November 12, 2006, www.nytimes.com; AFL-CIO, *Labor 2006*, "AFL-CIO 2006 Post-Election Survey/Hart Research," November 2006, www.aflcio.org.
2   Barb Kucera, *Workday Minnesota*, November 9, 2006, www.workdayminnesota.com.
3   Lichtenstein, 2002, pp. 100–132.

4   Robert Zieger, *The CIO, 1935–1955*, Chapel Hill NC, University of North Carolina Press, 1995, pp. 212–252.

5   Stephen Amberg, "The CIO Political Strategy in Historical Perspective: Creating a High-Road Economy in the Postwar Era," in Kevin Boyle (ed.), *Organized Labor and American Politics 1894–1994: The Liberal-Labor Alliance*, Albany NY, State University of New York Press, 1998, p. 173.

6   Gottschalk, pp. 16–22.

7   Amberg, p. 174.

8   Robert Zieger, "George Meany: Labor's Organization Man," in Melvyn Dubofsky and Warren Van Tine, *Labor Leaders in America*, Urbana, University of Illinois Press, 1987, p. 341.

9   Amberg, p. 175.

10   *Ibid.*, p. 175.

11   *Ibid.*

12   Peter Francia, "Protecting America's Workers in Hostile Territory: Unions and the Republican Congress," in Paul Herrnson, Ronald Shaiko, and Clyde Wilcox, *The Interest Group Connection: Electioneering, Lobbying, and Policymaking in Washington*, Washington DC, CQ Press, 2005, pp. 215–219.

13   Robert Biersack and Marianne Viray, "Interest Groups and Federal Campaign Finance: The Beginning of a New Era," in Herrnson, Shaiko and Wilcox, pp. 59–60.

14   Paul Herrnson, "Interest Groups and Campaigns: The Electoral Connection," in Herrnson, Shaiko, and Wilcox, pp. 32–33.

15   *Solidarity*, United Auto Workers, April 2000, p. 9.

16   Larry Sabato (ed.), *Divided States of America: The Slash and Burn Politics of the 2004 Presidential Election*, New York, Pearson Longman, 2006, pp. 54–55, 72–73.

17   Francia, p. 219.

18   Lichtenstein, 2002, p. 201.

19   Francia, pp. 220–223.

20   Moody, 1988, p. 128.

21   Lichtenstein, p. 229.

22   Marian Currinder, "Campaign Finance: Funding the Presidential and Congressional Elections," in Nelson, 2005, pp. 110–111.

23   Currinder, pp. 110–111.

24   Gary Jacobson, *The Politics of Congressional Elections*, sixth edition, New York, Pearson Longman, 2004, p. 64; *Statistical Abstract*, 2006, p. 266.

25   Jacobson, p. 65.

26   *Statistical Abstract*, 2001, p. 255; 2006, p. 266.

27   Currinder, pp. 109–116; Jacobson, pp. 60–73; Herrnson, Shaiko, and Wilcox, pp. 55–57; Biersack and Viray, p. 57.

28 Jacobson, pp. 63–75.
29 Roger Davidson and Walter Oleszek, *Congress and Its Members*, Tenth Edition, Washington DC, CQ Press, 2006, pp. 57.
30 Davidson and Oleszek, pp. 57–73.
31 Jacobson, p. 62.
32 Ronald Shaiko, "Making the Connection: Organized Interests, Political Representation, and the Changing Rules of the Game in Washington Politics," in Herrnson, Shaiko, and Wilcox, p. 7, 15–16.
33 Davidson and Oleszek, pp. 410–417;
34 John Wright, *Interest Groups and Congress: Lobbying, Contributions, and Influence*, New York, Longman, 2003, p. 14.
35 Davidson and Oleszek, pp. 198–199; Shaiko, pp. 6–19.
36 Gabriel Almond et al. (eds), *European Politics Today*, Third Edition, New York, Pearson Longman, 2006, pp. 109, 161; Anthony Birch, *The British System of Government*, Seventh Edition, Boston, Allen & Unwin, 1986, p. 93.
37 Metzgar, pp. 2–3.
38 Nicole Mellow, "Voting Behavior: The 2004 Election and the Roots of Republican Success," in Nelson, pp. 79–80.
39 Lichtenstein, 2002, pp. 141–177.
40 Zieger, 1995, p. 357.
41 Moody 1988, pp. 72–79; Foner 1976, pp. 312–331.
42 Moody 1988, pp. 83–94; Brecher, pp. 249–271.
43 Michael Nelson, "The Setting: George W. Bush, Majority President," in Nelson, pp. 7–8.
44 Moody 1988, pp. 135–156.
45 Stanley Greenberg, *The Two Americas: Our Current Deadlock and How to Break It*, New York, Thomas Dunne Books, 2005, pp. 134–135.
46 Thomas Frank, *What's the Matter With Kansas? How Conservatives Won the Heart of America*, New York, Henry Holt and Company, 2004, p. 128.
47 *Ibid.*, p. 129.
48 Eric Lee, "Q & A with Andy Stern," September 27, 2006, www.ericlee.info.
49 Greenberg, pp. 132–136, 355–360.
50 Wilson Carey McWilliams, "The Meaning of the Election: Ownership and Citizenship in American Life," in Nelson, p. 198.
51 Steven Lopez, "Overcoming Legacies of Business Unionism," in Milkman and Voss, pp. 120–121.
52 Edward Greenberg and Benjamin Page, *America's Democratic Republic*, New York, Pearson Longman, 2005, pp. 316–317; Davidson and Oleszek, p. 47; Jacobson, pp. 236–238.

53 Zieger 1995, pp. 230–231.

54 H. M. Gitelman, "Adolph Strasser and the Origins of Pure and Simple Unionism," in Daniel Leab (ed.), *The Labor History Reader*, Urbana, University of Illinois Press, 1985, pp. 156–164.

55 Mantsios, p. 46.

56 Buhle, pp. 211–212.

57 John H. M. Laslett, "Samuel Gompers and the Rise of American Business Unionism," in Dubofsky and Van Tine, pp. 84–85.

58 Philip Foner, *History of the Labor Movement in the United States*, Volume III, New York, International Publishers, 1964, p. 139.

59 Zieger, 1995, p. 15.

60 Nelson Lichtenstein, *The Most Dangerous Man in Detroit: Walter Reuther and the Fate of American Labor*, New York, Basic Books, 1995, p. 291.

61 Mantsios, p. 47.

62 Foner 1985, pp. 58–77.

63 Lenny Mendonca, "Shaking Up the Labor Movement: An interview with the Head of the Service Employees International Union," *The McKinsey Quarterly*, No. 1, 2006, pp. 53–60; *Labor Notes*, #316, July 2005, pp. 9–10.

64 Judd and Swanstrom, pp. 330–338.

65 Kim Moody, *Global City in Crisis: The Neoliberal Transformation of New York City 1975–2005*, New York, The New Press, 2007, *passim*.

66 John Mollenkopf, "How 9/11 Reshaped the Political Environment in New York," in John Mollenkopf (ed.), *Contentious City: The Politics of Recovery in New York City*, New York, Russell Sage Foundation, 2005, pp. 214–215; Capital Research Center, *Labor Watch*, July 2002, p. 6.

67 *The Chief*, May 27, 2005, pp. 1, 14; July 22, 2005, pp. 1, 7.

68 Discussions with union activists from independent and AFL-CIO unions in Puerto Rico in October 1998.

69 Fitch, pp. 306–307.

70 Discussion with North Carolina United Electrical Workers organizer, July 2006.

Chapter 9

1 *Labor Notes*, #295, October 2003.

2 *Labor Notes*, #285, December 2002, pp. 8–10; #286, January 2003, pp. 7–10.

3 Steve Lerner, "An Immodest Proposal: Rebuilding the House of Labor," *New Labor Forum*, Vol. 12, Issue 2, 2003, pp. 9–34; *Union Democracy Review*, #154, January/February 2005, p. 4.

4   Kate Bronfenbrenner, "What is Labor's True Purpose?" *New Labor Forum*, Vol. 14, Issue 2, Summer 2005, pp. 19–20.
5   *Union Democracy Review*, #154, January/February 2005, p. 4.
6   Bronfenbrenner 2005, pp. 20–21.
7   *Labor Notes*, #322, January 2006, pp. 11, 13.
8   *KeepMedia*, "Five Leading Unions For New Coalition to Rebuild American Labor Movement," June 15, 2005, www.keepmedia.com.
9   *KeepMedia*, "Carpenters Union Joins Change To Win Coalition," June 27, 2005, www.keepmedia.com.
10   *Labor Notes*, #318, September 2005, p. 9.
11   Jonathan Tasini, "After the Rift," *New Labor Forum*, Vol. 14, Issue 3, Fall 2005, pp. 8–9.
12   Mark Gruenberg, "Change to Win Establishes New Union Federation," PAI, November 8, 2005, p. 1, www.ilwu.org.
13   *Labor Notes*, #320, November 2005, pp. 3, 11.
14   Gruenberg, p. 2.
15   Eric Lee, "New Union Federation Born in the USA," www.ericlee.info.
16   PR Newswire, "Change to Win Unveils Major Initiative to Organize Millions of Workers," March 20, 2006, www.prnewswire.com.
17   *Labor Notes*, 320, November 2005, p. 3.
18   Olney p. 9.
19   *Ibid.*
20   NLRB *Election Report*, October 13, 2005, pp. 27–39.
21   Bronfenbrenner 2005, p. 23.
22   *Ibid.*, pp. 23–24.
23   Olney, p. 12.
24   Bronfenbrenner, 2005, p. 24.
25   *Ibid.*, p. 25.
26   Dan La Botz, *A Troublemakers Handbook: How to Fight Back Where You Work—and Win*, Detroit, Labor Notes, 1991, p. 3.
27   Olney, p. 13.
28   José La Luz and Paula Finn, "Getting Serious About Inclusion: A Comprehensive Approach," in Mantsios, pp. 177–179.
29   Roger Waldinger et al, "Helots No More: A Case Study of the Justice for Janitors Campaign in Los Angeles," in Kate Bronfenbrenner et al, *Organizing to Win: New Research on Union Strategies*, Ithaca, Cornell University Press, 1998, pp. 118–119.
30   *Labor Notes*, #285, December 2002, p. 9.
31   Parker and Gruelle, p. 1.
32   *Ibid.*, pp. 11–35.
33   Elaine Bernard, "Creating Democratic Communities in the Workplace," in Mantsios, p. 7.
34   Teresa Sharpe, "Union Democracy and Successful Campaigns: The

Dynamics of Staff Authority and Worker Participation in an Organizing Union," in Milkman and Voss, p. 63.

35   Parker and Gruelle, pp. 42–43.

36   Jeff Crosby, "Democracy, Density and Transformation: We Need Them All," March 17, 2005, p. 13, jcrosby@local201iuecwa.org.

37   Marshall Ganz, et al, "Against the Tide: Projections and Pathways of the New Generation of Union Leaders, 1984–2001," in Milkman and Voss, pp. 155–156.

38   Parkers and Gruelle, p. 69; BLS, "Union Members in 2005," *News*, USDL 06–99, January 20, 2006, Table 1, www.bls.gov.

39   Kate Bronfenbrenner and Tom Juravich, "It Takes More Than House Calls: Organizing to Win with a Comprehensive Union-Building Strategy," in Bronfenbrenner et al, pp. 32–33.

40   Bronfenbrenner and Juravich, 1998, pp. 25–33.

41   Bronfenbrenner and Hickey, p. 24.

42   Bill Fletcher, Jr. and Richard Hurd, "Beyond the Organizing Model: The Transformation Process in Local Unions," in Bronfenbrenner et al, pp. 37–53.

43   Steve Early, "Membership-Based Organizing," in Mantsios, pp. 85–87.

44   Slaughter, pp. 158, 350–351.

45   *Labor Notes*, 309, December 2004, pp. 10, 14.

46   *Labor Notes*, #329, August 2006, pp. 12–13; Paul Krehbiel, "Building a Committee to Work With Stewards," in Slaughter, p. 17.

47   William Fletcher Jr. and Richard Hurd, "Overcoming the Obstacles to Transformation," in Turner, Katz, and Hurd, 191–200.

48   Metzgar, p. 49.

49   SEIU, "Fast Facts," www.seiu.org.

50   Janice Fine, *Worker Centers: Organizing Communities at the Edge of the Dream*, Ithaca, Cornell University Press, 2006, p. 148.

51   US Department of Labor, "LM 2 (revised)," FY 2005, www.dol.gov/esa; "About SEIU," www.seiu.org.

52   Moody 2003, p. 43; Chaison 2001, p. 241; Michael Piore, "Unions: A Reorientation to Survive," in Clark Kerr and Paul Staudohar, *Labor Economic and Industrial Relations: Markets and Institutions*, Cambridge, Harvard University Press, 1994, p. 527; "SEIU History," www.seiu.org.

53   Piore, pp. 514–529.

54   *Ibid.*, pp. 522–529.

55   Ruth Milkman, "Women Workers, Feminism, and Labor since the 1960s," in Milkman, 1985, pp. 314–315; Early, p. 84.

56   Piore, p. 528.

57   Waldinger et al, pp. 105–118; Piore, p. 527; Catherine Fisk,

Daniel Mitchell, and Christopher Erickson, "Union Representation of Immigrant Janitors in Southern California: Economic and Legal Challenges," in Milkman 2000, pp. 199–211; Andy Banks, "The Power and Promise of Community Unionism," *Labor Research Review*, 18, Fall/Winter 1991/92, pp. 21–24.

58 Fletcher and Hurd, pp. 38–40.

59 *Labor Notes*, #205, April 1996, pp. 4, 14.

60 *Labor Notes*, #204, March 1996, pp. 8–9.

61 *Labor Notes*, #298, January 2004, p. 10.

62 SEIU, "SEIU History" and various pages on the website, www.seiu.org.

63 Fine, p. 148; *Union Democracy Review*, No. 159, November/December 2005, p. 1.

64 *Labor Notes*, #310, January 2005, p. 9.

65 Waldinger et al., p. 113.

66 Andrew L. Stern, "Memorandum," Re: IEB Decision on California Jurisdiction, June 11, 2006, p. 2; *Labor Notes*, #310, January 2005, p. 8; Capital Research Center, "Labor Watch," July 2002, p. 1.

67 SEIU, *Constitution and Bylaws*, 2004, p. 25, www.seiu.org.

68 Stern, p. 1.

69 "History," www.seiu32bj.org; discussion with SEIU organizer, July 2005.

70 Labor Research Association, "Union Mergers and Strategic Planning Deliver Results for SEIU 1199 Nursing Home Workers in New York," LRA Online, February 7, 2002, www.laborresearch. org; *The Health Care Employer*, Vol. 31, No. 3, Fall 2005, pp. 2–3; discussion with SEIU organizer, July 2005.

71 *St. Louis Post-Dispatch*, February 12, 2004, www.post-dispatch.com.

72 *Labor Notes*, #307, October 2004, p. 5; #314, May 2005, p. 7.

73 Stern, pp. 1–2.

74 *Santa Cruz Sentinel*, March 22, 2006, www.santacruzsentinel.com.

75 *Labor Notes*, #307, October 2004, pp. 5–6.

76 *Santa Cruz Sentinel*, March 22, 2006, www.santacruzsentinel.com.

77 *Labor Notes*, #323, February 2006, www.labornotes.org; *Union Democracy Review*, No. 161, March/April 2006, p. 3. For a detailed account of what was a complicated fight see Ferd Wulkan "How and Why SEIU Lost 2,300 Members at the University of Massachusetts," December 2005, 26 pages, www.zmag.org.

78 Discussions with British trade unionists and labor educators, June–July 2006.

79 *McKinsey Quarterly*, 2006, No. 1, pp. 60–61, www.mckinseyquarterly.com.

80 SEIU, *Steward's Manual*, www.seiu.org.

81 US Department of Labor, "LM–2, FY2000, FY 2005," www.dol.gov/esa.

82 SEIU, "Put Your Values to Work," "Jobs," www.seiu.org.

83 *Labor Notes*, #325, April 2006, p. 4.

84 *Statistical Abstract*, 1997, p. 436.

85 Fisk, Mitchell, and Erickson, pp. 200–209.

86 *Economic Report*, 2005, p. 266.

87 *New York Times*, April 24, 2000, p. A17.

88 *New York Times*, April 28, 2000, p. A12; *Labor Notes*, #255, June 2000, pp. 16, 14.

89 UNITE-HERE, "Successes of First Year a Model as Labor Debates Future and How to Grow," July 11, 2005, p. 3.

90 *Ibid.*, p. 1.

91 *Labor Notes*, #253, April 2000, pp. 16, 13.

92 *The Labor Educator*, September 20, 2006, info@laboreducator.org.

Chapter 10

1 For more on the Laborers see *Labor Notes*, #247, October 1999, p. 5, #278, May 2002, pp. 14, 16; for other such examples from other unions see Slaughter, *passim.*

2 *Union Democracy Review*, No. 155, March/April 2005, p. 7.

3 *Labor Notes*, #222, September 1997, pp. 1, 14–15; #224, November 1997, pp. 1, 10–11.

4 *Labor Notes*, #297, December 2003, pp. 1, 14; #298, January 2004, p. 1, 14; #299, February 2004, pp. 1, 14; #301, April 2004, pp. 1, 12.

5 *Labor Notes*, #311, February 2005, pp. 15, 16.

6 Peter Olney, "On the Waterfront: An Analysis of ILWU Lockout," *New Labor Forum*, Vol. 12, Issue 2, Summer 2003, pp. 33–40.

7 *The Chief*, December 30, 2005, p. 1,7; *New York Press*, April 19, 2006, www.nypress.com.

8 *Union Democracy Review*, No. 160, January/February 2006, pp. 1, 2; *Labor Notes*, #327, June 2006, pp. 1, 14.

9 *Labor Notes*, May 2005, www.labornotes.org.

10 *Labor Notes*, #316, July 2005, pp. 1, 14.

11 *Labor Notes*, #326, May 2006, p. 6.

12 *Ibid.*

13 *Labor Notes*, #322, January 2006, pp. 8–9.

14 Weir, p. 294.

15 Various issues, *Labor Notes* 1999–2006; *Union Democracy Review*, 1999–2006.

16 *Labor Notes*, #322, January 2006, pp. 1, 14.

17 *Labor Notes*, #313, April 2005, pp. 1, 11.

18 *Labor Notes*, #223, October 1997, pp. 14, 16; #226, January 1998, pp. 7–9, 11; #312, March 2005, pp. 1, 14

19 *Labor Notes*, #329, August 2006, p. 3;

20 *Labor Notes*, #236, November 1998, p. 3; #237, December 1998, p. 4; #238, January 1999, p. 6; #340, March 2000, p. 11; #341, April 2000; Fitch, pp. 162–165.

21 *Union Democracy Review*, No. 159, November/December 2005, p. 5; *Labor Notes*, #303, June 2004, p. 10.

22 *Union Democracy Review*, No. 161, March/April 2006, pp. 2, 7.

23 *Labor Notes*, #294, September 2003, p. 6.

24 *Union Democracy Review*, No. 152, September/October 2004, www.uniondemocracy.org.

25 *Union Democracy Review*, No. 154, January/February 2005, p. 5.

26 Longshore Workers Coalition, "Longshore Workers Coalition Responds to Government Racketeering Suit Against ILA," July 11, 2005, www.ilarankandfile.org.

27 *Labor Notes*, #263, February 2001, pp. 1, 14; *Union Democracy Review*, No. 161, March/April 2006, pp. 1, 4, 5.

28 For a history of AUD see Benson, 2005, *passim*; also www.union-democracy.org.

29 Chris Kutalik and William Johnson, "Twenty-five Years of Labor Notes History," *Z Magazine Online*, May 2004, Vol. 17 No. 5, www.zmagsite.zmag.org; also, www.labornotes.org.

30 For more information: www.unionist.org; www.newlaborforum.org; www.workingusa.org; www.labourstart.org; and for a discussion of shop floor newsletters, cartoons, and more see Slaughter, pp. 26–33.

31 *New York Times*, April 12, 2006, www.nytimes.com.

32 *New York Times*, May 2, 2006, www.nytimes.com; Brian Grow, "May Day: The Fight Behind the Protest," *Business Week Online*, April 28, 2006, www.businessweek.com.

33 *Los Angeles Times*, May 3, 2006, www.latimes.com.

34 *Labor Notes*, #253, April 2000, pp. 1, 14; #273, December 2001, pp. 15, 16.

35 Immanuel Ness, *Immigrants, Unions, and the New U.S. Labor Market*, Philadelphia, Temple University Press, 2005, p. 43.

36 *Labor Notes*, #332, November 2006, p. 13.

37 Migration Policy Institute, "Immigrant Union Members: Numbers and Trends," *Immigration Facts*, No. 7, May 2004, p.4.

38 Moody 1988, pp. 327–330.

39 Ruth Milkman and Kent Wong, "Organizing Immigrant Workers: Case Studies from Southern California," in Turner, Katz, and Hurd, pp. 104–107.

40 Ruth Milkman and Kent Wong, "Organizing the Wicked City: the 1992 Southern California Drywall Strike," in Milkman 2000, pp. 169–188.

41 Cited in Hector Delgado, "The Los Angeles Manufacturing Action Project: An Opportunity Squandered?" in Milkman 2000, pp. 228–229.

42 Milkman and Wong, in Turner et al., p. 111.

43 *Ibid.*, pp. 122–126.

44 *Labor Notes*, #327, June 2006, pp. 1, 6.

45 Biju Mathew, *Taxi! Cabs and Capitalism in New York City*, New York, The New Press, 2005, pp. 1–7, 68–69, 196–197.

46 Ness, pp. 150–161.

47 *Ibid.*, pp. 58–129.

48 Leon Fink, *The Maya of Morganton: Work and Community in the Nuevo New South*, Chapel Hill, University of North Carolina Press, 2003, pp. 2–6, 54–78, 96–97.

49 Fine, pp. 2–3, 11–14.

50 *Ibid.*, pp. 7–21.

51 Vanessa Tait, *Poor Workers' Unions: Rebuilding Labor From Below*, Cambridge, South End Press, 2005, pp. 165–169, 173–174; Fine, p. 9.

52 Tait, pp. 188–192; Fine, p. 9.

53 Fine, pp. 10–11.

54 Tait, pp. 178–181.

55 Make The Road By Walking, "Building Power in Brooklyn and Beyond," 2005 *Annual Report*, Brooklyn, NY, pp. 1–20.

56 Steve Jenkins, "Organizing, Advocacy, and Member Power," *Working USA: The Journal of Labor and Society*, Vol. 6, No. 2, Fall 2002, pp. 65–68.

57 Slaughter, pp. 262–263.

58 Make The Road, 2005 *Annual Report*, p. 12.

59 Fine, p. 11.

60 Saru Jayaraman, "In the Wake of 9–11: New York Restaurant Workers Explore New Strategies," August 2004, www.labornotes. org; Fine, p. 17.

61 *Labor Notes*, #289, April 2003, p. 5; #313, April 2005, pp. 1, 14; Slaughter, pp. 148–152; Fine, pp. 104–107.

62 Fox Piven and Cloward, pp. xiii–xvii.

63 Jenkins, p. 72.

64 Fine, pp. 120–125; Slaughter, pp. 251–254.

65 *Labor Notes*, #329, August 2006, pp. 10–11.

66 *Labor Notes*, #334, January 2007, pp. 1 and 14.

67 *Labor Notes*, #282, September 2002, pp. 8–9; Tait, pp. 188–192.

68 Slaughter, pp. 320–321.

Chapter 11

1 Crosby, pp. 1–21.
2 *Statistical Abstract*, 2006, p. 529.
3 *Statistical Abstract*, 2006, p. 399.
4 BLS, "Union Members in 2005," *News,* USDL 06–99, January 20, 2006, Table 5, www.bls.gov.
5 Foner, 1976, pp. 376–396.
6 Jack Bloom, *Class, Race, and the Civil Rights Movement: The Changing Political Economy of Southern Racism*, Bloomington, Indiana University Press, 1987, pp. 59–68, 103–104; Michael Goldfield, *The Color of Politics: Race and the Mainsprings of American Politics*, New York, The New Press, 1997, pp. 272–279.
7 Goldfield, pp. 244–249.
8 *Statistical Abstract*, 2006, pp. 29–31.
9 Goldfield, p. 279; *Statistical Abstract*, 2006, p. 27; 2001, p. 26.
10 BLS, "Foreign-Born Workers: Labor Force Characteristics in 2005," *News*, USDL 06–640, April 14, 2006, Table 6, www.bls.gov.
11 Fink, 2003, p. 2; *Labor Notes*, #329, August 2006, p. 10.
12 BLS, *State and Area Employment, Hours, and Earnings*, Customized Data Tables, September 16, 2006, www.bls.gov; *Statistical Abstract*, 2006, p. 416.
13 Mark Drabenstott, Mark Henry, and Kristin Mitchell, "Where Have All the Packing Plants Gone? The New Meat Geography in Rural America," *Economic Review*, Federal Reserve Bank of Kansas City, Third Quarter 1999, pp. 69, 74.
14 *Labor Notes*, #329, August 2006, p. 1.
15 REAP, "A Review of the US Meat Packing Industry," March 2006, p. 1, www.reapinc.org.
16 *Ibid.*
17 REAP, 2006, pp. 4–5; *Economic Report* 2005, p. 279.
18 REAP, 2006, p. 3.
19 Fink, p. 2; *Labor Notes*, #329, August 2006, p. 10.
20 Michael Broadway, "Beef Stew: Immigrants and Established Residents in a Kansas Beefpacking Town," in Louise Lamphere, Alex Stepick, and Guillermo Grenier, *Newcomers in the Workplace: Immigrants and the Restructuring of the U.S. Economy*, Philadelphia, Temple University Press, 1994, pp. 25–41.
21 *Statistical Abstract*, 2006, pp. 679.
22 BLS, "The Employment Situation," *News*, USDL 06–1542,

September 1, 2006, Table B–1, *www.bls.gov*; BLS, *Employment and Earnings from Current Employment Statistics*, September 15, 2006, www.data.bls.gov; United Auto Workers, "Statement of UAW President Ron Gettlefinger," *News*, July 18, 2006, www.uaw.org; *Guardian* (UK), September 16, 2006, p. 28.

23   Jeffrey Rothstein, "The Uncertain Future of the American Auto Industry," *New Labor Forum*, Vol. 15, Issue 2, Summer 2006, pp. 68–69.

24   BLS, *State and Area Employment, Hours, and Earnings*, Customized Data Tables, September 16, 2006, www.data.bls.gov.

25   BLS, *Employment, Hours, and Earnings from the Current Employment Statistics Survey*, "Truck Transportation," September 15, 2006, www.data.bls.gov.

26   BLS, "Union Members," Table 5, www.bls.gov.

27   Fine, pp. 8, 16–17, 278–279.

28   Tait, pp. 195–196; Fine, pp. 66–68.

29   James Andrews, "Pulling Together in North Carolina," *New Labor Forum*, Vol. 15, No. 2, Summer 2006, pp. 43–44.

30   Tait, pp. 188–192.

31   *Labor Notes*, #307, October 2004, pp. 1, 14.

32   MaryBe McMillan, "Letter to the Editor," *News Observer*, August 15, 2006, www.newsobserver.com; BLS, "Union Members in 2000," *News*, USDL 01–21, January 18, 2001; "Union Members in 2004," *News*, USDL, 05–112, January 27, 2005; BLS USDL 06–99, www.bls.gov; Andrews, p. 44.

33   Andrews, pp. 44–46.

34   Bronfenbrenner and Juravich, pp. 19–53; Bronfenbrenner and Hickey, pp. 17–55; Lopez, pp. 114–132.

35   Gruenberg.

36   Parker and Gruelle, pp. 14–15.

37   Hal Draper, *Karl Marx's Theory of Revolution: the Politics of Social Classes*, Vol. 2, New York, Monthly Review Press, 1978, pp. 97–98.

38   Stephanie Luce, "Life Support: Coalition Building and the Living Wage Movement," *New Labor Forum*, No. 10, Spring/Summer 2002, pp. 81–91.

39   For two recent expositions of this empire see, Chalmers Johnson, *The Sorrows of Empire: Militarism, Secrecy, and the End of the Republic*, New York, Henry Holt and Company, 2004, *passim*, David Harvey, *The New Imperialism*, New York, Oxford University Press, 2003, *passim*.

40   For some examples see Slaughter, pp. 339–350.

41   Moody 1997, pp. 227–268.

42   Joseph Stiglitz, *Globalization and Its Discontents*, New York, W.W. Norton & Co., 2003, p. 16, *passim*.

43   Kim Moody, "Unions," in Emma Bircham and John Charlton, *Anti-Capitalism: A Guide to the Movement*, London, Bookmarks, 2001, pp. 291–301.

44   Martin Shefter, *Political Parties and the State: The American Historical Experience*, Princeton, Princeton University Press, 1994, pp. 138–164.

45   Philip Foner, *History of the Labor Movement in the United States*, Vol. 9, New York, International Publishers, 1991, pp. 339–360.

46   Art Preis, *Labor's Giant Step: Twenty Years of the CIO*, New York, Pioneer Publishers, 1964, pp. 52, 364–365.

47   C. Wright Mills, *The New Men of Power: America's Labor Leaders*, Urbana, University of Illinois Press, 2001, pp. 211–213.

48   Eric Chester, *Socialists and the Ballot Box: A Historical Analysis*, New York, Praeger Publishers, 1985, p. 116.

49   Weir, pp. 305–306.

50   *Labor Notes*, #208, July 1996, pp. 8–9.

51   *Labor Notes*, #237, December 1998, pp. 3, 14.

52   *Labor Notes*, #208, July 1996, p. 9.

53   *Labor Notes*, #207, June 1996, p. 16.

54   *Labor Notes*, #234, September 1998, pp. 3, 12.

55   *Labor Notes*, #208, July 1996, p. 9.

56   Dan Clawson, *The Next Upsurge: Labor and New Social Movements*, Ithaca, Cornell University Press, 2003, p. 15.

57   Benson, p. 210.

58   Buhle, p. 196; Lichtenstein, 2002, p. 129.

INDEX

Figures in *italics* refer to tables.

Abernathy, William 15
Able, I.W. 109
Abozayd, Ahmed 190
Acevedo, Noel 209
Adams, Kirk 193–4
Adler, William 44
Advisory Committee on Trade Policy 112
affiliation 242, 243
African American Labor Center 69
African Americans 61; exclusion from
    politics 157–8; family income *84*,
    84–5; health benefits *82*; migration
    66, *66*, 87; militancy 64; pension
    plans *82*; poverty 87–8; segregation
    62; Southern population 62, 227;
    unemployment 85; union membership
    64, 66–7, *244*; values 160; voting
    patterns 146, 154; wages 81; in the
    workforce 66, 68, 70, *70*
agriculture 37
Alabama 45
Allied Industrial Workers 126
alternative work schedules (AWS) 34
Amalgamated Clothing and Textile
    Workers Union (ACTWU) *102*, 102
Amalgamated Meat Cutters 43–4, 103,
    115
Amalgamated Transit Union 125, 204–5
American Federation of Government
    Employees 243
American Federation of Labor (AFL) 61,
    63, 163
American Federation of Labor-Congress of
    Industrial Organizations (AFL-CIO):
    amnesty for undocumented workers
211–12; and business unionism 196–7;
and the Change to Win Federation
(CTW) 171–2, 173; and civil disobedience 121; Committee on
Political Education (COPE) 144;
creates A. Philip Randolph Institute
66; creation of 156–7; and El Salvador
73; electoral mobilization 143–9;
executive council 131–2; "institutions"
68–9; international work 136–7; and
the Kaiser Permanente partnership
111–12; leadership rebellion 129–33;
Legislative Department 144; and
mergers 114; and the mid-term elections 2006 143; National Day Laborer
Organizing Network 221; and the
NUP 169–71; organizational failure
137–42; political spending 146–8,
148, 150–1; shift to political activity
138; split 1, 3, 5, 198; Strategic
Organizing program 173; Sweeney's
record 133–7, 141, *142*; and the
Teamsters RICO suit 122
American Federation of State, Council
    and Municipal Employees (AFSCME)
    27, 116, *118*, *120*, 128, *128*, 130,
    167–8, 196, 206–7, 211
American Federation of Teachers (AFT)
    119, *120*, 128, *128*
American Institute for Free Labor
    Development (AIFLD) 69, 73
anti-Communism 68–9, 156, 227
apparel industry 21–2
Asian-American Free Labor Institute 69
Asian Women's Immigrant Association
    220
Asians 70, 71, *76*, 76, 214–15

Association for Union Democracy 209–10
AT&T 111
AT&T/Bell system 54
Atlanta 27
Auto Workers and Machinists 64, 98
automation 29
automobile industry 27, 113, 229–30;
  contract concessions 27; and imports
  14–15; in the South 45–6, 103–4,
  229–30; job losses 17; jointness 110–11;
  multi-tier wages 28; outsourcing 32;
  production 104; production workers
  102; restructuring 103–4
Axt, Deborah 218

bankruptcies 28
Banks, Andy 187
Bauer, Gary 160
benefits 81–3
Benitez, Lucas 3
Bennett, Mike 113
Bensinger, Richard 142
Benson, Herman 135, 209, 244
Bernard, Elaine 178
Bevona, Gus 132, 189
big labor 114–20
Biggs 55
Black/Brown Alliance 232
Black Power 157
Black Workers for Justice 217, 222,
  232
Blagojevich, Rod 168
Bloomberg, Michael 167
Bluestone, Barry 11–12
BMW 45
Botwinick, Howard 88
Braverman, Harry 39, 40
Brazil 73
Brecher, Jeremy 134, 135
Brenner, Robert 14, 17
Bronfenbrenner, Kate 19, 140, 170, 174,
  175, 180–1, 181, 233
Brooks, David H. 90
Brookwood Labor College 199
Brotherhood of Sleeping Car Porters and
  Maids 66
Bryan, William Jennings 151
Buhle, Paul 132
Bureau of Economic Analysis 46
Bureau of Labor Statistics 19, 38, 83–4
Burger, Anna 171
Burrus, William 131
Bush, George W. 168, 201
business corporate unionism 184,
  184–97

Business Roundtable 105, 149, 153
business services, mergers and acquisitions
  53–4

California 64, 180, 190, 200–1, 212–14
Canada 72, 211
capital 6–7; community of interest 164–5;
  and competition 15; export of 17, 18;
  fixed 47–8; and profit rates 13–14
capital investment 23–6, 24
Capital Moves (Cowie) 44
capitalism 58–9, 59
Carey, Ron 123, 130, 170, 179, 206
Caribbean Basin Initiative 74
Carolina Alliance for Fair Employment
  232
Carrefour 55
Carter, Jimmy 158
Caterpillar 125–6, 127, 200
Center for International Labor Solidarity
  (CILS) 136–7
Central America 72–3
Central Labor Councils 169, 199
centralization 189–94, 195–6
CEOs: compensation 90, 91, 92–3; perks
  93; retirement packages 92, 92; stocks
  and stock options 90–1, 91, 95
Chambers, John 91
Change to Win Federation (CTW) 1, 3,
  5, 101, 138, 142, 171–2, 172–3, 198,
  232–3
Chaves, César 68
Chavez, Hugo 136
Chavez-Thompson, Linda 130
Chicago 43, 67
Chief, the 208–9
childcare 86
Chile 73
China 19, 22–3, 44, 56, 63, 72, 148
Chinese Staff and Workers Association
  (CSWA) 217
Choosing Sides: Unions and the Team Concept
  (Parker and Slaughter) 210
Chrysler 27, 30–1, 104, 107–8, 109,
  110, 111
CIA 68, 69
civil rights movement 8, 64, 157
class 2, 58, 61–2, 154, 199–200
Clawson, Dan 244
Clinton, Bill 112, 129, 242
Coalition of Black Trade Unionists 131
Coalition of Immokolee Workers 2, 3–4,
  219–20
Coalition of Labor Union Women 65
coalitions 7–8, 202–3

Cohen, David 170
Cohen, Larry 175
Cold War 68–9, 129, 156
collective bargaining 109–10, 111, 113–14
Columbia 137
Committee for Real Change 206–7
Communication Workers of America
    (CWA) 27, 54, 108, 111, 114, 115,
    118, *118*, 119, *120*, 121–2, *128*, 140,
    173, 182, 196–7, 199, 213–14, 231,
    238
community based organizations 216
community of interest 164–5
competition 14–15, 52
computers 29
concessions 108, 109–10, 130
Concessions and How to Beat Them
    (Slaughter) 210
Congress 143, *148*, 148; committee
    system 149–50, 151, 153; reforms
    149–53
Congress of Industrial Organizations
    (CIO) 64, 162, 198–9, 227
consensus 111
Construction Users Anti-Inflation Round-
    table 105
construction industry 37, *42*, 46–7, *47*,
    61, 105–6
containerization 49–50
contingent work 12, 33–4
contract concessions 12, 26–8
contract terms 113–14
Convoy-Dispatch (Teamsters) 51
Coontz, Stephanie 65
Cordtz, Richard 187–8
Corporate Campaigns, Inc. 238
corporate culture 193–4
corporate power 6
corporate unionism 196
corporations, emergence of 61
corruption 104, 122, 132, 161, 206
Coss, Ken 126
Costello, Tom 134, 135
Cowie, Jefferson 44
Crawford, Edwin *91*
Crosby, Jeff 179–80, 224
CTV, Venezuelan Confederation of Labor
    136
Cuba 72, 73
cultural decay 159

Davidson, Richard *92*
"Day Without Immigrants" 3, 5–6, 49,
    211–12, 214
de-skilling 29

deal, politics of the 166–8
Debs, Gene 63
decentralization 32
Deloitte Research 19
Delphi 28, 32, 52, 205
"Democracy, Density and Transformation:
    We Need Them All" (Crosby) 224
Democracy Is Power (Parker and Gruelle)
    177–8, 179, 235
democracy, union 132, 177–9, 180, 194,
    224, 235–6
Democratic Leadership Council 158
Democratic Party 143, 145, 146, 148,
    149–53, 154, 154–62, 166, 240, 241,
    242
demography, industrial 58–9; 1870–1920
    59–63; 1941–70 64–9; post-1970s
    69–78
deregulation 50–2, 109, 149
Detroit 64, 66, 67, 200
Diop, Al 206
direct democracy 178, 180
displacement 89
divestitures *53*, 53
Dodge Revolutionary Union Movement
    (DRUM) 64, 67, 157
Dominican Republic 72, 73
Donahue, Tom 130–2, 131
Duffy, A. J. 205
Duke, David 241

Easterling, Barbara 130
Eastern Airlines 122, 124
economic activity: change in location 43–7;
    move to the South 44–7
Economic Leadership Dialogue on Citizen-
    ship 112
Economic Policy Institute 17, 22, 33–4,
    81, 83
economic trends, reversal of 11–12
education *42*, 42
El Salvador 72, 73
elections: Congressional 145, 146, 149;
    funding 150–2; mid-term (2006)
    143; NLRB 138–42, *139*, *140*, *141*;
    presidential 145, 147, 152, 156, 168;
    state and local 167–8; union member
    vote 143–9, *145*, 154–62
employee participation schemes 12
employer aggression 12
employer-employee relationships 6–7
employment: and FDI 20; Nonfarm
    industries *42*, 42–3; shifts in 37–43
employment agencies 41
Emspak, Frank 174

Engels, Frederick 236
equipment, capital investment in 24–5
ethnic queue effect 68
Euromarché 55
Exel 50
Experimental Negotiating Agreement 109
exports 20–1, *21*, 22

family income *84*, 84–7, 86, *93*, 94
Family Medical Leave Act (1993) 86, 148
Farm Labor Organizing Committee 4, 217, 232
farm laborers 3–4
Federal Election Campaign Act (1974) 150
Federal Reserve System 39
FedEx 51
feminism 65
Ferrer, Freddy 167
finance, insurance and real estate (FIRE) sector 41–2, 42, *42*
financial assets, distribution of 94–6
financial services 40
Fine, Janice 185, 218
Fishman, Mike 189
Fitzsimons, Frank 109
fixed assets per worker *25*, 25
fixed investments *24*, 24–5
Fletcher, Bill 181, 183, 187
Ford 27, 32, 52, 111, 230
foreign direct investment 16–19, *18*, 19–20, *20*, *46*, 46
foreign policy 238
Forester Research 19
France 55, 154
Frank, Thomas 159, 164
Fraser, Doug 104, 109
free trade 16–17, 19, 73–4, 154–5
free trade zones (FTZ) 73–4
freight volume 48

Galbraith, J.K. 26
Gates, Bill 96
General Electric 17, 28
General Motors 32, 45, 52, 103, 104, 109, 111, 113, 200, 230
Gerard, Leo 118
Germany 14, 16, 22
Gerrard, Leo 171
Global Insight 19
Global Positioning System (GPS) 33, 50
globalization 6, 11, 15–23, 37–8, 40, 49, 53, 71, 136, 237–9
goals, lack of 166

Gompers, Samuel 61, 63, 129, 133, 162, 163, 165
Gonzales, Juan 67
Gonzalez, Juan 125
Goodyear Tire & Rubber 28
Gordon, Jack 83–4
Gordon, Jennifer 218
Gordon, Suzanne 134, 135
government employment 37, *42*
Great Britain 72, 154, 167, 192
Great U-Turn, The (Harrison and Bluestone) 11–12
greed 11
Greenberg, Stanley 160
Grenada 73
grievance systems 183
gross domestic product 12, 14–15; by product type *38*, 38–9
gross national product, growth (1870–1920) 59–60, *60*
Gruelle, Martha 177–8, 179, 235
Guatemala 73
Guatemalans 215

Hanna, Mark 151, 165
Harrison, Bennett 11–12, 32
Hart-Cellars Act (1965) 70
Harvey, David 20, 48
Hasegawa, Bob 181–2
Hawaii 63
health benefits 12, 27–8, 81, *82*, 82–3, 132
Health Care Worker Recruitment and Retention Act 167
health care workers 116–17
health sector *42*
Health Security Act 129
Henriquez, Omar 218
HERE 116, 136, 169, 170, 173, 195–6, 217, 219
Heymann, Jody 86
hierarchy, culture of 208–9
Hill, Stanley 206
Hillman, Sidney 164
Hoffa, James P. 51, 104, 110, 170–1, 206
Honeycutt, Van 90
Hormel, Austin, Minnesota 27, 44, 103, 116
Huck, Gary 211
Hurd, Richard 181, 183, 187
Hurricane Katrina 47

IBEW 197
ideology 112–13, 162–6
immigrants and immigration 6, *60*, 61, 63; country of origin *71*, 71–4; "Day Without Immigrants" 3, 5–6, 49,

211–12, 214; European 59, 60; farm laborers 3–4; health benefits 81; Latin American 75, *75*; Mexican 75; militant action 211–16; numbers *71*, 71–2; organization 212–16; and poverty 88; power 5–6; problems facing 3; quota system ended 70–1; Southern states 229; strategic importance 212, 237–8; strikes 212–15; transport workers 49; undocumented *71*, 72, 218; union membership 77–8; and worker centers 217–20; in the workforce 72, *76*, 76–8
Immokolee, Florida 3–4
imperialism 63, 238
imports 14–15, 20–3, *21*, 22, 23, 49, 50, 237
income growth 96–7, *97*
Independent Coalition of Black Trade Unionists 67
India 19, 72
Industrial Production Index 39
industrialization 59
inequality, acceleration of 11
inflation 12, 23, 27, 79
information services *42*, 43
Inside the Circle: A Union Guide to QWL (Parker) 210
inter-modal transportation 49–50
interest rates 23
International Association of Machinists (IAM) 114, *118*, *120*
International Brotherhood of Electrical Workers (IBEW) *120*, 122
International Brotherhood of Teamsters (IBT). *see* Teamsters
international economic integration 15–16, *16*
International Ladies Garment Worker's Union (ILGWU) 102, *102*
International Longshore and Warehouse Union (ILWU) 201, 205, 243, 244
International Longshoremen's Association (ILA) 207
International Monetary Fund 74, 239
international monetary system 12–13
international production chains 17
international trade 14–15, 20–3, *21*
Interstate Commerce Commission 50
Iowa Beef Products (IBP) 44
Irani, Ray *91*
IT 19, 29

Jackson, Maynard 27
Jacobs, Irwin Mark *91*
James, Willie 208
Japan 14, 16, 22, 29, 30, 167

Jenkins, Steve 220
Jensen, Michael 91
job security 30–1, 112
jobs: competition for 6; and FDI 20; growth 83–4; growth in dead-end 83–4; and lean production 30–1; offshoring 19
Jobs with Justice 135, 219, 236
jointness 110–13
Juravich, Tom 180, 233
Just Health Care campaign 242
just-in-time delivery 49
Justice for Janitors campaign 124–5, 131, 132, 176, 186–7, 188, 191, 194–5, 199, 213

K-Mart 55
Kaiser Permanente 111–12, 112, 113
Kelly, Fernandez 89
Kilts, James 90
King, Martin Luther, Jr. 67, 157, 226
Kirkland, Lane 129, 129–30, 132, 146, 147–8, 163
knowledge, removal from labor process 29
Konopacki, Mike 211
Korea 72
Korean Immigrant Workers alliance 221
Krugman, Paul 92–3
Kutalik, Chris 202

La Botz, Dan 175–6
La Mujer Obrera 217
Labor Against the War 239
labor costs 25–6, 27, 44–5
Labor Council for Latin American Advancement 68
labor force. *see* workforce
labor law 12
labor-management cooperation 108, 110–13, 143
Labor Notes 17, 28, 31, 33, 125, 132, 134, 170, 172, 200, 210
Labor Party 240–5
labor process, removal of knowledge from 29
Labor Research Review 187, 211
Labor Start website 211
Laborers International Union of North America (LIUNA) 105–6, *120*
Lagginni, Bob 194
landbridge system 50
Latinos 67–8, 75, 213–14; family income *84*, 84–5; health benefits 81, *82*; pension plans *82*; poverty 87–8; unemployment 85; union member

voters 146; union membership 64, 68, 244; wages 81; in the workforce 68, 69–70, *70*, 75, *76*, 76–8
Le Blanc, Paul 61
lean production 28–36, 54–6, 175
Lease Drivers Coalition 214
Leedham, Tom 206
Legislative Action Committees 153
leisure & hospitality *42*, 42
Lens, Sidney 73
Lerner, Stephen 169–70, 177, 178
Lewis, John L. 198–9
Lewis, Kenneth *92*
Lichtenstein, Nelson 55, 67, 110, 127, 143, 156–7, 233–4
living agreement, the 111
living standards 2, 6–7, 79–87, 164–5
Lobby Disclosure Act (1995) 152
lobbyists 151, 152–3
local government 42, *42*, 43, 166–7
logistics 30, 32–3, 50, 231
Lorenzo, Frank 122
Los Angeles 205, 211
LTV Corporation 28
Luce, Stephanie 19

McCall, Carl 167
McCarron, Douglas 169, 171
McClure, Laura 132
McDonald, David 107
McDonalds 4
McEntee, Gerald 130
McFadden, Ian 190
McGovern, George 158
McGuire, William 90, 91, *91*, 92, *92*
McKinnell, Henry *92*
Make the Road by Walking 218
Make Work Pay campaign 172
management-by-stress 30
management rights 109
Mantsios, Greg 133
manufacturing industries: administration 40; cause of union decline 245; employees *42*; fall in profit rates 14–15, 17, 19; and FDI 16, *18*, 19–20, *20*, 46; fixed assets per worker 25, *25*; GDP share *38*, 38–9; growth 19–20; job losses 17, 19, 22, 31, 37, 101–4; and offshoring 19; union membership 64; value added *35*, 35, *44*, 45; wages 25–6; workforce growth (1870–1920) 59, *60*; working hours 34
Martinez, Maria 206
Marxism 162–3
Massachusetts 17

Mazzocchi, Tony 241, 242
Meany, George 66, 144–5, 157, 163, 164, 245
meatpacking 43–4, 103, 228–9, *229*, 230–1
Medicaid 87
Medicare 87
Mercedes 45
mergers and acquisitions (M&A) 52–4, *53*
Metaldyne 28
Metropolitan Transit Authority 201–2
Metzgar, Jack 155, 183, 187
Metzgar, Johnny 155
Mexicans 67–8, 72, 212–15
Mexico 44, 63, 71, 74, 74–5, 104
Michael F. Corbett & Associates 32
Microsoft 52, 152
Migration Policy Institute 212
militancy, suppression of 107–9
military interventions 73
Milkman, Ruth 77–8
Miners for Democracy 124
mining/natural resources *42*
Mitchell, John 165
modular production 32
Mollie's Job (Adler) 44
Monroe Doctrine 63
Montgomery, David 59, 60–1
motivation 30–1
Motor Carrier Act (1980) 50
Multi-fiber Agreement 22, 44
Murphy, Kevin 91
Muslims 215

Nardell, Robert *92*
National Civic Federation (NCF) 165
National Coalition for Dignity and Amnesty 212
National Day Laborer Organizing Network 221
National Education Association (NEA) 119, *120*
National Endowment for Democracy 136
National Interfaith Committee for Worker Justice 215
National Labor Relations Board (NLRB) 119, 172, 173, 246; elections 138–42, *139*, *140*, *141*
National Master Freight Agreement (NMFA) 104–5
Negro American Labor Council 66
neoliberalism 11
Netherlands, the 167
New Directions Movement 124, 208–9

New Jersey Department of Youth and Family Services 182
New Labor Forum 211
New Men of Power, The (Wright Mills) 240
New Unity Partnership (NUP) 169–71
New Voice program 131–3, 134, 142
New York City 2–3, 4–5, 27, 67, 77, 108, 124, 167, 189, 201–2, 206–7, 214–15, 240
New York Taxi Workers Alliance 214, 221
New York Times 101
9–to-5 186
Nissan 45
Nixon, Richard 149, 157–8
non-majority unionism 217, 222–3
nonstandard work 33–4
North American Free Trade Agreement (NAFTA) 16, 17, 50, 74, 129, 149
North Carolina 222, 232–3
Northland Poster collective 211
NUMMI plant 35
Nussbaum, Karen 186
NYMEX 27–8, 121–2

Occupational Safety and Health Act 151
offshoring 19
Oil, Chemical and Atomic Workers (OCAW) 241, 242–3
oil, prices 13
Olney, Peter 172, 176
Omaha Together One Community (OTOC) 220–1
OPEC 13
Open Door policy 69
Operation Dixie 227
organization, "new" forms of 7
Organizing Institute 136, 199
organizing model 187
Organizing to Win (Bronfenbrenner and Juravich) 180
O'Sullivan, Terrance 169
outsourcing 12, 30, 31–2, 166
overtime 34, 80–1, 85

Pacer Global Logistics 50
Pacific Maritime Association 201
Packinghouse Workers 102, 103
Paff, Ken 123, 170
Palmisano, Samuel 92
Panama 73
Panama Canal 50, 63
Parker, Mike 30, 31, 35, 177–8, 179, 210, 235

part-time work 12
partnership 165–6, 192
partnerships and mergers 108
Pataki, George 167, 172
pattern bargaining 27, 104–5, 175
Pension Benefits Guarantee Corporation 28
pension funds 95–6
pension plans 5, 12, 28, 81–2, *82*
Perkins, Julia 4
personal services 40–1
A. Philip Randolph Institute 66
Philippines, the 63, 72
Phillips, Kevin 96
Piore, Michael 186
Pittsburgh 67
Political Action Committee (PACs) 144, 150
political spending 146–8, *148*, 150–1
politics: business involvement 149–53; corporate money and 6; the deal 166–8; ethnic traditions 155–6; financial contributions 167–8; independent action 244–5; the Labor Party 240–5; racism in 156; two-party system 244; union mobilization 143–9; and values 160
poverty 87–9
Presser, Jackie 122–5, 187
Price Club 55
private sector: union density 19, 98, *100*; union membership 64, 98, *100*, 101, 106, 138
producer services 40
productivity 25–6, 83, 87
Professional and Business services 40, *42*, 42
Professional Air Traffic Controllers Organization (PATCO) 1, 107, 130
professionals 43
profit rates *13*, 13–14, 16, 17, 19, 23, 41–2, 88
Progressive Educators in Action (PEAC) 205–6
Progressive Party 241
public sector 27, 64
Puerto Ricans 67–8
Puerto Rico 63, 168
Pure and Simple Unionism 162–3

racism 87–8, 156, 157–8, 226, 227
Racketeer-Influenced, Corrupt Organizations Act (RICO) 122–3
railroads 33, 51–2, 117
Randolph, A. Philip 66, 157

rank-and-file rebellions 203–9
Raymond, Lee *92*
Raynor, Bruce 169
Reagan, Ronald 107, 130, 158, 239
Reagonomics 149
recession (1974–75) 1–2, 12–15, 75
recession (2000) 26, 45, 53
reengineering 31
reform movements: resources for 209–11;
  upsurge in 203–9, 246–7
Regional Bell Operating Companies
  (RBOC) 54
Rekindling the Movement (Fletcher and
  Hurd) 183
Remote Control Operation (RCO) 33
representation 183–4, 184, 192–3
Republican Party 146, 148, 151, 153,
  154–5, 155–6, 159–61
reserve army of labor 88
Restaurant Opportunities Centre 218–19
restructuring 103–4
retail 41
Retail Clerks 43–4, 115
retail trade *42*; Wal-Mart's domination of
  54–6
Retail, Wholesale and Department Store
  Union 218
Reuther, Walter 164
Rhode Island 190–1
Richardson, Charlie 29, 33
Riley, Ken 207
Riley, Leonard 207
Rivera, Dennis 167, 189
"Robber Barons" 61
Roberts, Brian *92*
Roberts, Lillian 167, 207
Rockefeller, John D. 63
Roediger, David 62
Rogers, Ray 126
Rollins, Kevin *91*
Romney, Edgar 171, 172
Roosevelt, Theodore 63
Rosenstein, Hetty 182
Rosselli, Sam 188
Ruben *92*

Sadlowski, Ed 107
Sassen, Saskia 40
Schermerhorn, Tim 124, 208
School of Americas 136
Seattle 181–2, 239
Segat, Susana 191
segregation 62, 63, 155
Semel, Terry *91*
Service Employees International Union

(SEIU) 101, 112, 114, 115, 116, 117,
  118, 119, *120*, *128*, 128, 130, 140,
  141, 167–8, 171, 172, 173, 181,
  182–3; activists 185–6; centralization
  189–94; Committee on the Future
  report 188; corporate culture 193–4;
  and the "Day Without Immigrants"
  211; decertifications 190–1; democracy
  194; International Executive Board
  189; international links 238; Justice
  for Janitors campaign 124–5, 131,
  132, 176, 186–7, 188, 191, 194–5,
  199, 213; local mergers 189–91;
  membership 185; New Strength Unity
  Plan 188–9; problems of new structure
  191–4; reform movements 205; shop
  stewards 192–3; social movement
  186–7; staff 193–4; structural
  development 185–8
service sector: GDP share *38*, 38–9;
  growth in 37–43; profit rates 41–2;
  union presence 42–3
servicing model 187
Shaikh, Anwar 13–14
Shailor, Barbara 136
shallow power 184–97
Shanker, Albert 129
shares *93*
Sharpe, Teresa 178, 181
shop stewards 192–3
Slaughter, Jane 30, 31, 35, 210, 242
social movement unionism 236–7
socialism, rejection of 163
Socialist Party 240
solidarity 4
Solidarity 147
solidarity pacts 202–3
South Carolina 45
South, the: African American population
  62, 227; African American poverty
  88; assets 231–3; automobile
  industry 45–6, 103–4, 229–30;
  construction contracts 46–7, *47*;
  demographic growth and diversity
  227; economic activity moves to
  44–7; and FDI 20, 46, *46*; immigrant employment 229; industrial
  diversity 227–8; industrialization
  225–31; meatpacking industry
  228–9, 230–1; Operation Dixie 227;
  political role 161–2; racism 156,
  157–8, 226, 227; transportation and
  logistics 231; union density 225–6,
  231–3; union membership 231–2;
  unionization efforts 226–31; value

added *44*, 45; wages 225–6, *226*, 228–9, *229*; worker centers 216–17; workforce 45
Spanish-American War 63
stagflation 23–6, 75
Staley, A.E. 116, 126, 132, 200
Stamford (Connecticut) Organizing Project 135
State Employees Association Of North Carolina 232
steel industry 109
Steelworkers Fight Back campaign 107
Steelworkers *see* USWA
Steier, Richard 209
Steininger, Daniel 93
Stern, Andy 115, 159, 169, 170, 178, 186, 187, 188, 189, 192, 194
Stigliz, Joseph 239
stocks and stock options 90–1, *91*, 95
Stone, Milan 125
Strasser, Adolph 162–3
strikes: 24–hour strike clause 109; 1945–46 64; 1950s 64, 107; 1960s 64; 1970s 64, 100–1, 107, 109; 1980s 107; 1989 121–2; 1990s 125–7, 199–200; California grocery strike (2003) 200–1; and concessions 28; coordinated structure 175; decline in numbers 98, *99*, 100; dockworkers (1971–72) 49; Dodge (1968) 67; GM (1970) 109; ILWU (2002) 201; immigrants 212–15; and merged unions 115–16; New York City transit workers 2–3, 4–5, 201–2; public employees 4; solidarity pacts 202–3; UPS 51, 200; and Wal-Mart 56; wildcat 7, 100–1, 109; workers striking 98, *99*, 100
Striking Steel (Metzgar) 155
supply chain management 50
sweatshops 88
Sweeney, John 112, 114, 130, 131–7, 141, 142, 146, 148, 150, 152, 165–6, 171, 176, 185–7, 197

Tabajadores en Acción 218
Taco Bell 2, 3–4, 219–20
Taft-Hartley Act (1947) 95, 144
Tarpinian, Greg 171–2
taxi drivers 214–15
Taylorism 29, 55
Teamsters 64, 98, 102–3, 104–5, 108, 109, 115, 117, 119, *120*, 122, *128*, 130, 140, 170–1, 171, 181–2, 200, 205, 206, 211, 231

Teamsters for a Democratic Union 51, 123, 175, 181–2, 200, 206
Teamster's National Master Freight Agreement 51
technology 11, 15, 26–8, 28–36
Telecommunications Act (1996) 54
telecommunications industry 54
Tennessee 45
textile industry 21–2, 44
Theodus, Sam 123
Third World Debt Crisis 74
Thompson, Heather 108
Thompson, John *91*
Thomson Financial 53
"Three Steps to Reorganizing and Rebuilding the Labor Movement" (Lerner) 169–70, 177
tire production 103, 105, 126
Tobin, James *91*
Tonak, Ahmet 14
Total Quality Management (TQM) 31
Toussaint, Roger 201–2, 208–9
Townsend, Chris 242
Toyota 34–5
Trade Union Educational League 240
Trade Union Leadership Council 66
trade unions: 1930s 7; African Americans in 64, 66–7, 244; assets 117–18, *118*; business organization 163–4, 184; call for reform 122–5; call to consolidate 169–70; competition for members 116–17; decline 1–2; decline 1989–95 125–9; decline in membership 1, 5, 11, 98, 101–6, *102*, 127–9, *128*, *137*, 137–8; density 19, 64, 98, *100*, 128, 170, 173–4, 191, 224, 225–6, 231–3, 245–6; exclusion of immigrants 61–2; failure of 245–7; failure to organize 245–6; gender bias 164; growth in membership 64; immigrant member-ship 77–8; independent political action 244–5; international links 238; Latinos in 64, 68, 244; leadership 107, 109–10, 129–37, 179–80, 198–9, 203–4, 246; leadership reform 203–9, 246; local organization 181–4, 184; member involvement 181–2; member-ship 98, *100*, 115, 118, 119, *120*, 185, 231–2, 244; mergers 114–20, 126, 128, 171, 243; power 173–6, 177, 178, 234–6, 244–5; private sector membership 64, 98, *100*, 101, 106, 138; service sector presence 42–3; situation 1989 121–5; staff 193–4; suppression of militancy 107–9;

survival strategies 106–14; transport industry representation 49; turning point 1; well-being indicators *128*; women in 64, 65, 244
transformation 224
transit workers 2–3, 4–5
transnational corporations (TNC) 16, 20, 52, 237
Transnational Information Exchange (TIE) 238
transport & utilities *42*, 43, 47
transport industry 47–52; consolidation 50–1; deregulation 50–2, 104–5; equipment 48; and the landbridge system 50; and the NMFA 104–5; volume 48; workforce 48, 51
Transport Workers Union (TWU) 4–5, 124, 201–2, 204, 208–9
Trumka, Rich 121, 124, 130, 131, 243
trusteeships 188–9
Tucker, Jerry 124, 125, 126, 172

undocumented workers, amnesty 211–12
unemployment 75, 85, 88
unemployment insurance 89
union avoidance 12
Union Cities program 135–6, 199
Union Communications Services 211
Union Democracy in Action (Benson) 209
Union Democracy Review 210
UNITE! 116, 169, 170, 181, 196, 215
UNITE-HERE 171, 195–6, 199
United Airlines 28
United Auto Workers International 28
United Automobile Workers of America (UAW) 102, 103–4, 107–8, 113, *120*, 124, 125–6, 127, *128*, 130, 147, 173, 175, 196, 205, 231, 232, 238, 241
United Brotherhood of Carpenters and Joiners of America (UBC) *118*, *120*, *128*, 140, 196, 204
United Electrical, Radio and Machine Workers (UE) 238, 243
United Electrical Workers 217
United Farm Workers 4, 64, 171
United Federation of Teachers 205
United Food and Commercial Workers (UFCW) 43–4, 103, 114, 115, 116, 117–18, 119, *120*, *128*, 140, 201, 215, 221, 228–9, 231, 232, 234
United Mine Workers of America (UMWA) 121, 123–4, 130, 198–9
United national Caucus 107
United Packinghouse Workers 43, 66

United Paper Worker International Union (UPIU) 126
United Rubber Workers 105, 126
United Service Workers for Democracy 190
United Teachers of Los Angeles 205
UPS 50, 51, 53, 175, 179, 200, 231
urbanization 60, 60–1
USWA 64, 98, 102, *102*, 105, 108, *118*, 118, 119, *120*, 126, *128*, 173, 196, 199, 238

Vanderbilt, Cornelius 96
Verizon 28
Vietnam 72
Vietnam War 68, 157
violence 161
Visteon 28, 32, 52
voting patterns 143–9, 147, 154–62

wages: CEO 90; contract concessions 27; decline in real value 11, 75, 79–81, *80*, 83–4, 85, 89, 103, 127; differentials 88–9; increase (1947–67) 68; meat-packing industry 228–9, *229*; minimum 89; and productivity gains 25–6, 83; race and gender differences 81; Southern states 225–6, *226*, 228–9, *229*; state comparisons *226*; two-tier schemes 12, 28; women 81, 85–6
Wages, Bob 241
Wal-Mart 30, 48, 50, 52, 54–6, 165, 225, 233–4, 237
Wall Street Internationalism 69
Wall, Suzanne 170
Wallace, George 156
Wallace, Henry 241
Washington Consensus 238–9
waste, elimination from production 29–30
Watsonville Canning, California 27
Watts, Dave 126
wealth 90–7
websites 211
Weir, Stan 50, 204, 213, 246
Welch, Jack 112
welfare 89
Welsh, Jack 92
What's the Matter With Kansas? (Frank) 159
Whitacre, Edward *92*
Whitman, Margaret *91*
wholesale trade *42*
Widening Gap, The (Heymann) 86
Wilhelm, John 169
William Levitt and sons 106

Wilson, Woodrow 63
Winning for Working Families 134–5
Winslow, Cal 100
women 62; health benefits 82; married 65, 65, 85–6; and nonstandard work 33–4; pension plans 82; union membership 64, 65, 244; wages 81, 85–6; in the workforce 65, 65, 68, 70
Woodruff, Tom 172
work, intensification of 34–5, 35
work measurement 34–5
work minutes 34–5, 35
work time 33–4
worker centers 216–22, 232, 236
Workers in a Lean World (Moody) 1, 15, 17, 37–8, 238
workforce 37–43, 69–70: African Americans in 66, 68, 70, 70; clerical worker numbers 39–40; by gender and race 70; growth (1870–1920) 59–60; immigrant 72, 76, 76–8; Latinos in 68, 69–70, 70, 75, 76, 76–8; shifts in 37–43; the South 45; tracking and control 33; trade union membership 5; transport industry 48, 51; women in 65, 65, 68, 70

working hours 12, 34, 85, 175
Working Smart: A Union Guide to Participation Programs and Reengineering (Parker and Slaughter) 210
working standards 2, 7
Working USA 211
Workingmen's Party 240
Workplace of the Future 111
Workplace Project 218
World Bank 239
World Trade Organization 16, 22, 239
World War 1 63
World War 2 64, 67, 114
Wright Mills, C. 240

Yellow-Roadway 51
Yettaw, Dave 124
Yokich, Steve 32
Yum! Brands 2, 3–4, 219

Zeller, Duke 176
Zieger, Robert 144, 157
Zinn, Howard 61

What Every
Woman
Should Know
About Her
Husband's
Money

Shelby White

TURTLE BAY BOOKS
A Division of Random House
New York   1992

All rights reserved under International and Pan-American
Copyright Conventions. Published in the United States by
Turtle Bay Books, a division of Random House, Inc., New
York, and simultaneously in Canada by Random House of
Canada Limited, Toronto

Library of Congress Cataloging-in-Publication Data

White, Shelby.
  What every woman should know about her husband's
money / Shelby White
    p. cm.
  ISBN 0-394-58721-9
  1. Married women—Finance, Personal. I. Title.
HG179.W524 1992
332.024′ 0655—dc20   91-50971

Manufactured in the United States of America on
acid-free paper
9 8 7 6 5 4 3 2
First Edition
Book design by Charlotte Staub

*To my mother and father who, after sixty
years of marriage, still share everything.
And, of course, to Leon and Tracy.*

Contents

1   Marriage Is Not an Equal
    Opportunity   3
2   I Do, I Do   15
3   Marriage, Inc.   30
4   "Honey, Just Sign Here"   48
5   Coming Apart   67
6   If You Thought Marriage Was Bad,
    Wait Until You Try Divorce   87
7   Retirement? For Whom?   119
8   Will Power: The American Way of
    Leaving   161
9   Cinderella Revised: The Rights of
    Children   200
10 What's It Worth?   213
11 1040   221

    Afterword   233
    Notes   237
    Bibliography   245
    Acknowledgments   253
    Index   255

WHAT EVERY WOMAN SHOULD KNOW
ABOUT HER HUSBAND'S MONEY

1.
Marriage Is Not an Equal Opportunity

When Barbara Walters signed her first million-dollar television contract, she reportedly said to her agent, "Promise me that in five years I won't have to marry for money." Curious about this comment, I once asked her if she had been quoted accurately. "Yes," she said, and then explained that, although she knew how to earn money, she didn't know how to manage it. She had accumulated some money and then turned it over to a friend, a highly regarded Wall Street expert, to invest for her. The results were disastrous. She lost a substantial amount and worried that it could happen again.

Barbara Walters, like many women, reflected the view that money was a man's domain and, in the end, a man will rescue a woman from financial woes. Barbara Walters also found out that this is not necessarily true. Yet many women, whether based on a tradition of dependence or the reality of lower wages, have a fear of financial ruin. Even women with substantial earnings power report "bag lady nightmare"—a feeling described as "a pervasive uneasiness that despite all their affluence and hard work they will end up destitute."[1]

When it comes to money and marriage, old stereotypes persist. Women have been coming out of the kitchen and going off to work for the past twenty-five years. We have had a sexual revolution, a divorce revolution, and a work revolution. The marriage revolution is not here yet. We have entered into an era of gender-neutral language that has attempted to eliminate the sexism in our vocabularies. Our legal system purports to make no distinction between males and females; our classrooms are enrolling more women than ever in areas previously reserved for males.[2]

Despite these changes, the promised equality has not materialized. Inside the home tradition takes root. We may have blended families and extended families, but we still have families. And in the privacy of our families, women are not equal. Women still take care of the inside of the house, pay the daily bills, and take care of the children. Their husbands do the outdoor work and manage the assets.[3] Men and women continue to define their roles in marriage according to traditional tasks. Men think of themselves as the breadwinners.[4] For men, the leading definition of masculinity is being "a good provider for his family." Men equate money with power and self-esteem, and women agree. Women think of men who earn a lot of money as masculine and powerful. In contrast, women think the definition of femininity is being able to balance work and home and caring for people. Men think femininity is defined as sexual attraction.[5]

This homage to tradition persists even though approximately 59 percent of couples who are not retired depend on two paychecks.[6] There are 8.4 million households with incomes above $75,000. Of this group, 68 percent of the moderately affluent are two-income couples. Fifty-nine percent of the very affluent are two-income couples.[7]

For generations American marriages were bound by a legal system that gave power to husbands. Now, the laws have changed. Modern marriage is supposed to be about equals. The problem is, men are resisting the change and continuing to use their higher earnings as a way to control their marriages. Women have adapted to working outside the home, but men have not as easily adapted to having working wives. Men are still reluctant to share the house-keeping. The more money a husband earns, the less willing he is to do the housework, no matter how many hours his wife works outside the home.[8] When children come along, the traditional roles are further entrenched.

What is control? How does it work in marriage? It means that a husband can make decisions to which his wife is afraid to object. As one woman said, "I was always afraid I would find myself out on the street with three children." She didn't feel she had any rights because she didn't earn the money.

Sometimes control is subtle. One example is the two-paycheck couple that argues about which one of them will pick up the children at school. The one with the lower paycheck usually picks up the children. The argument appears to be about time and responsibility, but it is really about power and control.

Sometimes the control is more direct. A typical example would be the husband who decides to buy an expensive stereo set even though his wife would prefer that the money be spent on clothes for the children. He earns the money so he gets to buy the stereo. It is not surprising to discover that the more money the man earns, the more likely that he will manage the assets.[9] The only leverage she has, said one wife, is to withhold sex.

For many women brought up to think they would be

equal financial partners in marriage, reality comes as an unpleasant surprise. Frequently there is a big change from when the couple dated and each paid their own way. When they married they probably continued to split expenses. For many women, the arrival of children means a dramatic shift in the balance of their marriages. For one thing, the husband may suddenly see his wife as a mother and want her to assume a more traditional role. Then too, a wife may discover that she can no longer keep up her end financially. This is especially true if she stops working, a decision both make together, but which has a much greater impact on the wife.

The equality women thought they would have at work hasn't really happened either. Women as a group are paid less than men. Notice, I said paid. Usually headlines read, women continue to "earn" less than men, making it seem as if women were somehow less deserving than men. In general women are paid 71 percent of what men are paid. Executive women do only 42 percent as well as executive men. The statistics vary, but rarely do women do better than men.[10] Women are more apt to interrupt their careers to raise their children. When they do, they are likely to fall behind men in the wage race. Women who go back to work, after they have taken time off, may have to accept a lower paying job, or they may lose some pension benefits or seniority at their former jobs. And this, fourteen years after the Pregnancy Discrimination Act was passed, that was supposed to protect women.

Many women take less demanding jobs in order to spend more time home with their children. Many women graduating from law school take jobs in legal departments of large corporations, instead of trying for more lucrative law firm partnerships. And guess what? Women who work as lawyers for large corporations are paid less than male lawyers in similar jobs.[11]

Women who enter fields formerly reserved for men also find resegregation; with women getting the caretaker jobs: more women doctors become pediatricians, the lowest paid field, than brain surgeons, one of the highest paid areas of medicine.

A growing number of women are discovering that they also must take care of their elderly parents, and their husband's elderly parents, as well. In February 1990, when Annalyn Swan, formerly editor of *Savvy* magazine, announced that she would leave her job, she told her readers, "Life has a way of making certain decisions for you. In my case it was the illness of a parent. Faced with the prospect of frequent travel and intensive care, I realized like many other women, just how much our society still depends for caregiving on women. For me, at least, the choice was clear. Life became a matter of being not just an editor but more importantly, a daughter." Swan is "sequencing," the term sociologists apply to the trading of office jobs for more independent projects. Swan writes that more women will opt to do this. Imagine reading a "swan song" like hers from a male editor in chief.

The income women have been bringing home has been a mixed blessing. Some men like it, but many men feel threatened when their wives work and become more independent.[12] And no wonder. Men have a lot to lose. When a wife works, she not only brings home a paycheck, but she also continues to do most of the housework and takes care of the kids. Not a bad deal for her husband. She also begins to have a separate life. Older husbands resent

7

wives who usurp their traditional role. Perhaps this is because many women work because their husbands do not earn enough. The husband already feels inadequate, since he is not fulfilling his expected role of supporting his family. Many women, capable of earning even more than their husbands, sense their husbands' discomfort. They decide they would rather have the marriage than the career, so they pull back.

Of course, husbands outearn their wives in almost 80 percent of families. Therefore, the wife's work is deemed less important and less essential. His salary is considered crucial, hers incidental. This frequently turns into the "I can't afford to work" syndrome. This means, after baby-sitters, transportation, clothing, and taxes are deducted from the wife's salary, the additional income is too small to warrant the time and effort. Many couples discover that up to two thirds of the second paycheck goes to child care, household help, clothing, food, and work-related expenses. The result—the wife stays home. The husband seldom gives up his job, because he is usually earning more money. Nor is the child-care cost considered as coming from the husband's salary.[13] Little economic value is given to the wife's unpaid household work of running the house, managing the children, or arranging the social schedule.

In lower income, younger families, when wives discover they are capable of earning a living—and maybe earning more than their husbands—it is the wife who becomes dissatisfied and often wants to leave the marriage.[14] Although there have been studies showing women plunging into poverty immediately after divorce, many women, liberated from the constraints of marriage, actually work harder and earn more than women who remain married. The marriage itself may be a reason women earn less money.

Sociologists, not surprisingly, have begun to discover a high correlation between women going to work and the divorce rate in America.[15]

Working part-time is not much of an improvement. June Ryan is typical.* Trained as a biologist, when I met her she was seven months pregnant. She and her husband bought a small house in the suburbs. June became a laboratory technician so that she could plan a work schedule that would allow her to be at home most of the time. In the three years since their daughter was born, June has continued to work at a job that pays her only an hourly wage with no benefits. Her husband Bill's career at a large corporation has continued to advance.

Although she was once able to support herself, the arrival of a baby and the overhead of a house have added expenses that June could no longer manage on her own. She has become financially dependent. Her lower earnings have put her in a position in which her husband can use his higher wages as a reason to handle the assets and otherwise control the finances of their marriage.

Many women, frustrated by a glass ceiling at the office, stay home and become just as dependent on their husbands as the mothers they had vowed not to imitate once did.

Only with a difference. Their mothers expected to stay home. In the nineties, women feel dependent, but they also feel guilty if they stay home with their children. On

*Not a real name. Throughout the book I have used fictitious names.

the other hand, women who try both to work and raise children are often too frazzled to do either job well. A wife finds herself with two careers: working mother and working woman. Her husband has only his career.

The wife who earns less or who has stayed home to take care of the children feels that she is not entitled to a say in the finances. One woman, now home caring for children, confided that her husband, sensing her unhappiness at feeling dependent, put money into her savings account every month. She only resented his attempt to "pay" her.

Today many women are saying no to this paternalism. While it is easier for the working woman to do this, because she has some economic leverage, the woman who stays home and cares for the children and helps her husband by entertaining his clients and otherwise freeing him from household chores to be able to devote himself to business, also has a right to share in the finances of the marriage, as partner and decision maker.

Obviously, there are some marriages that thrive on the powerful-husband/weak-and-protected-wife relationship. One woman said, "I always saw my husband as the merchant prince, and he always saw me as the student." When her husband had business losses neither one of them could discuss it because it would have destroyed the myths each had created about the other.

When people marry they bring their own attitudes about money with them. These attitudes tend to color the way they handle money in their marriages. The wife who was brought up in a home where her parents both worked and kept their money separate may feel guilty if her husband pays for her. The wife who was brought up in a more traditional household may feel uncomfortable if her husband doesn't pay for her. The woman who equates money with love may be disappointed if her husband doesn't buy her expensive presents.

Patterns of spending are also usually carried over from our own childhood. The wife who was brought up by thrifty parents hates to spend money unless she gets good value. The wife who hated eating in expensive restaurants ruined such occasions for her husband because she always looked at the prices and then calculated the cost of the ingredients.

The husband who saw his mother struggle after his father died and left the family with little money wants to put all his money into insurance. If he is married to a woman whose family never believed in worrying about that rainy day, conflicts can result.

Unfortunately, many couples who are easily able to discuss sex with each other, enter marriage without ever discussing just how they will manage their finances.

Money conflicts are different from control. You may want to save every penny for a house in five years, while your husband may want to spend more now and buy a less expensive house. You may want to invest in a new business; your husband may want to support his ailing mother. You may not mind owing money; your husband may hate it. These are legitimate conflicts open to discussion and compromise. And, let's face it, some pretty tense arguments. Control in the marriage is different. It means you may be forced to do things without discussion, without even knowing the facts.

Today, no woman should be ignorant of her husband's finances or her own. If a wife doesn't share financial decisions, regardless of who earns the money, her husband will act as the powerful daddy. By having to ask, you give up control and then money is used as a reward. Do what your husband would like and he will get you the car you want.

If your husband is reading this book he may be saying to himself, "I try and tell her, but every time I start to talk about taxes or my will her eyes glaze over." One man told me he would wait until he and his wife were taking a long car ride so that he knew his wife couldn't leave, and then he would try to explain his business to her.

I believe that the best marriages are those in which there is financial sharing. Women have a right to know about their husband's money. It is not "cute" not to know.

There are no rules in the marriage game. There is no best way to discuss money. Nor is there a best way to manage money. Some couples like to work on the checkbook together. In some homes neither one wants to tackle the chore. The point here is that you have to discuss your plan and reach a joint decision about how you will do it. Who really likes balancing a checkbook anyway? It's not a privilege; it's a responsibility. The same is true for spending and investing your money. If you are wondering what happens in other families, women tend to play a leading role in day-to-day management of household finances but back away from long-term financial planning issues including taxes, insurance, and investments.[16]

Sometimes, a wife must take things into her own hands. One woman borrowed $1,500 from a friend to use as a down payment on a house worth $40,000. The real estate broker, a woman, introduced her to a lawyer, also a woman. She was the lawyer's first client. She didn't tell her husband. She used her own credit to obtain a 7½ percent mortgage and showed her husband that they would pay less as owners than they did as renters while also building equity. Her husband was so impressed he urged her to handle all their money.

Experts usually give a few rules for managing the family money. The principal one is to talk about it. If this always leads to the same old arguments maybe you should consider counseling to break the pattern. Set aside a special time to talk over your finances. Each couple must make their own way. We start out with a lot of cultural baggage about roles, about power, and even about ability. But marriage is also about sharing and trust and responsibility. In the past women knew their role as bread baker, not breadwinner. Women were not supposed to know about money. Remember Geraldine Ferraro, the first woman to run for vice president as a major party candidate? When her husband was accused of financial wrongdoing Ms. Ferraro, a lawyer and a savvy politician, said she was "just an Italian housewife"—her husband dealt with the money.

Today women and men have to redefine their roles. Instead of staying home, women work and bring home money, in addition to taking care of their families. Marriage is supposed to be an economic partnership. Even if a woman is not bringing in the same amount, her contributions are important. Women must also take part in what was previously the man's domain, the finances. In the 1990s no woman should be ignorant about money— how it is earned, how it is spent, how it is invested. Knowing will not only help your marriage, but not knowing will leave you vulnerable while you are married and in trouble when you are no longer married.

And if you don't think this applies to you, just take a look at the facts.

Here Are Some Absolutely Frightening Statistics You Should Study No Matter How Long You Have Been Married, No Matter How Happy Your Marriage

- One third of all widows in 1985 were under age fifty when their husbands died.[17]
- Fifty percent of all women older than sixty-five in the United States are widows and will remain widows for fifteen years after their husbands die.[18]
- In 1990 there were 11.5 million widows between the ages of thirty and seventy with a median age of fifty-six.
- Two thirds of all recent first marriages will end in divorce.[19]
- The remarriage rate for divorced women aged forty-five through sixty-four is only about one tenth that for those under twenty-five.[20]
- Seventy-five percent of all nursing home occupants are women. (If he gets sick you will probably take care of him at home; you however will probably end up in a nursing home.)[21]

2.
I Do, I Do

Would you buy a house without reading the contract? Or take a job without knowing what you were expected to do, how many hours you would work, or what your salary would be? Probably not. Yet that is what you do when you sign a marriage license. Marriage is a legal contract between a man, a woman, and a third party—the state. Only states can issue marriage licenses, and these say very little about your marital rights. It's up to you and your husband to decide how you want to run your lives.

WOMEN, MARRIAGE, AND POWER: A BRIEF HISTORY

The role of the male as holder of power in a marriage goes back to the ancient Greeks and Romans. Marriage for the Greeks was governed by the need to protect the *oikos,* or family. The bride was given in marriage by her father. She was delivered over to the groom's house like a package. The husband became the keeper of his wife's property.

If she died, her sons got her property. Otherwise, it returned to her family.

The Romans continued this tradition. The term they used was *patria potestas.* So powerful was papa that he even had the right to kill his own sons. Women had far lower status, which is not to say that some of them didn't have great influence. Our word *marriage* comes originally from the Latin *maritus,* which means "provided with a bride." In the Roman marriage ritual, as depicted on Roman coins, the couples joined their right hands in a ceremony presided over by Concordia, the goddess who symbolized the union of citizens.

When Christianity began to replace the pagan empire, the Roman concept of marriage was simply incorporated into the new rites, but with a slight variation. Christ was now seen presiding over the marriage, and the bride and groom would no longer clasp hands. This has been seen as a change from a contractual idea to one of marriage as a more spiritual union.

The early Christian husband nevertheless assumed control of the wife's estate at marriage and accepted the concurrent obligation to provide support and maintenance during the marriage. The traditional Anglo-Saxon wedding didn't do much to change things. The ceremonial words used implied a giving of the bride to the husband. The wife and husband were then assumed to be one unit. This identity was further supported by the wife's assumption of her husband's name.

Until recently in America, women who married gave up their rights. During the colonial and revolutionary periods a husband had "control over the real property [land and buildings] a wife brought into marriage. He could use this property as he pleased but could not sell or give it away because it descended to his wife's legal heirs."[1] The law, however, gave him ownership of his wife's personal property—including her wages. These he could dispose of as he saw fit.

By the middle of the nineteenth century married women were making gains. In 1924 the League of Women Voters could proclaim "sixteen states [give] women an absolute right of contract, without any restrictions."[2] Today married women have the same rights as single women or men. A woman can make contracts, own property, and have credit in her own name.

Through the nineteenth century, because women gave up rights, they gained certain protections. Your husband had to support and maintain you. He was responsible for debts you had before you married and was responsible for "necessaries." Necessaries were defined as food, clothing, shelter, and medical needs. If your husband didn't provide food for you and the children he would then be liable to a merchant who gave you those items. These laws were written at a time when a wife had no recourse: She couldn't easily divorce. There was little she could do. The laws were written to protect the merchant who might help the indigent wife. In exchange for these guarantees, wives became dependent. Today state marriage laws are written in the new legal language that talks about "spouses" and equality. Courts have taken the position that "both spouses should be jointly held liable for each other's necessaries." Until the middle of this century a wife could not sue or be sued except through her husband. Nor could a wife sue her husband because that would have been like suing herself. This is a legal concept known as spousal immunity that is only gradually changing.

Marriage Laws and Marital Rights Today

Nothing in the marriage laws of the fifty American states mandates for a spouse who does not bring in his or her own income a minimum amount of spending money, a minimum sized home, a car, or anything else. It is only obligatory that each provide the other with "necessaries." Most states would also uphold each partner's marital right to sexual relations. Failure to engage in marital sex could lead to a charge of "constructive abandonment" or a "failure to fulfill this basic obligation of marriage." These are rights that are not specifically legislated but have come down through judicial interpretation, our so-called "common law."

This common law or law by tradition is the concept that also underlies common law marriage. Only thirteen states recognize a marriage that is not licensed.* The criteria for such marriages is the mutual agreement of man and woman that they will live as husband and wife. If you enter into a common law marriage in a state where it is valid, then other states must recognize it too. If you

---

*Alabama, Colorado, Georgia, Idaho, Iowa, Kansas, Montana, Ohio, Oklahoma, Pennsylvania, Rhode Island, South Carolina, Texas, and Washington, D.C.

establish a common law marriage, the rules for splitting up are the same as if you had gone ahead and gotten the license. Should you want to claim your marital rights, either in a divorce or under a will, you are probably better off having had a legal marriage.

The federal government plays a limited role in the laws of marriage. Pensions are regulated by federal laws and federal laws now mandate that women have a right to share in their husbands' pension funds, even if they didn't work. Federal laws supersede state laws in areas such as bankruptcy and federal taxes. These days both federal and state laws are constantly changing. If you are contemplating any significant changes in your life be sure you know the law, because what follows throughout the book is a general summary. Husbands, of course, can share in the pensions their wives receive. The federal government has also eliminated taxes on transfers of wealth between husband and wife.

Each state has its own qualifications for obtaining a marriage license. There are age restrictions. In Georgia you can marry at sixteen but you must have parental consent. If you are pregnant or already have a child, the age restrictions are waived. In New York you can marry as young as fourteen if your parents consent. There are restrictions on whom you can marry. Unlike Cleopatra, you cannot marry your brother. In some states you can't even marry (Habsburgs take note) your first cousin. But it's okay in California. Should you be greedy enough to want two husbands at the same time, the state will again say no. Should you be tying the knot for the second time, you will have to explain what you did with your first husband. Some states have a waiting period between the issuing of the license and the actual marriage ceremony. In Indiana you can even get married over the telephone, since both parties need not be present for the ceremony.[3] Most states have medical requirements. You may need a blood test. In California you may need a test for German measles if you are under the age of fifty.

Other than the cost of the license ($30 for New York City) there are no financial requirements. There are also no financial guarantees. Should you contemplate ending your marriage by divorce, you will discover that you have some very specific rights.

Should your husband die without a will, your right to inherit his property is clearly spelled out, again according to the laws of the state in which you live. For example, if you and your husband have no children you would receive three quarters of his property in Indiana, and one quarter would go to his parents if they were still alive. In Kentucky you would receive half of your husband's estate and the rest would go to his parents if they were still alive. In West Virginia you would inherit all your husband's property even if his parents were still alive.

Should your husband die and leave a will, each state spells out the minimum amount of his property that must be left to you, regardless of what the will says. This is known as your "dower" right, or forced share. Again it derives from Anglo-Saxon tradition. You had certain income rights that could not be taken away.

In fact, it is illegal for a man to disinherit his wife, although he can disinherit his children, except in Louisiana. Your husband also has rights to inherit from you, known as "curtesy." This too can be traced to Anglo-Saxon origins.

The most important determinant of your rights is the state in which you live. Nine states—Arizona, California, Idaho, Louisiana, New Mexico, Oregon, Texas, Washington, and Wisconsin—are community property states, which means you each own half of all the property you both amass during the marriage, regardless of who earns it or whose name is on the title. Wisconsin is a community property state, except for division of assets in a divorce. All the other states adhere to common law. Common law is not rigid and fixed but relies instead on broad principles, supposedly based on reason and common sense.

Our laws derive from two different traditions. Common law derives from the Anglo-Saxon idea that merged husband and wife into one entity and gave the husband all the power. He owned all the property and the wife became almost totally dependent.

In common law states the key to ownership of property during marriage depends on whose name is on the title. The titleholder has the right to sell the property or mortgage it, even if it is the home where you live. You do not have a right to your husband's earnings nor he to yours, except the right that each of you has to provide necessaries for each other. If your husband is the wage earner, he has control over his wages. He can dole out the money as he chooses.

The community property tradition comes from Spain—really from the Visigothic tribes that settled Spain. Supposedly, Visigoth men and women were partners who shared their rugged migratory life. The partnership meant that each partner owned half the property. But the Spanish, who were landowners, also wanted to protect the land, so they added their own stamp—the idea of separate property. If you entered the marriage with land, that land remained yours.

Community property means each spouse owns a one-half interest in any property acquired during the marriage, (except property that was inherited or received as a gift). Both husband and wife have the right to control the community property during marriage. This means that the consent of husband and wife would be required to pledge or sell any community property. California goes even further and states that a woman can spend 100 percent of her husband's community property share, but not land; both of you have to consent to sell real estate. You don't have to ask if you want to sell his yacht. Of course, he has the same right to spend yours.

Regardless of whether you live in a community property or a common property state, property is either considered marital property or separate property. These distinctions may not seem significant in a good marriage where you share your resources, but could become important under some circumstances.

For example, in a common law state, if you do not work and want a credit card, you must rely on your husband's credit, but in a community property state, if you do not work and want a credit card, half your husband's marital assets, including his salary, are considered your property. On the other hand, in a community property state you and your husband are jointly responsible for debts, even if only your husband signed the credit card. If the marriage ends and your husband had a pile of debts, they would be considered half yours. In a common law state, the debts would be his.

Your engagement ring is not marital property; it is a gift to you. It is your separate property. If you break the engagement, etiquette suggests you return it. As for wedding gifts, they were traditionally considered the property of the bride. In the new spirit of sharing, the wedding gifts are considered to be jointly owned—that is, unless a gift was clearly given to the bride or groom. In fact, a South Carolina court recently decided that a silver tea service, given by the bride's grandmother as a wedding present, was not marital property.[4] So you probably won't have to split the bridal negligee.

Just ask Abraham Ullah about the meaning of marital property. Mr. Ullah, a Brooklyn resident, purchased a $1 lottery ticket in 1986. His ticket came in—to the tune of $8 million. Both Ullah and his wife quit their jobs. Soon after, they filed for divorce. Mr. Ullah claimed the entire $8 million as his because he had purchased the ticket and picked the winning numbers. Furthermore, his wife was opposed to gambling. The judge in Brooklyn Supreme Court saw things differently and gave Mrs. Ullah half the winnings. Mr. Ullah appealed the decision, but the appellate court judge said the winnings were won "on a wager of a marital dollar."[5]

The New York Equitable Distribution Statute, known as Domestic Relations Law 236, defines the term as follows: "The term marital property shall mean all property acquired by either or both spouses during the marriage and before the execution of a separation agreement or the commencement of a matrimonial action, regardless of the form in which title is held . . . Marital property shall not include separate property as hereinafter defined. . . ." If you are working, your salary earned while you are married is marital property. If your husband buys a house with money he earned while you are married, the house is marital property.

The difference between owning that house in a community property state or a common law state is that during the marriage you are not a one-half owner of the house in a common law state unless your husband wants you to be. In a community property state such as California, the law requires that you are a half owner.

Separate property, at least according to the New York State code, is considered:

(1) property acquired before marriage or property acquired by bequest, devise, or descent, and gift from a party other than the spouse;

(2) compensation for personal injuries;

(3) property acquired in exchange for or the increase in value of separate property, except to the extent that such appreciation is due in part to the contributions of efforts of the other spouse;

(4) property described as separate property by written agreement of the parties . . .

If you owned a house before your marriage the house is your separate property. If you were hit by a truck and collected $100,000 that money is yours. If you bought a house with that money, the house is yours. If you and your husband signed a prenuptial agreement that clearly stated that the house is yours, then it's yours. However, if the house appreciates in value, that appreciation can become marital property. While this may seem simple, it is not. When you marry in a community property state, you and your husband split fifty-fifty everything that is earned during the marriage.

On the other hand, debts also become community property. If your husband borrows money that he then blows at a casino in Nevada, half the debt is yours. In a common law state, if he goes to the casino and loses, the debt is his. If you have a credit card and your husband uses it, the debt is yours.

In a common law state, death, divorce, or separation activates your rights.

In Arizona, Idaho, Nevada, Texas, and Wisconsin the laws change slightly about property division in a divorce—and division of property is based also on your ability to work, your age, etc. In Washington, community property laws apply during marriage and at death but upon divorce the courts may consider all property in making a division.

While this might not seem important in the throes of first love, consider what could happen: If you have no property in your name and you die, in a common law state you would have nothing to leave in your will for your parents or other relatives you might want to support. What if you die in an accident? Despite the best medical treatment, you do not survive. Your husband is distraught. He turns for comfort to a lovely divorcée. They marry. You had always planned to support your elderly mother, but of course you had no property to leave to her. What will your husband and his new wife do for her?

The point of this story is that if you live in a common law state and your home is owned in your husband's name, you will have nothing to leave to your mother. Had you lived in a community property state, half the house, even if your husband had earned all the money, would have been yours. You could have left your half to your mother.

If you live in a common law state, you don't automatically own half the property. You have to specify joint ownership when you buy it, and you should know the different types before you do. They are:

- *Joint Tenancy with Right of Survivorship.* Each of you owns the property. If one of you dies, the property goes to the other. This type of ownership would not help you if you wanted to leave your half of your house to your mother.
- *Joint Tenancy by the Entirety.* This is the same as above, only limited to ownership by husbands and wives—i.e., you must be married to qualify.
- *Joint Tenancy in Common.* This is closest to the type of ownership you would have in a community property state. You each own half the property and can leave your half in whatever way you choose. This is the best way to be sure your half of the house goes to your old mother.

Don't assume that the law will protect you. In the past few years state laws have changed drastically. For a long time laws were written to protect the family as a single legal entity with the husband as its head. The courts could not easily invade the sanctity of the home. But today the courts allow individual identity even within a marriage. You and your husband have separate rights, such as the right to have credit in your own name. While there are laws to govern asset distribution when you die or divorce, no legislation exists in common law states to control finances as long as a marriage is intact.

Should you divorce in a common law state, the law will

consider the property you and your husband acquired during your marriage "marital" property—to be divided. However, during the marriage the property is legally controlled by the spouse who earned the money. Often the majority of that money is earned by the husband. Sharing of that money during marriage must come from a private decision by husband and wife.

How you handle money and make financial decisions may be one of the important decisions you will make in your marriage. A willingness to share financially is really a part of the mutual trust that underlies a good marriage. The best time to plan what you will do is in the beginning. That is when you will, especially if you are marrying for the first time, have the least amount of money and be most willing to compromise. Knowing that you have some legal rights to your husband's money, and he to yours, can help you to participate in the family finances.

You may want to make some decisions with the help of your lawyer, especially if you are starting over (approximately 45 percent of recent marriages have one spouse who was previously wed). You may want a prenuptial agreement (see Chapter 4). This is nothing more than a contract, something a marriage license doesn't provide.

If you are already married—and this especially applies to women who are in long marriages—have never worked, and have been financially dependent on your husband, you should know as much about the family finances as possible. While there is no one way to handle the marital finances, there are a few things you might want to consider.

Ten Financial Rules for Marriage

1. Show him your finances. Naturally you'll expect to see his.
2. Don't forget to examine his debts, especially in community property states where you might both have to pay for each other's old debts. You should each check your credit ratings.* A bad loan in the past could mean trouble. One couple could not get a mortgage because he had skipped out on his student loan.
3. Decide whether or not you want to pool your assets. Making a conscious—and mutual—decision about this is highly recommended for first marriages.
4. Decide who will pay for what and how. When one of you makes much more than the other you may not be able to split expenses down the middle. One couple, in which the wife had more money than the husband, agreed that she would pay for certain things, but the husband never felt comfortable if his wife paid in public. So they arranged for him to always be the one who paid when they went out. Then the wife would reimburse him.

---

*To obtain a copy of your credit report you must contact the credit rating bureau that serves your area. The main credit bureaus are TRW Information Services (P.O. Box 2350, Chatsworth, Calif. 91313, 1-800-392-1122), Trans Union Credit Information Company (P.O. Box 5767, Wilmington, Del. 19808, 1-800-462-8054), and Equifax, Inc. (P.O. Box 740241, Atlanta, Ga. 30374, 1-800-685-1111). You may have to pay a small charge for your report. If you have been denied credit based on the bureau's report within the previous thirty days you are entitled to a free report. Most agencies require a written request, including your Social Security number, your birthdate, and current and previous residences. Include any required fee.

5. When only one of you earns the money, that one should not necessarily make all the decisions. Financial decisions should be joint.

6. No matter how you split finances and who earns what, make sure you each have some discretionary funds. One wife told me she had always managed her own finances before she married. When she married she and her husband decided on a joint checking account. Everything went into it. She hated having her husband know and question every expense. Things really got touchy when her husband questioned a hairdresser's bill that was large. He asked, "Why did you spend all that money; you don't look any different." She wisely replied, "That shows what a good job it was," and demanded her own account for personal expenses.

7. If you have separate property, think very carefully about whether you want to put it in a joint account. It's easy to give up control to show that you trust somebody. But you may regret it in the future. There is nothing wrong with having your own money.

8. Read the tax returns and ask questions. Don't worry about sounding ignorant. How else will you learn? You should speak to the accountant, too.

9. Never sign a contract that you don't understand.

10. Keep records—of everything. (See Chapter 3 for details on what to keep.)

3.
Marriage, Inc.

I remember my first wedding. I remember the shocking pink wool suit I wore for the ceremony; I remember the Raphael, the small Paris hotel with a view of the Eiffel Tower where we went on our wedding trip; and I remember all eight wedding guests. But, there is little I could have told you about our finances in those early days. Nobody should be as naïve as I was. Eight years later my husband died and I was alone with a one-year-old baby. It took me two years to even understand that I could not afford to live in the house that I owned.

Yet what happened to me isn't that extraordinary. Any woman married today is likely to fall victim to one of what I call The Three *D*'s: *D*eath, *D*ivorce, or other *D*isasters. If you are married now, your odds of being alone are high.

Recently, Betsy, a research librarian, became suspicious that her husband of twenty years was going to leave her. Before she could be sure, her husband had already spirited much of what she thought of as the family assets out of the country and into a Bahamian bank account. Although Betsy had signed joint tax returns, she had no idea exactly how much money her husband earned a year. Nor, to be perfectly fair, did she know how much money she spent. She didn't have a clue about the family finances.

Even if she never thought about divorce, she should have known about the money that was coming in and going out. In fact, one of the problems of the marriage was her refusal to stop spending money when her husband's business was losing money.

When it comes to knowing about the family money, most women probably fall somewhere between Betsy, who knew nothing, and those women we all know who handle all the family finances. Some of us may know our husband's salary, but not realize how much he has put into his pension plan; others may know all about the investments, but not realize how much the health insurance costs, because that is deducted from your husband's salary.

FIVE THINGS WOMEN DON'T USUALLY KNOW ABOUT THEIR HUSBAND'S MONEY

1. How much he has and how much he owes
2. How the assets are held (savings accounts, property, stocks, etc.)
3. How much insurance he has and what kind
4. How much he spends
5. How he's leaving it (the will)

There are two ways to discover the facts about your husband's finances. The good way is by sharing throughout the marriage. The other, and less pleasant way, is when financial disaster strikes and you discover that you are in debt, have worthless investments, or even face bankruptcy.

Studies have shown that women tend to abdicate a role in investment decisions. This is probably one of the biggest money mistakes any woman can make. Where is the evidence that men are better money managers? Even if you have had little experience in investing, you can learn. Take a course, read, and rely on your own common sense. Most of the time you will do as well as your husband, if not better. The big difference is probably that you don't think you can, or that you don't think you have a right to. You can, you do, and you should.

Of course, some women never find out about the facts of their husbands' finances until the marriage dissolves tragically—in divorce or death. Mary Elizabeth Murray, a retired schoolteacher, learned the hard way after her husband died. He had managed the investments, and when he died she let the broker handle her account. Before long Mrs. Murray had lost $125,000. Without asking her, the broker had sold her blue-chip securities and bought risky investments. Mrs. Murray took her case to an arbitration committee and was awarded $419,460. But it was a painful way to learn about investing.[1]

One way to begin learning about your husband's money, and your own, is to think of your family as a small corporation. Don't think that this means you have to have millions in the bank. It is merely a way to look at what you do have.

Corporations, large and small, generally prepare two types of reports. One is a net worth statement, the other a cash flow statement. Your net worth is really a record of what you have and what you owe—your assets and liabilities on a particular day. Corporations usually do an annual net worth report, but asset values such as stock prices can change quickly, so the net worth applies only to the day on which it is calculated. The cash flow statement lets you see how much money is coming in every month or year and how much is going out—in other words, income and expenses.

Start with a look at what you have. If you and your husband pool everything, you only need one, but you should include in your list how each asset is owned. If you have separate assets you may want to have separate accounts. If you don't want to approach your husband do it on your own. (See chart pages 34–35.)

Corporate financial reports also include what is called a cash flow statement: this really means the spendable income—the amount of cash you have coming in, and the amount of cash going out. If these two are not equal and the amount going out is greater than that coming in, you are spending too much. (See chart pages 36–37.)

The amount of money you and your husband spend is extremely important. Yet we go into marriage—or, for that matter, live on our own—with few rules about spending. One marriage I know of nearly broke up because the husband and wife could not agree on their spending. Nancy and Don are probably like many couples. Nancy turned over her paycheck to Don, who paid most of the bills. Nancy had a checking account that she used for everyday expenses. One day Nancy noticed a bank statement on Don's desk. She discovered that Don had taken a $10,000 loan to buy a camper. When Don came home

How to Calculate Your Net Worth*

ASSETS

Personal Property:
  house
  furniture and household effects (e.g., a wine collection, a
    library of books, compact disks)
  appliances, machines, and tools
  car, boat
Financial Assets:
  commodities
  stocks
  bonds
  checking and savings accounts
  mutual funds, money market funds, CDs
Real Estate
Business Partnerships
Hidden Assets:
  stock options
  pension funds, KEOGH, IRA, SEP
  insurance (cash and benefit value)
  possible inheritance
  deferred compensation (money you have earned but will
    receive in the future)

*Your net worth is the difference between your assets and your liabilities.

that evening she asked him about the loan. In the argument that ensued, Nancy discovered that she and Don had been living way over their incomes. Nancy even feared they could go bankrupt if they were to have any unexpected expenses.

Don thought Nancy was overreacting. After all, he explained, everything worked out perfectly when he ran the numbers through his computer. Don had used the

How to Calculate Your Net Worth *(Cont.)*

LIABILITIES

Outstanding Taxes:
   Social Security
   federal
   state and local
   real estate
Mortgages
Loans:
   business
   personal
   car
   home equity
Credit Card Debt
Installment Debt
Margin Debt on Stock Brokerage Accounts

computer to control and intimidate Nancy. Her fear of being in debt finally overcame her fear of challenging Don and the computer. "Everything was on the computer—it was his security," Nancy recalled. But not this time. After years of being intimidated by the authority that the computer numbers seemed to represent, Nancy demanded an accounting that she could understand— with pencil and paper.

How to Calculate Your Expenses

INCOME

Salary
Bonus
Dividends
Partnership Interest
Trust Income
Rental Income
Interest Income
  savings accounts
  money market funds
  CDs
Alimony

OUTGO

Mortgage and Amortization
  household repairs
  real estate taxes
Taxes and Charges
Debt Service on Credit Cards and Loans
Utilities:
  fuel and gas
  electricity
  telephone
Food and Liquor
Personal Care:
  hairdresser and health club
  books and magazines
Clothing:
  laundry
  dry cleaner
Automobile:
  fuel
  repairs
  insurance
  car payments

How to Calculate Your Expenses *(Cont.)*

OUTGO

Insurance:
  life
  personal and real property
  fire, theft, and liability
  medical/dental
  disability
  nursing home
Travel and Entertainment:
  nonreimbursed expenses
  reimbursed expenses
Vacations
Children:
  tuition
  child care
  clothing
Charity:
  religious organizations
  museum contributions
  alumnae associations
  health organizations
Savings and Investments
Miscellaneous Expenses:
  cigarettes
  office coffee breaks
  newspapers and magazines
  cosmetics
  (and don't forget those vet bills for Fido)
Alimony and Child Support

When Nancy began going over their expenses she real-ized that Don had developed a pattern of overspending. Each year he paid off the previous year's debts with his year-end bonus, but somehow the debts were never totally wiped out. They never started the year with a clean slate. With Don's company in financial trouble, there was a good chance that he wouldn't even get a bonus this year. Then what would they do?

Nancy took over the finances, including the check-book. She cut their expenses to the bone, putting them both on a food and clothing allowance. Gradually, over a six-month period, she began to cut their debt and their tendency to overspend. Don now admits that for the first time he no longer feels out of control. They are still vulnerable if a major disaster should hit them—say, need-ing a new roof for the house or a new car—but Nancy thinks they are on the right track.

The problem Nancy faced is not unusual. As in most of what we do in marriage, there are few guidelines. Spending just seems to happen. But it doesn't have to be like that.

CAN YOU AFFORD IT?

It's easy to figure out how much to spend. You just have to know that you can't pay out more than what comes in. The trouble is: credit. You can always buy just a little more than you can actually pay for, thanks to those little plastic credit cards. The problem comes when you find yourself charging on three or four cards. No one card will get you in trouble, but together they can begin to make a big dent in your monthly expenses. Add that to mortgages and car loans and pretty soon you could be like Nancy's husband Don—totally out of control, but under the illusion that everything is all right because you've put all the numbers in your computer.

What follows are some guidelines. If Nancy had known these figures she might have had the courage to stop Don before they had big problems. While most families have slightly different needs at different times, you might want to compare your family spending with those of other American families. (See below.)

But Nancy really needs to know more than average expenses. She also should know how much debt is consid-

AVERAGE BREAKDOWN OF EXPENSES
IN AMERICAN FAMILIES[2]

TYPE OF EXPENSE	PERCENTAGE OF TOTAL EXPENSES
Food:	15.1
at home	8.6
away from home	6.4
Housing	31.3
Apparel and Services	5.7
Transportation:	18.1
vehicles	7.5
gasoline and motor oil	3.7
other transportation	6.8
Health Care	5.2
Insurance and Pensions:	9.1
life and other	1.2
pensions and Social Security	7.9
All other—e.g., liquor, entertainment, personal care, cash contributions, education	15.4

ered tolerable. Even though Nancy thinks the only good debt is one that has been paid, Don is right to borrow money. It's one way to build assets. The problem with Don's borrowing was that it was going more to luxury goods—fancy restaurants and expensive suits and vacations—than it was toward building assets.

A reasonable amount of debt for a family is usually considered no more than 35 percent of your gross monthly income, which would include 25 percent for mortgage and housing expenses. But first you should have on hand enough liquid assets for three to six months of living expenses.

There are several computer programs that can help you keep track of all this information, but all you really need is a pencil and paper. You don't even need a calculator.

One of the most important reasons for knowing all the facts and figures is to be able to know what you would need if something happened to your husband. If you were left alone because of divorce or death, how would you manage? If you don't know now, you'll really have problems later on.

SHARING INCOME, EXPENSES, AND DEBTS

Not knowing about marital finances leaves you out of control of the situation. Yet many women like Nancy abdicate their financial role and let their husbands take over. Sometimes women do this because it's easier, because taking charge is taking responsibility. Sometimes women let their husbands take over because they feel they don't have the right to participate since they don't earn the money. Yet, in most cases, sharing the financial burden, either because you each earn some of the money or because you both decide and are responsible for the way money is spent, can improve marriages.

There are two kinds of money in marriage: first, the money that you and your husband earn and spend, your income, and second, the investments or other assets that you and your husband own and manage. You and your husband have to decide how you want to own and share your income and assets. If you live in a community property state, the state decides ownership for you; the assets and income you acquire during your marriage are owned jointly. But if you live in a common law state, the income or assets are owned by the person whose name is on the title.

There really isn't a best way to own assets or spend money. A lawyer who has seen many couples argue viciously about money during a divorce might advocate separate ownership of all property. A psychologist who has seen couples argue endlessly about money during their marriage might say that unless the assets are merged there will never be a true marriage.

At different times in your life you may want to do things differently. When I married my first husband we had few assets. We each earned a small salary, although his was much higher than mine. We shared everything. We owned our house jointly and we pooled our income. When I married for the second time, I had a child from my first marriage. My husband had his own family obligations. We also each had separate property. We have a much more complicated financial arrangement. As in most second marriages, not all of our expenses are joint.

(In 1988, the most recently available statistics from the National Center for Health Statistics, there were 2.4 million weddings. Of these, 10.7 percent were divorced men who married never-married women; 10.9 percent were divorced women and never-married men.[3]) Who actually writes the rent check or manages the stock portfolio may not be important at all, but you should both know what is going on. Most young couples in first marriages will probably share everything, so joint ownership is the most logical, regardless of who earns what. After all, isn't sharing why you got married? If you both work, you can share major expenses, share savings, and each keep some separate money for your own expenses.

If you have joint checking accounts and credit cards you should still have a credit card in your own name and a separate checking account, even if you have agreed to share all expenses.

If you do not have a credit card in your own name but have a card jointly with your husband, you can have your credit report in both names. You must request this when you apply for the card. That way, you will begin establishing your own credit history. If your account is old, you may have to write to the company to request a change in the way your credit is reported. If you have your own credit history, you can more easily get a credit card in your own name should you want one. If you are widowed and do not have earned income, obtaining a credit card can be difficult. You are better off having your own card before anything happens. If your husband is a bad credit risk, you definitely want only your own credit cards, not a joint account.

I had charge accounts in my husband's name and continued using them after my husband died. Nobody told me not to, and as long as I continued to pay my bills on time, I didn't have a problem. However, I felt insecure until I was able to change the cards into my own name. If you are only authorized to sign your husband's credit card, he can easily cancel it should you get divorced. One woman told of being totally humiliated in the small town where she lived when she went to the drugstore and was told her husband had closed the account. If you have a joint checking account, all the more reason to keep a separate checking account as well because he can clean out the account if he is planning a divorce.

As for responsibility for debts, each state differs. For example the California law says that you could even be responsible for some debts your husband had before marriage. In Maryland, however, neither spouse is liable for the other's debts incurred before marriage.

To Have and to Hold

Here is what you should absolutely keep handy in the house (I do this on one sheet of paper):

- Social Security numbers
- bank account numbers
- brokerage account numbers
- money market fund numbers
- insurance policy numbers

- credit card numbers (handy for catalogue ordering late at night and more important for reporting stolen cards)

I also keep all the numbers for our airline travel mileage so I can always tell the reservation clerk numbers when I make plane reservations.

Here is what you should keep close by:

- tax returns (last seven years)
- W-2 forms
- brokerage account statements (I keep the monthly statements for the current year and the yearly statements for the past seven years)
- bank statements (Canceled checks are always a problem—I keep a year's worth handy and store seven years of back checks)
- insurance policies—homeowners insurance, health insurance, life insurance
- copy of your will (original can be kept at your lawyer's office)
- inventory of all your possessions

Here is what you should keep in a safety deposit box:

- property deeds
- car title
- any IOUs
- marriage license
- divorce papers
- leases
- stocks and bonds

Money Mistakes Women Make[4]

While there are no rules for deciding how you and your husband should divide your money, many women who entered marriage thinking they would somehow work out the money without talking about it discovered years later that they had made some terrible mistakes. Below are nine common ones to avoid.

1. *Putting inherited money or property in a joint account.* Recently, my friends' daughter married. As a wedding gift, her parents gave the couple a house. This was very good, except for one thing: The new husband's first wife used this property as an excuse to try to get more money from her ex-husband. Keeping the house in the daughter's name would have simplified the situation.

2. *Using her money for expenses while her husband's investments increased.* For nine of the thirteen years of her marriage, Linda outearned her husband. They split expenses and used her extra earnings to pay taxes. Sounds reasonable. But all the time they were using her money, his separate investment account, which he had before they married, continued to grow.

3. *Not getting professional advice soon enough.* Remember Betsy, whose husband put the family assets into a Bahamian bank account? By the time Betsy thought to go to a divorce lawyer, her husband had set up investments that her lawyer was never able to find.

4. *Giving up control over her money to show faith and to*

bolster her husband's ego. Diane's husband took charge of the family finances, mainly her salary, while she worked and he stayed home. Too late she discovered that he put them in debt. She was stuck for the loans.

5. *Letting him keep all the family records.* When she and her husband divorced, Elaine didn't have the money to find out what there was, where it was, or how much it was worth.

6. *Trying to pay an equal share when she couldn't really afford to do so.* Esther's husband was much richer than Esther was. Yet they agreed to split everything. Problems developed when she lost her big earning job and dipped into her savings to try to keep up her end. She spent all her money, and because it was a second marriage had little to leave for her children from her first marriage.

7. *Using her separate money to buy something in joint name while her husband holds on to his separate investments.* When they split, Abby's husband got half the joint property, Abby got none of his separate investments.

8. *Not keeping records or receipts—especially for cash payments.* Gwen's husband was hiding income. She couldn't prove this and when they divorced she received a settlement based on his understated tax returns.

9. *The biggest mistake of all—thinking that talking about money is not romantic.* The very precautions that would help you at the time of a divorce or the death of your husband—prenuptial agreements, accurate records about property, knowing the value of stock

options—are viewed as unromantic. Not talking about money could lead to most of the above eight problems.

While many of these problems led to divorce, they were often problems that, handled differently, might have been resolved. In Diane's case, her husband plunged them into debt. Had they made joint decisions, they would probably still be married. But she began to lose faith in him when she saw how he handled what she had always thought of as their money.

The friend who paid an equal share of the expenses even though her husband was much richer began to resent every penny she had to give her husband. And frequently, it was pennies. When they went on a trip he would even record every bus fare in his little book. The final rupture came when he suggested that they invite her mother for dinner and then divided the check, one third, two thirds.

A possible divorce is not the only reason you should know about money, how it is spent, where it is kept, how it is invested, and how it is owed. It is equally important if you are widowed. Otherwise you will become a victim of what I have heard called "widowitis." Its chief symptom is the fear that ensues from not knowing what you can afford to do when you are on your own and not knowing how to do it.

But even more important, not knowing about the family money can leave you in a marriage in which you do not play an equal role in making decisions. It can leave you feeling dependent and vulnerable. Knowing about the assets, helping to keep the records, helping to make the decisions are all part of the economic partnership that modern marriage is supposed to be.

4.

"Honey, Just Sign Here"

When the history of New York in the 1980s is written, Donald and Ivana Trump will loom large as the quintessential twosome: she, a ravishing blonde from Czechoslovakia who wore beautiful clothes; he, a tall, brash real estate developer who owned hotels and gambling casinos. Magazines fed the public a continuous diet of Trump style. We saw their glittering triplex apartment, their yacht, and their palatial Palm Beach mansion. We knew their charities and their friends. We saw their helicopter whisking them to fabulous parties. What we didn't see was a young blonde from Georgia. When the papers broke the news of the Trumps' marital split, the banner headlines dwarfed those given to African leader Nelson Mandela, released after twenty years in prison.

While much was made of Mr. Trump's liaison with another woman, the main focus of the press was the revelation of the couple's premarital agreement. Details were quickly leaked alleging that Mrs. Trump was to receive $25 million, their Connecticut mansion, and custody of the children. Various sources further disclosed that the agreement, which had been written at the time of their marriage, had been revised three times since. His lawyers declared the agreement "ironclad"; her lawyers called it "unconscionable" and "fraudulent." Marital behavior that might have caused Mr. Trump to relinquish a large part of his fortune in the past was of no consequence. What counted was the premarital contract. In the end, you could not feel sorry for Ivana. She walked away with $10 million, a forty-five-room Connecticut mansion, a New York apartment, and use of the couple's 118-room Mar-a-Lago mansion in Florida for one month a year. And to be sure, the kids are okay; she gets $650,000 per year in alimony and child support.

Prenuptial agreements have been around for a long time. The Babylonians had them in the first millennium B.C. The agreements spelled out the dowry the bride would bring with her as well as the settlement should the marriage end in divorce. Often the inheritance rights of any children of the marriage were included. Agreements even allowed the wife's dowry to return to her father's estate should she die without children.

When Elizabeth I of England contemplated marriage, her agents tried to hammer out an agreement with the agents for the duke of Alençon, a Frenchman twenty years her junior. In June of 1579, Alençon's agents crossed the channel to work out the contract. They demanded the duke be crowned king immediately after the wedding, that a large pension be paid to him throughout his life, and that he would have the right to remain a practicing Catholic. The queen's agents asked Alençon to foreswear any contribution toward expenses should France go to war against the Netherlands. Queen Bess needed more than a lawyer; the entire Privy Council had to agree. They didn't and the marriage never took place.

In America, premarital agreements were considered the domain of the very rich, who used them mainly to limit the amount of money a husband or wife could inherit. Prior to the 1970s the courts would not uphold an agreement that spelled out conditions in the event of a divorce. Women were not allowed to waive their rights to alimony (it would have been unthinkable for men to receive alimony). Remember, property usually went to the owner—usually the husband—so alimony was the only point of negotiation in a divorce settlement. This was a way of protecting the little woman and preventing her from becoming a public charge.

Courts also worried that prenuptial contracts—also called antenuptial contracts—that waived alimony promoted divorce, because the husband would have no obligations if he left. But now that it's okay for women to work and for women to be considered equal, support is no longer a concern of the law.

Premarital agreements crop up everywhere these days, including the corporate world. When James Stewart, former chairman of Lone Star Industries, Inc., married one of his five wives, he billed the company $16,795 in legal fees for his prenuptial agreement and was reimbursed. When Charles Lazarus, who made a fortune as chief of Toys "R" Us, was accused by a shareholder of violating an obscure stock exchange trading rule, he denied the allegations. His explanation: The stock was owned by his wife, sex therapist Helen Kaplan, and they had a prenuptial agreement which kept her money separate from his. The court agreed with him.

The advent of equitable distribution laws, a rise in the divorce rate, a high number of second marriages, and an increase in the number of working women with their own assets have increased the number of prenuptial agreements. Many couples use the prenuptial agreement as a marriage contract, spelling out the consequences of a breakup or death much the way partners in a business would sign a contract. You might look at a prenuptial agreement as the economic contract of a marriage. All too often, however, it is an agreement made between unequals.

Prenuptial agreements are subject to state law. Many states have adopted a variation of the 1983 Uniform Premarital Agreement Act. States that have not adopted the Uniform Act have enacted some form of similar legislation which outlines the conditions under which an agreement should be signed, the settlement of property, and the conditions under which an agreement may not be enforceable. Check your state. In some, agreements must be notarized to be valid.

WHAT YOU GIVE UP WHEN YOU SIGN A PRENUPTIAL AGREEMENT

If you are getting married and your husband-to-be wants you to sign such an agreement, there are a few things you should know. Under the laws of the various states, you as the wife are legally entitled to certain "fruits" of the marriage should it end either in death or divorce. When you sign an agreement, you may give up some or all of these rights depending on the terms of the agreement.

1. You may be giving up your right to inherit property under your husband's will or under the intestate (having made no valid will) laws of your state. You are also giving up your elective share (the minimum amount of assets your husband must leave to you).
2. You may be giving up your right to an equitable distribution or a community property settlement should your marriage end in divorce.
3. You may be giving up other rights to which you are entitled in your state, such as the right to receive support, should your marriage end in divorce.
4. Some states also have homestead laws that would permit you to stay in the family home should you and your husband divorce.

If you are the one asking for an agreement, your husband is giving up the same rights to your assets. A prenuptial agreement supersedes state laws. When a Nebraska husband recently tried to claim his "elective" share under his wife's will, even though he had signed a prenuptial agreement, the courts ruled against him. The terms of the prenuptial agreement prevailed.

How Prenuptial Agreements Stand Up

Most state courts will uphold prenuptial agreements, providing they do not leave one spouse destitute (known as the public policy issue). Nor do some state laws permit agreements that are thought to facilitate divorce. For example, the courts would not uphold an agreement that required you and your husband to divorce in five years. A Utah judge recently overturned an agreement because he said it was "against public policy to facilitate the breakup of a marital relationship."[1]

Some states reserve the right to declare an agreement unenforceable if circumstances change drastically. In some states agreements must be "fair and reasonable" when made and not "unconscionable" at the time they are carried out. Needless to say, the terms are difficult to define. As a result more and more agreements are being decided by the courts.

A Texas judge ruled that "in determining whether a contract is unconscionable or not, the court must look to the entire atmosphere in which the agreement was made, the alternatives, if any, which were available to the parties at the time of the making of the contract, the non-bargaining ability of one party, whether the contract is illegal or against public policy and whether the contract is oppressive or unreasonable."[2]

The law does not protect you from signing a bad agreement. As one judge put it, "A party who knowingly has entered into a lawful contract which may be improvident . . . is not entitled to protection from the court(s) which are not free to change his contract for him or to avoid the results thereof."[3] The fact that an agreement may not seem fair doesn't help either—if you signed.

An agreement that violates a child's right to support will not stand up to court scrutiny.

Courts will also take a look at the way the agreement was executed. State laws may vary but there are four basic reasons an agreement can be invalidated: (1) fraud, (2) failure to disclose fully assets, (3) no separate representation (separate lawyer), (4) agreement was signed under physical duress.

Although any and all of these reasons could knock out

an agreement, a Wisconsin court recently found an agreement fair even though the wife didn't have her own lawyer and her husband hadn't disclosed his finances.

In other words, the rules are constantly changing.

A Florida court declared unenforceable an agreement signed when the husband "sprang" it upon the wife the day before a well-planned elaborate wedding was to occur in a large suite at the O'Hare International Airport in Chicago. He pulled the agreement from his pocket when the parties were at the jewelers picking up their wedding rings. Passage had already been booked for a honeymoon cruise to Europe, the wife's trousseau had been purchased, invitations for the large wedding had been sent. The husband had made no mention of the agreement prior to the surprise at the jewelery store. The wife certainly did not have independent counsel of her own choosing. "The only evidence of legal advice is that within twenty-four hours before the wedding, when the husband first presented the antenuptial agreement and she rebelled, she spoke on the telephone to his lawyers."[4]

As for signing your own handwritten agreement, this could be a problem. Steven Spielberg wrote one on a piece of paper without consulting a lawyer. Then he and his wife-to-be, Amy Irving, signed it. The agreement wouldn't hold up in court and Irving received one of the largest divorce settlements in Hollywood, reputed to be close to $100 million.

WHY A WOMAN MIGHT WANT
A PRENUPTIAL AGREEMENT

While the primary purpose of such agreements is still to protect the money of the wealthier spouse, agreements have also become almost mandatory for second marriages, where husband and wife want to keep their finances separate so that their children from a first marriage can inherit their property.

Couples who have been through terrible divorces the first time around may think things will be easier should the second marriage not pan out.

As the nature of marital property continues to expand to include professional degrees, pension funds, and even celebrity goodwill—more couples are drafting agreements that exclude these "assets" from division. Many lawyers report that when both husband and wife are starting marriage and are partners in professional practices they might decide ahead of time that their practices will remain separate and the only marital assets they will divide should there be a divorce would be personal property, their home, and any investments they held jointly.

Prenuptial agreements are also the place for some couples to hammer out potential child custody, child support, and visitation rights.

Sometimes couples who might not have considered a premarital agreement are asked to do so by what lawyers call "interested third parties." When there is family money, a parent or grandparent may put pressure on a daughter or grandson to obtain an agreement—sometimes even threatening to cut off the potential heir who does not want to ask his future bride to sign. Many times, partners in law firms or owners of small businesses now insist that all the partners have agreements to insure that a spouse who is a nonpartner will not be entitled to a chunk of the business as part of a divorce settlement.

Some couples want to use the prenuptial contract as the place to discuss the details of marriage, even going so far as to specify the number of times each week they will have sex. One can imagine a tired old couple in their bedroom, valiantly trying to live up to the obligations of their agreement. The courts are less interested in these personal details and are less likely to care about enforcing them. Premarital agreements serve as a plan for the dissolution of the marriage, not for the conduct of the marriage.

Here are some reasons why a woman might want a prenuptial agreement:

1. She has a lot more money than the man she is planning to marry and wants to keep control of her own money.
2. She is marrying for the second time and wants to protect whatever money she has.
3. She lives in a community property state and does not want to give up half of what she hopes to have.
4. She lives in an equitable distribution state and does not know how the courts might divide her assets should the marriage end in divorce, so she wants to establish her own terms.
5. She hopes it will eliminate problems should the marriage end in divorce.
6. She has children from a previous marriage and wants to be sure the children are protected.

7. She has a family business and doesn't want it to end up with his family.
8. She is a partner in a business and her partners want to be sure control of the business will not pass outside the firm.
9. She is the daughter of wealthy parents or has wealthy grandparents who insist she have such an agreement.

Agreements hit deep psychological nerves. Most lawyers can tell you of agreements that were never signed. One attorney tells of a couple who fought so bitterly that they stormed out of his office, never married, and his client never even paid him.

Prenuptials can imply a lack of trust, a signal that the one who wants the agreement doesn't want to share. If you are marrying a man who sees his money as his source of power, he may want you to sign the agreement so that he will not lose this power.

Women who have money may want agreements to be sure they are not being married because they are rich. The groom-to-be's willingness to sign an agreement may prove to her that he loves her for herself and not for her money.

In the not-so-distant past, especially in common law states, a woman virtually turned over her money to her husband. But now, a woman with her own income and assets has a choice. She can decide how she wants to handle her own money, even if she doesn't have a lot of it. A prenuptial agreement can be the place to iron out some of the financial details before marriage.

Inherited money can also play a role, especially if the money has been inherited by a woman from her father.

A woman may want to keep that inherited money for herself. It may be the only thing she got from her father who was incapable of giving her anything else.

A woman who saw her own parents fight bitterly over money when they divorced may want an agreement in the hopes of avoiding the kind of acrimony she witnessed.

Premarital agreements are signed before the wedding, at a time when couples are supposed to be most in love. For first marriages, especially, it's hard to think about the marriage ending.

So why do people sign them? A friend of mine, who signed an ultimately disastrous agreement—that is, disastrous for her—says, "I didn't want to show that I wanted anything. I thought it was a matter of principle." So she signed an agreement in which she gave up all rights to income and marital property, an agreement her lawyer advised her not to sign.

Another woman revealed that eight years after she signed an agreement she was still incensed about it. She says, "I will always be angry." But like many women, she didn't want to face the embarrassment of calling off the marriage.

Although the idea is repugnant to many women, I suspect few will react as did the fictional Pauline McAdoo in a recent novel by Dominick Dunne, *An Inconvenient Woman.* The beautiful, impeccably bred Pauline has been asked to sign an agreement by her soon-to-be-husband's lawyer. Instead of signing, Pauline flings an inkwell at the lawyer and storms off to Paris. Frightened of losing her, the groom-to-be fires the lawyer, rushes off to Paris, and presents her with a fabulous diamond engagement ring—and, just to make sure, immediately after the wedding presents her with an incredible van Gogh painting.

CHALLENGING A PRENUPTIAL AGREEMENT

Should you sign an agreement and then want to break it, you will have a hard time. Recently, Tim Peters, former husband of Sallie Bingham, the media heiress, tried to do just that. In the agreement, Mr. Peters waived all claims to alimony. When the couple divorced in 1990, Mr. Peters went to court in Louisville, Kentucky, to try and change the terms. The judge said that Mr. Peters "may now feel he made a bad bargain," but that was not sufficient grounds for revoking the agreement. In fact, the judge added that he thought Mr. Peters had married Miss Bingham "for her money and stayed married to her because of the material benefits that the relationship conferred."[5]

On the other hand, Jacqueline Onassis reportedly reopened negotiations with lawyers after the death of her husband Aristotle, and received more money than the original contract mandated.

If you want to challenge a prenuptial agreement in a state that follows the Uniform Premarital Agreement Act, you must prove that the agreement is not valid. For example, if you want to break an agreement because you say you were forced to sign it, you must be able to prove this to the court.

A Minnesota judge recently overturned a prenuptial agreement that provided that each party's earnings during the marriage were to remain separate property. One attorney drafted the agreement and testified that he advised both parties. During the marriage, all expenses were paid from the earnings of one spouse while the other spouse invested all earnings. The court ruled that not only full and fair disclosure is necessary, but each party must be advised by an independent attorney.[6]

An Alabama judge set aside a recent agreement after the bride testified that "she was presented with the document the evening before the wedding, was unable to contact an attorney, and signed it prior to leaving for church with the understanding it would be rewritten."[7]

If your husband-to-be says, "Oh, just sign it now; I'll change it later," run for the hills. He may leave you more in his will, but men seldom change their agreements.

How to Make the Best Deal

Only you can decide whether you are willing to sign a prenuptial agreement, but should you be asked, there are a few rules of the game that you would be wise to understand. Of course, you can always say no.

1. First of all, be sure you have your own lawyer, even if your husband-to-be is paying for it. (Of course, if you don't have proper counsel, the agreement could be voided at a later date, which may be exactly what you want. If this is the case, you already know the game and probably don't need this chapter.)
2. While agreements may be valid without it in some states, be sure your lawyer asks for and receives as much financial disclosure as possible.

3. If you are worried that there might not be any assets—remember even billionaires like Donald Trump can have financial problems—you might ask for some money to be put in escrow. Or you might ask for a noncancelable life insurance policy in case he dies.

4. Inflation is always a problem, so perhaps your lawyer could suggest a clause that will increase the amount of money you receive by the annual rate of inflation.

5. It's also a good idea to try and set conditions under which the agreement might be renegotiated—perhaps after a certain number of years or after the birth of a child. One woman who asked her husband to sign an agreement gave him 10 percent of her assets each year until he had 50 percent. Remember, if you want to change or revoke the terms of the contract, do it in writing.

6. Sometimes you might ask for up-front money. But the transfer should be made after the wedding. If you get the money before you are married, there would be a hefty gift tax. Once you are married, there is no tax on any money transferred between a husband and wife providing the one getting the money is a United States citizen.

7. If you and your husband are partners in business, you might include a buy-out agreement and a valuation agreement to avoid a messy battle in the event of a divorce. (See Chapter 11 for more about this.)

8. You might build into the agreements payout schedules that take into account tax laws. For example, if you and your husband own a house together and you will

end up with the house, the agreement should include the possible tax on the house should you decide to sell it.

Asking for an agreement can be hard. You have to bring up the realities of money at a time when you are only supposed to be thinking about love.

The late Roy Cohn, who drafted one of the three agreements signed by Donald and Ivana Trump, once told me he advised his clients, usually wealthy men, to resort to a series of white lies. Cohn proposed that Mister X go to his fiancée with the idea of a prenuptial agreement and if she says, "Oh, I'm shocked," Mister X can say, "I trust you completely, but my family won't allow it." Other lawyers suggest that the client put the blame on the lawyer.

While this is a somewhat cute approach that may have worked for some rich older men marrying attractive younger wives (seldom do you see a rich young woman marrying a poor old man), it is probably not an approach that bodes well for the success of the marriage. If you want an agreement because you want to be sure you will continue to have control over your own finances, it is better to say so directly.

One wealthy bride-to-be asked her future husband to sign an agreement. He objected. To avoid a fight, she placed all of her assets in a trust to be able to keep them separate when she married—a complicated legal procedure. Other brides may decide to take the risks that marriage entails rather than pursue the idea of an agreement.

One of the biggest problems with prenuptial agreements is the possibility that circumstances may change. You might sign an agreement that will not be enforced until twenty years later. Predicting your financial conditions that far in advance can be exceedingly difficult. As more and more agreements are being signed more and more case law is evolving that suggests that courts may eventually look at an agreement to see not only if it was fair when it was signed, but also if it is fair when it is enforced.

A recent Ohio decision addresses this issue. In this case a couple signed an agreement that was fair and reasonable at the time of the signing. After a fourteen-year marriage, the husband's assets had grown to $8 million. His income was $250,000 a year. The couple's standard of living had changed dramatically. The $200-a-month alimony that the wife had agreed to receive for ten years if the marriage ended was "unconscionable" because circumstances had changed. The judge felt this was grounds to set aside the agreement.[8]

The equality of earnings that you counted on might not materialize and you might have signed away your right to alimony. Women who do this should be extremely careful. Despite the gains women have made, men still continue to earn more, even in the same profession. If you don't consider and admit that your income might not keep pace, you could sign a mine-is-mine, yours-is-yours agreement that will be disastrous should something happen to your marriage.

Mistakes Women with Money Can Avoid

There is little hard evidence that men and women behave differently when it comes to signing prenuptial agreements. Men who are asked to sign such agreements by their future wives do not seem any happier about signing than women who are asked to sign. But many lawyers have anecdotal evidence that women, especially those who have earned their own money, are making mistakes that they don't think men are as likely to make when it comes to prenuptial agreements.

One common mistake occurs when women want to keep everything for themselves. One woman who was marrying for the second time had inherited several million dollars from her first husband. And she wasn't going to give any of it to number two—she wanted it all to go to her children. She insisted on an agreement whereby both parties waived their rights to the other's assets. Over the years her new husband took over a small company that he built into a business worth several hundred million dollars. They live in great style. To all their friends it is a great marriage. But underneath it all she is seething. Why? Well, it seems she went to her husband and asked him if he would, now that he is so rich, give her a few million dollars so she would have a little more to leave to her children. He has turned her down: an eye for an eye. While there could be a subtle psychological factor at work here, women, says one matrimonial lawyer, "tend to be so concerned about the money they earned that they try to protect it at the expense of a long-term gain."

Another common error women with money make is

that they will not take any risks. When a friend of mine married a few years ago, she now reluctantly admits, she signed an agreement with her husband to buy a large house in the country. The house was to be owned jointly. Each would contribute a certain amount of capital and expenses. You can probably guess the rest. They bought the house at an absolute low in the real estate market. They agreed that if they ever split, he would buy her out. This was just before a major real estate boom. When the split came, the house was worth several million dollars and she had to be satisfied with her original investment, which was a lot less.

Often women err just by getting plain bad advice. My friend Margaret was marrying for the second time. The man was from another state. He seemed ideal. He was a partner in a law firm in another state and appeared to be very prosperous.

Her lawyers advised her not to have a prenuptial agreement. They believed, but never checked, the man had more assets than Margaret and that an agreement would be detrimental to her should the marriage break up.

Her lawyers were wrong. And, when the marriage did break up, it turned out he was broke. In fact, he ended up suing her for some of her money and a lot of the marital property, including the sheets she had actually owned before they married.

Had she asked for an agreement he would have had to disclose his assets, for that is mandatory in New Jersey where the couple lived. Failure to do so invalidates the agreement. So unless the man had absolutely lied—which in itself would have been grounds to invalidate the agreement—my friend would have known the score.

If you are already married and don't have an agreement, there is always the "postnup." This works like the prenuptial agreement but might be more difficult to introduce into the marriage.

There are a variety of reasons for wanting one. A New Jersey lawyer reports preparing an agreement for a long-married couple. The wife thought the husband was taking a business risk she didn't like. She wanted an agreement that would safeguard a certain amount of assets.

You might inherit a great deal of money and want to be sure it won't become marital property.

You and your husband might decide to start a business. A postnuptial agreement could settle ahead of time what would happen in the event of either death or divorce.

Or, you might just be worried about the marriage.

In the end, no agreement will ensure a good marriage, and no agreement will mean that you won't have a messy fight should you divorce. If an agreement is made between unequals, there might always be resentment and anger that could even affect what might otherwise have been a good marriage. If you want an agreement because you think the marriage will not work out, maybe you should think again before marrying.

5.
Coming Apart

At the time of their divorce Gerarda Wilhel-mina Schoos Unkel Pommerenke and her husband Roger owned a home worth $125,000. When Mrs. Pommerenke was awarded only $7,500 as a divorce settlement she appealed the decision—and lost. Mrs. Pommerenke's practice of sunbathing "topless" in the presence of a male guest who "felt free to be in his 'underwear' or nude in the presence of his host's wife and in the absence of his host" did not influence the judge. Nor did it matter that Mrs. Pommerenke was guilty of adultery. What mattered was the $95,582 that Roger Pommerenke saved before their marriage and used for the down payment. Mr. Pommerenke kept his separate property. The marital property was divided equally. The judge decided the case accord-ing to modern divorce law—no more judgments about the good wife or the bad husband.

Welcome to the divorce revolution, a reversal of old rules that was supposed to eliminate the accusations and just divvy up the property. Divorce changed in four ways:

1. The grounds for divorce have changed.
2. Property settlements have changed.
3. Alimony has changed.
4. Child support and child custody have changed.

When I grew up, the kind of behavior exhibited by Mrs. Pommerenke would have been worthy of lurid headlines in the local paper. Adultery was one of the only reasons for a divorce. The others were desertion, alcoholism, and physical abuse; insanity was also a reason for divorce. If a wife was caught cheating, she was usually left with nothing. If it was her husband, he usually paid dearly for his errant ways.

Although a woman was recently prosecuted in Wisconsin for an extramarital affair and several states still consider adultery a punishable crime, moral judgments are increasingly removed from the financial decisions of divorce.

The word *divorce* comes from the Latin *divortium*, which allowed for the dissolution of a marriage by mutual consent. The ancient Romans had pretty well figured out the economics of divorce. If there was a divorce and no adulterous activity the wife could recover her dowry within one year. If the wife was guilty of adultery, the husband got to keep one sixth of the dowry. If the wife had done something less damaging, the husband only kept one eighth of the dowry. If the husband was fooling around, he had to return the dowry immediately. He could hang on to the dowry for six months if he had committed a less serious offense. If, said the Roman law, both parties had been guilty of the big A the law acted as if neither party was guilty—that is, the wife got her dowry back after one year.

By the twelfth century in England, divorce had become an absolute no-no. Ecclesiastic courts controlled divorce. Think of the trouble Henry VIII had when he wanted a divorce. In America where we didn't have church courts, divorce was the domain of the judicial courts or the legislatures. The first divorce in America was granted to Mrs. James Luxford in 1639 by a Massachusetts Bay colony court. The grounds: bigamy. Contrary to what many believe, divorce was allowed in most of the states with the exception of very Catholic South Carolina. After the Civil War divorce decrees accelerated at a frenzy, one divorce in every sixteen marriages by 1880, and one divorce in every six marriages in the late 1920s.[1] By 1990, almost two thirds of all marriages begun in the preceding fifteen years ended in divorce.

GROUNDS FOR DIVORCE

"Grounds" are reasons for wanting a divorce. Divorce changed dramatically on January 1, 1970, when California passed the first "no-fault" laws and changed centuries of thinking that a marriage could only end if one party had hurt the other party. Today all states have some form of no-fault law.

No-fault divorce eliminated the need for blame. When adultery was the principle grounds for divorce, the husband often staged an "assignation" in order to provide the necessary reason for the courts to dissolve a marriage. George Bernard Shaw, in his play *Getting Married*, depicts a scene in which a couple feign an argument that ends with the husband striking his wife in the presence of a witness so the wife could obtain a divorce on the grounds of physical cruelty.

Divorce reformers who supported no fault believed it would eliminate the need for "corroborated perjury."[2] No fault was meant to be a truth-in-divorce law. Couples could now obtain a divorce by mutual consent without trumped-up grounds. Psychological grounds such as irreconcilable differences and irretrievable breakdown can now be enough to qualify for a divorce.

How do you know if you have irreconcilable differences? In California, the leader in no fault, "The court will not consider evidence as to the existence or non-existence of the 'irreconcilable differences.' In fact, if one says there are irreconcilable differences and the other says there are not, that dispute, in and of itself, constitutes irreconcilable difference." Although the reform movement's detractors worried that "divorce on demand" would hurt women, other states rapidly followed California in adding no-fault clauses. Thirty-five states grant divorces for irreconcilable differences and irretrievable breakdown, six states allow incompatability, and nine states allow divorce by mutual consent. Georgia offers a choice of thirteen different reasons to abandon a marriage ranging from impotence to drug addiction to physical abuse.

1. Intermarriage by persons within the prohibited degrees of consanguinity and affinity
2. Mental incapacity at the time of the marriage
3. Impotency at the time of marriage
4. Force, menace, duress, or fraud in obtaining the marriage

5. Pregnancy of the wife by a man other than the husband at the time of the marriage, unknown by the husband [Notice that even in the gender neutral language of the law, this does not apply to husbands.]
6. Adultery in either of the parties after marriage
7. Willful and continued desertion by either of the parties for the term of one year
8. The conviction of either party for an offense involving moral turpitude and under which he or she is sentenced to imprisonment in a penal institution for a term of two years or longer
9. Habitual intoxication
10. Cruel treatment which shall consist of the willful infliction of pain, bodily or mental, upon the complaining party, such as reasonably justifies apprehension of danger to life, limb or health
11. Incurable mental illness
12. Habitual drug addiction
13. The marriage is irretrievably broken

In other words anyone can get a divorce. New York is one of the few states where, if a couple do not agree to a divorce, the one who wants the divorce must have "grounds" and be able to prove those grounds. In New York State either side can ask for a jury trial for a divorce.

Some states will grant a divorce if a couple have lived apart for a given number of years (Idaho, five years; Louisiana and Maryland, one year; Arkansas, Pennsylvania, Rhode Island, Tennessee, and Texas, three years) even if one party does not want the divorce.

If you cannot get a divorce in one state, you can move to a state with more lenient grounds. You would have to live in that state long enough to satisfy a residency requirement before you could seek a divorce. Your husband can do the same thing. You will get the divorce but you will be subject to the property settlement laws of the state where you lived. Nevada's six-week residency requirement has helped make it the divorce capital of America. Grounds for divorce in Nevada are either incompatability or living apart without cohabitation for one year. If you want sunshine, the Virgin Islands also has a six-week residency requirement.

If you want the divorce—and more and more women do—you can leave the marriage just as easily as your husband.

Some couples, for religious or other reasons, do not want to live together but do not want a divorce. They can agree to a legal separation. This is a formal document that sets out the rights and obligations such as support and child-custody arrangements the couple have with each other. If you have a legal separation, you cannot remarry.

Who Gets What?

While no-fault divorce made the actual dissolution of the marriage easy, some of the old "fault" concepts lingered when it came to the division of marital property. Some states still cling to the idea that the good wife or husband should be better rewarded than the bad. But even in those states where "fault" counts, the fault has to be really egregious to have an impact on the bottom line. Adultery may not be enough these days.

Eliminating marital fault from divorce did not eliminate fights between divorcing couples. With property at stake, divorcing couples began to battle over the value of property, ownership of property, and even what constituted property.

When it comes to divorce, there are several kinds of property. Yours, his, and ours. Lawyers refer to it as marital (ours) and separate (yours or his) property. Some states consider only marital property in divorce settlements. Other states look at all property without making a distinction between marital and separate property for divorce settlements. They are Alaska, Connecticut, Florida, Hawaii, Indiana, Iowa, Kansas, Massachusetts, Michigan, Montana, New Hampshire, North Dakota, Ohio, Oregon, South Dakota, Utah, Vermont, and Wyoming.

Some states exclude inherited property, gifts made to just one party, and income received from disability payments when dividing property in a divorce. Some states have quasi-marital property. This can be a real problem. Property can start out as separate property; for example, your house may have been purchased with money that you had before your marriage. But then your husband, by making repairs or helping with the upkeep, gradually may have transformed it into marital property.

Far more sweeping than the change toward easier divorce has been the change in the economics of divorce. A new concept of dividing marital property at the end of a marriage developed: equitable distribution. The common law states also began to move toward a concept of shared marital property. Before the laws changed, whoever held title to property—usually the husband—owned the property, even if his wife's money paid for it. The only property that the court could distribute in a divorce settlement was property jointly owned by the couple. Equitable distribution was an attempt to redress that situation in the states that do not have community property laws. Equitable distribution laws recognize for the first time the contribution of the housewife to the marriage and frequently to her husband's career. The new law proclaims marriage as an economic partnership, wiping out hundreds of years of dependency. Husband and wife are economic partners, regardless of which partner earned the money. Between 1970 and 1985 all states added some form of equitable or equal distribution of marital property upon divorce.

The old laws protected the state. The state did not want a man to walk out on his wife and children, leaving the state to support them. Sexist, gender-based rules, which were also written to protect the wife, have been abolished. The change in the law came as a result of changes in society. Women are working and can support themselves. Women are no longer seen as dependents. As more women have jobs and are protected by Social Security, medicaid, and unemployment insurance there is less incentive to keep the marriage together. If it ends in divorce, each partner has a right to an equitable, but not necessarily equal, share of the fruits of that marriage.

Equitable distribution was even introduced into some community property states as a means of distributing marital property in a divorce. The meaning of this idea can best be understood by looking at the actual law, as written into the New York State domestic relations law. Marital property shall be distributed equitably between the parties, considering the circumstances of the case and of the respective parties. The law lists the areas the judge must consider.

1. The income and property of each party at the time of marriage and at the time of the commencement of the action
2. The duration of the marriage and the age and health of both parties
3. The need of a custodial parent to occupy or own the marital residence and to use or own its household effects
4. The loss of inheritance and pension rights upon dissolution of the marriage as of the date of dissolution
5. Any award of maintenance under subdivision six of this part
6. Any equitable claim to, interest in, or direct or indirect contribution made to the acquisition of such marital property by the party not having title, including joint efforts or expenditures and contributions and services as a spouse, parent, wage earner, and homemaker, and to the career or career potential of the other party
7. The liquid or nonliquid character of all marital property
8. The probable future financial circumstances of each party
9. The impossibility or difficulty of evaluating any component asset or any interest in a business, corporation, or profession, and the economic desirability of retaining such asset or interest intact and free from any claim or interference by the other party

10. Tax consequences to each party
11. The wasteful dissipation of assets by either spouse
12. Any transfer or encumbrance made in contemplation of a matrimonial action without a fair consideration
13. Any other factor the court shall expressly find to be just and proper

Number 6, or its equivalent in other state codes, quickly became known as the "housewife's contribution." Modern divorce is about dividing assets, regardless of who earned the money and who holds title to the property. Although monetary contributions are important many state laws now mandate that nonmonetary contributions of a wife who stayed home and cared for the family be considered too.

Of course the new laws are written in the newspeak of the late twentieth century, the gender neutral. As one New Jersey judge explained it, "The common law must adapt to the progress of women in achieving economic equality and to the mutual sharing of all obligations by husbands and wives."[3]

The equitable distribution law and other laws gave the wife who stayed at home a claim on marital assets based on her contribution. Two different terms are designated: direct contribution and spousal contribution.

Direct contribution is fairly straightforward. If your husband owned a business before you married him and you worked in the business during the marriage, you made a direct contribution.

Spousal contribution basically says that if you were the wife who stayed at home and baked the bread, you were entitled to some of the marital dough.

Today, only a few state divorce laws omit the value of the housewife's contribution. They are Alabama, Hawaii, Idaho, Louisiana, Michigan, Nevada, New Hampshire, New Jersey, New Mexico, Oklahoma, South Carolina, Texas, Utah, Washington, and Wyoming.[4]

But equitable distribution did not solve some of the problems that its proponents believed it would. Equitable distribution laws only vaguely guided judges. What was equitable? Was it 50 percent of the assets to each, was it 64 percent? Without specific guidelines, equity was at the discretion of the judge.

To further complicate matters, there was a problem as to what even constituted property. Some things were obvious—the marital home, stocks and bonds, cash in the bank, and the family car. A business and the family silver were all fairly tangible assets. But other assets were less clear. What about a pension fund that would have a future value? Equitable distribution set into motion fights over the very nature of what constituted property.

As the divorce revolution has proceeded, the concept of marital property has expanded to include future earnings such as commissions on an insurance policy sold during the marriage, pension plans and other fringe benefits, and stock options. Intangibles such as professional goodwill and professional degrees are frequently defined as marital property.

Celebrity goodwill is another "intangible" that has been included in the division of marital assets. It is a problem most of us won't have. In 1988, the actress and model Marisa Berenson and her husband, Richard Golub, divorced. Golub claimed that the increased value of Ms. Berenson's career during the marriage was marital property and Golub was entitled to some of the proceeds. In a 1988 decision, the courts agreed with Golub that Ms. Berenson's celebrity status was indeed "marital property," although he was not awarded any money.

Consider the story of Loretta O'Brien. When she married in 1974 she was a teacher. Her husband was starting medical school. He received his medical degree almost ten years later. Two months after that he filed for divorce. In a landmark decision that may make Mrs. O'Brien the Rosa Parks of the matrimonial world, she demanded an interest in that license. The reasoning was simple: Even though the license didn't appear to be marital property, the license gave Dr. O'Brien a passport to future earnings. Mrs. O'Brien, who had supported her husband during those early years, would have none of those future earnings unless the license was deemed to be marital property. The New York Court of Appeals agreed with Mrs. O'Brien. She was awarded 40 percent of the value of his license.

Some states consider the professional degree property for the purposes of property division but not alimony. Some states have laws that mandate a division, and some states have case law without definite instructions. Some states are using the value of the degree as a substitute for alimony. An example is the case of a $100,000 award to a wife in Iowa based on her doctor husband's future earnings.

In some states the professional practice is also looked upon as an asset. In Oklahoma, the court considered the increase in value of the husband's practice during the marriage, even though the husband had been in practice before the marriage.[5] The trend would appear to be that the wife who helped her husband earn a professional degree is entitled to some compensation for this. Some states are calling for "equitable reimbursement,"—that is, giving back the money that was actually spent. (A good reason to keep accurate records.) But a Pennsylvania judge concluded that the wife was not entitled to be reimbursed for supporting her husband while he was in chiropractic school because she was legally required to support him.

Possibly the largest asset for most couples, besides the family home, is the husband's pension. Many states now treat pensions as marital property subject to equitable distribution. While many women have pensions, most do not. Or if they do, because they tend to leave jobs to have children the value of the wife's pension is generally much less than her husband's.

In New York, pension plans are considered marital property subject to equitable distribution, but recently in Nebraska the court did not consider the husband's pension plan as part of the marital assets. Even in states where a wife can share her husband's pension, she only shares that part of the pension that was earned during the marriage.

Gradually, some states are also beginning to look at the standard of living during marriage when making awards, and not just giving the wife of a long-term marriage a subsistence payment. Sandra Goldman is a good example. She was forty-six when, after a twenty-year marriage, she and her husband Peter, a neurosurgeon, divorced in 1987. The Goldmans have two children, Wendy and Gregory. Mrs. Goldman, a nurse, did not work during the marriage. Peter Goldman earned $478,560 in 1986. From time to time he receives bonuses and his corporate checking account pays for various personal expenses. He has a large pension fund into which his corporation has paid over $200,000 over the previous three years. The judge awarded Mrs. Goldman $1,000 per week for eight years, $700 alimony and $300 child support, and suggested that she brush up on her nursing skills. Said the judge, "Mrs. Sandra Goldman's opportunity for future acquisition of capital assets and income certainly will never approach that of Dr. Goldman. However, she has an opportunity to be gainfully employed and to invest wisely the distribution of assets pursuant to this judgment."[6] Oh yes, Mrs. Goldman was given the family home and its furniture, with the exception of her husband's guns and a gun cabinet, animal trophies, an elephant-foot fireplace fender, shotgun-shell loading equipment, gun cases, and daughter Wendy's Raggedy Ann doll. She was also given a lump-sum payment of $216,000, payable over five years.

Mrs. Goldman's lawyers appealed the decision. In the appeals court the judges said Mrs. Goldman's award should have been based on the standard of living she and her husband had during the marriage, thus expanding the interpretation of the Massachusetts divorce laws. When the case was retried, Mrs. Goldman was awarded lifetime alimony of $65,000 a year and most of her court fees.

Alimony? Don't Count on It

There is no question that many women, and a few men, who did not previously have title to property have benefited from the new property laws. But what happens when there is little property to divide? After property division, alimony looms as a major divorce problem. The concept of alimony has changed dramatically. Once again eliminating any distinction between husband and wife, the new statutes were enacted to eliminate the idea of the dependent wife getting a dole from her husband until she remarried, he died, or she committed some act, such as living with another man, that would deprive her of her stipend.

Alimony is awarded in only 15 percent of divorces these days. With or without fault, alimony is going the way of the dinosaur. The trend, say many lawyers, is for women to be self-supporting. Instead of the "permanent" alimony that used to be granted until a wife either died or remarried, alimony today, except in long-term marriages, if it is awarded at all is generally temporary. Lawyers frequently advise women who are contemplating a divorce to hang on for at least the ten-year mark, because that seems to be the magic number for "long-term" marriage, when alimony awards are considered. It is also the number of years you must be married in order to share in your husband's Social Security if you did not work long enough to qualify on your own.

The idea of alimony has changed, and so have the varieties. First of all, there is *rehabilitative alimony,* as if you, the wife, had just had a traumatic accident. This is generally defined as alimony that is given to a wife so that she will be able to learn a skill in order to be able to support herself. The problem here is that, most of the time, women who stayed home did so in order to take care of the children. Now you will be expected to continue to take care of the children while you learn how to support yourself—a good trick if you can do it.

Remunerative alimony is defined as alimony given to

compensate the wife for money spent during the marriage—especially in cases where the wife supported her husband while he earned an advanced degree. Naturally, if your husband supported you while you earned a degree, he is entitled to the same kind of remunerative alimony.

Permanent alimony is the old-fashioned type of alimony.

Lump-sum alimony may also be awarded. This is an amount that is based on the wife's future support requirements and loss of the wife's right of inheriting any part of her husband's estate. Wealthy women have also had to pay lump-sum alimony.

In California, where alimony is called "spousal support," there is a rough rule of thumb that alimony will last for half of the length of the marriage. In that state each county has support-guideline schedules. Here is a sample from one of them:

If the net earnings of one spouse are $300 to $600 per week, maximum support to the other spouse is one third of that income.

If the net earnings of one spouse are over $600 per week, maximum support to the other spouse shall not exceed 40 percent of that amount.

If there is both spousal and child support, the combined amount should not exceed 50 percent of the supporting spouse's net income.

No spousal support shall be provided to any spouse who, following dissolution, has income sufficient to maintain his or her standard of living.

Several state divorce laws eliminate alimony if there is fault. They are Georgia, Louisiana, North Carolina, Virginia, and Puerto Rico.

Then there are the states where you can get alimony, but fault counts against you. They are Alabama, Connecticut, Florida, Kentucky, Michigan, Missouri, Nevada, New Hampshire, North Dakota, Pennsylvania, Rhode Island, South Carolina, South Dakota, Tennessee, West Virginia, Wyoming, and Washington, D.C.

The payment of alimony and the distribution of assets assumes that couples have accumulated some assets during their marriage. Frequently, that is not the case; instead, they may have piled up the debts. In the latter case, divorce settlements become a question of dividing the debts. As the number of people filing for personal bankruptcy has increased, the impact of bankrutcy on divorce has come under more and more scrutiny. According to federal bankruptcy laws, alimony and child support awards are not wiped out by filing for bankruptcy. One bankruptcy question that has not been settled is whether creditors can confiscate property that might otherwise be used for alimony payments.

A big problem with alimony (and child support) can be collecting it. In California, a woman can get an "order of security." This means she can ask the court to order that her husband post a portion of his money for future support. If he does not pay support she can also get a lien placed on any property her husband owns in California so that if he tries to sell the property, the court won't let him transfer title.

In other states you might be able to get an alimony trust. Such a trust pays income to the wife assuring that her husband cannot squander the money. The remainder of the trust either reverts to the husband or to the children of the couple.

Would a woman fare better under the old system or is she better off today? Today the law assumes that a woman can go out and work. So women are more likely to be awarded the new "maintenance" rather than the old life-time alimony. A lot depends on your earnings capacity. To illustrate this, look what happened in a recent case in Oregon: "Jane Doe," an Oregon housewife whose eighteen-year marriage ended, was awarded payments by her husband of $1,000 per month for two years, $800 per month for six years following that, and $500 for the next sixty-nine months. When Mrs. Doe earned a teacher's license, the judge slashed her alimony by almost 25 percent: $1,000 per month for two years, $700 per month for four years, and $500 for four years.[7]

CHILD CUSTODY AND SUPPORT

No-fault divorce laws and equitable distribution challenged old assumptions about marriage. The new reform mood supposedly reflecting a change in society undermined centuries-old ideas about the need to preserve marriage and protect the family. But an even greater assumption was challenged with a series of new laws about child custody and child support (see Chapter 9).

In the past, a father had the responsibility for supporting his children; a mother was considered responsible for taking care of her children. So when a marriage dissolved, the mother was awarded custody and the father was ordered to pay child support and given visitation rights to his children. The new laws stress equity: Both mother and father had to support the children. And in an even greater break with tradition, fathers could have custody of their children, either joint physical custody, or joint legal custody. What this meant to some was that the best interests of the child should be considered. In some cases, courts were able to decide that the best interests of the child were served when the mother had custody part of the time and the father the other part, including arrangements that left parents driving their children back and forth to each other's houses on a weekly basis.

If joint custody is a possibility be sure you understand exactly what is meant both in your state and by your husband. States with joint custody laws are Alaska, Arizona, California, Colorado, Connecticut, Delaware, Florida, Hawaii, Idaho, Illinois, Indiana, Iowa, Kansas, Kentucky, Louisiana, Maine, Maryland, Massachusetts, Michigan, Minnesota, Mississippi, Missouri, Montana, Nevada, New Hampshire, New Jersey, New Mexico, North Carolina, Ohio, Oklahoma, Oregon, Pennsylvania, Tennessee, Texas, Utah, Vermont, and Wisconsin.

Were women better off before no-fault and equitable distribution? Probably not. The idea that women were taken care of by alimony prior to the change in divorce laws may be a myth. Critics of what some called divorce on demand cited as evidence statistics showing women plunged into poverty following the no-fault divorce laws. But these figures have since been challenged. Critics also point out that women's lower earnings not only are the result of divorce, but also the generally lower standing of women in the labor market.[8] And there is plenty of evidence that the old divorce days weren't so great either. Very few divorced women received any alimony under the old fault system. When they did, judges and ex-husbands used the doling out of alimony as a way to control the wife's behavior after a divorce. And, in those days, fault could be liberally defined. In one case, a fault—read "no alimony"—divorce was granted to a husband whose wife's "preoccupation with social and club activities and failure to prepare [her] husband's meals constituted marital cruelty. If a woman was at "fault" she didn't get any alimony at all. A woman who was awarded "permanent" alimony could have that money terminated or reduced, if her former husband remarried, because "the support obligations to his new spouse were more important than the claims of a former spouse."[9]

6.

If You Thought Marriage Was Bad, Wait Until You Try Divorce

In theory, divorce reform was supposed to liberate women and end the lying that previously surrounded it. Instead, the new divorce laws have sent women into battle on foot while their husbands have clobbered them from armored cars.

First, let's look at what divorce reform, that means no-fault divorce and equitable distribution of property, was meant to achieve. Guilt about divorce was to be eliminated, bitter fights were to end, and women would no longer be treated paternalistically, but would take their place as equals in the new economic partnership of marriage.

AND THEY DID NOT LIVE HAPPILY EVER AFTER

Instead of the promised equities, there have been increased inequities. Experts who promulgated the new laws are now taking a look at what they have brought about. Articles have begun to appear in learned journals about the unforeseen consequences of divorce reform.[1]

Most women who have been through a divorce in the last ten years don't need a sociologist to tell them the new system is fraught with problems and that women have been the biggest victims.

Sandra Goldman, about whom I talked in the last chapter is typical. The court proceedings in her divorce took over three years. Her lawyer, Peter Roth, believes there are several reasons Mrs. Goldman had problems.[2] One of her biggest problems was the lack of funds to adequately pursue her case. In Massachusetts, courts are reluctant to issue expert fee costs. These are fees paid to expert witnesses. Expert witnesses who testify as to the value of property usually must be paid at the time they give their opinions. A 1989 study of the Massachusetts court system revealed that judges rarely award expert witness fees.[3] Basically this cuts off a woman's chance to get what she needs, since many times it is the husband who has the information.

Sandra Goldman's plight revealed another inequity. Mrs. Goldman, who had not worked in years, was expected to retrain herself when she was in her fifties in order to work as a nurse. What many women have suspected is finally being acknowledged: "Judges devalue long-term homemakers' contributions to their families and make unrealistic assumptions about older women's opportunities in the paid work force. Thus, dissolution awards give women small shares of marital property and scant short-term alimony, leaving them in extremis financially while their ex-husbands enjoy their former, or even a more comfortable, standard of living."[4]

Another problem was that Mrs. Goldman didn't know about her husband's investments and had no idea of their value. Sandra Goldman's husband controlled the valuation of his assets. As one example, he invested $180,000 and then said it was worth only half. The court accepted his value. Frequently, with privately held stock, only insiders really know the valuation.

The problem, says one lawyer, is that today's fifty-year-old woman looks like what the judge thinks forty should look. She looks like she can go out and work. So that's what the judge is telling her. Women who stayed home and did not build their own careers have lost those years and are not duly compensated.

While housewives have lost out when it comes to splitting assets under the new rules of equitable distribution and no-fault divorce, many high-powered career women also discover that they have made mistakes that subsequently hurt them. Part of the problem is that the very laws that gave the nonworking wife a shot at the marital assets can now be applied to penalize the hardworking woman. Unthinkable as the notion would have been to our grandfathers, men are now demanding—and getting—support from and shares in the businesses of their wives. Lawyers who have dealt with the other side of the coin report that career women are often no more worldly when it comes to protecting themselves than their stay-at-home sisters.

It isn't only the stay-at-home wife who finds she has problems. Jane Smith, an office manager for a medical doctor, noticed one day a telephone call charge from Florida when her husband was supposed to be in Texas on a business trip. Other odd things happened but Jane ignored the signals. She couldn't believe anything was wrong with her twenty-year marriage. Jane's husband, a computer expert, managed everything. He even sold their house before Jane knew the marriage was in trouble. The house was in his name. In a common law state that meant he could use the money as he pleased. He spent much of it on his new girlfriend. When they divorced, Jane was left with furniture she had before the marriage, a trust for her son's education, and bitter memories. Her ignorance cost her dearly.

Jane's story underscores one of the biggest problems for women when their marriages end in divorce. For, while the law stipulates an equitable, or even an equal distribution of the assets accrued during the marriage, often women especially in common law states have no access to the marital assets before the divorce. A husband who wants to keep control of the purse strings can simply do so. If divorce occurs, finding out about the assets could be a problem, necessitating the long process of "discovery."

Discovery costs money. In addition, many women simply do not have adequate funds to even hire a lawyer. The funds are controlled by their husbands. So, despite the laws that declare marriage an economic partnership when the marriage is ending, a wife may find it hard to put her hands on any ready cash.

Instead of lying about fictitious romances in order to obtain divorces, some men now routinely understate the value of their investments. The 1989 Massachusetts study reported that lawyers who were surveyed said that only 35 percent of the financial statements filed by men were accurate. The survey reported that "the courts do not take discovery seriously. Discovery requests are often ignored by opposing counsel, and the courts do not enforce them as they do in other, nonfamily litigation."

Even community property states do not solve that problem of control of assets or access to funds for legal fees. And a recent decision in California has taken away one of the few means women in California had to raise money to finance their divorces. Since California is a community property state, each spouse is considered owner of half the marital property. So women were able to obtain funds by signing promissory notes for their half of the house. When a husband brought suit recently against the lawyer who accepted his wife's promissory note, the California supreme court declared the transaction void, thus eliminating a potential source of funds.

Sometimes, even a savvy wife does not get her fair share of the assets. While each divorce is a separate consideration, a pattern has emerged that to some degree is consistent. In court decisions, distribution of assets has been one third to the lower wage earner and two thirds to the higher wage earner. The wife, who stayed home with children in a long marriage, may receive 50 percent of the property, seldom more. In Texas, which has no alimony, a nonworking wife may receive more than 50 percent of the assets to offset the lack of alimony. But what happens when there are no marital assets?

If you worked with your husband to build a business, do not assume that it is equally yours and his unless you can prove it. Show that your money was used or keep track of the hours you worked. Be listed as a partner or an executive. When famed realtor Donald Trump announced that his wife, Ivana, would become president of New York's Plaza Hotel, Mr. Trump announced that her salary would be $1 a year plus all the dresses she could buy. While that may have sounded cute, Mrs. Trump would have been better off asking for stock.

When my friend Rhoda married her husband, a struggling artist, Rhoda was earning $50,000 a year. Her husband was a free-lance graphics designer. Pretty soon, however, he decided to open his own design firm. Rhoda helped finance it. She also took care of the books. They pooled their income. But that was all they pooled. Rhoda also did all the housework, while her husband began to play house with a beautiful architect who came in to order business cards. I'll skip all the details about Rhoda's attempt to ride out the affair and get right to the point. When Rhoda's husband finally left her, Rhoda lost her job and her husband had shut down his business in order to start a new one with his new companion. Rhoda is sure her husband diverted some cash from the old business to the new one but she can't prove a thing.

It is not unusual for a man to start a business with the help of his wife, who may use her earnings to support the household or may otherwise enable her husband to get started. When the marriage dissolves, it's usually the man who keeps the business.

The new laws do not make alimony a prime focus. There are 17 million divorced women in America. Only 15 percent receive alimony. In the past, alimony was all women really got no matter how long the marriage— property settlements were not part of the package. The premise of the new laws was that women didn't need alimony. They could leave a marriage and go out to work. When *Satanic Verses* author Salman Rushdie filed for divorce, his wife, Marianne Wiggins, declared that she didn't believe in alimony. In New Jersey one judge saw women as "lusting" after a permanent meal ticket. Feminists declared their opposition to the idea of being supported by former husbands. That was fine for the working woman. But it wasn't so great for the woman who had stayed home to take care of the children and had given up her career to help her husband. In cases where there is substantial property, alimony is important but not critical. Alimony is awarded less and less. In some states, there is no chance for alimony, only property division. So, if you and your husband spent all your money and didn't build any assets, there will be little to divide. Unless you can support yourself, you could have a difficult time.

The family home, which used to be automatically awarded to the wife, is now sometimes sold, and the proceeds are split. If there is an income-producing business it frequently goes to the husband. The wife might be given a lump-sum payment. While the initial division was equal, over time the wife loses out.

If the woman wants to keep the home, it could be equally disastrous. For example, if you live in California and your one asset is a house worth $200,000, in order to keep that house, you would have to come up with some way to give your husband his share of the money. You may end up bargaining away other things to keep the house, only to discover that you can't afford to maintain it. Or you may accept an appraised value of the house that turns out to be too high. When you try and sell the house, you will discover that you have lost money. You may accept the house and then discover, when you finally sell it, that you must pay a big tax because the house has risen in value. Chances are, that tax payment was not figured into your settlement.

And the worst of all catastrophes for most women now looms as a possibility. Equal rights language built into our laws suggests that a father has as much right to custody as a mother. Fear of losing her children has been added to the problems of divorce. While some men genuinely want custody of their children, lawyers across the country report that most men will use custody as a negotiating tool. They will threaten to seek custody of the children, then will agree to drop their demand for custody if the wife agrees to take a smaller property settlement or less alimony than she thought she deserved.

Matrimonial lawyers give several reasons why women do not end up with the stake they should after a divorce.

WHY WOMEN LOSE OUT

1. Women do not have records of the family finances before the divorce. When a divorce looms, they discover that "our" accountant has become "his" accountant.
2. Women do not know the value of the assets.
3. Women do not have the money to hire the experts to locate and value the assets during a divorce.
4. Women do not have the money to support themselves during the divorce process if their husbands refuse to send money, so they settle for less than they should.
5. Women do not have the money to pay for lawyers.

The reasons all add up to the same thing: a lack of financial equality at the bargaining table.

For some women, a divorce is their first experience with lawyers and negotiations. They may be married to men who are routinely involved with contracts, closings, and other details of business. For such women, the whole process of divorce can be more traumatic than for their husbands. Unfamiliarity with the process could also be a reason for settling for less.

The new laws have done little to reduce the acrimony of divorce. While divorce fights center around money and property, the fights manifest the emotional problems of the marriage. One couple fought bitterly in court about whether three African violets were marital or separate property. They were not fighting about money—the plants weren't even rare. They were fighting about control and winning, probably the same fights they had during their marriage.

Divorce is hell, no question. It's hell if you are Jane Doe or Jane Fonda with her looks, her fame, and her money. Fonda, who was divorced from her second husband after a seventeen-year marriage, described the process as "debilitating and frightening."

The same women who were dominated financially during their marriages allow themselves to be dominated in the divorce. They even hire lawyers who take on the role their husbands did, letting their lawyers make decisions for them. One woman, terrified of being alone, realized that she allowed her husband to talk her into giving up money by suggesting a reconciliation, which he never meant.

Should you be headed for a divorce, a compromising picture of your husband with another woman will not be nearly as important as a picture of his financial statement.

Some people who want a divorce begin making plans to bail out long before D day. Men have deferred bonuses or even postponed new positions until after a divorce in order to lessen the amount of money they might have to pay their wives. One trick for small business owners and professionals is to prepay expenses, while deferring income. Women who are contemplating a divorce are advised to stock up on groceries while their husbands are still paying the bills and to stash away cash. And while strategies for bailing out of a marriage are usually financial, one woman found her husband's "battle plan" in his briefcase. It called for him to begin body building to improve his pectorals in preparation for life with a younger woman.

If you already know about the family finances, you are way ahead of many women, especially those who are taken by surprise when their husbands want a divorce. Matrimonial lawyers suggest that if divorce is at all a possibility, you begin your preparations by ferreting out financial information. Of course, you are better off if you have been participating in the financial decisions of your marriage all along. You will need this information if you actually do get a divorce. If you don't get the divorce, having the information will still be helpful to you and beneficial to your marriage.

The hardest part of divorce, many women report, is making the decision that the marriage is over. How do you know when to even call a lawyer? There are several different situations, and each requires some thought. If you think the marriage is in trouble but are not sure you want a divorce, you should do the following:

1. Visit a therapist or marriage counselor. If you and your husband are able to discuss the problem, you can go together.

2. Begin gathering together all of the financial information you need if you haven't already done it.
3. Consult a lawyer. Don't worry that consulting a lawyer will lead you down the road to divorce. If you don't consult a lawyer, your husband may begin making secret divorce preparations and you will lose out.

If you think, as many women do, that your husband would never do anything underhanded, think again and pick up the phone. You don't have to commit yourself to a divorce. You can make perfectly clear the exploratory nature of your visit. The worst thing you can do is ignore the situation thinking that your husband would never do anything to hurt you. Believe me, he could. And you may find yourself doing things you never thought you could.

If your husband walks in one day, as happened to one woman shortly after she returned from a trip, and announces that he is leaving you, immediately proceed to step three. Your husband has already hired his lawyer.

If you have made up your mind that you want the divorce, you may only need steps two and three.

If you and your husband have agreed to a divorce, you may be able to choose less adversarial divorce methods.

If you heard about a vaccine for a disease that was bound to strike one out of three people, you would probably dash for the doctor to get a dose. Yet few of us are willing to take the same precautions about divorce.

If divorce is a possibility, plan carefully.

Divorce Battle Plan

1. Copy all bank records, real estate deeds, credit card statements, and tax returns you can find. This will help establish marital standard of living as well as marital property and debts (see step eight).
2. Some experts will advise women who have joint accounts to withdraw half the money, especially if there is a chance that you will have a hard time getting living expenses from your husband. It is not illegal for you to withdraw money from a joint account. That's what a joint account means—you both own it jointly. Many women who decide to do this discover that their husbands, having planned the divorce in advance, have already taken the money. Some experts, however, say that doing this can disrupt and exacerbate what otherwise might have been amicable divorce proceedings. Base your actions on your knowledge about how your husband is likely to react.
3. If you do not have credit in your own name, open charge accounts at department stores and with major credit card companies while you are still married. But if you go out on a spending spree with the cards, you could be liable for the debts. If you are just getting married, you do not legally have to change the names on all your charge accounts. You can keep some credit in your own name.
4. If you have children, begin a child-care diary: who feeds the children, who does the laundry, who plays with them. This can be helpful if there is a custody battle.
5. Try and accumulate enough cash for expenses for six months and enough to pay initial legal fees, if possible.

6. Many lawyers advise a woman who can do so to take some courses that will help prepare her for the job market if she is not working or for a better job if she is.

7. If you have stocks, call the broker and find out their value.

8. Be able to document your standard of living. If you and your husband traveled a lot, even though his business paid for it, that is part of your way of life. If you had a car and it was owned by your husband's business, or any other expenses that were paid for by your husband's business, include that information. This also helps in determining the value of your husband's business. He may have been charging expenses to the business that would therefore make the business appear less profitable.

9. Be able to document your "spousal contribution." If you traveled with your husband for his business, be able to explain the business nature of what you did, even if it is something as simple as giving suggestions to your husband when he prepared a speech. Business consultants charge money for things many wives do automatically. If you actually helped keep business records be able to show that too. And this does not apply just to women who are at home. Many highly successful women come home from their own offices to help entertain their husband's business clients. It seldom works the other way, except in TV commercials.

10. Try to establish a list of property that may be your separate property. (Some states—Connecticut and Massachusetts, for example—consider all property for distribution in a divorce.)

11. If you own the business and it was started with a loan from the bank in your name, or with a loan from your uncle Henry, be able to document this.
12. List your outstanding debts. If you have a credit line, find out what property is secured.
13. Some lawyers say that even when fault isn't supposed to count, if it exists, use it. Fault, by the way, doesn't have to mean a picture of your husband with that other woman. It can also mean economic fault. Your husband could have wasted the marital assets. If you can show that he did so, for example, by running up debts to finance a fancy trip for himself, that will be helpful when it comes to dividing the assets because his debts may be counted against his share. In 1988 Mark Gastineau, star New York Jets football player, abruptly retired to spend more time with actress Brigette Nielsen. As a result, Gastineau forfeited half his salary for that year. The judge awarded Mrs. Gastineau one third of the marital assets. He included in Mrs. Gastineau's share of the assets the one-third value of Mr. Gastineau's forfeited salary.[5]

Getting this information beforehand is invaluable. Once the battle lines of divorce are drawn it could be extremely expensive to go through the formal legal process called discovery for information that might be available to you.

If you don't know what's going on, your husband will have an advantage in negotiating a settlement. He will have a better idea of what assets you have and what they are worth. Despite all your initial hopes that your divorce will be different from those messy ones you heard about, you may have to fight dirty too. If you think your husband has been hiding assets you might have to hunt for them.

There are a lot of things you can do on your own. However, some people hire detectives to ferret out hidden funds. If you are feeling squeamish about this, know that you can buy a lot of information for $30 to $50 an hour. Here's a tip, however, for anyone thinking of hiring a professional. Work through your lawyer. If you hire the detective directly, there is no client-attorney privilege; your husband's lawyer can demand discovery and get a court order to look at the files. If your lawyer does the hiring, the detective is accountable only to your side. You wouldn't usually do this unless you were on the point of litigation.

How to Hunt for Hidden Assets

1. If you want to go the do-it-yourself route, you will need to invest in some equipment. A small tape recorder is a must for taping phone conversations. It's legal if you are taping conversations between you and your husband.
2. A prime source of information that is right in your house is the trash basket. Investigate it—you never know what you could find. Possible treasures that could turn up include old checks revealing bank accounts you didn't know about and credit card slips.
3. If your husband goes to the Cayman Islands a lot and he's not an avid fisherman, you could suspect that he has a bank account there.

4. Check the postmarks on the mail, in fact, check all mail.
5. If you find an unfamiliar key, it may be for a safe deposit box. Try and find out.
6. Illegal cash is risky. It is illegal. However, sometimes women use this as a negotiating point. Remember, if you knew about such cash when you signed joint tax returns, you will be in trouble too.
7. Your husband's office could be a treasure trove. If you can get inside long enough, copy as many documents as you can find, especially insurance policies, leases, and bank statements.

THERE IS MORE THAN ONE WAY OUT

Although most of the divorces that hit the newspapers pit one well-known divorce bomber against another, divorces do not have to be like that. There are several routes to divorce.

You can do it yourself. There are several books on the market. The do-it-yourself divorce is recommended for couples who have few assets, few debts, and a very brief marriage; where there is no question of child support or alimony; and where you each decided, if you have pension plans, to keep your own.

You can go to a legal clinic. You should be in somewhat the same situation as the do-it-yourself group: short marriage, few assets, no children, and few debts. This is a little more expensive than doing it yourself, but at least you have someone to answer any questions you may ask.

You can go to a mediator. Mediation is the hot buzzword of the divorce profession. As with the do-it-yourself divorce, some people are more suited to it than others. Mediation, or alternative dispute resolution (ADR), as it is also called, is an alternative to the traditional court resolution of disputes. A family mediator is a specially trained independent expert who sits down with a husband and wife and helps them come to an agreement. Many mediators started out as lawyers or therapists. The mediator does not make decisions or give legal advice. Unlike arbitration, where a couple would submit to a binding decision by a third party, a mediator tries to help a couple reach their own agreement. A settlement is not imposed. Mediation can be used to settle the whole divorce or a few sticky issues such as child custody, alimony, or property issues. Some states have court-mandated mediation for child custody and visitation issues.

The laws work differently in every state. For example, in California, parents who seek custody in the court must attempt mediation before taking their case before a judge. In Delaware, all contested custody, visitation, and support cases must be submitted for mediation. The Delaware laws specify a formula for support based on income and other criteria. The Kansas law recommends mediation of issues involving children and encourages the use of mediation in property settlements.

Divorce lawyers do not like mediation. Lawyers say that women are generally at a disadvantage in mediation. Says one, "I have seen women getting nailed in mediation, particularly when they have an imbalance of power with the spouse. I can give you countless examples of women who are married to high-powered, controlling men who push mediation because in the mediation sessions they can continue their intimidation and control where they cannot do that in a litigation setting." If this is true in your marriage, mediation is not for you.

Many lawyers say that mediators who were trained as therapists do not understand the financial complexities of divorce.

Mediation requires the voluntary participation of both husband and wife. If your husband refuses to go to a mediator, you can't go alone.

If you have little knowledge of the family assets, mediation will be a disaster. One couple who chose mediation after a twenty-year marriage were determined to avoid the conflicts they had seen in other divorces. They worked with a mediator to reach an agreement. Throughout their marriage they had always pooled their income, she as a lawyer, he as a stockbroker. During the marriage, money was seldom a problem. They had agreed early on that any money either one would inherit would go directly to their two children.

Their biggest asset was a house that they bought for $75,000. During the real estate boom of the eighties the house became worth $1,800,000. Their other major asset was his pension plan. They had very little in savings. They had some cash. They agreed that they would split everything and she would buy out her husband's share of the apartment. They showed the agreement to a lawyer who wrote the necessary legal documents and took care of the mechanics of the divorce. They decided to take their gross income as a basis for paying a proportionate share of the cost of supporting their two children. Presently, that is one third for her and two thirds for her husband. But the wife is hopeful her income will increase and that she will then pay more of the child support.

Cost for the whole process: $2,000 to the mediator and $500 for the lawyer.

The wife thinks that she might have gotten more money, but she had confidence that she would earn money and she and her husband agreed that they did not want fights about money. Most couples say that, but it doesn't work out that way. Possibly it worked in this case because they both knew exactly what the assets were and both felt confident of their ability to earn money.

If you are thinking about hiring a mediator, be sure the mediator is a member of the American Bar Association or the Academy of Family Mediators. The American Arbitration Association will also recommend mediators; you must pay a fee of $125 for the recommendation.

Divorce Really Hurts

The traditional way of divorcing is to hire a lawyer who guides you through the complicated procedure. Unlike mediation, which tries to bring parties together, traditional court-battle divorce is an adversary procedure: You and your husband have different interests, you and your lawyer have different interests, your husband's lawyer and your lawyer have different interests. Like war, it is treated as a battle to be won. Getting divorced, unlike getting married, is fraught with complex legal questions as well as emotional reactions. Regardless of your economic situation, whether you work, or have children, the questions you have are likely to be similar to those of other women. Divorce is like any other lawsuit: There is a plaintiff and a defendant. If you want the divorce and file the papers, you are the plaintiff, your husband is the defendant.

Temporary Support

It's nice to think that the man you married will, if he has supported you in the past, contribute to your support during the divorce negotiations. Sometimes that doesn't happen. You may have to go to court to force your husband to support you. Every state has its own form of temporary support. In Pennsylvania, for example, temporary support is based on a formula. If there are no children, the wife's income, if she is the lower earner, is subtracted from her husband's income. The difference is then multiplied by 40 percent.

Example:	Income of husband	$54,000
	Income of wife	20,000
	Difference	$34,000
		$\times$ .40
	Amount of temporary support	$13,600

The formula changes if there are children. In New York the court will award temporary support for necessaries and child support if a woman is without funds, but it is at the discretion of the court. In California, a wife with no children and no earnings capacity will be given 30 to 35 percent of her husband's take-home pay. If you are the worker, your husband can receive the same. If you have children, that figure climbs to 50 percent.

Sometimes the courts will award temporary support but husbands will not pay. Then you will have to go back to court. Lawyers suggest that this is done to wear down the resistance of the wife, who will then settle for less because she can't manage without anything. If this happens to you, and you borrow money to pay for groceries, keep a careful record of it.

As far as divorce itself, the legal process can take a long time. Many lawyers believe that couples need this emotional time in order to get through a divorce. Some lawyers suggest that there is a typical emotional pattern to a divorce. Couples begin by thinking they will be reasonable. Then, somewhere along the line, the situation turns bitter and angry. This, say many lawyers, is a necessary part of the separation process. Others, critical of the adversarial nature of conventional divorces, believe the sometimes hostile negotiations cause the anger.

One matrimonial lawyer, now turned mediator, explains negotiation. Lawyers for opposing parties play a "game of legal chess" with the object "to get as much as you can and give as little as you have to. The rules are that there are no rules." He believes that frequently lawyers raise clients' expectations because the lawyers are stating initial bargaining positions whereas the clients think they are being given final offers. The wife, thinking she has been given a final figure, becomes infuriated, if not insulted, by the paltry offer made by her husband. The husband, who may be the type who measures his self-esteem by his money, has now been asked to part with a huge chunk of his hard-earned cash. Naturally, his wife's lawyer doesn't think his client will get that figure. The husband is livid. Never, he says. And the fight is on. Sometimes it is only settled when the wife realizes that she cannot afford to play the game anymore because the attorney fees are too high. Sometimes it is only settled when the husband threatens to go to court and his wife suspects that he just might—something she cannot afford.

Questions to Ask Before You Hire a Divorce Lawyer

Let's assume that you have finally decided that you need a lawyer. Do not walk in and turn your case over to the first lawyer you meet. This is going to be a critical time and it is best to do some research. Get several recommendations from friends or call your local bar association for a list of matrimonial lawyers in your area. Ask if you will be billed for an initial consultation.

1. What type of practice do you have (e.g., matrimonial, corporate, litigation)?
2. Do you usually represent men?
3. What are the costs? Most lawyers will quote an hourly fee, usually between $75 an hour to as high as $350. The problem is, almost no lawyer will be able to estimate the number of hours your case will take.

    Your prospective lawyer will also try to assess you, to figure out how much your case will bring in legal fees. You must realize the longer your case takes, the more money your lawyer can earn. There is a built-in conflict of interest.

    Some lawyers will take a flat fee, but if the case takes much longer than anticipated will probably come to you to ask for more money. Nobody wants to work for nothing, so if you do not ante up more money, you may not be getting the best from your lawyer.

    Some lawyers will charge a percentage of whatever

you receive as your settlement. Be careful if they do; in most states it's illegal. Others may ask for a bonus if the case was settled very quickly and your settlement was substantial.

4. When will I be billed? Billing is extremely important—especially if you do not have much money available because your husband has taken most of it away. While some lawyers may work with you without asking for too much up front, if you need appraisers or experts, they are expensive and must be paid right away.

5. Will my husband pay my fees? Many women assume that their husbands will pay the legal fees and therefore it is not important to worry about the costs of the divorce. Do not make this assumption. Be very careful, even if your husband offers to pay your legal fees. One lawyer, David W. Belin, recalls learning a lesson when he was just starting his practice. His client was a wealthy man. The lawyer representing the wife was a well-known matrimonial lawyer. Belin's senior partner told him to contest every financial demand made by the wife's attorney—except for the fee. That was to be paid. In other words, the wife's lawyer would be willing to settle for less, on behalf of his client, the wife, as long as he knew that his fee would be paid. If at all possible, a wife is better off paying her own fees.[6]

6. Will you require a retainer (money that you give in advance)? Your lawyer then deducts the hourly fee from this until it is used up. Ask to be informed of how much money is being spent along the way.

7. Will you personally handle my case or will I work with one of your assistants?

8. Will I be able to reach you over the weekend (or at all)? This is often a big complaint. Not getting your

lawyer on the telephone can be extremely frustrating. One woman received a call from a neighbor while she was at work. Her husband was moving furniture out of their jointly owned home. As it was jointly owned, there was nothing to be done to stop him. By the time she reached her lawyer, it was too late—the furniture was gone.

9. Will I need to sign a contract? A good idea. Be sure to read it very carefully. It will set out the boundaries of the work your lawyer will do. Be sure to ask about any postdivorce settlement negotiations that may be necessary. One woman found, after she had reached a settlement with her husband, that he refused to turn over the specified property. Her lawyers told her they did not handle any after-divorce proceedings.

10. Will I be given copies of all documents and will you explain their meaning? Much of what goes on is the technical filing of motions. Many women complain that they are not told about this by their lawyers.

But above all, ask yourself, is this someone you will get along with, feel comfortable telling intimate details of your married life. Don't overlook any negative signs. Does your lawyer concentrate on you or constantly interrupt you to answer phone calls?

Are there any ways to minimize the cost of a divorce? Here are some tips from a top New York matrimonial lawyer:

1. Don't use your lawyer as a psychiatrist.
2. Have as much information as possible available.
3. Listen to what your lawyer says.

My own money-saving tip: Anytime you must call a lawyer on the telephone, have a list of questions that you want to ask. Write them down. Then arrange a time to speak with your lawyer. Remember that lawyers usually charge for telephone calls. Most often you will receive a minimum charge of fifteen minutes—whether you speak for five or fifteen the price will be the same. Wait until you have a few questions before you place your call. Keep a large clock nearby to remind you of the cost.

Another money-saving tip: Don't sleep with your lawyer. And if you do, make sure you're not being billed for the time. At least that's what Sherry Kantar, of Chicago, Illinois, claimed happened to her. A trial is pending. Her ex-lawyer says the allegations are "nonsensical."[7]

Above all, you have to help manage your case. You cannot just hire a lawyer and think you are being taken care of by a benevolent mother or father. Remember Rhoda, who didn't keep any records of the money she had put into her husband's business? Well, she made the same mistake when she hired a divorce lawyer.

Rhoda sent the lawyer a $5,000 retainer. Rhoda never saw any bills, never had a breakdown of expenses, and never asked a single question. When the lawyer called and asked for more money, Rhoda was astonished. Then she asked for an accounting and discovered lots of charges for late-night taxis and dinners. Rhoda demanded an explanation; after all, her case hardly required burning the midnight oil. The lawyer agreed, and Rhoda received credit for the taxis and dinners.

But managing your case means more than watching the legal bills. It means being realistic about when to fight and when to give in. One woman reports that she and her husband had agreed on almost everything. Then the lawyers stepped in, and she was too frightened to say anything when the lawyer escalated her original demands. She ended up with about the same settlement she had originally expected, but with much higher legal fees.

Sometimes, whatever you do, you will not end up as well as you would like. One reason may just be the state in which you live.

Here's what I mean. Recently, Amy and her husband decided to divorce after a ten-year marriage. During the marriage they managed to accumulate substantial assets. The trouble is, the assets were mainly his. In nine of the ten years of marriage Amy, a book editor, earned more than her husband, a professor. But, during those ten years, Amy free-lanced, while her husband taught at a large university. He had a pension plan. While she will share in the value of the plan, her share will be based only on the years during which they were married. She will not be able to continue to share in his plan. Her husband will continue to have his medical insurance, while she will have to find her own plan. True, she will be able to continue her husband's plan for eighteen months, but then she will have to buy her own insurance. But the most galling part of the split is the $150,000 her husband inherited from his uncle. In New York, that money is separate property. She gets none of it. Had they lived in Massachusetts, only a short drive away, that marital property distinction would not be made.

Your lawyers can give you a general idea of the way judges in your state or community are likely to decide various areas of a dispute, should your case go to court. Naturally you would like to avoid that. Once you have hired a lawyer, sit down and talk realistically about your chances.

IMPORTANT QUESTIONS TO ASK YOUR LAWYER

1. What are my state's general rules about property division? For example, in New York property is usually divided with the wife, usually the lower-earning spouse, getting between one third and one half of the marital assets. It will more likely be one half if there has been a long marriage, several children, and a wife who has not worked. In Pennsylvania, you are more likely to get a fifty-fifty split.
2. What happens in my state concerning a professional degree or professional practice? If you supported your husband while he went to medical school, will you be reimbursed for the actual money that was spent or will you be given a share in your husband's future earnings?
3. What are the laws in my state about alimony: lump-sum alimony; rehabilitative alimony—some states have abolished this form of alimony; remunerative alimony; and permanent alimony? (See pages 81–82 for definitions.)
4. How is a pension divided in my state? In some states the pension will be awarded as a lump-sum payout to the wife, immediately. In other states the pension will be awarded when the husband actually receives it. Since pensions are regulated by federal law you need a special document called a qualified domestic relations order (QDRO) to make sure you get what you're supposed to.

5. How is the family home likely to be divided? In some states the courts order the home to be sold and the proceeds to be divided, either in equitable distribution or in community property. Some states allow a wife to stay in the home with the children until the children reach a certain age, and then order the home to be sold. If you are awarded the family home, and there is appreciated value, make sure you know what the taxes will be. In some cases a judge will not make allowances for future taxes. For example, if you and your husband paid $100,000 for your house and you then sell it for $200,000, you will have to pay capital gains tax on the $100,000. If you and your husband split your assets fifty-fifty but you then have to pay taxes on your half, you have come away with a bad deal.

6. What about child support? Some states have a definite formula, frequently requiring support to come from both parents, depending on their ability to pay.

7. Will I be awarded medical insurance for myself or the children? If your husband has medical insurance from his company, you must be allowed to continue that coverage for at least thirty-six months after your divorce.

8. What about alimony trusts? If you have reason to believe your husband will not pay what he is supposed to, ask your lawyer about alimony trusts. Such trusts usually pay income to the wife and the remainder of the trust either reverts to the husband (usually the donor) or to the children of the couple.

9. How does my state consider standard of living? Remember the Goldman case because this is a new area of the law that is not really established. In California

recently, instead of awarding a wife support based on the couple's standard of living, the judge criticized the couple's high living, which he felt had been unrealistically maintained.[8]

10. What are the rules for temporary support in my state?

11. How can I make sure I collect what's due? Collecting can be a problem. If your husband also has title to the assets, even though you are awarded a property settlement you may have trouble collecting. In a 1988 New York divorce, Brenda Ritz was awarded $406,162, which she was to receive over a ten-year period. Three years later, Mrs. Ritz had not collected any of the money.

12. How can I keep my husband from transferring assets? If you have any reason to believe your husband is transferring assets, your lawyer may be able to get an injunction prohibiting your husband from moving the assets out.

WHEN TO SETTLE

A big problem in divorce is knowing when to settle. By the way, 90 percent of divorces do not reach the courts. Those that do, say many lawyers, are sometimes based on unrealistic expectations. Sometimes these expectations can be fueled at an early meeting with your lawyer when he suggests that you should receive a certain settlement. Sometimes they are brought about by a sense of anger or guilt, a feeling of being wronged and therefore wanting what you consider your rights.

The more you understand the financial realities, the more likely you will be to avoid these escalating battles. Often fights develop over an amount of money that, if split, would give each of you more than you will end up giving your lawyers. Yet many couples continue to wage war, ending in a pyrrhic victory for one of them and expanded fees for their lawyers.

If you and your husband are very far apart on what you think you should get, try to estimate what the court expenses might be plus your other legal fees. Then subtract that amount from what you think you are going to get. Then decide again whether you want the emotional strain of a court battle.

The emotional scars that these fights can leave may not be worth the struggle. Studies suggest that women who have been divorced for five years are happier than men who have been divorced for the same amount of time.

While the chances are unlikely that you will find yourself in a divorce court, you should know a few things about that. First of all, court cases are very expensive. The hourly fees that you will have to pay your lawyer will add up. In addition you may have to pay hefty fees to a variety of experts to help prove your point—expert appraisers, if there is a business, experts in stock options if those exist, and a myriad of other experts. In some states you may also have to pay for the costs of the court.

This doesn't mean that you should capitulate on every demand. It just means you don't want to end up like the couple in *The War of the Roses.*

Understanding the Bottom Line

1. If you are offered the house as an offset against other assets, know what taxes you will have to pay when you sell the house. This is true for other assets, such as stocks that you may acquire in a settlement.
2. Decide if you are better off with a lump-sum payment or a steady stream of income over a longer period of time. Ask your lawyer or accountant to help you figure out the differences.
3. Do not be tricked into settling on an amount and then discovering that the money is to be paid out over a long period of time, thereby lessening its actual value. If you do not understand the discounted value of money, you could be hurt. Briefly, this means the $1,000 that you get today is worth more than the $1,000 that you might get in five years. Over those five years the money will lose its purchasing power, depending on the rate of inflation. This is a figure that is easily calculated using a discount table.
4. Do not accept a property settlement that is then paid out over a ten-year period as alimony. There are two reasons not to do this. The first reason is that alimony is taxable to the recipient, so you are getting less than you thought. The second reason is that alimony can end for a variety of reasons—the court could reduce your alimony if you start working, alimony might end if you remarry, your husband could die or lose his money. If you have young children, an insurance policy might be appropriate; your husband pays it and you are the beneficiary.

5. If you have a lot of doubts about your settlement, get a second opinion.

It is unlikely that the laws will or should change. What will happen is more standards will develop in each state. And there may be some modifications. Some equitable distribution states may change the laws to assure a fifty-fifty split of marital property, for example. More states may become like Wisconsin, where a penalty is levied against the spouse who conceals an asset that is then uncovered. What can change, perhaps, is a woman's knowledge of her family assets. More property in joint name might also help women, because then you share more equally in the assets. Women will continue to work and have their own pensions and medical plans. As more women work they will approach divorce more as equals than as dependents. Then perhaps the laws will be truly equitable.

7.

Retirement? For Whom?

R etirement?" Carol Needham laughed. "We'll never be able to retire," she said. Carol, aged forty-three, and her husband Peter, aged fifty, have a ten-month-old baby. Carol, a computer programmer, has recently stopped work in order to be with her baby full-time. Peter's salary, as manager of a bookstore, has never been as much as Carol's. Now, as they try to live on Peter's salary and save for son Gregory's education, retirement seems remote, if not impossible.

This is a big change from earlier centuries. In the early Middle Ages, average life expectancy was forty-five years, but for women it was only thirty to forty years. There were few old people.[1] In 1990 there were 35,808 centenarians. Over 28,000 were women. Many of them will end up in financial trouble.[2]

Providing for retirement is a modern concept that grew out of the industrial revolution. The English Poor Law Statute of 1601 stated:

The father and grandfather, mother and grandmother, and children of every poor, old, blind, and impotent person, or other person not able to work, being of sufficient ability, shall at their own charges relieve and maintain every such poor person, in that manner, and according to that rate, as by the justices of that county where such sufficient persons dwell, in their sessions shall be assessed.[3]

Wealthy landowners were expected to take care of their peasants. The early idea of aid was of a service nature. You went to a poorhouse or to the old-age home. There was no system of paying money directly to the elderly or the sick. Otto von Bismarck introduced old-age pensions in the 1880s: It was part of his program of state socialism—not as a liberal measure but to forestall democratic socialism. Bismarck thought the ideal retirement age was sixty-five.[4] By coincidence that was the average life expectancy of the German worker.

For Americans life expectancy has far surpassed that of the German worker of 1880. Planning for retirement is an important concern of most couples. The ideal retirement plan would combine income from three sources: Social Security, private pension plans, and savings and investments.

SOCIAL SECURITY

Social Security is the retirement plan administered by the federal government, available to all workers who pay Social Security taxes (known as FICA on your paychecks). When you retire your Social Security benefits are determined by the amount of money you have paid into the system and the number of credits you have earned.

The number of credits depends on the number of years you have worked. For most women that is a lower number than for most men. In 1989 women received only 73 percent of the benefits men received.

While Social Security was never intended to provide all of your retirement income it is the only retirement fund for one out of five women over the age of sixty-five. You can begin collecting benefits when you are sixty-two, but you do not get maximum benefits until you are sixty-five. In the year 2000 the retirement age will begin to creep up. Anyone born between 1938 and 1959 will not collect benefits until age sixty-seven.

Social Security does provide benefits for nonworking wives or husbands. If you are married you can collect a retirement benefit equal to half of your husband's benefits. In other words, if your husband is entitled to $1,022 in monthly benefits when he retires, you would be entitled to receive a monthly benefit of $511. You and your husband would have a combined income of $1533 per month.

If you also worked, you will probably have your own Social Security benefits when you retire. However, you may discover that half of your husband's benefits are more than your own benefits, which are likely to be lower. (You can't get both your own benefits and benefits as a wife, but you can get the higher of the two.) In other words, you lose either your working benefit or your husband's survivor benefits.

If your husband dies and you were married at least nine months, you may be entitled to survivor's benefits provided by Social Security. As a widow you would receive the same amount your husband received when he was retired. If you have your own Social Security benefits, you would receive either your own benefit or your survivor benefit; you would not get both. If you and your husband had a combined Social Security income of $1,533 per month—$1,022 for your husband and $511 for you—and your husband died, you would receive his full benefit of $1,022 or your own full benefit if it was higher. If you remarry before age sixty, you lose your widow's benefits, no matter how long you were married. But in the eyes of Social Security, older is more valuable. If you remarry after you reach age sixty, you can continue to receive your widow's benefits and still remarry.

If you are divorced you may also be entitled to benefits based on your former husband's benefits if you were married for at least ten years, are sixty-two or older, and still unmarried. You can collect benefits if you have been divorced for at least two years, even if your ex is still working. But you will get a higher benefit if you can wait to start collecting. If your husband has more than one ex-wife collecting benefits on his account, well, even Uncle Sam draws the line and limits the amount that can be paid on each Social Security record to an amount usually equal to about 150 to 180 percent of an individual's retirement benefits. If there are two exes collecting, you may each get a reduced share.

To find out just what your benefits will be, call the toll free number, 1-800-772-1213, and request a Personal Earnings and Benefit Estimate Statement. Complete and return the form. You will receive back a computer printout that will give you all of your personal retirement information—past earnings, estimated retirement benefits, disability benefits, and even benefits that may go to your survivors.

PENSION PLANS

"Pension plan" is the umbrella term for a variety of retirement programs that private corporations provide for their employees. The benefits include retirement plans as well as health plans and stock option plans. In 1988 only 46 percent of full-time employees were covered by private pension plans, down from 50 percent in 1979. Only 12 percent of workers in companies with less than ten employees have pension plans.[5] Companies are not required to offer pension plans to their workers. However, those companies that do offer pension plans must comply with federal pension plan rules and in return are entitled to certain tax benefits. Pension plan benefits depend on the number of years you have worked.

Plans come in many varieties, but the premise is always the same: your employer puts money into a separate account where it can be invested and profits can accumulate, tax deferred, while you are working. Therefore, money that is credited to your pension fund is not reported as taxable income on your federal income tax return. You only pay taxes on the money when you retire and begin to take money out of your account. There are two different types of pension plans:

1. *Defined Benefit Plans*—The traditional plans offered by large companies. The benefit you get when you retire is fixed. The company itself contributes to an employee fund. The benefit you get when you retire is based on the number of years you worked, your salary, and your life expectancy. A rough rule of thumb for calculating your defined benefit retirement income

would be 1.5 percent of final pay for each year of service. If you worked for thirty years and your last year's salary was $50,000, your pension would be $22,500 a year. Because the company guarantees a certain payout when you retire, defined benefit plans have become very expensive. Many companies have discontinued them.

2. *Defined Contribution Plans*—The contribution put in, either cash or stock, is fixed, but the amount of benefits you receive at retirement is not; it is based on how well the money is invested. The big advantage to these plans is that your retirement money is growing tax deferred. Defined contribution plans include:

Profit-sharing plans—plans in which the employer's contributions are limited to 15 percent of its payroll with an annual dollar limit per participant of $30,000. The company decides on an annual percentage contribution, and each employee gets the same percentage. Companies are not required to make contributions every year. Don't expect any contributions in a bad year.

Money purchase plans—plans in which the annual contribution is fixed and can be no more than 25 percent of annual compensation. Once a company decides on a percentage to contribute, that amount must be contributed each year.

401(k) plans—plans to which you, the employee, contribute money that is deducted from your salary, thus lowering your income and reducing your taxes. In other words, you finance your own retirement, and the government gives you a tax break. The maximum amount of money that can be contributed each year is fixed. In 1992 the maximum amount was $8,728. Employers may, but do not have to, contribute to your plan. Usually, companies will match employee contributions; for example, if you put in one dollar they will put in twenty-five cents.

ESOPs—plans in which the employer contribution is only company stock.

Pension plans are also available for the self-employed and for employees of small companies. There are various plans called Simplified Employee Pension Plans (SEPs) that employers can establish and to which employees can contribute part of their salary. These are similar to defined contribution and defined benefit plans. There is a limit to the amount of money that can be contributed.

Government and civil service agencies also provide pension plans, usually similar to the 401(k), called the 403(b).

Other plans are available for partners in corporations, even if you are the sole owner. The most popular is the Keogh plan. It is like a 401(k) plan. If you own your own business, you can set up a Keogh plan. If you have employees they must also be allowed to participate in the plan. Your plan must have a sponsor, a bank, a mutual fund, or an insurance company. A professional or trade organization would also be a qualified sponsor.

The plan allows a self-employed person to put in $30,000 or 25 percent of your compensation up to $222,220.

If you have your own company and would like to start a Keogh plan, call the IRS (listed under Department of the Treasury in your telephone book) and request *Retirement Plans for the Self-Employed,* publication 500.

All plans regulated by the federal government must give you a plan summary and a yearly statement. Be sure you study yours and your husband's.

Individuals who work can also start their own personal pension plans, known as IRAs (Individual Retirement Accounts). Again, the principle is the same. You have a special account into which you put funds which are tax deductible and which can then accrue interest tax deferred. IRAs are tricky. The rule is that you can contribute up to $2,000 per year to an IRA. You can claim that $2,000 as a deduction against your federal income tax. However, you cannot claim a deduction if you earn more than $25,000, if you are single.

If you are married, and you want to contribute to an IRA, your husband's income is counted as well as your own. If your combined income is between $40,000 and $50,000, you can still get some of the tax deduction, but it stops when your combined income reaches $50,000. And, if you meet the salary requirements but your husband is covered by a pension plan, you can't take the deduction. A nice little wedding present from Uncle Sam. The working woman, who is not covered by a pension plan where she works, gets hurt the most by this. If a wife works and wants to open an IRA account because her company does not offer a pension plan, she will also be subject to that $40,000 rule. In other words, a wife can lose out on having a tax-deductible pension because of her husband's salary—a salary which may not be there for her, should they divorce.[6] You can contribute to your own IRA and not take the tax deduction. Your money would still accumulate tax deferred, and you would at least have a pension plan. You and your husband should each make your maximum contributions. It's a great way to save. You can probably do it automatically through a monthly accumulation plan at your bank.

If you are not working, you can still have an IRA, called a spousal IRA, really meant for the stay-at-home wife. Here's what you can do. In addition to the $2,000 that your husband can contribute to an IRA, an additional $250 can be contributed to the spousal IRA. But this does not have to be divided $2,000 to your husband, $250 to you. It can be divided in any proportion, as long as neither account receives more than $2,000. Whether this can be tax deducted depends on your husband's income. But, as with an IRA for a working woman, even if you can't get the tax deduction, once you have put the money away, it will increase tax deferred, an important way to build retirement funds.

If you are divorced and receive alimony, you can count that as earned income in order to establish an IRA. But the same income limits apply, so if your alimony is added to your earnings you may have too much income to deduct your IRA. Open one anyway, and let the money accumulate tax deferred.

How to Have Your Own IRA

Typical pension and savings plans might include a defined benefit plan, as well as a 401(k) and maybe some stock options. The defined benefit plan might be invested by the company money managers. For the 401(k) you might be able to choose a group of funds such as a bond fund, a stock fund, and maybe even an international fund.

How to Have Your Own Pension Benefits

1. If you are not working, you are entitled to a spousal IRA if you do not participate in another plan and if your husband earns less than $40,000. You can fund your IRA with tax-deductible dollars. Unfortunately, if you are working and your husband is covered under an active pension plan, you cannot get the tax deduction for opening your own IRA. You can, however, if you do not qualify for a tax-deductible IRA, still put money into an IRA. You should do this, even if it is a small amount and even if you have already paid some taxes on the money. The money that you put away will accumulate tax deferred and you will always have your own pension.

2. If you are working and your company offers a retirement plan such as a 401(k) that you have not joined because your husband has a plan, reconsider. Even if you lose some benefits by doing so, you should have your own pension plan. You and your husband may decide that you have $3,000 a year to invest in your combined plans. Do not have all of the money go into your husband's account. You are working and you should have your own account.

3. If you have a pension plan at your company and you leave to have a baby or to change jobs, you may be given a payout of your pension money. Frequently women do not invest that money in a roll-over IRA because it seems like an insignificant amount. If you don't roll over your distribution into an IRA, you have to pay taxes on it as income. Remember, left to accumulate that money can mount up. If you receive a pension payout as a distribution, immediately put it into a roll-over IRA.

4. If your husband already has a pension plan, there is nothing wrong with you having one too. That way, you are each protected.

If your husband works for a large company he will probably have some combination of benefits of this type.

SMART CHOICES

While the money in many benefit plans is invested by your employer, the trend lately has been a shift to defined contribution plans, which shift the decision-making responsibility to the employee. With defined benefit plans, your employer has to guarantee a certain result. With a defined contribution, the result could depend on your investment know-how.

Your employer may have opened the 401(k) through a mutual fund organization; your IRA may be with your local bank. No matter; you will need some basic investment strategy.

TAKING IT OUT WHEN RETIREMENT FINALLY COMES: IT'S NOT TAX FREE

When you and your husband retire, you may receive your retirement money as either a fixed monthly benefit—the usual way for pensions that are defined benefit—or as a lump-sum distribution from your company's retirement plan. If you receive a lump sum, you have just sixty days to make a critical decision. You and your husband can pay taxes on the money or you can defer taxes by putting the money into a special IRA called a rollover IRA. To decide requires careful analysis of the tax benefits of either choice. If either your company or your husband's gives a seminar on retirement tax planning, you should attend. If not, you should probably consult a professional. A mistake can be very costly.

Be sure to find out about Social Security integration. Social Security integration means that your employer can reduce what the company pays you by the amount you will get from Social Security; up to 50 percent of your pension can be deducted this way. If you and your husband are counting on both Social Security and pension income, be sure you check on this.

DON'T WAIVE GOOD-BYE TO YOUR PENSION

Since 1974 a series of laws has gradually mandated a spouse's right to share in a pension fund. If your husband has a private pension plan that is paid out in the form of a fixed monthly benefit you are also entitled to some benefits. When Congress passed the Employee Retirement Income Security Act in 1974 (ERISA) pension plans were required to provide married workers with survivors' benefits that must equal no less than half the retired worker's benefits. The trouble with the original law was that a husband did not have to tell his wife what he had done. Many widows discovered that their husband's pensions stopped when their husbands died. Since 1984 you and your husband must make this decision together. The law calls for a pension to be paid out as either a joint and survivor benefit or as a single benefit. If the benefit is a "single" benefit, it is higher than if it is a joint and survivor benefit. The single benefit stops with the death of the worker. The joint and survivor benefit pays a lower rate but continues during the lifetime of the nonworking spouse as well. Your husband cannot make the decision himself to chose a single benefit, leaving you without any benefits.

There are several ways you can receive your joint and survivor benefits. Here's a typical example. If the maximum payment for a pension is $3,500 per month, then a 50 percent survivor's payment might give a couple $3,000 a month, and when the husband died the wife would receive $1,500 monthly.

Some financial planners suggest that couples, when deciding whether to have a single, larger benefit or a joint and survivor benefit, which means a lower payout, also consider a plan known as pension maximization. It sounds great. You and your husband agree that you will take the higher monthly payout of your husband's pension. Then from the higher proceeds you buy a life insurance policy that will pay off when your husband dies.

There are several potential problems with this. The first problem is that you and your husband just might not get around to buying the insurance policy. There is also a chance that the price of the insurance will go up and you will not be able to get the amount you thought you could get.

Pension "max" as it is known, makes sense if you, the wife, have a pension plan that pays more than your husband's. You take the larger payout. Then buy an insurance policy on your life, which is a much cheaper policy because you are probably younger. Be very careful about signing off on a joint and survivor annuity under your husband's plan. The above is a simplified explanation of how pension plans and Social Security pay benefits. Every plan is different in its details.

While the federal pension laws protect the wife or

husband whose benefits are paid out in fixed monthly series, lump-sum distributions are not subject to such scrutiny. Your husband can take his money and run. If he is smart, however, he will put his lump-sum distribution into a rollover IRA while the two of you decide which is the best option for your money.

You can invest it in mutual funds, you can buy an annuity from an insurance company that will guarantee a fixed sum over a fixed period of years, or you can do a little of each. The main point is that you want the money to be around for both of you, and this requires careful planning.

The High Cost of Motherhood

When it comes to pensions, despite all the books that speak about you and your spouse, for women, the future can seem bleak. The higher wages and longer years of work that men experience and the lower wages and interrupted work years of most women culminate not surprisingly in gaps in their pension income when they retire. Consider the statistics: just 14 percent of women over sixty-five receive private pension benefits. For men the number doubles to 32 percent.[7] The average annual amount of women's pensions is $3,352. For men the figure is substantially higher, $5,727.

More women are employed in jobs that are not covered by pension plans. Women average 11.5 years away from the labor force; men average 1.3 years away.[8] A typical example is the woman who has worked for a few years. She leaves her job to have a baby. If she has begun putting money into a pension plan, chances are she has not worked long enough to assure a permanent pension (known as "vesting," regardless of whether you return to work for the same employer). If you leave a job and are not vested, you frequently get back your accrued benefits in a lump sum. If you act quickly (within sixty days) and put the money into an IRA, you pay no taxes and can continue to build a retirement war chest. If you spend the money instead to buy a new car, you have to pay taxes on the money and also a penalty for taking your money out of the pension plan early. Only 13 percent of the people under fifty-five who get lump-sum distributions put their money into IRAs. Since women are more frequent job changers they are more likely to lose out on building pensions.

Many women work part-time, not enough hours to be included in the pension plans of their companies. You must work at least twenty hours a week to be eligible for most company pension plans. Many women work in service industries that are least likely to have pension funds. There are no pension funds for the housewife.

If you have moved into formerly male-dominated work areas you are more likely to be covered. There tends to be greater pension coverage in older industries—manufacturing, mining, and communications. Retail business and other service businesses, such as finance and real estate tend not to offer pensions.[9]

Women tend to take off critical early years of their working lives in order to raise their children. But it is in those early years that they could be investing, letting their money accumulate. If you enter the workplace later in life, you've missed those capital building years.

Here's what I mean. If your husband started work when he was twenty-one and contributed $2,000 a year to a retirement savings plan and the money was tax deferred, he would have put into his account a grand total of $88,000. But if that money accumulated at 10 percent a year, when he was sixty-five he would have $985,387. You, on the other hand, take those first ten years of your life together to raise a few children. You don't start working until you are thirty-one. You put $2,000 a year into your account every year until you reach age sixty-five. At the end of that time, you would have put in actual dollars $70,000 into your account. If your money accumulated tax deferred at the same 10 percent, you would have $596,254. (For a look at how this really works, see the table on page 135.)

Clearly, the husband who starts early and lets his money accumulate in a retirement plan has a great advantage over the wife who delays her career. And this doesn't even consider the years you have lost in building your career. There's nothing wrong with making this kind of choice. What's wrong is then thinking you should not have a say in the money that your husband has been making.

To a great degree, pensions in most families are in the husband's name. The wife is either not working or works in a business that doesn't have a pension. Husbands have control of retirement planning. Frequently, pension planning for the wife is nonexistent; she gets survivor's benefits. As more women work and move into management positions in their companies, much of this disparity should change.

If you and your husband both work and have pensions,

THE HIGH COST OF MOTHERHOOD:
AT A 10 PERCENT YIELD, WHO HAS MORE AT 65?*

| AGE | HUSBAND | | WIFE | |
	CONTRIBU-TIONS	VALUE AT YR. END	CONTRIBU-TIONS	VALUE AT YR. END
21	$2,000	$2,200		$0
22	$2,000	$4,620		$0
23	$2,000	$7,282		$0
24	$2,000	$10,210		$0
25	$2,000	$13,431		$0
26	$2,000	$16,974		$0
27	$2,000	$20,872		$0
28	$2,000	$25,159		$0
29	$2,000	$29,875		$0
30	$2,000	$35,062		$0
31		$38,569	$2,000	$2,200
32		$42,425	$2,000	$4,620
33		$46,668	$2,000	$7,282
34		$51,335	$2,000	$10,210
35		$56,468	$2,000	$13,431
36		$62,115	$2,000	$16,974
37		$68,327	$2,000	$20,872
38		$75,159	$2,000	$25,159
39		$82,675	$2,000	$29,875
40		$90,943	$2,000	$35,062
41		$100,037	$2,000	$40,769
42		$110,041	$2,000	$47,045
43		$121,045	$2,000	$53,950
44		$133,149	$2,000	$61,545
45		$146,464	$2,000	$69,899
46		$161,110	$2,000	$79,089
47		$177,222	$2,000	$89,198
48		$194,944	$2,000	$100,318
49		$214,438	$2,000	$112,550
50		$235,882	$2,000	$126,005
51		$259,470	$2,000	$140,805
52		$285,417	$2,000	$157,086
53		$313,959	$2,000	$174,995
54		$345,355	$2,000	$194,694
55		$379,890	$2,000	$216,364
56		$417,879	$2,000	$240,200
57		$459,667	$2,000	$266,420
58		$505,634	$2,000	$295,262
59		$556,197	$2,000	$326,988
60		$611,817	$2,000	$361,887
61		$672,998	$2,000	$400,276
62		$740,298	$2,000	$442,503
63		$814,328	$2,000	$488,953
64		$895,761	$2,000	$540,049
65		$985,337	$2,000	$596,254
TOTAL	$20,000	$985,337	$70,000	$596,254

*Figures provided by Gary J Strum, senior vice president, Quest for Value Distribution.

you have an opportunity to build your retirement plans together.

MARRIED: HOW TO BLEND YOUR BENEFITS

1. Each of you should get copies of your benefit plan, IRA statements, and Social Security benefits.
2. If you both have pension plans be sure to check the beneficiaries. Naming a spouse is mandatory under some plans, unless you both sign waivers. You might want to leave your pension to your mother, but your husband would have to agree. For some plans you need a waiver, but on others—for example, IRAs—this is not mandatory. One woman's husband died and when she inquired about collecting his benefits, discovered that another woman already had. If you were previously married and your former husband is named as the beneficiary for a qualified pension plan, even though your current husband is entitled to collect survivor benefits, not changing the name could result in frustrating delays.
3. Find out what kinds of plans you both have available from your companies; if neither one of you has started to take advantage of retirement planning, get started. Consider building your retirement plans fifty-fifty. Otherwise you could end up with lopsided estates and have tax-planning problems

    Some companies make matching grants. If your husband's company matches contributions and gives fifty cents for every dollar he contributes and your company is only giving twenty-five cents on every dollar, it may seem wiser to put money into your husband's plan. But you should participate in your own company plan as well.

If you think you will take time off from your job to have children, start investing in your pension plan as soon as possible. Your money will accumulate tax deferred while you are not working.

If your company does not have a pension plan, contribute to an IRA, even if you have to do it with after-tax dollars.

4. If you and your husband have a long-term plan to buy a house, you can borrow against some pension plans. Check the loan provisions of the plans you are offered. If one of you has a loan provision in your plan, you might want to put more of your assets into the company plan with the loan provision. (Also note that your husband can borrow against a 401(k) plan without telling you. Naturally, you can do the same.)

5. Have a joint investment strategy. If your husband can only invest in fixed income through his plan, perhaps your plan can be put into equities to give you more investment flexibility. You and your husband should check the mix on a regular basis.

6. Know the payout choices. If you and your husband have defined benefit plans they must offer joint and survivor options. This means that when you are ready to retire you will have the choice of having your full benefits paid to each of you, or else you will each get reduced benefits paid in your lifetime and benefits that will continue to be paid to your spouse when you die. If your husband's full benefit is $20,000 he would get

that until he died, then his pension would stop completely. You would have just your own full benefit until you died. If you took a full benefit and your husband took a reduced benefit, you would continue to receive part of his benefits once you were on your own. Of course we never know who will die first, so a third option is for each of you to take a reduced payout.

7. You should also check out the payout options for any tax planning you might want to do. The type of distribution can make a difference in your tax planning. Remember, a big chunk of retirement income is taxable—all that tax-deferred money that you've been accumulating.

8. Be sure to find out whether your benefits or his are integrated with Social Security. If they are, your benefits will be reduced by the amount you receive from Social Security, *up to 50 percent of your total benefit.*

9. Check out the life insurance provisions of your pension plans. You might be able to buy life insurance at a good rate from your company. Also check whether the insurance would be transferrable if you leave your job. You might want to have some life insurance of your own. If you have a defined benefit plan and your husband dies before he reaches the age of fifty-five, his earliest retirement age, you might not get much of a payout. Life insurance, at least term, is a must in these cases. Term insurance is insurance purchased on a year-by-year basis. It does not accumulate any benefits and must be repurchased each year. The younger you are, the lower the premium. Term insurance, when you are young, is much less expensive than whole life.

10. Second marriages are a bit tricky. You and your husband may each have pensions that you would like to leave to your children from a first marriage. You might each want to waive your survivor rights as beneficiares of each other's plans. Some couples even include such waivers in prenuptial agreements.

   If this is a second marriage for your husband, find out if he has already promised part of his pension benefits to his first wife.

SAVINGS AND INVESTMENTS: THE THIRD PART OF YOUR RETIREMENT PLAN

If you and your husband have anything at all left over after putting money into your IRAs, Keoghs, 401(k) plans, and other tax-deferred investments, you will probably want to do some additional investing. Actually, your savings and investments should be a part of your retirement planning, because you probably will not have enough money if you rely on Social Security and your pension plans.

Women tend to let their husbands take over. Maybe it's tradition, because there is no evidence that women do not become successful money managers. In fact, where is the evidence that men are better? One woman was married to a CPA. She just assumed he knew what he was doing. When, sadly, he had a stroke, she was forced to take over the family finances. To her surprise, and that of her college-age son, she did much better than her husband. But don't wait for your husband to have a stroke. If you really know nothing about investing, take a course or begin reading some magazines. *Money* is a good one. Begin reading the business and finance pages of your newspapers. And use your own common sense. If you plan to hire a broker, both you and your husband should be in on the interview. Ask friends for recommendations—friends who are in similar financial situations. If you don't have millions, don't choose a broker who only handles accounts for the very rich.

If you are really neophytes, think about beginning to invest through mutual funds. But be sure you participate. Don't be intimidated. Ask even dumb questions. And if you don't like the answers don't invest. If someone promises too much too fast, zip your wallet and run. Don't invest because you heard that someone else did. Do your own homework. Understand what you are doing.

A Short Guide to Investments

First of all, you have to define the purpose of your investments. Of course, the primary purpose is to have more money, but sometimes you may be able to further refine your goals:

1. money for your old age
2. capital for a major project—a house, a business
3. money to leave for your children

The best way to achieve your goal has historically been investing in common stocks. Most people believe common stocks are risky because the value of stocks can fall. A stock is really a share in the ownership of a company. Stocks usually go up if a company does well, and down if a company does badly. Many people believe that by buying bonds that will pay a set rate of interest they are not taking any risk. A bond is really a loan that you are making to someone, either a corporation or a government agency or even Uncle Sam. You lend your money; in return you get back a set amount of interest over a fixed number of years. While it is true that if you buy a bond for $1,000 (the usual price for a bond) and hold it for ten years, you will at the end of those ten years get back your $1,000, but depending upon the rate of inflation, your money will have lost some of its purchasing power.

Your first goal when you invest should be to preserve the buying power of your money. The way to do that is to be sure you receive a return that is more than the rate of inflation. If, for example, inflation is 5 percent, you want your money to earn an amount that is more than 5 percent. Anything more than the inflation rate is your real profit. So, when we have periods of low inflation and high bond yields, as we have had for the later part of the 1980s, bonds can be a safe and profitable investment. When we have high inflation and low bond yields, as we did during the 1970s, bonds turned out to be a bad investment.

When you are young and are still earning money, you can afford to take more risk with your money. The older you are, however, the less concerned you may be with preserving the purchasing power of your money over a long-term period. Then bonds can also be a way to invest, because you know you will have a fixed rate of return that you can depend on every month. If you are not worried about leaving a lot of your money to your children you can also spend some of your money and not worry that at the end of ten years you will have less.

If you have an investment adviser with whom you feel

comfortable and with whom you have worked in the past, there is no reason not to continue. If you and your husband have a broker, you should get to know the broker or adviser; don't wait for something to go wrong.

If you have never invested, do not know an adviser, and suddenly receive a lump sum (life insurance checks could come within a month after your husband's death), put your money into a money market fund. Make sure it is one run by a large company, such as Fidelity or Dreyfus. You will receive interest and can take time deciding how you want to invest the money.

If the lump sum is a part of a pension split in a divorce, you can put that money into an IRA and keep the money tax deferred.

If you are ready to think about investing, try to define your goals. Then think about how you will invest. To me, mutual funds are the easiest and least expensive way to do this. There are two types of mutual funds: no load funds for which you do not pay a purchase fee and load funds which charge a commission. No load funds are usually sold by a broker, while no load funds are sold directly by the company that manages the fund. Many people say, only choose no load, but I think the most important feature in choosing a fund is how well the fund performs.

Money magazine and *Forbes* rate various mutual funds every year. This will give you an idea of past performance of the funds, but, needless to say, is not an indication of how well the funds will do in the future.

Once you have the information, purchase a small amount of one of the funds that seems to best fit your goals, such as income and growth, or just income. Do not invest more than 20 percent of your capital. Again, choose a big mutual fund company with a track record, even though no past record can tell you what will happen in the future.

The best type of common stock funds are those that provide some growth and income.

After you have put your first 20 percent to work, you can divide another 40 percent between two more funds so that you will have a total of 60 percent of your money invested in stocks. If this makes you nervous put only 50 or 55 percent of your money in common stocks.

Place 30 or 40 percent of your money in bond funds. There are many types of bond funds. You can buy government bond funds, municipal bond funds (usually tax free, and so pay a lower rate of interest) high-yield bond funds, and junk bond funds. The main point is to split your money in a few funds and to buy from big, well-known companies.

The remaining 10 percent of your money can be kept in a money market fund so you have immediate money should you need it.

You will be unlikely to get rich on this type of investing, but you will be able to sleep well at night and over the years will probably make a small profit above the rate of inflation.

This is a simple scheme. Your brother-in-law in the investment business will probably tell you to give him the money to invest for you. Don't do it.

One secret of successful investing is letting your money grow over a long period. It's not the only way to invest, but I think it is the best way for people who know little about the market.

How a Financial Planner Can Help

One way to plan for retirement is to visit a financial planner. The cost can range from a few hundred to a few thousand dollars, depending on the complexity of your assets. You can do it yourself with a workbook or plan provided by firms such as T. Rowe Price or Fidelity. WealthBuilder is a popular computer program that you can use. If you don't know too much about your retirement plans and your husband doesn't like to talk about it—because he doesn't like to think about retiring—suggesting that you visit a planner might be a great idea. Often a concerned wife brings her husband to a planner. Many planners will not see a husband without his wife or a wife without her husband. Word of mouth and company recommendations are good ways to find a planner. Remember, however, that this is an unlicensed field; just about anyone can hang up a financial-planning sign. Financial planners generally work in two different ways. One group charges a fee and does not sell products. The other group is usually affiliated with a company—either insurance or brokerage or tax shelter—and offers free advice, hoping to recoup on the products you subsequently buy. My own bias would be for the fee without the products.

Financial planning really forces you to focus on facts. The planning process can also bring out some hidden conflicts. Some of the problems are the recurrent financial fights in a marriage: you want to spend money on curtains, your husband wants to spend money on a wine refrigerator. But often deeper conflicts are revealed. One planner told of a husband who didn't want to have life insurance for his wife because he didn't "want some other guy spending his money." Sometimes, when a wife begins her career later in life than her husband, especially if she is a few years younger than he, she may not want to retire at all, preferring to continue working.

How much money you actually have, how much money you will need for retirement, and how you will get there are the basic questions of the planning business. The planner will need to know your expected Social Security and pension benefits as well as your other savings and investments. Computers make it easy to project a series of numbers to find out that you will need a certain amount of income when you retire. When you work with a planner you have to understand the assumptions.

While there are more scientific ways to figure out how much income you will need in order to retire, here are some guidelines. You will probably need 70 percent of the average of the last three years of your preretirement income. Of this, 15 percent will come from Social Security, and between 35 and 35 percent from a pension plan. The remaining dollars will have to come from investments. Planners use a rate of inflation and a rate of interest to figure out how much money you will need when you retire. They also use actuarial tables to figure out how many years you can expect to live.

You should know what those assumptions are in order to evaluate any advice you get.

QUESTIONS TO ASK A FINANCIAL PLANNER

1. What is the assumed rate of inflation?
2. What is the assumed rate of growth in assets?
3. What is the assumed yield?
4. Does the plan include spending assets?
5. Is the income taxable?

These questions are important. In this age of computers, numbers can do almost anything. Here's an example.

You and your husband would like to retire in eleven years with an annual income of $50,000 (70 percent of your current $70,000 income). The financial planner does a bit of calculating and determines that would need $89,793 if we have an inflation rate of 5 percent. Lately inflation has been low, but think back and remember what inflation was like a few years ago. Then ask the planner to tell you what would happen if inflation was higher or lower. Here is a little chart that will illustrate what the change in numbers can mean for that $50,000:

Your retirement income in 2003 dollars:	3% inflation	5% inflation	9% inflation
	$71,288	$89,793	$140,633

The planner looks at the amount of money you and your husband have socked away in savings and pensions and tells you that in order to get that $89,793 in eleven years, you would need a nest egg of $1.8 million if you could be assured of a 5 percent yield. But if you knew you could get 10 percent you would only need $1.1 million. The amount you have already saved will then be subtracted from the amount you will need. The planner will then suggest several ways to close the gap. You can decide you will manage on less. You can increase the amount of money you are putting away.

Many people consider buying annuities for their retirement. These are purchased from insurance companies. They function a little like pension plans in that you can build up tax-deferred investments that can begin paying money to you when you are ready to retire. You can buy fixed annuities, which pay a fixed rate; or you can buy variable rate annuities, which pay depending on how well the investments have performed.

There are a few drawbacks to buying annuities. They are expensive because there are high sales commissions and maintenance charges. Your money is locked away. And you have to be careful that the company offering them will be solvent when you are ready to retire.

Why bother to have them? They do offer the tax-deferred advantages of pension plans. They are a way to supplement a retirement account.

Other choices include deciding that you will sell your house and invest that money, assuming you can rent for less money than you could make by investing the proceeds from the sale of your house. You can also get a reverse mortgage that allows you to take money out based on the value of your house. You can decide that you will spend assets. This is known as spending down. You start with a fixed sum and then withdraw a certain amount each year, until you are left with zero. For example, if you started with $50,000 and withdrew $580 each month, your money would last for 10 years.[10]

There are several problems with financial planning.

Most financial plans do not take into account the likelihood of inflation eroding your standard of living because the plan never projects an increase in income while you are retired. If inflation is 7 percent, purchasing power will erode by half in just ten years. Nor does the plan usually project, as has happened in the early 1990s, a precipitous drop in interest rates. When this happens, projected income fails to materialize. Social Security does give you a cost-of-living increase, but the rule that most planners follow is that Social Security will only provide about 10 to 15 percent of your retirement income.

The second problem is that the plan changes when one of you dies. The early retirement years will probably be shared. Your Social Security and his, your pension plan and his, your joint investments—if you and your husband both worked and retire, you will each receive your maximum pension benefits; you will each get Social Security. If your husband dies, you will get your own Social Security. His will be discontinued. Your pension plan income will continue, and you will get the "survivor" benefits from his pension plan. If you never worked and your husband retires, you will still receive benefits from his Social Security and his pension plan. If your husband dies, however, you will receive smaller benefits from each, because you have no benefits of your own.

You, the wife, have to know what will happen to your income when you are alone. The purchasing power of the income you receive, unless your benefits are indexed to inflation as they are in Social Security, will erode. For women in second marriages, there are even greater problems because frequently some portion of their husbands' estates will be headed for his children from his first marriage. One financial planner who frequently works with couples getting ready to retire reports that discussing this with couples can lead to tremendous arguments.

Unintended Retirement

The 1990s began with a recession that has dragged on more and more. It is not unusual to pick up the paper and read a headline that says Corporation X will lay off 3,000 people. Yet few people are prepared for the financial dislocation this can cause. Of course, there is severance pay, usually tied to the length of time you have worked for the company. And, depending on the size of the company, there may be such "perks" as outplacement services and even the use of an office for a period of time.

These days, if you and your husband work, it is your husband who is likely to lose his job. What would happen to your finances if either of you were out of work for an extended period of time? Expenses don't change that much. Know how many weeks of severance pay you get. Know the expenses of finding another job. What happens to your health insurance?

You need savings and investments to see you through a crisis. Above all, you have to be supportive of each other. The wife who doesn't understand the finances can be a burden in troubled times. The wife who knows can help her husband.

Disability is another possible problem many couples may face. Sometimes, whatever you do, the unforeseen will arise. While it is hard to be prepared for all of life's blows, there are a few that can be softened.

When my friend Mary Green's husband was sixty, he suffered a stroke. She was suddenly plunged into a world of hospitals, doctors, and therapists. Fortunately, they had medical insurance. But as time elapsed and the exp nses continued to mount, the medical insurance cover d less and less. The insurance company rules chang d. The insurance company did not pay for private care. She had to hire nurses round-the-clock. She spent a lot of money on therapy, but her husband never regained his faculties.

Because her husband had the stroke before his sixty-fifth birthday, he was forced to retire with less than maximum pension benefits. Money became a problem. The income from her husband's two pension plans was not sufficient to cover expenses.

After some research, Mary Green found a solution. She sold their house and moved to a life care facility; another name is continuing care retirement community (CCRC). This is not a cheap or risk-free solution to your problems. You pay a lot to enter and then pay high monthly fees for services that can include meals, nursing care, and hospital availability. In 1988 the average entry fee was $45,000, and the monthly fee average was $715. (Two booklets that could be helpful are *Selecting Retirement Housing,* available free from AARP Fulfillment, 1909 K Street NE, Washington, D.C., or *The Blue Book of Continuing Care/Life Care Retirement Communities,* Wall and Ford, P.O. Box 1394, Princeton, N.J. 08542, $16.00.) Basically, life care facilities are a combination of retirement village and convalescent home. The big advantage of a life care facility is that once you have paid your dues, you can't be turned out.

Of course, not all disability is permanent. Divorce lawyer Raoul Felder may be accused of carving up his opponents in a courtroom, but when it came to carving a chicken he wasn't as skilled. While attempting to dismember the bird, he dropped a carving knife on his foot. The resulting injury kept him out of the courtroom for four months. With disability insurance, Felder was able to replace some of his lost income.

While the term "disability" has a variety of synonyms—including disadvantage, drawback, and handicap—the word has taken on a specific meaning in the lexicon of the American working world. It means to be hurt—either from illness or accident—in some way that means you can no longer work.

What are the odds that this will happen to your husband?

If your husband is over twenty-one, there's a one-in-three chance that he will become disabled at some time.

If your husband is forty or under, he is three times more likely to have a disability than he is to die.

If your husband is between the ages of thirty-five and sixty-five the chances of being unable to work for ninety days or more because of a disabling illness or injury are about equal to your chances of dying. "A twenty-five-year-old professional male stands a 34.8 percent chance of suffering a long-term disability by age sixty-five, and the average duration of the disability is twenty-six months. The odds decrease each year, reaching 17.6 percent by age fifty-five, but the average duration increases to fifty-three months."[11]

What You Should Know If Your Husband Can't Work

Does he have disability insurance? This insurance pays you some portion of your "earned income" should you be unable to work for a period of time. Disability insurance is income replacement. The standard rule is insurance covers 60 percent of what would have been your monthly income. If your husband pays the premium the income is not taxable. If his employer pays the premium, the income is taxable. Fewer than 20 percent of companies with 100 or fewer employees offer disability insurance.[12]

Find out the terms of your husband's disability insurance. How long must your husband be out of work before he will collect any money at all? Usually the longer you must be out of work before payments start, the lower the premium. Standard waiting times are between one month—the highest premium—and three months.

What percentage of his salary will be replaced by the disability payments? One couple was devastated to discover that the husband's disability insurance covered only his regular salary and not the bonus that he thought was part of his yearly earnings.

If your husband doesn't have disability insurance you may belong to a group that makes it available to its members. For example, the Archaeological Institute of America recently offered its members a disability insurance policy with a yearly premium of $47.50 for $500 in monthly benefits for those under thirty. As with most disability insurance there were restrictions and waiting periods.

Will your husband be eligible for Social Security payments as a result of his disability? You have to be unable to work for at least a year to qualify. Only about 20 percent of all disability claims are approved by Social Security.

What other sources of income do you have? Does your husband have a pension plan? If so, find out when he will be eligible to collect this and what percentage of his salary he will receive. Can he borrow against it?

Do you have a durable power of attorney that will allow you to act for your husband? If you don't and your property in not in joint name, you could spend time getting the court to appoint you as guardian. This could be granted as emergency powers, but it's much better to have a power of attorney on hand. You can prepare a power of attorney yourself by buying a form from a stationery store and then having it notarized. You should also have a durable power of attorney allowing your husband to act for you. (By the way, if you are taking care of elderly parents, be sure you have their signed durable powers of attorney.)

If your husband stops working because of a disability will you still be able to get medical insurance?

If your husband must stop working and he owns the company, how will the other employees be paid? If your husband has a small business, business overhead insurance, often referred to as key man insurance, covers rents, utilities, and salaries.

Of course, women can have accidents or get sick as well. And women are far less likely to have employee paid disability insurance. If you are working, you should also have some disability insurance to replace your lost income should something happen to you.

MEDICAL INSURANCE

Medical expenses are the wild card of retirement and old age.

Medicare is the federal government's health insurance program that provides medical insurance to those over sixty-five who are eligible for Social Security. Medicare is divided into two parts: Part A pays hospital insurance; part B pays doctor's bills. There is a monthly premium for part B. However, Medicare does not make any provisions for two of the largest expenses of old age—prescription medicines and custodial nursing home care. Medicare does cover nursing home care if it is rehabilitative. If you are hospitalized because you broke your hip and then must go to a nursing home, your bills would be paid by Medicare. Medicare does not pay for general dental work or foot care, both frequent problems as we age.

Many people choose to buy Medigap insurance. Medigap is private insurance available to pay for costs not covered by Medicare such as prescription medicine, hospital deductibles, a private-duty nurse in the hospital, and personal care at home.

Then there's Medicaid, a program meant for the needy which does provide nursing home coverage, but does not provide total health care. In order to qualify for Medicaid, however, you must have very few assets. Although Medicaid is a federal program it is administered by each state. State laws of eligibility vary. In some states the aid is provided only to those sixty-five or over or to disabled persons of any age. Other states allow Medicaid to be given in special situations where there are very high medical expenses to those whose income might otherwise disqualify them. The restrictions have led many people to protest that our national health care should provide more coverage. So far this is not a reality.

The best protection is to do it yourself. For most women, the preparation should mean a realistic look once again at the family assets. But this time you have to look at the possibility that an illness of your husband's will use up much of your combined assets, leaving you unable to get the care you need if you become ill. If you haven't gotten it by now, let me tell you once again: Women tend to outlive men. Women remain widows an average of fifteen years. By the year 2000, estimates project there will be 7.4 million widows; you may be among them. So you should be sure to check on nursing home insurance (see below) and life insurance for your husband.

NURSING HOMES: THE FACTS

By the third millennium over eight million Americans over the age of sixty-five will probably need some form of long-term care because of chronic illness. Of this group, 70 percent will probably be cared for by a family member—most probably you, the wife.

In 1985, 2.3 million people over age sixty-five spent at least part of a year in a nursing home. Two out of five people aged sixty-five or more risk entering a nursing home. The average length of stay in a nursing home is 2.5 years. Approximately 5 percent of the over-sixty-five population are now in nursing homes. About 25 percent of those over eighty-five live in nursing homes. Seventy-five percent of the nursing home population is female.

Nursing homes are not inexpensive. Costs vary from state to state. An average yearly cost could be $35,000. If you want deluxe care the price soars.

As more Americans live longer there has been a change in attitude about who should have to care for so many old folks. In the past it was considered normal for families to take care of their own. Now that isn't possible for many, leaving nursing home care the only option. The high cost of medical care means that funds are often spent for the husband's care, leaving the wife with a reduced income while her husband is ill, and even fewer assets to help her out when she is alone.

For a large part of the middle class, the money spent is part of the family's life savings. It may be a great part of what a couple had planned to bequeath to their children.

A growing group of Americans, including lawyers who specialize in elderly law, believe long-term health care should be paid by the government. They have developed strategies for clients to give away assets in order to qualify for public assistance, mainly Medicaid, which does pay for nursing home care. These strategies may change because while legally correct, they are against the spirit of the law. For more information write to The National Academy of Elder Law Attorneys, Inc., 655 N. Alvernon Way, Suite 108, Tuscon, Arizona 85711.

Should You Protect Your Assets and Qualify for Medicaid-Funded Nursing Home Care?

Several different strategies have evolved to help couples who would like to be able to qualify for publicly funded Medicaid to pay for nursing home care. Most of the Medicaid planning strategies involve giving up assets before you need nursing home care. Usually this involves creating trusts which transfer assets from one spouse to the other or from a couple to their children. Each state has a different standard.

Other solutions to the Medicaid qualifying problem include putting assets into annuities payable to the wife, whose income is not counted toward Medicaid eligibility, or putting assets into the family home, which does not count as an asset when computing your net worth for Medicaid. Oh yes, if you own your own burial plot that is not counted toward Medicaid eligibility.

Another possibility is to transfer all the assets to the healthy spouse, usually the wife, who then refuses to pay for her husband's nursing home care.

Some couples have taken an even more drastic step. Transferring all assets to the wife, for example, then getting a divorce. The sick husband can therefore be whisked straight to a nursing home paid for by Medicaid.

Of course, it isn't always the husband who gets sick. It can be the wife. This creates other problems, especially if the husband is older and realizes that he will not be around to take care of his wife and wants to be sure she will receive proper care should he die first.

Here is one way to handle that problem. If, as is sometimes the case, the assets are in the husband's name, he can create trusts in his will that will take care of his wife but will allow income to be cut off to allow his wife to qualify for Medicaid. Ultimately the assets would go to the couple's children.

Solutions to long-term care involving Medicaid are uncertain and involve giving up control of assets, something that may be psychologically and practically undesirable. What happens, for example, if your children divorce, are sued, or just spend your money? After all, you saved your money to take care of yourself in case of a rainy day, and, in a way, having to be in a nursing home is a rainy day. It's what you hoped would never happen, but if it does, maybe the money should be spent to assure your care. This is a question every couple will have to discuss and decide together.

Nursing Home Insurance

Of course, you can also prepare for the unwelcome by buying nursing home insurance. Nursing home insurance is a recent addition to the panoply of products peddled by insurance salespeople. If carefully chosen, it allows you the luxury of not worrying about being able to afford a nursing home.

Those who might benefit from nursing home insurance would be families with a net worth of between $250,000 and $400,000. If you get it before age sixty-five your premium will be much lower; it goes up as you get older. The biggest purchasers are usually those between sixty-five and seventy-nine. You can't buy it when you are over eighty.

The average premium is between $1200 and $4000 per year, which will probably pay as much as 80 percent of the cost. There are some pitfalls when buying nursing home insurance.[13] Insurance companies can claim all information was not supplied. Worse, the insurance company can go bankrupt.

Here's what to look for in nursing home insurance. First make sure the company is rated by A. M. Best, the leading insurance rating company, with a rating of A+ or A. Next see that the daily benefit is at least $80 with inflation protection and a minimum benefit period of two years. Normally, there will be a waiting period of ninety to one hundred days before your benefits begin. The longer the period that you wait before collecting, the lower your premium. Be sure that there is no prior hospitalization requirement—i.e., you don't have to first be in a hospital before going to the nursing home. And, finally, there should be no requirement of prior skilled care.[14]

TEN THINGS EVERY WOMAN SHOULD KNOW WHEN HER HUSBAND RETIRES

1. Should your husband continue to pay for life insurance? Of course a lot depends on your current assets.
2. Decide whether you will need nursing home insurance—usually recommended in cases of a net worth between $250,000 and $400,000. Remember the younger you are when you buy it, the cheaper your premiums.
3. If your husband would like to take a single annuity payout, instead of a joint but lower payout, be sure that

you will be able to continue medical insurance and that you will have enough income.

4. If your husband chooses a single life annuity remember that when you are alone you will receive no money from his pension.

5. Be careful of something called pension max (choosing a single annuity payment which gives you more money with the idea that you can then buy life insurance and still have more money to spend than if you chose a joint payout).

6. If you are working and not yet ready to retire, be very careful of retiring before you are eligible for maximum pension benefits.

7. Remember that all the money you and your husband spend together during retirement means there will be less for you when you are, as is more than likely, alone.

8. Remember that inflation, even at 5 percent, means the cost of everything will double in fourteen years.

9. If your husband is anxious to give everything to your children or, if it's a second marriage, his children, be careful. They may not help you when you need it.

10. Don't underestimate the amount of money you will both need when you retire.

Many women still think they do not have to plan for their own retirement—that their husbands will provide. When it comes to pensions, savings, and other plans for the future, every woman should know what her husband has and should plan for her own future as well.

8.
Will Power: The American Way of Leaving

What do John Lennon, king of music, and John Hay Whitney, king of America's old moneyed elite, have in common? For one thing, they both were very rich when they died. Even more important, they both wrote wills. Whitney's was an elaborate document with endless trusts, charitable bequests, specific personal bequests—his boathouse property and its contents (but not the yachts) to a friend; his paintings to his alma mater, Yale; and to his wife, his cooperative apartment in New York, $5 million in cash, his five-hundred-acre Long Island estate, an annual income of $500,000, and his art collection (just one of the paintings, *Au Moulin de la Galette,* sold at a New York auction for over $70 million). In short, it was the will of a wealthy man who died late in life and had a long time to think about what he wanted to do with the estimated quarter of a billion he was leaving behind. Lennon, as we all know, died in his prime. His will was simple. He left almost everything to his wife, Yoko Ono. His will was that of a man who had probably not spent a great deal of time thinking about the dispersal of his property. John Lennon was not atypical.

The oldest known will is that of Uah, an Egyptian who lived in the third millennium, B.C. American wills are rooted in the Anglo-Saxon tradition, as are much of our marital traditions. One of the earliest English wills on record was written by a wealthy woman named Wolgith way back in the eleventh century. Evidently a woman of considerable property, she divvied up her vast estates between her numerous children and her church—and offered up a solemn curse to any who would try and contest her wishes.

A will is the official document that tells the government and the public what to do with your property when you die. If you die without a will—*intestate* is the legal term—your property will be distributed in accordance with the laws of the state where you live. Federal laws do not govern wills, although the federal government swoops in to collect taxes on large estates.

Some couples think that if you do not have a will, the surviving spouse will inherit everything. But this is not true. Each state has its own laws about the way your money will be distributed if you die intestate. For example, in Oklahoma, if your husband died you would receive one half of your husband's entire estate. Any surviving children of your husband would receive the other half. You would receive the entire estate if your husband died and left neither parents, brother, sister, nor surviving children. If there are no surviving children, but a parent, brother, or sister of your husband's survives him, you, as the surviving spouse, would take all the marital property, plus an undivided one-third interest in the remaining estate. In Alaska, if your husband is survived by a parent you would inherit the first $50,000, plus one half the balance of the estate.

In a community-property state, you already own half the marital property. In California, if your husband died, you would inherit half of the marital property automatically as well as half of the community property of your husband. If there are no children, parents, sisters, or brothers, you would also receive all the separate property. If your husband leaves one child, you would receive only one half of the separate property. If your husband has more than one child, you would only receive one third of your husband's separate property. Your property would be treated the same way if you died first.

In ancient Rome, wills were read in public. If someone wanted to insult a despised enemy, he or she could put it in the will for all to hear.[1] Your will also becomes a public document; it is filed in the court system of your state.

A lot has been written about avoiding "probate" by not having a will. Probate really means "to prove" the will by having it approved in court. Avoiding probate gives you privacy. It also means eliminating probate fees, which vary from state to state. It does not, however, mean that you will avoid estate taxes that may be due.

Many people put all of their assets into what is called a "revocable living trust." This is a way to keep your assets out of the probate court. Assets in a living trust cannot be frozen for several months and can be managed without interruption. A living trust has a further advantage. If you become incapacitated, a successor trustee can easily manage your assets without the court appointing a guardian or a custodian. (A durable power of attorney can also be used to manage your assets easily without the court appointing a custodian.) However, putting all your assets in a living trust does entail legal fees. Avoiding pro-

bate does not mean you avoid estate taxes that may be
due.

Why Have a Will?

Many couples think they do not need a will if everything
is owned in joint name (as joint tenants with right of
survivorship). This is true up to a point. But what happens if you both die in an accident? The laws of your state
would then dictate how the money would be disbursed.
You could also lose some tax benefits. (See Chapter 2 on
advantages and disadvantages of joint ownership of property.) You and your husband may also think you do not
need a will because you have property that will not be part
of your estate—for example, insurance policies and retirement benefits that are paid directly to your beneficiaries
and do not become part of your estate. Having a will
allows for unlikely contingencies. You probably will not
die with a winning lottery ticket in your pocket, but what
if you do?

Many assets now pass outside people's wills because
they are disposed of by contracts or other agreements.
Having assets outside the will, by the way, does not mean
the assets are not part of your estate for death tax purposes. If your husband, for example, has a business and
an agreement to sell it should he die, he does not have
to leave the business in his will. If you or your husband
have a pension plan and have named beneficiaries, your
pension plan is not named in your will. Only property that
you own can be put in your will. If you and your husband
own your house jointly, with a right of survivorship, you

inherit the house if your husband dies first. His share of the house does not have to be left to you in his will, but if the house is in joint name, he can't leave his half to anyone else.

Wills let you give your property away as you wish. But only up to a point. Unless you have a prenuptial agreement that says you give up your inheritance rights to your husband's property, or he to yours, you must leave a certain amount to each other in all common law states except Georgia. This is known as the elective or forced share and is another holdover from our Anglo-Saxon traditions. In earlier times the husband would leave his wife the income from a portion of his land. More recently, the elective share could be satisfied by leaving the wife income from a trust, with assets usually not less than a third of the husband's probate estate.

Put simply, a husband or wife cannot disinherit a spouse who then might become a ward of the state. Each state has different rules for the so-called elective share. Your husband may have written a will before you were married and never revised his will to include you. If your husband dies and you discover that he wrote a will and left you out entirely, call a lawyer immediately. You usually have a limited time to file for your elective share. If your husband is very rich and left you very little, you may also be able to elect against the will. In some states the elective share is less than you would probably receive in a divorce settlement. New York's elective share law recently changed, allowing a wife or husband to claim an outright share instead of assets left in trust. In turn, your husband can claim a share of your estate, if you have cut him out.

Another important advantage to having a will is that it lets you name an executor—the person who is responsible for carrying out the terms of the will.

Moreover, a will is the place where you can name a guardian and make financial provisions for minor children. If you do not name a guardian, the court will appoint one for you. Many couples report that the naming of a guardian for young children is one of the biggest problems they face.

If you have children and die without a will, they may inherit money outright when they are eighteen in some states, twenty-one in others. Some children can deal with their newfound wealth; others do not do as well. Lawyers report seeing kids on great sprees and by twenty-five it is all gone, either on cars, boys or girls, or drugs.

A will is the place to disinherit your children, as well. State laws do not require that you leave a specific amount of money to your children. There is no forced share for children, except in Louisiana, where you must leave half your property to your children to be divided equally at your death. Lawyers advise that if you want to leave your children out, you must have a will to do this. You should make your intentions clear in case your child challenges your decision. Parents whose children have joined bizarre cults may want to be sure their hard-earned dollars do not end up supporting an ashram in India. While children do not automatically receive a share of the assets, if they are disinherited they are protected by various state laws if they are minors when you die.

If you are rich, a properly written will can help minimize federal estate taxes (which only begin on estates above $600,000 that are not left to a surviving spouse). States have different tax laws.

If you do not have a will and the court appoints an administrator, the estate may have to post a bond. Thus, having a will can save your estate unnecessary expenses.

Without a will it may take longer for the assets to be distributed.

A will also allows you to have the last word. When J. Paul Getty died, he left his villa in Italy to three of his girlfriends: One had the right to redecorate, one had the right to supervise the servants, and apparently all three had the right to live in it at the same time. Getty knew this would anger all three of the women.

Sometimes you might want to be sure a favorite, but not necessarily valuable, possession is in good hands. George Washington left "the gold-headed cane left me by Doctr. Franklin in his will" to his brother, Charles Washington. Washington's will also revealed him for the great statesman that he was. Unlike the legal language that is stuffed into the modern American will, rendering it basically indecipherable, Washington's handwritten document was clear and intelligent. In it he freed his slaves and, worried that some would not be able to support themselves, saw to it "that a regular and permanent fund be established for their support so long as there are subjects requiring it," and sought to establish a university in America so that "the youth of these United States" not be sent abroad where they were "contracting too frequently, not only habits of dissipation and extravagance, but principles unfriendly to Republican governm't and to the true and genuine liberties of mankind which thereafter are rarely overcome."[2]

Some lawyers advise, unless you have extremely valuable possessions, to list in a separate letter the personal property that you would like to give to friends or relatives.

This cuts down on legal costs and can avoid family arguments.

Men Without Will

Many men are reluctant to think about a will, let alone write one. Psychiatrists have long equated the reluctance to write a will with fear of death.[3] Pablo Picasso, who was ninety-one years old when he died on April 8, 1973, did not leave a will. In fact, he seems to have taken delight in predicting that the settling of his estate "will be worse than anyone imagines." The wrangling over his $260 million estate lasted almost four years. Eventually his assets were divided between his wife, his children, and his grandchildren. The government of France was given a large share of his paintings instead of death taxes. Lawyers fees consumed a huge chunk of the assets.[4]

Four U.S. presidents died without having written wills: Abraham Lincoln, Andrew Johnson, Ulysses S. Grant, and James A. Garfield.

Writing a will means having to admit one's mortality. It also means having to think about giving up control of one's assets. Some men are simply superstitious. They think writing a will will hasten their death. If a man's self-esteem is tied to his money, it is easy to understand that writing a will is anathema to him. A wealthy individual who leaves money in such a way that heirs can never gain control over it is probably quite different from the individual who leaves outright bequests to heirs. Sometimes men don't want to talk about a will because they then have to reveal how they value their property in relation to their wife and children. Recently, my friend Jane's husband, an advertising executive, died. Jane and Bill owned their home as tenants in common, which meant they could each name an heir for their share. When Bill died he left his half to his daughter from a previous marriage. His daughter wanted her money. So in addition to her grief, Jane had to sell her house. She also had to confront her anger at Bill. How could he have done this to her? Bill had felt that it was just a house. But Jane felt that it was her home.

For men there is an added problem. Those statistics that tell us that women will spend an average of fifteen years as widows are reminders to husbands that their wives will go on without them. Some men can contemplate this with reasonable humor; many cannot.

Surely Vincent Astor did. Mrs. Vincent Astor, speaking at a ceremony honoring her ninetieth birthday, recalled her husband telling her, "You're going to have a lot of fun with the foundation when I'm gone."[5] Mr. Astor was referring to the fact that his wife would, upon his death, become head of a foundation worth hundreds of millions of dollars. He felt that his wife would have an opportunity to use that money to good effect. And she has, becoming one of New York City's greatest philanthropists.

While you might suggest that your husband write a will, sometimes all of the reasons you can give are not enough to make your husband do it. One lawyer suggests that you should make an appointment to see the lawyer and then tell your husband the night before. Your husband may be waiting for just that little push.

Sometimes you can push too hard and then the will

won't count. At least that is what happened to Jean
Gerard. Mrs. Gerard, a former ambassador to Luxem-
bourg and a bigwig in the Republican party, inherited
$10 million from her husband James Gerard. There was
only one problem: Gerard signed the will in his hospital
bed only nine days before he died of bone cancer. In
Gerard's previous will written four months earlier, he had
left nothing outright to his wife but had left 40 percent
of his assets in trust for her and the balance of his estate
in trusts for his two children. After hearing thirty-five
witnesses, the judge ruled that Mrs. Gerard had unduly
influenced her husband, who was in no condition to think
about such things.

Little has been written about women's attitude toward
writing wills. One reason for this may be that women
have seldom in the past made their own money. When
they had money it was inherited, and usually left in such
a way that the women had little control over how the
money would be left after they died. Their husband's
wills generally took care of passing the money on to the
next generation. Today this is changing, and every
woman should have a will to pass on her own assets to her
husband and children and other heirs.

DEATH AND TAXES

While it's nice to know that your property will go where
you want, the big reason people have wills is to keep their
least favorite relative, Uncle Sam, from getting a penny
more than he has to. Naturally, the more money you and
your husband have, the more complicated this becomes.

You absolutely need a lawyer. The federal government plus your state government could claim a share of the money that you and your husband have saved, unless you have advice on the best way to take advantage of the current tax laws. Under current tax laws, only about six thousand estates each year owe any federal death taxes.

Since 1982 federal tax law permits a husband and wife to transfer to each other unlimited amounts of money without any taxes owed. (You must be a U.S. citizen to qualify for this transfer.) Before that, money left or given to a wife or husband above a certain amount was subject to an estate or gift tax. So if you and your husband have amassed a substantial amount of money, there are no taxes if you leave it all to each other when the first of you dies. But then that leaves the survivor with a large estate on which taxes would be owed, both to the federal and your state government.

If your combined net worth is less than $600,000 you do not have to worry. There will not be any taxes. If you are the survivor, one way to avoid any estate taxes would be to marry a younger man. You can then leave it all to him and no taxes would be due. This is not a plan most husbands will embrace with much enthusiasm.

Another way to avoid paying estate taxes is to give all your money away to charity. Or you can be like Charles Schwab. Charles Schwab was one of the great financiers of the twenties. Together with his partner, Andrew Carnegie, he founded the U.S. Steel Company. Andrew Carnegie left most of his money to a variety of philanthropic causes. Schwab, who died nearly broke in 1939, said, "I disagreed with Carnegie's ideas on how best to distribute his wealth. I spent mine."

While we can each leave unlimited amounts of money to our husbands, and they to us, without paying any taxes whatsoever, if we leave money to anyone else—to our children, other relatives, or friends—the federal government wants a share of any money you leave above your lifetime exemption of $600,000. If, therefore, you and your husband were to leave everything you owned to each other, no taxes are due. If you die first, no taxes will be owed on any money you left your husband. If your husband dies first, there is no tax on the money he leaves you. The problem comes with what lawyers call "the second to die." Assuming you haven't remarried, if there is more than $600,000 there will be taxes to pay. Estate taxes begin at 37 percent and move up to 55 percent on estates of $3 million, rising to 60 percent for transfers between $10 and $21 million. The time to plan for avoiding some of these taxes is before either one of you dies.

Avoiding the tax on that $600,000 is known as estate planning. There are several ways to do it. The one I like best is to equalize your assets. If you and your husband each have $600,000, you can each leave your heirs $600,000 without incurring any estate taxes. If all of your assets are in your husband's name and you die first, your $600,000 exemption is lost. If your husband doesn't remarry and dies with an estate of $1.2 million, he can only leave $600,000 tax free—a heavy tax will be due on the second $600,000. In other words, if either of you dies with the entire $1.2 million in your estate you will have to pay estate taxes. Each of you should create a marital trust into which you put $600,000. Your husband names you the beneficiary of his trust: You have all the income and when you die the trust then goes to your children. You do the same thing with your $600,000.

While owning all of your property in joint name is highly desirable and epitomizes the sharing aspects of marriage, it could mean that the spouse who dies first will lose the $600,000 exemption.

Federal tax laws offer another option for reducing estate taxes. Each of us can give $10,000, or for a couple $20,000, to as many people as we would like, each year, without incurring any gift taxes. If you have two kids and three grandchildren, you can kick $100,000 a year out of your estate each year. That way, you can keep your assets down to the $600,000. All good, but sometimes you can worry too much about taxes. The money you give to your children could be needed to take care of illnesses in your old age, or could give you and your husband a chance to take trips and enjoy extras.

Another way to take money out of your estate is to pay for your grandchildren's college education. If you pay the tuition directly to the school, you do not have to pay a gift tax. This is in addition to the $10,000 a year you can give each child without gift taxes.

DIFFERENT WILLS FOR DIFFERENT TIMES

A good will is the best way you and your husband can protect each other and your children when death comes. Unlike prenuptial agreements and divorces, most wills are not areas of major battle. If you and your husband discuss and make financial decisions together, it is more than likely that you will discuss wills. If you and your husband contribute to the family income, it is important that each of you knows how you will manage without that income.

If you are a woman who has never handled the family

finances, your husband may think he is protecting you by keeping you in the dark about his plans and leaving everything in the hands of a trustee. This really isn't fair to you. The husband who says "If anything happens to me, just call Fred, the accountant," may not realize that you would prefer to know what will happen to you ahead of time. You should know. You should ask. One lawyer reports, "After a widow goes through a mourning process [she] blooms. They start out doubting their own capabilities. They end up being competent and even enjoy handling their own finances." Think about Katharine Graham. She inherited *The Washington Post* from her husband when he died in 1963. Mrs. Graham, a housewife, took over. She said, "I quickly learned that things don't stand still—you have to make decisions." She made enough of the right ones to make her family one of America's wealthiest, with an estimated net worth of $360 million.[6]

Wills play a slightly different role in second marriages. Many couples, especially if they have children from first marriages, want prenuptial agreements in order to be sure that money will go to their children from a first marriage. If your husband is leaving money in trust—where you get the interest and his children get the principal—conflicts can easily develop. Sometimes you don't need a second marriage for that to happen. One widow tells of wanting to buy a condominium in Florida to spend time there with her second husband. Her children were enraged that she was spending what they considered their money on another man.

If it's a second marriage and you and your husband have old wills that left assets to your previous mates, divorce usually automatically cancels out the first wife or husband in a previously written will—but not always. In Iowa, for example, if a will refers to a former wife by her name, Jane Smith, but not as "my wife, Jane Smith," the will would stand despite a divorce. And in Louisiana and Mississippi, divorce does not automatically revoke a will. So if you or your husband had wills when you were previously married to others, be sure to change them.

Wills are probably one of the last bastions of tradition, written by lawyers who were educated under old laws and with old attitudes that continue to assume that a woman must be protected, that a woman must have money doled out to her. Not infrequently, men write wills that give control of family businesses to their sons, while leaving money in trust for their wives and daughters.

Trust Me

Frequently, in common law states, assets are owned by the husband. He consults a lawyer. The lawyer urges him to write a will that protects the money more than it protects his wife. Typically this involves leaving the money in a trust. Unfortunately, the planning that gives the least amount of money to the government also sometimes gives you, the widow, the least amount of control over the money. The planning starts with a careful calculation of your net worth and your husbands', as well as a look at the way in which property is owned jointly, separately, in common, etc.

Here's how it was described in one recently published book.

Ned's plan had been carefully prepared, but he had made one major miscalculation. When left on her own, Ned's wife proved to be a very poor manager of money. Between her grief at having become a widow at such a young age and her lack of familiarity with the specifics of investments Ned's estate was wiped out within a few short years.[7]

The message is implicit: Women are incapable; do not leave them money outright. It is a message that seems to pervade the legal profession as well as the estate-planning contingent. And the best way not to leave money directly to your wife, child, or husband is by leaving money in trust.

Trusts are, as far as I am concerned, a misnomer. My dictionary defines *trust* as complete assurance, faith, and dependence. But there is also a submeaning of guarding and preserving. This definition is generally applied to trusts.

Trusts are great in certain situations. If you and your husband die in an accident, you would certainly want money left in trust for your minor children.

If you or your husband have elderly parents, you might want to establish trusts to take care of them in the event that something would happen to either of you. Trusts are not as advisable until you have assets of at least $600,000 each. If you and your husband are young, leaving money to each other in trust may not make sense. Why lock up the money for years?

You can establish a trust while you are alive. This is called an inter vivos trust. A trust that is established after you die is called a testamentary trust. Trusts are revocable or irrevocable. There are usually tax advantages to an irrevocable trust, but not to a revocable trust. While you are alive, you might want revocable trusts in case you change your mind about the trustee.

When you die your executor is responsible for setting up any testamentary trusts called for by your will. The trust then becomes a separate legal entity that pays taxes. Our tax laws make the trust an attractive way to leave money. The more money you and your husband have accumulated, the more likely your wills will include various trusts. Here are some of the current favorites.

First of all, there is the QTIP trust—the Qualified Terminable Interest Property trust. This trust seems to have been custom-made for the controlling husband. It is also ideal for second marriages. Your husband puts his money in trust. You the wife are allowed some income, but the ultimate beneficiaries of the trust are decided by your husband in his will. You are, in effect, treated like a child on an allowance.

Lawyers love this one, especially when they are named as trustees and can collect a fee for doling out the income to you.

The bypass trust (also called a credit shelter trust) is another estate planners' favorite. Your husband, who controls the assets, puts $600,000—his lifetime exemption—into a bypass trust. You can get the income and the trustee can also have the power to give you principal from the trust. The rest of your husband's money can be yours tax free because of the unlimited marital deduction.

There is also the classic marital deduction trust, not much used since the creation of QTIPs. Here's how this one works, as described in a financial planning book. The "surviving spouse is provided with income for life and the power to appoint who will receive the trust principal. There's lots of flexibility regarding the powers of the trustee to withdraw principal or even for the surviving spouse to withdraw principal." The part I like is the following: "The big feature of the classic marital trust is that the management of the fund is taken out of the spouse's hands. A surviving spouse can be protected from the manipulations of children and relatives because control ultimately rests with the trustee."[8] Notice the gender-neutral language. But the implication is clear: Keep the money out of the hands of the little woman. The irony here is that when the wife dies her trust will usually go to her children or her husband's children from a previous marriage—outright—even if the children are only in their early twenties.

Tax experts have also figured out how you can have your money and give it away to charity as well. There are several types of charitable trusts that can help. The main idea is that you can get a tax deduction for giving assets to a charity while at the same time retaining some of the income for you or your heirs.

Charitable Lead Trust. You establish a trust with a fixed sum of money and receive a tax deduction for a portion of the contributed amount. The money produces income. That income goes to the charity for a fixed number of years. At the end of the fixed period the trust goes back to the beneficiary, either you, the donor, or your heirs. In other words, you get a tax deduction and then get your money back.

Charitable Remainder Trust. This is almost the opposite of the charitable lead trust. You or your husband establish a trust, you get the income, then when you die, the charity you designate gets the remainder. Many public charities offer donors ways to donate money through such trusts. In one type of trust, the charitable remainder annuity trust, the donor knows ahead of time the rate of income that will be generated. In another type, the charitable remainder unitrust, the payout fluctuates.

The drawback to such trusts is that they are irrevocable.[9]

So what should you do? Know as much as possible about your family finances. Discuss your intentions and your husband's. If your husband can't think about writing a will, make the appointment with the lawyer yourself, then tell your husband what you've done. He'll probably go with you. Above all, discuss possible trustees with your husband if either of you plans to establish trusts. Trustees can wield great power. There's a reason for all those cartoons about bank trust departments and weeping widows.

Trusts and How They Work

A *trust* is an arrangement in which someone holds assets for the benefit of someone else.

The *grantor* is the person who sets up the trust (also called the settlor, the donor, the creator, or the trustor).

The *beneficiary* is the person, or persons, who receives the economic benefits. There are two types.

The *income beneficiary* is the person who gets the income (frequently the wife, especially with older husbands).

The *ultimate beneficiary,* also called the remainder

beneficiary, is the person, or persons, who gets the assets of the trust when the trust ends (frequently your children or a designated charity).

The *trustee* is the person, or institution, who has legal title to the assets that are in the trust.

The most important of the above for you to understand is the trustee. The trustee must carry out the obligations set forth in the trust agreement—such as managing the assets by investing them, paying out the income, running a business, or paying the necessary taxes. Choosing a trustee is crucial if you plan to leave money in trust for your children, your parents, or your husband. It's also important if your husband plans to leave money in trust for you.

The trustee is the person who manages the trust. Trustees are paid for doing this. The fee varies depending on the size of the trust and its complexity. If you are planning to establish a trust in your will or your husband in his, you can establish the fee before you write the trust. The person who establishes the trust can give the trustee broad or narrow powers. If you give the trustee broad powers you want to be sure the trustee is somebody with good judgment.

There are two types of trustees: the professional trustee, from a law firm or bank trust department, or the trusted friend. My own preference would be for the trusted friend. The professional trustee—the lawyer or banker—will usually try to suggest that the bank or the law firm will be there long after your trusted friend is gone. The number of banks and law firms that have either merged or failed over the past few years makes that argument somewhat less forceful than it used to be. Furthermore, when you appoint a bank as a trustee, you can never be sure who in the bank will actually manage your trust. It could be a recent MBA graduate learning the ropes on your trust, or it could be a venerable old gentlemen who never made it out of the trust department.

A capable friend who acts as trustee has a big advantage over the bank trust department named in a will. The friend trustee can pick and choose how the trust should be invested and can change investment advisors should the performance be less than satisfactory. If a trust is locked into a bank trust department you have little chance to make a change.

You have to be careful not to pick a trustee who will love the control. You also have to understand the possible conflict a trustee has. If you have a trust with $1 million in it and the trustee is paid a 1 percent fee for managing it, that means the trustee earns $10,000 a year. If you, the wife, would like to yank a few hundred thousand dollars out of your trust to buy an apartment, the trustee may decide it is not a good idea—after all, the trustee's fee will drop if the assets diminish.

There is another problem with trusts that should be pointed out. Most of the time trusts are supposed to pay out the income. That's very good if trust assets are invested in CDs paying 9 percent. But it is not very good if they are invested in CDs that only yield 5 percent. You would suddenly have a big drop in income. Trusts must allow for this kind of shift and therefore must be flexible in the way they invest as well as in the way they pay out money. The trustee should have some idea that the donor of the trust, your husband, would rather see the trust diminish and have you maintain your standard of living.

There are many ways to leave money, but trying to be too restrictive for too long can result in unexpected consequences.

A trust agreement that is too rigid could turn out to be a disaster. In one case, a man set up a trust and his wife was to receive only the interest. The balance was to go to charity when he died. His wife outlived him by thirty years. Inflation totally eroded the buying power of her income and she had to spend her old age living on very little.

A big question is: Should you name your husband as a trustee and should he name you? Were there no tax implications, the answer would be easy. Name your husband; ask your husband to name you as trustee. You should also name a co-trustee and a successor trustee. It doesn't matter that you may not know how to invest money. Nobody will be more concerned about hiring good money managers for your money than you. If you don't know, you will learn. My first husband never had a will until I refused to travel with him unless we both made wills to name a guardian for our daughter. Then the unlikely happened. My husband drowned while on a fishing trip leaving me alone with our one-year-old daughter. His will named me as one of his executors. My husband's will also established a trust and named me and one of his business partners as trustees. It was a decision for which I will always be grateful. Having a friend, instead of a bank or lawyer whom I hardly knew, at a time when I was so devastated meant a great deal to me. As an executor and trustee I also had to make decisions. This sense of being in control helped me gradually to rebuild my own shattered life.

Tax implications are important in the naming of trustees. One of the main purposes of setting up certain trusts is to avoid having to pay estate taxes. But there's a catch. For example, if you, the wife, were the trustee of a credit shelter trust and had the power to invade the trust, the tax advantage would be lost.

THINGS TO KNOW BEFORE WRITING A WILL

You and your husband will have to decide about executors for your wills. The executor's role is slightly different from that of the trustee's. The executor is really the stage manager for your estate. (The estate, by the way, is everything you left behind.) The basic job of the executor is to carry out the instructions in your will. While this calls for many technical and legal responsibilities, you do not have to name a lawyer or a professional for the job. If you become the executor you can hire a lawyer to do the work. Executors are paid fees based on a percentage of the assets of the estate. In California, executors' fees are set by statutes: 4.9 percent of the first $15 thousand, 3 percent of the next $85 thousand, 2 percent of the next $900 thousand, 1 percent of the next $9 million, .5 percent of the next $15 million. Above that, the court decides. Lawyers can be hired to do the specific tasks for a lot less, in some cases. If you serve as executor you are entitled to that fee. However, if you receive an executor's fee, it is taxable income for you.

The executor files the will for probate, pays any debts that are due, pays the funeral expenses, and lists the assets and liabilities. (This is the kind of information you and your husband should already have.)

The executor also must file the federal and state death

tax returns. The federal estate tax return is due nine months after the date of death, regardless of whether any taxes are owed, although extensions are possible.

As with trustees you can name a close friend or a professional institution. If you do name a friend, be sure to tell the friend. Being an executor is time consuming and not everyone wants to take on the job. Be careful about naming a bank, which may only take an estate of a minimum size.

The best choice of an executor is probably your husband for your will and you for your husband's will. You might also consider a coexecutor for large estates. Usually you would also name a successor executor. You can also spell out fees for executors in your will that will override state laws. Be sure the potential executors agree in advance.

What You Should Know About Your Husband's Will

Here are six basic things you should know:

1. Where it is
2. If there is a trust, what type of trust and what its terms are
3. What happens to the trust
4. What, if anything, is left for the children
5. Who the trustees are
6. Who the executors are

While these are the things that will be part of the will, there is other information that you should also know

What taxes, if any, will be due to Uncle Sam and to the state and when will they be due? The death of your husband does not mean Uncle Sam does not claim income taxes that were due on any income earned up until the day your husband died.

If your husband's assets are mainly real estate and not left only to you, you should find out whether you will have to sell property in order to pay the estate taxes. There are some provisions for extending the time frame for making these payments. Another way not to have to force the sale of property in order to pay the taxes is to create an insurance trust. If your husband has insurance, but he is the owner of that insurance, it goes into his estate and taxes are due. If a trust owns the insurance and is the beneficiary, the money goes to the trust; there are no taxes due. The insurance money can be used to pay estate taxes. This is very important if you want to avoid selling a property or a family business.

If your husband runs his own business, will you know what to do to keep it running? Will you be able to meet the immediate payroll? Is there someone who can step in to take over, and have you discussed this with your husband? If you and your husband are in business together or the business is yours, there are several routes to take. If it's your business or your husband's and you have partners, you could have a buy-sell agreement. This usually establishes a fixed price at which one of you buys out the other. If your husband has a buy-sell agreement, you should know about it. The big problem here is not revaluing the business. You could end up having your husband's share bought out by his partners, at a price that was established years ago, while the business has continued to grow. Or, worse still, you might have to buy out a partner at an overvalued price that was established when things were going well, but since then the business has collapsed.

Frequently, the way to provide for buying out a partner in such a situation is with an insurance trust.

You might have a family business that you would like to keep in the family. There are ways to do that, too. The usual way is to give your children stock when the business is just beginning. That way they become owners at low cost. If the children are very young, the stock is put into trust.

There is yet another method called the estate freeze. This is complicated, tricky, and requires the advice of highly specialized experts. It involves two classes of stock. One class appreciates in value, the other has a value that is fixed, or frozen. You or your husband keep the frozen-value stock and give the stock that appreciates to your children.

While all of this may seem remote, especially if you are young, believe me—this can happen to anyone. Knowing a little about your situation can take away the anxiety and fear that you will be unable to manage.

If despite everything you and your husband refuse to write wills, all is not totally lost—well, at least to some extent. There is a little lawyer's trick known as post-mortem tax planning. Suppose your husband forgot to write a will. You inherit everything. Your husband's $600,000 exemption is lost, ordinarily. But you can "disclaim" an amount up to $600,000 and let it go directly to your children. It's risky, however, because not all states allow a disclaimer, especially for jointly owned property.

WHAT IF YOU WERE SUDDENLY WIDOWED?

Here's a list of questions you and your husband might try and answer. You will probably think of many more.

1. How would you meet the monthly expenses that are now paid by your husband's income and your income? Most couples cover this gap by having life insurance—term insurance when you are young, whole life when you get older.
2. Would you have cash for funeral expenses? Here's where a separate account that can't be frozen is helpful. Funeral expenses vary but on average can be $3,000.
3. If you are insured under your husband's health plan, could you continue it? Most companies give you thirty-six months in which you can continue to pay for coverage. During that time you should find out whether you will be able to convert the policy to keep it on your own or can find another insurer. Don't forget to ask; the company may not call to tell you.
4. Would you be eligible for Social Security benefits? You would be if your husband was covered. You can get widow's benefits as well as benefits for your children. The trouble here is that the benefits stop when your children are sixteen. Then you are not eligible for benefits again until you are sixty-two, when you can get retirement benefits. But if you begin drawing benefits at age sixty-two you will receive a lower amount than if you wait until you are sixty-five. If you remarry before age sixty, you lose the right to widow's benefits;

marry after sixty and you keep your benefits and your new husband.

5. Would you be able to continue living in your house? Frequently couples have mortgage insurance that pays off the house if the husband dies. This may not be the best way to insure your house. You would be better off having life insurance for the amount of the mortgage. Coverage would be cheaper. In addition, the insurance would go directly to you, and you could continue the mortgage payments. You would have more control over making a decision about your house than if the mortgage were automatically paid.

6. How would you pay for your children's education?

7. What if you have a lot of debts?

These are hard questions to think about, let alone plan for. If you and your husband do nothing else, you should at least know the basics—where your assets are, how they are owned, and how much of them will be yours, should something happen to him. If he has lawyers, brokers, or other advisers get to know them too. The main point should be that you end up with as much control over your assets as possible, and feel comfortable managing them.

A Guide to Being Alone

If your husband dies you are a widow. The word comes from the old English. In addition to its primary meaning as a woman who has lost her husband, the word is defined as "empty" or "extra hand at the card table." Unfortunately, that is also the way many people, even friends, will sometimes regard you once you are no longer part of a couple. The implication that widow conjures up for many people is deeply rooted in earlier times. Then, and even today, widows were often entitled only to their "dower" rights. This generally meant the "income" from a part of their husbands' estates.

When the Time Comes

I can tell you that nothing in life prepares you for the trauma of losing your husband. Nevertheless you should try to plan the funeral. This is not one of life's easier tasks. Remember, an expensive service is probably not the best use of your money, especially if you are uncertain of your future finances. Your local funeral director will be able to tell you the proper procedures. But you can have whatever touches you would like. My husband and I recently attended a service where a favorite shawl was draped over the casket of the friend who had died. It was a simple and lovely gesture, and a very personal reminder of our friend. Costs average around $3,000. Much depends on the elaborateness of the casket you choose and the number of cars you rent for the cemetery. Flowers are another consideration. You may also want to place a notice in your local newspaper. The clergyman is generally paid a small amount, in cash.

Some people choose to plan funerals in advance. There are even prepaid plans. If you want to do this, here are a few tips. You can check prices at a few funeral homes before making a decision. You can even have a trust where your money will accumulate, until needed, and earn interest. Here you have to be careful as to what happens to any excess money. In some states, that money could go to the funeral director. You also have to be sure that inflation is figured into your plan so that there will be no extra charges.

During the First Month

Find the will. If there is a will, it will have to be probated. While you can go through the probate process alone if you are the executor, you are probably better off hiring a lawyer.

There is more than one kind of probate and the process differs in each state. Some states have a special small-estate process when the total estate is a maximum ranging anywhere from $2,000 to as much as $100,000. Probate does not have to be done immediately, but it should be done in the first few weeks. The ultimate goal of probate is to be sure debts are paid and heirs get what they should.

During the First Three Months

You will also need copies of the death certificate; in some cases these must be certified. You may need as many as twelve. The funeral director can help you with this. You need the certificates in order to collect life insurance and anything else for which you may be the beneficiary. You also need it to transfer assets to your name, to probate a will, and for other purposes as well.

Here is a list of items that will need to be transferred into your name.

- Title to your house, if it was jointly owned
- Bank Accounts—Joint accounts could be frozen, which is one reason you should have an account in your own name.
- Credit Cards—If you have credit cards in your own name you can continue to use them. If your credit cards are all in your husband's name, and you signed on them, you can probably continue to use them. As long as you continue to pay on time, you will not have any problems. But at some point you will probably want to notify the company and have the cards changed to your name. Be sure you have records to document that you were an authorized signer. If you had a joint credit card, notify the company that the card should be in your name only.
- Automobile title
- Auto insurance
- Securities

You should also review your will. If your husband was the executor, you will need to name somebody else. Sign a durable power of attorney. Sign a health-care power of attorney. (Actually, you and your husband should both have them.)

If your husband was the beneficiary of your pension or life insurance, change this.

If your husband worked with lawyers, accountants, or other advisers, meet with them. Decide whether you want to continue working with them. You don't have to. Even if it is the lawyer who drew his will, you can hire your own.

If you were working, go back to work, not only for the

income, but because having something to do every day will lessen some of your grief.

Take a look at your finances during the first three months and redo your net worth (asset and liability) statement as well as your cash-flow statement. (See pages 34–35 and 36–37.)

Review your insurance needs. If you have young children, you may need life insurance. If you are working, you may need disability insurance. If your husband was the beneficiary of your life insurance, you may not need it anymore.

Social Security: You are eligible to collect if your husband had paid into Social Security and you are a surviving spouse with minor children. As noted earlier, you and your children can collect benefits until the children reach sixteen. Then all benefits to you stop unless you are at least sixty-two years old. You are also eligible to collect as a widow, without children, when you reach the age of sixty-two. You will receive benefits based on either your own earnings or your husband's, whichever is higher. If you and your husband were already collecting benefits, you will have to notify the Social Security office of his death. You will continue to receive benefits, but they will decrease. The toll-free number for Social Security is 1(800)772-1213. Documentation you will require:

- Your husband's Social Security number
- Your Social Security number
- Your children's Social Security numbers if they are minor children
- Your children's birth certificates
- Your marriage certificate

• Your husband's W-2 form or a federal self-employ-
ment tax return for the most recent year

Life insurance: Notify the insurance company, either
directly or through your insurance agent. The named
beneficiary is paid directly, usually in two to three weeks.
You will need a death certificate.

Pensions: If you and your husband were receiving pension benefits under his pension and it was a single annuity, your benefits will stop. If you and your husband were
receiving benefits from your husband's pension and it was
a joint and survivor plan, the amount might change depending on the type of benefits you were receiving. If
your husband was not yet retired, notify his employer and
find out about any lump-sum payouts that may be due to
you.

Investments: If you are unfamiliar with your husband's
investments, call the broker and have the statements sent
to you. Then ask the broker to explain the reasons various
stocks and bonds were chosen by your husband. If your
husband always invested your money, and you suddenly
find that you have received the proceeds from his life
insurance in a lump sum, immediately put the money into
a money market fund. Don't even think about doing
anything else—no matter who recommends it. It's your
money now. You will have plenty of time later to decide
how to invest. If you are getting pension proceeds or life
insurance in a lump sum, you will possibly have to make
a choice as to how to invest this money. One possibility
is an annuity. While annuities can offer a certain amount
of safety in the short run, they are usually paid out in fixed

sums, so are less likely to keep pace with inflation. In addition, you give up control over your money.

Debts. Usually a notice placed in the local newspaper announces the death so that anyone with outstanding claims can come forward. A specific number of days is usually allowed in which claims may be filed. If debts were in his name only, the executor must pay them. If they were in joint name, you may have to pay them.

Medical Insurance: If your husband was working and had medical insurance, call the company to find out about continuing the policy to extend to you and your family. Under COBRA laws, you must be given the chance to continue the policy for thirty-six months. After that you may be able to get a conversion policy. Find out if you will have to requalify for the conversion policy.

Estate taxes: There are no federal taxes if money is left just to you. Taxes are owed, however, on amounts that exceed $600,000 left to other beneficiaries. Many states have inheritance or estate taxes. Most states have no taxes beyond the amount the federal government allows as a credit against federal estate-tax payments.

Income taxes: You will have to file a return as usual, and can continue to file a joint return for the year in which your husband died. If you have dependent children, you can file a joint return for two years. If money is being paid to you from an annuity, you must pay income tax on it.

What Not to Do

1. Do not make decisions about selling your house, unless this is something you and your husband carefully planned.

2. Do not buy anything from anybody that the seller claims will give you an income for life.

During the First Year

Think about whether you want to keep your house. This should not just be based on economics, but on your feelings as well.

The finances are easy to calculate. You have to decide, if your income is less than when you were married, if you are making a sacrifice out of some loyalty to the marital home or to your children who do not want you to sell.

Keep in mind how the taxation works when you inherit the house, providing you did not own it outright but received it as either half of a joint tenancy with your husband or inherited it from your husband. You inherit your husband's part of the house—either his half or the entire house at what is called the "stepped-up" basis in value. No taxes are due when you inherit the house. Taxes would be due if you decided to sell the house. That's when cost basis counts.

Here's an example.

Original cost of the house:	$100,000
Value of the house when your husband dies:	$250,000
Your basis if your husband owned the house:	$250,000

If you sold the house for $250,000 there would not be a capital-gains tax. Your basis if you owned the house jointly would be:

Your half:	$50,000
His half:	$125,000
Your new basis:	$175,000

If the house was owned jointly and you sold it for $250,000 you would have a taxable profit of $75,000. If you are fifty-five or over you would have a onetime exclusion of $125,000 so you would not have a tax. If you had rolled over gains from a previous sale, your basis would be reduced by the amount of the earlier gain.

You have to decide whether you will do better with a smaller house and some income from the proceeds of your sale. If you decide to sell and have anything of value—say, worth over $1,000—you might want to consult a dealer or an auction house. Otherwise, you might want to have a tag sale to reduce the accumulation of several years that you would otherwise have to cart away with you.

Special Advice for Older Women

You want to be sure that you will be all right should you become ill and incapacitated in your old age. Many of my friends have parents who are now getting old. The situation is often the same—everything is fine until the father dies and the mother is alone. The mother is fine for the first few years. Then many begin to fail. Sometimes it is her health, sometimes her mind. One friend's mother, living alone in a Florida condominium, began to imagine that people were trying to break into her apartment. My friend and her two sisters pooled their money and bought a small house that one sister and her husband lived in with the mother. This worked for a while, but eventually the mother needed the care of a nursing home. If you have children, discuss the possibilities with them of what might happen to you and how you would like things handled.

Here are a few things to consider:

- Possibly buying into a retirement community
- Selling your house while you still have the energy to move and the house has not gotten to be too much of a burden to you
- Making funeral arrangements—One woman I know even purchased her own casket because, she said, if she left it to her son, an artist, he would try and build one and she might never be buried.

If you do not have children, or feel that they are too far away to be of help should you have problems, find an elder-care attorney with whom you can discuss your future. Check on the elder care services in your community. You may want to consider giving away some of your assets in order to qualify for nursing home care. You may want to consider nursing home insurance. If you are managing your own assets, you may want to put them in a living trust to make it easier for someone else to take over, or else sign a durable power of attorney. A power of attorney is an appointment to let someone else act for you. A durable power of attorney lets someone else act for you even if you become incapacitated. A springing power of attorney is only activated if you become incapacitated.

Many women who are alone and faced for the first time with having to handle their own money seem to make some of the same mistakes.

The Five Most Common Mistakes Made by Women Whose Husbands Always Did Everything for Them

1. Thinking if her husband did it a particular way, it must be right. An example is the woman who inherited a

portfolio of CDs that had been yielding 9 percent. When yields dropped, she refused to change her husband's plan.

2. Being unwilling to take any investment risk. By not taking any risk a woman's investments do not keep pace with inflation and she keeps having to reduce her expenses because her dollars buy less and less. Your money has to generate increasing, not diminishing, income.

3. Giving loans to her children. This leaves her with even less money, thus making her more fearful and unable to manage. Often, women left alone after long marriages feel life is not going to offer much anymore, or they feel guilty for surviving, and are therefore vulnerable to requests from their children, who frequently promise to pay back, but often have problems doing so. Resist the temptation.

4. Meeting a new man and letting him take charge because she feels she cannot handle money. Most women can, and should, handle their own investments—if not on a daily basis, at least by frequently consulting a broker or advisor.

5. Being unable to understand the reality of her new situation and thus failing to cut expenses. An example of what can happen is a couple where the husband's income had been $75,000. The wife didn't work. After her husband died she was left with assets of $250,000. Her income dropped to below $25,000. This was a drastic change, which she could not accept.

Many women have been faced with the same problems, although each person's situation is different. The more knowledge you have beforehand, the better equipped you will be. But even if you are starting out with little awareness, you can learn quickly. One woman said she learned the most by asking her friends. She never asked for general advice. She always asked for specific information. If one friend knew about automobiles, she asked that friend about cars. If another friend knew about insurance, she would address her insurance questions to that friend. You may not have such competent friends, but you can do a lot of your own research, and you can learn.

9.
Cinderella Revised: The Rights of Children

We all know the story of Cinderella. While modern writers have accused women of having a Cinderella complex—waiting for their prince to rescue them—few people seem to have concentrated on the real villain: not the wicked stepmother, but the wicked father. Haven't you wondered what kind of man would allow a woman into his life who would do such terrible things to his children? Haven't you wondered why his right to do this is never questioned?

CHILD'S RITES

Children's rights have changed dramatically over the centuries. In ancient Rome, children were raised at the whim of the father. When the child was born, the father could either keep the baby or order that it be left exposed to the elements. When a baby was born the midwife placed the child on the ground. The father could either lift up the child, signifying his intention of raising the child, or leave it on the ground to die. Often children were left to die in order to preserve intact the inheritance of the children already living. They were also frequently given up for adoption, particularly when the natural parents could not afford to give the child advantages. Octavius, who became the emperor Augustus, was the adopted son of Julius Caesar. Children were used in order to form political alliances, make advantageous marriages, or to serve the aims of their parents in other ways.[1]

Roman sons remained subject to their fathers' rule until the fathers died. (Roman women were under the thumb of first their fathers and then their husbands.) The earnings of the son belonged to the father, and fathers could disinherit their sons. And since Roman women often died in childbirth, a stepmother who could influence the father could prove to be a great threat to the children of a first marriage.

Americans have moved a long way from pagan Rome. The rights of children are increasingly protected by federal and state laws. The official definition of *child* is a person who has not reached the age of majority, usually eighteen, who is not married, and is still at home. American children have specific rights. Children are, at least theoretically, protected from the abuse of parents. This means a court order can remove children from a home where abuse is suspected. After "emancipation" parents are no longer responsible for their children, although in some states parents are responsible for their disabled children, even after the age of emancipation.

Unlike the Romans, Americans have long believed in the maternal right. Until fairly recently, mothers were awarded custody of their children unless there was an extremely unusual circumstance. Fathers paid support in the event of divorce. In the last few decades, however, fathers, claiming equal rights, have begun to seek custody of their children.[2] The increasing number of stepparents has further complicated the idea of custody, throwing doubt into the once-sacred doctrine that the "natural parent" should raise a child. One example is the child who was raised by a mother and stepfather. In the past, if the mother died, the natural father would automatically be given custody of the child, even if he had previously abandoned that child. Today, the best interests of the child are considered, and custody might be awarded to the stepfather who had raised the child.[3]

Children have the right to make contracts with adults, and to have these contracts enforced. On the other hand, children cannot have contracts with adults enforced against them.

American parents also have certain legal obligations toward their children. Children are entitled to support and education. Children also have the right to medical care. Sometimes this right is enforced by courts when the religious beliefs of parents may prohibit medical intervention.

The money that children earn or inherit is also protected. An example might be a child actress who earns a high salary. Her salary must be used only for her support. In one situation, the mother of a young actress became ill and had no health insurance. The mother, who had guided her daughter's career, could not use any of her daughter's money for medical expenses, even though the daughter would have wanted to help her mother. Parents must consider themselves guardians of the money. Occasionally, children have sued parents and accused them of mismanaging funds left for them.

If you and your husband die intestate, your children have certain rights to inherit money from your estates. However, except in Louisiana, you do not have to leave money to your children.

Should you or your husband die, your children may also be eligible to receive survivors' benefits from Social Security. If your husband died and he had paid into Social Security, your children would be entitled to benefits from the time your husband died until they reach the age of eighteen. They would be able to receive benefits until they are nineteen if they are full-time high school students. The benefits would be based on your husband's benefits. Your children would also be entitled to benefits based on your Social Security if you died.

If you or your husband retire and are entitled to receive Social Security benefits, your children may also be entitled to benefits under special circumstances—if they are under age eighteen, or if they are over eighteen and disabled. If you or your husband retire and are entitled to a maximum benefit, each of your children can receive up to half of your benefit. (The government does draw the line, however, with something known as Family Limits.)

MOTHERHOOD

Should you and your husband divorce, the law becomes quite specific about your obligations to your children. Child support and child custody are carefully spelled out in divorce and separation agreements. However, during marriage parents must make their own rules about how to raise their children.

For many couples, the decision to have children is the most important decision they will make. The decision may be even more critical for many women than for men. No matter how equally a couple may decide to divide marital obligations and no matter how willing the father is to help, it is still the mother who must physically give birth to the child. The mother is also most often the person who remains responsible for that child. More often than not it is the mother who cuts back on her career and forfeits some of her earlier goals in order to take care of her child. And, should the marriage end in divorce, mothers, not fathers, end up with custody and responsibility for the children.

CHILD SUPPORT IN DIVORCE

While the law in general says children are entitled to support, when a couple divorces, laws become much more specific about a child's rights. Since 1984, all states have been required to have specific child-support guidelines. Basically, these guidelines consider the income of the parents and the standard of living that the income of the parents should afford the children. Often the support guidelines are some percentage of the gross income of the noncustodial parent, or else a percentage of the combined incomes of both parents. The different methods of computing child support can lead to a big difference in the type of award the custodial parent will be given.[4]

One problem with child-support awards is the nonmonetary costs—usually borne by the mother. Studies estimate that divorced mothers spend between 19.6 and 26.6 hours each week taking care of their children. If a monetary value is put on that time, studies have come up with a figure of $123,553 as the nonmonetary cost of caring for a child until the age of eighteen.[5]

So much for the theory. In practice, fathers frequently underreport income when awards are made, and then fail to pay the necessary support after the divorce. In some situations, no child support is awarded at all. In a recent study of 670 Connecticut divorces, no support was ordered in 20 percent of the families studied. The average weekly support ordered for each child was $49.58. A further Connecticut study reported that 82 percent of the mothers were awarded sole custody of their children, yet 26 percent reported that the fathers were not paying the ordered support.[6] Nationally, uncollected payments of $19 billion have been estimated.[7] According to a 1989 Census Bureau study, only half of the 5 million women entitled to child support received it in full.[8] On the other hand, there are fathers who go the other way, using their time with the children to lavish material goods on them. Often when parents divorce, mothers find that they must struggle on a limited budget all week. Then children visit a more affluent father on weekends, who buys them elaborate toys and clothing the mother cannot afford. One example was a father who stopped paying support to the children's mother, then entertained the children at a hotel on weekends, allowing them to run up large room-service charges.

The large number of stepfamilies in America has led to some complications in the laws of child support and child custody. Sometimes fathers, just like Cinderella's, will form another family and not take as much care of their children from their first marriage.

If you and your husband divorce, you may find your husband reluctant to agree about some items of support for your mutual children. Sometimes this is your husband's way of getting back at you. Other times it merely reflects something you knew for a long time while you were married—your husband likes to control spending. This can lead to scores of petty arguments with a former husband. You may assume an interpretation of support that may be different from your husband's. Don't assume anything. When Mary and her husband, Jim, divorced, the decree said her husband would take care of medical expenses.[9] Although he could have perfectly well afforded it, her husband refused to pay dental expenses. Mary had assumed that medical and dental were one and the same. She could not have imagined that her husband would be reluctant to pay for the braces necessary for their two daughters. However, her divorce decree did not specify.

Her husband was using his money to control a situation, the same thing he had done during Mary and Jim's marriage. If you expect your husband to help pay for your children's education, be sure you are specific: Do you mean college? Graduate school?

If you are divorced and your husband has not paid child support, trying to collect can be frustrating. You can hire a private attorney. But frequently women cannot afford to do that. You can go to various state agencies to try and collect. The state agencies that help women collect back child support are often tied to the welfare departments of the state, and many women are reluctant to go to such bureaus. One of the most effective ways of getting child support that is owed to you is to get a payroll deduction order: The money is taken from your husband's salary and he cannot stop it. But getting any results takes a lot of time and energy. A delinquent father can say he has paid. Then the agencies have to weigh your word against his. Enforcement of payment of child support is also regulated by the courts, including the right to garnish wages to collect unpaid support. Many states also have so-called long-arm laws that allow a father who has left his home state to be pursued for child support. (Note the use of *father* here, instead of the currently popular usage *noncustodial parent;* 90 percent of the nonpayers are the fathers.) Credit agencies that request the information can report unpaid child support as debt, thus giving delinquent fathers bad credit ratings.

Fathers who do not pay child support are often supporting another family. Then they use the second family as an excuse for not paying the children of their first family. Not even Solomon would be able to solve some of the complicated financial problems of the modern American blended family. In New York State, if a father has one set of children from a first family, his first wife can get an order to deduct money from his salary, which takes priority over the needs of his second family—that is, unless he can show that the children of the second family will be worse off than the children from the first family.

Do You Want Your Children to Be Rich?

Child support, at least until the age of majority, is a "right" of American children, but inheritance is left to the largess of the parents.

In America, unlike France, it is not illegal for a man to disinherit his children, except in formerly French Louisiana. Reasons for disinheriting children can be complex. One Manhattan lawyer, Fred, originally from Oklahoma, moved to New York with his wife and two children. Then his wife left him for one of his best friends. Fred eventually met a lawyer who had children of her own. When Fred died of a heart attack after a vigorous tennis game, he was in his early forties. His two sons were in their teens. His will left all his money to his new girlfriend, trusting her to take care of his children.

If you decide you do not want to leave money to your children, you had better prepare a will saying so. Without a will the intestate laws of your state will provide for your children. This usually means children will inherit between one third and one half of your estate. Should your children inherit money when they are below the age of majority—between the ages of eighteen and twenty-one, depending on the state—that money would be put into a trust.

Chances are, unlike Cinderella's mother, you will outlive your husband, and therefore be able to provide for your children. But what if you die first? Here's where property ownership can become extremely important. If you and your husband live in a common law state the situation is as follows. If all of your property is in your husband's name, then you cannot designate how any of it should be dispersed should you die. If you and your husband own your property jointly, as many couples do, and it is as joint ownership with right of survivorship, it will go to your husband. *Tenants in common* means you own the property together, although not necessarily equally. But you can each leave your share to anyone you want at death. In other words, if you own your house as tenants in common, you could leave your half to your children, in trust if they are minors.

If you live in a community property state, you have rights to half the marital property, and can leave your half to your children. Your husband can do the same. Sometimes this can create problems, however. Be sure your husband hasn't put you in a position where you might be forced to sell your house before you want to because he gave his share to his children.

While you probably don't want to see your children left with nothing, it's important to balance your own needs with what you would like to leave to them. Americans are living for a very long time and spending much of their money on their own retirement and medical care. Many parents also spend a great deal of money on their children's education. Many also help their married children buy a house. So, often, there is not that much money left to leave to children. But as your assets increase, it's a good idea to talk with your husband about exactly what you would like to do for them.

If you each have children from a first marriage, you may again discover very different money attitudes that could cause problems. You may think children should have a regular allowance, no strings attached, while your husband may think an allowance is something that a child must earn. You may want to scrimp and save to send your children to an Ivy League college; your husband may think a state school like the one he attended is good enough. He may be of the "I did it myself" school and believe very little money should be left for the children. You may believe that children could greatly benefit from the security of some money that they knew would be theirs.

Money left for a child by a parent can also be interpreted by the child as a token of the parent's love. Not leaving money can send a message that a parent may not have intended.

Some months ago, my husband and I were talking to an English friend of ours who had twin boys. We were surprised to discover that our friend planned to leave more to the first-born twin. Unlike the French, who divide property equally among their children, the English adopted primogeniture—leaving all the property to the first-born son. When the English came to the New World they too adopted the system. Thomas Jefferson abolished primogeniture. Americans tend to want to leave equal amounts to each child. Of course, one does hear stories of parents who left unequal amounts of money thinking one child was well provided for. Not infrequently the well-off child suffers financial reverses when it is too late to change the will.

Should you decide to leave money for your children, you also have to decide how old they should be when they get the money. Lawyers have a tendency to suggest money be left in trust for a long time. A good solution is to leave the money so that it is gradually given to your children, say one half at age thirty and the balance at age forty. Leaving money outright to children could pose a problem should the children divorce. If you know that you will leave money to a son or daughter, you might discuss with your children the way in which they would like the money left. Remember, in some states there is no distinction between separate and marital property when couples divorce. You might suggest that they have prenuptial agreements so that they can keep their inherited money separate. And depending on how the money is used, separate money can quickly become marital. When leaving money for your children, there is also a question of trustees. You need to pick people who will outlive you and be able to manage that money for a long time. Naming one child as trustee for another child may not be the best solution.

Many men still think women are not capable of handling money. Most daughters still can't persuade their fathers to let them take over the family business. When there are family businesses, fathers frequently think of bringing in their sons, but only bring in daughters as a last resort.[10]

Despite the changes made in women's lives, fathers tend to see their daughters as producers of grandchildren. They leave wills that put money in trust for their daughters while leaving money outright to their sons.

If you are remarried and have children from your first marriage, remember that the law requires certain money to go to your current husband. If you have a pension, you must name your husband as a beneficiary and he must name you. That means that a husband of a short marriage will take precedence in receiving your pension benefits over your children from a first, long marriage.[11] The only way to avoid this is by having your husband sign a waiver of his survivor's rights to your pension money. You should discuss this before you marry. You also must check to be sure your particular pension plan will allow you to name someone other than your husband as a beneficiary.

Your husband is also entitled to a minimum share of your assets under the elective share laws of the state in which you live. If you want to leave all your money to your children, be sure you have a signed agreement from your husband—before you marry.

10.
What's It Worth?

When Samuel Newhouse, the publisher, died in 1979 the IRS claimed that his estate owed an additional $609 million in taxes, based on their appraisals of the value of Mr. Newhouse's minority interest in Advance Publications, Inc., and Newhouse Broadcasting, Inc. Eleven years later, U. S. Tax Court Judge B. John Williams, Jr., ruled against the IRS and settled for the $48 million the estate had originally submitted. The deciding factor was the judge's acceptance of the valuation placed on the stock as defined by the experts brought in by the Newhouse tax consultants.[1]

While the tax act of 1984 has eliminated any taxes on transfers of property between husband and wife, valuation of property still plays an important role in estate and divorce decisions.

Valuation becomes especially important if your husband is a partner in a small business. For example, if the partnership agreement states that the wife of a deceased partner is to be paid out in cash, how the partnership is valued can make an extraordinary difference in the amount of money you will receive.

When George Davidson died recently, he left shares of a privately owned company as part of his estate. Under the terms of his divorce agreement from a previous marriage, George had left one third of his estate rather than a specific dollar amount to his first wife. The remainder went to his second wife.

His first wife wanted to see a high value placed on the shares because, although they could not be sold publicly, she would be paid out in cash based on the value of the shares.

Still another group had an interest in the valuing of the shares. The stock brokerage firm that issued the stock wanted the value of the stocks to remain high. If not, the brokerage firm would have to devalue its net worth, a substantial portion of which is based on the stock. The company had been sold shortly before George's death. It went from being a company with substantial assets to being a company with a considerable debt. The husband had exchanged his shares for shares in the acquiring company.

An initial evaluation of the company made by the new owners valued the shares at $600,000. The brokerage firm revalued the shares at $400,000. When the executors hired an independent evaluation company, the stock was revalued as being worthless. In the meantime, the first wife had been paid her share of the stock, based on the second evaluation ($125,000).

If you and your husband divorce, his pension and yours could be your largest assets other than your home. Yet determining what it is worth for purposes of division in a divorce is not as simple as might be thought.

In many states, pensions are considered marital property when they are accumulated during the marriage. In a few states pensions are considered earnings and not marital property. Some states consider a pension as alimony, and other states regard it as a property award. If a pension is a property award, you would receive your share of it even if you remarried, but if a pension is considered alimony and you remarried, your payments would stop. Nevertheless, when it comes to evaluation many problems arise.

Even the date to use for determining the value of a pension plan, since the benefits are in the future, is a cause for conflict. Do you use:

The date of marital separation?
The date of filing of complaint?
The date of hearing or trial?

In Indiana, Richard N. Skirvin's pension vested thirty-two days after his divorce decree was entered. Even though his marriage lasted twenty-three years, his pension was not considered marital property and his wife received no part of it.[2]

Many other variables must be considered when trying to determine the value of a pension plan. For instance, what rate of interest should be used? What age will be used for the husband's retirement?

In a defined benefit plan, the pension amount is constantly accruing and has a value that is determinable at any time, including into the future. But, again, with future figures there can be variables such as fluctuating interest rates.

Frequently, when it comes to the division of pensions,

women lose out. In Massachusetts, for example, the husband is generally awarded his pension as part of the division of property: The usual practice is to value the benefits as of the date of divorce and treat them as a setoff for other assets that will be assigned to the wife. The result is that the wife often receives no retirement benefits from the marriage; instead she gets 50 percent of the present value.

You must also remember that if you are paid out for a pension plan that your husband will not collect for ten years, you are given a discounted value of the money. In other words, the value of a dollar that will be paid in ten years is less today. Experts use tables called discounted or present value tables to determine what that amount will be.

Here is an example of how a seemingly large pension award can vanish.

Amount of pension ten years out	Rate of interest	Amount you get
$100	5%	$61.39

In the past few years as more and more states have recognized the marital property value of pensions three basic methods of valuing pensions for divorce have evolved.

In the first method, the value of the pension is simply the amount of money that the employee has contributed, plus the accrued interest. The second method looks at the future benefits and then discounts those benefits to arrive at a present value. There are a number of variables in this method, including whether or not the employer will actually still be in business, and how long after retirement the employee will continue to live.

In a recent Maryland divorce, the husband's pension was valued at $122,936.87 because only his contributions to the plan and interest were considered. Had the second valuation method been used, the pension would have had a value of $358,034.22.[3] The wife was able to appeal the original valuation of her husband's pension. But for many women, the high cost of such an appeal would rule out any chance of doing so.

Another way that a woman can lose out when dividing pension benefits is on the assumption of a retirement date. The longer your husband works at his job, the more money he can accumulate in his pension. Yet many pension evaluations are made based on the earliest age at which your husband might retire, usually age sixty-two. This means the amount of money you might be awarded would be less than the amount your husband will actually receive.

Valuation of stocks that are listed on a stock exchange is simple. There is a definite price for a particular day.

Valuation of a stock option—an agreement to buy a stock at a specific price at a future date—is not as easy. Do the options have any value before they are exercised? That is one question that could arise in a divorce action. Naturally, experts for your husband would try and say that an unexercised option has no value. If this happens, ask your husband to give you all of his valueless options. The hope is that the price of the stock will rise. The option will allow you to buy the stock at a lower price and you will have a built-in profit.

Not having access to the company records puts one at

a great disadvantage. In a divorce it is generally the wife who therefore suffers. If a wife who did not work in a business is paid out by her late husband's partners, not having all the records could also be a disadvantage when it comes to valuing inventory.

Valuation of a privately held company or a professional practice differ in divorce or estate appraisals.

If your husband is the key person running the business and he suddenly dies, the value of the company may diminish considerably. But, if you divorce, the value of the company wouldn't change. Experts refer to this as the multiple—the number that would be used to establish the company's fair market value. There are several methods that can be used. Sometimes it is a multiple of earnings. If the man who ran the business dies, that number might drop to 2, whereas if he is still alive and running the company, in a divorce action, the multiple might be 6. In other words, the business would be worth more or less depending on the key person. Of course, in a divorce action your husband's lawyers would say, "Mr. Jones is very valuable. If something happened to him there would be no business." Your husband's lawyers would want to use a low multiple. Your lawyer would claim that "the business could be run by a monkey." He would try and establish a high multiple by suggesting "There's no cult of personality."

Some businesses have what are called buy-sell agreements. One partner agrees to buy out the other at a specific price. Often these agreements are written with the tax collector in mind, and so have values that are considerably lower than the actual worth of the business. If you own a business and the partners have agreed to pay your estate should you die, you must be sure you have an up-to-date buy-sell agreement that truly reflects the value of the business—otherwise your heirs could lose out. If your husband has a business, be sure he has taken a recent look at the buy-sell agreement. It may have to be revalued.

Medical and legal practices are assets that must frequently be valued in a divorce settlement, unless you and your husband have agreed in a prenuptial agreement that you will keep your practices out of any divorce negotiations. If a medical or legal practice is part of a divorce agreement, be sure you have an appraiser who specializes in evaluating medical practices, not just a general appraiser. When a medical practice is evaluated for a divorce, "goodwill" is often disputed. Goodwill is the value imputed to the business, above and beyond the actual assets. In other words, if your husband is a doctor, how much are his actual reputation, client list, and special skills worth, above the actual medical equipment, accounts receivable, value of the office lease, etc.? Obviously, medical and legal practices are worth more when your husband is alive and able to practice than if your husband dies and you try to sell his practice to another doctor. In a divorce, the goodwill would have some value, but without your husband, the practice would be worth much less; there would be no goodwill.

Valuing works of art can also be extremely difficult. For one thing you have to value a work that is unique.[4] Different definitions can apply. If a work of art is given as a charitable contribution, the IRS will look to a comparable work of art. For estate taxes, the criterion is for a fair market value. For insurance purposes, you might want to know the replacement value. This is not the value you would use for estate tax purposes or equitable distribution in a divorce case.

Questions to ask an appraiser:

1. Have you dealt specifically with this field before? You would not want a jewelry appraiser to value your African sculpture.
2. How will you substantiate the price—e.g., auction catalogues, other dealers?
3. How will you charge? Be careful of the art appraiser who is charging a percentage of the appraised value. According to Victor Wiener of the Appraisers Association of America, the IRS will not accept an appraisal that is based on a percentage of the appraised value unless it's for estate or gift taxes.[5]

The more information you have about the work, the better. For example, if you know that a work was published, and you can provide its provenance, you may be able to show that the work has a greater value. Remember, too, that just because a dealer asks a high price for a work of art, does not mean that the work will be sold at that price. The same technique would apply to all types of appraisal.

11.
1040

Q. And you saw the tax returns on an annual basis. Is that right?

A. Yes.

Q. I take it you reviewed the returns before you signed them, didn't you?

A. Frankly, I didn't. I trusted [my husband] completely.

Q. Weren't you curious, whether you trusted him or not, as to the state of the family finances?

A. Frankly, no.

Q. Did you ever keep copies of the returns which you signed?

A. I didn't have them.

The speaker in the above dialogue is a female executive with an annual salary of over $300,000. This is a transcript from her divorce proceedings. When it came to finances, like many women she reverted to the traditional role of the wife. No matter that in her own job she oversaw huge budgets and made financial commitments affecting hundreds of employees. At home her husband managed the finances, hired the accountants, and she signed on the appropriate lines.

The tax return is frequently the husband's job, just as mowing the lawn is considered his domain. Husbands don't necessarily do the taxes because they want to keep things from their wives. They do the taxes because their wives don't want to touch them.

As a result, the tax return has become a mystery to many women and therefore a great weapon when it comes time for a divorce. Smart lawyers pore over the tax return looking for hidden assets and income. The discovery of an outstanding loan might signify the existence of a net worth statement that could be used to demand more in divorce settlements. Many women don't even have copies of a tax return for which they are jointly liable should there be a problem with underpayment.

By the way, if you do not have copies of your tax returns, you can get them from the IRS. To request a copy of a return you need Form 4506 available by calling a local office. The problem is, getting the returns could take months, which you don't want to waste if you are getting a divorce, and the government might only go back three or four years; your lawyer, on the other hand, might need more.

These days, you just might be the family member who prepares the tax returns, or you might do them with your husband. If you are not interested in the tax returns, you should be: It's part of the marriage.

The tax return can give you a good insight into your husband's attitude about money. Does he try to take business deductions for personal expenses? Is this how you would handle it? If it's not, knowing early on in your marriage could be helpful.

. . .

Here are three reasons you should read your tax return:

1. You might discover that your husband has less income than you thought.
2. You might discover that your husband has more income than you thought.
3. You might discover that your husband is cheating the government and because you are signing the returns you could be in trouble.

What the Tax Return Can Reveal: A Short Course in Reading Tax Returns[1]

The basic form 1040 is the clue to what's going on. It tells about taxable income and related investments. What follows is based on the 1040 as it appeared in 1991.

Income: This section of the tax return is on the first page. It lists different forms of income. Most are straightforward:

- wages, salaries, and tips
- taxable interest income (There is also a line for tax-exempt interest income that has been added to the return recently, but isn't always reported accurately.)
- dividend income
- capital gains (capital losses also would be listed here)— If your husband dabbled in the market and dropped a bundle, here's where it will appear.
- partnership income (This is of particular interest to

your divorce lawyer but it's also good to know about if your husband dies or is disabled.)
- pensions and annuities
- business income or loss
- income from estates and trusts

What you won't find on the 1040 are some tax-free investments. You would need the state income tax return to find this. You also will not find investments that do not pay interest. Foreign investment income, although it is supposed to be listed on the 1040 and then filed as a separate Form 90.22.1, may not be filed by everyone. The existence of a life insurance policy does not show up on a tax return either.

Adjustments to Income: This is the second most interesting section of the tax return: Here you may find an IRA or a KEOGH plan that your husband hadn't mentioned. You might even find alimony payments for a wife you hadn't known about (including her Social Security number). You should also check your husband's W-2 form to see if the box for any retirement plans is checked.

If you find a sudden increase in your husband's donation to a Keogh, it could mean he wants to reduce the amount of his income—a possible sign that he could be planning to leave the marriage.

You will not find any deferred compensation or deferred bonuses on a tax return.

Form 2106, Employee Business Expenses, is also an interesting part of the tax return. Some of these expenses may contribute to your family's standard of living. They could include food, entertainment, telephone, and auto expenses. It's important to understand what part of your living expenses come from your husband's job and yours, if you both work, because in the event of a divorce your lawyer will want to figure this into the settlement.

Schedule D. Capital Gains and Losses. There's a lot to look at here. You are supposed to report the gain and loss you have from the sale of stocks, bonds, real estate, partnerships, the sale of your home, and income from trusts. What you are looking at is a number that does not always tell you about the underlying asset.

If, for example, you see that stock has been sold for $8,000 and there is a $2,000 loss, you want to be sure you know what happened to the proceeds of that sale. The return will just tell you about the loss, but not what happened to the $8,000.

You might see that there is partnership income but you will not be able to tell the value of the underlying property.

There might be income of $4,000 from a trust, but the trust could be worth $100,000 and your husband could control the assets.

If you see interest income from bonds, you can sometimes work backwards to get an approximate idea of their underlying value. If you see $3,600 in income and you use a rate of interest of 6 percent, you would know that there had to be an asset worth around $60,000.

If you and your husband both work and you are planning to take time off to have a family, looking at reimbursed expenses, in addition to your salary, will give you a better idea of how much different your way of life might be on only one income.

If you and your husband divorce and you are asking for support, the amount of support is often based on the standard of living. If your lawyer can show that you and your husband had a way of life that was based partly on his salary and partly on expenses that were reimbursed by his employer, you might receive more support.

If you and your husband are divorcing, you should also look at some of the deductions that might artificially reduce income. These would include noncash charitable contributions or any type of casualty or theft loss. This could be important for alimony.

If you and your husband are planning to retire and you want to consider how much money you will spend, just looking at your salaries might lead you to underestimate the amount of money you would both need. Adding in your reimbursed expenses to your salaries would give you a more realistic amount.

If you and your husband are also taking a look at how you might manage as a widow, you would also want to consider these expenses.

How Taxes Work If You Are Divorced

You can transfer tax-free money between husband and wife. What you can't do is pass off alimony, which would require tax payments, as marital exchange. Alimony is usually tax deductible by the payor and taxable to the recipient. If you, the wife, receive alimony, you must pay taxes on it. If you, the wife, pay alimony to your former husband, you deduct it and he pays the taxes.

So as not to disguise cash transfer (not tax-deductible by the payee) as alimony (deductible by the payor), the laws are quite specific about what counts as alimony. For example, if you receive a lump-sum payment of $100,000 and it is given in three years, you can be paid in equal installments for three years or you can be paid in decreasing amounts, providing it is not more than $15,000 each year. Thus many alimony settlements are really property settlements in disguise. Alimony must stop when the payor dies, and can only be paid when husband and wife are living separately.

If one spouse has a very low income and the other a very high income, you can negotiate which of you gets the deduction. Sometimes this is a point of negotiations in a divorce proceeding.

If you keep the marital home as part of your divorce settlement and you then sell it, you will have to pay the taxes if there are any capital gains. The cost of the house will be considered the price you paid when you and your husband bought the house, not the price the house may have been when you and your husband divorced. Courts often do not figure the capital gains taxes when dividing property. So what seems like an equal split can cost you money. Remember that you do have two options that could blunt the blow: You could roll over the profits into another house within two years and not pay taxes on the appreciation, or you could, if you are over fifty-five, take advantage of the $125,000 exclusion.

If you get a cash payment of part of your husband's pension before his retirement age, that money must be rolled over into an IRA—within sixty days, or you will have to pay taxes on it. If you are getting this pension money and need to use it right away, you will be getting less money than you thought. A cash settlement of $100,000 and a pension settlement of $100,000 have different tax implications. The $100,000 in cash is a transfer, no taxes due. The $100,000 in pension money has income tax consequences when you eventually take the money out. You would have to pay a 10 percent penalty for using the money before he is fifty-nine and a half. You would also have to pay any income tax that was due.

Property settlements are not taxable because they are treated as a transfer between husband and wife. But if there is appreciated value, the tax would have to be paid when the property is sold. For example, if you transfer stock from husband to wife that cost $60,000 and is now worth $100,000, the wife would have to pay the taxes on the $40,000. This has to be figured into the settlement.

Child support is not tax deductible. The government does allow you to deduct children as dependents. Sometimes the deduction is negotiated as part of the settlement.

RETIREMENT TAXES[2]

Money that is stashed away in a tax-deferred account—such as an IRA or a KEOGH plan—becomes taxable income when it is withdrawn upon your retirement. If you withdraw the money before you retire, you not only pay the income taxes but you pay a penalty for taking the money out before you should. (In 1992 the magic number is fifty-nine and a half years.) The theory here is that you will be in a lower tax bracket when you retire than when you are working so the taxes won't be so bad.

If you change jobs, are fired, or are part of a retirement

plan that is ending, you could also receive a lump-sum payout. As mentioned, this money has to be reinvested in another plan or a roll-over IRA in order for you to avoid paying income taxes and a penalty.

If you receive your money in a lump-sum payout and are over fifty-nine and a half you can take advantage of forward averaging tax breaks.

If your husband had an IRA and you are the beneficiary, you will receive a lump-sum payment. If this is rolled over into another IRA you will not have to pay taxes. When you retire you can receive all of your IRA funds in a lump sum.

You will have to pay taxes on your Social Security benefits if your overall joint income is $32,000. If you are single, you pay taxes on Social Security if your income is over $25,000. The tax system does not give a break to double-income childless couples.

If you are over fifty-five and you sell your house, you do not have to pay capital gains on up to $125,000 of profit. Remember, however, this is a one-shot, one-house-per-couple deal. If you are married to someone who has taken his onetime write-off, you and he as a couple cannot claim this benefit again. If you know you are going to remarry and have not taken your benefit but your husband-to-be has already used his, sell your house before you remarry. You must have lived in the house for three years. Remember, too, that if you had previously deferred profits on a house sale, by buying another house your tax base would be reduced by that amount. Here's an example of how this works.

If you and your husband are eligible to receive your retirement money in a lump sum, known as lump sum

House A was purchased for:	$ 50,000
House A was sold for:	$100,000
House B was purchased for:	$150,000 (tax basis for House B is $100,000)
House B was sold for:	$350,000 (gain would be $250,000)
The exclusion would be:	$125,000
Taxes would be due on:	$125,000

distribution, you can put it into a roll-over IRA within sixty days of the payout, and keep that money tax deferred. You would pay income taxes on the amounts you withdraw, but presumably at a rate lower than you paid when you were working.

ESTATE AND INHERITANCE TAXES

No estate taxes are owed to the federal government on any amount a husband leaves to a wife or a wife to a husband. State governments have different rules; in some states you may have taxes to pay.

Each of us is entitled to a lifetime exemption of $600,000 to leave money without incurring any federal estate taxes. This is known as the unified gift and estate tax. If you have $700,000 and leave it to your husband, he pays no taxes when you die. When he dies, he can leave $600,000 tax free, but estate taxes will be due on the other $100,000. Not all states conform to the federal lifetime exemption.

Estate taxes owed to the federal government must be paid nine months after the date of death, except for closely held businesses or in cases where hardship can be shown. If you have commercial real estate that has suffered a substantial drop in value the government might not force you to sell at a loss in order to pay taxes. You might be able to make a deal to defer payment.

If you inherit the family house from your husband, you own the house at the amount it is worth when your husband died, not at the price your husband paid for it. This is known as getting a step-up basis in value. Therefore, you do not pay any taxes on the appreciation between the time your husband bought the house and you inherited it.

Tax laws are constantly changing and difficult to understand. A good accountant is probably the best person to ask about taxes. If you don't have one, ask friends for suggestions, make appointments, interview a few, and then make your choice.

Afterword

In the 1970s Barbara Walters could speculate about whether she would have to marry for money. But in the 1990s Joan Lunden can tell her the answer. A Westchester County court recently ordered Joan Lunden, TV anchorwoman, to pay her husband of fourteen years $18,000 a month in temporary support. Miss Lunden wondered why her husband couldn't just go out and get a job.

The nineties could be the decade when women finally come into their own. And while this doesn't mean the end of the wife who stays home to take care of her family, it should mean the end of the wife who doesn't know what is going on. Taking financial responsibility is part of the process. It would be naïve to suggest that the laws work perfectly, but at least they exist. The direction is right. The laws are in place to allow us an equal stake in the workplace. Women also have equal property rights. Now, the battle that was waged by so many women to secure these rights must be waged by individual women in their homes.

Marriage is here to stay. And while our legal system continues to define the property rights for death and divorce, we must make our own rules for our marriages. We must reeducate our husbands and sons to see a different role for women. But, equally important, we must educate our daughters to their responsibilities as well.

I believe that knowledge of family finances will help. Women have to participate in financial decisions. And women have to take responsibility for their own financial futures. Every woman should know about her pension, her will, her health insurance as well as her husband's. Every woman should recognize that even in the best of marriages, her financial interests may differ from her husband's. You should know how the decisions you and your husband make will affect your future. If you have children from a previous marriage and assets you want to leave them, you should know how the laws of your state about marriage, divorce, and death can affect your ownership of property.

It doesn't mean that you have to be able to invest money like a pro, but it does mean you should know when you need a pro, who the pros are, and how to choose them. If your husband is good at it, let him do it. But if he's not, you must not be afraid to ask questions and to participate in the process of his decisions.

It doesn't even mean that you have to earn big bucks, but you should know about the money you and your husband have accumulated.

Women have spent their years taking care of their homes, their husbands, their children, and, increasingly, their parents. It's time women started taking care of their finances. It doesn't mean that you are planning a divorce;

it merely means that you are realistic about the possibility and prepared should it happen.

The key is knowledge and participation, instead of control and abdication.

Remember, it's your money too. Think of it that way.

Notes

1. Marriage Is Not an Equal Opportunity

1. Kagan, Julia, and Rosalind C. Barnett, "Money Mastery," *Working Woman* (December 1986), p. 71.

2. In 1960, 230 women and 9,010 men were awarded law degrees. In 1988, women received 14,345 law degrees, men 35,469. In 1960 women received 387 medical degrees from American schools; men received 6,645. In 1988, women received 4,984 medical degrees, men received 10,107.

3. Voydanoff, Patricia, "Economic Distress and Family Relations: A Review of the Eighties," *Journal of Marriage and the Family* (November 1990), p. 1100.

4. Potuchek, Jean L., "Who's Responsible for Supporting the Family? Employed Wives and the Breadwinner Role," Wellesley College, Center for Research on Women (1988), p. 3.

5. Interview, Susan Hayward, senior vice president, Yankelovitch, Monitor (August 7, 1992).

6. U.S. Bureau of Census Population Reports P-20 No. 458, *Household and Family Characteristics.* Washington, D.C.: U.S. Government Printing Office, 1991, p. 247.

7. "The Rich Are Different from One Another," *Wall Street Journal* (November 12, 1990), p. C1.

8. Shelton, Beth Ann, "The Distribution of Household Tasks, Does Wife's Employment Make a Difference," *Journal of Family Issues* (June 1990), pp. 131–32.

9. Blumberg, Rae Lesser, and Marion Tolbert Coleman, "A Theoretical Look at the Gender Balance of Power in the American Couple," *Journal of Family Issues* (June 1990), p. 241.

10. Morris, Michelle, and Alexandria Siegel, "The Thirteenth Annual *Working Woman* Salary Survey 1992," *Working Woman* (January 1992), p. 53.

11. Bernstein, Daniel, "For In-House Women, the Story Differs," *National Law Journal* (1992).

12. Crouter, Ann, in Menghan and Parcel, p. 1090; and Stanley, Sandra C., Janet G. Hunt, and Larry L. Hunt, "The Relative Deprivation of Husbands in Dual-Earner Households," *Journal of Family Issues* (March 1986), pp. 3–20.

13. Lewin, Tamar, "For Some Two-Paycheck Families, the Economics Don't Add Up," *New York Times* (April 21, 1991) p. 18; Johnson, Elizabeth Ritchies, "I Couldn't Afford My Job," *Redbook* (April 1991), p. 89; and Potuchek, p. 7.

14. White, Lynn K., and Shengming Tang, "The Economic Foundations of Marital Happiness and Divorce," paper presented at Midwest Sociological Society, St. Louis, Mo. (April 1991), unpublished.

15. White and Tang, ibid.

16. Survey, Oppenheimer Management Corporation (March 1992), unpublished.

17. Bumpass, Larry, James Sweet, and Teresa Castro, "Changing Patterns of Remarriage." University of Wisconsin (August 1988), unpublished paper, p. 4.

18. Schoen, Robert, et al., "Marriage and Divorce in Twentieth Century American Cohorts," *Demography* (February 1985) p. 101.

19. Bumpass, p. 1.

20. Uhlenberg, Peter, Teresa Cooney, and Robert Boyd, "Divorce for Women After Midlife," unpublished paper, pp. 11–12.

21. Dobris, Joel C., "Medicaid Asset Planning by the Elderly: A Policy View of Expectations, Entitlement and Inheritance," *Real Property, Probate and Trust Journal* (Spring 1989), p. 3.

2. I Do, I Do

1. Wortman, Marlene Stein, ed. *Women in American Law,* Vol. 1, *From Colonial Times to the New Deal.* New York: Holmes and Meier, 1985, p. 112.
2. Wortman, p. 372. An excellent article to read about women's rights is by Mary Moers Wenig, "The Marital Property Law of Connecticut: Past, Present and Future," *Wisconsin Law Review* (1990), pp. 807–879.
3. Weisbert, Lynn, "A Marriage Made . . . by Satellite?" *National Law Journal* (March 4, 1991), p. 39.
4. *Pappas* v. *Pappas,* 300 S. C. 62, 386 S. E. 2d 468, South Carolina Court Appeal, 1989.
5. *Ullah* v. *Ullah* Decisions, Second Judicial Department Kings County, 1A Part 5, Justice Rigler, November 8, 1988.

3. Marriage, Inc.

1. Schultz, Ellen, "When It's the Wrong Time for Big Financial Decisions," *The Wall Street Journal* (October 29, 1991), p. C3.
2. Consumer Expenditures in 1990, Bureau of Labor Statistics.
3. "Study: Her 2nd trip down the aisle likely to be his first," *New York Post* (August 26, 1991), p. 15.
4. Helene Brezinsky, New York, shared her list of mistakes with me. This list incorporates some of her material.

4. "Honey, Just Sign Here"

1. *Neilson* v. *Neilson,* 780 P. 2d 1264 (Utah, 1989); Freed, Doris Jonas, and Timothy B. Walker, eds., "Family Law in the Fifty States: An Overview," *Family Law Quarterly* (Winter 1991), p. 392.
2. *Baylor Law Review* (1990), p. 830; *Wade* v. *Austin,* 5243 Wnd at 86.
3. *D'Amato* v. *D'Amato,* 176 So. 2d 907.
4. *Lutgert* v. *Lutgert,* 338 So. 2d 1111 October 27, 1976.

5. "Chronicle," *New York Times* (January 1, 1991), p. 59.

6. *McKee-Johnson* v. *Johnson*, 444 N.W. 2d 259 (Minnesota 1989), in Freed and Walker, p. 391.

7. *Mixon* v. *Mixon*, 550 So. 2d 999 (Alabama Civil Appeals, 1989), in Freed and Walker, p. 393.

8. *Gross v. Gross*, 464 NE Reporter Second Series, 11 Ohio St 3d 99 No 83-564, Supreme Court of Ohio, June 13, 1984, p. 500.

5. COMING APART

1. Riley, Glenda. *Divorce: An American Tradition.* New York: Oxford University Press, 1991, pp. 12–16, 133.

2. Sheppard, Annamay, T., "Women, Families and Equality: Was Divorce Reform a Mistake?" *Women's Rights Law Reporter* (Fall 1990), p. 144.

3. *New Jersey Shore Medical Center–Fitkin Hospital* v. *Baum's Estate*, 84 N. J. 137, 417 A. 2d 1003 (1980), in Sheppard, p. 145.

4. While these states do not have specific statutes that recognize the so-called "housewife's" contribution, the courts may still consider the contribution when dividing marital assets; Timothy Walker, editor, "Family Law in the Fifty States," *Family Law Quarterly*, (Winter 1990), p. 539.

5. *Ford* v. *Ford*, 766 p. 2d 950.

6. Interview with Peter Roth, lawyer for Mrs. Goldman, July 28, 1991; *Goldman* v. *Goldman*, "Findings of Fact and Conclusions of Law," Department of the Trial Court, Probate and Family Court, Docket No. 86D-0125-D1 (May 10, 1988).

7. Brown, Ronald L. "Case Developments," *Fairshare* (January 1990), p. 25.

8. Abraham, Jed H., *"The Divorce Revolution* Revisted: A Counterrevolutionary Critique," *American Journal of Family Law* (Summer 1989), p. 103.

9. Singer, Jana B., "Divorce Reform and Gender Justice," *The North Carolina Law Review* (June 1989), pp. 1103–5.

6. IF YOU THOUGHT MARRIAGE WAS BAD . . .

1. Wardle, Lynn D., "No-Fault Divorce and the Divorce Conundrum," *Brigham Young University Law Review* (1991), pp. 79–142; Sheppard, Annamay T., "Women, Families and Equality: Was Divorce Reform a Mistake?" *Women's Rights Law Reporter* (Fall 1990), pp. 143–152.
2. Interviews with Peter Roth, September 27, 1990.
3. Report of the Gender Bias Study of the Supreme Judicial Court, Commonwealth of Massachusetts, 1989. The Massachusetts gender bias study revealed that "Eighty-five percent of the lawyers responding to the family law survey said that courts rarely or never award adequate counsel fees in advance. Sixty-eight percent reported that judges rarely or never award adequate expert witness fees."
4. Scharfan, Lynn Hecht, "Gender Bias in the Courts: An Emerging Focus for Judicial Reform," *Arizona State Law Journal* (1989), p. 239.
5. Anderson, Cerisse, "Football Player's Retirement Held a Waste of Marital Asset," *New York Law Journal* (July 1989), p. 1.
6. Belin, David W. *Leaving Money Wisely: Creative Estate Planning for Middle and Upper-Income Americans for the 1990s.* New York: Charles Scribner's Sons, 1990, p. 98.
7. Sherman, Rorie, "Billed for Sex?" *National Law Journal* (August 1991).
8. *Smith* v. *Smith*, 90 Daily Journal DAR 13732, *Matrimonial Strategist* (January 1991), p. 2.

7. RETIREMENT? FOR WHOM?

1. Aries, Philippe, and Georges, Duby, eds. *A History of Private Life from Pagan Rome to Byzantium,* Vol. I. Cambridge, Mass.: The Belknap Press of Harvard University Press, 1987, p. 459.
2. 1990 Census, CPH-L-74, Age, Sex, Race and Hispanic Origin Information, August 7, 1990, US. Bureau of the Census.
3. Dobris, Joel C., "Medicaid Asset Planning by the Elderly: A Policy View of Expectations, Entitlement and Inheritance," *Real Property, Probate and Trust Journal* (Spring 1989), p. 7.
4. Stern, Fritz. *Gold and Iron.* New York: Alfred A. Knopf, 1977, pp. 208–209.

5. Bernstein, Aaron, "In Search of the Vanishing Nest Egg," *Business Week,* July 30, 1990, p. 46.

6. Congress established Individual Retirement Accounts in 1986. At that time, you could deduct from your income, thus lowering your tax bracket, the amount of money you put into your IRA. The money could then be invested tax free. Recently, however, the rules for IRAs changed. If your income is above $40,000, you cannot deduct the amount put into your IRA from your income. The only advantage to an IRA that now remains is that the money can grow tax free. A husband and wife's income is counted jointly. If a wife wants to open her own pension fund account because she works for a company that does not provide a pension plan, she would have to count her husband's income as well as her own in establishing eligibility to deduct her contribution from her salary.

7. Topolnicki, Denise M., "How to Get What's Coming to You," *Savvy* (November 1989), p. 44.

8. "Heading for Hardship: Retirement Income for American Women in the Next Century," *Older Women's League* (May 1990), p. 8.

9. Bernstein, *Business Week* (July 30, 1990).

10. Rosefsky, Bob. *Money Talks.* New York: McGraw-Hill Publishing Company, 1989, p. 535.

11. Health Insurance Association of America. *The Consumers Guide to Disability Insurance,* p. 1. [Statistics from Guardian Life, as quoted in "Disability Insurance," *Changing Times* (August 1990), p. 56.

12. *Changing Times* (August 1990), p. 53.

13. "The Unaffordability of Nursing Home Insurance," A Families USA Foundation Report (January 1990), p. 4; *Consumers Guide to Long-Term Care Insurance.* Washington, D.C.: Health Insurance Association of America (April 1989).

14. "The Unaffordability of Nursing Home Insurance," p. 2.

8. WILL POWER

1. Aries, Philippe, and Georges Duby, eds. *A History of Private Life from Pagan Rome to Byzantium,* Vol. I. Cambridge, Mass.: The Belknap Press of Harvard University Press, 1987, p. 31.

2. Collins, Herbert R., and David B. Weaver. *Wills of the Presidents of the United States.* New York: Communication Channels, Inc., 1976, pp. 19–28.

3. Roth, Nathan, M.D. *The Psychiatry of Writing a Will.* Springfield, Ill.: Charles C. Thomas, 1989, pp. 52–53.

4. Huffington, Arianna Stassinopoulos. *Picasso, Creator and Destroyer.* New York: Simon and Schuster, 1988, pp. 471–72.

5. Luncheon honoring Mrs. Vincent Astor, sponsored by the World Monuments Association, October 22, 1991.

6. Seneker, Harold, ed., with Dolores Lataniotis, "The Richest People in America," *Forbes* (October 21, 1991), p. 281.

7. Rosefsky, Bob. *Money Talks.* New York: McGraw-Hill, 1989, p. 568.

8. Tillman, Fred, and Susan G. Parker. *Your Will and Estate Planning.* Boston: Houghton Mifflin, 1990, p. 49.

9. Based on proposals from the New York Public Library.

9. Cinderella Revised

1. Aries, Philippe, and Georges Duby eds. *A History of Private Life from Pagan Rome to Byzantium,* Vol. I. Cambridge, Mass.: The Belknap Press of Harvard University Press, 1987, pp. 9–11.

2. Czapanskiy, Karen, "Volunteers and Draftees: The Struggle for Parental Equality," *UCLA Law Review* (1991), pp. 1415ff.

3. Buser, Paul J. "Introduction: The First Generation of Stepchildren," *Family Law Quarterly* (Spring 1991), p. 6.

4. Munsterman, Janice T., Claire B. Grimm, and Thomas A. Henderson, "A Summary of Child Support Guidelines," National Center for State Courts (February 1, 1990), p. 3.

5. Dodson, Diane, "A Guide to the Guidelines," *Family Advocate* (Spring 1988), p. 8.

6. Brett, Leslie J., Sharon Toffey Shepela, and Janet Kniffin, eds. "Women and Children Beware: The Economic Consequences of Divorce in Connecticut," Hartford College for Women, Women's Research Institute, Hartford, Conn. (1990), pp. 32–33.

7. Waldman, Steven, "Deadbeat Dads," *Newsweek* (May 4, 1992), p. 46.

8. Lester, Gordon H., "Child Support and Alimony: 1989," *Current Pop-*

ulation Reports, Consumer Income Series P-60, No. 173, Washington, D.C.: U.S. Government Printing Office, 1991, p. 1.

9. In 1990, only 40 percent of mothers receiving child support were also awarded health insurance benefits. Of these only two thirds complied. Lester, pp. 8–10.

10. Interview with John Messervey, family business consultant, Lake Forest, Illinois, 1982.

11. Wenig, Mary, "The Marital Property Law of Connecticut," *Wisconsin Law Review* (1990), pp. 807–79.

10. WHAT'S IT WORTH?

1. Garniau, George, "Newhouse Wins Tax Case," *Editor and Publisher* (March 10, 1990), pp. 12, 31.

2. *Skirvin* v. *Skirvin,* 560 NE2d 1263 (Indiana Appeals 1 District 1990).

3. *Imagnu* v. *Wodajo,* 582 Atlantic reporter, 2d Series, December 4, 1990. 85 Md. App. 208.

4. Lerner, Ralph E., "Putting a Price on Art," *The National Law Journal* (June 17, 1991).

5. Wiener, Victor, "Recent Cases Highlight Complications Involved in Selecting an Appraiser," *The National Law Journal* (June 17, 1991), p. S7.

11. 1040

1. Podell, Peggy, and M. Dee Samuels, eds. *The 1040 Handbook: A Guide to Income and Asset Discovery.* Chicago: American Bar Association, 1990.

2. An excellent guide to the retirement tax maze is *Maximizing Your Retirement Plan Distribution,* available at this writing from Charles Schwab, 101 Montgomery Street, San Francisco, Cal. 94104.

Bibliography

Books

Appel, Jens C. III, and F. Bruce Gentry. *The Complete Will Kit.* New York: John Wiley and Sons, 1990.

Aries, Philippe, and Duby, George, eds. *A History of Private Life from Pagan Rome to Byzantium,* Vol. I. Cambridge Mass.: The Belknap Press of Harvard University Press, 1987.

Belin, David W. *Leaving Money Wisely: Creative Estate Planning for Middle- and Upper-Income Americans for the 1990s.* New York: Charles Scribner's Sons, 1990.

Collins, Herbert R., and David B. Weaver. *Wills of the Presidents of the United States.* New York: Communications Channels, Inc., 1976.

Huffington, Arianna Stassinopoulus. *Picasso, Creator and Destroyer.* New York: Simon and Schuster, 1988.

Lewis, Naphtali, and Meyer Reinhold, eds. *Roman Civilization.* Vol. 1, *Selected Readings, the Republic and the Augustan Age.* New York: Columbia University Press, 1990.

McConaughey, Dan E. *Georgia Divorce, Alimony, and Child Custody.* Norcross, Ga.: The Harrison Company, 1990.

Podell, Peggy, and M. Dee Samuels, eds. *The 1040 Handbook: A Guide to Income and Asset Discovery.* Chicago, Ill.: American Bar Association, 1990.

Raggio, Grier, Jr., Lowell K. Halverson, and John W. Kydd. *Divorce in New York: How to Negotiate Your Divorce Without Tears or Trial.* New York: Rutledge Books, 1987.

Riley, Glenda D. *Divorce: An American Tradition.* New York: Oxford University Press, 1991.

Rosefsky, Bob. *Money Talks.* New York: McGraw Hill, 1989.

Roth, Nathan, M.D. *The Psychiatry of Writing a Will.* Springfield, Ill.: Charles C. Thomas, 1989.

Roth, T. *Babylonian Marriage Agreements, Seventh–Third Centuries, B.C.* Germany: Verlag, Butzon and Becker Kevelaer, 1989.

Shaw, Bernard. *Collected Plays with Their Preface: Definitive Edition.* New York: Dodd, Mead & Company, 1971.

Stern, Fritz. *Gold and Iron.* New York: Alfred A. Knopf, 1977.

Weitzman, Lenore J. *The Marriage Contract: A Guide to Living with Lovers and Spouses.* New York: The Free Press, 1981.

Wortman, Marlene Stein, ed. *Women in American Law.* Vol. 1, *From Colonial Times to the New Deal.* New York: Holmes and Meier Publishers, 1985.

The World Almanac. New York: World Almanac Publications, 1992.

GOVERNMENT REPORTS

Bureau of the Census. Current Population Report. *Child Support and Alimony, 1989.* Consumer Income Series P60–173. 1989.

Bureau of the Census. Current Population Report. *Child Support and Alimony.* Consumer Income Series P23–154. 1985.

Department of Health and Human Services, Social Security Administration. *Retirement.* SSA Publication No. 05-10035. January 1991.

Department of Labor, Pension and Welfare Benefits Administration. *What You Should Know About the Pension Law: A Guide to the Employees Retirement Income Security Act of 1974, as Amended by the Retirement Equity Act of 1984, and the Tax Reform Act of 1986.* May 1988.

Supreme Judical Court, Commonwealth of Massachusetts. *Gender Bias Study of the Court System in Massachusetts.* 1989.

REPORTS

Brett, Leslie, Sharon Toffrey Shepela, and Janet Kniffin. *Women and Children Beware: The Economic Consequences of Divorce in Connecticut.* Women's Research Institute, Hartford College for Women. Summer, 1990.

Families USA Foundation. *The Unaffordability of Nursing Home Insurance.* Washington, D.C. January 1990.

Health Insurance Association of America. *Consumers Guide to Long-term Care Insurance.* Washington, D.C. April 1989.

———. *Consumers Guide to Disability Insurance.* Washington, D.C. July 1989.

McLanahan, Sara S., and Renee A. Monson. "Caring for the Elderly: Prevalence and Consequences," unpublished, 1989.

Munsterman, Janice T., Claire B. Grimm, and Thomas A. Henderson, *A Summary of Child Support Guidelines.* National Center for State Courts. February 1, 1990.

Older Women's League. *Heading for Hardship: Retirement Income for American Women in the Next Century.* Washington, D.C. May 1990.

ARTICLES

Staff of *American Demographics* magazine. "The Rich Are Different from One Another." *Wall Street Journal* (November 12, 1990).

Barron, James. "In *Trump* v. *Trump,* the Focus Is on Lots of Fine Print." *The New York Times* (February 15, 1990).

Bernstein, Aaron. "In Search of the Vanishing Nest Egg: For Young Workers, Pensions May Be Going the Way of the Dodo." *Business Week* (July 30, 1990).

Bernstein, Daniel. "For In-House Women, the Story Differs." *National Law Journal* (1992).

Blumberg, Rae Lesser, and Marion Tolbert Coleman. "A Theoretical Look at the Gender Balance of Power in the American Couple." *Journal of Family Issues* (June 1990).

Brown, Ronald L., ed. "Partially Rehabilitated Spouse." *Fairshare: The Matrimonial Law Monthly* (January 1990).

Buser, Paul J. "Introduction: The First Generation of Stepchildren." *Family Law Quarterly* (Spring 1991).

Collins, Robert Kirkman, ed. "Style to Which They Were Accustomed." *The Matrimonial Strategist* (January 1991).

Czapanskiy, Karen. "Volunteers and Draftees: The Struggle for Parental Equality." *UCLA Law Review* (1991).

Dobris, Joel C. "Medicaid Asset Planning by the Elderly: A Policy View of Expectations, Entitlement and Inheritance." *Real Property, Probate, and Trust Journal* (Spring 1989).

Dodson, Diane. "A Guide to the Guidelines." *Family Advocate* (Spring 1988).

Freed, Doris Jonas, and Timothy B. Walker, eds. "Family Law in the Fifty States: An Overview." *Family Law Quarterly* (Winter 1991).

Garneau, George. "Newhouse Wins Tax Case." *Editor and Publisher* (March 10, 1990).

Johnson, Elizabeth Richie. "I Couldn't Afford My Job." *Redbook* (April 21, 1991).

Kagan, Julia, and Rosalind C. Barnett. "Money Mastery." *Working Woman* (December 1986).

Lerner, Ralph E. "Putting a Price on Art." *The National Law Journal* (June 17, 1991).

Lewin, Tamar. "For Some Two-Paycheck Families, the Economics Don't Add Up." *The New York Times* (April 21, 1991).

Morris, Michele, and Alexandria Siegel. "The Thirteenth Annual *Working Woman* Salary Survey 1992." *Working Woman* (January 1992).

Otten, Alan L. "Farm Belt Holds Onto Its Oldest Americans." *Wall Street Journal* (September 4, 1991).

Paulson, C. Morton. "What If You Couldn't Work Anymore?" *Changing Times* (August, 1990).

Potuchek, Jean L. "Who's Responsible for Supporting the Family? Employed Wives and the Breadwinner Role." Working Paper No. 186, Wellesley College, Center for Research on Women, 1988.

Schafran, Lynn Hecht. "Gender Bias in the Courts: An Emerging Focus for Judicial Reform." *Arizona State Law Journal* 21 (1989).

Schoen, Robert, William Urton, Karen Woodrow, and John Baj. "Marriage and Divorce in Twentieth Century American Cohorts." *Demography* (February 1985).

Schultz, Ellen C. "When It's the Wrong Time for Big Financial Decisions." *Wall Street Journal* (October 29, 1991).

Schultz, Marjorie Maguire. "Contractual Ordering of Marriage: A New Model for State Policy." *California Law Review* (March 1982).

Seneker, Harold, ed., with Dolores Lataniotis. "The Richest People in America." *Forbes* (October 21, 1991).

Shelton, Beth Ann. "The Distribution of Household Tasks: Does Wife's Employment Make a Difference?" *Journal of Family Issues* (June 1990).

Sherman, Rorie. "Billed for Sex?" *National Law Journal* (August 1991).

Sheppard, Annamay T. "Women, Families and Equality: Was Divorce Reform a Mistake?" *Women's Rights Law Reporter* (Fall 1990).

Somerset, Lady Anne. "Elizabeth I." *Connoisseur* (November 1991).

Stanley, Sandra C., Janet G. Hunt, and Larry L. Hunt. "The Relative Deprivation of Husbands in Dual-Earner Households." *Journal of Family Issues* (March 1986).

Tobias, Carl. "Interspousal Tort Immunity in America." *Georgia Law Review* 23 (1989).

Topolnicki, Denise M. "How to Get What's Coming to You." *Savvy* (November 1989).

Vikan, Gary. "Art and Marriage in Early Christianity." *The Walters Art Gallery Monthly Bulletin* (October 1991).

Voydanoff, Patricia. "Economic Distress and Family Relations: A Review of the Eighties." *Journal of Marriage and the Family* (November 1990).

Waldman, Steven. "Deadbeat Dads." *Newsweek* (May 4, 1992).

Walker, Timothy B. "Family Law in the Fifty States: An Overview." *Family Law Quarterly* (Winter 1992).

Wardle, Lynn D. "No-Fault Divorce and the Divorce Conundrum." *Brigham Young University Law Review* (1991).

Wenig, Mary Moers. "The Marital Property Law of Connecticut: Past, Present and Future." *Wisconsin Law Review* 3 (1990).

White, Lynn K., and Shenming Tang. "The Economic Foundations of Marital Happiness and Divorce." Paper presented at the 1991 meetings of Midwest Sociological Society, Des Moines, Iowa, March 1992.

Weisbert, Lynn. "A Marriage Made . . . by Satellite?" *National Law Journal* (March 4, 1991).

Younger, Judith T. "Perspectives on Antenuptial Agreements." *Rutgers Law Review* 40 (1988).

Wiener, Victor. "Recent Cases Highlight Complications Involved in Selecting an Appraiser." *The National Law Journal* (June 17, 1991).

Additional Readings

Marriage

American Bar Association, Public Education Division. *Your Legal Guide to Marriage.* Chicago: American Bar Association, 1983.

Felton-Collins, Victoria. *Couples & Money: Why Money Interferes with Love & What to Do About It.* New York: Bantam Books, 1990.

Sager, Clifford, and Bernice Hunt. *Intimate Partners: Hidden Patterns in Love Relationships.* New York: McGraw-Hill, 1979.

Warner, Ralph, Toni Ihara, and Stephen Elias. *California Marriage & Divorce Law.* Berkeley, Calif.: Nolo Press, 1990.

Divorce

Briles, Judith. *The Dollars and Sense of Divorce: The Financial Guide for Women.* New York: Master Media Limited, 1988.

De Angelis, Sidney M. *You're Entitled!: A Divorce Lawyer Talks to Women.* Chicago: Contemporary Books, Inc. 1989.

Engel, Margorie L., and Diana D. Gould. *The Divorce Decisions Workbook: A Planning and Action Guide.* New York: McGraw-Hill, 1992.

Friedman, James T. *The Divorce Handbook: Your Basic Guide to Divorce Updated.* New York: Random House, 1982.

Harwood, Norma. *A Woman's Legal Guide to Separation and Divorce in All 50 States.* New York: Charles Scribner's Sons, 1985.

Jacob, Herbert. *Silent Revolution: The Transformation of Divorce Law in the United States.* Chicago: University of Chicago Press, 1988.

Lake, Steven R. *Rematch: Winning Legal Battles with Your Ex.* Chicago: Chicago Review Press, 1989.

McConaughey, Dan E. *Georgia: Divorce, Alimony and Child Custody.* Norcross, Ga.: The Harrison Company, 1990.

Robertson, Christina. *A Woman's Guide to Divorce and Decision Making.* New York: Simon and Schuster, 1988.

Samuelson, Elliot D. *The Divorce Law Handbook: A Comprehensive Guide to Matrimonial Practice.* New York: Insight Books, 1988.

Woodhouse, Violet, Victoria Felton-Collins, and M. C. Blakeman. *Divorce & Money: Everything You Need to Know About Dividing Property.* Berkeley, Calif.: Nolo Press, 1992.

Retirement and Estate Planning

American Association of Retired Persons. *How to Plan Your Successful Retirement.* San Francisco: ACCESS Press/The Understanding Business, 1988.

American Bar Association, Section of General Practice. *All-States Wills and Estate Planning Guide.* Chicago: American Bar Association, 1990.

Appel, Jens C., and F. Bruce Gentry. *The Complete Will Kit.* New York: John Wiley & Sons, 1990.

Lester, Toni P. *How to Settle an Estate or Prepare Your Will.* New York: Perigee Books, 1988.

Quinn, Jane Bryant. *Making the Most of Your Money.* New York: Simon and Schuster, 1991.

Money Management

Card, Emily. *The Ms. Money Book: Strategies for Prospering in the Coming Decade.* New York: E.P. Dutton, 1990.

Leonard, Robin. *Money Troubles: Legal Strategies to Cope with Your Debts.* Berkeley, Calif.: Nolo Press, 1991.

Status and History of Women

Aries, Philippe, and Georges Duby, eds. *A History of Private Life from Pagan Rome to Byzantium,* Vol. I. Cambridge, Mass.: The Belknap Press of Harvard University Press, 1987.

Fuchs, Victor R. *Women's Quest for Economic Equality.* Cambridge, Mass.: Havard University Press, 1988.

Leonard, Frances. *Women and Money: The Independent Woman's Guide to Financial Security for Life.* New York: Addison-Wesley Publishing Company, Inc., 1991.

Mason, Mary Ann. *The Equality Trap.* New York: Simon and Schuster, 1988.

Acknowledgments

Thanks to so many.

Writing a book about marriage and money means you are writing a book to which just about everyone will have something to add—some little anecdote, some personal experience that helped enrich my perspective. Throughout the book, I refer to many of my friends who were willing to entrust their stories to me. I have changed their names and their situations to ensure their privacy. But I thank them all for their help.

Many others helped me as well. Geraldine Fabrikant, of *The New York Times* gets my first thanks, for she knew I had an outline for a book stuck away in a drawer and encouraged me to meet Ed Victor who became my agent. Ed Victor's belief, from the start, that my one-page outline could become a book was the catalyst I needed. Joni Evans, my editor, publisher, and friend, never failed to steer me in the right direction. She patiently coped with my anxieties, and was always there when I needed her.

Much of the work on this book was done at the Writer's Room in New York, a sanctuary that provided the atmosphere I needed in order to complete my work.

I was also fortunate in being able to call upon many of the outstanding practitioners in the fields of law, insurance, money management, marital counseling, and financial planning. I would like to thank especially Robert Wittes who patiently read many chapters, as well as William Zabel, Robert Cohen, Connie Chen, and Peter Roth.

Alan Wachtel shared his insights gleaned from many years of family therapy practice. Gary Strum cheerfully crunched many numbers for me. The late Ernest Sommer was a guide through the financial world for many years.

Especially helpful whenever I called were the various experts at the Bureau of the Census who were willing to supply any number of statistics that are cited in the notes.

Natasha Gray, who toiled as research assistant, gets special mention for all her efforts.

Then there were the many who were willing to answer my questions, strangers who were kind enough to take time from their own busy schedules to find a reference, send me an article, or otherwise give me information.

Linda Barbanel, Dr. Clifford Sager, and Violet Woodhouse answered many questions about money and marriage. Stanley L. Goodman gave a straightforward account of the problems of evaluation. Eleanor Alter, Harriet Newman Cohen, Thomas M. Mulroy, and Barry Meadows were all experts on the problems of women and divorce. Peter Strauss and Yisroel Schulman were guides to the world of elder care law. Family Planners, Janet Kovanda, Maxine Hyrkas, Claire S. Langden, Mary McGrath, and Margaret Tracy were among those who provided great help.

Vincent Gandolfo, William Lockwood, Lenard Marlow, Glen Henkel, Mary Moers Wenig, Alexander Folger, Marvin Snyder, Stanley Lipton, Deborah Batts, and Robert George all contributed, and The Stuart Planning Seminar kindly allowed me to attend a seminar.

The Turtle Bay Books staff were all always a pleasure to work with, and particular thanks to my copy editor, Gail Bradney.

Index

Academy of Family Mediators,
    105
Adultery
    as grounds for divorce, 67–68
Alimony, 80–84
    before no-fault laws, 85–86
    as earned income, to establish
        an IRA, 127
    and income taxes, 226–27
    lump-sum, 82
    percent of women receiving,
        92–93
    permanent, 82
    rehabilitative, 81
    remunerative, 81–82
    states that award, 83
    trying to collect, 83
Alternative dispute resolution
    (ADR). *See* Mediation
American Arbitration Association,
    105
Annuities, 132
    when you are widowed, 193–94
Appraisers Association of
    America, 220
Assets
    building, 40
    calculating your net worth,
        34–35, 192

cash-flow statement, 192
    hidden, how to hunt for, 101–2
    outside the will, 164–65
Astor, Vincent, 169
Attorneys
    for estate planning, 171
    for prenuptial agreements, 60

Bank accounts
    in your own name, 191
Bankruptcy
    impact of, on divorce, 83
Bigamy, 69
*Blue Book of Continuing
        Care/Life Care Retirement
        Communities*, 150
Brezinsky, Helene, 45, 239
Buy-sell agreements, 218–19

Capital gains and losses on tax
        returns, 225–26
Cash-flow statement, 33
Checking accounts
    in your own name, 42–43
Child care cost, 8
Children
    and child support, 84–86,
        204–7
        collecting back, 206–7

Children *(cont'd)*
　　long-arm laws, 207
　　taxes on, 228
　definition of child, 201
　"emancipation" of, 201
　fathers seeking custody, 202
　and inheritance, 208–12
　　disinheriting, 208
　　primogeniture, 210
　　joint custody of, 85
　motherhood, and responsibility
　　for, 203–4
　prenuptial agreements and, 55
　rights of, 200–3
　　making contracts, 202
　　stepparents and, 202
　survivor's benefits and, 203
Cohn, Roy, 62
Community property states
　and prenuptial agreements, 56
Continuing care retirement
　　community (CCRC), 150
Contracts
　signing, 29
"Corroborated perjury," 70
Credit cards, 22
　problems with, 38–39
　in your own name, 42–43, 191
Credit reports
　how to obtain a copy of, 28
"Curtesy," 20

Debt
　and divorce, 83
　reasonable, 40
　responsibility for, 43
　　when you are widowed, 194
Disability, 149–51
　insurance, 152–53
Discretionary funds, 29
Divorce
　and alimony, 80–84, 85–86
　and current standard of living,
　　79–80

battle plan for, 98–101
and child custody-support,
　　84–86, 204–7
　collecting back, 206–7
　"corroborated perjury," 70
　the court-battle, 105
　deciding if you want one,
　　96–97
defined, 68
and dividing the debt, 83
and division of property, 72–80
effect of, on previous will, 175
equitable distribution, 73, 74
　direct and spousal, 76–77
　laws of, 75–76
and "equitable
　　reimbursement," 79
grounds for, 67, 68, 69–70
how to hunt for hidden assets,
　　101–2
and your husband's pension, 79
and intangible property, 77–78
legal separation, 72
minimizing the cost of, 110–13
"no-fault" laws, 69
　and division of marital
　　property, 72–80
questions to ask the lawyer
　after you hire him, 113–15
　before you hire him, 108–10
rate, 9
reform, 87–94
routes to, 102–5
and taxes, 226–27
and temporary support, 106–8
understanding the bottom line,
　　117–18
when to settle, 115–16
Divorce problems
　the family home, 93
　father has as much right to
　　custody, 94
　increased inequities, 87
　lack of funds, 88, 90–91

no access to marital assets, 90
no funds for legal fees, 91
penalizing the working woman,
89
reasons women lose out, 94–97
"Dower" rights, 20
Durable power of attorney, 153

Eldercare, 7
Employee Retirement Income
Security Act (ERISA), 130
English Poor Law Statute of
1601, 119–20
Equality of working women, 6–7
Equitable distribution
laws of, 73–76
direct contribution
and prenuptial agreements,
56
and spousal contribution, 76–77
Expenses
guidelines for, 39
how to calculate, 36–37

Fears
of women, of being financially
destitute, 3
Femininity
defined as sexual attraction, 4
FICA. *See* Social Security
Fidelity WealthBuilder, 144
Financial decisions
dependence of women and, 9
importance of, in marriage, 27
taking responsibility for,
234–35
ten rules for, in marriage, 28–29
Financial planners, 144–51
questions to ask, 146
Financial reports
cash flow statement, 33
net worth statement, 32–33
Fonda, Jane, 95
Forbes, 142

401(k) plans, 124–25

Gastineau, Mark, 100
Gender-neutral language, 4
Gerard, Jean, 170
Getting Married, 69–70
Getty, J. Paul, 167

Health insurance. *See* Medical
insurance
Homestead laws, 52
Household work
economic value of, 8

Income taxes. *See* Taxes
Income vs. outgo, 36–37
Independence of women
as threat to men, 8–9
Inflation
effect on retirement dollars,
146–48
Information
important, to keep in the
house, 43–44
Inheritance rights, 165
Inherited money
and prenuptial agreements,
57–58
Insurance
life, 138, 193
disability, 149–51
medical, 149, 153–55
when you are widowed, 194
nursing home, 158–59
trusts, 185–86
Investments. *See* Savings and
investments
IRAs (Individual Retirement
Accounts), 126–27, 142
as earned income, if you
receive alimony, 127
how to have your own, 127
rollover, 129, 132
spousal, 127

Irreconcilable differences, 70
Irretrievable breakdown, 70
Irving, Amy, 54

Joint tenancy ownership of
    property, 26

Kaplan, Helen, 50
Keogh plans, 125–26

Laws. *See* Marriage laws
Lazarus, Charles, 50
League of Women Voters, 17
Legal separation, 72
Lennon, John, 161
Life expectancy, 119–20
Lunden, Joan, 233

Masculinity
    defined as being the "good
        provider," 4
Marriage
    control in, 5, 11–12
    effect on, when children come,
        6
    financial sharing and
        responsibility in, 12
    and money, old stereotypes
        about, 4
    powerful husband/
        weak-and-protected wife,
        10, 11
    statistics about, 14
    ten financial rules for, 28–29
    traditional roles in, 4
    and women who work outside
        the home, 5
Marriage laws. *See also*
        Prenuptial agreements
    "common law," 18–19
    after divorce, 26–27
    and ownership of property,
        21–22, 26
    in community property states,
        22–23

"curtesy," 20
    and debts, 25
    "dower" rights, 20
    and dying intestate, 20
    and effect of divorce on, 25
    qualifications for a marriage
        license, 19–20
    and sexual relations, 18
Mediation, 102–5
Medicaid, 154–55, 156
    protecting your assets, to
        qualify for, 157–58
Medical insurance, 149, 153–55
    if your husband can't work,
        153
    Medicaid, 154–58
    Medicare, 154
    Medigap, 154
Money, 139–40, 142
Money management. *See also*
        Savings and investments
    calculating your net worth,
        34–35
    checking accounts, 42–43
    conflicts and control, 10–11
    credit cards, 42–43
    debts, responsibility for, 43
    five things women don't know
        about, 31
    how to calculate your expenses,
        36–37
    how to discover the facts
        about, 31–32
    investing, 32
    mistakes to avoid in, 45–47
    rules for, 13–14, 28–29
        in second marriages, 41–42
    sharing income, expenses, and
        debts, 40–44
Mutual funds, 132, 142.
    See also Savings and
        investments

"Necessaries," 17, 18
Net-worth statement, 32–33

New York Equitable Distribution
Statute Domestic
Relations Law, 23
Nielsen, Brigette, 100
"No-fault" laws. *See* Divorce:
"no-fault"
Nursing Homes
facts about, 155–56
insurance, 158–59
protecting your assets, to
qualify for, 157–58

Onassis, Jacqueline, 59
Ono, Yoko, 161

Pension plans. *See* Retirement:
pension plans
Personal Earnings and Benefit
Estimate Statement, 122
Picasso, Pablo, 168
Power, women, and marriage,
15–18
Power of attorney, 191
durable, 163, 197
springing, 197
Pregnancy Discrimination Act, 6
Prenuptial agreements, 27, 48–66
challenging, 59–60
history of, 49–50
how they stand up in court,
52–54
and unconscionable contract,
53
invalidating, 53–54
signing a bad agreement, 53
increase in, 51
and inheritance rights, 165
making the best deal, 60–63
and marrying for the second
time, 64–65, 212
mistakes to avoid, if you have
money, 64–66
"postnup," 66
problems with, 62–63
reasons for, 55–59

and state laws, 51, 52
waiving pension rights in, 139
what you give up when you
sign one, 51–52
Property
equitable distribution of, 77
intangible, 77–78
marital, 22–24
defined, 23–24
in divorce settlements, 72–80
ownership of
in common law states, 21, 26
in community property
states, 21–22
types of, 26
rights
in ancient Greece and
Rome, 15–16
Christian concept of, 16
during the 19th century,
16–17
today, 17–18
separate, 22, 23
defined, 24
in divorce settlements, 72–80
valuation of, 213–20
husband's business, 218–19
medical and legal practices,
219
pensions, 214–17
questions to ask the
appraiser, 220
stocks, 217
works of art, 219–20
when you own separate, 29
Public policy issue, 52

Recordkeeping, 29
Retirement, 119–60
amount of income needed for,
145–46
pension plans, 123–29
defined benefit, 123–24
defined contribution 401(k),
124–25

Retirement *(cont'd)*
  government and civil service,
    125
  IRAs, 126–27, 129, 132
  Keogh, 125–26
  money purchase, 124
  profit sharing, 124
  (SEPs), 125
  determining the value of,
    214–17
  first old-age, 120
  how to blend your benefits,
    136–39
  how to have your own, 128–29
  life-insurance provisions of, 138
  lump-sum distribution, 129
  naming beneficiaries, 136
  pension maximization, 131
  Social Security, 120–22
  spouse's right to share in,
    130–32
  taking it out, 129–30
  taxes on, 227–30
  vesting, 133
  women's vs. men's, 132–36
  ten things to know when your
    husband retires, 159–60
*Retirement Plans for the
    Self-Employed, 125*
Rushdie, Salman, 92

Safety deposit box
  what to keep in it, 44
Savings and investments, 32,
    139–43
  amount of income needed for
    retirement, 145–46
  annuities, 147
  bonds, 141, 143
  common stocks, 143
  effect of disabilities on, 149–51
  effect of inflation on, 146–48
  guide to, 140–43
  money market funds, 142, 143

  mutual funds, 140, 142
  problems with, when one
    spouse dies, 148–51,
    193–94
  using a financial advisor,
    141–42
  using a financial planner,
    144–51
Selecting Retirement Housing,
    150
Shaw, G. B., 69
Simplified Employee Pension
    Plans (SEPs), 125
Social Security, 120–22
  benefits for nonworking spouse,
    121
  for divorced wives, 81
  integration, 130
  survivor's benefits, 121–22,
    192–93
    for children, 203
Spending
  patterns of, carried over from
    childhood, 11
Spielberg, Steven, 54
"Spousal support." *See* Alimony
Stereotypes
  about money and marriage, 4
Stewart, James, 50
Swan, Annalyn, 7

Taxes, 221–31
  capital gains, on your house,
    195–96
  death tax returns, 183–84
  estate, 194, 230–31
  estate planning, to avoid death
    taxes, 170–73
  getting copies of returns, 222
  if you are divorced, 226–27
  income, after death of spouse,
    194
  on child support, 228
  on pensions, 227–28

and property settlements, 228
returns
  Employee Business Expenses,
    form 2106, 224–25
  how to read, 223–26
  reasons to read, 223
  Schedule D Capital gains
    and losses, 225–26
  signing the returns, 221
  unified gift and estate tax, 230
Tenancy by the Entirety
  ownership of property, 26
T. Rowe Price, 144
Trump, Donald and Ivana,
  48–49, 61, 62
Trusts, 175–83
  bypass (credit shelter), 177
  charitable, 178–79
  defined, 179
  how they work, 179–83
    beneficiaries, 179–80
    grantor, 179
    trustee, 180–83
  insurance, 185–86
  inter vivos, 176
  irrevocable, 176–77
  marital deduction, 177–78
  QTIP (Qualified Terminable
    Interest Property), 177
  revocable, 176–77
    living trust, 163–64
  and taxes, 183
  testamentary, 176–77
Two-income couples, 4, 5
  and costs of child care, 8

Unemployment. *See* Disability
Uniform Premarital Agreement
  Act of 1983, 51, 59

Walters, Barbara, 3, 233
Washington, George, 167
Whitney, John Hay, 161
Widowhood

advice for older women,
  196–97
defined, 188–89
five common mistakes women
  make, 197–99
the house, what to do with it,
  195–96
planning the funeral, 189–90
questions to think about before,
  187–88
signing power of attorney, 191,
  197
things to do
  during the first month, 190
  during the first three
    months, 190–94
  during the first year, 195–96
what not to do, 194–95
Wiener, Victor, 220
Wiggins, Marianne, 92
Wills and estate planning,
  161–99.
  See also Trusts
before you write your will,
  things to know, 183–84
children, naming guardian for,
  166
death tax returns, 183–84
different wills for different
  times, 173–75
dying intestate, 162–63
effect of divorce, on previous
  will, 175
effect of tax laws on, 170–73
  federal and state taxes and,
    166
  ways to avoid taxes, 172–73
elective share, 165
estate freeze, 186
executors, 166, 183–84
history of, 162
inheritance rights, 165
men without wills, 168–70
powers of attorney, 163

Wills and estate planning *(cont'd)*
  probate, 163–64
  questions to think about before
      you are widowed, 187–88
  revocable living trust, 163–64
  in second marriages, 174–75
  what to know about your
      husband's will, 184–86
  why you should have a will,
      164–68
Women. *See also* Widowhood
  and financial dependence, 9
  working mother vs. working
      woman, 10
Work
  equality of women and, 4, 6, 9
  the "glass ceiling," 9
  part-time, 9

ABOUT THE AUTHOR

SHELBY WHITE is a financial journalist who has written and lectured on the subject of women and money. Her articles have appeared in many publications, including *Forbes, Barron's, The New York Times, Institutional Investor,* and *Corporate Finance.* She and her husband live in New York City.